D1606271

DESTRUCTION

OF THE STEAMBOAT

SULTANA

DESTRUCTION
OF THE STEAMBOAT
SULTANA
THE WORST MARITIME DISASTER
IN AMERICAN HISTORY

GENE ERIC SALECKER

NAVAL INSTITUTE PRESS

ANNAPOLIS, MARYLAND

This book has been brought to publication with the generous assistance of the *Sultana* Disaster Museum in Marion, Arkansas.

Naval Institute Press,
291 Wood Road
Annapolis, MD 21402

Library of Congress Cataloging-in-Publication Data
Names: Salecker, Gene Eric, 1957- author. | Naval Institute Press, publisher.
Title: Destruction of the Steamboat Sultana : the worst maritime disaster in American history / Gene Eric Salecker.
Description: Annapolis, Maryland : Naval Institute Press, [2021] | Includes bibliographical references and index.
Identifiers: LCCN 2021049931 (print) | LCCN 2021049932 (ebook)
ISBN 9781682477434 (hardcover) | ISBN 9781682477441 (ebook)
Subjects: LCSH: Sultana (Steamboat) | Steamboat disasters—Mississippi River—History—19th century. | United States—History—Civil War, 1861-1865—Prisoners and prisons.
Classification: LCC E595.S84 S245 2021 (print) | LCC E595.S84 (ebook) | DDC 973.7/71—dc23/eng/20211018
LC record available at https://lccn.loc.gov/2021049931
LC ebook record available at https://lccn.loc.gov/2021049932

∞ Print editions meet the requirements of ANSI/NISO z39.48-1992
(Permanence of Paper).
Printed in the United States of America.

30 29 28 27 26 25 24 23 22   9 8 7 6 5 4 3 2 1
First printing

To my wife, Susan, and my father, Roy

CONTENTS

PREFACE

I n the early morning hours of April 27, 1865, the steamboat *Sultana* exploded, caught fire, and sank in the Mississippi River. Among her passengers the *Sultana* was carrying nearly two thousand newly released Union prisoners of war who were going home at last. Some of those men were killed in the explosion, others died in the fire, and many drowned in the icy waters of the river. But some survived to tell their stories.

The *Sultana* disaster left a great many questions unanswered: What caused the explosion? Exactly how many people were on board at the time? How many people survived, and how many people died? And, perhaps most perplexing of all, who were these people? Although a great many authors have tried to answer these questions over the past 150 years, most of them have relied on legends and unverified "facts" that grew up around the disaster. Very few of them examined the records in the National Archives in Washington, DC, looked through the handwritten transcripts of the three official bodies that investigated the disaster, or pored over the handwritten testimony from the court-martial of Capt. Frederic Speed, the only person tried for the disaster. Most authors take as fact the unverified information that has been passed down over the years, and as a result, a great deal of secondhand and thirdhand information has become established as part of the *Sultana* legend. I hope to change that.

In 1992, my friend Jerry O. Potter wrote his ground-breaking book, *The* Sultana *Tragedy: America's Greatest Maritime Disaster*, using actual transcripts and material from the National Archives. When he was finished, he passed his material to me and encouraged me to write my own book. And so I did. In 1996, using Jerry's material as well as dozens of firsthand accounts I had gleaned from state archives and state libraries, my book *Disaster on the Mississippi: The* Sultana *Explosion, April 27, 1865* was published. These two books are perhaps the best-researched books on the *Sultana* ever written.

As well researched as our books were, though, we got a few things wrong. In doing our research we physically had to go to the various archives and state libraries and pore over hundreds of pages of microfilm and microfiche. Inevitably, there were errors. Today, most of the sources—newspapers and government documents, including pension records and service records—have been digitized and are available online. Researchers can sit at home and search burial records and headstone applications. It is now possible to write a work of historical nonfiction without ever leaving home. It is also much easier to look into the facts, myths, and legends surrounding the *Sultana* disaster.

In 2015, I began an exhaustive two-year search to determine conclusively how many people were on board the *Sultana* from April 24 to April 27, 1865; how many people perished in the disaster; and how many people survived. At the same time that I was researching the numbers connected with the *Sultana* I was also trying to determine the source of the facts and myths that are accepted as part of the official history of the *Sultana* disaster. By taking my investigation back to primary sources, I have been able to dispel many of those myths and also to add a great deal to the true story of the *Sultana*.

This work looks at the events, incidents, and people connected to the terrible disaster, and proves or disproves the "facts," myths, and legends that have grown up around it. Wherever possible I have let those involved—the paroled prisoners, civilian passengers, guards, crew members, rescuers, and eyewitnesses—tell their stories in their own words. I am hoping that the truth about the *Sultana* and the complete story of the disaster are finally told here.

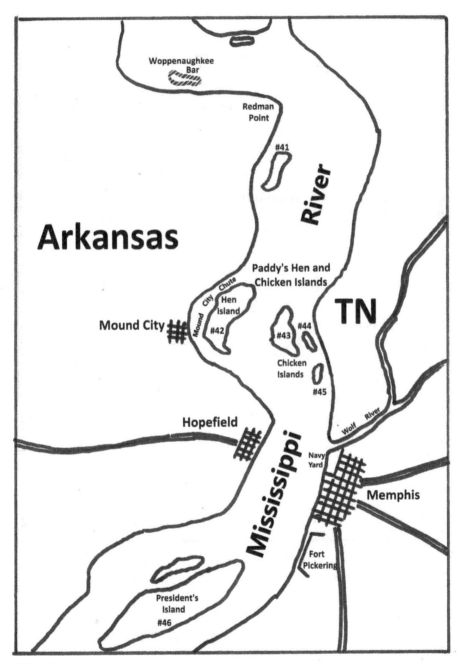

Memphis area

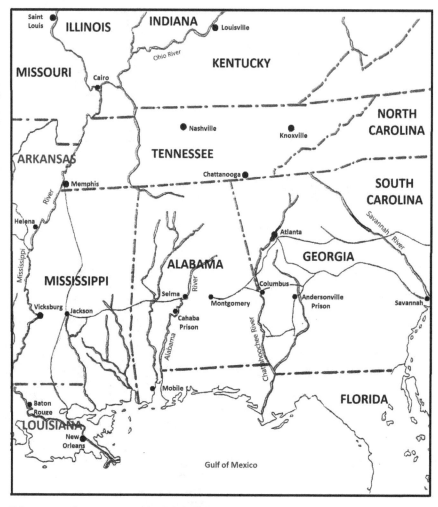

Mississippi River area in the Middle South

1

THE *SULTANAS*

"As some particulars have been published of the destruction by fire, lately, of the steamer *Sultana*, on the Mississippi river, it may not be uninteresting to your readers to learn the whole of the circumstances as they occurred under the eye of one of her passengers." The *New Albany Daily Ledger* went on to quote this eyewitness: "[S]omething like a thrill of horror came over me, as I looked around and saw the hideous fate we were escaping. By this time the fire had rapidly advanced, and the greater portion of the vessel was enveloped in flames." It was March 25, 1857, near Hickman, Kentucky. The entire steamboat burned to the waterline, although most of those on board were saved. The fourth steamboat named *Sultana* had come to a fiery end.[1] It would be six years before another Mississippi steamboat carried the name *Sultana*.

The first steamboat named *Sultana* (a sultana is the wife or concubine of a sultan) was built in Cincinnati, Ohio, in 1836 by Capt. A. W. Tufts. A fast boat, *Sultana* (No. 1) set a couple of speed records going between Louisville, Kentucky, and New Orleans, Louisiana. At the time she was retired in February 1843, *Sultana* (No. 1) had run the Mississippi for seven years, almost unheard of on a river where the average lifespan of a steamboat was between four and five years due to accidents, snags, or fire.[2]

In August 1843 a second steamboat named *Sultana* was launched across the river from Louisville for Capt. Horace Pease.[3] Another fast boat, *Sultana* (No. 2) set records twice in 1844 and again in 1845; but when a new boat named *Sultana* came along in November 1847, Captain Pease retired his boat.[4]

Sultana (No. 3) was built more for work than glamor, and at 306 feet in length was one of the largest boats on the river. Carrying six boilers and "one engine expressly for lifting and lowering freight," the third *Sultana* was owned by Capt. Henry J. Moore and two St. Louis businessmen.[5] Though not fast, *Sultana* (No. 3) set a record for carrying 1,600 tons of freight from Quincy, Illinois, down to New Orleans in 1849.[6] On June 12, 1851, the two-and-a-half-year-old steamboat was docked at St. Louis when a spark from her blacksmith shop set her on fire. Three people died in the fire, and the boat was a total loss.[7]

In August 1851, a new *Sultana* was built at Paducah, Kentucky. Owned by four different individuals over her lifetime, it was *Sultana* (No. 4) that burned to the waterline some three miles below Hickman, Kentucky, on the night of March 25, 1857.[8] For the first time in twenty-one years, there was no *Sultana* on the Mississippi. Then, in the winter of 1862, in the middle of the Civil War, a new steamboat named *Sultana* was built at John Litherbury's boatyard near Cincinnati at a cost of $60,000.[9]

The fifth *Sultana*, still lacking her smokestacks, pilothouse, and other essential parts, was launched into the Ohio River on January 2, 1863. Many authors have incorrectly called the *Sultana* built in 1863 the SS *Sultana*. The *Sultana* was not a steamship, however; she was a privately owned Mississippi River steamboat; and she was a boat (i.e., she had a flat bottom and a low freeboard), not a ship. Built side by side with her twin sister, *Luminary*, and launched on the same date, the two vessels—the *Sultana*, owned by Capt. Preston Lodwick, and the *Luminary*, owned by Capt. John A. Williamson—were described as "large and splendid steamers designed for the New Orleans trade."[10] Although Confederate forces still blocked the Mississippi River, both captains knew that the South could not hold onto the river much longer and that the lucrative cotton trade with the lower South would soon be wide open.

Captain Lodwick was fifty-two years old when he approached the commission firm of David Gibson & Company with the idea of building the new *Sultana*.[11] Generally speaking, steamboats were not built from blueprints. Most sidewheelers were identical and varied only in their measurements and fancy work. Atop the hull was the main deck, which held the coal or wood bins, the furnace and boilers, and the engines. On either side of the hull, situated about two-thirds back from the bow, was a paddlewheel. Wide guards built out over the water from the paddlewheel housings prevented the paddlewheels from "sticking out" from the sides of the hull and also provided additional cargo space. Behind the engines was an enclosed cargo area for livestock or deck passengers.

A wide stairway at the front of the main deck led up to the second deck, or boiler deck—a misnomer because the boilers were actually on the main deck. The main cabin, or main saloon, which occupied most of the second deck, was a long, cavernous social hall flanked on both sides by staterooms, most for single passengers but a few for families. The steamboat office and bar were at the forward end of the main saloon, and the last fifty feet or so could be closed off with a curtain for a ladies' parlor where the gentler sex could seek refuge.

Plain stairways led up to the next deck, the wide-open hurricane deck, which was actually the roof over the main saloon. The hurricane deck was covered with tar and felt, mixed with sawdust or sand, to help reduce the possibility of fire from a live spark thrown from the chimneys, as river folk called the smokestacks. The center of the hurricane deck was raised to form a skylight over the main saloon. Set atop the raised skylight roof was the texas cabin where the steamboat's officers lived. High on top of the texas cabin roof was the all-important pilothouse.[12]

Sultana (No. 5) was 260 feet long, with a 42-foot beam and a 7-foot-deep hold. Litherbury had her hull "extra fastened" to protect against damage from snags and floating debris. The twin paddlewheels, 34 feet in diameter with 11-foot-long buckets, or paddles, gave *Sultana* (No. 5) an overall width of perhaps 70 feet. Rated to carry 1,000 tons of cargo, she would draw roughly 5 feet of water when fully loaded.[13]

During the early 1860s, steamboat builders began to install tubular boilers rather than the old-style flue boilers earlier steamboats had carried. Flue boilers were built horizontally side by side and had two to five return flues, or tubes, running the length of the boilers. The draft of the chimneys pulled the superheated air under the boilers to the back, then forward through the return flues down the center of the boilers, then out the front and up the chimney. As the hot air rushed through the flues, the water in the boilers boiled and turned to steam. The steam then rose up into a steam drum sitting atop the boilers and passed down the main steam line to the engines.

By contrast, tubular boilers, also arranged horizontally side by side on the main deck, each had a dozen or more smaller flues or tubes running through the boiler, thereby greatly increasing the amount of heat being transferred to the water. An engineer noted that they were "smaller and consequently much lighter and less cumbersome and consume less fuel, and . . . therefore especially adapted to our Western rivers where a light draft of water and deck room is so desirable."[14] The *Sultana's* four high-pressure boilers, manufactured by Gaylord, Son & Company, Forge Iron Works of Cincinnati, were only 18 feet long by 46 inches in diameter, "of cylindrical form," each containing twenty-four 5-inch-diameter return flues.[15] Each boiler was constructed of charcoal-hammered No. 1 iron, 17/48 inch thick, while the tubes were ⅛ inch thick.[16] The two high-pressure engines were manufactured by Moore & Richardson, Locomotive and Marine Engine Builders, with cylinders 25 inches in diameter and an 8-foot stroke.[17]

Sultana (No. 5) had thirty-eight staterooms with two berths in each, allowing her to carry seventy-six cabin passengers. A "good piano" sat in the ladies' cabin in the rear of the main saloon. The boat and all its furnishing had been built by Cincinnati suppliers. The cabin, staterooms, and carpentry work were done by the Marine Railway and Dry Dock Company; the carpet was manufactured by John Shillito & Company; the upholstery, mattresses, and bedding came from Charles B. Prather; and the glassware, china, and tableware were from Hunnewell, Hill & Company. The ornate gas chandeliers were from McHenry & Carson, wholesalers in gas fixtures and lamps. Even the outside guy lines and metalwork were manufactured in Cincinnati. The rigging, lines, and blocks came from Harcourt & Meek, while the tin, copper, and sheet iron were by William H. Lape and Company.[18] *Sultana* (No. 5) was the pride of Cincinnati both inside and out.

In terms of safety, the new *Sultana* carried two lifebelts per state-room. Three fire pumps and thirty round-bottom fire buckets marked "Fire Only" were placed at strategic points throughout the steamer. (The round bottom prevented them from being used as regular mop-ping buckets because they wouldn't stand upright.) *Sultana* (No. 5) carried five axes and one metal lifeboat (usually stored upside-down on the hurricane deck so it wouldn't fill with rainwater). A small sounding yawl, which hung from the stern, was mainly used by the crew to sound the depth of the river.[19]

The boilers, always the worry of any steamboat captain or owner, had their own safety devices. The set of four boilers had two weighted safety valves set to open and let out excess steam if the internal pres-sure rose above 145 pounds per square inch (psi). Two water supply pipes three inches in diameter had "sufficient means to keep the water [inside the boilers] at all times and under all circumstances up to four inches over the flues." A metal alloy "safety guard" fused open auto-matically at 150 psi and could not be closed again, unlike the safety valves.[20] In terms of both luxury and safety, the new *Sultana* seemed to have it all.

While the *Sultana* was under construction, Captain Lodwick began recruiting a crew. Steamboat crews fell into three distinct groups: officers, cabin crew, and deck crew. Captain Lodwick himself would act as the master, giving "his attention primarily to over-all direction, particularly to the management of the boat as a business enterprise." "On the western rivers," steamboat historian Louis C. Hunter explained, " . . . the captain was often less skilled in the han-dling of boat and machinery than the other officers and in practice if not in law, his authority under some conditions was subordinate to that of the pilot."[21]

The first and second mates had the job of getting the unskilled deckhands to load and unload freight in a fast and efficient manner. "To place the cargo in the hold and deck room and above the guards so as to distribute the strain evenly over the hull and supporting chains, keep the boat in trim, and give it easy running qualities," Hunter noted, "called for both skill and intelligence. If the cargo were badly distributed the boat's draft would be increased, the effectiveness of the paddle wheels diminished, and the tendency to list and roll accentuated."[22]

The pilot of a steamboat, usually the most skilled officer on board, was one of only two individuals on the boat requiring a license. Once the boat was under way, his word was law. A captain could suggest a certain route or ask for a stop at a certain landing, but if the pilot read the water and felt that the course would put the boat in peril or that the stop would be too hazardous, he could overrule the captain. It was the pilot, and the pilot alone, who set the course of the steamboat. Each steamboat carried two pilots who worked in shifts, six hours on and six hours off. Each pilot had to know the river in bright daylight, in the dark of night, in heavy rain, and in thick fog, because the safety of the passengers and other crew members was literally in the hands that rested on the pilot wheel.[23]

The other officer requiring a license was the engineer. There were usually two engineers on each boat, working in four-hour shifts. "His job was a hot, greasy, and generally thankless one," Hunter noted, "performed out of the public view and commanding little attention or interest save when something went wrong."[24]

The most worrisome part of an engineer's job was the care of the boat's boilers. Since steamboats on the lower Mississippi pumped in dirty river water to feed their boilers, the boilers often filled with mud, which settled in the bottom of the boilers and "lowered the efficiency of the engine, added to the hazards of operation, and necessitated frequent boiler cleanings."[25]

Historian Ken Watson described the job of cleaning a boiler:

> As soon as the boat was made fast the "mud valves" were opened, the fires drawn, the water released from the boilers, then the process of cleaning began. Entering the boiler shell through a manhole [at the top rear of each boiler], thus equipped with a hammer and a sharp-linked chain, the [engineer or, preferably, a young boy] chipped away at the hard scale by pounding it with the hammer, and by using

the chain with a sawing motion he cleaned the flues. The loose mud and sediment was then flushed out by a stream of water from a hose, connected to a hand-operated force pump.[26]

The chipping and sawing had to be done to each flue and to the bottom and sides of the boiler. It was a hard, painstaking job and one of the least glamorous of the engineers' trade, but it was essential if the engineers wanted to keep their vessel safe and in top operating condition.

The first clerk and second clerk worked in the steamboat office and were responsible for the overall management of the passengers and the steamboat's books. "The clerk was freight as well as passenger agent," Hunter noted, "soliciting cargo, fixing rates, bargaining with shippers, making out waybills, checking cargo, and the like. He also purchased fuel and supplies, handled the payroll, shared in the hiring and dismissal of the ordinary crew members, and performed a variety of other functions related to the management of the boat." At every landing, the clerk stood at the foot of the stageplank checking passengers and freight on board or off. At the worst landings, the second clerk handled the process, thereby gaining the unenviable nickname "mud clerk" because he sometimes stood ankle-deep in mud.[27]

Most steamboats carried a cabin crew resembling a hotel staff: stewards, cooks, waiters, cabin boys, and chambermaids. The deck crew, who made up about one-half of the entire crew, were confined to the lower deck and consisted of the firemen who stoked the big furnaces beneath the boilers and the deckhands who wrestled the freight.[28]

By the time *Sultana* (No. 5) was ready to take on passengers and freight for her first trip, Captain Lodwick had a robust crew for his beautiful new vessel. "The *Sultana* is one of the largest and best business steamers ever constructed," proclaimed the *Cincinnati Commercial Tribune* on February 4, 1863. "Passengers . . . may anticipate an agreeable trip on the *Sultana*."[29]

2

THE FIRST TWO YEARS

S*ultana* (No. 5) ran into trouble right away. On February 11, 1863, she set off from Cincinnati for Pittsburgh on her maiden voyage carrying six hundred tons of freight and a fair number of passengers. The *Commercial Tribune* reported that "the *Sultana* glided off gracefully from the levee, her machinery working beautifully, and her movement indicating something more than ordinary speed." Unfortunately, the river was rising, and the new boat could not get under the suspension bridge at Wheeling, Virginia (West Virginia would not become a state until June 20, 1863). Because he had built his boat for the cotton trade, Captain Lodwick had installed extra-tall smokestacks to prevent any sparks from falling onto his intended cargo. The *Sultana* unloaded at Wheeling, took on coffee and sugar, and returned downriver to Cincinnati.[1]

For her first four weeks, the *Sultana* ran between Cincinnati and Wheeling, but in mid-March she was tabbed for "government service," and Captain Lodwick took her downriver toward the Cumberland River and then Nashville, Tennessee, earning a government paycheck. Most steamboat captains did not like having their vessels requisitioned by the government, because they could make more money carrying regular passengers and regular freight and cargo on scheduled runs. And when the government took over a boat, rules and regulations regarding passengers and cargo went by the wayside. The number of troops crowded on board was often three or four times the boat's legal carrying capacity. While oceangoing vessels were bound by national and international laws and regulations regarding what and how much they could carry, no such law governed inland river vessels. In 1825, the U.S. Supreme Court had ruled that "admiralty jurisdiction was limited to tidewater." That is, maritime laws did not apply to inland river commerce.

With the influx of river traffic after Robert Fulton's first commercial steamboat appeared in 1807, accidents began to occur with much greater frequency. When the federal government refused to act, several individual states passed laws intended to prevent such accidents and to hold steamboat captains and their owners responsible. When rivers ran through several states, however, there were difficult jurisdictional problems.[2]

After a boiler explosion on the steamboat *Moselle* killed 160 people in 1838, Congress finally got involved. The Steamboat Act of 1838, enacted for "the better security of the lives of passengers," stipulated that engineers had to be licensed, that owners and captains were responsible for all disasters unless they could prove otherwise, and that steamboat boilers had to be inspected. Unfortunately, the act proved almost useless. Federal inspectors were given no standards, and many were unqualified. Congress, unwilling to interfere with a growing industry, hoped that the steamboat captains and owners would regulate themselves by a "law of discretion" and let their moral convictions guide them toward better control and management.[3]

In the following years, however, the "law of discretion" proved almost nonexistent. Boiler explosions and steamboat fires and collisions continued with regularity. In early 1852, after several steamboat boiler explosions resulted in the deaths of about 250 people, Senator Thomas Jefferson Rusk of Texas had had enough. "This is the only country in the world, which has not passed stringent laws to regulate the manner in which that powerful agent, steam, is to be employed by individuals; this is the only country in the world where human life would be recklessly and wantonly sacrificed to the cupidity of steamboat proprietors."[4] In August, Congress passed the Steamboat Act of 1852, calling for, among other things, hydrostatic testing of boilers and placing limits on the amount of steam pressure allowed in them. New safety regulations required steamboats to carry lifebelts and firehoses.

The new act also stipulated that not only engineers but also pilots had to be licensed, and that both had to pass an examination before getting their license. Furthermore, the act stated that these licensed individuals had the exclusive power to override instructions from the steamboat captain if they perceived danger in their areas of operation. Steamboat inspectors likewise had to be federally licensed and trained and were given the exclusive power to sideline a steamboat indefinitely until the captain or owner had repaired any disclosed violations of the regulations.[5]

Perhaps because of the new act, accidents and loss of life on the western rivers declined between 1853 and 1860. But the start of the Civil War in 1861 changed that. Viewing rivers as the quickest and easiest way to move troops from point A to point B, the Union and Confederate governments often requisitioned steamboats over the protests of owners, captains, and even passengers.[6] Neither government paid much attention to the Steamboat Acts of 1838 and 1852. Legal carrying capacities were routinely ignored. U.S. Supervising Inspector of Steam Vessels John J. Witzig complained, "I have frequently protested, and the military commander would tell me 'it was a necessity.'" The number of accidents on the western rivers increased throughout the war.[7]

When the war first began, the federal government chartered boats in order to have them immediately available for service. Assistant Quartermaster Capt. F. S. Winslow wrote that chartering boats "gave the Government officers absolute control over floating storehouses, ready, at a moment's notice, to go in all imaginable directions." Soon, however, chartering was seen as an unnecessary cost. Maj. Gen. James L. Donaldson, supervising quartermaster of the Department of the Cumberland, noted that "whether boats were working or lying up, delaying along the rivers, or hurrying back and forward, as they should do, the pay was the same, and it was too lucrative to be will-ingly yielded."[8]

Instead of chartering boats, the chief of rail and river transporta-tion, Maj. Gen. Lewis B. Parsons Jr., "made temporary contracts by the hundred pounds or by the piece for government transportation, and discharged all boats from charter." Under the contract system, owners and captains would be paid a set amount for each trip depend-ing on the amount of freight or troops carried. "By the change from charter by the day to service by the pounds," General Donaldson said, "it can be easily shown that the Government saved one to two million dollars in its operations."[9]

Operating under the contract system, steamboat owners began charging the government per person to ship troops along the river, sometimes at exorbitant rates.[10] Eventually, the government began regulating the amount of money that could be charged for the trans-portation of troops and freight. In due course, the average cost to ship troops was settled at "one-third of one cent per man per mile."[11]

After Captain Lodwick delivered his government freight to Nashville in mid-March 1863, the *Sultana* returned to Cincinnati. Throughout the rest of March and early April she shipped back and forth between Wheeling and Nashville.[12] On May 8, the *Sultana* headed toward Memphis on her first Mississippi River run. The *Daily Missouri Republican* of St. Louis described "this beautiful steamer" as "another model of Cincinnati boat building [that] reflects credit on the builders and furnishers. . . . She is a light draught boat, and intended for the St. Louis and New Orleans trade. We wish Capt. Pres success and good luck and trust he will make a 'pocket full of rocks.'"[13]

Once he reached Memphis, Captain Lodwick decided to see just how fast his new steamer was. The *Memphis Daily Bulletin* reported: "One of the most exciting events to river men which has occurred at the landing during the war took place yesterday. It was the departure of three magnificent packets for up river ports. It was supposed that a race would take place on the Mississippi river last night that would awaken more interest than any other similar event which has taken place in years." The three steamboats—the *City of Alton*, the *Sultana*, and the *Belle Memphis*, the latter mastered by thirty-two-year-old Capt. James Cass Mason—set off at 6 p.m. on May 9 for Cairo, Illinois. The *Belle Memphis* got to Cairo first, laid over there for fifty minutes, and left before the other two boats even came into sight.[14]

The *Sultana* was not in sight because she had been stopped at Columbus, Kentucky, by U.S. government officials and ordered to carry federal troops back downriver to Memphis. On May 18 the *Sultana* was still under government contract. Along with her sister the *Luminary* and three other steamboats, she was carrying troops down to Vicksburg when a Confederate artillery battery fired on the boats and an escorting gunboat, the *Linden*, just above Greenville, Mississippi. The Confederate shells tore into the lead steamboat, injuring twelve people, before the *Linden* could respond. After firing about twenty-five shells at the battery, the *Linden* landed Union infantry who went in pursuit and eventually burned the town of Greenville.[15]

When Maj. Gen. Ulysses S. Grant began the siege of Vicksburg on May 18, the *Sultana* and *Luminary* were there. Both vessels carried "stores for the army" downriver and "the wounded and prisoners" back upriver to Memphis. On one trip, the *Sultana* returned upriver carrying a Confederate prisoner who had deserted with important correspondence meant for a Confederate commander bringing reinforcements to Vicksburg. The *Sultana* remained "on Government account" throughout all of June and until Vicksburg capitulated on July 4, 1863.[16] Five days later, the last Confederate bastion on the Mississippi, Port Hudson, Louisiana, fell and President Lincoln proclaimed, "The Father of Waters again goes unvexed to the sea." On July 18, the *Sultana*, still in government service and "with a load of government horses and mules on board," finally went all the way upriver to St. Louis. It was her first visit to the city that would eventually become her home port.[17]

On July 29, 1863, the *Sultana* was near Island No. 53, about forty-five miles below Memphis, headed upriver toward St. Louis carrying three Union generals and troops from the XIII Army Corps when about thirty Confederates soldiers fired on her. The shots "damaged [the *Sultana*'s] upper works," and although none of the generals was injured, a private of the 29th Wisconsin Infantry was mortally wounded.[18]

By August 1863 the *Sultana* was back in private business. Captain Lodwick left St. Louis for New Orleans on August 7 and arrived there eleven days later, completing the first of the boat's many trips down to the Crescent City.[19]

In October, the eight-month-old *Sultana* was moved up to Mound City, Illinois, just above Cairo on the Ohio River, for moderate repairs and a coat of white paint that "made a great improvement in her appearance."[20] By early November she was ready to resume her travels. With Captain Lodwick commanding, the *Sultana* left St. Louis on November 18 carrying a load of government supplies for Memphis and troops from the 42nd Ohio Infantry for New Orleans. Just below the mouth of the Red River, Confederate guerrillas once again fired into Captain Lodwick's boat. A few of the lady passengers "fainted and fell into the arms of any who chanced to be near," and the infantrymen of the 42nd Ohio "delivered a few volleys . . . before the boat had passed out of danger." No one was injured, and the *Sultana* continued on to Memphis and New Orleans.[21]

During December 1863 and the first part of January 1864, the *Sultana* sat idle at Cairo because the river near St. Louis was blocked by ice. "There are now fifty-four steamers at [Cairo], . . . laid up to await the opening of navigation," a St. Louis newspaper reported. By the third week of the new year the ice had melted, and river commerce continued, with the *Sultana* once again doing government work. She remained in government service throughout February.[22]

Then, on March 1, 1864, a Louisville newspaper reported that Preston Lodwick had sold his fine steamer to four individuals from St. Louis. William A. Thornburgh of R. & W. A. Thornburg, house and steamboat painters, and Logan D. Dameron of Nanson, Dameron & Company, commission and forwarding agents in the grain trade, bought a one-quarter share each. John H. Bowen of Bowen and Martin, commission merchants, bought a one-eighth share, and Capt. James Cass Mason, formerly of the *Belle Memphis*, the victor in the three-boat race back in May 1863, bought a three-eighths share. On March 31, John Bowen would sell his one-eighth interest to Logan

Dameron, giving Dameron a three-eighths share equal to Mason's holding. "Capt. Lodwick has sold the *Sultana* to Capt. J. C. Mason and others, of St. Louis, for $85,000," the *Louisville Daily Democrat* reported.[23] After owning *Sultana* (No. 5) for a little more than a year, sixty-four-year-old Preston Lodwick had made a nice little profit of $20,000.

Of the four buyers, Captain Mason had the most interesting background. Born in Lynchburg, Virginia, around 1831, he was raised in Missouri and grew up beside the river. His first work on steamboats was as a clerk, then as master or owner on boats primarily running on the Missouri River. On November 27, 1860, Mason married Rowena Mary Dozier, the second daughter of wealthy farmer and steamboat owner James Dozier. James Dozier had contracted for the construction of the steamboat *Rowena* in 1858, and his son Frank Dozier was her master. James Cass Mason worked as a clerk on the boat until October 11, 1861, when he bought out the interest of his brother-in-law Capt. Frank Dozier and became the master of his wife's namesake boat.[24]

In mid-June 1862, Mason took the boat down the Mississippi for the first time. Mason and the *Rowena* traveled back and forth between St. Louis and Memphis until early February 1863, when the boat was stopped near Island No. 10 and inspected for contraband goods. In the subsequent search, the crew of the gunboat *New Era* discovered a passenger concealing two hundred ounces of quinine intended for the Confederacy. A navy prize crew took the *Rowena* the rest of the way down to Memphis. When her cargo was being unloaded, "[a] further examination revealed that some of the cases entered as dry goods on the permits of shipment contained gray clothing." In all, two thousand pairs of trousers destined for Confederate soldiers were discovered, along with a few revolvers. The *Rowena*'s officers were arrested, and the *Rowena* was sent to Cairo for adjudication.[25] Captain Mason had been caught aiding and abetting the Confederacy.

Although Mason and the others were eventually released, the *Rowena* remained in government hands, along with several other steamboats that had been seized. For the next few weeks, the confiscated boats, with government crews, ran supplies down to Grant's army in Mississippi. On March 20, a U.S. marshal announced that the U.S. district attorney for the Southern District of Illinois had filed suit "against the steamer *Rowena*, her engines, boats, tackle, apparel and furniture, in a cause of condemnation and forfeiture." The *Rowena* was to be sold at public auction in April.[26]

The sale never took place. On April 18, while still in government service, the *Rowena* hit a snag and sank about thirty miles above Cairo. "She was coming out from St. Louis with a load of supplies for the fleet," the *Cincinnati Commercial Tribune* reported. In July, a public auction was held for her remains and machinery. The auction advertisement noted that the U.S. government was selling "the wreck of the steamer *Rowena*, as it now lies in the Mississippi River [and] the Engines, Boilers, &c., of the steamer *Rowena*, as they now lay on the levee at Cairo."[27] After the seizure and then the total loss of the *Rowena*, James Dozier cut off all interaction with his irresponsible son-in-law.

The resilient Mason landed on his feet. On March 30, 1863, within weeks of his release by Union authorities, he was back in command of another steamboat, the *Belle Memphis*. For the next year, Mason ran back and forth between St. Louis and the downriver towns, eventually taking the *Belle Memphis* all the way to New Orleans after Vicksburg and Port Hudson fell. Known for his recklessness, Mason was not against running his boat at top speed or engaging in an occasional race, as he did against *Sultana* (No. 5) and the *City of Alton* in May 1863. In February 1864, when he left the *Belle Memphis* and bought into the *Sultana*, his officers presented him with "an unusually fine diamond ring." Captain Mason was described as "spare-built, about five feet ten inches in height, light complexion, sandy whiskers and moustache."[28]

Mason took command of the *Sultana* for the first time on March 9, 1864, and made a government run down to New Orleans and back again at the end of March.[29] By the time the *Sultana* returned to St. Louis, General Parsons of the Quartermaster's Department had set a new transport rate. From St. Louis to New Orleans, the rate for "commissioned officers, horses and cattle" was now set at $2 for the first 100 miles, and then $1 each hundred for the next 600 miles. For miles

800–900 the rate dropped to 50 cents for each hundred miles, and for miles 1,000– 1,200 the cost was 25 cents each hundred. The rate went back up to 50 cents for the final 100 miles. If an officer, horse, or cattle traveled the full 1,250 miles from St. Louis to New Orleans, the government paid the steamboat captain $10.25 per officer or animal for the entire trip.[30]

The rates for transportation of enlisted men were set at $1 for the first 100 miles and 50 cents for the second hundred. After that, all additional miles were paid at 25 cents per 100 miles. For the same 1,250-mile trip from St. Louis to New Orleans, the captain of a steamboat could expect to receive $4.25 per man. To ship freight the same distance, the aggregate cost for the entire trip would be 50 cents per 100 pounds.[31]

Before Captain Mason could set off on his second trip as master of the *Sultana*, however, he was summoned to Washington, DC, along with the secretary for the steamboat line that had managed the *Rowena*. In the meantime, the *Sultana*, commanded by Capt. William Thompson, carried government supplies and troops on numerous occasions through April, May, and the first week of June.[32] On June 10, the steamboat was released from government work, and Captain Thompson took her downriver to New Orleans. Without any government freight, and competing for passengers and cargo with dozens of other steamboats plying the Mississippi, "the *Sultana* came in from St. Louis rather light."[33]

Captain Mason took over command of the *Sultana* when he returned from Washington and set out for New Orleans on July 2. When the *Sultana* returned to St. Louis on July 16, she carried "a goodly number of passengers, but no freight."[34] Instead of the business boom that most steamboat owners expected once the Mississippi River opened up, the opposite occurred. There were suddenly too many boats and not enough business.[35]

On July 29, 1864, when the *Sultana* was six miles above Cairo on another trip down to New Orleans, with the river at low stage, Captain Mason came upon the steamboat *Henry Ames*, which had struck a snag and was sinking fast. The *Sultana*, along with the steamers *Olive Branch* and *Emperor*, took off all of the sinking boat's deck load, which included two hundred head of cattle and a number of passengers, but could do nothing to stop her from sinking. As she continued on toward Cairo with the rescued cattle and passengers, the *Sultana* herself struck a rock as she rounded out from the Mississippi into the Ohio River. "The rock forced its way partly through the hull on her starboard knuckle, and she shipped so much water that the lower tier of freight in her hull was damaged," reported a St. Louis newspaper. Always the daredevil, Captain Mason was not going to let a hole in the bow of his boat keep him from making a profit. "A bulkhead was immediately built, the water pumped out . . . [and the *Sultana* was] under way to complete her trip in six hours."[36]

On August 18, Captain Mason put his vessel "on the docks" at Daggett & Morse Sectional Dock Company at Carondelet, Missouri, immediately south of St. Louis to make permanent repairs to the damaged hull. By September 3 she was ready for another trip downriver. "The *Sultana* has been repaired and refitted, and is one of the handsomest steamers afloat," crowed the *Daily Missouri Democrat*.[37]

On October 4, while coming upriver from New Orleans carrying a paltry 316 barrels of flour and a few boxes of maize, the *Sultana* was nearing Cape Girardeau, Missouri, when she came upon the steamboat *M. S. Mepham*, which had just struck a snag. Taking the crippled boat in tow, the *Sultana* pulled the *Mepham* down to a wood yard below the Cape and then started upriver again. Unbelievably, the *Sultana* hit the same snag "and was so damaged" that she once again had to go in for repairs.[38] For the second time in less than four months, Mason's steamer needed costly repairs at a time when steamboats in general were suffering financially.

After the second hole was repaired, the *Sultana* set off for New Orleans on October 23 carrying a sizable amount of freight and livestock and a good number of passengers. Once again, however, the boat ran into trouble in low water, grounding out about twenty-five miles above Cape Girardeau. The crew put the livestock ashore to lighten the load but had to wait until November 1 to get their boat afloat again, reload the livestock, and continue downriver to New Orleans. By the time Captain Mason started back upriver on November 12, his fellow owners in St. Louis—William Thornburgh and Logan Dameron—had enrolled the *Sultana* in a new steamboat organization, the Merchants' and People's Line. Boats belonging to the group would compete against those of a rival line, the Atlantic and Mississippi Steamship Company. The latter carried freight destined for New York City and the east coast via New Orleans. The Merchants' and People's Line would deal only with service between St. Louis and New Orleans, forgoing any freight destined for the eastern seaboard.[39]

The *Sultana* made her last trip of the season on December 4, once again going downriver to New Orleans.[40] On coming back upriver with "very light freight and scarcely any people," she "ran in heavy ice from [Cairo] to Commerce [Street in St. Louis]," a St. Louis newspaper reported. "The ice was very heavy and ran slowly, but there was no gorge." Although the ice was not "a gorge" (i.e., it did not solidly block navigation), steamboats risked damage coming through it. The *Daily Missouri Democrat* reported on December 31, "Steamers actually arrived here yesterday direct from Cairo, having encountered no gorge, but with their wheels more or less demolished from the heavy ice through which they ran." One of the boats fighting through the heavy ice was the *Sultana*.[41] Once again, the impetuous Captain Mason had pushed his boat beyond the limit. He finished 1864 facing more costly repairs, this time to *Sultana*'s paddlewheel buckets.

3

HARD FINANCIAL
TIMES

lthough Mason had advertised for a January 5, 1865, trip to
New Orleans, a huge ice gorge blocked the entire Mississippi
River twenty-five miles above Cairo until late January.[1] Finally,
on February 5, with newly repaired paddlewheel buckets, *Sultana* (No.
5) left St. Louis. On board was a new first clerk, "Mr. W. J. Gambrel,
late a merchant of Kansas City."[2]

William Jordan Gambrel had been born in Virginia in 1825
and brought up in St. Louis. He eventually moved to Kansas City,
Missouri, and worked in a commission business. In 1855, at age
thirty, he married seventeen-year-old Ida R. Brown. William Jordan
Gambrel Jr. was born three years later, and in 1861 a daughter came
into the family. Her name, Rowena Mason Gambrel, suggests that
William and Ida had more than a passing friendship with James and
Rowena Mason. In 1863 the Gambrel family moved to St. Louis, and
in early 1865 William became first clerk on the *Sultana*, with William
D. Shanks of St. Louis as the mud clerk.[3]

As Captain Mason started out on this first trip of 1865 he was
hurting for money. He had made no trips—and thus received no
income—for the past six weeks, and the recent repairs to the *Sultana*

had been expensive. Times were rough for all the steamboats. There were now two competing steamboat lines carrying freight and passengers down to New Orleans. "An interesting season may be expected on the Mississippi," the *Daily Missouri Democrat* noted on February 8, "with two such excellent packet lines as the 'Merchants' and People's' and the 'Atlantic and Mississippi Steamship.'" It was no wonder, then, that Mason got under way as soon as the ice block below St. Louis broke, becoming "the first boat . . . since the close of navigation, by the gorge."[4]

The daring Captain Mason pushed his steamboat hard, reaching New Orleans on February 13 and returning to the Gateway City on February 20. Within three days he was on his way again. As the *Sultana* moved downriver, the Mississippi got noticeably higher as the heavy winter snows and rains farther north swelled its tributary rivers. Two days after the *Sultana* reached New Orleans, on March 2, the *Times-Picayune* was warning its readers, "There is an abundance of water coming."[5]

On March 4, the *New-Orleans Times* reported that Captain Mason's *Sultana* and Capt. Benjamin P. Tabor's *Olive Branch* would leave simultaneously for St. Louis on March 5, suggesting that perhaps a race was in store. Like the *Sultana*, the *Olive Branch* had been built in 1863, but at 283 feet she was 23 feet longer, and she carried 6 regular flue boilers instead of the *Sultana*'s 4 tubular boilers. Mason was never one to turn down a challenge. The clerk of the *Olive Branch* later reported, "At Stock Yard we found the hitherto invincible steamer *Sultana*, waiting for us to come up, she having boasted while in port that she would pass the *Olive Branch* under way." The two steamboats left New Orleans "side by side . . . with the intention of trying the power of steam."[6]

The *Olive Branch* shot into the lead and stopped at Donaldsonville, Louisiana, seventy-eight miles upriver from New Orleans, well ahead of the *Sultana*. Captain Mason's boat passed her at Donaldsonville and took a one-mile lead, but the *Olive Branch* caught up, and the two boats pulled into Baton Rouge, 130 miles from New Orleans, side by side. When the *Olive Branch* was detained in New Orleans and left twenty-five minutes after the *Sultana*, Mason shot into the lead again.

The *Sultana* was five miles ahead of the *Olive Branch* as she passed Morganza, Louisiana, but the race soon tightened. A passenger on the *Sultana* reported that she "was delayed three minutes at Red River, [and] also delayed six minutes at Fort Adams, where the *Olive Branch* overtook and passed the *Sultana* before she stopped her wheels. When the *Sultana* started again she was but a few lengths astern of the *Olive Branch*, yet did not arrive at Natchez until after the *Olive Branch* had been landed thirty-seven minutes."[7]

At Natchez, the federal government stepped in and ended the race. "At this port Uncle Sam had use for us," the clerk of the *Olive Branch* explained, "and we returned to New Orleans under orders." Captain Mason was having trouble with his boilers and was forced to lay over at Natchez for repairs, which may be one of the reasons why the government requisitioned only the *Olive Branch*.

Henry J. Lyda, a steward on the *Sultana*, reported that the boat "stopped at Natchez and Vicksburg on the last two trips . . . to patch and repair her boilers," indicating that the *Sultana* had repairs on two different trips. However, departure and arrival times printed in New Orleans and St. Louis newspapers show that the *Sultana* had only one extended trip in 1865, taking thirteen days going upriver between March 5 and March 18, the dates of the race. All other trips, both upriver and down, averaged between six and seven days, so Lyda may have been mistaken. The length of time taken indicates that all the repairs were made on the March 5–18 trip, with temporary repairs being made at Natchez and then more permanent repairs being made at Vicksburg, where qualified boiler mechanics could be found.[8]

Although tubular boilers like those the *Sultana* carried were just as safe and reliable as regular flue boilers under most conditions, they needed constant cleaning, which was difficult because of the many flues running through each boiler. While conventional flue boilers were generally cleaned at least once or twice per round trip, tubular boilers were supposed to be "cleaned about every five days." The boilers were filled with water taken directly from the river, which was always clouded with sediment. That was particularly the case "[d]uring the flood seasons of spring and fall," Louis Hunter noted, when "even the ordinarily clear water of the upper Mississippi and the

Ohio was turbid with suspended sand and silt, and in streams such as the Missouri and lower Mississippi the water was always muddy." If not removed frequently, the sediment that settled on the bottom of the boilers could cause pockets of hard sediment to form between the outer shell and the water inside the boiler. This in turn could cause problems, including an explosion.[9]

On March 18, the date the *Sultana* finally reached St. Louis, the *Memphis Argus* reported that the river was "at a stand at last, and much higher than it has been for years before. On this side it has narrowed the levee until there is not room enough for a dray to pass between the waters edge and the Government warehouse [directly above the levee]; and on the other side it covers the former site of the town of Hopefield." (Hopefield, Arkansas, directly opposite Memphis, had been burned on February 19, 1863, because it was suspected to be "a mere shelter for guerrillas." Only the charred shells of its few buildings remained.) "Opposite us the river is away out of the bank," the *Argus* said on March 23, "and overflowing the Arkansas country, for miles back. The water is so deep in the streets of Hopefield that good sized steamers can steam along without much difficulty."[10] The Mississippi was well out of its banks that spring. The Army Corps of Engineers, which in peacetime maintained the levees holding back the river, had been occupied elsewhere during the war, and many of the levees had given way. Opposite Memphis, the flooded river stretched three miles wide over the Arkansas bank.[11]

On March 24, Captain Mason registered the *Sultana* at the U.S. customs house in St. Louis by filling out the necessary Form C Enrollment, which licensed the boat to ply the Mississippi River system. The form listed William A. Thornburgh as a one-fourth owner of the *Sultana*, with Logan D. Dameron and Captain Mason owning three-eighths each. Shortly thereafter, however, Mason sold one-eighth of his interest to his first clerk, William J. Gambrel. But with two young children and another expected in October, Gambrel did not have the ready cash to pay Mason.[12] The money Mason needed was not coming from his new partner.

Within the next month, James Cass Mason, who now owned only a one-fourth share of the *Sultana*, would split his stocks twice. First, he sold a one-eighth interest in the steamboat to Samuel De Bow, a steamboat agent in New Orleans. A little while later, now owning only a one-eighth share himself, Mason split his stock again and sold one-half to William Shanks, his mud clerk, giving each man a one-sixteenth share. In a matter of only a few months, Mason had gone from owning a three-eighths controlling share in the *Sultana* to minority ownership.[13]

"Business remains in a very dull condition," the *Daily Missouri Democrat* reported on March 23 as Captain Mason made ready for another trip. There were just too many boats and not enough business. The St. Louis correspondent to the *Cincinnati Commercial Tribune* noted that "the *Sultana* has been loading for nearly a week, and has not yet completed her cargo."[14] The *Sultana* finally left St. Louis on March 26, arriving at New Orleans on April 1. Within two days Captain Mason was headed back upriver, carrying "a few passengers and but little freight." With the river at flood stage, Mason's two pilots, George J. Cayton and Henry Inghram, both of St. Louis, cut some corners on the river, going over flooded bends and thus shortening the route by dozens of miles, and the steamer arrived back in St. Louis on April 8 in record time. A Cairo newspaper clocked the trip at "4 days and 7 hours, the best trip of the season."[15]

Even with troublesome boilers, Mason's two-year-old boat could still fly. That record-setting trip earned Mason the coveted elk's antlers signifying the fastest boat on the river. He immediately mounted the antlers in the center of the lower set of two spreader bars holding his twin smokestacks apart, announcing to passengers wanting a fast trip and businessmen hoping to send their freight on the fastest steamboat that this was the boat they wanted.[16] Captain Mason was hoping that his speed record would pay off in cold, hard cash.

While Mason was making his record-setting trip, a couple of items appeared in St. Louis newspapers that would have a connection to the *Sultana* in the long run. The "once popular steamer" *Bostona* (No. 2) had been purchased by Capt. John Watson for $40,000. The 260-foot-long steamboat had been built at Cincinnati in 1860 and had seen better days, but Watson planned to "repair and thoroughly refit and refurnish the *Bostona* before she start[ed] south."[17] Captain

Watson's first trip downriver with his refurbished boat would have a great impact on the *Sultana*.

The other newsworthy article appeared in the *Daily Missouri Republican* on April 1. Titled "From Vicksburg: An Appeal for an Exchange of Prisoners," the article told how Brig. Gen. Morgan Lewis Smith, USA, commanding the Post and District of Vicksburg, had met with a representative of the Confederate government to work out an exchange of the prisoners of war both sides held. Under the agreement, "all Federal prisoners now in Georgia, Alabama and Mississippi [were] to be placed in a camp within four miles of the post of Vicksburg, Miss.," where they would await the arrival of Confederate soldiers held by the North for a man-for-man exchange. Although the Union soldiers would still be prisoners of the Confederacy, they would be clothed, fed, and cared for by the federal government until the official exchange. Between April 4 and April 21, the *Daily Missouri Democrat* published 3,792 names of Union prisoners who had arrived at the parole camp. The names had been forwarded to St. Louis by the assistant adjutant general at Vicksburg, Capt. Frederic Speed.[18] Before long, the destinies of Captain Speed, some of the prisoners, and the *Sultana* would intersect.

Fortunately for the cash-strapped Captain Mason, the Merchants' and People's Line had signed a contract with the U.S. government to be the sole company to transport Union troops. Although boats from the rival Atlantic and Mississippi Steamship Company could carry troops if no Merchants' and People's Line boats were available, the Merchants' line would get preference if steamboats from both lines were in port at the same time.[19] This contract would play a big role in the next few weeks in regard to the *Sultana*.

Hoping to make a quick turnaround after his record-setting trip, Captain Mason began advertising for an April 11 run down to New Orleans. The trip was delayed after John Schaffer and John Magwire, "Inspectors of Hulls and Steam Boilers for the District of St. Louis," boarded the *Sultana* on April 12 to conduct her annual inspection. The two inspectors subjected each of the four tubular boilers to a hydrostatic pressure of 210 psi, far above the prescribed working pressure of 145 psi. They also checked the two safety valves and noted that both were set to blow open if the pressure rose above 145 psi and that the safety guard of "alloyed metal" would fuse open if the pressure rose above 150 psi. Schaffer and Magwire were satisfied with what they found and turned the findings over to head customs collector Richard J. Howard and deputy collector John Samson, who signed off on the certificate.[20] The *Sultana*, up to date in all safety and machinery matters, was free to cruise for another year.

On April 13, Captain Mason and the *Sultana* were finally ready to set off for New Orleans. Ten hours before departure, however, steward Henry J. Lyda resigned his position. The boilers had passed inspection and the safety certificate had been signed, but Lyda had lost confidence in the *Sultana*'s boilers—and in her officers. Well aware that the boat had undergone multiple repairs on previous trips, Lyda reasoned that "the *Sultana*'s boilers were not fit for duty." He also felt that Mason and his engineers were careless. Unwilling to spend another trip on the unsafe vessel, Lyda left. He was replaced by Walter B. Smith.[21]

The *Sultana*'s first stop would be Cairo. In addition to having William Jordan Gambrel as his first clerk, Mason had young William "Willie" Stratton of St. Louis as his mud clerk, replacing William Shanks. The same two pilots who had set the most recent speed record for the *Sultana*, twenty-nine-year-old George J. Cayton, a licensed pilot for eight years, and twenty-two-year-old Henry Inghram, were once again in the pilothouse. Tending the boilers were thirty-four-year-old First Engineer Nathan Wintringer of Steubenville, Ohio, and forty-nine-year-old Second Engineer Samuel Clemens (not to be confused with the well-known author), a married man with five children and some twenty-five years of experience. Captain Mason's first mate was English-born William Rowberry, a thirty-seven-year-old married man with four children. Second Mate William Butler assisted him in keeping the unruly deckhands in line. Stewards Henry Cross and George Slater saw to the needs of the passengers, James Murphy and Sam McQueene took care of the pantry, and the bar was tended by affable barkeeps James O'Hara and Thomas McGinty. Junior stewards Alexander Durst (age fifteen) and George Mountain (age fourteen), helped out in the main saloon. Counting officers, cabin boys, firemen, chambermaids, and deckhands, the *Sultana* carried a crew of eighty-five as she started downriver toward Cairo.[22]

At 1 a.m. on Good Friday, April 14, the *Sultana* docked at the Cairo wharf boat. Mason found freight waiting at Cairo, shipped down the Ohio for destinations farther south, and was told that the *Sultana* could take "all she can carry." Planning on spending all day Friday in port loading the much-needed freight, Mason advertised in the *Cairo War Eagle* that the "regular and unsurpassed passenger packet" *Sultana* would be departing for New Orleans at 10 a.m. on Saturday, April 15, 1865.[23]

4

MESSENGER OF DEATH

Near 10:15 p.m. on the night of Friday, April 14, 1865, President Abraham Lincoln was shot at Ford's Theater in Washington, DC, by John Wilkes Booth. At almost the same time, another assassin attacked, but was unable to kill, Secretary of State William Seward in the secretary's home. A third assassin backed away from his assignment to assassinate Vice President Andrew Johnson at the Kirkwood House hotel. At 7:22 a.m. on April 15, Lincoln passed into eternity. Word of the president's death went out via telegraph immediately.[1]

When the news reached Cairo, the "bells on the boats and public buildings" began a slow, mournful tolling. Both of Cairo's newspapers—the *Democrat* and the *War Eagle*—came out with special editions in heavy black ink.[2] Grabbing up an armload of both papers, Captain Mason set off at about 5 a.m. (Cairo time) for New Orleans. Since the start of the Civil War, telegraphic communications below Cairo had been spotty because of severed telegraph lines. During these last few days of the war, as the Confederacy was coming apart, telegraphic communications with many areas of the South were nonexistent. The quickest way to spread news was along the rivers. The

Sultana set off from Cairo with her flag at half-staff and her railings draped with black bunting. Captain Mason intended to go down in history as the first boat to spread the news of Lincoln's death.[3]

The *Sultana* made the 259-mile trip downriver to Memphis in just over a day, arriving in the wee hours of Easter Sunday, April 16. All along the way, at every landing and way station, news of the assassination was shouted ashore. At Memphis, Mason and the crew spread the word and passed out a few copies of the special Cairo editions. A reporter with the *St. Louis Daily Missouri Republican* reported from Memphis that "news of the assassination of Pres. Lincoln and Sec. Seward has created intense excitement [the telegraph message from Washington had erroneously reported that William Seward had also been killed, and the Cairo newspapers repeated the message]. The city is to be draped in mourning."[4]

The residents of Memphis had been under Union occupation for almost three years by now and had made their peace with federal authorities. The city was home to almost a dozen Union hospitals and was a supply base for federal soldiers, and the citizens took the news of Lincoln's murder hard. The *Memphis Daily Bulletin* reported, "By order of the commanding General, all business will be suspended today, from sunrise to sunset, as a mark of respect to the memory of Mr. Lincoln. The *Sultana* was the first to bring the news of his assassination. She came in with flags at half-mast and decked in mourning."[5]

Leaving Memphis after only a short stop, trying to stay ahead of other steamboats, Mason raced downriver and reached Helena, Arkansas, near noon on April 17. Assistant Surgeon Daniel Berry (87th IL Inf) recalled her approach:

> One morning, from my quarters, I saw a long, low lying, side-wheel boat coming around the upper bend in the river. With us idlers every passing boat was an object of interest and speculation, particularly so if coming down the river as we were always hungry for news from home. With my glass I made out the name *Sultana*, and also that her flag was flying at half-mast. A flag at half-mast is a thing of evil. It is a daunting grief, a sign of distress or disaster. . . .

Wishing to know more of its story I hastened down to the wharf boat, and was one of the first to reach the clerk's office, where I was confronted with the startling proclamations announcing the assassination of President Lincoln. I distinctly recollect the shock those headlines produced on me. Had I myself received a mortal blow I could not have felt greater surprise.[6]

After telling the terrible news at Helena, Mason pushed off downriver again. Near sunset on Monday, April 17, the *Sultana* docked at the Vicksburg wharf boat, and once again Mason announced the tragedy. Within minutes, Capt. Reuben Benton Hatch, one of the many Union army officers in the city, came down to the levee to see Captain Mason.[7] Although Hatch was a personal friend of Lincoln, he was not there to talk of the assassination. He had something else to discuss.

By the time the *Sultana* reached Vicksburg, Confederate authorities had finally released the thousands of Union prisoners of war being held in the exchange camp outside the city, despite the fact that no Confederate prisoners were coming down from the North for the specified one-for-one exchange. With the Confederacy collapsing, the rebel government had agreed to release the men without the exchange. Within days, the paroled Union prisoners would be sent home on steamboats going upriver. The federal government was paying boat captains to carry the men north just as it would for the transportation of any troops. In these hard times, carrying a large load of prisoners could mean a nice windfall for a boat captain. It was with this in mind that Captain Hatch arrived at the *Sultana* that Monday night looking for the cash-strapped Captain Mason.[8]

Sultana survivor Rev. Chester D. Berry, in his monumental work *Loss of the* Sultana *and Reminiscences of Survivors* (1892), claimed that after the fall of Vicksburg in July 1863 General Grant had implemented a system in which steamboat captains were paid $10 for every officer and $5 for every enlisted man using river transportation. Survivor 1st Sgt. Nicholas Homer Karns (Co. B, 18th OH Inf) repeated Berry's claim in a series of reminiscences published in March and April 1898 in the *Lewisburg* (Ohio) *Leader.* Unfortunately, no official documents verifying these figures have been found, either in the 127 volumes of *The War of the Rebellion: A Compilation of the Official Records of the Union and Confederate Armies* or the 32 volumes of *The Papers of Ulysses S. Grant.*[9]

Capt. William Franklin Kerns, assistant quartermaster in charge of transportation at Vicksburg, remembered that the government had a contract that paid "so much per man, per hundred miles." As explained in chapter 3, the federal government would pay a certain amount per hundred miles up to a total of $10.25 per each officer and $4.25 per each enlisted man for the entire 1,250-mile trip from New Orleans to St. Louis.[10]

The newly released prisoners would be traveling from Vicksburg to St. Louis, a total of 880 river miles, so under the terms of the contract established by General Parsons, the chief of rail and river transportation, the government would pay $9 per officer and $3.25 per enlisted man for the trip.

When Captain Hatch went on board the *Sultana* on the evening of April 17, he undoubtedly knew the transportation rates being paid by the government. He also undoubtedly knew James Cass Mason. From November 1862 until February 1863 Hatch had been the assistant quartermaster at St. Louis, in charge of requisitioning boats for the federal government, while Mason was master of the *Rowena.* Then, from February to August 1863, Hatch was the chief quartermaster of the District of Eastern Arkansas, headquartered at Helena on the Mississippi River, while Mason was master of the *Belle Memphis.* Although there is no documentary evidence to prove that the men knew one another prior to their April 17, 1865, meeting on board the *Sultana,* they would have had ample opportunity to interact during the previous years. Subsequent circumstances suggest that they were at least acquaintances.

A few minutes before Captain Hatch boarded the *Sultana,* Miles Sells, the *Sultana's* agent in Vicksburg and a friend of Captain Mason, boarded the steamer and was told the terrible news of Lincoln's death. Mason and Sells were standing together when Captain Hatch, whom Sells also knew, came on board to see Mason. Although Sells was not privy to the conversation that took place when Hatch and Mason stepped aside, he later testified that Hatch told Mason that "there was a good deal of government freight and prisoners to ship." Hatch may also have offered the cash-strapped Mason a tempting deal.[11]

Both men were in financial straits at the time. In November 1863, the large merchandising store of R. B. Hatch & Company in Hatch's hometown of Griggsville, Illinois, had burned to the ground with all its stock. A Springfield, Illinois, newspaper reported, "The insurance is only partial, and the loss very heavy."[12] By April 1865, Hatch had still not recovered financially from the loss, and one look at the *Sultana*, which obviously needed paint and some major repair work, would have told Hatch that Mason was also in need of funds. Additionally, Hatch would have known that the *Sultana*'s boilers had been repaired in Vicksburg only a month earlier, since all steamboat arrivals had to be reported to the Quartermaster's Department. Hatch took Captain Mason aside, out of earshot from Miles Sells, to discuss a plan that could benefit them both.

If Hatch could guarantee Mason one thousand paroled prisoners to take back north, would Mason be willing to give Hatch a percentage of the earnings? Mason could be looking at a tidy sum if Hatch could guarantee one thousand men, but Hatch would provide them only if Mason agreed to a kickback. Although Sells did not hear the particulars of the conversation, he had the distinct impression that some type of a deal was made. After taking a copy of one of the Cairo "extras," Hatch left the *Sultana* secure in the belief that he and Mason had just agreed to a lucrative deal.[13]

Mason and Sells continued in conversation until Gen. Morgan Smith, the commander of the Post and District of Vicksburg, hobbled on board. The forty-four-year-old Smith had been wounded in the left hip in December 1862, and his left leg was now partially paralyzed. Smith was a river man himself. For fifteen years before the war he had worked on the Ohio and Mississippi in command of "a half dozen different steamers." Although Smith may have already known Captain Mason, the connection between the two men is less certain than the one between Mason and Hatch. Smith may have come on board the *Sultana* to inquire about the death of President Lincoln, but according to Sells, Captain Mason immediately "asked General Smith if he could give him a load [of released prisoners]" when he came back upriver. Mason already had Captain Hatch's assurance of that, of course, so perhaps Mason was hedging his bet. Sells recalled that "Smith promised he would."

After a time, General Smith climbed into his waiting buggy and offered Sells a lift to his lodgings. Sells would later claim that as they moved along, "Smith told me he could give Captain Mason a load as he came up, back [from New Orleans], and that if Hatch and Captain Speed didn't turn the men out to him, give him a load, to let him know." Sells agreed he would.[14]

Still trying to stay ahead of all of the other boats with the news, the *Sultana* took on a load of coal and set off from Vicksburg near 8 p.m. By sunup on Tuesday, April 18, she was 110 miles downriver from Vicksburg, nearing Natchez, Mississippi, still bearing news of Lincoln's death. On the bluffs overlooking the river was Cpl. Edwin L. Hobart (Co. D, 28th IL Inf), whose unit was doing provost duty in the city. Hobart recalled:

> Near me on the bluffs were two gentlemen—civilians—and our attention was attracted to the steamer *Sultana* descending the stream; her flag was half-masted, and she was tolling her bells at intervals of perhaps 30 seconds. I approached the two gentlemen, and remember of hearing them say that the steamer possibly had dispatches announcing the death of Secretary Seward, then known to be sick [from a buggy accident]. At any rate, it was ominous of some great National loss, and as the war was practically over it could not be a battle loss.
>
> As [the *Sultana*] rounded up to the levee a voice on board shouted, in reply to an inquiry, that *President Lincoln had been assassinated*. The *Sultana* had received the dispatches at Memphis [*sic*], and in those days of meager telegraphic facilities was the pioneer which brought us this sad announcement.[15]

A short while later, the *Sultana* was off again.

At 10 p.m. on April 18, the *Sultana* completed the 135-mile run from Natchez to Baton Rouge. "The President of the United States

Assassinated Friday Evening, April 14th," ran the morning head-lines. "Secretary Seward's Throat Cut the Same Night. The Actor John Wilkes Booth the Assassin of President Lincoln. . . . We are indebted . . . for a copy of the *Vicksburg Daily Herald*, brought down by the steamer *Sultana*." Newspapers reported that "the news created immense excitement. Business was entirely suspended, public offices closed, and flags placed at half-mast." Captain Mason stayed at Baton Rouge only a short time before turning the *Sultana*'s bow downriver for the last 133 miles to New Orleans.[16]

The *Sultana*—and the news—reached New Orleans at mid-morning on April 19, 1865. The *New-Orleans Times* lined its columns with bold black ink and thanked "Mr. Wm. J. Gambrel, the ever-attentive clerk of the *Sultana*, for the late river favors" (i.e., the Cairo newspapers). "Business on the landing yesterday was suspended throughout, and the steamers at the landing displayed their colors at half mast, in respect to the sudden demise of the President." On April 20, the *New-Orleans Times* lined its columns in black and on the first page published a poem entitled "Midnight Walk on Deck of the Steamer *Sultana*, Opposite Vicksburg, in April, 1865," dedicated to "Captain J. C. Mason, of the steamer *Sultana*, in memoriam of her being the first boat which carried the sad news of the assassination of President Lincoln and Secretary Seward into Dixie."[17]

National tragedy or not, Captain Mason continued on with his business. The *Sultana*'s boilers were thoroughly cleaned that very day under the immediate supervision of her first engineer, Nathan Wintringer, and the newspapers were advertising the departure of the steamer for 5 p.m. the next evening, April 20. Notwithstanding the *Sultana*'s distinction as the "Messenger of Death," Mason had a hard time acquiring a load of passengers and freight. Only one boat actually left New Orleans on April 20—Mason's old rival the *Olive Branch*, under Ben Tabor, the same captain Mason had raced in March. "The *Olive Branch* took out everything that offered for the West," the *Times-Picayune* noted. The steamboats *Lady Gay* and *Pauline Carroll* also remained in port, unable to get cargo. Hoping to add to his small load of passengers and freight, Mason decided to delay his departure for twenty-four hours, until 10 a.m. on April 21.[18]

A few more passengers boarded the *Sultana* during the delay, including Seth William Hardin Jr. (twenty-nine) and his lovely new wife, Hannah Sophia Osborne. Hardin, late an adjutant with the 53rd Illinois Infantry, was a partner in the banking house of Cushman, Hardin & Brothers in Chicago. He and his twenty-two-year-old bride had married on December 22, 1864, but delayed their wedding tour until the spring of 1865. Having finally honeymooned in New Orleans, the happy couple boarded the *Sultana* for their return trip to Illinois.[19]

A lone woman coming on board was thirty-five-year-old Jennie A. Perry, the wife of Acting Third Assistant Engineer William C. Perry of the ram *Tennessee*, then stationed near New Orleans. After a visit with her husband, she was now returning home to Cincinnati.[20] Another lone female passenger was thirty-nine-year-old widow Sarah "Sallie" Bowman Woolfolk from Lexington, Kentucky. In 1844, at the age of seventeen, Sallie had married her first cousin, Dudley Mitchum Woolfolk of Yazoo County, Mississippi, and gone to live on his two-thousand-acre plantation. In 1861 Dudley died of unspecified causes, leaving Sallie childless and fairly well off. When General Grant's Union army swept into Yazoo County during its move against Vicksburg, Sallie fled back to Lexington. Now, after visiting relatives in New Orleans, she boarded the *Sultana* carrying a gold watch and chain, $250 in gold in her purse, and a stack of well-read letters.[21]

Coming on board with a more substantial amount of gold were Samuel D. Spikes (fifty) from Assumption Parish, Louisiana, and his wife, Elethia (forty-two), along with their six children (Louisa, twenty-six; Lurany, twenty-three; DeWitt Clinton, nineteen; Elizabeth "Lizzie," seventeen; Susan E., seventeen; and a son whose name and age are not recorded), and a niece (Adeline). The family was moving from Louisiana to the North. They brought along the family Bible and $17,000 in gold, which was quickly deposited in the clerk's safe next to $15,000 in cash from the wholesale grocers and commercial merchant firm of Nanson, Ober & Company of St. Louis.[22]

Another person making his way onto the *Sultana* with a "large sum of money" was James Augustus B. Butterfield (twenty-nine), late a sergeant with Company A, 2nd Illinois Cavalry. Butterfield had enlisted in August 1861 and served with the regiment until he was discharged in August 1864 at the expiration of his three-year enlistment. He remained in government service as "chief citizen clerk for a Division Quartermaster" in Louisiana until April 1865, earning "a considerable salary." With the war drawing to a close, Butterfield "resigned his position and started home with the intention of announcing his candidacy for Sheriff of Ogle County, [Illinois]." Butterfield intended to use his savings to help his sixty-five-year-old widowed mother in Massachusetts.[23]

Not quite as wealthy was Canadian-born Daniel McLeod (twenty-two), late a private of Company F, 18th Illinois Infantry, who had been wounded in the right knee at Shiloh in April 1862. He had been taken to a Cincinnati hospital, where doctors had removed the musket ball and had wanted to remove the leg but for some reason refrained from doing so. McLeod was shuttled from hospital to hospital until he was finally mustered out of the service in June 1864. A butcher by trade, McLeod "was never able to make any use of that leg" afterward. He was receiving a pension of $8 per month, "the full pension at that time for entire disability."[24]

Robinson Hackleman (forty-four), a blacksmith by trade, was another ex-soldier who hobbled on board the *Sultana*. In August 1862 Hackleman had left his wife and seven children, including one newborn, to join Company C, 16th Indiana Infantry. On October 30, 1864, while the regiment was stationed near Berwick City, Louisiana, the constant "heavy picketing, scouting, &c., proved too heavy for his physical strength." Hackleman contracted chronic dysentery and suffered from "a large hydrocele" (a swollen scrotum), and was finally discharged at Thibodeaux, Louisiana, on April 7, 1865. He painfully made his way up the stageplank of the *Sultana* in New Orleans to head home to Rush County, Indiana.[25]

Booking passage on board the *Sultana* with a heavy heart was English-born Enoch Bent (fifty-three), a newly elected justice of the peace from Randall, Wisconsin. The father of seven had traveled down to New Orleans to bury his eldest son. Twenty-five-year-old Elijah Bent had waited until late September 1864 before joining the 95th Illinois Infantry. After the regiment moved to New Orleans in February 1865, Elijah was taken ill and passed away on April 14. Enoch had traveled down to New Orleans to see his son buried in Monument Cemetery.[26]

Also coming on board the *Sultana* in New Orleans was Lt. Col. Charles Elmer Compton (twenty-nine), 53rd US Colored Troops (USCT), bound for Memphis. After joining the 1st Indiana Infantry in May 1861, Compton had been in a couple of different regiments before becoming a lieutenant colonel of the 53rd USCT on December 9, 1864.[27] Passengers J. D. Fontaine (twenty-two) of Dallas City, Illinois, and William Long also boarded in New Orleans. Long was shown to Stateroom 10, close to the front of the main saloon. Perhaps getting rooms nearby were good friends Peter Martin and Pat Gray, both residents of New Orleans.[28]

By the time the *Sultana* was ready to leave on her upriver trip on April 21, she carried a crew of about 85 men and women, some 40 paying passengers, and a cargo of about 225 hogsheads of sugar (weighing about 1,200 pounds each, for a total of almost 135 tons). The cargo also included 97 boxes of wine (about 50 pounds each, for a total of about 2.5 tons), about 60 "fat hogs," and perhaps 40 or 50 "condemned horses and mules" deemed unfit for government service. Additionally, somewhere along the line the *Sultana* had acquired a mascot—a large pet alligator that was kept in a sturdy wooden box inside one of the paddlewheel housings.[29] The load was not a large one, but Captain Mason was hoping to pick up his promised 1,000 paroled Union prisoners of war at Vicksburg, making the trip well worthwhile.

After leaving New Orleans on the morning of Friday, April 21, the *Sultana* moved steadily upriver that day and all day Saturday, April 22, in spite of the heavy spring flooding. The *Vicksburg Daily Herald* noted,

> The flood is perhaps as great this year as it was [in 1862]; but owing to the loss of the levees, the water has a wider scope of country over which to spread. . . . DeSoto [opposite Vicksburg,] however is getting the free benefit of the rise. We do not suppose there is an acre of dry ground upon the peninsula opposite Vicksburg, and over most of it a

steamboat could float easily. Some of the houses are in the water up to their roofs, and none are tenable except for the fishes of the sea."[30]

The river was so high at most places that the steamboat *Ruth* went "from New Orleans to Cairo in three days and twenty-three hours . . . against a rising river the entire distance." By passing over flooded fields and cutting off twisting, curving bends, the *Ruth* had bettered the *Sultana*'s seasonal record by eight hours.[31] When Captain Mason and the *Sultana* returned to St. Louis, he would have to relinquish the coveted elk's antlers to Capt. George Pegram and the *Ruth*.

Like any good first engineer, Nathan Wintringer watched his machinery and gauges as the *Sultana* fought the strong flood current. "The boilers were in perfect condition," he remembered. Lieutenant Colonel Compton recalled, "From New Orleans to Natchez . . . she ran at usual rate of speed," about nine miles per hour. At Natchez, the *Sultana* took on one more passenger, Miss Lucy Smith of Illinois, who "had been down to meet her lover who was an officer and was stationed at Natchez. She had come down from the north to marry him but he told her that he would soon be mustered out and that she had better go back and they would be married at home."[32]

All seemed fine on the *Sultana* until she unexpectedly slowed down about one hundred miles below Vicksburg. "[I]t was stated to us by some of the boat that there was a defect in one of the boilers," Lieutenant Colonel Compton recalled. "That either . . . it could not be used or else under very low pressure of steam. The passage therefore was unusually tedious . . . on account of the slowness."[33]

Wintringer later recounted that he had discovered "a small leak" in the "larboard [far left-hand] boiler at the third sheet from the forward end, a few inches below the horizontal diameter of the boiler where it was exposed to fire." In layman's terms, "a leak on a side seam on the larboard boiler." The pressure was reduced in all four boilers, since they were all interconnected, and the *Sultana* "carried low steam and worked along moderately."[34]

Near 8:45 p.m. on Sunday, April 23, 1865, the *Sultana* limped up to the Vicksburg wharf boat. While Wintringer went into town to look for a boiler mechanic, Second Engineer Samuel Clemens and the firemen began to let the water out of the boilers. Captain Mason met up with Miles Sells and went in search of Captain Hatch and the promised load of one thousand ex-prisoners.[35]

5

THE VICKSBURG OFFICERS

Of all the Union officers at Vicksburg who would be involved with the *Sultana*, Reuben Benton Hatch had the most troubled background. His family had moved from his hometown, Hillsborough, New Hampshire, to Griggsville, Illinois, when he was fifteen years old. As an adult, he made good connections. He owned merchandising stores in Pittsfield and Quincy, Illinois, along the upper Mississippi River and met and befriended many steamboat captains and a number of prominent Illinoisans, including Abraham Lincoln.[1]

When the war began in April 1861, forty-one-year-old Hatch joined the 8th Illinois Infantry and was soon made regimental quartermaster. Leaning upon his prominent friends, including his older brother Ozias, who was now the Illinois secretary of state, and President Lincoln, Hatch was soon made a captain and assistant quartermaster for the Union army gathering at Cairo.[2]

Almost immediately Hatch and his two civilian clerks began using the Quartermaster's Department to line their own pockets. Among their many schemes, they bought various supplies for the government at low prices and then charged the government higher prices. In

September 1861, Hatch, always a drinking man, became a full-blown alcoholic when he returned to Griggsville to bury two of his children—his oldest and second youngest—who had both died of diphtheria.[3]

When Hatch returned to Cairo, he had a new commanding officer. Brig. Gen. Ulysses S. Grant soon discovered the fraudulent practices of his quartermaster. Reuben Hatch and his two clerks were arrested, and Hatch faced a court-martial for his offenses. Hatch quickly called upon his friends in Springfield and Washington, including the president, to come to his rescue.[4]

President Lincoln appointed a presidential commission to look into Hatch's affairs. When the commission eventually reported finding many mistakes in the Quartermaster's Department but very little fraud, Lincoln and others sent letters to Secretary of War Edwin M. Stanton endorsing the reinstatement of Captain Hatch. Although Stanton bristled, he eventually released Hatch from arrest on October 6, 1862, and appointed him chief quartermaster for the District of Eastern Arkansas, headquartered at Helena.[5]

In August 1863 Hatch resigned from the service because of some trouble at home. It was during this time that a fire tore through an entire block in Griggsville and completely destroyed Hatch's merchandising store.[6] Having lost his main source of income, Hatch wanted back into the army, where he could make more money, both legally and illegally. He got his friends and President Lincoln to lobby for him with the quartermaster general in Washington and reentered the army on March 12, 1864, as the chief quartermaster of the XIII Army Corps.[7]

While in Louisiana during the disastrous Red River Campaign, Hatch developed a fistula-in-ano, an extremely painful and annoying abnormality in the connection between the anal canal and the skin, which bothered him for the rest of his life.[8] In December 1864, after burying another child, and plagued by his alcoholism and ailment, Hatch once again tendered his resignation. Before it could be accepted, Hatch and all the other quartermasters were ordered to stand before a military examining board verifying their knowledge and qualifications. Hatch failed miserably.[9]

"Of the 60 officers who have appeared before this board not more than 1 or 2 can compare with Capt. Hatch in degree of deficiency," the examining officers noted.[10] "His accounting deficiency, in view of his long period of service, must be ascribed either to culpable negligence, or to incapacity. In either case he is totally unfit to discharge the duties of assistant quartermaster." The board recommended that Hatch be removed from the service.[11]

While that recommendation was wending its way through government channels, Hatch was assigned as the assistant quartermaster of volunteers at Vicksburg on February 11, 1865.[12] When Hatch arrived at Vicksburg, he found himself under the command of Maj. Gen. Napoleon Jackson Tecumseh Dana, an 1842 graduate of West Point now commanding the Department of Mississippi. Dana had been severely wounded in the hip at the Battle of Cerro Gordo on April 18, 1847, during the war with Mexico. After the war, Dana worked as a banker in St. Paul, Minnesota, until the Civil War started and he accepted a commission as colonel of the 1st Minnesota Infantry.[13]

At the Battle of Antietam on September 17, 1862, Dana was again severely wounded, this time in the left leg. He was promoted to major general of volunteers on November 29, 1862, and in December 1864, now sufficiently recovered, was named head of the Department of Mississippi.[14]

Immediately under General Dana was Brig. Gen. Morgan Lewis Smith, commander of the Post of Vicksburg. Born in Mexico, New York, on March 8, 1822, Smith had been a drill instructor during the Mexican War.[15] Afterward he lived in St. Louis and captained a number of steamboats. When the Civil War began, Smith recruited and organized the 8th Missouri Volunteer Infantry. He was severely wounded in the hip at Chickasaw Bayou, Mississippi, on December 28, 1862, and was out of duty for almost a year. Still forced to use a buggy because of his nagging hip wound, Smith was made the commander of the Post and District of Vicksburg on September 27, 1864.[16]

Capt. George Augustus Williams, like Reuben Hatch, had a troubled military past. Born in 1831 in Newburgh, New York, Williams graduated from West Point in 1852. In March 1862, while with the 1st U.S. Infantry, Captain Williams suffered a hernia while helping place siege guns around New Madrid, Missouri. A year later, during General Grant's Vicksburg campaign, Williams suffered an additional strain that left him unfit for combat duty. In June 1863 he was appointed provost marshal in charge of the military prison in Memphis.[17]

While he was at Memphis, Captain Williams came under the influence of the corrupt Maj. Gen. Stephen A. Hurlbut and allegedly began accepting bribes to speed the release of political prisoners suspected of being Confederate sympathizers. After Maj. Gen. Cadwallader C. Washburn replaced Hurlbut, a prison inspector found the prison to be "the filthiest place [he] . . . ever saw occupied by human beings." Upon receiving the inspector's report, Secretary of War Stanton wanted Captain Williams removed from the service.

Perhaps frightened at the prospect of losing his career, his honor, and his prestige, and having gained the backing of General Washburn, Williams seemed to turn a corner. In October 1864 he wrote Secretary Stanton requesting that an entirely new facility be built to house the Memphis prisoners. The current prison, he said, was too old to maintain and was not a proper facility. Shortly thereafter, however, on October 24, 1864, Williams was transferred to Vicksburg as commissary of musters under General Dana.[18]

Capt. Frederic Speed was another of General Dana's staff officers who would gain notoriety in connection with the *Sultana*. Born in Ithaca, New York, in 1841 but raised near Gorham, Maine, Speed enlisted in the 5th Maine Infantry at the beginning of the Civil War. He was eventually promoted to captain and made adjutant for the First Division, XIX Army Corps in late 1862. In January 1864 he was promoted to assistant adjutant general of the entire XIX Army Corps; and in August he became assistant adjutant general of volunteers for the defenses of New Orleans. Speed had worked with a number of generals during his time in the army and had won their praise for his competence. On February 28, 1865, he was ordered to Vicksburg for duty as an assistant adjutant general under General Dana.[19]

The last of the officers at Vicksburg who would have an impact on what happened with the *Sultana* was Capt. William Franklin Kerns, who was born in Indiana in 1839 but grew up in Minnesota. Kerns enlisted in the 9th Minnesota Infantry in August 1862 and was made a clerk in the Quartermaster's Department. His hard work and skill earned Private Kerns promotion to captain on February 29, 1864, and he was ordered to St. Louis as an assistant quartermaster in charge of transportation. Four months later Kerns was ordered to Vicksburg, and in February 1865 he came under the immediate supervision of Captain Hatch when Hatch became the chief quartermaster at that post. Although the two men developed a working relationship, they were never friends. For the most part, Captain Kerns was left alone to arrange transportation for troops and supplies up and down the Mississippi River because Captain Hatch "did not care to see this class of orders."[20]

On April 23, 1865, when the *Sultana* finally came back upriver to Vicksburg, all the major players were in place. Major General Dana, perhaps walking with a slight limp because of his wounded hip, was the head of the Department of Mississippi. Under him, in charge of the Post and District of Vicksburg, was Major General Smith, forced by his hip wound to ride in a buggy. On Dana's staff was Commissary of Musters Captain Williams, who had managed to remain in the army by the skin of his teeth, and Chief Quartermaster Captain Hatch, an alcoholic with a painful physical condition who had managed to remain in the army through the influence of powerful family and friends. Dana's staff also included Assistant Adjutant General Captain Speed and Assistant Quartermaster of Transportation Captain Kerns. It was a mixed lot of individuals, and all would play a hand in loading the paroled prisoners of war onto the steamer *Sultana*.

6

CAPTURED

With the exception of the small Union army guard unit, all of the soldiers who would be placed on board the *Sultana* were paroled prisoners of war. All of them had survived the rigors of training camp, where thousands had died of disease; and most had survived long, hard campaigns and the terrors of battle. A few had been captured without a fight—during a quick cavalry raid on their camp, perhaps, or while out foraging for supplies—but all of them had faced and survived the humiliation of captivity. Some had been prisoners for only a few weeks and were in good shape; others had been prisoners for years and were physical and emotional wrecks. All were happy to be released and on their way back north.

One of the longest held was Pvt. George W. Henry (Co. M, 2nd TN Cav), who had been captured on February 22, 1863, at Okolona, Mississippi. Pvt. Wilson Ganze and Pvt. William Marvin (both Co. C, 47th IN Inf) had been captured at Champion's Hill, Mississippi, on May 16, 1863. Pvt. James Wesley Thompson (Co. C, 4th MI Inf), Pvt. Newman A. Easlick (Co. G, 4th MI Inf), and Pvt. Edward K. Sorgen (Co. G, 4th OH Inf) had been captured at Gettysburg on July 2, 1863. At least ninety-six of the men who would go on the *Sultana* had been captured at the bloody two-day battle of Chickamauga, Georgia, on September 19–20, 1863.[1]

There were at least fifty-eight men who had been captured at Brice's Cross Roads (Guntown), Mississippi, on June 10, 1864, and another thirteen captured the next day at Ripley, Mississippi. All of them had been part of a Union raid out of Memphis meant to draw Maj. Gen. Nathan Bedford Forrest and his Confederate cavalry away from General Sherman's advance toward Atlanta.[2] Thirty-four cavalrymen from the 6th Kentucky Cavalry and the 7th Kentucky Cavalry (both Union) and four artillerists from the 24th Indiana Battery were captured on June 24, 1864, at Lafayette, Georgia, while protecting Sherman's right flank. Confederate cavalry raids staged on Sherman's Atlanta campaign between July 23 and August 8, 1864, accounted for at least another seventy-five prisoners.

The largest cohort had been captured by Major General Forrest during his September 1864 raids through northern Alabama and middle Tennessee along the Tennessee and Alabama Central Railroad. On September 24, Forrest led 4,500 men to the town of Athens in northern Alabama. Protecting the town was a small fort garrisoned by about 470 men from three U.S. colored infantry regiments and about 130 men of the 3rd Tennessee Cavalry (Union), who had been left behind when their regiment went out on a patrol because they were either convalescing or without mounts.[3]

Forrest's men appeared late on the evening of September 23 and drove the defenders back into the fort. The next morning Forrest began a lengthy bombardment. Convinced that he was opposed by at least ten thousand Confederate troops, the commander of the fort surrendered.[4]

Sgt. Samuel Abraham Dyer (Co. C, 3rd TN Cav) was inside the fort when the Confederates took possession. "They captured me the 24 of September 1864," he wrote home, "and they took all of my money and all of my close but what I had on my back." Pvt. Charles M. Eldridge (Co. G, 3rd TN Cav) had been trapped outside the fort and had spent the morning hiding in the crook of a rail fence. The Confederates spotted him after the fort surrendered: "[T]hey soon found me . . . [and] began to take what I had so I don't know how many there was pulling me around trying to get my pistol, while that was going on, someone snatched my hat off, while another pulled my coat from me[.] [W]hen that was done I was ordered to sit down, when they began to drag me around by the feet trying to get my boots."[5]

General Forrest had acted quickly to force the surrender because his scouts had reported that a relief train was rushing to the rescue from Decatur, Alabama, about fifteen miles south of Athens. A relief column consisting of 163 officers and men from the 102nd Ohio Infantry and 215 men of the 18th Michigan Infantry fought to within a couple hundred yards of the fort before noticing the rebel flag now flying from the ramparts.[6] "We fought them three and a half hours," wrote Pvt. Jacob Homer (Co. A, 102nd OH Inf). "When we were about 200 yards from the fort, we discovered that it had been surrendered and we scarcely knew what to do. . . . [W]e all thought it best to surrender or we might all be killed."[7]

The Confederate horsemen "robbed us of our blankets, watches and all valuables," Sgt. Hosea C. Aldrich (Co. G, 18th MI Inf) wrote. Pvt. William Columbus "Billy" Lockhart (Co. E, 102nd OH Inf) recalled, "a Johny full cocked [a] revolver and struck me with the muzzle end, and called me a sun of a Bitch. I afterwards Learned that He was a Capt. and told me to surrender. I said to Him you have captured us so you will Have to take From me what you want. . . . He went through me like a Dose of Double strength Horse salts."[8] Of the nearly 1,000 men Forrest's troops captured on September 24, 1864, at least 417 would end up on the *Sultana*.

But Forrest did not stop in Athens. On September 25, his 4,500 men attacked the earthen fort guarding a huge railroad trestle bridge over Sulphur Creek, nine miles north of Athens. Inside the enclosure were 400 African American infantrymen of the 110th USCT along with about 150 troopers from the 9th and the 10th Indiana Cavalry and about 400 mounted men of the 3rd Tennessee Cavalry (Union) who had sought refuge there. Forrest's troopers attacked the fort throughout the day, getting cannon onto higher ground and sending plunging fire into the fortification. After more than 200 defenders were killed and ammunition ran low, the fort finally surrendered.[9] Of roughly 800 men captured at Sulphur Creek Trestle, at least 371, mostly from the Indiana and Tennessee cavalry units, would end up on the *Sultana*.

Confederate troops under Maj. Gen. John Bell Hood moving into central Tennessee in November 1864 captured more men who ended up on the *Sultana*. Sixteen members of the 175th Ohio were swept up at Bridge No. 16 and Blockhouse No. 14 on November 24 and 25 near Columbia, Tennessee, while guarding the Tennessee and Alabama Railroad. The defense of the bridge and blockhouse was the first, and last, engagement of the newly organized 175th Ohio.[10]

Major General Hood's army continued pressing northward through Tennessee, capturing almost four dozen more Union soldiers who would embark on the *Sultana*, taking them between November 27 and 30. Second Lt. Joseph Taylor Elliott (Co. C, 124th IN Inf) was among those taken prisoner. "My entire company was captured by Hood near Springhill [*sic*], Tenn., on November 30, 1864," he lamented. "The company was left on picket duty and the regiment moved off. This was done as a military necessity, our duty being to maintain the picket line in order to give the regiment time to withdraw."[11]

On November 30, the Confederates finally caught up with the Union army south of Franklin, Tennessee, where they had managed to throw up defensive works. A thin line of soldiers protecting the main Union battle line were awaiting the order to retire back to the main line when the Confederates attacked. Unfortunately, the order never came. When 20,000 screaming rebels rushed forward, the men fired a volley and then raced back toward the main Union earthworks.[12]

Cpl. Ira B. Horner (Co. K, 65th OH Inf) was quickly gobbled up in the Confederate charge: "Soon after capture we were stripped of our clothes, robbed of our shoes we wore, and left to stand or lie about in the mud and made to march over rough roads in unshod feet, unfed, the sick allowed no more care than the strongest were allowed; no care indeed except to prevent escape."[13]

Cpl. Erastus Winters (Co. K, 50th OH Inf) was in the center of the main Union battle line when the Confederates broke through: "Saw [our forward troops] break for our lines with the grey coats right among them. From that on till they reached our lines it was a confused mass of blue and grey, in a mad rush for our lines." Winters too was taken prisoner.[14]

Counterattacking units were rushed forward to blunt the Confederate breakthrough. Hood failed to destroy the Union army at Franklin, but thousands of blue-clad soldiers were killed or wounded in the battle, and hundreds were captured. At least 166 of the men captured at Franklin would end up on the *Sultana*.

Although terribly mauled at Franklin, the Confederates continued to pursue the retreating Union army, eventually besieging them in Nashville. On December 3, after Hood sent Major General Forrest's cavalry on a raid to destroy the Nashville & Chattanooga Railroad, Forrest captured about two dozen men from Company F, 115th Ohio Infantry at Blockhouses Nos. 1 and 3 between Nashville and Murfreesboro, Tennessee. The next day he captured two more companies of the 115th Ohio in Blockhouse No. 4 and La Vergne, Tennessee. First Sgt. John Clark Ely (Co. C) turned thirty-nine that day while defending Blockhouse No. 4. "Rebs came in sight early in large force under Gen. Forrest," Ely wrote in his diary for December 5. "Capt. [Lewis Frederick] Hake [Co. B] surrendered the fort and Co. C are prisoners."[15] Some eighty officers and enlisted men of the 115th Ohio Infantry would eventually be placed on board the *Sultana*.

The last of the Union soldiers to end up on the *Sultana* were members of a Union cavalry raid that swept through northern Alabama in late March and early April 1865. Some seventy-eight soldiers, including fifty-six men from the 6th Kentucky Cavalry (Union), were taken in small groups, some after sharp firefights and others too exhausted to fight after riding for days on end. Brothers Francis Marion and James Wallace McDaniel (both privates in Co. I, 6th KY Cav) were asleep in a corn crib when Confederate cavalrymen surprised them. Cpl. Simeon Dickens Chelf (Co. G, 6th KY Cav) was forced to surrender after a short skirmish near Tuscaloosa. He recalled, "Oh, well do I remember a rebel who traded me a pair of shoes for a good pair of boots, and all the difference I got was: 'Set down you Yank, or I'll put my bayonet through you, while I pull them boots off.'"[16]

Many of the captured Union soldiers who wound up on the *Sultana*, stripped of their clothing and equipment but not their dignity, were marched south to one of the dreaded prison pens where the Confederates confined their captives.

Private Eldridge, captured in the crook of a rail fence at Athens and deprived of his hat, coat, and boots, remembered his trek south. "[T]he next morning they had us going by sun-up, without anything to eat. [S]o the first cornfield we came to the guards gave us some corn to eat and we had to eat it raw just like a pig, so that was all we got to eat that day." After marching two days without shoes, Eldridge began to give out. "I did not see how I could travel another day barefooted, but they didn't consult my feelings about that." When the column finally reached the railroad, each man was given a piece of hardtack that "looked like it was made from corn-meal and cow-peas ground together, but never-the-less it tasted good to a man who hadn't had but three ears of corn in four days."[17]

Sergeant Aldrich, also captured at Athens, recalled similar experiences. "We were marched over rough roads and through rivers, our feet sore and our stomachs empty. By rail we were but little better off. I well remember one dark, stormy night we were crowded into dirty box cars that they had used for shipping stock and left in a filthy condition. We stood up all night, and the cars were run at such a rapid rate we were thrown against each other and against the sides of the car, for our tired limbs could hardly hold us up."[18]

Food was a problem for every prisoner being moved toward a Southern prison. Pvt. Montgomery W. Jordan (Co. G, 3rd TN Cav), who was also captured at Athens, recalled, "We crossed the Tennessee River . . . and all we had to eat was green pumpkins. We ate them smoked, without salt or grease."[19] Half-naked and hungry, they trudged on, dreading what lay ahead.

7

PRISONERS

Captured Union soldiers were usually taken to a temporary holding stockade at Meridian, Mississippi, about ninety miles east of Jackson, before they were moved to a more permanent prison. Most of the men who ended up on the *Sultana* were taken to either Castle Morgan at Cahaba, Alabama, or Camp Sumter at Andersonville, Georgia.

The prison enclosure at Cahaba (or Cahawba), twenty-seven miles southwest of Selma, sat alongside the Alabama River just downriver from where the Cahaba River joined the Alabama. The main structure, an unfinished brick warehouse with a partial roof on each end, measured 193 feet by 116 feet, with walls 16 feet high. There was a smaller room at the northeast corner of the warehouse and a small four-seater toilet just outside the southeast corner. Wooden bunks built one above the other under the roofed portions of the warehouse could accommodate 432 men.[1]

A fourteen-foot-high wooden stockade fence surrounded the warehouse, with an elevated walkway for guards along the outside. The warehouse was situated at the back two-thirds of the stockade, and a large front area measuring approximately 100 feet by 180 feet served as a cook yard. This front area could be accessed only during the day, because the men were locked inside the warehouse at night. Water came into the stockade, and then under the walls of the warehouse, via a small stream that flowed west to east and then into the Alabama River. Unfortunately for the prisoners, the stream first ran through the small nearby town of Cahaba. Pvt. Perry Samuel Summerville (Co. K, 2nd IN Cav) recalled, "The water passed through the city in pipes to a hydrant outside the prison where the stock came to drink. The people would wash there and then the water would pass down through the prison for us to drink and cook with, but it was one of the purest articles we got."[2]

Like most Civil War prisons, in both North and South, Cahaba had a deadline—a line of stakes stuck a few feet inside the stockade fence topped with a thin rail. Any prisoner who crossed the deadline was risking his life. Private Summerville remembered "standing near a comrade one day who happened to get his foot on the dead line, the guard above shot at his foot, barely missing it." A second deadline was established inside the warehouse. "At night we were always driven into the square [brick] enclosure," Pvt. John Lowry Walker (Co. B, 50th OH Inf) explained, "and inside this enclosure was another dead line with about twenty Confederate soldiers on guard."[3]

On July 30, 1863, after the Confederacy had refused to exchange captured Black soldiers, President Lincoln issued General Orders No. 252, effectively suspending all exchanges until the Confederates agreed to treat Black prisoners the same as white prisoners. When the exchanges stopped, prison compounds on both sides filled to capacity. The Confederacy built a bigger facility at Andersonville, Georgia, 125 miles south of Atlanta, to hold them. On February 17, 1864, the first men were transferred out of Cahaba and sent to Camp Sumter, the official name of the Andersonville prison pen. By the end of April 1864, only the few Union men deemed too sick to travel were still at Cahaba.[4]

The spring 1864 campaigns brought in new captives, however, and Cahaba began to fill once again. While the Confederacy eventually agreed to return Black soldiers on the agreed man-for-man basis, General Grant, who was now in charge of all Union forces, refused to reinstitute the man-for-man exchanges that had taken place prior to General Orders No. 252. "If we commence a system of exchange which liberates all prisoners taken," Grant pointed out, "we will have to fight on until the whole South is exterminated." Men in prisons, on the other hand, "amount to no more than dead men." Grant knew that he was condemning Union soldiers held in Confederate hands to remain in prison until the end of the war, but he felt it was necessary. By the time Grant made his decision on August 18, 1864, Andersonville prison already held 30,000 men, and newly captured Yankees were soon being sent to Cahaba again.[5]

By the fall of 1864, Cahaba was already crowded with perhaps a thousand men. Private Walker remembered entering Cahaba in late fall of 1864: "We were taken to the prison, the gates were opened and we were pushed in like so many cattle. The familiar greeting of 'Fresh fish!' came from our comrades who had been there for some time previous to our arrival."[6]

Private Eldridge, who had been stripped almost naked after he was captured, "did not see how I could live if I had to stay here being bareheaded, no coat, and barefooted, so I took a long cry over the matter." Fortunately, three comrades shared their blankets with Eldridge. Likewise lacking a blanket, Private Homer kept warm by sleeping "in spoon fashion, ten or a dozen in a row. When one turned over—we all turned over."[7]

With the Civil War in its third year and the Union naval blockade keeping precious supplies from entering Southern ports, Confederate soldiers were finding rations hard to come by. Food for the Union prisoners was even scarcer. "Our fare consisted of corn and cob chopped together," noted Pvt. William Harmon Christine (Co. H, 102nd OH Inf), "and once in a while some poor beef that you could smell before it reached the inside of the prison fence." Private Homer remembered that "[o]ne piece of meat they brought had an abscess as large as the crown of my hat. The pus or matter ran out over the meat as we cut close to it. I tell you it was a bad piece."[8]

The starving prisoners at Cahaba inevitably lost weight. Pvt. Philip L. Horn (Co. I, 102nd OH Inf) was a "gaunt frame of bones" when he finally returned home: "I was a big boy when I went in the war at the age of 17. Two hundred pounds is my normal weight. But when I arrived home after seven months in prison . . . I weighed less than 100 pounds." Pvt. Commodore Smith (Co. F, 18th MI Inf) was in

Cahaba only six months: "My weight when captured [on September 24, 1864] was 175 pounds, and when I [was released on] March 16, 1865, my weight was 94 pounds, although I had not been sick a day while in prison."[9]

Besides thinking about food, the men spent their time picking body lice off themselves and their clothing. With everyone kept in close confinement, no bathing facilities, and no way to attend to personal hygiene, the men were crawling with lice. "We had to skirmish every day," Sergeant Aldrich recalled; "that is, to sit down on the ground, take off our garments one at a time, hunt the seams over, and between our thumb nails demolish the nits and older ones that we could find, and that generally was a large number; to feel them crawl and bite was additional creeping torture."[10]

In spite of the poor food and lousy conditions, Cahaba was perhaps the best-run prison on either side. Much of that was due to the administrator, Capt. Howard Andrew Millet "Ham" Henderson. Henderson had been a Methodist minister before the war and took a genuine interest in those assigned to his care. The death rate at Cahaba was only about 2 percent, the lowest of any Civil War prison (the average death rate in Northern prisons was 12 percent, while that in Southern prisons was 15.5 percent). Henderson was one of the few prison commandants on either side to gain the respect of the men he held in captivity. "He was a man who was held in the highest esteem by all the prisoners for his kind and considerate manner toward them at all times," Private Walker recalled.[11]

In September 1864, knowing that winter was coming and many of his charges lacked adequate clothing and supplies, Captain Henderson traveled to Memphis under a flag of truce and met with Major General Washburn. Acting as an agent of exchange, Henderson proposed the release of 350 men from Cahaba for the release of a like number from Northern prisons. Because the cessation of the exchange was still in force, however, Union authorities would not agree to the exchange. Instead, Washburn and Henderson arranged to send Union clothing and supplies through the lines to the prisoners at Cahaba.

In December 1864, a steamboat carrying all kinds of clothing and supplies, including a "sufficient supply of medicine," docked next to the prison.[12] Pvt. John M. Phillips (Co. F, 5th TN Cav) remembered that many men in the prison were "barefooted, bareheaded, and otherwise destitute of clothing, till the day before Christmas, when the Government sent us each a pair of socks, pants, cap, two blankets for every three men, and a blue blouse."[13]

Lack of clothing was not the only problem the men faced at Cahaba. "On or about the 1st of March, 1865," reported Pvt. Daniel Garber (Co. E, 102nd OH Inf), "the Alabama river got very high, owing to the incessant rain for the past few days and consequently overflowed the prison to the depths of two feet, at the highest place, making it very disagreeable, for we had no place to stand up or lie down but in the water."[14] Explained Pvt. Henry Koon (Co. A, 18th MI Inf),

> Although we thought we were on the highest point of land, the rise of water was such that it overflowed the whole grounds of our prison, and remained so about six days, varying in depth from knee to waist deep. . . . Our privies were located at the lower end of the prison, and as the water backed up it raised all the human excrement and filth to mingle with the water, which all floated up into our prison, remaining there for several days.[15]

Lt. Col. Sam Jones, who had temporary charge of Cahaba while Henderson was away, waited several days before he decided to send 1,000 prisoners upriver to a temporary holding pen in Selma. The 1,700 who remained had to deal with the water as best they could.[16]

On March 6, the prisoners remaining at Cahaba were told that they were about to be released. Pvt. James Robert Collins (Co. F, 3rd TN Cav) remembered, "Finally to our intense joy and relief, word came that we were to be sent to the exchange camp at Vicksburg, Miss., to be exchanged. Words cannot begin to express our feelings when we knew that we were again to leave that horrible hole. Hearts full of gratitude and thanksgiving to the great Almighty beat riotously in the bosom of every prisoner and the tears coursed unrestrainedly down every cheek when the glad news was made known." Steamboats began to appear at the Cahaba landing within days, and by April 12, 1865, almost all of the Union soldiers had been removed from the prison.[17]

Thousands of men were leaving the Confederate prison at Andersonville, Georgia, at the same time. Although Cahaba was bad, Andersonville prison had earned an even worse reputation. The first prisoners had entered Camp Sumter in February 1864, many transferred from prisons in Richmond. First Sergeant Karns was among the first arrivals.

> I do not remember the exact time but sometime between the 20 and 28th of Feb., our train pulled up to a little station called Andersonville, on the Macon and Albany railroad. . . . I could see the outline of a huge wall or stockade, and over inside of this stockade everything looked dark and dismal. . . . After fifteen or twenty minutes delay on the outside, I noticed the huge gates swing back on their massive hinges and we marched as it were into the gates of —. Everything being in darkness on the inside we lay down promiscuously for the remainder of the night, and in the morning awoke to behold the interior of Andersonville prison. . . . [Fifteen] feet from the stockade [wall] was the ever dreaded dead-line, this consisting of stakes drove in the ground to the height of 3 feet with a slat nailed on top, on top of the stockade were the sentry boxes and in there the confederate guards were stationed . . . having instructions to shoot anyone crossing the dead line.[18]

Karns went on to describe how a sluggish little stream, "about 8 feet wide and 6 to 8 inches deep," ran through the center of the stockade and was used for "washing, bathing and drinking purposes."[19]

Another prisoner who came from Richmond, fifteen-year-old Pvt. William A. McFarland (Co. A, 42nd IN Inf), recalled, "The cover we had overhead was the blue canopy of heaven, while we were surrounded on the four sides by a high wall and a strong armed guard. When sleeping we were obliged to huddle together to keep warm in the winter." Pvt. Isaac Noah "Ike" Davenport (Co. C, 7th TN Cav) had similar memories: "During our prison life . . . our beds was only the sandy hills of andersonville prison, some thare of us who had a few raged [*sic*] blankets in which we would role ourselves in at night and trust god to watch over us while we slept."[20]

Andersonville, like Cahaba, was rife with body lice. Karns remembered, "One day as I was taking a stroll through the stockade, . . . I came across a number of prisoners, who were seated down on the ground engaged in skirmishing (or killing gray-backs); each individual had disrobed himself of some article of clothing, and judging by the stains on their thumb nails and fingers, they were having good success."[21]

Food at Andersonville was at least as bad as that at any other Southern prison. Pvt. Chester Dawson Berry (Co. D, 20th MI Inf) arrived at Andersonville from Richmond in late June 1864: "Here the rations, which at first were small enough, kept diminishing, until the 1st of September, 1864, there were but two tablespoons of very coarse corn meal, the same of stock peas, with about two ounces of fresh beef."[22]

Karns was not likely to forget the meat:

> At times they issued us meat which the best experts among the prisoners were unable to tell what it was. However the general belief was that it was mule meat. . . . When they issued us fresh beef there was nothing thrown away but the intestines of the animal. I have seen beef heads (minus the tongue) brought in with the eyes in and the horns on and issued to so many men as so many rations. The shin-bones with the hoofs on were issued. I remember one day of receiving a portion of the stomach for my share, and upon this were particles of the food yet which it had contained.[23]

With such poor rations, it was inevitable that most of the prisoners lost weight. Pvt. Harrison Parker Hunt (Co. E, 36th IN Inf) weighed 186 pounds when he arrived at Andersonville and 90 pounds on his release. Eppenetus Washington McIntosh (Co. E, 14th IL Inf) lost 110 pounds in Andersonville. He entered weighing 175 pounds and left 6 months later, in March 1865, weighing "only 65 pounds, and almost destitute of clothing."[24]

The poor food and overcrowding led to rampant disease. Cpl. Thomas W. Horan (Co. H, 65th OH Inf), who called Andersonville "Hell on Earth," said, "I have saw men lying not able to help themselves with Maggots working in their eyes and nose and them alive." Remembered Private Davenport, "We could only help the pore sick keep the flies off of them and off of there sors for sum of the boys legs and feete was sweld so tite tha busted." Each day, the sick prisoners were collected and taken to the camp hospital just outside the stockade wall.[25]

When a small group of sadistic men began to prey upon the sick and weak, the other prisoners rebelled and put six of the most notorious on trial. They were found guilty and hanged from gallows built inside the stockade. Wrote Private Davenport, "I saw six men hung ded on one pole tha was called radars but I called them thieves and murders tha had kild and robed sevrel of the por boys for what little money the had. The boys stood that but a short time till there was a stop put to it." Added Sgt. Joseph Stevens (Co. B, 1st MI Sharpshooters), "[They hung there] until sun down, so everyone could have an opportunity of seeing them, as a warning for the rest of the gang."[26]

Originally built to hold about 10,000 men, the prison held more than 22,000 by June 1864, 5 months after it opened. The prison compound was expanded to 27 acres to accommodate them. By July, the number had risen to 29,000; the number peaked at 33,114 in August. The overcrowding, diseases, lack of medicines, bad sanitation, and poor rations killed men at a rapid rate. In Andersonville prison, the death rate was 29 percent.[27]

Andersonville's commander, Capt. Heinrich "Henry" Wirz, was likely one reason for the high death rate. Unlike Captain Henderson at Cahaba, Captain Wirz despised the men under his care, and the men returned the sentiment. Although he had inherited a bad situation, he did little to improve it. Capt. James Walter Elliott (Co. F, 44th USCT) called Wirz "his Satanic Majesty's most loyal representative on earth."[28]

In September 1864, fearful that General Sherman would swerve toward the prison when he started his March to the Sea, the Confederate authorities began to move the Andersonville prisoners to other compounds.[29] In mid-March 1865 there were only four thousand prisoners left at Camp Sumter to be sent to the exchange camp outside Vicksburg. Captain Elliott, who had been kept in a separate officers' stockade, remembered the moment. "'Get ready for exchange,' came the order. Oh! the joyous shout that made the castle walls ring out. How each of us laughed and cried, shook hands with and hugged his fellows. . . . The joy of that hour more than repaid for all past retributions." The sixty-five officers were taken to the Andersonville railroad depot to await the men from the main stockade.[30]

Capt. William L. Coleman (Co. D, 40th IN Inf) had never seen "[a] more miserable set of men. . . . Ragged—so ragged—many with nothing better than an old and tattered piece of a blanket to cover their haggard and emaciated bodies. A great many of the men were so weak and poor, through disease and starvation, that they had to be carried to the [train] cars by their comrades." "One might have thought that the grave and the sea had given up their dead," Lieutenant Elliott said.[31]

As the first train pulled away from Andersonville heading toward Vicksburg, Private Horan summed up the feelings of his fellow prisoners: "God forbid I should ever be taken into bondage again."[32]

8

CAMP FISK

In January 1865, a group of about twenty Confederate officers and civilians, including two agents of exchange—Col. Nathaniel G. Watts and the recently promoted Lt. Col. Howard A. M. Henderson—appeared at Vicksburg under a flag of truce. Henderson had earlier arranged for a load of clothing to be delivered to the Union prisoners at Cahaba. Now, in January 1865, he and the others hoped to get more aid. The Confederate agents met with Union Capt. Archie C. Fisk, assistant adjutant general under Gen. Morgan Smith, and admitted to the "dire straits of their prisoners of war . . . and . . . asked the North [to] send clothing and medical supplies to them." Captain Fisk "replied that they could have what they wanted if they would deliver to me our men then confined in their prisons so that I, and not they, might see them properly fed and clothed."[1]

On February 21, a formal agreement was approved by General Smith, representing the United States, and Colonel Watts and Lieutenant Colonel Henderson, representing the Confederacy. The agreement stipulated that the Union prisoners held in Meridian, Cahaba, and Andersonville were to be brought to Vicksburg and would "remain there at the expense of the United States Government" until Confederate prisoners in the North could be brought down for a man-for-man exchange. This "parole camp" would be guarded by Union soldiers, but the prisoners would remain under Confederate control until properly exchanged.[2] With the signing of the agreement, General Smith and the two Confederate colonels set in motion the eventual release of thousands of Union prisoners.[3]

The Big Black River, eight miles east of Vicksburg, was stipulated as the dividing line between the Union and the Confederacy. The Union would build a pontoon bridge across the Big Black, with Confederates guarding the east end and Union soldiers guarding the west. A tract of land one and one-half miles wide on each side of a railroad running from the Big Black west toward Vicksburg would be considered neutral territory.[4]

Unofficially, the Confederate camp on the east bank of the Big Black was named Camp Townsend, and the Union parole camp, near Four-Mile Bridge, a railroad trestle located four miles outside of Vicksburg, was called Camp Fisk in honor of Captain Fisk. Guarding Camp Fisk would be the 66th USCT under the command of twenty-two-year-old Maj. Franklin Ellis Miller, who had been "Apptd. major from civil[ian] life . . . by order of the President" and had been in the service for only a little more than two months.[5]

The men from Meridian and Cahaba began arriving at the Big Black around March 16. It was not an easy journey. Some eight hundred men from Cahaba had been brought down the Alabama River to the mouth of the Tombigbee River by steamboat. The boat turned up the Tombigbee and continued, according to Pvt. Samuel B. Stubberfield (Co. F, 18th MI Inf), "as far as navigable, and then by rail to Meridian." From Meridian, the men were transported west toward Jackson, Mississippi, the end of the rail line. The prisoners had to walk the last forty miles to the Big Black River because the railroad had been destroyed.[6]

It took the men two days to walk the forty miles. As the column neared the river, Private Eldridge heard the men in the front suddenly begin to cheer: "About 4 o'clock in the evening I heard those in front began to holler and run, so I didn't understand what it meant, until I got further where I could see, and it was because they had gotten sight of the old stars and stripes again." The flag was flying high upon a flagpole erected on the west (Union) side of the pontoon bridge. "I can't express my feelings," Eldridge continued. "I hollered until I was completely exhausted, my strength being all gone from joy to think I was out of prison and would soon be free again." Because they arrived late in the day, the men were kept on the Confederate (east) side of the river overnight.[7]

Within eyesight of Union lines, the eight hundred men had to endure one more night without food. Pvt. George Washington Stewart Jr. (Co. D, 40th IN Inf) complained, "I never can forgive the quartermaster [at Vicksburg] for not giving us rations on the night we arrived at Black river. He held the rations on one side of the river and us on the other side fourteen hours without anything to eat." The quartermaster at Vicksburg was Capt. Reuben Hatch.[8]

Early the next morning, the men began crossing over. As the name of each prisoner was called, the man crossed the pontoon bridge and his name was entered into the Union books. Many had not been on Union-controlled soil for more than a year. Men laughed and cried and hugged one another as tears streamed unabashedly down their cheeks. "When I got to the other side," Eldridge said, "I went to where the old flag was standing a way up 40 feet in the air, I stood there and looked at that big 20 ft. silk flag, and thought it was the prettiest thing my eyes ever beheld."[9]

The men were taken four miles by train to Camp Fisk, where they were finally given food, shelter, and medical attention. Pvt. Adam Farmer (Co. A, 3rd TN Cav) wrote home on March 19, "We are not exchanged yet, nor we don't know when we will be. . . . We have a nice camp and plenty to eat. And will draw clothing today." Farmer was issued one blue blouse, one pair of trousers, one shirt, and one pair of socks. Private Eldridge also got new clothes: "You don't know how much better I felt after being washed and getting on clean clothes."[10]

Pvt. William N. Goodrich (Co. E, 18th MI Inf) was in the second group to reach the Big Black. "After riding in dirty box cars and then marching, we arrived at Big Black river on the 21st of March, 1865." As before, the march from Jackson to the Big Black took two days. "The first day the weather was nice," remembered Corporal Winters. "The second day it set in to rain, and soon the roads became muddy and slippery, and our old, ragged clothing became thoroughly wet through. . . . My old shoes were so worn that they became an incumbrance to me, so I cast them aside and marched in my sock feet."[11] Knowing that salvation lay before him, Winters "took a fresh chew of tobacco and forged ahead."

Around sundown on March 21 the head of the straggling column reached the Big Black River. Although the men were forced to spend one more night on Confederate-controlled soil, they were up bright and early the next morning. "[T]he officers were soon busy calling the roll," Winters said, "and as fast as we answered to our names, we passed over the pontoon bridge to freedom, into God's country, under the bright folds of Old Glory, where we yelled and shouted ourselves hoarse with thankfulness and joy."[12]

The new arrivals "drew tents, blankets, clothing and a full supply of rations. At first some heartless commissary [officer], thinking we were so near starved that we would eat any old thing, issued us some stale, wormy hardtack, but we soon gave them to understand that that kind of business had to be cut out at once, and after that our rations were all right." Private Walker also remembered the disgusting hardtack. "After we had passed through all the hardships and hunger of Southern prisons," he said, "our quartermaster at Vicksburg could not resist the temptation to make some money by feeding us on condemned hardtack so alive with vermin as to be almost unfit for a dog to eat. On the morning of the second or third day some of the boys showed these crackers to general Dana, commander at Vicksburg, who had come out to see us, and after that fresh bread was furnished to us daily."[13] The wormy hardtack, of course, had been issued by Chief Quartermaster Reuben Hatch, who was apparently following his old practice of purchasing poor rations at a low price while charging the government for fresh crackers, with the difference going into his pockets.

About March 20, General Dana ordered his commissary of musters, Capt. George Williams, to "superintend the exchange of the paroled prisoners." Three days later, Confederate commissioner Colonel Watts informed Williams that the first group of men from Andersonville was about to arrive at Jackson, and that many were sick and feeble and would not survive the forty-mile walk to the Big Black River. General Dana arranged for Lt. Col. George S. Kemble, chief medical director of the Department of Mississippi, to take twenty wagons and retrieve the sick and lame. "The very day of [Kemble's] arrival [at Jackson], the Andersonville prisoners came toward evening," reported a New Orleans newspaper. "During the night, eleven of the poor sufferers died. . . . Six more died before the [wagon] train reached the Big Black." The men were "but moving skeletons, if perchance they can move."[14]

The Andersonville men were in far worse shape than those from Meridian and Cahaba. Corporal Winters was at Camp Fisk when they arrived: "Poor boys! What a sad plight they were in; many of them so weak and emaciated we had to lead them from the [train] cars to camp." Assistant Adjutant General Speed wrote home a few days later that "about three thousand have arrived so far—Those from Cahaba are well and hearty—those from Andersonville are more dead than alive."[15]

Among the first group of Andersonville men who walked to the Big Black was Capt. James Walter Elliott. "On March 26 we hailed the glorious flag of our country as it floated on the breeze. Tears flowed at sight of that proud emblem." When his name was called, Elliott crossed over to the Union side of the pontoon bridge: "We crossed; we gathered at the river; we sang and danced and rested under the shade of the trees. Out from the gates of hell—out from the jaws of death—going home."[16]

Corporal Horan, who was also in that first group from Andersonville, remembered that after the prisoners crossed the Big Black, "they gave us plenty of crackers to eat and whisky to drink." The men were taken to Camp Fisk and given more to eat. Captain Elliott joyfully recalled that "barrel after barrel of pickled-cabbage [sauerkraut] was rolled out and the heads knocked in, and we, marching round and round, gobbled out and ravenously devoured the cabbage and licked the vinegar from our fingers, the sweetest dainty to my bleeding gums that I ever tasted."[17]

Small groups of Andersonville prisoners continued to arrive at the Big Black throughout March. The second large group appeared on April 1. First Sergeant Karns was in that group. When the men spotted the American flag on the opposite side of the river,

[t]he few remaining hats and caps went high in the air, . . .
we shouted and cheered until the valley and hills echoed
and re-echoed with our rejoicing. After we had shouted
ourselves hoarse, we were marched across the pontoon
bridge . . . in single file between a Union and Confederate
officer. . . . As we reached the further end of the bridge, we
scrambled up the bank, every fellow for himself, until we
reached the camp of the Union soldiers. Some fell down on
their faces beneath the flag and wept. Some laughed, while
others joined in singing "The Star Spangled Banner."

The newcomers were herded toward the cook tent, where each was
given a tin cup full of coffee and a single hardtack cracker. "We
remonstrated at first on not getting more than one cracker," Karns
said, "but we were told that the first lot which came through had been
given all they could eat and the result was that a number of them died
by over eating, so we concluded it was for our own good."[18]
    On April 5, with more and more men arriving every day but no
Confederate captives arriving from the North, General Smith asked
General Dana to take control of the entire endeavor. Perhaps he felt
that Dana, who was in charge of the entire Department of Mississippi,
might have better luck getting the Union authorities to release the
Southern prisoners held in the North for the man-for-man exchange.
Dana quickly wrote to General Grant informing him that there were
"about 5,000 of our prisoners under flag of truce awaiting exchange"
and asking "that a sufficient number of rebel prisoners be sent me . . .
for exchange." On April 8 Dana sent Captain Williams to Cairo, site
of the closest working telegraph, to help expedite the process and
communicate directly with Grant.[19]
    Before Captain Williams returned, the Confederates released
almost four hundred critically ill prisoners, who were quickly sent
upriver to St. Louis on hospital boats. On April 11, the assistant commissary of musters, 1st Lt. Edwin L. Davenport (Co. F, 52nd USCT),
who was acting as the assistant commissioner of exchange while
Captain Williams was away, was ordered to release all government
employees and civilian prisoners at Camp Fisk. At the bottom of the

order was written, "The Quartermaster's Department will furnish the necessary transportation."[20] The release of prisoners had begun, and Captain Hatch's department was ordered to furnish the necessary steamboat.

Captain Williams was still in Cairo when a telegram reached Vicksburg on April 13 with orders to begin releasing all of the Union prisoners at Camp Fisk. On April 9, Gen. Robert E. Lee had surrendered to General Grant at Appomattox Court House, Virginia. Grant immediately ordered Confederate veterans paroled without the man-for-man exchange, and the same was to be done with the Union prisoners being held at Camp Fisk. "No equivalents are to be demanded," wrote Col. Robert Ould, the overall Confederate agent of exchange.[21] The stumbling block that had slowed the prisoner exchange at Vicksburg had finally been cleared.

For the men waiting at Camp Fisk, time had been passing slowly. Upon reaching the camp, most had received pen and paper from the U.S. Sanitary Commission, a civilian organization started in 1861 to provide medical care and personal items to the soldiers, and immediately wrote home, some for the first time since their capture. On April 7, Pvt. Samuel W. Poysell (Co. E, 95th OH Inf), who had been in Andersonville, wrote, "Oh my dear Wife I still love you and hope Soon to be with you. . . . Oh wont that be a happy time wen I can come home to Stay with my loving family. . . . I have almost forgot how you and the children look for I have not Saw you for over two years." Sergeant Dyer wrote to his wife, "I want to see you & the children the worst I ever did in all my life, but I expect that there will bee but few of you that would know me if I was there to-day for I am near the grave today than any of you ever saw me before in my life." Sgt. Richard Jourdan Foley (Co. A, 6th KY Cav) wrote to his sister, "You know not, nor can you imagine the yearnings of my heart to hear from or see the loved ones at home."[22]

Most men praised the Sanitary Commission and the U.S. Christian Commission, an organization that furnished medical services, religious tracts, and personal items to the Union troops. Poysell wrote, "the Sanitary & Christian Commission are doing lots for us they give us paper ink & pens to write our friends and Potatoes & onions &

Crout to Eat and we ar doing very well." Teamster Henry Marshall Misemer (Co. F, 3rd TN Cav) wrote to his wife on March 28 that "the Sanitary Commission have furnished us in papers, envelopes, pens, ink, Postage stamps, tobacco, paper, combs, towels, handkerchiefs, thread, tin cups, news papers, testaments and many other things."[23]

The Sanitary Commission did not have a branch office in Vicksburg, but representatives had come down from the North with shirts, drawers, and socks enough for eight thousand men at Camp Fisk. "Every man as he came in had shirt, drawers, and socks given him, and thousands of towels, handkerchiefs, combs, suspenders, and other needed articles were distributed," a Sanitary Commission manager reported. The commission also provided 2,100 bushels of potatoes, 200 barrels of sauerkraut, 300 barrels of soft crackers, fruit, tobacco, and "nearly every other article they needed."[24] To his sister, Sergeant Foley announced, "I am healthy, hearty, fat and saucy; always able to consume my rations, have nothing to do but eat, drink and sleep."[25]

While awaiting exchange, Corporal Winters remembered, "We had no duty to perform but to keep ourselves and our quarters neat and clean, and cook and eat, and soon we began to fill out and look like men once more." A few men managed to get passes to see Vicksburg and inspected the 1863 siege lines. "With the choice of positions the rebels had, and the natural advantages presented," noted Lieutenant Elliott, "it was almost a mystery how the troops under General Grant could have advanced as close as they did to the rebel line." Sgt. Thomas Josiah Hinds (Co. K, 18th MI Inf) agreed: "[I]t is the greatest wonder, how Grant took this place for it is a fortress."[26]

When word of Lee's surrender reached Camp Fisk, a celebration followed. "While I write the sound of artillery is reverberating through the air and great joy prevails over the news of the entire capture of General Lee and his army on the 9th, of this month," Sergeant Foley wrote. First Sergeant Ely wrote in his diary for April 13, "Heavy cannonading in Vicksburg. . . . War news glorious, Lee caved to Grant, bully, bully, glorious bully, if any man can save the union, why General Grant is the man."[27]

Two days later, on April 15, with Captain Williams still away, Capt. Frederic Speed became the acting commissioner of exchange.

General Dana and Assistant Adjutant General Capt. Joseph Warren Miller would remember that Speed volunteered for the job. "I feel quite sure that there never were any written orders assigning Captain Speed to the place," Miller stated. "The business was given into his own charge on his own suggestion." Dana wrote, "During [Williams'] absence Capt. Frederic Speed, Assistant Adjutant General of this Department, at his own suggestion, was assigned by me, to the performance of Captain Williams duties and took entire charge of the receiving of prisoners from the rebel agents and of sending them to the parole camps at the North."[28]

Captain Speed, however, remembered that he was ordered to take over as the acting exchange commissioner. "I should have had nothing to do with the prisoners, and I should not have had, if I had not been ordered to do so," he later claimed. Capt. William H. H. Emmons, a junior assistant adjutant general, agreed. When Emmons was asked "by whose orders" Speed was made acting commissioner of exchange, he replied, "By those of Major General Dana." And in fact, General Dana did eventually admit to ordering Speed to take on the exchange job. "I had first intrusted [sic] the whole exchange business to Captain Williams," Dana explained, "but he having left, Capt. Speed was placed in charge of it in addition to his other duties, *by my orders*" (emphasis added).[29] As will be seen, it was not unusual for people connected with the *Sultana* disaster to change their stories from time to time.

In fact, no official order was ever issued. As the senior assistant adjutant general in the Department of Mississippi, Speed had already been sending the lists of prisoners' names to St. Louis and had already established a working relationship with Colonel Watts and Colonel Henderson. It seemed only natural that he would take over as the agent of exchange while Williams was away. "I simply assumed the duties while Capt. Williams was absent," Speed recalled. "The original order [placing Captain Williams in charge] was not revoked."[30]

With Captain Speed acting as the commissioner of exchange, General Dana began the process of shipping the men at Camp Fisk upriver to the North. "I ordered Captain Speed to prepare their rolls as rapidly as possible," Dana wrote, "and send them north as rapidly as the rolls could be prepared, calculating, as near as circumstances would permit, about a thousand at a load for the regular packets as they passed."[31] Dana's orders called for the men to be shipped north in lots of about one thousand, and that was the number of men Captain Hatch had offered Captain Mason on April 17 when the *Sultana* came downriver spreading the news of Lincoln's assassination.

Speed was forced to work with badly jumbled Confederate records. The names were not listed in alphabetical order or by state or regiment. The Confederate prison authorities had simply entered the names into the different prison camps' books and rolls as each man arrived. By April 17 Speed had managed to copy the names of all of the Illinois prisoners and regular army soldiers into a separate book, and General Dana subsequently issued Special Orders No. 133 sending all the prisoners from Illinois home as soon as possible. "The Illinois men were Parrolled today and getting ready for going North to Benton Barracks St. Louis," Sergeant Ely wrote in his diary. As usual, Captain Hatch's Quartermaster Department was to furnish transportation.[32]

The *Henry Ames* of the Merchants' and People's Line, which held the government transportation contract, was expected to carry the Illinois men upriver. The *Ames* had struck a snag and sank back in July 1864 (with the *Sultana* rescuing her cargo) but had since been raised and repaired. With Capt. Thomas C. Crawford in command, the *Henry Ames* was expected to take about one thousand men to Benton Barracks. When the *Ames* was late arriving in Vicksburg, Captain Speed and his assistants continued adding more men to the first batch as they worked on the prison books and rolls.[33]

While the paroling officers waited for the *Henry Ames*, a runner from another steamboat line, almost certainly the Atlantic and Mississippi Steamship Company Line (AMSCL), which did not hold a government contract, came into the Quartermaster Department in the headquarters building of General Dana in search of a batch of prisoners. "If it takes money to get them, we have as much as anybody," the runner blurted out. Civilian clerk George B. Dunton, one of the men who had been arrested as an accomplice to Captain Hatch for his fraudulent schemes in 1861–62, was still working with Hatch. He later claimed that he was shocked by the insinuation that people in the Quartermaster Department would be willing to take a bribe to put the men on a noncontract boat. "I replied that it did not take any money in *this* office."[34] Apparently that was not the case, since Captain Hatch met with Captain Mason of the *Sultana* on the night of April 17 to arrange that very thing.

Well aware that General Dana had ordered the paroled prisoners to be taken upriver in batches of one thousand, Captain Hatch went down to the riverfront to offer a deal to Captain Mason. He promised to guarantee Mason a full load of one thousand men if Mason would agree to return a percentage of the government transport fees to Hatch. Despite the recent news of Lincoln's death, Captain Hatch had left the waterfront a happy man as the *Sultana* continued downriver toward New Orleans.

9

HIDDEN OFFERS

In spite of the tragic news the *Sultana* had brought to Vicksburg, the prisoner exchange had to go on. Around April 18, William C. Jones, an agent for the Atlantic and Mississippi Steamship Company Line, went into the riverfront office of Capt. William Kerns, assistant quartermaster in charge of transportation, and met with civilian clerk G. Gordon Adams. Jones was there to offer a deal. According to Adams, Jones said, "I understand there is a premium offered to get these troops and if there is anything of that kind, we are willing to pay as much as anybody." Taken aback by the offered bribe, Adams recalled, "I immediately closed his mouth on that subject by telling him it was useless to talk in that way at our office."[1]

A day later, April 19, Adams told Captain Hatch and his chief civilian clerk, George B. Dunton, about Jones' offer. Dunton remembered that "allusion was made to these paroled prisoners who were to be sent north. I think he [Adams] asked if there were any to go, saying there seems to be a great desire to take them, adding, they are offering 50 cts. per head for the contract of transportation." In his own recollection, Adams spoke of the offers "openly and in a joking way so that anyone could have heard it in the office."[2] Neither Adams nor Dunton knew that at least one such deal had already been completed.

Before the contract boat *Henry Ames* arrived, the noncontract steamer *W. R. Arthur* nosed in at Vicksburg on April 22, having left

70

New Orleans fifteen hours ahead of the *Ames*.[3] AMSCL agent Jones approached James P. McGuire, a steamboat passenger agent, and offered him "ten cents a head for the prisoners" if McGuire could use his influence to get the first load placed on the *Arthur*. Jones would later call this offer "a regular business transaction." Others might call it a bribe. McGuire agreed and sought out the acting assistant quartermaster, 2nd Lt. William H. Tillinghast (Co. E, 66th USCT), to put the deal in motion.[4]

Tillinghast was a good man to approach. Arrested for forgery at age eighteen, he had skipped bail and enlisted as a private in the 72nd Illinois Infantry on February 17, 1864. Because his parents were "persons of the highest respectability" (his father was a prominent music professor in Chicago), it seemed likely that he would be saved "from the penitentiary," but Tillinghast didn't wait around to find out.[5] He was now working under Capt. Reuben Hatch, suggesting that birds of a feather do flock together.

McGuire admitted that he "made application for [the shipment of the paroled prisoners] to Lieut. Tillinghast, asking him who was the proper person to apply to. He told me he was shipping them. I thought this was the fact from his having been at the parole camp." Without mentioning Jones' name, McGuire told Tillinghast that he "was employed by one of the Atlantic's line. I told him what I was to receive for the prisoners and also told him that if I got them through his efforts he should lose nothing by it, or words to that effect." In other words, if Tillinghast could get the prisoners for the *W. R. Arthur*, McGuire was willing to share a bit of his earnings with the lieutenant. Tillinghast remembered, "The substance of it was that he supposed that I had sufficient influence to secure the shipment of the men on any boat."[6]

Realizing that he was "unexperienced in the business," Tillinghast went to the office of Captain Kerns, who was in charge of river transportation, and asked about the upcoming shipment. Kerns told him that the men "would all go with the People's Lines" (the contract line). Unable to secure any men for McGuire and the *W. R. Arthur*, Tillinghast left the office but did not tell McGuire that he had been unsuccessful.[7]

After the *Henry Ames* finally arrived on April 22, Jones, still hoping to get some men for the *Arthur*, approached Tillinghast in person and asked "what boat would get [the prisoners] and what the rate was." Jones undoubtedly knew that the *Henry Ames* had already been selected to take the first lot of prisoners and that the government was paying $9 per officer and $3.25 per enlisted man from Vicksburg to St. Louis. In using the term "rate," he was actually trying to see what bribe Tillinghast would require to put the men on a noncontract boat. Tillinghast said that he "knew nothing about it," meaning that he knew nothing about the "rate" necessary to bribe a Union officer. He then told Jones that "the men would go with the People's Line." Realizing that he was wasting his time with Tillinghast, Jones departed.[8]

Word of the arrival of the *Henry Ames* was immediately telegraphed to the parole camp. In the extra day that it had taken for the *Ames* to arrive, Captain Speed had been able to complete the rolls for the men from Iowa, Louisiana, Minnesota, Missouri, and Wisconsin, and they were ordered to join the men from Illinois on the *Ames*. The men rode the train into Vicksburg and then walked the short distance from the depot to the wharf boat. Eventually, 1,315 men crowded onto the *Ames*, 315 more than General Dana had envisioned sending at one time. Still, when Dana came down to the riverfront to see the boat depart on the evening of April 22, he said nothing about the boat being overloaded beyond the one thousand men he had stipulated. "I had taken great interest in expediting the departure of these brave fellows to their homes," he explained.[9]

By allowing more than one thousand paroled prisoners on the *Henry Ames*, General Dana became complicit with the disregard to his wishes his junior officers had shown. If Dana had acted on his authority and chastised or punished the officers responsible, there might not have been any more overloaded boats. Instead, he gave tacit approval to the overloading. His junior officers now assumed that it was okay to overload the steamboat transports. It might be four hundred more next time, or even five hundred.

While the *Henry Ames* was being loaded and the *W. R. Arthur* was still at the waterfront, agent McGuire, still believing that Lieutenant

Tillinghast controlled the loading, accosted Tillinghast. "God damn it why did not the *Arthur* get those men," McGuire demanded; "you could have done it." At that point, Tillinghast finally admitted that he had nothing to do with the loading of the men. "I told him that I had no men to give to any boat and that I could not give them if I wanted to do so." Tillinghast would later say that McGuire became angry and blamed it all on the *"Ames* men" and the agents of the Merchants' and People's Line, claiming that they "were trying to beat me and that he would fix them." McGuire then turned to him and asked, "Are you going to stand by and see me beat?" Undoubtedly intimidated by the angry steamboat agent, Tillinghast recalled, "I said that I would stand by him."[10]

A short time later, agent Jones cornered Tillinghast again, but this time he was more straightforward. "He [Jones] took me to one side and said if I could secure the men for his line of boats, I should be remunerated," Tillinghast remembered. This time, when the two parted, Jones probably felt that he finally had Tillinghast on the hook.[11]

On the evening of April 22, Captain Speed sent an orderly, Pvt. Jameson Cox (Co. B, 2nd NJ Cav), to the Quartermaster Department to tell Hatch "that Captain Speed wanted [Hatch] to inform him when any boat should come for prisoners . . . so that he could get the men off as early in the morning as possible." Speed and his assistants had been working hard on the prison books and had the names of about seven hundred more men—from the northeastern states and Alabama, Kansas, and Mississippi—completed. All he needed was for Hatch to inform him when the next boat arrived. Cox remembered that "Hatch said he would let him know."[12]

About the time that Hatch was promising to inform Speed when the next boat arrived, Captain Ben Tabor's *Olive Branch*, the *Sultana's* old rival, came into Vicksburg. A noncontract boat, the *Olive Branch* was docking at the company's wharf boat when AMSCL agent Jones showed up and spoke to Tabor. "[K]nowing that troops were to be shipped, I advised the captain to lie over until Sunday morning" (April 23, 1865), Jones later testified. Hoping to get some men, although his boat had no government contract, Captain Tabor went to see Captain Hatch. What was said between the two was not recorded, but it is definitely known that on the night of April 22 Captain Hatch knew that the *Olive Branch* was in Vicksburg. Captain Tabor came away from the meeting having decided to lay over until the morrow.[13]

It is almost certain that Captain Hatch cut a deal with Captain Tabor to put men on the *Olive Branch* in return for a kickback. Jones confirmed that "the arrangement was made between Captain Tabor and Hatch."[14] Although Hatch had agreed to inform Captain Speed immediately when boats arrived, he failed to tell him about the *Olive Branch*. He also failed to notify Captain Kerns, who was in charge of river transportation in Vicksburg. Captain Hatch had just set a devious plan into motion.

The next morning, April 23, Captain Speed sent Private Cox over to the Quartermaster Department to find out if any new boats had arrived. Cox recalled that "Hatch said there was none." This was a bold-faced lie. Hatch knew full well that the *Olive Branch* was in because he had talked to her captain just the night before. Private Cox returned to Speed and informed him that no boats had come in during the night.[15]

About 8 a.m. Captain Hatch finally informed Captain Speed that the *Olive Branch* had come in the night before. A shocked Speed rushed over to the Quartermaster Department and complained, but Hatch innocently informed Speed that he himself "had but just before learned of her arrival" and claimed that he had known nothing about the *Olive Branch* being in port overnight. He then turned the blame on his master of transportation, saying, "Capt. Kerns is required to report all boats upon their arrival to me. He failed to report the arrival of the *Olive Branch*. . . . I do not know why he so failed to report her."[16]

With men ready to send home, Speed was incensed that Captain Kerns had failed to report the arrival of the *Olive Branch*. At this point, according to Speed, Hatch suggested that bribery was involved. Speed believed him. By believing that Kerns had taken a bribe from the contract boat line and had failed to announce the arrival of the noncontract *Olive Branch* until a contract boat could arrive, Speed was playing right into Hatch's hands. Speed decided to thwart Kerns and, according to Hatch, "ordered the [*Olive Branch*] to receive fourteen hundred (1,400) prisoners," even though she was a noncontract boat.[17]

Hatch would later claim that in doing so, Captain Speed had taken the selection of the transport out of the hands of the Quartermaster Department, even though it was Hatch's job to select the next boat. More than likely, however, Hatch wholeheartedly agreed with Speed. He already had a deal with Captain Tabor to send the next big lot of prisoners on the *Olive Branch*. Why should he protest the usurpation of his authority?

Speed rushed out to Camp Fisk and spent the rest of the day gathering men from the eastern states and from Kansas, Alabama, and Mississippi and sending them into Vicksburg. At the end of the day, when the *Olive Branch* was ready to leave, she was detained for some unspecified reason, which Speed unaccountably attributed to Captain Kerns. When the *Olive Branch* finally pulled away in the late afternoon, she had on board "619 paroled prisoners," all the men whose names Speed could get ready. It was not an overly large number, but it was enough to make Captain Tabor, and in turn Captain Hatch, happy.[18]

The *Olive Branch* was not even out of sight before Captain Speed showed up at department headquarters to lodge a formal complaint against Captain Kerns. General Dana recalled that Speed was in "considerable indignation" and "asked for authority to place Captain Kerns, the Quartermaster of Transportation at this post, in arrest." Speed then explained the facts as told to him by Hatch: Kerns had failed to report the arrival of the *Olive Branch* to his superior (Hatch), and the boat had been unnecessarily detained after the men had been put on board. As Dana recollected their conversation, Speed told him that he "had been informed that this delay was made because she did not belong to the line which had the Government contract; and that the contract line had offered a pecuniary consideration, per capita, for the men to be kept for their boats; and the intention was to detain the *Olive Branch* till one of the contract line came along to take the load from her." Speed would later state, "[I]n consequence of an intimation I had had the day previously by Hatch . . . I thought there was something going on wrong and I mentioned to [General Dana] the remarkable detention of the steamer *Olive Branch* as tending to confirm my suspicion."[19]

Surprised by these allegations, General Dana immediately sent for Kerns and directed him to "make a written explanation of the detention of the steamer." Kerns explained that he didn't know the *Olive Branch* had been detained until after she had left Vicksburg. Apparently, Dana accepted Kerns' explanation, because he took no action again the assistant quartermaster.[20]

Captain Kerns was surprised as well by Speed's allegations. Although he was the person in charge of river transportation, Kerns had not been consulted in the selection of the *Henry Ames* or the *Olive Branch*. Hatch had selected the *Henry Ames*, and Speed had selected the *Olive Branch* with the tacit approval of Hatch. Kerns had likewise known nothing about the number of men placed on the steamers until runners from the boats came to his office for a transportation pass after all the men were on board.[21]

After meeting with General Dana, Speed was in the adjutant general's office when Chief Quartermaster Hatch approached him to discuss the next shipment. The only men left at Camp Fisk belonged to units from Indiana, Kentucky, Michigan, Ohio, Tennessee, and Virginia (or West Virginia) and would be shipped to Camp Chase, Ohio, near Columbus instead of Benton Barracks, Missouri, to be mustered out. A steamboat, or steamboats, would carry the men to Cairo, where they would be put on a train for transport to Ohio. Hatch said that he believed the men would be ready to go in about two days, on Tuesday, April 25. Speed said no, the lists were not ready yet, but he should have all of the rolls deciphered and made out in four days' time, by Thursday, April 27.

Hatch then brought up the subject of transportation. He "named several boats that were coming up," Speed recalled. "The *Sultana* was one of them." Hatch reminded Speed that the *Sultana* was a contract boat and was entitled to take as many men as could be made available. He also reminded Speed of the rumors of bribery by agents for noncontract boats. By the time the conversation ended, Hatch had convinced Speed that "the *Sultana* was intended to take part of the troops."[22] With one conversation between the man responsible for selecting the transportation and the man currently responsible for delivering the prisoners to the waterfront, Captain Hatch had managed to ensure that the *Sultana* would get a load of men, and that he himself would get his cut of government money.

Near 8:45 p.m. on April 23, the *Sultana* finally limped into Vicksburg with her leaky boiler. Perhaps trying to make sure that there was no oversight this time, Captain Kerns immediately reported the steamer's arrival to department headquarters, making sure that Hatch's clerk George Dunton was aware of her arrival.[23]

Captain Speed was still at department headquarters when the *Sultana*'s arrival was announced. General Dana would later say, "The next boat was the *Sultana* and she arrived so soon after the departure of the *Olive Branch* that Captain Speed reported to me that rolls for only about 300 men could be prepared and that therefore, none would go by her, but they would wait for the next boat."[24] Although Speed had initially told Hatch that the *Sultana* would get some men, she had arrived so soon after the *Olive Branch* left that he now felt otherwise.

While Chief Engineer Wintringer sought out a boiler mechanic, Captain Mason and agent Miles Sells went to see Captain Hatch. According to Sells, Mason said that "he wanted all the men he could ship on his boat and asked [Hatch] if he had any ready." Hatch "said they had the men to ship," Sells recalled, meaning there were at least the one thousand promised prisoners, but "[Hatch] didn't know whether Speed could have the rolls made up." Hatch complained that Speed "seemed very slow in getting up the rolls," and told Mason and Sells that Speed had only "about three hundred or perhaps five hundred that he would be able to ship the next day." Mason immediately complained that "it would hardly pay him to wait until the next day for that number of men and claimed that if the men were ready he was entitled to them, being one of the boats carrying government freight."[25] Mason did not mention that he would be detained anyway because his boiler needed repairs.

Mason must also have been angry when he discovered that this last group of prisoners would be going to Cairo, only about 670 miles away, instead of the 880 miles to St. Louis. Rather than the $9 per officer and $3.25 per enlisted man he was expecting to receive, Mason would get only $8 per officer and $2.75 per enlisted man. In order to make up the difference, he would need a larger load of prisoners.

Hoping to mollify Mason, Hatch, who was also in charge of land transportation, told him "that if Speed could get them ready and bring them in, he, Capt. Speed, could have the transportation"; that is, Hatch would make sure the trains to bring the men in from Camp Fisk would be available. Sells also said that Hatch suggested that Mason and Sells go over to Speed's boardinghouse to talk to the captain himself. Hurting for money, especially with an upcoming repair bill, and determined to get his promised load of one thousand prisoners, Mason set out with Sells to talk to Speed. "[B]ut as we left," Sells remembered, "[Captain] Hatch remarked that he did not think (Speed) would ship them, for the reason that he (Speed) wanted to put them all on one boat and would not have them ready before Thursday morning."[26]

At Speed's boardinghouse, Sells introduced Mason as the "Captain of the steamer *Sultana*" and told Speed that Hatch had sent them "to see how many men he could give the boat." Speed said that he badly wanted to ship the prisoners, but "he couldn't get the trains" on account of a court-martial taking place the next day that required their use. After informing Speed that Hatch had agreed to provide the necessary trains, Mason declared that "he was entitled to these men, as his boat was one of the People's Line that had the contract for carrying [them]."[27]

Mason wanted to "pin [Speed] down to a certain number," but Speed refused. Captain Mason "appeared to be very much disappointed when I told him that no men were ready to go," Speed recalled, " . . . as the rolls for but between three and four hundred men had been completed and I did not think it would be possible to get even that number checked and into Vicksburg before he would want to leave, but told him that if he wanted to wait that as far as I was concerned he could have all the men that could be got ready to go." Sells confirmed that Speed "said he would give all the men he could, but couldn't say how fast he could get the rolls made out."[28]

Captain Mason once again failed to mention that he wasn't going anywhere because of the boiler repair. Frustrated that he might be delayed in getting his promised one thousand men—and his government stipend—Mason set out by himself to see General Smith, who had promised to help him if he had trouble getting a load of prisoners.[29]

While Mason was working hard to get his promised load, Chief Engineer Wintringer had brought R. G. Taylor, a boilermaker from Klein's Foundry with twenty-eight years' experience, to inspect the leaky boiler. Taylor recalled that "the middle larboard [left] boiler had bulged out on the straight seam on the third sheet." That is curious, because Wintringer stated the leak was in the "larboard boiler." The middle larboard boiler would be the number 3 boiler in the bank of four, while the larboard boiler would be the number 4 boiler. Since he was the chief engineer and would be the one keeping an eye on the patch as the boat traveled upriver from Vicksburg, Wintringer's memory is probably the correct one. It was the number 4 boiler, then, the outside left-hand boiler, that was in need of repair.

After thoroughly inspecting the bulge and leak, Taylor told Wintringer that it would be necessary to cut out the two bulged-out sheets of iron and replace them with new sheets. This was a major job that would sideline the boat for a couple of days at least. Aware that Captain Mason had gone into town to obtain a load of paroled prisoners, Wintringer knew that the *Sultana* could not be sidelined for two days. Taylor remembered Wintringer asking "if I could repair her in any way so they could get to St. Louis." The experienced Taylor told Wintringer, "[I]f I done anything at all I would make a job of it or have nothing to do with it." Taylor then left the *Sultana* "with the intentions of having nothing to do with her." Before he could get off the wharf boat, Wintringer called him back and asked him "to do the best I could and get them out as soon as I could." Perhaps against his better judgment, Taylor relented and began work on the defective boiler.[30]

When Mason arrived at department headquarters he ran into Captain Williams, who had just returned from Cairo. On reporting back to headquarters, Williams had been informed that Captain Speed was the acting assistant exchange commissioner and "that all but 1,300 or 1,400 of [the prisoners] had been paroled and sent North." Williams had just received this information when Captain Mason arrived and announced that he was going to make a formal complaint to Washington "against the exchange office" because the second large load of men had been put on a noncontract boat. He also told Williams that Captain Speed was refusing to give him a large group of prisoners. Because he had just returned to Vicksburg and was not familiar with the circumstances, Williams sent for Speed to explain.[31]

When Speed arrived, Williams asked him "if it was not possible to get the men off on the *Sultana*," stating that he was "anxious to have the matter closed up." Speed told Williams what he had just told Mason: he had only "three or four hundred men for whom the rolls had been made out." Speed then agreed to send the four hundred on the *Sultana* rather than hold them until he could make up a larger load. When Mason complained that the number was too small, Captain Williams "suggested that the names could perhaps be checked on the [Confederate] books of the parole camp and the [Union] rolls completed afterward." If this were done, the *Sultana* should be able to get a good-sized load. The "proper way to do it," Williams said, "would be to check the men as they went on board the boat."[32]

Captain Williams apparently was once again acting as the authorized commissioner of exchange and was making the decision to ship all the men at Camp Fisk north immediately and work on the rolls afterward. Names could be called from the Confederate books and a checkmark made next to each name. Later, the names with the checkmarks could be recorded on the Union rolls, since any remaining unchecked names would be of prisoners who had already gone North on the *Henry Ames* or *Olive Branch* and had already been transferred to the Union rolls. Apparently, Captain Mason was pleased with the arrangement, because Miles Sells recalled that Mason told him "there would be no trouble about getting all the men he wanted."[33]

After Mason left department headquarters, Williams told Speed that he "did not intend to be mixed up in steamboat quarrels." Speed recalled that Williams also said that "the Quartermaster Department had all to do with the transportation and that they could do as they chose about it, or they could arrange it, something of that kind." Williams remembered that "Captain Speed expressed that, as his opinion, also."[34]

Williams also remembered that Speed proposed a special working arrangement between the two of them: "[Speed] informed me that there was only thirteen (13) or fourteen (14) hundred now to be exchanged, and that [since] he was familiar with the affairs (and I was not) he proposed that he should continue and finish up the work[,] which I consented to." Speed himself remembered that he and Williams "thought [it] advisable that I should continue on active supervision in as much as I had taken so active a part heretofore and was more familiar with it than it was possible for Capt. Williams to be." Accordingly, Williams would remain as the overall commissioner of exchange, but Speed would continue as acting commissioner and would continue reconciling the Confederate books and the Union rolls. Finally, Williams agreed to accompany Speed to Camp Fisk the next morning and help with hastening the last group into Vicksburg.[35]

Satisfied that they had worked out an agreeable solution, Williams and Speed went to Captain Hatch's office to inform him about the arrangement and to make sure that trains would be available to bring the men into the city. Perhaps with dollar signs flashing before his eyes, Hatch suggested that the *Sultana* should take all the remaining prisoners instead of only one thousand. Captain Williams recalled that Speed objected "on account of the rolls not being made out so as to call their names."[36] Speed was willing to send some men on the *Sultana*, but certainly not all of them.

Rolls had already been completed for about three or four hundred men from Ohio, but it would take a long time to go through the jumbled Confederate books to ferret out the names of the rest of the men from Ohio, put a checkmark next to the names, get them on the trains, and get them down to the *Sultana*. If *all* the remaining men at Camp Fisk were to be sent on the *Sultana*, the process would have to be repeated for the men from Indiana, Kentucky, Michigan, Tennessee, and West Virginia as well. Captain Speed doubted that it could be done in one day. However, with Captain Hatch promising to furnish the necessary rail transportation and Captain Williams promising to help, Speed finally relented. "It was decided that this could be done," Speed testified, "and orders were sent to the camp to have all the men rationed, organized and prepared to go as soon as possible."[37]

After the three officers parted, Captain Williams ran into his assistant commissioner of exchange, Lieutenant Davenport, and informed him about the arrangements worked out between Mason, Hatch, Speed, and himself. Wishing to get started as soon as possible, Williams, in his capacity as commissioner of exchange, sent Davenport to Camp Fisk "that evening to get the men ready for shipment as fast as they could be got ready."[38]

Meanwhile, Captain Speed went to department headquarters to explain to General Dana what had just transpired. "Captain Speed came to my office and reported that he had consulted with Captain Williams and had decided to ship all the balance of prisoners on the *Sultana*, as Capt. Williams had advised that they [could] be counted and checked as they went on board and he would prepare the rolls afterward." Dana was satisfied with the arrangement and asked Speed how many prisoners would be involved. Speed "replied about 1,300— not to exceed 1,400, that the exact number could not be stated owing to discrepancies in the rebel rolls."[39]

Originally, General Dana had stipulated that the prisoners were to be sent home at "about a thousand at a load." Although the number now promised for the *Sultana* was once again larger than that, General Dana made no objection to Captain Speed. About that same number had already been shipped north on the *Henry Ames* and Dana had made no objection. How could he protest now?

As a final act for Sunday, April 23, 1865, General Dana directed Captain Speed to send Special Orders No. 139 to General Smith, instructing him to form a detail of "one officer, three non-commissioned officers, and eighteen privates . . . to be sent as guards, with [the] paroled prisoners to Camp Chase, Ohio." The selected officer was to take his command and report "to the senior officer on board the steamer *Sultana* at 12 o'clock tomorrow."[40] The final decision had been made. The *Sultana* had been selected by Captain Hatch and approved by General Dana to take the last group of men from Camp Fisk, estimated at between 1,300 and 1,400 men. Everything was falling in line for Captain Hatch.

10

THE LOADING
BEGINS

Captain Hatch showed up at Captain Speed's boardinghouse before 7 a.m. on April 24, 1865, to see him "in reference to the shipment of the prisoners which was to take place on that day." Perhaps making sure that the men—and his money—were still guaranteed, Captain Hatch spent "about twenty minutes" in conversation with Speed and came away understanding "that the prisoners should go on the steamer *Sultana*." Speed recalled that Hatch "asked . . . about the shipment of the prisoners and [was told] that it had been decided by myself and Capt. Williams to send them all forward on that day."[1] Hatch surely could not have been happier.

Shortly after Hatch left, Speed went to department headquarters and had the officer on duty, Assistant Adjutant General Capt. Joseph Warren Miller, write up Special Orders No. 140 stipulating, "All of the prisoners of war, officers and enlisted men, remaining at the Parole Camp, at Four-Mile Bridge, and those which have been sent to Hospital at Big Black, from the States of Virginia, Tennessee, Kentucky, Ohio, Indiana, and Michigan, have been paroled by Lieutenant Colonel H. A. M. Henderson, Assistant Special Agent of Exchange, C.S.A." The order also stipulated that "Major W. H.

Fidler, 6th Kentucky Cavalry, will take charge of the men, now in camp at Four-Mile Bridge, and will organize them into companies, and assign the officers and non-commissioned officers, and will proceed with them to Camp Chase, Ohio, where he will report to the commanding officer for further instruction." Maj. Frank Miller was ordered to provide the 1,400 or so men with rations for seven days. As usual, the order specified, "The Quartermaster's Department will furnish transportation." A notation at the bottom of the order stated, "Copy furnished Captain of the *Sultana*," indicating that the transporting vessel had already been selected.[2]

No order issued prior to this one had included a notation about a specific boat or steamboat captain. When Captain Kerns, master of river transportation, was later asked if it was "usual or customary to find a notification upon the orders you received for the transportation of troops, that the captain or master of a certain vessel would be, or had been, furnished with a copy of the order," Kerns answered, "No sir, it was not." Captain Miller, however, recalled that "captains of steamboats were frequently in the habit of visiting headquarters in reference to the shipment of troops, that on some such visit I furnished him, Captain Mason, with a copy as a matter of information." Although it was not the regular practice, it was not prohibited for steamboat captains to be given copies of orders of transportation.[3]

Out at Camp Fisk, Major Miller and his assistants were already hard at work, having been informed by Lieutenant Davenport the previous evening that the men were to be prepared for transportation. Pvt. George S. Schmutz (Co. I, 102nd OH Inf) remembered, "Glad shouts of joy rent the air when the news came to us to pull up camp at Vicksburg on the 24th of April, 1865, and embark on the boat on our homeward journey. We had been lying in Parole Camp . . . for about four weeks, expecting orders every day to tear up quarters." "We did not wait for the second order," Sergeant Karns said. "As we had no knapsacks to pack or accoutrements to get ready, we were over to the railroad in a very short notice."[4]

As the sun rose, Maj. William H. Fidler (Field and Staff, 6th KY Cav), the senior officer among the prisoners and the man placed in charge per Special Orders No. 140, began to organize the men for the trip home. They were first organized by state and then into companies of one hundred men each, with an officer placed in charge of each company, although Major Fidler's aide, Capt. James M. McCown (Co. K, 6th KY Cav), recalled that not all the companies had an officer accompanying them. For instance, the 432 Tennessee prisoners put on the *Sultana* should have been accompanied by 5 officers, yet there were only 2 officers among the group. Three of the companies were commanded by noncommissioned officers, more than likely three of the seven first sergeants.[5]

Since the rolls for the Ohio soldiers were already complete, the Ohio prisoners assembled first, moving into a large field in front of the train depot. After sorting them into companies, the officers had the men sit on the ground to await the arrival of the train that would take them into Vicksburg. While they waited, Lieutenant Davenport continued working on the rolls, looking for the names of the Indiana soldiers in the messy Confederate books and transferring them to the orderly Union rolls.[6]

At the waterfront, boilermaker R. G. Taylor continued repairing the leak on the *Sultana*'s left-hand boiler. While cutting out a section of the boiler, he noted that the twenty-four flues running from front to rear were in "perfect condition." However, he also noticed that the inside of the boiler was scorched. "I think the iron was burned," Taylor recalled, "and that the boilers were used with little water."[7] Such usage was dangerous indeed. When a boiler was operated with too little water, the flues above the waterline would get red hot. Should more water be suddenly introduced into the boiler, either via a water pump or because the boat tilted to one side, the water would come in contact with the superheated flues and instantly turn to steam, dramatically increasing the pressure inside the boiler. If the boiler was not strong enough to withstand the sudden increase of pressure, an explosion could result.

While the boilers were being repaired, Chief Engineer Wintringer took the opportunity to clean them. Although the spring floods had churned up the sediment in the Mississippi, Wintringer found that "not a great amount" of sediment had collected inside the boilers during the trip upriver from New Orleans, where the boilers had also been cleaned.[8] By early morning on Monday, April 24, the cleaning was done. All that remained was the completion of the repair and the loading of the prisoners.

Boilermaker Taylor had worked throughout the night. "I cut out a patch of 11 by 26 including the lap," he recalled afterward. "I desired to set the sheet back to which I intended to rivet, and was prevented from doing so by the engineer." Instead of being allowed to flatten the bulged-out plating before applying the patch, Taylor was instructed to rivet the patch directly over the bulge. When Taylor was later asked, "Did you consider that the patch was only a temporary one?" He answered, "I did consider it temporary. The Captain said to me that he would have the entire two sheets cut out at St. Louis." When asked, "Was it necessary in your opinion that the bulge on the boiler should be forced back for the safety of the boilers," Taylor replied, "Yes it was." Taylor added, "I had to fit my patch to it." The body of the boiler itself was made of charcoal-hammered No. 1 iron, $17/48$ inch thick. The patch, according to Taylor, was "No. 1 charcoal iron, a full ¼ [inch thick.]" One-quarter inch equals $12/48$ inch, which means that the patch placed on the boiler was $5/48$ inch thinner than the body of the boiler. John Witzig, the supervising inspector of steam vessels at St. Louis, later testified, "According to law, that boiler was allowed one hundred and forty-two (142), or one hundred and forty-five (145) pounds of steam, with the thickness of seventeen forty-eighths ($17/48$) inches." With the thinner patch, Witzig explained, "the law would only have allowed one hundred and forty-three hundredths pounds (100.43 lbs) [of pressure]." Although Wintringer supervised the entire repair, he made no protest over the use of the thinner material.[9]

While the repair job was under way, Lieutenant Tillinghast, who had agreed to be "remunerated" by agent William Jones of the non-contract Atlantic and Mississippi Steamboat Company Line, went on board the *Sultana* and unexpectedly ran into Jones. Almost immediately Jones asked Tillinghast how many men would be going on the *Sultana*. "I said that I knew not," Tillinghast remembered replying. When Jones asked if all of the remaining men at Camp Fisk would go on the *Sultana*, Tillinghast "again said that I did not know but supposed they would not." Apparently, Tillinghast had better knowledge of the number of men still remaining at Camp Fisk than Captain Speed did. While Captain Speed thought that the remaining men at Camp Fisk could all fit comfortably on the *Sultana*, Lieutenant Tillinghast "supposed they would not."[10]

Jones informed Tillinghast that the noncontract steamboat *Pauline Carroll* would be arriving in the late afternoon and, according to Tillinghast, said he "would pay me 15 cts for every man that I would secure for his boat." Tillinghast later admitted, "I think I told him all right, that I would see him again." Although rumors of bribery had been swirling around for the past few days, this was the first confirmed amount and acceptance of a bribe. While Captain Hatch had been able to keep his activities with the *Olive Branch* and with Captain Mason quiet, Lieutenant Tillinghast would readily admit that he had been offered and had accepted a bribe to try to get some prisoners placed on board a rival company's steamboat.[11]

After talking with Tillinghast, Jones went to department head-quarters and "spoke to [Capt.] Hatch, Q.M., on that morning and stated that the *Pauline Carroll* would be here on that evening." Jones told Hatch that he "had been informed that some 2,000 to 2,500 prisoners were to be sent North and asked if we could not get a portion of them." Perhaps because of what he had learned from Tillinghast, Jones thought that the number of men remaining at Camp Fisk was much larger than the 1,300 to 1,400 quoted by Captain Speed. If that were true, they could not all fit comfortably on the *Sultana*. Surely a large number would be available for the *Pauline Carroll* as well.

Jones then offered Captain Hatch, the man charged with selecting the transportation for the prisoners, an incentive to place any overflow on board the *Pauline Carroll*. Hatch was already getting a percentage of Captain Mason's government payout; now he would be guaranteed a payout even if the men were separated and the overflow placed on the *Pauline Carroll*.[12] It was a win–win situation.

Captain Kerns was in his office early on the morning of the sched-uled shipment when Captain Mason came by. In testimony given six days after the event, Kerns said that on the night of April 23 he had "received word from my superintendent [Captain Hatch] that the *Sultana* would not leave this port until the next day [the 24th] as they expected to take a number of paroled prisoners up the river. On the morning of the 24th of April Mr. Mason . . . came to my office and told me he was going to take a lot of paroled prisoners north." Then, for the first time since arriving in Vicksburg, Mason finally told one of the military authorities that the *Sultana* was undergoing repairs. Said Kerns, "He also informed me that he was having his boiler patched, and he expected to have it done by the time the prisoners were loaded."[13] Since Kerns had gotten word the night before that the *Sultana* had been selected as a transport, the appearance of Captain Mason at his office aroused no suspicions.

Eight months later, however, in January 1866, Kerns changed his story and claimed, "The first that I knew that the *Sultana* was going to take prisoners at all was from Captain Mason, who came into my office on the morning of the 24th of April. . . . Knowing that the boat had been in port some time, I asked him when he would leave or why he did not leave. He said he was waiting for a load of paroled prisoners or expected to get a load that day."[14] As was true for many of the officers connected with the loading of the *Sultana*, Kern's story changed after he had time to think about the consequences of his answers.

Near 8:30 a.m., Speed and Williams left department headquarters in company with the orderly Pvt. Jameson Cox and set out for Camp Fisk. When another orderly asked Speed "what boat was going up," Speed answered, "The *Sultana*." Remembered Cox, "By that we understood the prisoners were going on that boat."[15]

While the three were walking the five blocks up Cherry Street to the train tracks, Speed filled Williams in on the previous two large shipments and informed him of the trouble between "the contract [boats] and the other line of steamers." Speed said, "I mentioned to him that in consequence of an intimation I had had the day previously by [Captain] Hatch, [that Captain Kerns had taken a bribe,] that I thought there was something going on wrong and I mentioned to him the remarkable detention of the steamer *Olive Branch* as tending to confirm my suspicion." Speed continued, "I told Capt. Williams that I was very much inclined to think that the People's Line, being the contract line, were entitled to any favors that the Govt. had to dispense, provided that they offered equal facilities." Speed recalled

Williams replying that "as there were stories of bribery, the men had better be delivered at the contract boat, and then the Quartermaster might send them by that or take the responsibility of doing otherwise." In other words, both men agreed that it was their job to get the men from Camp Fisk to the riverfront. After that, it was the job of the Quartermaster Department and Captain Hatch to put them on any boat deemed qualified, contract or not.[16]

When they arrived at the train tracks the three men discovered that the train waiting to take them out to Camp Fisk consisted of only one passenger car and a few boxcars. Since Hatch had promised to provide them with "the best cars on the line," Speed, Williams, and Cox rode the train to the engine house to get two idle passenger cars. They informed the superintendent of military railroads at Vicksburg, Edward D. Butler, of Hatch's promise, and Butler had the two passenger cars attached to the other cars and then joined the others for the four-mile trip out to Camp Fisk.[17]

When the train arrived at the parole camp, the eager Ohio men crowded up to the small platform. With the appearance of Captain Williams in the camp, Lieutenant Davenport understood that Williams was once again in charge. When later asked specifically who was "acting as Commissioner of Exchange on that day," Davenport replied, "I understood Captain George A. Williams to be. That was my understanding of it."[18]

As soon as they reached the camp, Williams and Speed began to load the train. "I think that there was but one state called from the [Union] rolls," Davenport remembered. "That was Ohio. The balance from the [Confederate] books. As each state was called, the names of each man was called from the rolls and the books, and they went on board the cars." Speed and Davenport took turns calling the rolls and checking off names while Williams, Cox, and others helped get the men onto the trains. Cox recalled that Williams was "superintending the loading [of] some of the men on the first train. . . . There were several officiating, among them myself."[19]

Although both Speed and Williams had agreed that Speed should continue to supervise the loading of the trains, most of those who later testified thought that Williams was now in overall charge of the exchange. Colonel Henderson, the Confederate exchange agent, said, "I had recognized Capt. G. A. Williams as the federal commissioner. . . . I regarded all others as agents, adjutants, or clerks of Captain Williams. No other one having been appointed, I always recognized him, of course." Regarding Captain Speed, Henderson wrote, "during [Williams'] absence I had arranged all preliminaries on the Confederate side with Capt. Speed, as temporarily representing Capt. Williams."[20]

Every man who heard his name called and hurried toward the train had first to pass by Surgeon Henry Clay Huntsman (50th USCT), the man in charge of the military hospitals in Vicksburg. It was Huntsman's job to make sure that every man who boarded the train was physically able to make the trip to Cairo. "I was present when the men were selected," Dr. Huntsman later said, "and sorted out the sick men. I designated those who should not go. That was my duty." Huntsman sent about forty-five men back to camp, but many of them circled around and climbed on the train anyway. Dr. Huntsman remembered that "only fifteen (15) reported to me in the evening," suggesting that at least thirty sick prisoners boarded the *Sultana* with their mates.[21]

Around 10 a.m., Capt. William Shields Friesner (Co. A, 58th OH Inf.) was working on some long-overdue reports in his regimental camp outside Vicksburg when a courier handed him an order telling him that he had been selected to head the guard unit of "one officer, three non-commissioned officers, and eighteen privates" who were to accompany the paroled prisoners on the *Sultana*. Perturbed because he was behind in his paperwork, Friesner quickly rode over to General Smith's headquarters to see if he could have the order rescinded. Instead, he was informed that he would not have to report to the *Sultana* until 7 p.m., giving him plenty of time to complete his reports. Left with no option, Friesner headed back to the 58th Ohio encampment to finish his paperwork and get ready for the trip to Cairo.[22]

It was also about 10 a.m. when another contract boat, the beautiful one-month-old *Lady Gay* under Captain John A. Williamson, nosed up to the Vicksburg wharf boat. Captain Kerns was on duty when the 286-foot-long steamboat pulled in. Kerns had "heard from someone, but cannot state who, that all the prisoners at the parole camp near this post, were to go on [the *Sultana*]. I thought there were more men in camp than could be carried with comfort on one boat. [So when the] *Lady Gay* came into port . . . I immediately notified [Captain] Hatch, Chief Quartermaster of this Department, of the fact, and asked him if it would not be advisable to detain the boat and place part of the prisoners on [the *Lady Gay*]." Kerns, of course, was unaware that Hatch had cut a deal with Captain Mason to get a kickback for every man placed on board the *Sultana* and did not want even one prisoner placed on the *Lady Gay*.

Hatch told Kerns "that he had nothing to do with it particularly but said that he would telegraph Capt. Speed . . . asking him whether the steamer *Lady Gay* should be detained to take part of the prisoners."[23] Hatch was in charge of selecting the transport steamboats, of course, and it was his job to have something "to do with it." He could have easily selected the *Lady Gay* to take some of the paroled prisoners, but he wanted a large group to go on the *Sultana*, with any overflow going on the *Pauline Carroll* when she arrived. The more men Captain Mason carried, the more money Hatch got. To appease Kerns, however, Hatch told Kerns that he could detain the *Lady Gay* while he sent a telegram out to Camp Fisk to see about dividing the men. Kerns detained the *Lady Gay* on the word of Captain Hatch, although her captain told him that he "was anxious to proceed and did not wish to stop."[24]

It took more than an hour for Hatch to send the telegram, for Speed to respond, and for Hatch to notify Kerns that all the men would go on the *Sultana*. Both Speed and Williams were still under the impression that there were only about 1,400 men left at Camp Fisk, a large but not unprecedented number. "A few moments after that dispatch from Hatch," Kerns recalled, "Brigadier General Morgan L. Smith . . . and Captain Williamson of the *Lady Gay* came to my office. General Smith asked me if I had heard from Hatch, if so, let [Williamson] off. I informed him of the contents of the telegram, or showed it to him. He then directed me to let [the *Lady Gay*] proceed." Perhaps wishing to allay Kerns' fears about an overcrowded *Sultana*,

Williamson added that the *Pauline Carroll* would be up during the afternoon and should be available to take any overflow.[25] The *Lady Gay* left Vicksburg just before noon without a single paroled prisoner on board.

When the officers at Camp Fisk had finished loading almost 650 Ohio men on the train, they began loading some of the Indiana men, whose rolls they had begun working on. The names of fifty-one Indiana soldiers culled from the Confederate books were called, and those men came forward and were placed on the train. With approximately seven hundred people crowded into the three passenger cars and the few boxcars, Superintendent Butler protested that that was enough. "I told [Speed] the train had on as many men as it could carry and he still put on more men," recalled Butler. "He must have put on a hundred and fifty (150) or two hundred (200), to the best of my recollection, after I told him the train was full." By the time Speed was through, he had crowded another 150 Indiana soldiers on board the train, for a total of about 850 men.[26]

The officers needed to know the exact number of men going on board the *Sultana* both in order to obtain a transportation pass and to ensure that Captain Mason received the correct government stipend. Since no one at Camp Fisk had been counting the men as they boarded the train, Speed told Williams that he would go "to town to attend to the shipping of the men." Instead, Williams suggested that Speed should stay at Camp Fisk and he would go. "I was not well," Williams recalled, "and I said that I would come into the post. [Speed] asked me as I went in to count the men as they went on board." Along with William Butler, Confederate Commissioner of Exchange Henderson, Major Miller, and Major Fidler (the ranking officer among the prisoners), Captain Williams climbed on board the train and left the parole camp around noon.[27]

When the train arrived at the Vicksburg depot, the men disembarked and assembled for the five-block walk down to the levee. As they marched in fours along Mulberry Street, they got their first glimpse of the *Sultana*. Cpl. Michael M. Brunner (Co. C, 59th OH Inf.) thought she "was a good boat, as Mississippi river boats went in those days." One of the officers noted, "To the soldiers, she had a

record. For it was the *Sultana* . . . draped in mourning and bell tolling, that bore to Vicksburg the startling news of the assassination of
President Lincoln."[28]

Led by Captain Williams and Major Fidler, the column reached
the forward gangway of the lower wharf boat docked near the foot of
Clay Street and stopped. According to Williams, he was willing to
take the responsibility of placing the men on board the wharf boat,
but he was not willing to put them on board the *Sultana*. "[I] directed
[the] men to remain on the wharf boat," he recalled. "Neither I nor
Captain Speed had anything to do with transportation. It was the
duty of the quartermaster entirely."[29]

While there is no conclusive evidence that Captain Williams was
responsible for moving the men from the wharf boat onto the *Sultana*,
there is definite proof that the prisoners themselves needed no special
invitation. "It was not at all necessary to be invited to go on board,"
stated Sgt. Arthur Alexander Jones (Co. C, 115th OH Inf), "and as
we did so we noticed the repairing of the boilers." Another Ohioan
who noticed the ongoing repairs was Sgt. William Boor (Co. D, 64th
OH Inf), whose "attention was attracted by the noise and work at
the boilers going on at that time. We were marched to the hurricane
deck and informed that this was to be our place of abode . . . I went
below and looked at the boilers, which were not very favorable to my
mind."[30]

Sgt. Alexander C. Brown (Co. I, 2nd OH Inf) received a pleasant surprise as he boarded the *Sultana*: "I stepped on the ill-fated
steamer and was introduced to the first clerk, when I was informed
that my fare was paid to Cairo." Back in Camp Fisk, an express agent
had called upon Brown to inform him that friends in Cincinnati had
asked the agent "to render me any assistance I required in cash or
otherwise." At the time, the only thing Brown wanted was "cabin
passage to be procured for me" when he finally shipped home. Now,
as he boarded the *Sultana*, the express agent proved true to his word.
Instead of sleeping on the decks with the others, Sergeant Brown
would be in a private stateroom.[31]

Brown was delighted to sit down with the other cabin passengers
for lunch at "a table filled with all the substantials and pastry. . . . After

eating a very light meal of the plainest food on the table, I helped myself to more than some would think proper under the circumstances and carried out to my comrades quite an armful of victuals." He passed out the pilfered delicacies to friends eating hardtack and became the hero of the moment.[32]

Being the first on board, the Ohio soldiers grabbed the best spots available. Dozens of men from the 115th Ohio Infantry gathered at the very front center of the hurricane deck, around the steamer's big bell. Congregating nearby were the men of the 50th Ohio Infantry. Dozens of men from the 102nd Ohio Infantry moved to the rear of the hurricane deck and spread out around the boat's one metal lifeboat. One deck below, more men from the 102nd gathered on the left side of the boat, near the wheelhouse and outside the railing, on the wide, flat guard. Others from the 102nd, mostly from Company A, settled down on the front of the second deck near the sturdy railings around the twin openings of the main stairway.

The Indiana men settled in beside the Ohio boys. Men from the 9th Indiana Cavalry grabbed space on the hurricane deck in front of the wheelhouses and crowded around the texas cabin. Some even climbed up on the roof of the texas and claimed spaces in front of and behind the pilothouse. Men from the 40th Indiana Infantry took up spots near the left-hand wheelhouse and behind the texas cabin. Down on the second deck, some Indiana boys moved in among the lads from Ohio and spread their blankets in the wide-open space between the front of the main cabin and the main stairway openings, and on the left-hand guards outside the railings.[33]

Out at the parole camp, the first train had been gone only a short time when 1st Lt. Joseph Stockton McHarg (47th USCT), who had been at Camp Fisk as an acting assistant quartermaster helping Lieutenant Tillinghast for the past few weeks, approached Captain Speed. McHarg had "learned from Lieutenant Tillinghast that the men were all going on one boat, though [he] did not know which boat it was." Having assisted Tillinghast in feeding and supplying the prisoners for almost a month, McHarg was convinced that all of the remaining men could not fit on one boat. "I went to Captain Speed and asked him if these men were all going on one boat. He said they were. I made the remark to the captain that I thought there were too many men to go on one boat." Speed responded, "Officers . . . sometimes get dismissed from the service for meddling with that which is none of their business." Rebuked, McHarg said nothing more and walked away.[34]

While Speed and some of the other officers were away having lunch, a second train unexpectedly arrived. "Not more than twenty (20) minutes after the first train left, the regular passenger train came in from Big Black, and those men which stood on the platform ready to go were put on board of it," recalled Private Cox. "There were three (3) passenger and one (1) baggage car on this train, and those seats which were not occupied by the regular passengers were filled, the passengers being sent into the rear cars. There were, I think, no men standing."[35]

This second train carried the remainder of the Indiana troops, approximately 200 men, and 100 or so men from Michigan. In all, about 310 men were crowded onto the cars with the paying passengers. "The second train was a passenger train and the men were only put into the seats," continued Cox. "There were only two (2) in a seat. . . . More men were not put on because the engine was short of water and the train could not wait."[36] The train left for Vicksburg between 1 and 1:30 p.m.

In Vicksburg, Captain Williams was standing at the starboard gangway of the wharf boat, counting the last of the men from the first trainload, when an officer approached and informed him that Captain Speed "was receiving pay for sending the men on some boat. I could not ascertain which. I was very angry at the idea that Capt. Speed was using me as his tool in his fraud." When asked if he knew which officer had provided the information, Williams answered, "I think Lieut. Tillinghast was the officer who informed me that Capt. Speed was receiving 50 cts. a head for furnishing these troops to boats for transportation." As soon as the last man was counted and on the wharf boat, an angry Williams hurried toward department headquarters.[37]

Shortly after Williams left for headquarters, Dr. Kemble, the department's medical director, arrived with twenty-three sick men confined to cots. Kemble later testified, "I put the sick men on board with the general understanding with Captain Speed that it was the desire to send all the paroled prisoners to their home as rapidly as possible. . . . I received no special instructions to put them on the *Sultana*. I was going to put them on that boat so that they, the paroled men, should all go together. It had been my privilege to send my convalescents whenever able to travel on any boat without orders." The cots were placed on the second deck in front of the main cabin. The *Sultana* had been constructed with the main cabin set farther back than was the case on most boats, leaving a large open space between the end of the cabin and the railings around the two openings of the main stairway. Not only was this space wide open, it was also above the fireboxes of the steamer and would provide a warm spot for the sick men.[38]

All of the men from the first train were already on the *Sultana* when Dr. Kemble brought on his sick men. He later said that the boat "was not crowded" at the time, "but I was told that seven hundred more men were coming in from camp." Realizing that the *Sultana* would be overcrowded with another seven hundred men jammed on board, Dr. Kemble headed uptown to see General Dana, hoping to get orders to remove the men he had just placed on board.[39]

Kemble found General Dana "at his residence" and asked him "for permission to remove my sick men from the *Sultana* and take them back to the hospitals. For the reason that in my opinion that with the men already on the boat, and those coming from Parole Camp, the boat would have been too much crowded for the comfort and safety of the sick men." Bowing to the doctor's expertise, Dana gave Kemble permission to remove his patients and stop any more convalescents from going on board.[40]

While Dr. Kemble was talking to General Dana at his residence, Captain Williams was at headquarters looking for the general. When he discovered that Dana was not in, Williams sent a quick telegram to Lieutenant Davenport, his assistant commissioner of exchange at Camp Fisk, "to hurry in the men as fast as possible." Williams later claimed that he sent the telegram because he "had received information that Captain Speed was receiving bribes for them and I wished to check [i.e., stop] Captain Speed in it." The telegram simply read,

"Lieutenant Davenport hurry up the men as fast as possible. The *Sultana* is waiting for them." When Davenport received the telegram, he did not understand the reason for it. Not knowing how to answer, Davenport took the telegram to Captain Speed.[41]

By the time the telegram reached the parole camp, Captain Speed and the others had returned from lunch, having missed the entire loading of the second train. It is highly unlikely, however, that they were not informed by Cox and others that a second train had come, been loaded with about three hundred men, and had then gone. As Speed made his way back to the train platform, Lieutenant Davenport showed him the telegram from Captain Williams because he wanted to "ask [Speed's] advice whether it would be necessary to answer it or not. I believe [Speed] told me it did not need any answer. That we were doing all we could to get the men ready."[42]

Speed, who was working as fast as possible to process the men, resented Williams' interference: "Lieut. Davenport, who was Capt. Williams and my assistant in the movement of the prisoners, showed me a telegram from Capt. Williams asking how long it would be before the men would be in and asked me what reply he should make. I was somewhat irritated at the time and at a loss to understand why Lieut. Davenport was called upon to give this information when Capt. Williams knew that I was at the spot." Speed told Davenport to reply, "when Capt. Speed gets ready."[43] It was a snap reply but not altogether unwarranted under the circumstances.

After sending the telegram to Davenport, Captain Williams went to lunch at "the saloon under the theater." There he met Major Miller and the Confederate commissioner of exchange, Colonel Henderson, who had both accompanied him into Vicksburg on the first train. During the meal, Williams called Miller outside for a private conversation. As Miller remembered it, Williams "stated that there were two lines of boats, one of which was in the employ of the government and the other not, and it was the wish of certain parties to place the prisoners on a different boat from that on which it was intended that they should go. He requested that I should tell Lieutenant Davenport to hurry up the work at camp. He said he had telegraphed to him but lest he might not get the dispatch he wanted to send word by me also."

Miller, who had also heard rumors of bribery, agreed to return to
Camp Fisk to speak directly to Lieutenant Davenport.[44]

The second train reached the Vicksburg depot at about 2:15 p.m.
No officers were present to meet it, but the officers among the prisoners formed them into columns and moved them north on Mulberry
Street to the levee. Although Captain Williams was not present to
count them, other officers and orderlies counted the men as they went
on board the wharf boat and then boarded the *Sultana*.[45]

The remaining men from Indiana and the one hundred or so men
from Michigan were placed on the main deck. "We marched on her
in fours, filling up the boat as we marched," wrote Pvt. Benjamin
Franklin Johnston (Co. A, 5th MI Cav). Cpl. Murry S. Baker (Co.
D, 4th MI Cav) "tried to get close to the boiler, but it was full there,
so I laid down by the stern door." Dozens of prisoners from the various Michigan cavalry units as well as dozens of men from the 18th
Michigan Infantry crowded into the stern cargo room, sharing space
with a few cows and some of the "condemned horses and mules" taken
on board at New Orleans. The rest of the horses and the sixty hogs
were "on the after guards" outside the stern cargo room. Only a few
men, mostly from Indiana, claimed spaces on the open bow.[46]

After finishing his lunch, Captain Williams went back to department headquarters to meet with General Dana and lodge a complaint
against Captain Speed. Assistant Adjutant General Capt. Joseph
Miller intercepted him as he arrived. "Captain Williams . . . [was] in
a state of some excitement, [and] said that he had just been informed
that Captain Speed had been induced for a consideration to detain a
considerable portion of the prisoners at the Camp that evening so that
they should not be sent on the *Sultana*, but should be given to another
boat that desired them," Miller remembered. Having already sent
a telegram to Lieutenant Davenport and asked Major Miller to go
out to hurry the men into Vicksburg, Captain Williams now sought
more official means. "Captain Williams desired me to send an order
to Captain Speed that all those prisoners should be brought in immediately," Captain Miller testified. Miller told Williams not to bring
his allegation to General Dana "unless he could immediately prove
it." As Williams went into General Dana's office, Miller told him that

Captain Mason had just left the office after stating that the *Sultana* "would leave in two hours."[47]

Confident in his charge against Captain Speed, Williams lodged his formal complaint with General Dana. The general later described the visit.

> About the middle of the day Captain Williams came and reported that the captain of the *Sultana* said he would leave in an hour or two and that a large proportion of the men were still out at the parole camp and he did not believe that proper exertions were being made to get them off and that he had been informed that a pecuniary consideration had been offered, per capita, for the detention of the men, and shipment of them on the other line and that he thought Capt. Speed was practicing delay purposely for the detention of the men till the *Sultana* should leave and a boat of the other line arrive.[48]

Once again surprised by an allegation of bribery, General Dana recalled, "I then informed Captain Williams of what Captain Speed had previously reported regarding Captain Kerns and his clerks, and stated that I thought he had the rumor wrong. He [Williams] promised to investigate it."[49]

As a confused Captain Williams left headquarters, Captain Miller showed General Dana the telegram that Williams wanted him to send to Camp Fisk. Miller later said that he "submitted the telegram, as a matter of course, to the General before sending it. I should say that the General approved the sending of the telegram." Without further ado, Miller sent the following telegram to Captain Speed: "Will all troops now at the camp be sent on the *Sultana*? How soon will they be in? Captain of the *Sultana* has been here and says he will be able to leave in two hours. The General wishes to go to the boat to see them off." The telegram was sent about 4 p.m., the third telegram sent to Camp Fisk in the past few hours.[50] In the meantime, Captain Speed was readying the last of the men for their trip into Vicksburg.

11

LIKE DAMNED HOGS

After two trains had transported paroled prisoners to Vicksburg, only about 150 men from Michigan and all the men from Tennessee, Kentucky, and West Virginia remained at Camp Fisk. Cpl. George Marshal Clinger (Co. E, 16th KY Inf) recalled, "We received orders to pack up, which occupation did not take long for there was not much to pack." Capt. James McCown was in charge of organizing the remaining troops: "The Tennessee troops were formed into five (5) companies [of about one hundred men each], Kentucky had two (2), [and] Virginia had one (1) squad of twenty-six (26) men, I think."[1]

Sometime in the early afternoon, the train that had taken the first group into Vicksburg—consisting of the engine, three passenger cars, and a few boxcars—returned to pick up the last remaining men. Arriving with the train was Maj. Frank Miller, who was returning to Camp Fisk at the request of Captain Williams to see Lieutenant Davenport and get him "to hurry up the work at camp." As soon as the train arrived, Captain Speed, Major Miller, Lieutenant Davenport, and the others began calling the last of the names, adding checkmarks to the Confederate rolls before assisting the men onto the cars.[2]

Captain Speed was busy with the loading when he received the telegram sent through General Dana. "I received a dispatch from [headquarters] . . . stating that the Captain of the *Sultana* had told the General that he would go in two hours and asked if the men would be in in that time. I think that I replied that they could not be got in so soon," reported Speed.[3] Since the train had just arrived, Speed knew that he had more than two hours of work ahead of him.

Down at the waterfront, at around 4 p.m., the fourteen-month-old steamboat *Pauline Carroll*, Capt. Hugh L. White commanding, arrived and was duly reported to the Quartermaster Department by Captain Kerns. Still believing that there were more men at Camp Fisk than could comfortably fit on one boat, Kerns tried once again to see if he could get the men divided. "I went to [Captain] Hatch and told him that the *Pauline Carroll* was in and asked him if I should not detain her," Kerns remembered, "and asked him to give me an order to do so. He informed me, in effect, that he had nothing to do with the matter, that he had telegraphed Captain Speed [earlier in the day] and had his answer and that he should not interfere in the matter."[4]

That is surprising. If too many men were being loaded on the *Sultana*, Hatch had the authority—indeed the duty—to put some of them on another boat. Both Captain Speed and Captain Williams had professed that they would deliver the men to "the contract boat, and then the Quartermaster might send them by that [boat] or take the responsibility of doing otherwise." Yet, when he was told that there would be too many men to go comfortably on one boat, Hatch shirked his duty and declared that "he should not interfere in the matter."

At the waterfront, William H. Geins, a passenger on the *Pauline Carroll*, was about to accompany the boat's first clerk, F. Delgado, to department headquarters to see about getting some troops for the *Carroll* when Captain Hatch suddenly showed up. "As we were going off the gangway plank," Geins wrote, "we met [Capt.] R. B. Hatch General Dana's Chief Quartermaster. Mr. Delgado said H. was just the man he wanted." Apparently, Hatch had hurried down to the *Pauline Carroll* right after Kerns informed him of her arrival. After a few minutes of conversation, Hatch and Delgado met with

Captain White. Captain Hatch later reported, "The boat was anxious to get some of the troops, but I told [White and Delgado] that the matter was beyond my control." That was Hatch's official statement. More likely, Hatch was checking on the deal he had made with agent William Jones the day before to get a kickback from Captain White if an overflow of men could somehow be sent on board the *Carroll*. After ascertaining that the deal still stood, Hatch headed over to the *Sultana*.[5]

"I saw Capt. Mason of the *Sultana* just after [meeting with Captain White] and he insisted that all the men could go on his boat," Hatch stated. "I think they were not then all on board but he knew the number. I did start to see if there was sufficient room on the boat but effecting that the business was taken out of my hands, I turned about and left her."[6] Without a thorough inspection of the steamer Hatch had no way of knowing how crowded the boat already was and how crowded she would soon be. By simply taking Mason's word, Hatch once again shirked his responsibility.

While Hatch was down at the waterfront, a frustrated Captain Kerns met with General Smith, the commander of the District of Vicksburg. "I went to General Smith . . . and stated the case to him, and asked him for instructions or advice as to whether I should detain the *Pauline Carroll* or not. He told me that he had nothing to do with these paroled prisoners, that the business had been taken out of his hands by the Department commander [General Dana] but that if I wished to detain the *Carroll* I could do so and whatever I did on the matter would meet his approval." General Smith had indeed given the responsibility for the exchanges over to Dana on April 5. Still, as post commander, General Smith had the authority to detain a second boat and have the men divided, or at least to make that recommendation to General Dana. Unfortunately, like so many others involved with the loading of the *Sultana*, he shirked his duty and did nothing. Nevertheless, Captain Kerns felt that he had been given the power to detain the *Pauline Carroll*.[7]

Kerns returned to the levee and boarded the waiting steamer. "Mr. Jones, the agent, asked me if he could get any men for the *Pauline Carroll*," Kerns remembered. "I told him I did not know. I could not

tell until the men came in, but that I rather thought he could get some."
When Captain White complained that he was already behind schedule and would remain only if guaranteed a load of prisoners, Kerns
threatened to order him to remain in port if he had to. Although he
was not pleased, Captain White consented. Captain Kerns then hurried over to the *Sultana*.[8]

Kerns met with Captain Mason and his first clerk, William
Gambrel, and asked the two "how many men they had on board and
how many more they expected. . . . [Mason], or both of them, told me
that they had about a thousand (1,000) men on board and that they
expected, on the train, about six hundred (600) more." Fearing that
1,600 men would be too many for the *Sultana*, Kerns "asked them
if they thought they had room for all of them comfortably, and they
assured me that they had and assured me that they had carried more
men than they expected that day and were anxious to take them, that
these men, without arms or equipments, would take up much less
room than men armed and equipped that they had carried before."
Perhaps silently questioning the truthfulness of that answer, Kerns
next rushed uptown to see if he could find somebody willing to take
the responsibility of dividing the last expected load of prisoners.[9]

Upon reaching headquarters Kerns met again with General Smith
and Captain Hatch. Kerns "asked General Smith . . . if he would
not go down to the boats when the last trainload came in, so that, if
he thought the men ought to be divided, that he could give instructions on the spot. [Captain] Hatch also informed me that he would
be there." Hoping he had finally convinced somebody to go down to
the river and see how the loading was going, Kerns left headquarters
and returned to the waterfront, unaware that Hatch had just returned
from there.[10]

General Smith recalled that he "started to go to the boat to see
about it [but] I met some man connected with the Q.M. Dept. at the
parole camp, near Hatch's office. I learned from him that there were
only three hundred to go. I concluded that they could be very comfortable on the *Sultana* and immediately returned to my office."[11] The officer he spoke with was undoubtedly Lieutenant Tillinghast. It seems
puzzling that Tillinghast stopped General Smith from going down to

the waterfront to divide the men. Tillinghast had been offered fifteen cents per man to put some prisoners on a noncontract boat such as the *Pauline Carroll*. Tillinghast may have been double-dipping. Passenger agent McGuire later said that Tillinghast told him "that the captain of the *Sultana* was a gentleman and although he [Tillinghast] had tried to keep the prisoners off of that boat (the *Sultana*) Capt. Mason had said to him that if he had his measure, it should cost him nothing for clothing for a whole year and that not having his measure, he had made it all right anyhow."[12] It appears, then, that while Tillinghast had agreed to put men on the *Pauline Carroll* for a kickback of fifteen cents per man, he had also agreed to put men on board the *Sultana* to get free clothing "for a whole year."

Also double-dipping, after making a deal with Captain Mason of the *Sultana* and Captain White of the *Pauline Carroll*, Captain Hatch knew that he had nothing to lose if the men were divided. Hatch's chief clerk, George Dunton, recalled that late in the afternoon "Hatch telegraphed to Capt. Speed, who was then at the Four Mile Bridge, asking if he should detain the *Pauline Carroll* to receive a portion of these men."[13] When Speed received the telegram, the fourth one of the day, the last train was almost loaded. Speed recollected that the telegram said: "Is there more prisoners than can go on the *Sultana*? If so the *Pauline Carroll* has arrived. Shall I detain her?" Speed "answered him, under the impression that there was about fourteen hundred men in [a] carefully worded dispatch, 'No the *Sultana* can take them all' or words to that effect."[14] When the answer came back, Captain Hatch washed his hands of the whole affair. If all the men went onto the *Sultana*, he was guaranteed a kickback. If some went onto the *Pauline Carroll*, he was guaranteed a kickback. He was covered either way.

Private Cox recalled that a short time after the fourth telegram arrived, "Captain Speed, Lieutenant Davenport and some other officer whose name I do not know [probably Major Miller], got on the train and came into town." This last train carried some 800 men: the remaining men from Michigan (about 150), all of the men from Tennessee (429), all of the men from Kentucky (194), and the handful of men from West Virginia (20). "We got away from camp with the last man about three quarters of an hour before dark," remembered Captain Speed.[15]

Having put all the men who remained in Camp Fisk on the final train to Vicksburg, Speed felt that his duties were done. He asked the conductor if he could be dropped off at the foot of Cherry Street so that he could go directly to headquarters and begin the final preparation of the rolls. Lieutenant Davenport heard the request: "There was a conversation between [Speed and the conductor, and] to the best of my knowledge and as near as I can remember, Captain Speed wanted him to stop to let him off at the foot of this street, Cherry Street. The train could not stop on account of the heavy grade and curve just above the street. . . . The reason why he wanted to get off was because Headquarters was on the street." Speed thus had to remain with the men all the way to the depot.[16]

It was nearly 5 p.m. when the last train pulled up to the Vicksburg depot. "Major Fidler was in command at the depot when the last train reached town," Captain McCown noted. In the gathering darkness Major Fidler had the men form into columns of fours before heading down to the *Sultana*. While this was going on, Captain Speed and Lieutenant Davenport took a seat on the tracks and talked. "We set down on the railroad track together," Davenport stated. "He expressed a desire that he wanted to go to headquarters. . . . I asked him to go down [to the *Sultana*]." Captain Emmons, Speed's roommate, later recalled, "Captain Speed informed me that on his arrival in Vicksburg he did not intend to go on the *Sultana* at all but finally concluded that he would go down and see how they were getting along." Although Speed felt that he had discharged his responsibility, he agreed to go down to the *Sultana* with the men.[17]

Captain Williams had intended to meet the third train at the depot, but he was back at the wharf boat confronting Dr. Kemble when it arrived. Dr. Kemble had returned to the *Sultana* with permission from General Dana to remove his twenty-three cot-ridden patients. "It was nearly dark," Kemble stated. "I went on the cabin forward, where my sick men were. My impression on looking at the outside was the boat was not full and I would have been willing to have put my three hundred sick men [from the hospitals] on had it not been for the seven hundred [*sic*] which I saw was coming in from the Railroad Depot."

Kemble "immediately removed the sick men confined to cots." As they were leaving the boat, Captain Williams stopped them, claiming that he had already recorded their names on his roster. Kemble "convinced him that he was wrong, that the rolls had not yet left my home, and were held by me to be turned over to Captain Speed. He presented no further objections to my removing them." The names of the twenty-three cot-ridden patients had never been given to Speed, the doctor explained, so their removal from the *Sultana* would not spoil Williams' count. Satisfied with Kemble's explanation, Williams let the doctor and his patients leave. As Dr. Kemble was returning to the hospital, he ran into about three hundred convalescent patients coming to the boat from the hospital and "turned them back to hospital also."[18] There would be no hospital patients going on the *Sultana*.

By the time all the cot-ridden patients were removed from the *Sultana*, the last group of prisoners, with Major Fidler and Captain Speed leading them, was approaching the wharf boat. Pvt. Ike Davenport of Tennessee was with this last group. "[W]e marcht thrue Vicksburg a set of glad harted boys for we was now to be embarked on the *Sultana* which was wating at the warf for us." Cpl. Thomas R. Sharp (Co. F, 2nd WV Cav) remembered "passing through a part of the city till we came to the brink of the Father of Waters." He thought the *Sultana* was "a fine looking specimen of the western steamboat."[19]

Captain Kerns was on the wharf boat when the men started coming up the gangplank. He was still convinced that there were too many men to go comfortably on one boat and was still trying to get the men divided. Kerns testified that he

> met Captain Speed just as he was coming in onto the wharfboat and told him that the *Pauline Carroll* was then going up, and asked if he did not think a part of the men had better go on her. [Speed] said he thought not, that the rolls were made for the men to go together and that it was too late to divide them. I asked if there was not two (2) majors going up, and asked if one major could not go with

each boat or division, if the men were divided. He said that made no difference, that the rolls and papers were all made for them to go together.[20]

Although Captain Speed had earlier agreed to leave the selection of the steamboats to the Quartermaster Department, it seemed to Kerns that he was now objecting to the selection of a second boat and interfering with the division of the men.

Speed remembered otherwise. "When I myself had got about half way across [the wharf boat] a gentleman whom I supposed to be Capt. Kerns, whom I did not then know personally, accosted me with the question, 'Would it not be better to put some of the men on the *Pauline Carroll*?' I replied, 'I don't know.' [Kerns] then said, '[Capt.] Hatch, Genl. Smith and . . . Capt. Williams have been here and wanted it done.'" Having agreed to leave the selection of transports to the Quartermaster Department, Speed decided to check with Captain Williams before letting the men proceed.[21]

Speed said that he approached Williams and "told him what Capt. Kerns had told me. He replied substantially in these words, 'No. I have been on board. There is plenty of room and they can all go comfortably.' He said this in rather an irritable tone that, together with the telegraphic dispatches I had received in the afternoon somewhat displeased me. I left him and told the men to go on the *Sultana* and passed aboard the boat myself."[22] According to Speed, he would have been willing to send the last trainload to the *Pauline Carroll*, but when the man he recognized as the commissioner of exchange sharply rebuked him, he turned away, feeling that Williams had made the decision to keep the men together and ship them all on the *Sultana*.

Shortly thereafter, Captain Williams was approached by Captain Kerns. "While I was counting [the men] Capt. Kerns came to me and said something about the *Pauline Carroll*. I told him that I was counting and could not then talk," Williams recalled. Kerns, however, recalled the conversation as being not so short and not so civil:

Captain Williams was at that time, as I understood Commissioner of Exchange of Prisoners and seemed to me to have as much to do with the men in directing them as

anyone else. I asked Captain Williams if part of the men
could not go on the *Pauline Carroll* lying there or if he did
not think it would be better to put a part of them on her.
He said, no, that they could all go very well on the *Sultana*.
That the *Pauline Carroll* had offered 20 per cent or twenty
(20) cents per man . . . and for that reason she could not
have a man, or words to that effect, and that I would hear
more about it by and by.

Rebuffed by an irritated Captain Williams, Kerns turned away,
unaware that Williams was operating under the belief that somebody,
perhaps Kerns himself, had accepted a bribe.[23]

Agent Jones, lingering nearby and still determined to get some
men and government money for the *Pauline Carroll*, approached
Lieutenant Tillinghast, who had already agreed to accept fifteen
cents per man to put prisoners on a noncontract boat. "[A]s the boat
was filling up," Tillinghast later testified, Jones "asked me again why
all these men were going on this boat. I said . . . I would ask Capt.
Speed and he would tell me." The young lieutenant crossed the wharf
boat and approached Captain Speed. "I remarked to Capt. Speed
that the *Pauline Carroll* was here and would like to take the men,"
Tillinghast later told investigators. "I told Capt. Speed that there were
more men than should go on one boat. He remarked that there was
sufficient room." Passenger agent McGuire recalled that later, "Lieut.
Tillinghast told me that he tried to get the last eight hundred prisoners on the *Pauline Carroll*, that Jennings and Jones had offered from 10
to 25 cts. a head for the prisoners, but that Capt. Speed had told him
(Lieut. Tillinghast) that as they had all come together they had better
all go together."[24] Apparently, Tillinghast decided that free clothing
for a year was better than fifteen cents a head and stopped trying to
divide the men.

But while Tillinghast had given up, Jones had not. After speaking
with Tillinghast, he approached Captain Kerns. Jones reported that
Kerns "said . . . he did not think it possible that the *Sultana* could
take them all. That he had protested against this thing to no avail."
Jones admitted, "I was anxious as Agent of the *Pauline Carroll* to get

a portion of these troops and so said to Capt. Kerns, remarking at the time that I thought it a shame that so many should be carried on one boat." Kerns said only, "[I] told Mr. Jones that the men would have to go on the *Sultana*."[25] He had repeatedly tried to separate the men but had failed.

Although Speed and Kerns could not get the prisoners divided, it seemed for a time that the men themselves might do it. "When about one third of the last party that came in had got on board, they made a stop and the remainder swore they would not go on board," William Butler, a shipping agent on the *Pauline Carroll* stated. "They said they were going to be packed on the boat like damned hogs; that there was no room for them to lie down, or place to attend to calls of nature. There was much indignation felt among them and among others who were about the boats." Saddler Louis Bean (Co. A, 6th KY Cav), who was in the last group to board, recalled, "As we were going on board, I heard Major Fidler, who was in command, tell the captain of the boat that there were too many men on board, they were too much crowded. The Captain [Mason] said he could not help it, the men were all to go on and he thought he could carry them through."[26]

Cpl. Jeremiah Mahoney (Co. I, 2nd MI Cav) believed he knew the reason why nobody went on the *Pauline Carroll*: "Some of them did attempt to go on her, but they were told she had the small-pox aboard to keep them off."[27] In their weakened physical condition, the men knew that they would never be able to survive a bout of smallpox. So they continued to board the *Sultana*.

While the soldiers were crowding on board the *Sultana*, a handful of civilian passengers also came on board. The "Fourteen Star Performers" of the Chicago Opera Troupe, a traveling minstrel company known for their "Music, Dancing, Songs and Jokes," were going as far as Memphis. Two more paying passengers, J. T. Farris and sixty-year-old James M. Safford Sr., both agents for the Indiana Sanitary Commission, boarded as well, satisfied that they had done their best for the prisoners from Indiana. Among that group was Safford's son, Pvt. George M. Safford (Co. H, 10th IN Cav). With the last of the prisoners finally going home on the *Sultana*, the two men booked passage as well.[28]

Also coming on board were forty-one-year-old 2nd Lt. Harvey Annis (Co. G, 51st USCT), his forty-eight-year-old wife Ann, and their seven-year-old daughter Isabella "Belle." In late 1864, when his regiment had been stationed in Vicksburg, Annis had begun "suffering from Chills and Fever," which eventually led to "enlargement of the spleen . . . render[ing] him unfit for field service." When the 51st USCT moved to New Orleans, Annis had stayed behind awaiting a medical discharge. Ann and Belle had come down from Oshkosh, Wisconsin, to nurse him and were finally taking him home.[29]

As the Annises were checking in with William Gambrel, they commented on the large number of soldiers on board. Ann later wrote, "The clerk or mate pointed out to my husband and myself the sagging down of the hurricane deck in spite of extra stanchions which were put in a great many places." The hurricane deck, which was actually the roof of the second deck, had begun to sag under the weight of the men, and heavy wooden braces had been put in place to keep it from caving in. Although Ann remembered that the "boat was very much crowded," she also noted that "the men behaved very well indeed." And that was a good thing. Any carousing or mischief might have caused the hurricane deck to collapse beneath them.[30]

Perhaps because of the sagging deck, Captain Mason finally approached an unnamed Union officer and protested the overcrowding. Although Mason had wanted a large load of prisoners, he did not want his boat damaged by their weight. Pvt. Levi George Morgan (Co. B, 21st OH Inf.), who was sitting near the bow, recalled, "When about half of us were on board the captain of the boat stopped us and said that he had enough, for he did not consider the boat safe enough to take so many as he had just had the boiler patched a few days before [sic]. The [officer], however, who had charge of us, swore that he was loading the boat and would put as many men on as he pleased."[31] The Steamboat Acts of 1838 and 1852, which regulated the legal carrying capacity of steamboats, were being ignored with impunity.

Captain McCown recalled that when he boarded the *Sultana*, Major Fidler ordered him "to take two (2) companies of Kentucky troops and place them around the boilers of the boat, to remain there." Saddler Louis Bean, who was among those Kentuckians, "went to a spot near the left-hand engine and remained there. . . . The boat was so crowded that I couldn't get to any other place." While McCown was placing the Kentucky troops, he noted Major Fidler leading the others up to the hurricane deck.[32]

Among the men following Major Fidler were the last of the men from Michigan and those from Tennessee. "I went on board with the last party, and went up on the hurricane deck," remembered Michigan cavalryman Corporal Mahoney, "but finding it so much crowded that I could not get through the men, I returned to the boiler [main] deck where I found a place to lie down near the wheelhouse, and occupied it during the voyage." Tennessean Private Eldridge felt lucky to find a warm place on the hurricane deck, where his "comrades . . . had got us a place up on top of the boat just behind the smokestacks, right over the boilers."[33]

Many Tennessee soldiers left the crowded hurricane deck and found a spot on the main deck. Seventeen-year-old Pvt. John Thomas Lesley (Co. K, 3rd TN Cav) and six others with whom he "had buddied for twenty long and weary months were sleeping on top of the wood rack, for in those days they used wood for fuel instead of coal, the wood being stacked alongside the boilers." (Lesley was wrong about the wood being the boat's main fuel, but even coal-burners like the *Sultana* burned some cordwood to help aerate the coal.) Private Collins and his father, Pvt. Joseph Henry Collins (Co. G, 3rd TN Cav), were also on the main deck. "Hundreds of other soldiers were sleeping on this deck," the younger Collins said, "crowded together as thick as they could find room to lie. The other two decks—the upper and hurricane—were likewise crowded with sleeping men."[34]

Around 5 p.m., boiler mechanic R. G. Taylor finally finished patching the leaky boiler. "I was about 20 hours in doing the work," he remembered. "I considered it a good job before I had left. I did consider it temporary. I think the iron was burned, and that the boilers were used with little water." When asked if he considered the boilers safe when he was finished, he replied, "I did not." Had he informed the chief engineer, Nathan Wintringer, what he thought? "He should have known as well as I," Taylor answered.[35]

As the prisoners settled down on the main deck, they suddenly noticed the large crate containing the *Sultana*'s mascot. "I guess everyone that was on the *Sultana* knew something about the monstrous alligator that was on the boat," Pvt. Benjamin G. Davis (Co. L, 7th KY Cav) recalled. Cpl. Ira Horner also noticed the creature. "[T]here was an alligator seven and one-half feet long," he remembered. Added Pvt. Daniel William Lugenbeal (Co. F, 135th OH Inf), "He was kept in the wheelhouse. It was a curiosity for us to see such a large one."[36] For the time being, the crew left their mascot where he was and went about the business of getting under way.

There was little room for the men to spread their blankets and lie down. "We were driven on like so many hogs until every foot of standing room was occupied," Corporal Clinger remembered. "A thousand passengers would have crowded her comfortably," Pvt. Edward Fredrich Hedrich (Co. B, 9th IN Cav) said; "with over 2,000 she was like a hive of bees about to swarm."[37]

While the crowding would have been bad enough for physically fit individuals, these men had just come from cramped, filthy Confederate prisons. Already rumors were spreading about the reason behind the overcrowding. "It was openly charged at the time that the Quartermaster at Vicksburg [Capt. Reuben Hatch] and the Captain of the *Sultana*, [James] Cass Mason, had made money by placing six or eight hundred more men on the boat than her capacity would stand," noted Private Safford.[38]

After helping to place the Kentucky prisoners around the boilers, Captain McCown went looking for Major Fidler. Instead, he ran into Captain Mason in the main saloon. "Captain, you are going to have a pretty good load," McCown stated. "Yes, a pretty good load," Mason replied. McCown noted that Mason "seemed not unwilling" about that.[39]

McCown was then approached by a worried William Gambrel, who was also looking for Major Fidler. McCown recalled Gambrel saying that "if they placed many more on the top of the cabin roof, . . . it would give way and fall through." Perhaps noticing the supports already in place, McCown hurried up to the hurricane deck to find Major Fidler and tell him what Gambrel had said. "He commenced moving the men to the side, off the cabin roof, below, as fast as he could."[40] For the time being, disaster had been averted.

It was around 6 p.m. when the last man came on board. Captain Williams began to tally his numbers, using the totals from only the first and third trains, which he had counted himself, and came up with between 1,300 and 1,400 men. One of the other officers who had been counting the men informed him that he had missed the second group. "There was some person, I do not know who . . . told me that some three (3) or four hundred (400) [more] had been placed on board. . . . My impression was that they came from the hospital." Making a quick recalculation, Williams came up with the new total of "nineteen hundred and sixty-six (1,966)."[41]

The three or four hundred men the other officer mentioned were not from the hospital, of course. They were the four hundred from the second train, which Captain Williams had missed because he was in town lodging complaints and sending telegrams. Although the officers assisting him with the loading knew about these additional men, Captain Williams did not. Much has been made about the fact that neither Captain Speed nor Captain Williams was present when the second train arrived in Vicksburg. Captain Speed was not interested in counting the men; his responsibility had ended when the men from Camp Fisk reached Vicksburg. How many there were and which boat they boarded were not his concern. On the other hand, it *was* Captain Williams' responsibility to count them. Still, other officers were there to count the men, and when it came time to tally the numbers, they did their job and informed Captain Williams of those he had missed.

After he learned the new tally, Captain Williams went on board the *Sultana* for the first time. When later asked if he had gone on board the *Sultana* at any time during the loading, he answered, "I do not think I was aboard of her. I am pretty certain I was not aboard of her until all the prisoners were on board."[42] Had Captain Williams been present to inspect the boat after the men from the second train boarded, he would have seen how crowded she already was and might have been inclined to send the third trainload of men over to the *Pauline Carroll*, as Captain Kerns had asked him to do. Williams' inadvertent ignorance and his failure to inspect the *Sultana* during the loading resulted in almost two thousand paroled prisoners being placed on board.

As Williams was about to go on board the *Sultana*, he spotted Captain Kerns. Williams recalled, "I spoke to him and as near as I can remember my words said, 'You spoke to me about transportation. I have nothing to do with it. I am creditably informed that offers have been made to officers by the boats of 50 cts. per head for all sent by their boats, that I do not intend to be mixed up in the matter, that I will deliver the men at the contract boat and you can do as you choose.'" In his subsequent testimony, Williams said, "I [had] learned that Capt. Kerns was the quartermaster so accused, and that was the reason I spoke to him on the wharf boat about officers receiving pay &ct."[43]

When he finally boarded the *Sultana*, Williams went up to the main saloon, where he found Captain Speed. "I went to him and I told him that I had done him an injury," Williams professed, "that I had understood that he was taking bribes for putting men on board of boats, and had reported the fact to General Dana, but that General Dana had informed me that Captain Speed had already reported some quartermaster for it and that I sought this opportunity for apologizing to him for it." Captain Speed recalled the conversation:

> [Captain Williams] told me then he had an apology to make and told me he had done me an injury by saying to the General that he believed that I had received a bribe for putting the men on some particular boat, but that since, he had become satisfied that such was not the case. He also told me that his authority was an officer whom he did not know and told me he would hunt him up. I told him this must be done, that all I had gained from four years' service was my good name. He promised this should be done.[44]

The officer who had directed the suspicion toward Captain Speed was, of course, Lieutenant Tillinghast.

When Captain Williams informed him that there were close to two thousand men on board the *Sultana*, Speed "was greatly surprised as it largely exceeded my expectations. I had supposed, judging from the number which had been realized in the two previous detachments that were previously sent off, that there would be between fourteen and fifteen hundred men." Williams remembered Speed then asking him "if I thought the men were comfortable." Williams answered, "I said that I thought that they were, that I had asked several of them and they said they were." Williams, who had boarded the boat for the first time only a few minutes before and could have spoken to only a few men while working his way up to the main saloon, felt confident enough to make a blanket statement about the comfort of all the men. Williams would later insist, "I had seen during the war quite as many men on board of boats as she had and apparently comfortable. . . . She was a first-class boat and one of peculiar construction. I did observe something unusual. Her cabin terminated aft of her smokestacks and gave her forty (40) or forty-five (45) feet more of boiler [second] deck than most other boats." When Captain Speed was asked if he had ever inspected the *Sultana*, he replied, "No sir, but when I was on board, I observed casually, that she was very roomy, and that there was a fine place for the men in front of the cabin, capable of holding, I should judge, five hundred men, under shelter, and that she was otherwise roomy."[45] That "roomy" space was on the second deck, around the twin openings of the main stairway and in front of the main saloon. This was along the only path that both Speed and Williams could have taken to get to the main cabin.

From this point, the responsibility of getting the men safely to Cairo was in the hands of Captain Mason. Speed recalled saying to Mason, " 'Now Capt. you will take good care of the men because they are deserving of it and you know what a trouble we had to get them to you.' His reply was in substance, 'I will take as good care of them as any other men. You see we have a good boat here.' He expressed himself that they would go through comfortably and safely."[46] That was apparently adequate for Speed and Williams.

At some point Captain Kerns also went into the main saloon:

> I went up to the office of the boat where I saw Captain Mason and the clerk, and asked them if they did not think they had a pretty big load and if they thought the men

could go comfortably. They said, "Yes," or intimating that it was a good-sized load and Captain Mason told me he had carried as many, if not more, men than he had on board with comfort. He gave me to understand that he was glad to get the men and that he had no doubt that they could go with entire comfort. . . . Afterward Captain Williams, Captain Mason, and the clerk, and I think, Captain Speed and myself, were standing near each other talking with each other, and they all expressed themselves as being of the opinion that the men were very comfortable and would go with entire comfort, or words to that effect.[47]

Kerns went on to testify, "I think I told Captain Williams . . . to send up the number of men and officers to my office by the clerk of the boat, that my transportation clerk would issue the transportation pass for the men. This was about eight o'clock, I think." Captain Kerns had also noticed the unusual configuration of the deck space between the main saloon and the main stairway openings on the *Sultana*: "[H]er cabin was shorter than is usual in boats, her cabin not coming forward within ten (10) or twelve (12) feet of her chimneys, giving a very large space forward for the accommodation of troops. Her lower decks or guards were entirely free from freight or anything I could see with the exception of twenty-five (25) or thirty (30) head of mules, or horses, on her rear guard."[48]

After asking for a runner to be sent to his office for the transportation pass, Kerns left the boat. "I then came down from the *Sultana* onto the wharf boat, and met Mr. Jones, agent of the *Pauline Carroll* and remarked to him I had done all I could to get some of the men on the *Pauline Carroll*, but that it was no go . . . that the men could not be divided and that the *Pauline Carroll* might go."[49]

The *Pauline Carroll* had been waiting at Vicksburg for the past few hours, but as the last of the paroled prisoners filed on board the *Sultana*, Captain White knew that his wait had been in vain. Shipping agent William Butler was watching the loading from the *Carroll*. "A loyal gentleman who was standing by me, Judge Burwell, said it was a damned shame to crowd men on board a boat in that way; that he did not believe the men would have as much room to lie down as was allowed to slaves on slave ships." The *Pauline Carroll* left Vicksburg with "very little freight and . . . seventeen passengers."[50]

Captain Williams provided his tally of men to the *Sultana*'s second clerk, Willie Stratton, and then, "after cautioning the men to be careful about fire," departed. When Stratton reached the transportation office to get the pass, Captain Kerns was not there. Kerns recalled, "while [I was] at supper, the 2nd Clerk of the boat went up to the office, with the number given him by Captain Williams or Captain Speed, and my clerk gave him the transportation pass." The clerk, civilian employee Elias Shull, later testified that he issued the pass for "35 officers and 1,931 enlisted men."[51]

Although the exact number of paroled prisoners placed on board the *Sultana* has been debated over the years, the transportation pass for the *Sultana* specified a total of 1,966 officers and men. During two years of extensive research among every known list of prisoners placed on board the *Sultana*, including hospital lists, newspaper lists, state adjutant generals' reports, regimental histories, and handwritten lists in the National Archives, I have been able to identify 35 officers and 1,918 enlisted men, for a total of 1,953, only 13 short of the number on the official transportation pass.

It was just before 8 p.m. when Captain Friesner arrived with his small guard detachment from the 58th Ohio Infantry: "When I went on board, the boat was just ready to shove off. I don't know that anyone got on board the boat after I did." Friesner reported immediately to Major Fidler for instructions and then began stationing his men around the boat.[52]

About that same time, Captain Speed left the *Sultana* in company with Lieutenant Davenport, who thought they left about fifteen or twenty minutes before the boat shoved off. Speed recalled, "As I left the boat I noticed that she had very large accommodations for men in front of the cabin, and that it seemed to be a favorite place with the men, and that a great many were straining to get places there. As I passed below on the main deck I noticed the men passing backward and forward of the boilers. I did not see any [live]stock on board of her. I left the boat at that time, about 8 o'clock P.M."[53]

Around 9 p.m., after about twenty-four hours in port, the *Sultana* backed away from the wharf boat. Sergeant Karns was among the men who "cheered and shouted" as the boat pulled away. Private Safford found the departure a moving experience: "As the boat swung out into the river and we realized that at last we were bound for God's country, home and friends, we lustily cheered the grand old flag that floated defiantly from the jack-staff. That old flag never seemed so dear before, and many an old veteran who had borne the horrors of Andersonville without a sign of weakening broke down and cried like a child."[54]

The *Sultana* made a stop or two before actually leaving Vicksburg. After backing away from the wharf boat, she went downriver a short way and loaded rations for the men and coal for the boat. QM Sgt. Hiram C. Wells (Co. E, 8th MI Cav) remembered that "about dark, [the *Sultana*] dropt down river and took on 100 lbs of hardtack and a quanity of Bacon then dropt [down] the river for coal got Sta[r]ted up the river about 11 oc at night." The food taken on board included "[hog] Jowels, shoulders, Fresh Beef, Pork, pilot bread, soft bread, beans, Rice, hominy, coffee, sugar, vinegar, candles, soap, salt, [and] pepper." The Sanitary Commission put on some additional food items.[55]

Apparently, all of the foodstuffs were stored in the hold because the bow and the stern cargo room were completely filled with soldiers. "The *Sultana* had no freight on her boiler deck excepting 40 head condemned government stock [i.e., horses]," reported Sgt. Christian M. Nisley (Co. D, 40th IN Inf). The sixty "fat hogs" that had been taken on at New Orleans and two or three cows used for fresh milk and butter were quartered inside the stern cargo room.

After all her passengers, the food, and enough coal to take them to Memphis were on board, the *Sultana* backed into the swift waters of the Mississippi and turned her bow upriver. "Left Vicksburg Tuesday about 1 o'c A.M.," recorded her pilot, George Cayton. Pvt. Nathaniel M. Foglesang (Co. A, 18th MI Inf) agreed on the timing: "The overloaded boat steamed out of Vicksburg at one o'clock a.m., on the 25th of April."[56] The overcrowded, but overjoyed, soldiers were finally on their way home.

12

ON THE RIVER

"We were a merry-hearted, jolly set of men and boys as the *Sultana* was turned loose from the wharf at Vicksburg, swung out into midstream, and turned her prow toward the North with her living freight of human beings," Corporal Winters remembered.[1]

As the *Sultana* finally pulled away from Vicksburg, Sergeant Brown, who had been given a stateroom, visited with the first clerk, William Gambrel.

> The clerk and myself had quite a chat and he seemed to take quite an interest in having me relate some of my prison experiences. I broke in on his questioning to find out how many there were on board the boat. (The *Sultana* was one of the largest boats on the Mississippi river.) The clerk replied that if we arrived safe at Cairo it would be the greatest trip ever made on the western waters, as there were more people on board than were ever carried on one boat on the Mississippi river. He stated that there were 2,400 soldiers, 100 citizen passengers, and a crew of about eighty—in all over 2,500.[2]

Gambrel was exaggerating. As first clerk, he had been given a copy of the transportation pass for 1,966 officers and men, so he knew the actual numbers. His total of 2,400 may have been his way of padding the boat's bill to the U.S. government. Captain Mason would receive a voucher for carrying the paroled prisoners from Vicksburg to Cairo at a cost of $8 per officer and $2.75 per enlisted man. With a reported 35 officers and 1,931 men, he could expect close to $5,600. However, if Mason and Gambrel, both part owners of the *Sultana*, could bring the total up to 2,400 men, they could expect $6,600, out of which Captain Hatch would receive his kickback.

As the *Sultana* started upriver with her precious cargo, many of the men were still looking for a place to bed down. Sergeant Karns "crowded up the stairway leading to the cabin deck, and finding every space taken up, I edged my way up to the hurricane deck, though I found it crowded nearly as bad as below. By this time we had lost sight of the lights of Vicksburg and were gliding along at a merry rate." Karns eventually found a spot on the second deck, to the left of the main stairway opening but close to the outside railing. "Many of us put in the time for an hour or two of social conversation, chatting of home and friends and the many good things we would have to eat. We consoled ourselves that we had lived through it all, and were now in the land of the free and the home of the brave. We possessed no thought other than in a few days we would be at home, surrounded by friends and feasting on the fat of the land. Thus the night passed."[3]

Corporal Winters was philosophical about the crowding:

> When we marched aboard the *Sultana* we saw that we were
> crowded, but we were all anxious to get home so did not
> pay very much attention to our crowded condition. We had
> been crowded in prison, hence it was nothing new for us to
> be crowded on the boat, in fact we were thinking of more
> pleasant things. . . . Thoughts of home and the loved ones
> they expected to meet there, took possession of every mind,
> crowding out all thoughts of danger or disaster, a four years
> cruel war was coming to a close, peace was almost in sight.
> We were going home to God's country. . . . [N]o south,
> no north, no east, no west but all would soon be at home
> to mingle with those we love and to receive their warm

welcome and receive the sweet kisses of affection of wives, mothers, sisters, and sweethearts.[4]

While the enlisted men were forced to find room out on the open decks, the officers were able to bed down in the main saloon. First Lt. Elbert Jerome Squire (Co. D, 101st OH Inf) recalled that "the commissioned officers occupied cots that were placed in two rows and two tiers that were placed one above the other through the cabin."[5] As always, rank had its privilege.

As it turned out, there were not enough cots for every officer. Some of the civilian passengers had paid for "deck passage," meaning that they would normally have to stay below on the main deck. "Cabin passengers," in contrast, were given staterooms on the second deck. Since the boat had been invaded by almost two thousand paroled prisoners and the main deck was jammed, the deck passengers were apparently being allowed to sleep on the cots set up down the center of the main saloon. Indeed, "the passengers were provided for first," Lieutenant Elliott noted, "and some of us [officers] were left unprovided for."[6] Officers without cots slept in chairs or on the floor. Still, it was better than being outside on the cool, windswept decks.

Before falling asleep that first night, Louis Bean, who had claimed a spot near the engines, noticed the chief engineer checking the recently repaired boilers. Wintringer "went up several times to look at the patch which was put on the boiler at Vicksburg."[7] Although Wintringer considered the work "well done and sufficient," he was taking no chances.

When the sun rose on Tuesday, April 25, the *Sultana* was perhaps seventy miles upriver from Vicksburg. Private Eldridge had slept on the exposed hurricane deck.

> The sun came out bright and beautiful the next morning, it was real chilly for me not being well tho I had gained some strength while at Vicksburg. I sat by one of the smoke stacks leaning back against it to keep warm. The river was very high, and with me on top [of] the boat it looked to me like I was higher than all the surrounding country. I sat there looking at the beautiful scenery as we plowed up thru

the rolling tumbling muddy water of the Mississippi River, knowing the war was over, and thinking if God would spare my life a few days longer I would be at home where my mother and sisters would tenderly take care of me. Oh, it was the happiest day of all my life, and the other men were sitting around talking of home and singing with joy.[8]

As the sun rose, the men were able to see the immensity of the spring flooding. "The river was extremely high and in many places the country was submerged to such an extent that we appeared to be sailing on a lake," commented Lieutenant Squire. First Sergeant Ely, who was undoubtedly with the 115th Ohio Infantry men who were crowded around the bell on the front of the hurricane deck, penned in his diary for April 25, "Fine day, still going up, river very high over country everywhere."[9]

With the coming of daylight the men also began thinking about breakfast. As the *Sultana's* stewards began removing the cots and setting up the dining tables that would run down the center of the main saloon, the officers went below to retrieve rations for their men. Captain McCown drew the rations for the companies that had no officers and were led by sergeants. One of those sergeants was Franklin Barker from Michigan, who "had charge of a company of 90 men." Barker remembered that he "drew the rations on the lower deck and issued them on the upper deck. Except for this purpose I rarely left my place."[10]

Although the *Sultana* carried enough food for every soldier, many of the two thousand men did not get a full ration of meat and hardtack. McCown reported that he issued "[i]n the neighborhood of eighteen hundred. . . . They were issued every morning at nine o'clock." If this was true, then about two hundred men were probably sharing their friends' food instead of receiving their own allotment. Bean thought "there were some two hundred men who were complaining of not being fed very well."[11]

Hardtack and raw salt pork were not very satisfying. "[W]e couldn't get to cook or boil any coffee on board the boat. Ate the meat raw and drank water," Captain McCown said. "We had rations of all kinds that the government issued but we couldn't cook any of them on account of the crowd." A few of the men managed to find ways to heat the meat and boil their coffee. Sergeant Barker remembered that "there was a small stove on the after-main-deck where some of the men made their coffee, but generally, as far as I know, there was very little cooking, and the men lived on hard bread and raw salt pork or bacon." Sgt. David Hites (Co. G, 102nd OH Inf) agreed: "The cooking was done at the boilers and at a stove on the after main deck. We had no camp kettles or mess pans, and the cooking was done by small messes with such utensils as they had."[12]

Some of the soldiers discovered that they could cook their rations in the furnaces under the boilers or boil their beef and coffee in the boiling water drawn directly from the boilers. "The cooking was done for small messes of five or ten men, by the hot water taken from the boilers," Bean recalled. "Only one party could cook at a time and it took all day to get through." Wintringer admitted that "[t]he soldiers were somewhat in the way of the firemen, not to any great extent. They were somewhat in the way as they are on all boats that have troops on, a quantity of troops. In their way wanting to be cooking around the furnace."[13]

Fortunately, as Lieutenant Squire noted, "the Sanitary Commission issued some provisions which did not require cooking—crackers and pickled vegetables." Major Fiddler assigned Captain McCown "to see that the Sanitary rations were equally issued to the different companies on board the boat."[14] The officers did not have to worry about cooking their own rations. They dined in the main saloon and ate the same fare as the paying passengers.[15]

Dealing with "calls of nature" was difficult on the packed steamboat. Generally, steamboats had two toilets on the lower deck directly behind each paddlewheel housing for the deck passengers, and two on the cabin deck: the ladies' room located behind the larboard paddlewheel housing and the gentlemen's in front. The hurricane deck, however, had no facilities at all. Normally, that deck would be unoccupied; but the men crowded onto the *Sultana* had taken almost every available space. Louis Bean, who seemed to see everything, noted, "For calls of nature the men had places aft of the wheelhouses on the main deck, the water closets on the cabin deck, and holes cut in the top of the wheel-houses for the men on the hurricane deck." Since it would take too long for a soldier to move from the top deck down to the bathroom on the second deck, especially if he was suffering from diarrhea or dysentery, the men broke holes in the top of the paddle-wheel housings and went there.[16]

Perhaps, too, the men used the fire buckets filled with sand or water that were stored in racks at different locations around the steamboat. Since the men on the upper deck lacked any real restroom facility, they may have used some of the fire buckets as chamber pots and dumped the contents over the sides of the paddlewheel housing. A photo of the overcrowded *Sultana* taken at Helena, Arkansas, on April 26, 1865, unmistakably shows the holes torn in the top of the paddlewheel box as well as dark stains running down the side of the housing left by the contents of the buckets.[17]

The men found the fire buckets useful for getting drinking water from the Mississippi as well. It was easy to take a bucket from its rack, tie a rope to the handle, and lower it from the upper deck into the river. The buckets were rarely returned to their racks.[18]

Back in Vicksburg, Captain Speed and Captain Williams were already at department headquarters when General Dana arrived on Tuesday morning. Dana "inquired of Captain Speed whether the boat had left and was informed she had," and "then inquired as to the exact number of men she had taken, and was astonished to hear that there were nineteen hundred (1,900). Having never seen the boat I inquired as to her capacity and as to the comfort of the men and was assured by both Capt. Speed and Capt. Williams that the load was not large for the boat, that the men were comfortable and not overcrowded and that there were very few boats which had so much room for troops as the *Sultana*."[19] Both captains were lying—or at least neither had seen enough of conditions on the boat to say otherwise. The boat *was* overcrowded and the men were *not* comfortable. Had General Dana gone down to the river while the boat was being loaded, he would have seen that for himself.[20] As was the case with so many others connected to the *Sultana*, however, he had shirked his duty.

Like Dana, General Smith did not know how many paroled prisoners the *Sultana* was carrying when she left Vicksburg. When later asked about the overcrowding, however, he did not condemn it, saying simply, "Had I been master of transportation, I am not sure that the importunities of those poor fellows to go together would not have prevailed on me to let them all go on the *Sultana*."[21] Had he been in charge, in other words, he probably would have listened to the men's pleas to stay together and would have allowed them all to go together on the *Sultana*. General Smith *was* in charge, however, and although he was not the "master of transportation," he *was* the commander of the Post and District of Vicksburg. When the actual master of transportation, Captain Kerns, asked for Smith's help to get the men divided, General Smith had also shirked his duty.

As the *Sultana* steamed northward, far upriver at Memphis the Union picket boat *Pocahontas* was going about her duties. The crew of the small steamboat spent April 25 moving up and down the Mississippi in the vicinity of Memphis "destroy[ing] everything found in the form of water craft." The Union authorities were having trouble with local guerrillas and believed that destroying all the small rivercraft would curtail the activities of these night raiders. By the end of the day, all known yawls, rowboats, and skiffs had been "sunk or hacked into pieces."[22]

As the first day went on and the *Sultana* continued to churn upriver, it was discovered that several of the men on board were ill, even though the authorities had tried to prevent sick men from boarding. First Lt. Simeon W. Dickinson (Co. E, 2nd MI Cav) noted, "There were fifteen or twenty men who were quite unwell with diarrhea, and these men collected on the deck forward of the [main] cabin where such care was taken of them as was possible under the circumstances. No medicines or supplies for sick men were sent on board for the command and we had to depend upon what the boat could furnish, and such articles as the Sanitary Commission had on board."[23]

Major Fidler, who was responsible for all of the men under his charge, did his best for the sick ones. On Fidler's orders Captain McCown "got a doctor [who was] on board the boat to attend to them." The ever-observant Louis Bean confirmed that "[a] citizen doctor who was on board gave one man a dose of medicine, and I don't know that any more was given. There was no medical officer with the command." The "citizen doctor" may have been ex-major John Hill, late an assistant surgeon with the 41st Ohio Infantry, who had been discharged from the service and had booked passage home as a private citizen.[24]

In the absence of an official doctor, Cpl. Samuel F. Sanders (Co. I, 137th IL Inf) acted as a hospital steward. When the other men from Illinois had been sent home on the *Henry Ames*, Sanders had been kept behind. "I was nursing the sick in the barracks," he later explained, "and did not leave Vicksburg until the last boat load. . . . I had charge of sixteen sick comrades, who were sleeping in front of the cabin."[25]

At some point over the years the *Sultana* saga acquired an apocryphal story that "among the passengers on board were twelve ladies, most of them belonging to the Christian Commission," a branch of the Young Men's Christian Association (YMCA), who went on board the *Sultana* at Vicksburg to take care of the sick. According to the story, after the explosion, one of these ladies calmed the struggling masses in the water below the bow and then refused to jump into the water herself for fear that she would lose her "presence of mind and be the means of the death of some of [the men]," so she calmly folded her hands over her bosom and "burned, a voluntary martyr to the men she had so lately quieted."

It is a charming story, but it is also a fabrication. Only two of those connected with the disaster mentioned some Christian Commission ladies being on board the *Sultana* at all: survivor Chester Berry and rescuer William H. C. Michael, acting ensign of the timberclad *Tyler*. Oddly, Private Berry mentioned these women in the introduction to his monumental 1892 book, *Loss of the* Sultana *and Reminiscences of Survivors*, but did not mention them in his own personal reminiscence. Six years later, in 1898, Ensign Michael, who had corresponded and visited with the survivors and may have read Berry's book, repeated the story in an article on the disaster. Ensign Michael was never on board the *Sultana*, however, so his reporting must be considered secondhand.[26]

Not one of the more than two hundred first-person accounts from soldiers, civilians, and crew members who were on board the *Sultana* from April 24 to April 27, 1865, makes reference to the "ladies belonging to the Christian Commission" being on board the steamboat either prior to or during the disaster, including Private Berry's personal narrative. The obvious conclusion is that no ladies of the Christian Commission got on board the *Sultana* at Vicksburg or anywhere else on that trip up the Mississippi. In fact, when it was rumored that "Mrs. O. E. Hosmer, one of the ladies connected with the Sanitary Commission, was on the steamer *Sultana*, at the time of the late explosion," the *Chicago Tribune* reported, "We are reliably informed that this is not so. No ladies took passage at Memphis."[27]

There were women on board for that trip, although exactly how many is hard to determine. Private Walker said that there were seventeen. Pvt. Jacob Rush (Co. L, 3rd OH Cav) agreed that there were "seventeen lady passengers on board," but added "[and] several of the wives of the deck hands." Second Lt. William French Dixon (Co. A, 10th IN Cav) thought there were nineteen women on the boat, and Pvt. George C. Loy (Co. D, 1st WV Lt. Art) recalled that there were "about twenty wommin and children." We can positively identify thirteen women passengers, ranging in age from the two seventeen-year-old Spikes girls, Elizabeth and Susan, to forty-eight-year-old Ann Annis. And as Private Rush indicated, the wives of several of the deckhands were on board as well, perhaps employed as chambermaids, laundresses, and so on, and must be included in the total number of women.[28]

It is likewise difficult to determine how many children were on board the *Sultana* between April 24 and April 27. We know of seven-year-old Belle Annis; and Adeline Spikes, the Spikes family's niece, may have been a child. Private Rush recalled seeing "two small children," and Private Safford saw "six small children." There also seems to have been at least one infant. Private Foglesang recalled seeing a mother with a "little baby about two-month-old." Additionally, the crew included several "cabin boys." All in all, we know that there were approximately seventy paying passengers and eighty-five crew members, most of the latter being adult males.[29]

In addition to people, there were also government horses and mules on board the *Sultana*. The men's estimates of their numbers varied from Bean's "eight or ten" to Homer's "thirty or forty" to McCown's "fifty or sixty," but William Rowberry, the *Sultana*'s first mate, who was responsible for the storage of cargo, both animate and inanimate, should have the final word: "We had no cargo on the boat [at the time of the explosion] except 60 head of mules and horses."[30]

Far upriver, the *Henry Ames*, the first steamboat to leave Vicksburg with a large load of paroled prisoners, reached St. Louis in the early afternoon of April 25. "Thirteen hundred and fifteen paroled Federal prisoners arrived here yesterday, by the steamer *Henry Ames*," the *Daily Missouri Republican* reported. "The men left the boat about 2 o'clock, and marched in a body out to Benton Barracks." The *Cleveland Leader* added the information that "the men belong to Illinois, Iowa, Wisconsin, and Minnesota."[31]

Sometime on April 25, a few of the soldiers on the *Sultana* returned to tease the crew's pet alligator in its sturdy wooden crate inside the wheelhouse. Private Lugenbeal remembered, "We would punch him with sticks to see him open his mouth. [Finally] the boatmen got tired of this and put him in the closet under the stairway."[32]

The overcrowding made it difficult—and unwise—for the soldiers to move around. Bean recalled that "the men generally remained in their places day and night. If a man gave up his place once, he would find it difficult to find another one." Lieutenant Dixon commented, "They were huddled on all the decks so thick that there was no passageway between them." Captain McCown noted that "the men were everywhere in the boat, where they could get a chance to hold on, to stand up or sit down. The boat was very crowded." In spite of the crowding, however, the men seemed well behaved. "The men were very quiet on the boat all the way up," recalled Corporal Mahoney. Passenger Ann Annis likewise thought "the men behaved very well indeed. There was no carousing or quarreling, and only little moving about."[33]

The men had little to do as the boat steamed upriver, so when the *Sultana* passed downstream-bound steamboats or riverside towns, they would generally crowd to one side or the other to see the sight. Bean wrote, "On several different occasions when other boats were passing us, the men would gather in masses to one side of the boat which careened her over very much and two or three times she was very near dipping, or taking water in the guards." When the men crowded to one side, Captain McCown said, "at times the boat moved only with one wheel, the other being out of the water. The flag staff also inclined from perpendicular from same cause."[34]

Captain Mason did his best to stop such moving about. Lieutenant Elliott, who "became quite well acquainted with" Mason and called the captain "a careful man," wrote, "I remember his cautioning the men not to crowd on one side of the boat when making a landing, because the tilting of the boat and its return to a level position would endanger the boilers." McCown added, "At every landing of the river, the guards and officers were both instructed to keep the men quiet in their places, and not let the men rush over to the side of the boat for fear of capsizing her and smashing her in."[35]

Chief Engineer Wintringer was well aware of the dangers careening posed to a boat's boilers, and he was also aware that "the boat was top heavy and was consequently inclined to careen over from side to side." Because of this he kept a careful eye on the boilers, especially the patched left-hand boiler. But he did not think the tilting was "so much so as to cause the water in any of the boilers to be so much lowered as to expose any part of it to the fire unprotected by water."[36]

And that was the danger. Should the water inside the four boilers be too low, the tilting of the boat would cause one or more of the flues within each boiler to be exposed above the surface of the water. Without the surrounding water to absorb the heat, the exposed flues might become red hot. When the boat returned to an even keel, the water would level out and flow over these superheated flues. When the water came in contact with the heated flues it would instantly turn to steam. This, of course, would cause an instantaneous rise in steam pressure. Normally, the safety valves would blow and release the pressure (unless they were tied down, which engineers sometimes did to allow for an overload of pressure). If the increase in pressure was too great and if there was a weak spot in the boiler, the steam would blow right through it.

In the right combination, careening, low water in the boilers, and a weak spot were a recipe for disaster. Part owners James Cass Mason and William Gambrel were both concerned about the number of people crowded onto their vessel. Captain McCown recalled that Gambrel had told Major Fidler that "there were so many men aboard and on the roof of the cabin, that if they made any quick movement in mass, the roof would give way; also, if they moved rapidly from one side of the boat to the other, they would sink her or cause some accident." A reporter who interviewed civilian passenger J. T. Farris after the disaster wrote, "Mr. Farris represents that Captain Mason appeared to be uneasy and troubled in mind, all the way up the river, and remarked in the presence of Mr. Farris, that the passengers little knew the danger they were in, and that [Mason] would give all he was worth if he had them safely in port."[37] Although Mason was in desperate need of money, it would do him no good if his steamboat was crushed underfoot or exploded due to the overcrowded soldiers.

Mason may have turned to alcohol when the responsibility of carrying so large a load of men lay heavily on his mind. Opinions vary on that subject. Wintringer claimed not to know how much the captain drank. He did admit to having the impression that Mason "was not strictly temperate," quickly adding, however, "I never saw him under the influence of liquor." Lieutenant Squire, who was quartered in the main saloon, agreed: "I noticed that the man who was pointed out as the captain of the boat, drank very frequently at the bar, though I never saw him as I thought under the influence of liquor. I wondered that he could drink so much and not show it." Captain Hake disagreed: "I noticed the man whom I afterward found to be the Captain drinking very frequently and took him to be one of the passengers. To the best of my belief I saw the Captain under the influence of liquor . . . so much so that it was difficult for him to balance himself."[38] If Mason was indeed so much "under the influence" that it was "difficult for him to balance himself," he was joining the long list of individuals connected with the *Sultana* who were shirking their duties.

As the day streamed by and the *Sultana* brought the men closer to their homes, Cpl. John Fox Jr. (Co. A, 50th OH Inf) recalled that their "hearts [were] filled with joyful anticipations of the pleasures we expected to enjoy with our friends and loved ones when we would reach there." Pvt. George Hass (Co. A, 102nd OH Inf.) likewise remembered the fervent anticipation: "Many of the soldiers on board had not seen home and friends for years, and having just been released from captivity, their hearts were filled with joy at the prospective meeting of father, mother, brothers, sisters, or per chance she who was soon to become the bride of the returned soldier."[39]

Sgt. William A. Buchanan (Co. D, 93rd IN Inf) summed up the men's feelings in the flowery prose popular at that time:

> These poor men had just been released from the worst of Rebel prisons, after months untold suffering, and at last were nearing home. "Home," Ah, God! how that word sustained them; how they had longed for it by day and dreamed of it by night; through months of pain and starvation the thought of it had kept them alive, and now they were almost there. They could almost feel the longed for arms of wife, the clinging kiss of child, see the tear-dimmed eyes of the loyal old mother, who, when they had started to help protect the dear old flag, had bravely said: "Go, my son, and God go with you," and feel again the father's hand clasp.[40]

As darkness came on, the men began to settle in for the night. "[T]he excitement was so intense among us it was hard for us to settle down for rest and sleep," wrote Corporal Winters, "but when we finally did settle every available space on the boat from the boiler deck to the hurricane roof was occupied. It was impossible after we all lay down for one to walk anywhere on the boat without stepping on someone." Although the boat had careened from side to side a few times during the day when the men moved about, Captain Friesner of the guard unit noted, "The boat ran more steady when the men were lying down."[41]

"Many a weary soldier lay at night in the ill-fated boat dreaming of home and loved ones," wrote Private Collins, "full of inexpressible happiness that at last all dangers and hardships were over, and that the white dove of peace had perched upon the flags of hostile armies, and song and laughter would take the place of groans and tears of agony."[42]

13

HELENA AND MEMPHIS

When the first rays of the sun peeked over the horizon on Wednesday, April 26, 1865, the *Sultana* began to come to life. As Captain Friesner noted, the boat had "a population equal to that of a flourishing country town"—a town crammed into a very small space. In spite of the overcrowding, the men felt safe. Farrier Josiah Watson (Co. M, 9th IN Cav) thought the "*Sultana* was undoubtedly a staunch and good reliable craft as was fully demonstrated by her carrying an immense cargo of sugar and other freight . . . besides the 2,200 paroled soldiers and a crew of eighty men—she made good time under an experienced and skillful crew."[1]

The company commanders lined up on the main deck to receive and distribute the morning meal and coffee. After breakfast the men settled back and let the miles go by. Corporal Winters and his friends "whiled away the time gazing at the shifting scenes along the shore, playing little tricks on each other, singing little songs, telling little jokes; laughing and talking about the happy times we expected to have when we reached our homes in receiving the warm and welcome caresses of fathers, mothers, brothers, sisters, wives, sweethearts, and friends."[2]

"A happier crowd I never saw," Sergeant Brown recalled; "we all felt that a few more hours would land us at home where anxious friends were awaiting our return. Our names had already been forwarded by telegraph to the press North, and many hearts were made light by the prospect of meeting a son, a husband, brother or sweetheart." Commissary Sgt. Uriah James Mavity (Co. H, 9th IN Cav) wrote, "Our hearts grew lighter and visions of home more vivid as we drew nearer and nearer to our destination."[3]

The *Sultana* was approaching Helena, Arkansas, and once again Captain Mason was worried about the men shifting about. William Gambrel asked Captain McCown to caution them against rushing to one side, and McCown recalled Captain Mason making "a similar statement to Major Fidler, who got on the pilot house and calling 'attention' to the men, told them to keep quiet especially in case of an accident and not to change places when the boat was stopped." The *Sultana* was finally within sight of the east Arkansas town, and Mason didn't want the men moving to that side of the boat.[4]

In the nearby encampment of the 87th Illinois Infantry was Assistant Surgeon Berry, who had witnessed the *Sultana* on her down-river trip spreading the news of Lincoln's assassination. "The next time I saw the boat was on her return trip up the river. She was loaded down with such a mass of human freight as I had never seen before. She was black with men—how many, no one ever seemed to know. Her cabins, her decks, her guards, hurricane roof, wheel-houses, every available spot where a man could attain foothold, was occupied." As the boat appeared, dozens of soldiers from the 87th Illinois rushed to the riverbank "to salute the cloud of 'returning braves' as they passed up the river."[5] It was about 7 a.m. when the *Sultana* finally tied up at the Helena wharf boat.

Despite the warnings, the paroled prisoners rushed to the landward side of the vessel to get a look at the little Arkansas town. And it was an unusual sight. The rising Mississippi River had inundated the streets, and the residents and the garrison of Union soldiers had to use small rowboats to get around town. Private Schmutz remembered "the street covered with water—people could only pass through the streets on boats. All rushed to the side and the officers pleaded with the men to get back, fearing the [*Sultana*] would capsize, it was so heavily loaded." Lieutenant Elliott, who had heard Captain Mason warn the men against crowding to one side, noted that "the men managed very well except at a few places, especially Helena, Arkansas, where they all tried to get a view of the place."[6]

If the prisoners wanted to see the spectacle of the flooded town, the people of Helena were just as curious to see the overcrowded *Sultana*. "[T]he spectacle of the mass of humanity covering the boat like so many insects aroused curiosity and brought out almost the whole population," Friesner explained, "and with them an enterprising photographer who wished to take a picture of the boat. This caused a general crowding to one side and the boat careened to one side, whereupon the captain and clerk [Gambrel] came begging me to have the men stand back and trim ship or they would blow up the boat."[7]

The Helena photographer was Thomas W. Bankes, a thirty-five-year-old Englishman who had come to America as a teacher before the war and had taken up photography in 1863. After taking a few pictures of the flooded streets, he stood perhaps fifty feet from the stern of the *Sultana*, on the port side, and focused his camera on the vessel.[8]

As soon as the men on the *Sultana* spotted Bankes setting up his tripod camera, they rushed to get into the picture. "[E]ach soldier seemed to be bent on having his face discernible in the picture," recalled Captain Elliott. "I entreated and exhorted prudence, while I sat on the roof, my feet pendant and my hands on a float, momentarily expecting a capsizing and sinking."[9] Friesner, too, "was very much afraid that she would be blown up by the crowding of the troops to the side. But, by the exertions of the officers and guards, the danger was averted."[10]

Bankes' photograph is an amazing record. The Helena wharf boat is to the left, the steamboat to the right. Dark smoke is coming out of the larboard smokestack, perhaps indicating that the *Sultana* was keeping her paddlewheels going to counteract the strong current. Human beings swarm over all the decks like ants. Men sit on the stern railing on the main deck, their feet hanging over the rails. Black mourning bunting appears to be hanging behind them. The heads of at least two horses are visible behind the railing on the afterguard.

On the second, or cabin, deck, the wide guard in front of the left paddlewheel housing is also crowded with soldiers. A string of laundry hangs from a diagonal line next to them. The hurricane deck above is black with people.

On the back part of the hurricane deck, one soldier stands high above the others, undoubtedly because he was standing atop the *Sultana*'s metal lifeboat. There are prisoners on top of the texas cabin roof, and someone who might be Captain Mason is in the pilothouse door. A dozen or more soldiers are on top of the left paddlewheel box, most sitting but one soldier standing tall, hands in his pants pockets, looking away from the camera, probably at the flooded streets of Helena. Holes are visible in the top of the housing, and dark streaks run down the side of the paddlewheel box. And above it all, perched triumphantly in the center of the lowest of two braces holding the smokestacks apart, are the coveted elk's antlers, the prize awarded to the fastest steamboat on the river.

As Bankes looked through his lens, he saw prisoners everywhere— except on the second deck, directly behind the paddlewheel housing. The photograph clearly shows two of the *Sultana*'s civilian passengers: a man holding a top hat at the railing and, to his left, a woman with long, dark hair. To their left is a solitary soldier, probably a member of the guard unit. The lack of paroled prisoners in this area, plus the appearance of the civilian passengers, may indicate that the area was off-limits to the men. With paying passengers on board, and all of the rest of the boat crowded with soldiers, this area may have been designated a refuge for the civilian passengers.

The woman at the rail is Lucy Smith. Pvt. Charles J. Lahue (Co. D, 13th IN Cav), who owned a copy of the photograph, explained years later, "I find a doleful kind of pleasure in picking out the figures of my comrades who posed in that happy group. Prominent in the foreground stands a Miss Smith, a woman whom the soldiers loved, with a voice of a nightingale and the soul like an angel. She had gone to Natchez to meet and welcome her lover from the strife and was then on her way home in anticipation of the sound of wedding bells."[11]

When Bankes clicked his shutter, he knew that he had captured the *Sultana* at her proudest moment. Besides being famous as the

Messenger of Death bearing news of Lincoln's assassination, the *Sultana* would go down in history as the boat that carried almost two thousand Union prisoners home from the notorious Confederate prisons. Her image had been captured for all eternity.[12]

After an hour at Helena, the *Sultana* started back upriver near 8 a.m.[13] Once again the soldiers settled back and watched the scenery go by. Captain Friesner described that part of the trip.

> After leaving Helena, we went merrily up the river past homes with wide verandas, dark with the shade of protecting trees; groups of deserted Negro cabins near; past ugly mouths of swampy bayous with their rotting snags and slimy, pestilential waters; past miles of cottonwood brakes that could only raise their leafy tops above the water—for the flood of the Mississippi was on—the leaves so dense we could not see beyond, and we seemed sailing along the edge of the world and all the rest was shoreless water and its leafy inflorescence. On the boat, all was animation, gladness and joyous expectation as the black pipes spread their dark feathery vapors far down the river until they mingled with the dim sky. . . . Hasten! Hasten! Good boat! Strain every iron nerve and let your great, fiery heart glow with the huge mass of love you carry and let the glad wheels sing at their work for the love that awaits us. Tonight Memphis—in the morning Cairo—tomorrow's sun and we will breathe the air again of a free land in our own beloved homes.[14]

Miles ahead, at Memphis, eighteen-year-old William Hazel Woodridge was looking for a skiff to take to his mother's livestock farm about seven miles above the city on the Tennessee side. Woodridge and his mother lived in Memphis, but their overseer, R. K. Hill, had sent word that he needed a boat because of the floodwaters. "Only a few dry places of land were out of water," Woodbridge explained. "My mother's farm was one. There was a great deal of stock sheltered under the barns there and scattered about the place. The only way to go around the farm . . . was by skiff." Since the crew of the Union picket boat *Pocahontas* had destroyed all the small watercraft in the area, Hill needed a new boat to get to the animals.

Woodridge had to search for "several hours" before he found a skiff. Its owner was William Boardman, of the "first wood yard above the city." Woodridge continued, "The river was very high when I left Memphis that day. The water was over the Arkansas shores, extending back several miles, and pickets of Union soldiers had been thrown out to watch any progress on the river. . . . [W]e left Memphis early in the afternoon of the 26th. As the pickets along the river front in the vicinity of the city were very strict, we had to slip out the best way we could. So we went up Wolf River to Hatchie and then through the overflow to the farm, arriving there about sundown."[15]

Far to the north, at around 2 p.m., the *Olive Branch* finally reached Cairo with "200 cabin passengers and 800 on deck, including 619 paroled prisoners from Vicksburg." She remained at Cairo only a few hours before continuing on to St. Louis, where she arrived early on the morning of April 27.[16]

The sun was low in the western sky as the *Sultana* closed in on Memphis. Pvt. Joseph R. Ratekin (Co. I, 11th IL Cav), who was in an encampment south of the city, remembered the incredible sight as the boat passed. "At the time my regiment, the 11th Illinois Cav., was in camp on a high cliff about three miles below Memphis, and I well remember this boat sweeping past up the river about 5 o'clock in the evening. The boat came within a stone's throw of where I and perhaps 200 others were standing, and we gave a loud cheer, which was returned by those brave boys, many of whom had lain in rebel prison pens for months."[17]

Union forces had occupied Memphis shortly after their victory at the Battle of Memphis on June 6, 1862, and the city had been turned into a Union supply base. The base included a branch office of the U.S. Sanitary Commission and the Soldiers' Home run by the commission. On the riverbank two miles south of the city was Fort Pickering, a large earthen fortification guarding the southern water approach to Memphis. Any vessel approaching the city from the south would have to slow down as it entered a sharp 90-degree turn, leaving itself vulnerable to the fort's cannon.[18]

Just upriver from the city wharf near the mouth of the Wolf River was the Memphis Navy Yard, where the ironclad *Essex* was anchored. An unnamed petty officer saw the *Sultana* arrive at Memphis: "I first saw the *Sultana* as she rounded the point below Fort Pickering, in plain view from our deck, and she presented the appearance of an immense mass of human beings; it seemed as if every foot of space, from her hurricane deck down, was crowded. She was loudly cheered by crowds of people, who lined the wharves and levees."[19]

It was near 7 p.m. on Wednesday, April 26, when the *Sultana* finally docked at the foot of Court Avenue. She stopped in Memphis for two reasons: to offload the 225 hogsheads of sugar, 97 boxes of wine, and 60 "fat hogs" that had been taken on at New Orleans; and to take on coal for the last leg of the journey to Cairo.[20]

The men took advantage of the stop. "The moment the boat touched the wharf at Memphis, Tenn., the boys began to jump off," recalled Pvt. Walter Glazier Porter (Co. C, 18th MI Inf). "I went with the rest and roamed about town until ten o'clock in the evening of the 26th of April when we went back to the boat." Although Private Foglesang remembered that "a guard was stationed at the edge of the boat with orders not to let any of the prisoners get off," none of the other soldiers reported seeing such a guard. Captain Friesner, who was in charge of the guards on the *Sultana*, did not mention placing a guard at the landing. In fact, he went to bed before the boat left Memphis, so he must not have been worried about the men getting off.[21]

Many of those who went into Memphis were looking for a good meal to supplement the meager rations doled out on the *Sultana*. Pvt. Truman Marion Smith (Co. B, 8th MI Cav) "went to the 'Soldiers' Rest' [and] got something to eat," and Pvt. James Payne (Co. C, 124th IN Inf) recalled that "[a] number of the boys, myself being one of them, got off here and went up into the town to see if they could get something to eat, and at least get some fresh air."[22]

C. W. Christy, superintendent of the Memphis Sanitary Commission, had a busy night:

> From sunset till near 10 o'clock, the night of her arrival, we plied our hands and feet at the Lodge [i.e., Soldiers' Home]

giving the men such fare as we had. The pickled onions and curried cabbage were better than gold to their sight and taste. Of course, out of such a host, it was but a handful we could feed, but we did our best. The men were in good spirits. They were getting nearer home each day. They spoke earnestly of their good treatment at Vicksburg, and said that the further North they got the better seemed the people and the better seemed the fare. We all went to bed that night tired, but glad to have ministered to the physical wants of such men—the heroes and martyrs of the war; and glad in their gladness that home and friends, at last, lay so little way and so few days off.[23]

Private Payne's commanding officer, Lieutenant Elliott, also went into town: "It being reported among the men that the boat would be at Memphis for some time, and there being no control over us, a number of us took advantage of the occasion to go into the city in search of amusement." Elliott calculated that "about 150 of the men had gone up into the city to see the sights." Among them was Pvt. Mathew Boner (Co. F, 4th KY Cav), who along with "two other soldiers attended a theatre."[24]

Since each of the 225 hogsheads of sugar weighed about 1,200 pounds, Captain Mason sought assistance from the soldiers in unloading the huge barrels. Mason asked Major Fidler for "a detail of men to unload the 250 hogsheads of sugar," Private Kennedy recalled. Pvt. Robert Wesley Gilbreath (Co. E, 9th IN Cav) remembered that Mason added an incentive. Any soldier who helped would be given "a little money, a fair supper and, for those who wanted it, all the whiskey they could drink." Pvt. Samuel Henry Raudebaugh (Co. K, 65th OH Inf) "helped unload the sugar and received seventy-five cents an hour for the time I worked." Perhaps more than the food or money, Pvt. Albert Norris reasoned that it was the need to get home that drove the men to help: "We were so eager to speed the trip that we threw off our coats and helped the roustabouts."[25]

Sergeant Aldrich admitted he used the opportunity to get into town for a good meal: "[T]hey called for volunteers to help roll them ashore. It took a dozen of us to roll one, and when we got ashore we struck up town and let a dozen more roll the next one. I went up town and found the Soldiers' Home, and got supper which I long will remember for it was the first table I had seen spread in a long while, nearly three years. About 9 or 10 o'clock that evening I went back to the boat well fed, but tired."[26]

During the unloading of the hogshead, one of the barrels cracked open and spilled its contents onto the cobblestone levee. Corporal Winters wrote that "a number of men and boys had quite a picnic eating sugar, and carrying off more for future use. Comrade Pouder [Pvt. Andrew Jackson Pouder, Co. K, 50th OH Inf.] was one among the number; besides bringing up all we wanted to eat at the time, he filled our ever-ready three-quart bucket, with the expectation of having it for future use." Another soldier who thought of the future was fifteen-year-old Stephen Millard Gaston (musician, Co. K, 9th IN Cav): "I found a hogshead of sugar broken (as soldiers always do find) and my comrade, [Pvt.] Wm. Block [Co. K, 9th IN Cav.], and I filled everything we could find with sugar, intending to eat the sugar and hard tack while going up the river to our destination. We stored our sugar in front of the pilot house at our heads, for we had made this our bunk and turned in for the night. Our evening dreams were sweet, for we had eaten about two pounds of sugar each."[27]

With the sugar (about 135 tons) and the 97 boxes of wine (combined weight 2.5 tons) removed from her hold, the *Sultana* had just lost almost 140 tons of ballast. Although the combined weight of the 2,130 people on board was not excessive, the fact that most of them were high up on the hurricane deck and that there was nothing left in the hold except the barrels and boxes of rations meant that the boat's center of gravity had shifted upward. If the boat had a tendency to careen with nearly 140 tons of ballast in her hold, what would happen now that the hold was practically empty?

All of this should have been evident to First Mate William Rowberry, who was in charge of the distribution of freight; to Captain Mason, who had been on the river in charge of steamboats long enough to know what could happen to a top-heavy vessel; and to Chief Engineer Wintringer, who should have known that a top-heavy steamboat will tend to careen, which in turn might create a problem with the boilers. Yet, none of them acted to redistribute the weight left on board. In all fairness, there was not much they could have done. Every inch of space on the lower decks of the *Sultana* was already occupied. They could not insist that the men come down from the hurricane deck and pack more tightly onto the main deck; nor did they insist that some of the men go down into the dark hold for the last leg of the journey to Cairo, although some men did. Quite simply, Captain Mason and the others had set the stage for a disaster when they had taken on almost two thousand paroled prisoners with no place to put them but the wide-open hurricane deck high above the water. When the boat had 140 tons of cargo in her hold, the decision to place most of the men on the upper-most deck made little difference. With the removal of that cargo, the decision had suddenly become far more important.

A few people were coming and going as the *Sultana*'s cargo was offloaded. Getting off were Lieutenant Colonel Compton, who had gotten on at New Orleans, and the fourteen members of the Chicago Opera Troupe. After the disaster, a Memphis newspaper claimed that the troupe's "members knew many of the returning soldiers, and on the trip up, gave several concerts on the boat." Not a single soldier wrote of being entertained by the troupe, though, and like so many other "facts" connected with the *Sultana* disaster, this story seems to be baseless.[28]

Among the others coming on board the crowded *Sultana* was Senator-elect William Dunham Snow from Arkansas, who was on his way to claim his seat in Congress. The Massachusetts-born Snow had settled in Pine Bluff, Arkansas, in 1860 and had helped to raise three Union regiments from Arkansas.[29]

Near 9 p.m., as they had done on the previous two nights, the stewards began setting up two rows of double-decker cots down the center of the main saloon. Lt. Joseph Taylor Elliott, who had spent the previous two nights sleeping on the cabin's floor, was determined to get a cot this night. He threw his hat "in the first cot toward the bow of the boat," and then went to get his few belongings from his old sleeping spot. "On coming back," he said, "I found my cot occupied by Captain [William Henry] McCoy [Co. F, 175th OH Inf] . . . who refused to give it up." The two officers nearly came to blows before 1st Sgt. Lewis C. Keeler (Co. D, 58th USCT) persuaded Elliott to take an empty cot at the back of the cabin, just in front of the ladies' cabin, beneath the one Keeler had taken.[30]

Before retiring for the night, Elliott spoke with Captain Mason. "[I]f I believed in presentiments," Elliott later said, "I would believe that he had one that something dreadful was going to happen, for in our conversation he said that he would give all the interest he had in the boat if it were safely landed in Cairo. I was impressed at the time by what he said but in a few minutes it wore off."[31]

About this same time, Capt. James Walter Elliott was also looking for a cot. He had spent the previous night in a chair after giving his cot from the first night to another officer. As soon as the cots were set up, Elliott placed his hat on a cot near the front of the main saloon. A little later, when the officer to whom he had given his cot the night before asked him if he had found a cot, Elliott pointed to the one with his hat. The officer "said that one was in a hot, unpleasant and danger-ous place over the boilers, and that he had reserved one for me in the ladies' cabin. 'Give it to some poor fellow who had none last night,' I said; but a moment afterward he came and told me he had removed my hat to the cot selected by him, and that I would have to take that or none. Soon I retired to the cot, read until weary, fell asleep, was partly aroused by the boat leaving the wharf a little after midnight, but relapsed into sweet slumber."[32]

Around 10:30, Senator-elect Snow ran into First Clerk Gambrel and commented about the number of men on the *Sultana*. Gambrel replied that "he thought it was the largest number ever carried up the river," Snow recalled. Having already set a speed record on their last run between New Orleans and St. Louis, the *Sultana* was now ready to set another record by carrying the largest number of people ever assembled on one boat on the Mississippi. Gambrel showed Snow a "certificate of some authorized quartermaster" that listed the 1,966 paroled officers and enlisted men. According to Snow, the list also included "seventy (70) Cabin Passengers and eighty-five (85) hands belonging to the boat."

Gambrel told Snow that the trip to Cairo usually took about twenty-three hours and "that he expected to reach that City in time for the 12 o'clock midnight train the next evening." Gambrel's tone turned somber when he told Snow that "he felt the responsibility of having so many on board. 'Suppose there should be a fire.'" That, to Snow, indicated that Gambrel "realized his position."[33]

The unloading of the freight was completed just before 11 p.m., and the *Sultana*'s bell rang to signal that she would be leaving in a few minutes. Private Porter returned to discover that he would have to find a new sleeping spot.

> [S]everal of us [had] slept on the boiler deck in a coalbin as the other decks were so crowded, [but] as they were going to take on coal enough for the rest of our journey we had to find new sleeping quarters. After roaming around on the cabin deck as best I could among the sleepers, I found a place between the smokestacks, and spread down my blanket and was about to lie down, when one of the men nearby said that he was holding that place for another man. I took up my blanket and found another vacant place large enough to lie down, but before I laid down was informed that it was being held for another man. . . . I made my way back to the stairs and found room enough by sticking my feet over the steps, laid down and was soon lost in sleep.[34]

Pvt. Louis Schirmeyer (Co. A, 32nd IN Inf) had also gone into town, where he and a friend "filled up with beer and almost missed the boat." Another soldier who took on some beer was a tall Tennessean. "He was a thin seven-footer," sixteen-year-old Private McFarland remembered, "and he came down to the boat, shouting and cursing, at the point of bayonets, so drunk he could hardly walk. He was brought up to the hurricane deck, where he caused considerable disturbance. I was quite young at that time, and it pleased me very much to tease this fellow. He tried to get at me, but the men were so thick he had to run over a number in trying to get me, and received a number of licks for his trouble."[35] Some have identified this "tall Tennessean" as Richard Morgan Pierce (Co. D, 3rd TN Cav), but Pierce's Volunteer Enlistment record indicates that he was five feet, eleven inches tall, only three inches taller than the average height of a Civil War soldier.[36]

Pvt. Eppenetus McIntosh of Illinois was a new addition to the *Sultana*'s manifest. McIntosh departed Vicksburg on the *Henry Ames* but was left behind when that boat stopped in Memphis. "I, supposing she would remain some time, went into town to look around and buy some articles I needed, and while gone she moved off and left me," McIntosh explained. "Along in the evening the steamer *Sultana* landed loaded with another lot of prisoners, so I embarked intending to go to Benton Barracks and join the comrades I left on the *Henry Aims* [*sic*]." With almost two thousand paroled prisoners already on her crowded decks, who would notice one more?[37]

As the men began to settle down for the night, Captain Friesner decided to do the same: "I went to bed about 10 o'c P.M. Everything being very quiet and no bar open to my knowledge at any rate there was no drinking when I went to bed." He retired to his stateroom, removed his outer garments, and stretched out on his bunk.[38]

The *Sultana* backed away from the Memphis levee at around 11 p.m., swung into the flooded Mississippi, and headed upriver to take on coal. A number of the paroled prisoners who had gone into town missed her departure. Private Payne and his comrade Pvt. Thomas Wright (Co. C, 124th IN Inf) "wandered around until we heard the signal to start and then we ran for the boat, but we were too late. . . . We saw that the *Sultana* was going to stop at some coal barges and take on some coal, and we in our desperation tried to get aboard here; but . . . we were again unsuccessful. While we were standing on the wharf, or rather in the sand, we were watching the *Sultana*, our hope, joy, and pride, steam away, feeling our hearts sink within us."[39]

Private Boner and two friends who had attended the theater also missed the boat. "When they started toward the dock they heard . . . the signal announcing that it was ready to resume its journey up the Mississippi River. They broke into a run, but arrived at the dock too late to board the vessel." Pvt. George Downing (Co. G, 9th IN Cav) missed the boat but managed to get back on board anyway. "Comrade Downey [*sic*] had sent home for money from Vicksburg," Pvt. Henry Josiah V. Kline (Co. G, 9th IN Cav) remembered. "He went ashore at Memphis to see some friends, but the boat left him and he gave a man two dollars for bringing him in a skiff to the mouth of Wolf

River where the boat stopped to coal. When he laid down he said: 'If I had not sent home for that money I would have been left.'" In all, according to Pvt. Hugh M. Kinzer (Co. E, 50th OH Inf), "about two hundred failed to make their appearance and were consequently left in Memphis."[40]

Over the years, confusion has arisen as to where the *Sultana* went to take on coal after leaving Memphis. Some thought that she crossed the river to take on coal from coal barges anchored off the Arkansas bank, but with the river at tremendous flood stage, the barges would have appeared to be anchored in the middle of the river. Instead, the records indicate that she got her coal from Brown & Jones' fleet of coal barges anchored on the Tennessee side near the mouth of the Wolf River.

A panoramic photograph of the Memphis levee taken in 1864 shows a number of barges in the foreground, upriver from the steamboat landing. A sign high on the bluff behind them distinctly reads "CO AL," with Pittsburgh Coal's castle symbol between the "CO" and "AL." A wartime photograph of the ironclad *Essex*, docked near the same location, shows the same sign clearly proclaiming "Pittsburgh CO AL." Cpl. Robert M. Elza (Co. E, 3rd TN Cav) also thought that the boat went to the Wolf River site: "After Memphis we were to the mouth of Wolf River, where the steamer coaled." Chief Engineer Wintringer, who was on duty at the time and should have known where the *Sultana* went, wrote, "We left Memphis about eleven o'clock . . . and went up to the coal yard, which is about a mile above the city wharf and took aboard one thousand bushels of coal."[41]

An unnamed petty officer on board the ironclad *Essex*, which was tied up at the Memphis Navy Yard near the mouth of the Wolf River, confirmed that "she steamed up by us, slowly, and tied up alongside of a coal barge, just above where we were moored. I could distinctly hear the merry song of the roustabouts, as they trundled the coal on board, mingled with the merry making of the soldiers."[42]

The *Sultana* also took on a small load of wood at this time. It was customary to burn wood along with coal because the burning wood was thought to help break up the coal and allow for better aeration and hotter combustion. The wood was kept on the main deck not far from the coal bins and furnaces. Private Bean remembered that "the main deck was pretty much filled with wood"; and Corporal Mahoney saw "coal and wood both on this deck." Sgt. Robert Franklin Talkington (Co. A, 9th IN Cav) saw "several cords of four feet engine wood" stacked on the deck.[43]

When Nathan Wintringer ended his four-hour watch at midnight, all seemed to be well:

> I noticed the boilers particularly at Memphis and they seemed to be in good condition. We kept up from ninety to one hundred pounds of steam while there. I was on watch when we left there, and continued in charge of the engines until we stopped at the coal-boats, about half a mile above the city landing, where I was relieved by Mr. Samuel Clemens, the 2nd Engineer. At that time the boilers were, as far as I could judge, all right. . . . I talked with [Clemens] about the patch and he agreed with me that the boilers were as safe with it as before the fracture took place. . . . [T]here was nothing wrong, nor was there a sign of a leak or a defect about the boilers up to that time.[44]

Wintringer retired to his room in the forward part of the texas cabin.

At about the same time, Captain Mason turned command of the *Sultana* over to First Mate William Rowberry and headed to his cabin in the very front of the texas. Although Private Walker reported that "the officers and crew of the boat [had been drinking] whiskey," and "that every man connected with the boat was filled with it, the captain being so 'overloaded' that he had to be carried to his stateroom," that does not seem to have been the case. Private Walker was slightly scalded in the disaster and may have had a personal score to settle with the crew of the *Sultana*. No other person wrote of the officers and crew drinking whiskey while the boat was at Memphis. Captain Mason may have had some drinks on the trip up to Memphis, but there is no evidence that he was drunk and had "to be carried to his stateroom" on the night of April 26, 1865.[45]

Several soldiers saw Mason trying to get to his cabin without stepping on the reclining soldiers. Sgt. William Fies Jr. (Co. B, 64th OH

Inf), who had bedded down on the second deck near the starboard railing, wrote, "I remember, just before I fell asleep, Captain Mason, in command of the boat, came up from below, to go to his stateroom I presume, and was compelled to crawl around on the rail, as the deck was so crowded with men lying down that he could not find room to step, and was in consequence made the subject of several jokes." When he got to the hurricane deck, Captain Mason was spotted by Private Rush. "Saw the Captain a few moments after we were under way and he appeared perfectly sober."[46] The senior officers also retired for the night, confident that the steamboat was in very capable hands.

14

EXPLOSION

THE CAUSE

A round 1 a.m. on April 27, 1865, the *Sultana* finally moved away from the coal barges and started back up the river. George Cayton was in the pilothouse steering the boat, having come on watch at midnight. A low bank of clouds had settled over the Memphis area, blotting out the moon. Commissary Sergeant Mavity remembered that "the dark clouds fringed the sky and keen flashes of lightning darted fitfully across the heavens." Private Horn added, "The night was pitchy dark and some rain was falling."[1]

A few of the men were still moving around in spite of the late hour. Farrier Josiah Watson was one of them.

> The men laid down wherever there was laying room. The forecastle and lower deck were crowded with sleeping forms. I was looking for a place to lay down but could find no room below so I went up the stairway to the cabin deck. Here again I found every foot of space occupied, so I again took the stairs to the hurricane deck. This also was nearly all filled with sleeping men, but I found some six of my

company near the escape pipes who kindly offered me a share of their sky blanket, so I laid down for a rest.

Watson noticed that "the escape pipes were working as regular as a man's pulse, so I knew that all was well."[2]

Pvt. George A. Clarkson (Co. H, 5th MI Cav) had found a place to bed down on the main deck but could not sleep: "I was suffering with diarrhea and scurvy. The men lay so thick that I could not see any of the deck. All was peace and no sign of disaster. I spoke to the engineer [Clemens] of how nicely we were going and then returned to my place on the deck, which was about twelve or fifteen feet forward of the boilers next to the guard or railing of the boat." It was a chilly night, and Clarkson wrapped himself in his blanket and was soon asleep.[3]

Inside the main saloon, deck passenger William McLeod, who had been allowed into the main saloon because of the overcrowding outside, missed out on getting a cot and could not fall asleep. Instead, he "sat up reading at a table in the center of the cabin." One deck above him, Private Davis also could not sleep: "[It was] two o'clock in the morning [when] I got up to have a smoke. I went [down] to the boilers to get a light for my pipe and going back to the hurricane deck, where I had been sleeping, I sat down for about ten minutes."[4]

After leaving the coal barges, Cayton kept the boat to the right, near the Tennessee side, as he steered past Paddy's Hen and Chicken Islands (Islands Nos. 42–45). Only the treetops on the islands were visible above the high water. When he was seven miles upriver from Memphis, Cayton entered a left-hand turn at Rodman's Point. Woppenaughkee Bar was up ahead near the Arkansas shore, but it was well below the water and offered no obstacle. After entering the left-hand turn, Cayton started to cut diagonally across the swollen river from the Tennessee to the Arkansas side looking for slack, or at least slower, water. The strong current hit the *Sultana* directly in her starboard side, tilting her a little to port. Either nobody remembered or nobody would say just how much she tilted. Cayton said that she "was running steadily without careening, and, as near as I could tell, on an even keel. The men were in their quarters [i.e., asleep on the decks] and therefore the boat was setting level on the water."[5]

In his spot down near the engines, the ever-watchful Louis Bean had noticed that both engineers had checked the patched boiler frequently after leaving Vicksburg, although he didn't remember if Clemens checked it on the night of April 26–27. At about 2 a.m., high up above, on the hurricane deck, Corporal Brunner "was lying in the pile of sleeping men near the pilot house out on deck . . . when we heard a peculiar hissing coming up through the [steam escape] pipes. Everyone was awakened, around where I was sleeping. Then we heard other noises from below that convinced us that something was wrong in the engine room."[6]

Corporal Elza was on the main deck "near the boiler."

> I was sitting on the steps talking to J. F. Haun [Pvt. Joshua F. Haun, Co. E, 3rd TN Cav], as we were going around the northwest side of Hen and Chickens' Island, endeavoring to enter what is known as Shute No. 40 to Mississippi rivermen. At this juncture I heard the engineer [Samuel Clemens] complain of his boilers being too full of water to make Shute No. 40 as it took a great deal of steam. He then blew some of the water out and closed the valve and struck the gauge, the boiler being still full of water. The engineer said, "D—n it, that is not enough," blowing the water out the second time. He closed the valve and struck the gauge, and a dry steam whistle began to sound.
>
> At once I realized the danger, and went to my partner [Pvt. Nathan Marcum, Co. D, 4th KY Mt'd. Inf] and woke him, at the same time starting to tell Whittenbarger [Pvt. Drury A. Witenbarger, Co. E, 3rd TN Cav] of the danger of the explosion. I said, "The engineer had—" and at this juncture she blew up.[7]

The *Sultana* had just reached slack water on the Arkansas side and come back on an even keel when the boilers blew. Or as Captain McCown put it, "The fated steamer had obeyed her helm and righted herself in the current when the surrounding gloom was lighted up as by a torch from the infernal regions."[8]

Up on the hurricane deck, Private Davis had finished his smoke and taken up his canteen: "[I] was about to take a drink when the boiler exploded and the canteen flew out of my hand. I never saw it again."[9]

In a split second the overcrowded *Sultana* was mortally wounded. It would take more than five hours for her to die, but die she would. And she would take many lives with her.

The exact cause of the explosion has been debated for more than 150 years, but despite much speculation, there has been no definitive answer. The paroled prisoners on board did not know. "[I]t seems that no one knows exactly the cause of the disaster," Private Homer noted, while Cpl. Isaac Van Nuys (Co. D, 57th IN Inf) said that "[t]he steamer was running at her proper speed (nine or ten miles an hour). No peril seemed imminent and the event remains yet a mystery."[10] Still, we can conclude that the explosion was the result of a combination of factors rather than one single thing.

A leading factor was the metal used to fabricate the *Sultana*'s four horizontal tubular boilers. The boilers had been made from no. 1 charcoal iron. In 2014–15, Patrick Jennings, principal engineer at the Hartford Steam Boiler Inspection and Insurance Company, conducted extensive experiments on this iron and determined that while it was the best available material of the day, it was not suitable boiler material. This type of iron gets brittle when it is overheated and cooled repeatedly."[11]

The author of *A Practical Treatise on High Pressure Steam Boilers: Including Results of Recent Experimental Test of Boiler Materials* came to the same conclusion in 1880: "C. No. 1 iron, or C. H. iron (charcoal hammered, as it is oftener known) . . . very much resembles the common iron in its general qualities, having but little elasticity and breaking with a sudden jerk." This type of iron "becomes very brittle by repeated heating and cooling. . . . It is not a suitable iron for boiler construction."[12]

Unfortunately, nobody knew this in 1863 when the *Sultana*'s boilers were manufactured. The steamer's boilers had been repeatedly heated and cooled each time the *Sultana* was in port for a few days. Each time this was done, as Mr. Jennings would later prove, tiny hairline fractures developed throughout the iron. Indeed, it was only a matter of time before the boilers blew. By the mid-1880s charcoal-hammered no. 1 was no longer being used in boiler construction.

Another factor Jennings examined, and experts at the time of the disaster also mentioned, was the quality of water used in the *Sultana*'s boilers. Every steamboat plying the Mississippi River pumped unfiltered, muddy river water into the boilers. Jennings pointed out that "[t]he mud in the water settled on the plates and surfaces acting as an insulator between the water and the iron. This caused the iron to repeatedly overheat and burn [and] . . . this iron gets brittle when it is overheated and cooled repeatedly."[13]

An engineer who had once worked on the *Sultana*, Robert Long, stated in 1902, "She ran like a snake in the water and made steam so easily that the firemen sat on the coal and sang but the river water was so riley that her boilers would get scaley and go to leaking."[14] Add to that the fact that the river was at flood stage and the sediment normally sitting on the bottom would have been churned up and suspended in the water, and it is indisputable that the water being pumped into the *Sultana*'s boilers in April 1865 carried more sediment than normal.

A third factor in the cause of the explosion was the design of the boiler, which was recognized even at the time to be problematic. Jennings' later experiments would confirm the flaws. In 1865, many steamboats had moved away from the old-fashioned standard horizontal flue boilers and were using tubular boilers. The *Sultana* carried four horizontal tubular boilers, each of which contained twenty-four smaller flues, or tubes. While this design may have increased the amount of heat being transferred to the water inside the boilers, it also made it extremely hard to clean the Mississippi mud out of the tubes. An article published in the *Daily Missouri Democrat* in February 1866 explained: "[There are] two causes for explosion . . . one of insufficiency of water in the boiler, and the other the want of care in keeping the boilers thoroughly cleaned. It is the duty of the engineer to attend to these two points especially, and the only additional care required in the tubular boiler is that it requires to be cleaned oftener." A later investigation showed "that the [*Sultana*'s] boilers were foul . . . so foul that the mass at the bottom of the boiler had to be removed by an iron bar."[15]

After the tubular boilers exploded on the steamboats *Missouri* on January 30, 1866 (80 lives lost), and *W. R. Carter* on February 9, 1866 (125 lives and $250,000 in property lost) many owners of boats with tubular boilers decided to replace their boilers with "a new set of the old-fashioned flue-boilers." Before the year was out, tubular boilers were outlawed on steamboats (see chapter 29).[16]

While poor-quality iron, dirty water, and poor design were indisputable factors in the explosion, other factors may have been involved as well.

Some people believed that the *Sultana* was operating with low water in her boilers. Although Clemens was mortally scalded in the explosion, he was able to give a sworn statement before he died. He said that the boilers were carrying about 135 pounds of steam when they exploded, 10 pounds less than their normal running pressure. Clemens also managed to speak with the chief engineer, Wintringer, who reported afterward that "[Clemens] said he could assign no cause for [the explosion]; everything, he said, was right; there was plenty of water in the boilers, and there was not an extra pressure of steam."[17]

Pilot Cayton and First Mate William Rowberry, who had charge of the *Sultana* at the time of the explosion, both stated that the steamboat was running at her "usual rate [of] about nine or ten miles per hour." If the *Sultana* was going upriver against one of the worst floods in recent times at her "usual rate," Clemens must have had the pressure in the boilers much higher than the 135 psi that he claimed. And if, as Corporal Elza claimed, Clemens "blew some of the water out" of the boilers not once but twice, then the pressure within the boiler would have increased dramatically.

Even after blowing some of the water out of the boilers to increase his pressure, Clemens may have felt that enough water remained in the boilers for safety purposes when in fact there was not. In 1865, the only way to check the level of the water inside the boilers while the boat was in motion was by viewing the two glass water gauges and the one steam gauge. Unfortunately, the gauges could be very inaccurate. Wintringer later explained: "The water in the boilers sometimes 'foams' as it is called, giving the appearance of plenty of water when there is little or none, but I never knew it to occur in the boilers of the *Sultana*."[18] Still, if the water was foaming and Clemens was getting a false reading, he might have mistakenly believed that there was too much water in the boilers each time he blew out some water.

In 1866, experienced consulting engineer Norman Wiard wrote about the hazards of foaming in boilers:

> It is not generally known to engineers that sufficient water may *appear* to be in the boiler by the water gauges and "low water detectors," when there is not proper quantity. There are two kinds of foaming or ebullition [bubbling] in the water in a boiler; surface ebullition, as shown in water boiling in an open vessel, caused by the rapid passage upward from the bottom of the vessel and bursting at the surface of numerous bubbles or spheres of steam; and foaming, or the collection of such spheres of steam at the bottom of the boiler, which rise with such velocity through narrow water spaces as to raise up the whole body of water above the narrowest part of the water space, between the flues and keep it up at that level. It is a common experience of engineers to find solid water come out of the upper water-gauges upon opening them, and dry steam from the lowest gauge.[19]

Cincinnati engineer and boilermaker Isaac West was interviewed on May 14, 1865, and gave the following testimony.

> Boilers may be destroyed either by bursting or destroying. . . . In the second case, one or more boilers of the set are entirely destroyed by the sudden development of steam by some unusual cause, which acts on the boilers like the ignition of so much gunpowder. This explosion is in all cases occasioned by the want of sufficient water in the boilers, in which case the boilers or the flues become heated to redness, and when the water is again forced into them, the sudden development of steam, which is caused by the water coming in contact with the heated iron, acts like the burning of a mass of gunpowder, and the immediate destruction of the boilers is the consequence. In the case of the *Sultana*, . . . I am inclined to believe that the explosion took place from a deficiency of water in the boilers. . . . The *Sultana*'s boilers were of the tubular kind, having about twenty [flues] in

each boiler, and if at any time the water should be below the upper tier for a few minutes, they would become red-hot, and on the return of the water to its proper level, they would in all probability collapse which would probably result immediately in the explosion of the boilers."[20]

If Corporal Elza was correct, then the *Sultana* was indeed running with a "deficiency of water" because Clemens had blown water out of the boilers not once but twice.

Inspector Witzig speculated that if the *Sultana* had only one-half inch of water above the flues, the boat would have had to careen only "four and a half inches . . . to uncover the top of the flues."[21] When the boat came back on an even keel, which the *Sultana* did after crossing to the Arkansas side, the superheated metal contacted the water and instantly turned to steam.

Steamboat historian Louis Hunter noted that "a cubic foot of heated water under a pressure of [just] sixty or seventy pounds has about the same energy as a pound of gunpowder, and that a western steamboat boiler . . . contained in its contents at 150 pounds' pressure enough energy to hurl the boiler over two miles into the air."[22] And according to steamboat expert Alan Bates, "When a boiler is ruptured, the release of restraint allows all the water to instantly convert to steam—steam that occupies a couple of thousand times the volume of the water. A violent explosion ensues."[23]

So, if Clemens had gotten a false reading on the amount of water within the boilers because of foaming, and had "blown out" some of the excess, as Elza recalled hearing him do, just before the *Sultana* cut across the river near Rodman's Point, the water level in the boilers may have been below or just slightly above the top flues. When the boat cut across the river and took the current directly in her side, she may have careened just a little, exposing the uppermost flues inside each of the four interconnected boilers. According to Witzig, if the water level in the boilers was too low, even a tilt of only four and one-half inches would have exposed the top flues of the boilers to the superheated air of the furnace while the steamer was making her way across the river. Cayton and Rowberry might not have even noticed this slight tilt.

We can only speculate that the water in the *Sultana*'s boilers was lower than it should have been, although boiler repairman R. G. Taylor, who riveted the patch onto the *Sultana*'s larboard boiler at Vicksburg, had noted that "the iron was burned" and thought that "the boilers were used with little water."[24] Perhaps that was a common occurrence on the *Sultana*. We will never know.

Patrick Jennings postulated a pressure drop as being responsible for the explosion. He suggested that the *Sultana*'s boilers may have contained more than enough water to cover the tubes even when the boat careened, and noted that there is a "tremendous amount of energy stored in a boiler under pressure, [and] almost all of this energy is in the water. A sudden drop in pressure will cause a portion of water to instantly boil, creating steam which expands rapidly. This expansive power is what creates catastrophic explosions." He went on to say that "a boiler full of water has more energy stored and available for explosive power than a boiler low on water."[25]

> If there is a break or leak in the boiler, the pressure inside immediately drops. With this drop in pressure, the temperature at which water boils also drops. The water temperature in the boiler will then be greater than the boiling temperature. Therefore, some of the water will flash to steam, expanding and re-pressurizing the boiler.
>
> If the opening is small and the boiler is strong enough, the pressure will be contained and the water or steam will steadily leak out as the boiler remains intact. If, however, the boiler cannot contain the pressure due to a weakened condition, the result will be an explosion as more and more water flashes to steam and rips the openings wider almost instantaneously. Overall, the weaker or more brittle the boiler, the larger the explosion will be.[26]

Only one of the people called before investigators in 1865 testified that a boiler full of water could be dangerous. Brig. Gen. Morgan Smith, a former steamboat captain himself, stated, "I have known instances where boilers were exploded when they were carrying the required amount of water. The supposition is that the explosion is caused by the sudden generation of gases. It has never been positively accounted for."[27] This corresponds with the findings of both Bates and Jennings. Since most of the energy inside a boiler is stored in the water, a full boiler is potentially more dangerous than a partially full boiler. A small break in the outer skin would cause a sudden reduction of pressure, which in turn would cause the "sudden generation of gases" (i.e., steam) that would rip through the small break and blow away everything before it, as occurred on the *Sultana*.

The overcrowding may also have been a contributing factor. The overcrowded, top-heavy *Sultana* may have been careening more than just four and one-half inches right before the explosion, although there is no hard evidence to support that conjecture. Witzig, Wintringer, and a few other steamboat men believed that might have been the case.[28] Pilot Cayton, who was on duty at the very top of the boat at the time of the explosion, testified that the boat was on an even keel. If the boat had careened significantly, he would have felt it. When asked point-blank "whether or not the explosion of the boilers on the steamer *Sultana* was caused from the careening of the boat," Cayton responded, "I think it was not, sir."[29] Likewise, the few prisoners who were awake just prior to the explosion and survived never mentioned a strong tilt.

A final possible cause of the explosion is sabotage. Some newspapers at the time speculated that a Confederate saboteur had smuggled a bomb disguised to look like a lump of coal onto the *Sultana*. The physical evidence, however, as well as other information, tends to disprove this theory (see chapter 29 for a thorough discussion).

In all probability, then, a number of factors contributed to the explosion of the *Sultana*'s boilers. To summarize: the poor-quality iron used in the boilers was known to weaken and become brittle when repeatedly heated and cooled; the river water used in the boilers was filled with silt, which tended to settle on the bottom of the boilers, forming hot pockets; the *Sultana*'s boilers may have been foaming at the time of the disaster, making the gauges show more water than the boilers actually contained, a problem that would have been exacerbated if Clemens did actually blow out some of the water to increase the steam pressure; finally, as the *Sultana* moved diagonally across the river and took the full force of the strong flood current in her side, she may have careened enough to expose the upper tubes within the four boilers to the heated air from the furnaces. When the *Sultana* got across the river and righted herself, the water would have leveled out, come in contact with the superheated tubes, and generated an excess of steam, which found a weak spot in the brittle metal and blew through it in a tremendous, deadly explosion.

15

EXPLOSION

THE STRUCTURAL DAMAGE

The explosion came from the top back of the boilers and tore upward through the floor of the main saloon, the main saloon itself, the ceiling of the main saloon (the hurricane deck), the texas cabin, and the pilothouse. Normally during a steamboat accident, the pilot would run the boat into the bank and let the passengers rush to safety, as was done with *Sultana* (No. 4). Without a pilothouse, however, the *Sultana* was a floating, helpless wreck. Private Homer wondered "why the pilot did not steer the boat to the shore, but some of the boys said the boat was disabled and could not land. The boat was floating and drifting with the current." Cpl. William Harrison Norton (Co. C, 115th OH Inf) reported that "[t]he boat became unmanageable as soon as it blew up."[1]

The fact that the explosion came from the back of the boilers and went upward is proof that the patch installed at Vicksburg on the forward, bottom part of the left-hand boiler was indeed "a good job" and had nothing to do with the explosion. The brittle metal gave way somewhere else.

The first boiler explosion was followed a millisecond later by the explosion of two more boilers. On October 20, 1865, a wrecking company doing salvage work on the remains of the *Sultana* "removed one boiler, which was the only one unharmed, and [confirmed] that the other three were blown to atoms." Unbelievably, one of the middle boilers remained intact, perhaps because of the sudden decrease in pressure from the rupture of the other three.[2]

The tremendous force generated by the explosion went upward at roughly a 45-degree angle. Since the main saloon on the *Sultana* was set about fifteen feet behind the chimneys, the blast tore a hole through the second deck from about a few feet in front of the front wall of the cabin to about one-third of the way back. The back two-thirds of the saloon were undamaged. Civilian passenger William Long was in Stateroom 10, about one-third of the way back in the main saloon: "I jumped up and saw that the [forward] partition separating my stateroom from the next room was knocked all to pieces. I ran out in the cabin with nothing on but my shirt, and ran back to the stern."[3]

Lieutenant Squire was sleeping in a cot set about one-third of the way back in the saloon. The explosion tore through the deck directly in front of Squire, covering him with wreckage. "Rubbish was falling around me and all was dark. I endeavored to crawl out one way but could not. Turned in the opposite direction and kept going on my hands and knees until I was free from the rubbish and found myself nearly in the rear of the Ladies Cabin where one lamp was burning."[4]

For the men sleeping immediately in front of the main saloon's bulkhead, the explosion was catastrophic. Private Hass and four of his friends were asleep on the open deck between the main saloon and the two stairway openings leading down to the main deck: "Not more than three feet from where I was lying was a hole clear through the boat. It seemed as if the explosion of the boilers had torn everything out from top to bottom. Many of the boys who were sleeping over and directly by the boilers were either torn into atoms or blown into the river."[5] Most of the men sleeping in this area above the boilers had been sick and had been placed there because it was warm.

The blast spread outward as it went up. "Part of the cabin and deck kitchen were blown off into the river," Cpl. Jonathan Wesley

Vanscoyoc (Co. A, 64th OH Inf) noted. The deck kitchen was in front of the starboard paddlewheel housing, on the second deck. On the larboard side, Pvt. Jotham W. Maes (Co. B, 47th OH Inf) and his comrades were sleeping "just back of the left wheel house, on the middle deck. . . . About three by ten feet of the portion of the deck upon which we were sleeping [was] blown with its occupants into the river."[6]

Some of the men near the railings or even outside the second deck railings were catapulted into the river. Pvt. John Henry Kochenderfer (Co. D, 102nd OH Inf) and five others were asleep "outside the railing in front of the left wheel on the middle or cabin deck floor. We were outside and over the four great boilers. . . . The first I realized after the explosion, I found myself about 300 feet from the boat shrouded in total darkness and in what appeared to be an ocean of water." Private Schmutz, also on the cabin deck, "was lying with my head to the stairs leading to the hurricane deck, and three of my comrades were lying with their heads to the cabin. I was asleep at the time of the explosion, and only remember crying, 'What's the matter?' and feeling a burning sensation, when I found myself in water." Private Horn, another man blown off the cabin deck, reported that "hundreds of men were thrown overboard by the explosion, and plunged, still asleep, into the icy waters."[7]

After tearing through the cabin deck and the main saloon, the blast continued upward through the hurricane deck. Because the blast was traveling at a 45-degree angle, the forward one-third of the hurricane deck was not damaged. Private Gilbreath and two friends were "sleeping together on the hurricane deck, about half way between the pilot house and the bow of the boat." The explosion reached as far forward as Gilbreath's position. "The first thing I knew of the explosion, [I] was standing on my feet, looking right down into the boiler room. The whole of the vessel, amidships, was torn in pieces."[8]

Sgt. John E. Norton (Co. E, 5th MI Cav) had gone to sleep "in the center of the upper deck and ten feet in front of the smokestack." He awoke to find himself "pinned or held down by the timbers or materials of some sort," but he correctly reasoned that his location in front of the smokestacks had saved his life because "the boilers being back of the smokestack prevented my being thrown into the water." Pvt. Christian Ray (Co. C, 50th OH Inf) was also sleeping on the front part of the hurricane deck just forward of the chimneys. The explosion "blew the pilothouse and everything off within three feet of where my partner and I lay. The rubbish fell down on us and pinned us there for awhile."[9]

As the explosion tore through the hurricane deck, it threw some men forward and some backward. Pvt. Asa Ebenezer Lee (Co. A, 6th IN Cav) was "on the hurricane deck, near the pilothouse" (probably the texas cabin) and "was thrown to the forecastle [of the main deck,] striking my back and shoulders and was severely bruised by the fall." Sergeant Buchanan, who was also "lying on the hurricane deck, near the pilot house [texas cabin] . . . was blown back to the wheel house and covered with debris." Hundreds of men were blown upward and outward at the same time.[10]

Private Eldridge and his friends were sleeping "up on top of the boat just behind the smokestacks, right over the boilers." He awoke to find himself "flying thru the air . . . whirling over and over." Pvt. George C. Anderson (Co. F, 102nd OH Inf), "on the hurricane deck, near the pilot house [texas cabin]" with two of his friends, "was thrown out of reach of anybody and saw nothing of my comrades after the explosion."[11]

The hole that tore through the *Sultana* did not go as far back as the twin paddlewheels and paddlewheel housings, which were situated just behind the middle of the boat. Pvt. Manly C. White (Co. B, 8th MI Cav) "was asleep on the hurricane deck, aft of the wheelhouse, on the Arkansas side, and was not injured by the explosion."[12]

Private Kline was sleeping in front of one of the wheelhouses between Pvt. Charles William M. King (Co. G, 9th IN Cav) and Private Downing, the soldier who had been left behind in Memphis and had paid someone to row him out to the *Sultana*. "Comrade King sprang up at the first shock, exclaiming 'O God, Oh mother! I am lost, I am gone,'" Kline said. King ran across the deck and jumped overboard. As for Private Downing, Kline "never heard him speak again." Both King and Downing perished.[13]

The concussions shook the two paddlewheel housings, which were supported by a bottom-chord cantilever system that counterweighted

one against the other. The explosion loosened the cross-chains forming the system, and each housing tilted outward. The right wheelhouse pulled away from the superstructure only slightly, while the
left wheelhouse tilted far out but remained attached at the bottom.
Corporal Clinger was sleeping "aft the boat on the Tennessee side.
The wheelhouse broke loose and I came near going down with it."
Private Berry saw that "the wheelhouse . . . had broken away partially
from the hurricane deck. When it reached an angle of about forty-five
degrees it stopped."[14]

After tearing through the hurricane deck, the explosive blast,
still traveling upward at an ever-widening 45-degree angle, ripped
through the middle of the texas cabin. Chief Engineer Wintringer, in
his cabin "about mid-ships on the larboard side of the texas, was not at
all injured, and I do not know how much, if any, of the texas in front
of my room was injured, but most of it behind my room appeared to
have sunk down on the cabin or lower deck."[15] Captain Mason, in
his room in the very forward part of the texas, was not injured by the
explosion.[16]

The force continued up through the texas cabin and ripped through
the pilothouse. The front part of the small pilothouse remained intact,
but the back two-thirds was torn off and blown skyward. It came back
down at the spot where the boilers had been. Two men were inside
the pilothouse at the time: George Cayton, who was holding the
huge pilot wheel, and First Mate Rowberry. Rowberry was thrown
outward and away from the boat, and Cayton went straight up and
came straight down. Both survived. "We were about seven miles up
the river when the boilers exploded and I found myself in the river,"
Rowberry told investigators. Cayton said, "I was at the wheel and fell
on top of the boilers where I was wedged in by the wreck. I crawled
out [from] under the pilot house."[17]

When the huge hole was blown through the deck behind the twin
smokestacks, there was not enough support left to keep the extra-tall
stacks upright and they began to fall. The two heavy spreader bars
between the chimneys held them together as they fell. Instead of falling in the same direction, however, they twisted, with the left stack
falling forward and the right one falling backward. Eventually, the

spreader bars broke. The left stack fell squarely onto the center of the forward part of the hurricane deck, smashing into the bell and actually splitting in two; the right stack fell backward into the opening that had been blown through the center of the boat and smashed through what was left of the pilothouse.

Corporal Sharp, who had been sleeping on the main deck below, saw the smokestacks fall, "killing and crippling many. The larboard [left] smokestack fell forward reaching the forecastle of the lower deck. The starboard stack fell up on the hurricane deck." Pvt. Lewis Allen Deerman (Co. K, 3rd TN Cav), who had been sleeping "halfway back on the deck," awoke to find "one of the smokestacks lying in front of me. I saw at once that [the deck] was torn to fragments."[18]

Many members of the 115th Ohio Infantry had crowded around the bell near the front of the hurricane deck. The left chimney came down directly on top of them. Pvt. John J. "Jack" Zaiser (Co. F) awoke to find himself "covered with the smokestack which had fallen lengthways on the upper deck. It had burst in two and half of it had dropped on me. Comrade Smith [Sgt. William H. H. Smith, Co. F], who slept beside me was killed by being struck by the stack in its descent. I was almost smothered by the soot and smoke."[19]

Pvt. William P. Madden (Co. I, 8th OH Cav), sleeping near the men of the 115th Ohio Infantry, had a particularly terrifying experience.

> Suddenly I was awakened by an upheaval and crashing of timbers. I attempted to arise from my recumbent position and as I threw up my hands to explore my surroundings I got them severely burned, and was horrified to find that my efforts to extricate myself were fruitless and the heat was stifling. . . . I wrapped my blanket about me in order to protect myself from further violence from my hot environments. I called in the name of my Divine Master for someone to remove whatever hindered my escape, and may God bless whoever he may be that removed the obstruction—I know him not. I crawled out as black and begrimed as a coal digger. I then discovered that I had been under a piece

of the boiler iron about a half of a circle, both ends being blocked with timber and debris thrown hither and thither by the force of the explosion.[20]

Madden was lucky. Instead of being held down by a "piece of the boiler," he had actually been trapped inside half of the splintered chimney. The inside of a boiler would not have been "black and begrimed," since a boiler is filled with water, not coal dust. However, the inside of the smokestack would have been.

Pvt. William Crisp (Co. D, 18th MI Inf) was not so lucky. "I was asleep on the Boiler deck [i.e., main deck] about sixteen feet from the Boiler and the great side of the Boiler was Blown out and shut down over me breaking my left shoulder and the heat was so intense I seemed to be nailed to the floor[.] I could not stir hand or foot[.] I thought I should be roasted alive then and there[.] I was scalded and Burned to death almost[.]"[21]

When the heavy left smokestack hit the forward part of the hurricane deck, the thin stanchions on the second deck that had been supporting the upper deck splintered, and the whole front section of the hurricane deck crashed down onto the deck below. Dozens of men were crushed or trapped in the wreckage. Those sleeping near the two main stairway openings were saved because the sturdy railings around the openings remained upright and stopped the upper deck from crashing down on them. Cpl. William A. Hulit (Co. A, 64th OH Inf), who had been sleeping near the stairway openings, was "aroused by the shock of the explosion and hot steam on my face and hands, which seemed for a time would smother me, on raising up my head [I] came in contact with the hurricane deck, which had crushed down onto the banisters, which protected me from being crushed to death." Pvt. Wesley Lee (Co. A, 102nd OH Inf) also struck the fallen upper deck. "I bunked on the front part of the cabin deck, between the two stairways, and was asleep when the explosion took place. I sprang to my feet at the noise, and in doing so struck my head against the deck above, which had been smashed down and was supported by the railing around the stairs."[22]

The main stairway below the two openings was not damaged, and the men who now lay between the hurricane deck and the cabin deck were able to crawl out from under the wreckage and down the main stairway to the bow. "On my hands and knees I made my way to and down the stairway to the boiler deck and out onto the bow of the boat," reported Corporal Hulit. The many soldiers who could not reach the stair openings were obliged to get down to the bow as best they could. Private Wesley Lee "slid down a fender to a lower deck." Cpl. Peter Frederic Rosselot (Co. E, 50th OH Inf) "climbed down on the lower deck, by means of ropes and spikes, to the front part of the boat."[23]

The men sleeping between the back end of the stairway banisters and the front of the main saloon received the full force of the falling upper deck. When the stanchions on the main deck let go, the upper decks slanted down onto the main deck. After the three boilers disintegrated in the explosion, the furnaces below the front part of those boilers were wide open on top. When the upper decks canted downward, the debris slid into the exposed coals of the furnace and became kindling for a developing fire.

Private Walker witnessed the horror: "[T]he central portion of the boat had fallen in on top of the boiler, forming a funnel, which was filled with a mass of our unfortunate comrades." Sgt. James Harvey Kimberlin (Co. C, 124th IN Inf) saw the dreadful sight as well: "The force of the explosion was so great that the boilers were thrown . . . off the furnace, leaving a great mass of burning coal exposed. . . . [T]he wreckage with its human freight, mangled and torn, many of them killed outright, dropp[ed] into the open uncovered furnace." Pvt. Albert Norris (Co. A, 76th OH Inf) was one of those who slid downward with the debris: "I was lying asleep on the cabin deck of the boat, just in front and nearly over the furnace. I fell to the boiler deck upon the hot irons of the furnace, burning my left arm and shoulder to a crisp. The men on the hurricane deck fell upon me, and it was some time before I became conscious of my surroundings." Lieutenant Elliott, who had slept on one of the cots at the rear of the main saloon because a higher-ranking officer had taken his cot in the front, went forward and saw that "[t]he cabin floor had dropped down at the front, without breaking off, and now made an inclined plane to the lower deck. The cots . . . had disappeared."[24]

Strangely enough, Private Crisp, who awoke to find himself trapped under a portion of a boiler, survived because of that:

"[W]hen the heat got out some I found I could move and I cralled [*sic*] out of that Hell to the front of the Boat and then it was I saw what happened[.] I could look into the fire and see hundreds of men burning up among the Timbers[.] [T]hat Boiler saved me from being crushed to death by the falling timbers[.]"[25]

The right smokestack, falling backward, crashed down onto the forward remains of the pilothouse and into the hole blasted through the decks. Fifteen-year-old musician Stephen Gaston, who had been asleep "in front of the pilothouse," saw that "the smokestack had fallen directly on the pilothouse crushing it down almost on us. . . . I was a prisoner again, for a network of rubbish surrounded me." Cpl. William Henry Peacock (Co. G, 9th IN Cav) was sleeping nearby "on that part of the boat where the officers' berths were located, called the 'Texas,' in front of the pilot house. There were four of my comrades with me . . . when the explosion took place, [we] fell back on the boat together and were covered with the flying debris."[26]

The explosion did not damage the stern cargo room on the main deck, but the concussive force blew debris, bodies, and body parts from the shattered decks above onto the room's sleeping occupants. Private Foglesang "was lying on the lower deck near the stern of the boat. Everything came down upon me and others around me." Cpl. Albert W. King (Co. D, 100th OH Inf) was sleeping "about twenty feet from the stern of the boat. . . . Men, coal, wood and timbers from the boat were thrown over and beyond us. The steam and ashes smothered us so we could scarcely breathe." Pvt. Commodore Smith "was nearly buried with dead and wounded comrades, legs, arms, heads, and all parts of human bodies, and fragments of the wrecked upper decks. I struggled to my feet and tried to go forward on the boat, but could not on account of the wreckage and carnage of human freight which now covered the lower deck."[27]

The men sleeping in front of the boilers faced the twin dangers of boiling water and steam from the exploded boilers plus the falling debris from the upper decks. Private Collins awoke to find himself "fastened tightly by the mass of timber that had fallen from above, so that I could hardly move. . . . Hundreds of poor fellows sleeping on the lower deck where I was were securely pinned down by the great heap of wrecked timbers that fell upon them." Instead of being buried in debris, Pvt. William T. Shumard (Co. A, 7th OH Cav) was propelled forward by the concussion. "I and twelve comrades lay side by side asleep, just in front of the boilers, on the lower deck. The first that I knew, I was holding to a chain [hanging from] the bow of the boat."[28]

While the explosion tore apart the center of the boat and collapsed the upper decks down into the blasted hole, it was still possible to move from the back of the *Sultana* to the front. Sgt. Andrew Thomas Peery (Co. B, 3rd TN Cav) was "on the lower deck, about the center of the boat" with several other members of his regiment: "I . . . started for the bow of the boat. . . . The lower deck for a considerable distance all around the boilers was covered with the dead and wounded. . . . As we passed, the fire was getting a start and we had to pass it. I got onto the wreck and got my feet snagged on nails or something. I then stepped on one of the smokestacks [probably a piece of a boiler] and got my feet burned. Somehow I . . . got to the bow of the boat."[29]

While every survivor could recall the destruction caused by the explosion, only a few could recall the sound. Captain Friesner, in his stateroom, heard "a dull, heavy sound." Ann Annis, who was in her stateroom with her husband and daughter, remembered hearing "a loud noise, something like the rattling of iron." Some men likened the noise to the sound of artillery. Cpl. Winfield Scott Colvin (Co. F, 6th KY Cav), sleeping on the rear of the hurricane deck, heard "an explosion, louder and more terrible than the largest piece of artillery is capable of making." Captain Elliott, inside the main saloon, remembered "a report as of the discharge of a park of artillery, [and] a shock as of a railroad collision." Private Johnston, at the bow of the main deck, described the sound as "a report exceeding any artillery that I had ever heard, and I had heard some that was very heavy, especially at Gettysburg."[30]

While some thought that the explosion *sounded* like artillery fire, others believed that it actually was. Pvt. Manly White, who was up on the hurricane deck, "first thought that a rebel battery had fired on us, and a shell had exploded on board." Pvt. Samuel Cornelius Haines (Co. G, 40th IN Inf), also on the top deck, said, "About the first thing

I thought of was that some raiding rebel battery had thrown a shell into the boat." Pvt. Truman Marion Smith, asleep on a wheelhouse, remembered, "Someone cried out that the rebels had fired onto us. I thought a shell had exploded near me, but found it was hot steam." And Corporal Chelf, down on the bow of the main deck, recalled, "A piece of iron glanced my head, and in the excitement I thought the rebels had fired a battery at us."[31]

Oddly enough, many survivors said they heard nothing at all. Lieutenant Elliott, whose cot was near the ladies' cabin, wrote, "Curiously enough, although the cots and staterooms were full of men, the explosion did not seem to have awakened them." Senator-elect Snow, in a stateroom, "was awakened by a sensible tremor or shudder passing over the boat, but heard no explosion." Commissary Sergeant Mavity was up on the rear part of the hurricane deck: "So deep had been my sleep that I had not heard the report of the bursting boiler." "Soldiers are sound sleepers," Lieutenant Elliott explained.[32]

Since the explosion came from the boilers rather than the furnace, there was no fire at first, just a killing steam. After hearing the loud noise, Lieutenant Annis looked out into the main saloon and told his wife that there was "a considerable steam there." Corporal Hulit, trapped under the wreckage of the collapsed hurricane deck, remembered that "steam was hissing and pouring from every part of the wreck." Private Safford was sleeping on the cabin deck when the boilers exploded: "The boat trembled like a leaf, and in an instant the white steam had enveloped her from stem to stern."[33]

Corporal Winters, who had slept "just forward of the smokestacks on the cabin deck," slid down the inclined deck when the left chimney smashed the decks downward and landed "on the coal pile in front of the furnaces. The steam was so stifling, I could scarcely breathe where I was, so I carefully treaded my way out onto the bow of the boat." Private Rush was one deck higher, on the hurricane deck, near one of the wheelhouses. "The upper decks appeared to have been shattered and to have sunken down on the lower deck. . . . [T]he hot steam was coming up through the deck."[34]

Many soldiers were seriously scalded or killed by the hot steam and boiling water that was thrown from the exploded boilers. Captain

McCown, who had been sleeping near the center of the main saloon, suffered terrible injuries. The explosion threw him from his bunk bed and enveloped him in a cloud of scalding steam. On his later pension application he reported that he was "severely scalded both externally and internally . . . was fearfully scalded about head and face & down one side of body. . . . Mouth, throat and lungs badly effected [*sic*], mucous membrane coming off tongue and lips . . . inhaled hot steam and had the thumb of left hand crushed. . . . scald of right arm." He also reported, "my eyelids were closed for five (5) days before I saw anything. I also inhaled some steam and I couldn't speak for seven (7) days."[35]

Private Garber was asleep near the stern on the hurricane deck with the other members of the 102nd Ohio Infantry when the cloud of hot steam poured out of the blasted hole. "I was on my feet and enveloped in a cloud of hot steam, and was considerably scalded in the face," he remembered. Sgt. Maj. Van Buren Jolley (Field & Staff, 10th IN Cav) reported on his invalid pension application that he "inhaled into his lungs hot steam from the bursting boilers [so that] both lungs have been affected."[36]

The debris that slid down into the open furnaces quickly caught fire. Lieutenant Squire remembered hearing "that the boiler had exploded, but that if no fire occurred we should be saved. A moment later a bright flame shot up in the front part of the cabin." Sergeant Norton heard people shouting, "Put out that fire, put out that fire! I looked and discovered a fire breaking out above the deck about the size of the crown of a hat. It grew rapidly and soon illuminated the awful scene." Private Berry, who had bedded down on the main deck, watched the fire start: "The upper decks of the boat were a complete wreck, and the dry casings of the cabins falling in upon the hot bed of coal was burning like tinder. A few pailsful of water would have put the fire out." Corporal Sharp, also on the main deck, agreed. "[T]he fire started from the wreckage in the furnace pit. Three or four men with buckets could have kept the wreck from burning. If there had been no panic there need have been no loss of life, except those killed in the explosion."[37]

Although many men raced to the racks that held the round-bottomed red fire buckets, there were no buckets there. Some supposed that the buckets had all been blown overboard by the explosion, but the blast had nothing to do with it. The men themselves had removed them earlier and used them to scoop drinking water from the river or as slop buckets.[38]

Corporal King, who was on the main deck, recalled, "Men called for buckets, but none were left on the boat, and in a few minutes later the fire assumed great proportions." Among all the men looking for the missing fire buckets, Private Morgan perhaps put forth the greatest effort. "My first thought was to get some buckets and put the fire out, but not seeing any and being afraid to venture over the wreck I jumped off [from the second deck] and swam to the stern of the boat, then got on again, but could not find any." Finally concluding that there were no buckets anywhere, Morgan turned "to help throw off the dead men, for it looked hard to see them burn."[39]

Although no buckets could be found on the lower deck, Sergeant Fies saw "a number of men trying to extinguish the fire by throwing water with buckets" up on the hurricane deck. After jumping into the water, Corporal Norton looked back at the hurricane deck and saw "a few brave men fighting the fire with buckets of water." Unfortunately, the only way to refill the buckets was directly from the Mississippi, which was about twenty-five feet below the hurricane deck, or from big red fire barrels positioned about the deck and filled with water for that specific purpose. Chances are, however, that the fire barrels had long since been drained dry by thirsty soldiers.[40]

"Had the boat not caught fire, those imprisoned by the wreckage could have been rescued, but the flames which quickly gained an uncontrollable headway, made it imperative for every man who could to save himself," explained Private Collins. Captain Friesner noted that "the hull and afterpart of the boat were uninjured." Had the men been able to extinguish the fire, only those killed by the explosion or crushed to death in the wreckage would have died. A few more might have died of their injuries, but the majority would have survived because there would have been no need to leave the boat. But when the fire suddenly took hold, the *Sultana* and most of her occupants were doomed. As First Sergeant Karns would later say, every person on board now had the "choice of two things . . . to either burn to death or drown."[41]

16

THE EXODUS

People began to leave the *Sultana* even before the fire started. Among the first to go were five deckhands. Private Rush, who was on the hurricane deck near the pilothouse when the explosion occurred, immediately raced to the stern. "As I reached the stern of the boat I saw a yawl launched from the lower deck with four or five persons in it, all of whom, I believe, were deck hands. I presume they were parties who were on watch at that time. There was a woman who begged piteously to be let into the boat, and from the conversation that took place, I think she was the wife of one of them, but they realized the situation and got away from the boat as quickly as possible and left her." Private Safford also commented on seeing the small sounding yawl "appropriated by what was left of the crew, who made off with it at once."[1]

The sounding yawl was gone, but there was still a lifeboat near the stern up on the hurricane deck. "Our heads were resting on the sloping side of a metallic life-boat when the steamer blew up," Corporal Fast remembered. "In a minute or two it seemed that a hundred men were tugging at the boat. It was thrown overboard, and after it, making a plunge of perhaps twenty feet into the dark water, went from a hundred to a hundred and fifty men. My chums followed that boat and lost their lives." Private Rush was among those who helped to launch the lifeboat: "Not being able to get into the yawl, Steward

[Pvt. George Washington Stewart Jr., Co. D, 40th IN Inf] and I then turned to and helped launch the life-boats [*sic*] from the upper deck, but as soon as a boat struck the water, crowds from each deck jumped into it, striking upon one another, and the boat was capsized."[2]

Although the boat landed upside-down in the water, dozens of people fought to get onto it. Watching from the second deck, Senator-elect Snow noticed that the lifeboat "was launched bottom up from the hurricane deck upon the heads of those below, and afforded support for a few in that condition." The boat "turned over and over," Rush wrote, "and many were drowned in trying to get into [it], as every time [the lifeboat] would turn bottom side up [it] would bury from fifty to seventy-five." Someone soon put an end to the entire affair. Pvt. William Henry Ross (Co. A, 102nd OH Inf) reported that "one of the small boats was thrown from the hurricane deck, and it landed bottom side up, and there was a fellow jumped down from the same deck, and he had a stick in his hand, and he ran or punched a hole in that boat." The boat sank without saving a single life.[3]

Some people who were startled awake by the explosion and the immense cloud of steam panicked and raced for the safety of the river. First Sergeant Karns recorded the first seconds after the explosion when "instantly the air was full of splinters and fragments, slumber and quiet which reigned but a moment ago, is now turned into the wildest confusion, the shrieks and cries of the women and children, the oaths and prayers of the soldiers and crew, the neighing of horses, the braying of mules, mingled with the heavy thud of the bodies and fragments as they fall into the water is beyond conception. The once magnificent *Sultana* now a wreck."[4]

After the huge hogsheads of sugar had been unloaded at Memphis, many men had slipped into the empty hold for the last part of the voyage to Cairo. After the explosion, the men in the hold clamored for those above to open the heavy hatches. "The hold of the boat was full of comrades," Pvt. Ogilvie E. Hamblin (Co. E, 2nd MI Cav) remembered. Hamblin had been wounded in the "arm near the shoulder" and captured at Racoon Ford, Georgia, on October 30, 1864. He claimed that Confederate doctors had amputated the shattered limb "for practice." He used the arm he had left to help the men trapped in the hold. "They cried for the door of the hold to be opened. My chum (Frank Perkins) [Sgt. Francis Marion Perkins, Co. E, 2nd MI Cav] and I pulled the door away, when they came rushing out of the hold like bees out of a hive, followed by dense clouds of steam and smoke."[5]

That act of supreme kindness by a one-armed man and his comrade was replicated a few minutes later by Pvt. Otto Clem Bardon (Co. H, 102nd OH Inf). Bardon was in the stern cargo room "lying by the side of the hatch-hole" when the explosion woke him. He "stood at this hatch-hole to keep comrades from falling in, for the top was blown off by the explosion."[6] Bardon, Hamblin, and Perkins thought of their comrades at a time when most others were thinking only of themselves.

"Veterans who had faced death on the field of battle without flinching were rushing about wildly, with the madness of fear depicted on their countenances," Private Hass recalled. "It was an awful moment— far more terrible than the crash and roar of battle." Pvt. DeMarquis Lafayette Githens (Co. F, 50th OH Inf) concurred. "In all my experience in war, I never saw anything more frightful than the scene on the boat—the horror came upon the sleeping hundreds on the boat like a bolt of lightning."[7]

Sergeant Kimberlin watched men push and shove to get into the water.

> Those on the top or hurricane deck were twenty-two or twenty-five feet above the water. The poor crazed fellows never paused to look, but plunged as far from the vessel as possible, alighting in the midst of dozens who had preceded them—the water around the boat for twenty to forty feet was a solid, seething mass of humanity, clinging one to another. Of those who went into the water with the first mad rush not more than one in ten escaped drowning; but of those who went into the water later, first taking off all their heavy clothing, including their shoes or boots, and securing some sort of a float, about one-half escaped and lived to return home.[8]

Some men on the bow, either wounded by the explosion or just unlucky, were trampled when they lost their footing and fell to the deck in front of their stampeding comrades. Pvt. James Knox Polk Brady (Co. B, 64th OH Inf) remembered that dead and wounded men alike were "being trampled upon." Immediately after the explosion, Corporal Chelf had seen a dead man lying on the bow. After avoiding the men pushing their way into the river, Chelf looked at the man again. "He was still there but all of his clothing was torn off him by the men running over his body."[9]

In spite of multiple injuries, many soldiers survived. Corporal Horner "was jammed among the debris; my left shoulder was dislocated; my left breast crushed in; my teeth crashed out; my left leg scalded; my hearing permanently impaired." Pvt. James McKendry (Battery D, 1st WV Lt Art) "sustained severe injuries to bones, limbs, fractured skull, left temple and injury to right shoulder and arm." Cpl. Stewart Oxley (Co. I, 51st OH Inf), reported, "My ribs on one side were cracked and broken, my back was badly injured, and the right side of my face and head scalded."[10]

The small fire that could have been extinguished with only a few buckets of water was soon out of control. Built of the lightest material possible to make her fast, and coated repeatedly with oil-based paint, the *Sultana* was a kindling box waiting for a spark. "[T]he flames which quickly gained an uncontrollable headway, made it imperative for every man who could to save himself," Private Collins said. Private Kochenderfer agreed: "[T]here being no effort made to check this little flame in very short time it became a fierce conflagration."[11]

Private Safford was on the cabin deck. "The flames, like huge serpents, darted up the woodwork, snapping in our faces. The dry timbers, the painted and oiled panels and cabins burned like paper. In ten minutes' time the craft was one sheet of flame, driving the survivors into the water." Inside the main saloon, Lieutenant Elliott "looked up to the ceiling and saw the fire jumping along from one cross-piece to another in a way that made me think of a lizard running along a fence."[12]

An unforeseen problem with having the officers stay in the main saloon separate from the enlisted men was that in case of an emergency there was nobody out on deck to take charge and give orders. Most of the men on the *Sultana* had been in the army long enough to become accustomed to following orders, but as Pvt. Benjamin Davis concluded, "In the confusion there was no command whatever."[13]

Without an officer present to tell them what to do, most of the men headed for the expected safety of the water. The overcrowding made the problem worse. "[T]he flames whipped down on them and those nearest the fire could not stand it and crowded back so that a great many near the edge of the boat were pushed overboard," said Private Porter. "The fire broke out in the vicinity of the boilers, which caused the soldiers to rush with tiger-like fury to the opposite extremity of the boat, or to that part of the boat farthest from the flames," wrote Pvt. Joshua S. Patterson (Co. F, 104th OH Inf). "Thus many poor hapless beings were pushed overboard by the pressure of the horrified and stricken mass of humanity. Being one of the number who were pushed overboard, and not versed in the art of swimming . . . I realized that life would soon be extinct, and that it did not seem uncertain for what fate Providence intended me."[14]

The men rushing to the water grabbed anything they thought could help them stay afloat. Corporal Rosselot, on the forward part of the cabin deck looked down into the water and "saw many men . . . fighting over a piece of timber or plank, and some crying and praying, some jumping in the water to escape from the fire and drowning." Sergeant Talkington was on the bow when he witnessed "two men pick up a large board probably two by twelve inches and perhaps twelve feet long, carry it to the edge of the boat and drop it overboard among the crowd of men in the water. They immediately jumped in after it. The board and the two men both disappeared under a mass of humanity struggling to get hold of it." Sickened by the fighting in the water, Talkington and other men "threw several cords of four feet engine wood overboard for the men in the water to hold to."[15]

Even a piece of the *Sultana* to help keep them afloat was no guarantee of survival in the fighting mob. Sergeant Boor saw "hundreds of men in the water pleading for help, clinching one another while they would hold onto each other—going down by the dozens at a time." Lieutenant Dixon was horrified: "Such as were not blown overboard jumped, and to their destruction, for they seemed to go in heaps and were drowned in groups and hundreds, as, instead of separating, they clung to one another, and so each helped to drown himself and his fellow."[16]

Even the best swimmers were in danger among the struggling mass of humanity. Corporal Norton "tried to swim, but others jumping from the burning boat pushed me under the surface time and time again." Private Ray saw men who could swim "fighting and kicking to keep off those unfortunates who could not swim, but all in vain. They clustered together and went down." "[N]o matter how good a swimmer a man might be," Private Maes said, "if he got into one of those crowds his doom was sealed and he would go down with the clutching mass." Young Stephen Gaston believed that "many a bold swimmer was drowned that night who could have saved himself if alone."[17]

Added to the horrendous sights those on board the *Sultana* witnessed that night were the terrible sounds. "Such screaming and yelling I never heard before or since," Private Robinson recalled. Corporal Norton "could hear the cries of those that were burned and scalded screaming with pain at every breath, and men all along the river were calling for help. I stood for a few minutes and listened to the awful wail of hundreds of human beings burning alive in the cabin and under the fallen timbers."[18]

As he waited on the hurricane deck for the water to clear, Corporal Fast

> saw many men standing on the debris and on the edge of the boat, just ready for the final leap, indulging their vocal and oratorical powers in a great variety of ways. Some were praying, some singing, and some swearing a "blue streak." Some would curse Abe Lincoln, Jeff Davis, General Grant any and everybody prominently connected with the war. Some were crying like children. Some muttered curses on everything in heaven above or on the earth below. Some prayed very loud, and most passionately; others were getting off very formal and graceful prayers all in dead earnest.

"Even the animals . . . uttered the most dreadful cries," Private Patterson said.[19]

While the men on the hurricane deck tried to save themselves with the metal lifeboat, those clustered on the bow sought safety with the boat's two heavy stageplanks. Sergeant Karns explained, "for those who do not understand the capacity of a gangplank (or stageplank as some call it) I will say that they are of framework, about 20 or 25 ft. long and about 4 ft. wide. The *Sultana* had two of these: one lay on the bow of the boat, while the other was strung up with rope and tackle even with the cabin deck. The first gangplank which lay on the bow of the boat, was thrown off in the first of the excitement and I do not know if any were saved by it or not."[20]

Corporal Sharp was there when the first stageplank was launched overboard. "There were two large cotton stages on board that would have floated 1,000 men. I saw one of them launched with a crowd of men on it and when in the water they all tried to stay on top of it. It got to turning over and over, and I think all got away from it and were drowned."[21]

After safely making his way from under the collapsed hurricane deck, Corporal Winters helped launch the first stageplank.

> It was just at this time, my attention was attracted to some men who were trying to launch a large stageplank, and also to the voice of someone, who was saying, "You men that can't swim better follow this plank." That appealed to me, for I knew no more about swimming than a year-old child, so I took hold, and helped shove the plank overboard, and jumped after it.
>
> The plank shot down under the water, but soon came to the surface, and righted itself with just as many men on it and around it, as was possible to get near it.
>
> I was one among the number that thought the only place of safety for me was on top of the plank. We only drifted a short distance till the plank was turned completely over. I was not looking for anything of that kind to happen, and taken off my guard, I lost my hold on the plank, and sunk beneath the water.

Winters managed to find the stageplank again and pleaded with the others "to be more quiet, and though the plank was turned over a number of times, I always managed to retain my hold on it. But every time it would turn over a number would be washed off who would never reach it again."[22]

Shortly after the first stageplank was launched, the remaining men on the bow turned to the second one, which was suspended above the bow. While they were cutting it down, some soldiers from the upper decks jumped onto it to escape the spreading flames. "I was on the outside of the cabin deck near the stairway at the time of the explosion and jumped on a stageplank and remained on it until it broke down, crushing many prisoners under it," stated Corporal Brunner. Sergeant Karns was also on the cabin deck.

> My attention was attracted to some comrades who were cutting the ropes that suspended the second gangplank, and something impressed me that I must go with it. I only had time to step over the railing on[to] the plank, when plank and all went crushing down on the heads of those on the bow of the boat below. The result of this did not come into mind at the time, but I have been impressed since with the thought that it must have been fatal to a great number, if not all that were underneath the plank.[23]

Private Phillips watched from the bow as the plank was cut down: "Someone called attention to a long gangway plank tied up with ropes some ten or twelve feet above our heads. The plank was very heavy, about twenty-five feet long. They cut it loose and it fell on the heads of the mass of men below, killing several."[24]

"As soon as we rallied from the fall," Karns said, "as many as could cling to the plank shoved it off into the water." Private Walker remembered that "every inch of space was seized by frantic men who refuse[d] to leave so it was pushed into the water with its human freight. I stepped off, as I knew to remain meant sure death." Sergeant Fies noted that "about as many as could get hold of it were trying to launch it, first on one side then on the other, finally it went overboard carrying with it a great number, but as it was heavily bound with iron it sank, and must have carried down with it a great many who had a hold of it."[25]

Made of solid wood reinforced with iron bands, the stageplank sank quickly and took a long time to come up. The shock of the cold water took Karns' breath away as he sank with the plank. "The combined weight of the plank and those hanging to it, sent it far below the surface. I soon let go and came to the top for breath. In my efforts to get to the top I struck several poor fellows on their way to the bottom." Private Walker, who remained on the bow, was shocked by what he saw after the plank hit the water: "[E]veryone was swept off, and never in my life have I witnessed such a struggle as there took place. I thought the sights on the battlefields terrible, and they were, but they were not to be compared with the sights of that night when the animal nature of man came to the surface in the desperate struggle to save himself regardless of the life of others."[26]

When the second stageplank finally surfaced, a number of men quickly grabbed hold of it, including Pvt. Henry Harrison Gambill (Co. B, 14th KY Inf), who "got upon it, with twenty-five other comrades. One of them caught me by the shoulders. I finally succeeded in getting him to release his hold in time to save my own life, but he was drowned. I then beseeched my comrades to get off the stageplank and rest themselves on its edges. By so doing it would not turn over, hold us all up and we would be safe, but my pleadings availed nothing. Finally, they all drowned but myself and four others."[27]

In addition to the two main stageplanks, a few smaller stageplanks were also thrown overboard. Immediately after the explosion, Private Ray and a friend left the hurricane deck and descended to the stern cargo room.

> As we passed along we came across a stageplank about six feet long, three feet wide and two inches thick. My partner knew I could not swim. We then carried the plank to the edge of the boat and threw it off. My partner said to me, "This is all I can do for you, jump on it." I never exchanged a word, but jumped on the plank, struck one edge of the board and it turned over with me two or three times. Finally, I got my breast fixed on one end of it and held on with one hand and worked away with the other.[28]

Nathan Wintringer was also saved by one of the smaller planks. After fighting a losing battle to get the soldiers to put out the fire, the chief engineer took to the water with a window blind. "I was not in the water long until I came across a gangway plank about thirty feet long and fifteen inches wide. I abandoned my shutter for it. I was not there long until four others kept me company. There was just about enough buoyancy in the plank to keep our heads above water, and that was all."[29]

In addition to the stageplanks, men threw "cordwood, boxes, bales of hay, pieces of wreckage of the boat that could be got loose—anything that would do to float with," Corporal Hulit recalled. Private Rush agreed: "Doors, boards, planks, bales of hay, &c., were thrown overboard by those less excited."[30]

Many looked to the sixty horses and mules tied along the stern guards or in the stern cargo room for survival. Private Hedrich remembered,

> A big crowd of passengers had flocked to the stern, where a lot of mules were quartered. Many of the mules had broken loose and were stamping up and down the deck. Several of us seized one and threw him overboard intending to jump over ourselves and let him swim us ashore. But the water was black with heads and arms of drowning passengers, and the mule sank instantly with a dozen men under and on top of him. We threw in several more, all with the same result.

Sergeant Buchanan was also hoping that a mule could save his life: "I found two mules hitched on the other side of the wreck and thought I would let one loose, take him by the tail, make him jump overboard and tow me ashore, but before taking a 'tail holt' I thought I would let one go first to see how he performed. Just as he jumped he kicked mule fashion, and I saw that my plan would not work. Some comrade in the water got this mule by the tail and sang out for me to turn them all loose."[31]

Harvey, Ann, and Belle Annis were in their stateroom "near the center of the vessel" when the boilers exploded. After Lieutenant

Annis looked out the cabin door and saw the steam in the main saloon, "he closed the door and tried to open the one leading out to the guards, but this was jammed by something, and someone outside said we were all stove in." Fearing the worst, Harvey put a life belt on his wife and one on himself. Ann later said that he did not put one on seven-year-old Belle because the belts were too large. Instead he picked up his daughter, still wearing her pink nightgown, and led his wife through the steam-filled main saloon to the stern transom windows. "He let himself down to the lower deck with the child, and I followed him," Ann stated, "but as I was descending the rope a man from above jumped on me and knocked me into the hold of the vessel."

When she described her experience Ann simply wrote, "From this I was extricated." But it was not that easy. A newspaper reporter later embellished the story: "[W]hen Mrs. Annis slid down this line she fell through a hatchway into the hold of the vessel. Her horror of the situation may well be imagined. . . . Fortunately, however, she was pulled out of this dismal pit onto the deck from which she was expected to jump into the water." Her husband and child had already jumped overboard, and Ann was getting ready to follow when "she was stepped upon by a mule . . . and was firmly held for a considerable length of time. In the meanwhile, also, many of the human passengers, half frantic from the effects of their burns, fell around her upon the deck, where she was pinioned, and Mrs. Annis was soon more securely held by this network of suffering humanity." Ann struggled free and immediately jumped overboard, hoping to catch up with her husband and daughter, but discovered that her lifebelt was askew. She clung to the rudder as she tried to straighten it.[32]

During this time Harvey Annis seems to have procured a door with a window in the upper half for himself and Belle. A survivor later reported that he saw "a man and little girl, the latter upon a window, going down the stream. The child seemed to have on a pink dress." A newspaper article about the disaster noted, "Mrs. Annis is of the opinion that the window which the soldier spoke of was the glass portion on the door upon which her daughter was riding as the child would most likely have been clinging or sitting upon the wooden portion of the door and the glass part would probably have projected out of the water." Also, "the fact that the daughter of Mrs. Annis was attired in a night gown of that color at the time of the accident leads the mother to believe that the people whom the soldier said he observed were the husband and child, struggling for life." Unfortunately, the soldier also reported that "the man and child were seen about the time they were nearing an eddy and that soon the child fell off the door and that when she sank the man dove after her. . . . [B]oth husband and child were drowned at this point. The former had been in the army and having been sick was coming home with his wife at the time the disaster occurred. He was consequently not very strong and it is considered remarkable that he braved life as long as he did."[33]

Ann clung to the rudder as long as possible. As the fire swept back through the stern cargo room, a barrel of oil or grease may have exploded, because she remembered hearing another explosion. "By this explosion there seemed to be a great deal of fire thrown all over the water about the boat to a considerable distance from her. [She] was obliged to take a small piece of board." It may have been at this time that Ann received severe burns to her arms and hands. One of her descendants noted that she "was burned from the backs of both hands up to her shoulders. . . . She wore long sleeves for the rest of her life and attached lace to the cuff so her hands and arms would be covered."[34]

Another woman who left the main saloon was Jennie Perry. Immediately upon hearing the explosion, Jennie "fastened on a life preserver and sprang into the river, at the stern of the boat." She "immediately found herself floating in the midst of soldiers, horses, and all the debris incident to the wreck. . . . Together with several soldiers, she managed to secure a door, which helped to sustain them in the water as they floated down the deep and rapid current of the mighty river."[35]

Daniel McLeod, crippled at the Battle of Shiloh by a musket ball through his right knee, was seated at a table in the main saloon when the boilers exploded. "[W]hen the explosion took place I was blown over the table being, as it were, on the outer edge of the crater. Both my legs were broken at the ankle." A few minutes later, McLeod spotted Captain Elliott peering down through the gaping hole in the middle of the saloon's ceiling and asked for his help.

Elliott "turned in the direction of the voice, so polite, so cool and calm amid this confusion. There, on the head of the last cot on this side [of] the breach, which was covered with pieces of the wreck, sat a man, bruised, cut, scalded in various places, both ankles broken and bones protruding. With his suspenders he had improvised tourniquets for both legs, to prevent bleeding to death."

"I am powerless to help you; I can't swim," Elliott replied, to which McLeod calmly answered, "Throw me in the river is all I ask, else I shall burn to death here."

With assistance from Capt. William L. Coleman (Co. D, 40th IN Inf), Elliott carried the terribly wounded man out to the promenade guard. McLeod "at once climbed down on the hog chains to where they had been broken off and let myself drop into the water, which was full of the wreck and men trying to escape, but not so many as there were shortly afterward when the flames forced them to take to the water. I had been brought up near the water and was a good swimmer, so I floated down the river."[36]

Newlyweds Seth and Hannah Hardin were also in the main saloon when the boilers exploded. They "remained on the wreck until compelled by the flames to jump overboard, the cabins fell in with a crash, and simultaneously several hundred persons sprang into the river, causing a confusion by which husband and wife became separated." Hannah Sophia Hardin was never seen again.[37]

There may have been another bridal party on board the boat. Captain McCown remembered seeing "a bride, her bridesmaid, the groom, and his best man." Major Fidler and the badly injured McCown found themselves out on the bow after making an unsuccessful attempt to put out the fire. McCown had just said to Fidler, "Major we can do no good here. We cannot restore any order—it is every man for himself, and God for us all, and we must look out for ourselves." The next instant, McCown heard a woman scream from the hurricane deck, "My mother! Oh! My mother!" Then a "white-robed figure leaped into the dark and angry waters. It was the young and beautiful bridesmaid. In an instant the major was over the guards and to the rescue. He lifted his burden to the surface of the frowning waters, but the wild and excited crowd, thinking of self only and seeing their leader in the water, rushed headlong upon him and the beautiful girl. They all sunk beneath the murky waters to rise no more."[38]

There were other women and children on board the *Sultana* that terrible morning. Pvt. Alonzo Adelbert Van Vlack (Co. F, 18th MI Inf) was asleep on the hurricane deck when the explosion woke him. "My first thought was to get a door out of the cabin," he said. "I looked down into the cabin and there saw women and children running to and fro and screaming for help. I shouted to them that they would try and run the boat on shore but there was so much confusion they could not hear me." Pvt. Friend E. Alvord (Co. A, 2nd MI Cav), who had slept near the wheelhouse, "saw two ladies who had thrown themselves into the water, they having nothing to keep them up, and sank, when I saw them no more." Down inside the main saloon, Senator-elect Snow "saw several husbands fasten life preservers to their wives and children and throw them overboard into the struggling mass below."[39]

Private Safford immediately tried to find his father, who was in a stateroom off the main saloon:

[K]nowing where the life-preservers were kept, I found one for myself and another for my [father], and assisted five of the ladies over the side of the boat from the cabin deck, after buckling on life preservers. I had fastened a preserver under the arms of a very handsome little lady from Columbus, Ohio, who displayed more grit than half the men, and as I turned to help another, a man, or the semblance of a man, jerked the life-preserver from the Columbus lady and she sank before his eyes. Thank God, the cowardly dog was not a soldier, but was one of the crew.[40]

Private McFarland was already in the water when he "saw a woman rush out of a stateroom in her night clothes with a little child in her arms. In a moment she had fastened a life preserver about its waist and threw it overboard. The preserver had evidently been fastened on too low, for when the little one hit the water it turned wrong end up. The mother rushed into the stateroom in an instant and was then out and sprang into the water and grabbed the child—all of which occurred in the space of a couple of minutes." While McFarland watched, the woman righted the child and pushed her way through the struggling crowd.[41]

17

THE GROWING
FIRE

The *Sultana* was heading upriver into a strong breeze when her boilers exploded. Without her pilothouse, she was a floating, burning wreck at the mercy of wind and current. After the fire started, the strong breeze forced the flames toward the stern, pushing everyone in their path ahead of them. "[T]he wind coming downstream drew the flames down the center of the boat," Captain Friesner said, "and the cabin caught fire."[1]

After the first mad rush for the water, the people who remained on the bow soon realized that the flames were not coming their way. Sergeant Fies noticed that the "slight barrier formed by portions of the upper decks which had fallen down . . . kept most of the flames from reaching those of us who were on the bow of the boat." For a few minutes, at least, the bow was the safest place to be.[2]

But that suddenly changed. Perhaps twenty minutes after the explosion, the twin paddlewheel housings, which the blast had loosened and canted outward, finally broke away from the upper superstructure and fell on the sides of the boat. The left paddlewheel housing, which had been tilted away at about a 45-degree angle, toppled first but remained attached to the hull at its base. The huge paddlewheel

187

box stuck out from the *Sultana* at the perpendicular and formed an outrigger. As the strong flood current struck this box, the steamer began to turn. When the right wheel housing also broke loose and toppled into the river, the left box broke away from the hull as well, but the damage had already been done. The *Sultana* was turned completely around, and the stiff wind was pushing the flames from the stern toward the bow. All those who had found safety on the bow were now in grave danger.

Lieutenant Squire had left the main saloon—the last person out—and thrown himself into the water. After thrashing about for a while he made his way toward what must have been the left paddlewheel while it was still upright:

> I came up directly under the wheel and seized hold of one of its arms or paddles. I tried to pull myself up but could not. On one side of the wheel were quite a number of men while others were holding on to them and trying to get out of the water. This destroyed the balance and the wheel partially revolved. Clinging to the arm, I was carried up until the arm I had hold of became the top arm. As the wheel revolved, those on the side were carried down into the water and relinquishing their hold were swept away by the current.

Still clinging to the paddle, Squire managed to divest himself of his clothes and was wondering what to do next when the entire paddle-wheel housing broke loose and fell sideways into the water.

"The rush of water broke my hold, and I was carried along, nearly drowned," Squire continued. "It appeared I was caught in the wheelhouse like a rat in an open box inverted, but the side of the wheel house that when in proper place was next the boat was soon uppermost and was badly charred by the fire." Somehow Squire managed to remain calm. "Floating on my back in this prison, I discovered a small hole at the top, burned through by the fire. . . . I thrust my hand through and broke the opening large enough to crawl through, splashing water on the burning boards and crawled through, burning my hands somewhat in doing so. The heat from the burning boat was

almost intolerable and I was obliged to let myself down in the water
and splash water onto my head and neck to prevent burning." Once
he was back in the water, Squire clung to the side of the wheelhouse,
which was still attached to the *Sultana*. He "secured a window blind
to use when the boat and the wreckage upon which I floated should
sink, which was liable to occur at any moment."[3]

On the other side of the boat, Corporal Colvin managed to get
inside the right paddlewheel housing while it was still upright. Flames
shooting out of a cabin window had forced him to drop into the river
while he was climbing down from the hurricane deck. He

> cought [*sic*] holt of a large trunk over another mans shoulder
> and held to it until it floated into the wheelhouse. Then we
> let go of the trunk and took holt of the wheel. In a short
> time the wheelhouse burnt loose and fell over on its side.
> There were about a dozen men in the wheelhouse when it
> fell and if any of them got out except myself I do not know
> it. I was almost gone when I came up with the wheelhouse
> and it was sometime before I was able to get on top of it.

The right wheel housing had broken completely away from the
Sultana's superstructure but continued to float. "After I had been on
the wheelhouse some time two other men . . . got on the wreck of the
wheelhouse with me," Colvin said. "We floated along by the side of
the hull till it sunk. Then we floated on down the river."[4]

When the left paddlewheel housing fell into the water and forced
the boat to turn, the men who had thought themselves safe on the
bow, in front of the firebreak, now found themselves in the path of
the fire. "A dense mass, estimated at about five hundred, took refuge
on the bow of the boat while the flames were driven aft by the wind,"
Senator-elect Snow recalled. "A few moments afterward the wheel-
houses, loosened by the concussion and the flames, fell off outward,
and the boat turned bow downstream, reversing the flames. The
largest part of this number then must have perished, as they had no
material at hand to throw over to sustain themselves, except a few
bales of hay which were immediately seized on the turning of the
boat."[5]

Cpl. Adam Leak (Co. B, 3rd TN Cav) had gone forward after the explosion and "was standing near the jackstaff, when the wind veered and sent the flames in a solid mass against us, sending us in a body overboard." Private Walker had also remained on the bow: "There were perhaps eighty or one hundred of us . . . 'waiting for something to turn up,' but we were not kept waiting long, for the boat soon swung around and the wind blew the flames directly on us, which so scorched our naked bodies that we all made a frantic rush for the water. Being in about the center of the crowd I pushed those in front, those behind pushed us, and we all went into the river in a bunch. When I touched the water it was a great relief to my scorched body."[6]

When he tried to surface, Walker was forced back under by others who jumped after him: "I could feel arms and legs and bodies of men all around me, but I was fortunate enough to know what I was doing all the time, and I struck out with the best effort I could make at swimming. After a few strokes I came to the surface. Just at that time a part of the wreck, a piece of studding four or five feet long, floated within my reach, and another man and I seized hold of it at the same time." Corporal Leak had managed to grasp "the cables in a coil and when going down continued to pay them out until I had secured a hold on their length that kept me above the water and thus saved myself, as I could not swim at all."[7]

The explosion that tore off the back half of the texas deck killed most of the *Sultana*'s senior crew members, but five survived the initial blast. Second Engineer Samuel Clemens was standing beside the boiler and was mortally scalded. He was rescued but lived only "about fourteen hours." George Cayton was at the wheel in the pilothouse. He was blown straight up and came straight down, then "crawled out under the pilothouse and endeavored to prevent the passengers from jumping into the river, telling them to hold onto the wreck as long as possible." When the fire got out of control, Cayton gave up and headed for the water: "I got a plank and swam to the island called Hen and Chickens."[8]

First Mate William Rowberry was also in the pilothouse, but he was blown upward and outward along with the back three-quarters of the house. He and a few other men managed to grab onto a plank.

Chief Engineer Wintringer was sound asleep in his berth and was uninjured by the explosion: "I worked my way down on to the lower deck. I tried to get where the fire was to see if it could not be put out, but could not get near for the rubbish, and there was so much confusion. . . . I remained on the boat only about twenty minutes, in which time she was pretty much enveloped in flames. . . . I managed to get hold of a shutter and . . . took my chances and jumped into the river."[9]

The other *Sultana* officer to survive the explosion was Captain Mason, who was in his cabin in the very forward part of the texas cabin, in front of the huge hole blasted through his boat. Mason left his cabin and at first tried to calm everyone down since there was no immediate fire. "We saw Captain Mason, master of the boat, in his shirt-sleeves and bare-headed, trying to restore order, and asking the crowd to quiet down and be patient, as he thought we would receive assistance very shortly," wrote Private Rush, "but to quiet the excitement under such circumstances was impossible. . . . I believe Captain Mason did all that any person could do under the circumstances." First Sgt. Jacob Helminger (Co. B, 50th OH Inf) said that Mason "told us to come to order, that the hull was not hurt and we would land. Now, if the fire could be put out I would have thought this order very advisable."[10]

Once the fire started and smoke replaced the steam, Mason knew that his boat was doomed and began trying to save his passengers. Private Homer, on the hurricane deck, remembered that "Capt. Mason . . . was all the time busy throwing down things for the boys to get hold of, barrels, boxes and bales of hay and cabin doors." Private Rush saw Mason helping "breaking off doors, & etc. & throwing them off into the river to assist those in the water."[11]

Undoubtedly James Cass Mason felt responsible for the fate of all of the paroled prisoners on board the *Sultana* since it had been his backhanded dealings with Captain Hatch that had placed so many men on a boat with faulty boilers. After helping out all that he could on the hurricane deck, Mason continued his efforts on the second deck promenade. Sergeant Stevens was already in the water when he saw Mason on the cabin deck. "I came to the surface again and saw the captain tearing off window shutters and throwing them into the river for the boys," the sergeant wrote.[12]

Captain Friesner was on the second deck and was about to leap overboard when he suddenly stopped. "Seeing a pair of Army pants sticking out from between the fallen roof, I touched them. They kicked. I tried to lift the roof but could not. I called for help. Capt. Mason came, but was so exhausted he could not lift twenty pounds, and exclaiming 'I can't, I can't,' left me." Undaunted, Friesner continued in his efforts to free the trapped soldier. "Inspired by the approaching fire and the efforts of the imprisoned man, I excelled myself lifting the roof and he began to squirm out. . . . He crawled out, said nothing but rushed headlong overboard. I recognized him, I thought, as James Suller of Co. K."[13] Pvt. James Stuller (Co. A, 58th OH Inf.—Guard Unit) had, in fact, transferred from Company K in December 1864.

Captain Mason apparently left the cabin deck and went down to the bow, but got there after the boat had begun to turn and after the second mad rush for the water had already begun. The *Daily Missouri Republican* of St. Louis reported that "[s]everal soldiers stated that the last they saw of the Captain he was standing on the forecastle advising every-body to keep cool and use the best efforts to save themselves." Sergeant Nisley had fallen through the crashed decks after the explosion, suffering injuries to his back as well as burns from the fire and steam. After getting out from under the wreckage, Nisley "immediately set about helping to extricate those who were caught fast by pieces of the boat. After this, in company with Capt. Mason, of the *Sultana*, I threw over broken pieces of the boat and other materials for those already in the water, but after a little time the fire became so hot that I was obliged to take to the water. A great many had sunk to rise no more, and there were but few floating and swimming about that would be liable to drag me down. Capt. Mason was the last man I talked with while on board the boat, and he was still on the boat when I left." Sergeant Nisley may have been the last person to see James Cass Mason alive. He was never seen to leave the burning vessel or spotted in the water. His body was never recovered.[14]

One other member of the "crew" was known to have survived the explosion: the *Sultana*'s alligator. The crew had put the sturdy wooden box holding the alligator inside a closet beneath the main stairway to keep the soldiers from tormenting their mascot. Since the main stairs were a good distance in front of the boilers and furnace, the box was in front of the firebreak of debris that had collapsed downward from the upper decks, and it was well in front of the fire that started in the furnaces and swept toward the stern. As the disaster unfolded, many soldiers thought of the alligator. Corporal Horner had been thrown into the water by the explosion. "Although I felt that I would not drown," he later said, ". . . I did not feel comfortable from the fact that there was an alligator seven and one-half feet long keeping me company." Seventeen-year-old Pvt. John Harrison Simpson (Co. I, 3rd TN Cav), also catapulted into the water, "kept thinking about that alligator. . . . I wondered if it would grab my leg." Private Davis admitted that "the alligator troubled me almost as much as the fire."[15]

While many remembered the alligator, Private Lugenbeal was more interested in the sturdy box. "I thought of the box that contained the alligator, so I got it out of the closet and took him out and ran the bayonet through him three times." Planning to use the box as his own personal lifeboat, Lugenbeal

> took off all my clothing except my drawers, drew the box to the end of the boat, threw it overboard and jumped after it but missed it and went down somewhere in the mighty deep. When I came up I got hold of the box, but slipped off and went down again. When I arose to the surface again I got a good hold of it and drew myself into it with my feet out behind, so that I could kick, the edges of the box coming under each arm as it was just wide enough for my breast and my arms coming over each edge of the box; so you see I was about as large as an alligator.

Balancing himself chest down, Lugenbeal began kicking and paddling.[16] The others in the water with him were determined not to let him—and the box—get away. "There were hundreds of men in the water and they would reach for anything they could see," Lugenbeal continued. "When a man would get close enough I would kick him off, then turn quick as I could and kick someone else to keep them from getting hold of me. They would call out 'don't kick, for I am drowning,' but if they had got hold of me we would both have drowned."

Lugenbeal managed to paddle his little boat all the way down to Memphis, although his chest and underarms were rubbed raw by the time he arrived. For the rest of his life he would be remembered as the man who was "Saved by a Alligator."[17]

Although Lugenbeal thought that he had killed the alligator, Private Zaiser and a few of his friends found otherwise. After working their way down from the forward part of the hurricane deck to the forward part of the main deck before the fire became a roaring inferno, Zaiser told his friends, "Suppose we see whether the fire cannot be put out." The group "started back toward the furnace. When we came to the coal pit we found that the alligator which had been in a box the day before was lying on the coal at liberty. On our arrival at his side he turned toward us and we decided that we had better not stay there any longer." Zaiser and his friends fled, but that movement may have been the alligator's last, for it never bothered a single person in the water—or at least no one who lived to tell about it.[18]

While most men fought only to save themselves, some fought desperately to save others by throwing debris into the water for the drowning men. Cpl. Jesse Martin (Co. D, 35th IN Inf) came across "one man who seemed to be taking things coolly. I went to him and asked him if he would help me throw things to those in the water to swim on. We went to work throwing over anything we could find that would float excepting a large plank. This we saved for ourselves."[19]

Up on the second deck, Lieutenant Elliott also tried to help the struggling men in the water. "A number were tearing the sheathing from the boat and throwing it into the river as floats, [and] I joined them in this work. This employment quieted me and gave me time to consider the situation." Nearby, Private Rush and Private Stewart were also helping out. "Steward [sic] and I kept ourselves occupied in throwing overboard such things as we could manage to tear loose from the state-rooms—doors, blinds, etc."[20]

Just as heartbreaking as watching the struggling men in the water fight among themselves was watching and listening to the men trapped in the wreckage or wounded by the explosion and collapse of the decks. First Sergeant Karns recalled the suffering: "It was no uncommon thing to hear the cries of those who were so mangled as to

be unable to crawl, for others to throw them overboard, as they preferred death by drowning rather than by fire. The pleadings of some
of these were heeded to, while others were left to either be trampled
to death or consumed by the fire." Corporal Winters recalled that "[a]
number were crippled by the explosion so that it was impossible for
them to be saved and they begged their comrades to throw them overboard and allow them to drown rather than burn to death, and this
was done. When all hope of saving them was gone, the poor victims
thanked those whose hard lot it was to perform this sad task."[21]

Sgt. Michael H. Sprinkle (Co. K, 102nd OH Inf) and Private
Lockhart were among those on the hurricane deck helping to throw
injured men overboard. When "a sergeant of the 1st Ohio called for
help, to help throw these men over who were caught under the stack,"
Lockhart and Sprinkle went over to assist. Lockhart remembered
that he "threw over ten or twelve, but one survived, that was all, and
one that had both limbs broken and he got out." Sergeant Sprinkle
thought they helped more than ten or twelve: "The boat soon took
fire and Billy Lockhart and myself threw at least fifty of those who
had been wounded in the explosion overboard, thinking it better that
they should take their chances of drowning than be left to burn up,
which they would do if left on the boat." Cpl. John W. Divelbiss (Co.
E, 102nd OH Inf) did not survive after Lockhart threw him into the
water. Private Homer, his friend, said that Divelbuss "was burned or
scalded so that he was disabled from swimming and knew it, so he
begged for God's sake for Billy Lockhart to throw him overboard, he
preferred to drown rather than remain on board and burn to death, so
there was another good-natured soldier found a water grave."[22]

Pvt. Commodore Smith, on the main deck in the stern cargo room,
was also assisting injured and dying men:

> I remained on board the hull of the boat for perhaps twenty
> or thirty minutes, throwing overboard all the loose boards
> and timbers and everything that would float to assist those
> in the water and save them from drowning if possible.
>
> And now occurred the hardest task of my life. The boat
> was on fire and the wounded begged us to throw them

overboard, choosing to drown instead of being roasted
to death. While our hearts went out in sympathy for our
suffering and dying comrades we performed our sad but
solemn duty. I say we because there were others besides
myself who were fortunate enough not to be hurt or blown
overboard by the explosion, and they too were doing all
they could to alleviate the sufferings of their unfortunate
comrades.

[W]e proceeded to perform carefully, but hurriedly, the
most heartrending tasks that human beings could be called
upon to perform—that of throwing overboard into the jaws
of certain death by drowning those comrades who were
unable on account of broken bones and limbs to help themselves. Some were so badly scalded by the hot water and
steam from the exploded boiler that the flesh was falling
from their bones.[23]

At a time when most of the people on board the *Sultana*—men,
women and children—were thinking only of their own survival,
Elliott, Sprinkle, Martin, Lockhart, Rush, Smith, Stewart, and a few
others thought of their comrades and did all in their power to help.

18

THE RIVER

The number of people who died immediately when the boilers exploded at about 2 a.m. on April 27, 1865, is unknown. Private Rush calculated "that the explosion itself did not Kill or throw from the boat more than 200 persons." The force of the explosion catapulted many people into the dark, cold Mississippi. "I was sound asleep when it happened, waking up feeling myself flying through the air," Private Eldridge said. "At first I could not imagine what had happened . . . but when I hit the water the first thought came to me was to swim back to the boat, so I swam around several times, but could not see it."[1]

Many of the soldiers who woke in midair or in the water had no idea what had happened. Private Summerville thought he "must have been thrown fully one hundred feet. I sank only once. My first thought was that the steamer had been running close to shore, and I had been dragged off by a limb." Private Schmutz "did not have the slightest notion that the boat had blown up" and thought someone had thrown him overboard. "That the boiler had exploded never entered my mind. . . . Being in the water I did not know how badly I was scalded, but knew that my face was burned, for now and then I had to dip my face in the cooling water to allay the burning sensation." It was only after being rescued that Schmutz discovered the extent of his injuries. "My entire left side was one blister, and such agonies I never wish again to experience."[2]

Those who found themselves in the water in almost total darkness had to be lucky to find something to help stay afloat. Private Anderson "was thrown out of reach of anybody and saw nothing of my comrades after the explosion. I swam about in the water for a time, and finally got a piece of railing that was thrown from the boat and stuck to that and floated down the river with Mr. Horn from Wooster, and two others."[3]

Pvt. Philip Horn had been "lying on the left side of the boat at the foot of the stairs that went to the hurricane deck. I was either blown through the stairway or thrust out sidewise into the air. I struck the water feet first and went down twice. I could not swim but I attempted to paddle dog fashion. When I came to the surface of the water after the second time down I encountered a piece of wreckage which I seized." Although Horn did not mention Anderson by name, he did recall that "there were seven of us clinging to this one floating timber."[4]

Another soldier who found himself unexpectedly catapulted into the water from the hurricane deck was Eppenetus McIntosh, the soldier from Illinois who had been left behind at Memphis by the *Henry Ames* and was hitchhiking upriver on the *Sultana*: "I was awakened by a sudden push, and discovered I was flying through the black night air. I struck the water forty or fifty feet from the boat; I soon came to the surface and began swimming, not being able to understand just what had happened. Coming in contact with a floating scantling, with a few shattered boards attached, I clung to it." McIntosh had suffered greatly in Andersonville prison, going from 175 pounds down to 65, but he attributed his survival to this dramatic weight loss: "[B]eing reduced to a mere skeleton through being confined in rebel prisons was in my favor, as I could never have survived that awful disaster [clinging to a few small boards] had I weighed as much as I did before my prison experience."[5]

Although many men perished when they could find nothing to cling to in the darkness, some managed to survive without a float. Cpl. Pleasant Lafayette Atchley (Co. K, 3rd TN Cav) "was thrown into the surging waves of that mighty river, into the jaws of death, and life depended on one grand effort, expert swimming, which I did successfully, and after swimming six or seven miles . . . landed on the Arkansas shore without any assistance whatever."[6] Corporal Atchley was an exception to the rule.

Several men who were forced into the river ended up clinging to chains and lines hanging over the edge of the bow. Commissary Sergeant Mavity had jumped into the water with a "stick of wood" but immediately ran into trouble. "Several times was I pulled under water by others drowning and, finding that the wood could not aid me and spying a cable chain, I grasped the latter as a last means of hope. Holding firmly to this with my hands, and catching my toes in the lower links, I managed to keep my head above the water." Farrier Samuel Jackson Thrasher (Co. G, 6th KY Cav) and Pvt. Abraham Rhodes (Co. I, 6th KY Cav) were still on the boat when they spotted a rope and a chain hanging over the bow. "When the heat became so intense we could not stay on the boat any longer," Thrasher said, "we went down into the water, under the bow of the boat, holding to the rope and chain until the cabin burned down."[7]

A handful of people found refuge clinging to the rudder at the stern, including Ann Annis. One of the others, Private Foglesang, recalled,

> While I was hanging to the rudder a man cried: "Get off from me." There were nine of us that had hold of that rudder and I, being the top one, kept quiet. Soon the coals from above began to fall on my head and shoulders and I began to think that I must get out. A part of the deck burned off and fell into the water and I tried to get those who were under me to swim but they were afraid to let go lest they drown. The coals came thicker and faster; so that I had to brush them off my head and hang onto the rudder with the other. I had to do something and made up my mind to jump into the water.

Although Foglesang did not reach the fallen deck piece, he did find a floating door and with one other person started downriver toward Memphis.[8]

The *Sultana* disaster occurred in late April, after the winter snowmelt had begun in the North. Pvt. William Faulkner (Co. E, 12th NY

Inf) reported that "[t]he weather was not very cold that night, but water coming down from the North was icy cold." Private Madden believed that "many a good swimmer lost his life by being made powerless by the icy waters of the northwest with which the Mississippi river is flushed at that time of the year."[9] With his usual flair for words, Lieutenant Elliott recalled that the water "was colder than 'Greenland's icy mountains'"; and Pvt. Joseph D. Bringman (Co. D, 102nd OH Inf) said that "in every direction men were shivering and calling for help, while the water was carrying us swiftly down the stream."[10]

As the men floated along in the swift current, the cold began to have a telling effect on their thin bodies. "I became very cold and my limbs began to cramp," said Pvt. Franklin A. Clapsaddle (Co. F, 115th OH Inf). When he was finally rescued, Private Summerville "had been two hours in the river and was so chilled and numb that I could not stand." Sgt. James Thomas Wolverton (Co. G, 6th TN Cav) thought it "remarkable that any of us could be alive after such great exposier [sic] in the ice cold water."[11]

Although almost every survivor complained about the long exposure to the cold water, one man thought it was therapeutic. Private McIntosh explained that "[b]eing in the cold water so long had reduced the swelling in my ankles and feet, and they looked like scalded beef; the scurvy ulcers were thoroughly cleansed by their prolonged bath in the sandy water, and I believe now that terrible bath had much to do with saving my feet from amputation."[12]

Although it was not called hypothermia in 1865, many of the soldiers suffered from the drop in body temperature they experienced in the cold water. Simply put, hypothermia occurs when the body loses heat faster than it can produce it. When the body temperature drops below about 95 degrees, drowsiness and loss of consciousness can result, ending in heart and respiratory failure if the victim gets no relief.[13] In their weakened, emaciated condition, with very little body fat to insulate them, many of the paroled prisoners began to suffer from hypothermia within minutes of their immersion in the icy cold water. Most of the *Sultana* passengers were in the water for four or five hours, and many were naked because they had stripped off their clothing to prevent others from grabbing it and drowning them.

"During the long three and a half or four hours' struggle in the water my greatest difficulty toward the end was in keeping awake," Private Walker recalled. "I found myself going to sleep a number of times, and I would then work hard with my arms and legs to arouse myself." Private Bringman "was so chilled that I was powerless, and a kind of drowsiness came over me. I felt that I was going to sleep and I seemed as comfortable as if in a downy bed. I soon dropped to sleep, or to unconsciousness." Pvt. Joseph H. Mayes (Co. H, 40th IN Inf) was holding to a ten-foot-long plank with a man from Michigan: "[W]e were so cold that we stopped trying to get out. We could not move hand or foot, and the Michigan man swore that he could not hold on any longer. . . . We became unconscious and did not remember when we were picked up. We came to about nine o'clock that day."[14]

Lieutenant Dixon, who was holding onto a couple of small planks, began to lose his grasp on reality. "I was getting very cold and numb, my mind was wandering blank. . . . It seemed like everything was becoming blank. . . . It seemed like a dream." Even after climbing into the top of a submerged tree, Private Johnston suffered from the effects of hypothermia. "Being obliged to remain in the water, holding fast to a tree for some time, I began to get cold and sleepy."[15] It will never be known how many of the *Sultana*'s passengers died from hypothermia.

Many people encountered swirling eddies and whirlpools in the strong floodwaters, especially as they tried to get close to shore. Sergeant Stevens "could not swim to the shore" in the swift current, "the eddies carrying you away each time you attempted it." Private Walker, who did not know how to swim, "was caught in an eddy, whirling around several times and forced out again into the current. I realized that since I was not a swimmer I was but wasting my strength in those efforts, and concluded to float with the current." Pvt. Commodore Smith, who *was* a swimmer, tried to keep his head when he encountered a whirlpool. "[A]fter encountering several whirlpools and being carried around and around in them, each time being carried back into the center of the river, by hard struggling, keeping a cool head, and using my dexterity as a swimmer I finally reached a point half a mile above the city of Memphis where I lodged in a tree out in the flats of the river."[16]

Many of the people clinging to debris witnessed the death of a friend or comrade whose float was caught in an eddy or whirlpool. Private Christine was holding onto a couple of planks when he was joined by two other soldiers. "The first that got on became so bad that he did not know anything, and finally fell off, when we got into a whirligig, which carried us around pretty fast," he reported. Lieutenant Elliott was clinging to a set of stairs with three other soldiers when they ran into a whirlpool. "Into this we went, and such twisting and turning round, upside down and every other way, was never seen; but I held on to the steps with an iron grip. In my boyhood days I had read 'Faust,' and the description of the devil dragging him down into hell came pretty near fitting me. But Satan, who then claimed me as his own, finally let loose his icy hold, and we shot out into the current and on down the river, less one man who was left in the whirlpool and drowned."[17]

Private Kinzer and another man were floating along with a piece of board when they got into an eddy near a semi-submerged tree and had a brief visitor. "At this point the swift current and dead water formed an eddy and we went whirling around. As we were going around a person caught on to our board, who said that she was a woman. After going around once or twice she let go and floated down on her own board, at the same time we floated out of this swift current and swam directly to the timber."[18] The woman may have been Ann Annis. She was alone as she floated down the river and recalled clinging to "a small piece of board."[19]

Thirty-five-year-old Jennie Perry had put on a lifebelt before leaving the *Sultana*. After Corporal King jumped into the water over the stern railing, he surfaced to find that "a lady was beside me grasping me and calling for help. I managed to get away but on getting a hold on some wreckage I returned and assisted her." The woman was Jennie Perry, and the wreckage King grabbed was a stateroom door. Eventually, the two were joined by several others.[20]

The *Cincinnati Commercial Tribune* of May 11, 1865, mentioned King and Perry.

Of the gloomy half-dozen companions, the lady and a young soldier [i.e., Corporal King], boyish in years, but manly and noble in deed, were the most self-possessed, for they alone raised their voices in words of encouragement or advice. The others, men who had faced death on battle-fields and in rebel prisons, were as babes in that trying hour. They wept aloud, and the waters echoed back their shrieks of utter despair. One of [the soldiers] crawled upon the door and remained there, to the imminent peril of the others. . . . Another, who observed that Mrs. Perry had on a life-preserver, let go of the door, and grasped her arm, forcing her under the water. She managed to shake him off and regain the door, he taking his place by her side again. [H]e repeated the operation three different times, on each occasion dragging Mrs. Perry under the water, and nearly strangling her. Happening to perceive another door floating near them, Mrs. Perry attempted to secure it, but as she was about to lay hands on it, a soldier, who had been clinging to it, arose to the surface and warned her off. She . . . attempted to catch hold of the door, but the soldier thrust her off into the water, and compelled her to return to the other.[21]

Mrs. Perry was back with her first float for only a short time when the door drifted among "a few logs which had been caught near a small submerged island." Corporal King "now saw that we were among small trees and brush, but my feet would not reach bottom. . . . I soon discovered a log among the drift which I mounted. It sank partly, and I had no trouble in seating my companion. I held her with one hand grasping the little tree next to me with the other. Our weight upon the log brought it down and we were in the water to our shoulders." Although partly submerged, Jennie Perry and Corporal King were at least alive.[22]

Ever more desperate, people snatched at doors, planks, pieces of the *Sultana*, and anything else that floated by. Sergeant Norton had left the *Sultana* with a small box but decided that he needed something more substantial: "About fifteen feet away from me I saw a bale of hay with a soldier boy lying across it, which I made the greatest physical effort to reach. I finally made it and putting my arm upon one corner, and with my box under the other arm, I was soon able to disgorge some of the water from my lungs. As soon as I could speak I assured the soldier boy that I would not sink his bale of hay. He was piteously begging me not to as he could not swim. I told him to keep a look out and not let anyone get on with us."[23]

Sergeant Stevens was also saved by a bale of hay. He had remained on the bow of the *Sultana* until the boat turned, then went into the water. "I now commenced swimming dog fashion, but my strength soon gave out and I began to strangle. I yelled for help, and comrade Charles Tabor [Sgt. Clark P. Tabor, Co. I, 2nd MI Cav], one whose life I had saved while in prison, heard and knew my voice, and swam away from the bale of hay on which he was floating, caught me by the hair and with the aid of the other men who were on the bale, pulled me on top, and thus in turn saving my life."[24]

The tightly packed bales of hay stayed afloat even with several men clinging to them. Private Van Vlack grabbed onto one that had "three or four men hanging onto it." Quartermaster Sergeant Wells saw "five boyes come floting along hang[ing] to a bale of hay. I caught on as they Sed it was a free raft and would float all that could hang on."[25]

Barrels also proved useful—for some people. Pvt. James Wiley Hodges (Co. F, 3rd TN Cav) left the boat with a small plank but "soon found that it was not sufficient to hold me out of the water so I caught hold of a floating barrel, but after turning it over a few times concluded I did not want it and let it go. I then turned back to the boat and obtained three planks." Apparently, most people with a barrel had the same problem because they were hard to manage in the strong current. Sergeant Fies explained, "I saw a number of men bringing from the hold empty cracker barrels and jumping overboard with them, but I saw they were worse than useless in keeping the heads of the men above water, having only one head in them they would not balance."[26]

Lieutenant Elliott, floating down the dark river on a set of stairs with three others, witnessed someone else on a barrel. "One man who passed us was bobbing up and down in a way that reminded me of a frog in the game of leapfrog. As he came within a few feet of us, I asked him what he was on, and he answered me, 'Don't touch me; I am on a barrel.' He actually was astraddle a barrel, holding on to the rim, and at any other time his queer motion would have been laughable." Private Robinson saw another soldier struggling with a barrel: "[The soldier] would crawl up on it and pray. He got up a little too far and over he went still hanging to it. He came up on the other side of it and the first thing I heard him say was 'd—m this thing, it will drown me yet.'"[27]

Only slightly less difficult to manage were the horses and mules that had been on board the *Sultana*. Once forced overboard, each animal was grabbed by dozens of men. Unfortunately, just as a horse will run back into a burning barn if not led far away, many of the horses and mules swam back toward the *Sultana*. "Some of the mules on board took to the water and were seized by soldiers," Private Zaiser recalled. "The mules turned toward the burning ship [*sic*] and toward the people and the boys had a hard time trying to turn them around."[28]

Pvt. Pleasant Marion Keeble (Co. H, 3rd TN Cav), who lost his older brother Pvt. John Harrison Keeble (Co. A, 3rd TN Cav) on the *Sultana*, found some amusement in the antics of his friend Pvt. Samuel Pickens (Co. A, 3rd TN Cav): "Sam was on a horse in the water. The horse wouldn't swim away from the boat. A dead mule came floating by. Sam got onto the dead mule. We afterward laughed with Sam about this. Sam said that his swapping a live horse for a dead mule was the best trade he ever made."[29]

Cavalryman Pvt. William Marshall Pryor (Co. B, 3rd TN Cav) made a similar "best trade" in the swirling waters. A letter written by one of his descendants passed along the story: "When [the *Sultana*] blew up, it threw him out in the water and he couldn't swim. He grabbed the tail of a live horse swimming by. As the horse began to tire, Pryor saw a dead horse floating by and he grabbed it because he knew it would float and the live horse would sink. Eventually the dead horse floated to the bank, and Pryor was saved." Another cavalryman, Private Robinson, did not have to trade a live horse for a dead one, but he did survive through the help of one of the dead animals. "I was almost a goner," he recalled, "when I saw a dark object in the water and made for it, and it was a dead mule, one that was blown off the boat. He was dead but not quite cold. I crawled up on him and was there when I was picked up."[30]

In most cases, a dead horse or mule was better than a live one. If the animal was blown from the boat and died with oxygen in its lungs, it would remain afloat. If it was alive and drowning and inhaled water, it would sink. Also, as Private Robinson indicated, the natural body heat of the animal, although dissipating rapidly in the cold water, provided some warmth to the person clinging to it. Dead or alive, the army horses and mules saved a few lives—and almost took a few as well.

Sergeant Peery enjoyed talking about Private Keeble's own encounter with a mule. "I saw Pleasant Keeble on a part of [the] wheelhouse fighting a mule. The mule would get its front feet on the raft and Pleas would knock it off with a club. It would come again. Several times the mule almost capsized the raft. I don't think I ever saw a more earnest fight. The mule finally gave up or was killed."[31]

Although it was no laughing matter at the time, Lieutenant Elliott recalled with some amusement another incident with a horse that took place on that dark morning. "There were . . . several men who were floating down the river on a log, when a horse that had been on the boat swam up and stuck his nose over the log. The boys nearest him took it to be an alligator, and rather than keep his company they let loose and gave him full possession."[32]

Whether they were clinging to a horse or mule, a barrel, a hay bale, or some other wreckage from the *Sultana*, there were now hundreds of people in the dark water being swiftly borne downstream toward Memphis. "The river, from the boat to Memphis, was full of struggling men and dead bodies," Private Gilbreath said.[33] It was only a matter of time before someone on the riverbank noticed.

19

THE RESCUES

It was fortunate that the disaster occurred close to a major city whose inhabitants had become accustomed to interacting peacefully with federal authorities. When the *Sultana* exploded, sending hundreds of men, women, and children into the swirling waters of the Mississippi, dozens of people around the Memphis area—Union personnel stationed in and around the city as well as citizens of Memphis and Arkansas—unhesitatingly rushed to their assistance.

One of the first rescuers on the scene was eighteen-year-old William Woodridge, who had taken a borrowed skiff up to his mother's livestock farm seven miles above Memphis, near where the *Sultana* exploded. Woodridge was sound asleep when the explosion occurred. "It sounded like a hundred earthquakes. The noise rolled and re-echoed for minutes in the woodlands." Woodridge, the overseer, Mr. Hill, and the owner of the small boat, William Boardman, rushed outside to the front porch. "Quite a distance out in the river we saw a steamer burning. . . . The flame was shooting far up into the sky when I first saw her. It was so bright in our front yard I could have picked up a pin," Woodridge said. "It was fortunate we had that skiff. Mr. Hill . . . and myself started out in it to save all we could. I did the best I could for a little fellow, helped guide the skiff and occasionally giving a lift to a struggling fellow who was fighting for his life." The rescuers took the living to dry land and built a fire to warm them. The dead they laid "across logs in the driftwood, so that they might be taken off below." Woodridge thought they plucked forty-five men from the water.[1]

While Woodridge and Hill were in the small skiff, the sidewheel steamboat *Bostona* (No. 2) was coming downriver from St. Louis on her first trip since owner John Watson had refurbished her. Her first mate, William B. Alvord Jr., spotted "the light of the fire of the Steamer *Sultana*" at around 3 a.m. "We were coming down the river. We discovered the light some five or six miles from where we found the wreck. . . . We first thought it a fire at Memphis." As the *Bostona* drew nearer, the crew realized that they were looking at a burning steamboat. "When we first discovered the boat it was completely in flames," continued Alvord, "and the river appeared almost black with persons. When we neared it, I think all the passengers who were saved at all had left the wreck."[2]

Ames Fisher, the *Bostona*'s first clerk, recalled that "the *Bostona* was run near the burning steamboat; we found that she was the *Sultana*; the water for a long distance all around her was as light as day, and thickly dotted with heads of human beings; we all set to work to try to save as many as we could." Immediately Captain Watson ordered the sounding yawl to be put out and then "directed that stageplank, tables, chairs, and anything that would be of assistance be thrown overboard. The entire crew, officers, and deck hands worked their utmost to save the drowning." A Mr. Deson, one of the passengers, "took one of the foot planks . . . and went out on it, and succeeded in saving the lives of no less than eight persons."[3]

"The *Bostona* first floated down with the current, and everybody on her tried to save the drowning men," Fisher said. "I myself took off several doors and shutters and threw them to persons in the water; a great deal of loose stuff was thrown overboard; when we could see a chance to save a man's life we threw him anything we could get hold of . . . as fast as we got the men out of the water we helped them into the cabin, gave them a glass of spirits and some hot coffee; we put some into the staterooms and others on the cabin floor; some were badly scalded and mangled."[4]

Private Rush recalled the approach of the *Bostona*. "She came about the time the last of the passengers were leaving the wreck . . . and rendered all the assistance possible, by throwing over hay, launching their yawls and life-boats, in which they carried a torch in the bow of the boat, and throwing ropes, and picking up such as came in their wake." Holding to some debris with one other soldier, Rush tried to maneuver toward the rescue boat. "A yawl came near us when I called for help, and a rope was thrown to me," Rush went on, "but as I reached with my right hand for the rope, my companion reached for me and got hold of my hair, which at the time was very long. He seized my hair with a grasp firm enough to pull me on my back and get me under water, but his hold soon relaxed, and as I came up the yawl passed out of sight, and I was again left in darkness and drifted along with the current of the river."[5]

Sergeant Karns was drifting in the light of the burning *Sultana*, clinging to the second large stageplank with several others, when they saw the lights of the approaching *Bostona*. "How eagerly we watched her lights as she glided down the river, and as she steamed on, a hundred or more voices could be heard up and down the river calling to her for help," Karns said. "Our cries from the gangplank mingled with the pleadings of the others until the last hope vanished as she moved on down the river, picking up only a few, if any, who came in her immediate course."[6]

In all, the crew and passengers on the *Bostona* rescued perhaps 100–150 people. "Our yawl made nine trips while we were floating downstream bringing at each trip from four to nine persons," Alvord proudly proclaimed. "We also used our lines in bringing persons to the boat. Cord wood was thrown over liberally, and it afforded much assistance. Many persons, perhaps fifty or sixty were brought in by the assistance of our lines." Among those rescued was the *Sultana*'s first mate, William Rowberry: "Myself and five others got hold of a plank and was picked up by the Steamer *Bostonia* [*sic*]."[7]

The men who were brought on board were given a stimulating drink of whiskey. "It sure tasted good after drinking a gallon of muddy Mississippi water," Private Norris remembered. Knowing that he had to get the injured ashore and spread the word of the disaster to Memphis, Captain Watson made the difficult decision to leave the scene of the disaster and continue downstream. "After she passed some distance she appeared to put on Steam and put on to Memphis," Rush said. Although he was one of those left behind, he later agreed that the *Bostona* "adopted the best plan to save men, as she kept the steam and picked up those who were being carried off by the current, while those who had made the shore and the timber were safe anyway."[8]

Nevertheless, those left behind were crushed when they saw the steamer heading downriver away from them. Private Hedrich had been sure that the *Bostona* would pick him up: "When I was nearly worn out a steamer came by picking up floating passengers so near that I thought of course she would take me on. But the wind was in the wrong direction. They couldn't hear me, and I gave myself up for lost." Sergeant Karns, who was also bypassed, "eagerly watched the steamer's lights as they disappeared down the river, and as the last glimmer vanished in the distance below, I heaved a sigh of sad disappointment, and thought to myself that all must be over soon. As the boat disappeared, so did our last hope and we became discouraged, so much so that we had ceased our efforts to steer our plank to a landing and were drifting along in darkness."[9]

Shortly after the *Bostona* left the scene, the little *Grey Eagle* miraculously appeared. The *Grey Eagle* and the steamboat *Home* had been lashed together towing a raft of barges packed with 1,200 horses. The two boats and the barges "were laying to above the mouth of Wolf river" when the *Sultana* exploded. Capt. James H. Ray of the *Grey Eagle* "immediately called to Captain [S. B.] Burdsal [of the *Home*], telling him that I proposed to let go [of the barges] and try to save some of the people, and he answered back, and said, 'I'll stay with the tows.'" Just about the time the *Grey Eagle* had built up enough steam to go to the rescue, the *Bostona* arrived at Memphis with her precious load.[10]

Many of the people on the *Sultana* had stripped off their clothing before jumping into the river and were completely naked when pulled from the water. The *Bostona*'s clerk remarked that when the rescued passengers were put ashore in Memphis, "they took with them a great deal of [the *Bostona's*] bedding, for covering, . . . they took sheets and comforts and blankets; and a great many of the badly scalded and bruised were carried ashore on mattresses."[11] It would take some time to get everybody off the *Bostona* safely, but while the crew was preparing the vessel for a return trip to the *Sultana*, the *Grey Eagle* was rushing upriver toward the scene of the disaster.

Pvt. James Stuart Cook (Co. C, 115th OH Inf) was clinging to a "little board" when the small steamboat arrived: "The scenes of my life were passing through my mind and I was about to give up all hope when I saw downstream a dim light; this gave me new courage. As it approached me I saw that it was a steamer, and as she neared me I shouted with all the strength of a drowning man for help. When they heard me they stopped and threw me a rope, by which I was helped on board." The crew "made me drink two horns of whiskey, about fifteen minutes apart. This is the only time that I felt that whiskey did me any good," Cook admitted.[12]

Just below the Memphis Navy Yard, near the mouth of the Wolf River, a watchman on one of the coal barges spotted a man in the dark water. John J. Barry, the checking clerk, recalled, "About 2 o'clock . . . the watchman on the fleet came down and woke me, and said there was a man drowning and had gone under the barges. A few minutes later he came back and said the whole river was full of men. I hurriedly dressed myself and went on deck." The thirty-five men who worked on the coal barges were alerted. "Pretty soon we had every skiff we could lay hands on out in the river. We worked all night and picked up 125 or 130 people. Some of them were alive and all right, some of them were half dead. Many were scalded terribly, and cries could be heard from all over the river. It was terrible."[13]

One of the first men to be rescued at Memphis was Pvt. Wesley Lee: "When I came in front of the wharf boat, two men came out with a lantern and I called for help. One of them jumped in a skiff and was soon by my side, took me in, and in a short time I was by a fire in the wharf boat, where I was given some clothing. . . . I informed them the *Sultana* had blown up and her crew was in the water."[14]

Almost immediately the bells on the docked steamboats pealed out the news, rousing the townspeople. Unable to set out immediately because their boilers lacked steam, the large steamboats sent out their small boats while they stoked the furnaces and hurried to bring the water in their boilers to a boil. Pvt. Fenton Andrew Hussey (Co. C, 5th IL Cav), one of those who aided in the rescue, wrote home that "the People immediately Lowered all the Small boats from the Steamboats and Set forth to help the Unfortunate the darkness hindered a great deal nevertheless the Search was Successful." The *Memphis Daily Bulletin* reported that "a yawl was immediately sent out from the *Marble City*, and in a few minutes seventeen persons were picked out of the water and brought ashore. Two were afterward found clinging to the wheel and they were also saved."[15]

Private Schmutz recalled his own approach to Memphis: "In due time I arrived in front of the city, and then I sent up such a cry that soon brought some small boats, in one of which I was taken, and landed on shore. I then realized that I had been terribly scalded." Suffering "the most excruciating pain," Schmutz "ran up and down in the cool air to relieve the pain. I felt easy going against the wind, but returning it was excruciating. I was urged to lie down, but for a time refused; finally I yielded after putting on a pair of cotton drawers and shirt. I laid down on a cot that had been prepared for me. Soon afterward an ambulance came and took me to Gayoso Hospital."[16]

Lieutenant Dixon was likewise rescued by a small boat from one of the steamers. "I drifted with the current and was floated back by the eddies, so that after five of the longest hours mortal ever spent, as it seemed to me, I found myself off Memphis, and would have passed on without knowing it had I not heard the voices of rescuers who had been picking up bodies and swimmers from the wreck. I called to them and they came out to me and hauled me in the boat, when I collapsed. I was practically dead from cold and numbness, and I am satisfied I could not have held out ten minutes longer."[17]

Docked at the Memphis Navy Yard near the mouth of the Wolf River, upriver from the coal barges and the city wharf, were three Union naval vessels: the tinclad *Grosbeak*, the timberclad *Tyler*, and the ironclad *Essex*. Acting Master's Mate William B. Floyd of the *Grosbeak* was perhaps the first among the three crews to realize that something had happened to the *Sultana*. Floyd had watched the heavily laden steamboat pass upriver. "Shortly after she passed out of sight behind one of the islands, I noticed a red glow in the sky, which very soon showed plainly as a fire. I cannot describe the horror I felt at the thought that perhaps it was the *Sultana* on fire."

Floyd took a telescope and watched the glow for a while. "I watched her closely and to steady my glass held it against a stanchion; I then discovered she drifted past the glass, which showed that she was floating and not lying in shore." Fearing the worst and beginning to hear the cries of people who had drifted downriver, Floyd ran across the deck shouting, "All hands on deck and away cutters, away! . . . in a very few minutes I was seated with six good oarsmen and a boy in the bow, and we were on our way out in the river in the direction of the cries for help." Finding a piece of wreckage holding twelve survivors, Floyd and his crew began rescuing the men. "One was missed and was floating by; at the risk of being pulled overboard, I leaned out as far as I could, and grabbed him by the hair of the head and pulled him in."[18]

The timberclad *Tyler* was the northernmost of the government vessels tied up at the Navy Yard and was therefore the "nearest of any vessel to the scene of the disaster." Acting Ensign William H. C. Michael recalled what he saw and heard: "At the time there was a dense fog and this, combined with the darkness . . . made it impossible to distinguish any object more than a few yards distant. Our boats were at once manned and my cutter was the first out. The wails, cries, and prayers for help could be heard distinctly all around us, but we could not see any one for a while. What an awful situation that was. Hundreds of dying men pleading for aid and we, ready and willing, unable to do a thing." Acting Master Charles Ackley said of the men's cries: "[O]f all the sounds and noises I ever heard that was the most sorrowful; some cursing, calling for help, and shrieking. I will never forget those awful sounds."[19]

As the fog lifted and the sky became lighter, Michael and his crew in Cutter 1 finally began pulling people from the river. In all, Cutter 1 rescued sixty-five people. "Of this number not one was free from severe bodily injuries or painful scalds," Michaels wrote. "One poor boy . . . was so badly scalded that the flesh came off when we pulled him over the gunwale of the boat." Among the number saved was one unnamed woman. "A woman was rescued who held on to a plank with one hand while she kept her babe above water with the other. The babe was dead, but the half-dead mother did not know the awful truth till hours after she was saved."[20]

The *Tyler* was undergoing repairs at the time, and much of the crew was ashore. Frances L. "Frannie" Ackley, who was visiting her husband, the executive officer, left her little baby in their cabin and followed her husband into Cutter 2, placing herself in the bow with a boat hook. Minutes later, while Ensign Michael watched from Cutter 1, Mrs. Ackley snagged the clothing of a man clinging to driftwood and drew him on board her cutter. "Bless your brave and devoted soul," Michael shouted, and his crew said aloud, "Amen!"[21]

One of the men Frannie Ackley rescued was Private Lahue, who was among the last to leave the *Sultana*. Lahue swam downriver and eventually climbed upon a log wedged against the top of a submerged tree. "I remained there until daylight," Lahue wrote. "A lady discovered me and pointed me out to the captain of a boat, saying that there was a little boy on a log, in the brush, out on the river. The lady and two of the crew came in a boat and rescued me, and placed me on board the gunboat and wrapped me in blankets." Mrs. Ackley reportedly "continued this hazardous work until the end of the tragedy, the boat in which she personally took part in the rescue saving between 40 and 50 men." Even afterward on shore she "took a place among those who were administering aid to the sick and continued this work for days thereafter." In 1902, Congress awarded Frances L. Ackley a private pension of $20 per month for her actions.[22]

On the ironclad *Essex*, Lt. James H. Berry was awakened by a call from the night watchman informing him that the *Sultana* had exploded and the water was full of drowning men. "I ordered all the boats manned," Berry reported, "which was done immediately, and I went in the cutter, which was the first ready, and we went out to the middle of the river. The morning was very dark, it being about one hour before daylight and the weather overcast, and the shrieks of the wounded and drowning men was the only guide we had."[23]

A petty officer on board the *Essex* recalled what happened next.

> The shrill pipe of the boatswain's whistle sounded through the ship, accompanied by the hoarse call: "Turn out all hands!" "Man the boats!" and before I could get on deck, all the boats had been manned, and shot out in the murky darkness, it being impossible to see anything a cable's length ahead; but a more appalling scene can hardly be conceived. The river seemed to be alive with drowning men, some praying for assistance, some cursing the fate which, after a day or two of liberty, had condemned them to a horrible death, others shrieking aloud in agony, while ever and anon you could hear the last gulp of some miserable wretch as he screaming for assistance, sank to rise no more.[24]

Coxswain Thomas G. Love was in one of the *Essex*'s small boats. "All that day we found men almost dead, hanging to the trees about two miles out into the river," Love said, "and among those that I rescued was one man so badly scalded that when I took hold of his arms to help him into the boat the skin and flesh came off his arms like a cooked beet. I lost my hold on him but soon caught him again, and with help he was got into the boat and saved from a watery grave." Love's boat was credited with rescuing seventy-six people.[25]

"When all our boats were gone except the market boat, called the 'dingey,' our six messenger boys took it and saved the only woman that was saved who was on board the *Sultana*," Love added. The petty officer in command of the market boat reported: "I saw floating toward us what was evidently the head of a lady just above the water; all the support she had was a side casing to a stateroom door. As she came up to the bow of the boat, I seized her and drew her aboard; she murmured a faint 'My God, is that you!' and immediately became insensible. She was so benumbed with cold that her form was perfectly rigid; the sailors immediately proffered round jackets and overshirts, in which I wrapped her, until we could pull ashore and deliver her to the good Sisters of Charity." The unnamed woman may have been Ann Annis, who was rescued near Memphis "about five o'clock in the morning . . . [by] a party in a passing boat."[26]

Private Safford was one of the men the *Essex*'s small boats rescued. Just after the explosion, Captain Elliott had run into Safford inside the shattered main saloon: "I met young Safford, whose father had joined us at Vicksburg as a Sanitary Commissioner. The father's arms were both badly scalded, and he was otherwise injured. The son put two life-preservers on his father and one on himself, and they hastily got upon a stateroom door in the water. A horse, leaping from the boat, struck the door, knocking father and son off and separating them." Private Safford confirmed, "We were separated the instant we touched the water. I was [eventually] picked up by a rowboat from the gunboat *Essex*."[27]

Lieutenant Berry's Cutter 1 had been picking up soldiers and drifting with the current when they plucked Private Horn and a handful of others from some wreckage. Horn later recalled the rescue:

> [We] floated down the river, passing the city of Memphis. . . . It was now just before daybreak and the darkness was terrible. Nevertheless, we sounded the loudest possible alarm, which was heard by men in a gunboat lying near and we were picked up by a skiff. As we were helped into the skiff, I saw my bunkmate, Joe McKelvey [Pvt. Joseph M. McKelvey (Co. C, 102nd OH Inf)], for the first time since the explosion, although he had been clinging to the same bit of wreckage as I had. As I got into the skiff McKelvey recognized me and said, "For God's sake help me in." I asked him if he were hurt and he said, "Yes, scalded from head to foot."[28]

Eventually, Lieutenant Berry's cutter drifted south of Memphis opposite Fort Pickering, the Union fortification guarding the downriver approach to the city and manned by the 3rd U.S. Colored Heavy Artillery. The guards had orders to fire on any boat that did not heed the call to pull into shore and be identified. When a sentry noticed a few boats out on the river in the early morning fog, he instantly hailed them. When no reply came from the boat crews, who were preoccupied with rescuing *Sultana* victims, the sentry fired a warning shot at the boats. Private Horn remembered the incident. "We started up the river toward Memphis and when crossing the river to the Arkansas side we were fired on by some negro guards, Union men who thought we were Confederates." Lieutenant Berry went ashore and confronted the guard. Telling him that he was in the act of rescuing drowning individuals from the *Sultana*, Berry explained that he had not heard the call to come ashore. Berry set out again and had reached the middle of the river when "another shot was fired from the fort and came whistling over our heads." When Berry went ashore this time, he was furious.[29]

Berry confronted Lt. Daniel P. Yates, the white officer in charge of the Black sentries. Understandably irritated, Berry asked Yates why he had been fired upon a second time. Could he not hear the cries of the men in the water? Yates likewise grew angry and said "that his orders were to fire on all skiffs." In language Yates would later describe as "discourteous," Berry countered that the boats "were not skiffs; that they were [a] man-of-war's gig and cutter." The two men nearly came to blows before Berry got back into the cutter and returned to rescuing the *Sultana* victims.[30]

According to Yates, however, the garrison at Fort Pickering "rendered instantly such assistance as we could for the poor sufferers." He had "a good fire" built and "ordered coffee made, then gave them all the whiskey and blankets happening to be on hand." Private Gilbreath and a soldier from Michigan were among those brought ashore at Fort Pickering, "numbed by the cold and exposure" and barely able to walk. Gilbreath added, "Our rescuers took us up the steep bank of the river into the Fort and gave each of us a half pint of whiskey, supplied us with breakfast and lent us clothing." Another rescued soldier, Private Ray, "was nearly chilled to death, and was carried up to the barracks. Here I was placed in front of a roaring hot fire and given enough alcohol to kill three men in a common condition." An estimated one hundred men were brought ashore at Fort Pickering.[31]

As strange as it seems, the guards at Fort Pickering were not the only sentries firing on the *Sultana* victims. Before he reached even Memphis, Corporal Horner was shot at by guards above the city. "We floated gently and peacefully along until we came to where the city guards were stationed, [and] they fired upon us not knowing what was the matter. Soon we arrived in sight of the city lights." While Horner managed to avoid the guards, Pvt. Truman Smith did not. He and an unnamed comrade

> kept swimming till near daylight, when someone cried "Halt!" We swam toward shore and as we came closer the command to "Halt," was repeated. I replied that we could not as we were in the water. Finally we got to shore and we were told to get out, but my limbs were so benumbed that I could not. The man came to the water's edge, took me by the arm and pulled me ashore, but I could not stand on my feet. He called his comrade who was in a tent and they together picked me up and put me in their bed, and then went back and rescued my comrade. They built a fire and rubbed us and gave us some clothes. After awhile we saw a boat coming up the river and we hailed it.[32]

Private Eldridge ended up before a roaring fire as well, but only after he had floated past Memphis. He and two others had clung to a ladder blown off the *Sultana* as they watched the lights of Memphis pass by.

> We drifted on four miles farther down the river where there was a farmer living near the river, who had a good skiff. It was then about seven o'clock. He had heard the cries for help and he got into his skiff and took fifteen of us to the river bank. I didn't know anything more, they said when they pulled me in the skiff and lay me on the bottom of the boat I lay perfectly still like I was dead. They thought I was dead, and when we got to shore my two comrades carried me out on shore one taking me by the hands and the other by my feet, they said while they were carrying me they could feel my nerves quivering and jerking and when they layed me down they saw I was not dead so they made a big fire and warmed me up.

Eldridge's unnamed rescuer clothed him in a Confederate officer's jacket while his two comrades began rubbing his arms and chest to "start blood circulating." After two hours, Eldridge finally regained consciousness. "I remember that when I saw the fire I was so cold that I tried to crawl right into it. But the boys held me back. I told them to let me go, that I was freezing. Along after a while when I came to realize a little more I noticed that I had a Rebel officer's uniform on, well it made me so mad I wanted to pull them off right then, but they laughed at me and said I would have to let them alone until I could get some more, that my clothes had been lost in the river." Years later, Eldridge felt differently about his rescuer. "I don't care if that man had been an officer in the Rebel army he was a good man and did all he could for us. I have wished many times I could have met him and thanked him for his kindness to me."[33]

Farther downriver around President's Island (Island No. 46), James M. Safford Sr. was rescued by a group of African Americans after he had floated twelve miles. Private Keeble, having successfully fought off the pesky mule, was another person that group rescued: "As we came to a bend in the river we were over near the shore. In the half-darkness we could see a negro running along the bank with a pole. He told us to try to get as near the shore as possible, because the water was swifter around the bend. Then he waded in up to his neck and reached out for us with a long pole, something like a hook. We took hold of the pole and he swung us into the shore. He saved our lives."[34]

Sergeant Talkington may have floated the farthest:

> About twelve miles below Memphis I floated nearer the shore. There was an army post at a small town there. I began to cry for help. Someone heard me and answered back. We called to each other several times, then I heard someone throw an oar into a rowboat. I thought at the time that was the best sound I had ever heard. I guided them by shouting and in a few minutes my rescuers caught up with me. They hauled me into the boat and landed me safely in the little town I had just passed among Union soldiers and friends.[35]

Meanwhile, back in Memphis, dozens of people were rushing down to the cobblestone wharf in response to the ringing bells.

Forty-eight-year-old Eliza "Aunt Lizzie" Aiken, a nurse at Adams Hospital at the southwest corner of Adams and Second Street, heard the bells and ran through the nurses' ward calling for the other nurses to "dress as quickly as possible, for something fearful was coming." As she reached the front door of the hospital, "news ran through the halls that the *Sultana* had exploded, some distance up the river, and that the stream was full of drowned and drowning men." She hurried down to the riverbank "in company with half the inhabitants of the city."

"The whole river was alive with human beings, scalded and drowning," Aunt Lizzie remembered; "hundreds were hanging to pieces of timber, the banks were strewn for miles with the dead, and from the whole struggling, suffering mass went up a heart-rending cry that froze the blood of those who heard it." She had those still alive carried to the city's hospitals. After seeing the terrible injuries the passengers had suffered, she returned to Adams Hospital to prepare "liniment for the burned."[36]

One of the soldiers taken to Adams Hospital was Corporal Winters. "I was furnished a pair of drawers, placed in an ambulance, and taken to Adams general hospital. Here I was furnished dry hospital clothes, and given a cot. . . . I was slightly scalded on face, neck, hands, feet and left arm." Sergeant Fies "was placed in a ward with quite a number who were severely scalded, or otherwise badly injured, and such misery and intense suffering as I witnessed while there is beyond my power to describe. The agonizing cries and groans of the burned and scalded were heartrending and almost unendurable." Private McKelvey, who was "scalded from head to foot" in the explosion, was taken to Adams Hospital as well but died before the day was through.[37] In all, about 176 people were treated at Adams Hospital.

Equally as active as Aunt Lizzie on the cobblestone waterfront was Dr. Bernard J. D. Irwin, medical director and superintendent of U.S. hospitals in Memphis. When he got word of the disaster, Dr. Irwin ordered all "ambulances and medical attendants" to the river. When he reached the waterfront and learned that victims were scattered up and down the bank, Irwin ordered that all—living and dead—were to be "collected and brought to the landing." Dr. Irwin had the injured rushed off to hospitals and the dead laid out on the cobblestones.[38]

Gayoso Hospital, near Main and Gayoso Street, was the destination for some of the survivors. Army nurse Margaret Meseroll Hays from Mendota, Illinois, was appalled at the former prisoners' condition: "The poor fellows were so emaciated and weak." Ann Annis was rescued opposite Memphis and taken to Gayoso Hospital, as was Pvt. Jason M. Elliott (Co. F, 3rd TN Cav). Elliott's friend Pvt. Robert N. Hamilton (Co. F, 3rd TN Cav) wrote, "He was scalded all over and unable to help himself, but was perfectly composed and bore his sufferings with great fortitude. He had his army badge which he requested me give to his parents. He died that night at Gayoso Hospital, Memphis, Tenn."[39] Gayoso would handle 103 *Sultana* victims.

Private Walker was taken to Washington Hospital, only a block north of Gayoso, near Union and Main. Walker was completely naked when his rescuers pulled him from the water. "Nearly every hack in the city was there to meet us," he recalled, "but as most of us had no clothing, we had to remain on board until some was supplied us. The best we could do to make a presentable appearance was to attire ourselves in white drawers and undershirts brought by the Christian Commission. With nothing on but these garments I took a seat beside the driver on top of the hack and was driven through the city to Washington Hospital." Cpl. Thomas Dunn Moore (Co. F, 50th OH Inf) sent a letter home from Washington Hospital on the day of the disaster: "My hands are both badly scalded, so a delegate of the Christian Commission writes this. My feet also much burned, especially my left foot. I was walking on hot coals and was thrown up by the explosion."[40] Washington Hospital treated 143 people from the *Sultana*.

The last of the major hospitals to get a large number of *Sultana* survivors was Overton Hospital at the southeast corner of Poplar and Main. Private Foglesang was helped into a waiting hack by two Memphis women after he came ashore. "They took me to the Overton hospital," he remarked, "and as I went into a ward . . . [it] was quite filled with the boys that were on the boat, some of them nearly dead and dying with the injuries received from the exposure."[41]

Sergeant Karns was rescued by the small steamboat *Jenny Lind*.

> I knew nothing more until aroused at Memphis by one of the
> crew. I was told to get off and we would be taken to the hos-
> pitals. As I walked out on the cabin deck I saw multitudes of
> people; men, women and children of all classes had gathered
> to see the few remaining survivors of the ill-fated *Sultana*.
>
> As we marched out in single file through the surging
> throng of people brushing elbows with some of the finest
> dressed people of Memphis, I was somewhat overcome.
> I could not tell whether it was my destitute condition or
> whether it was for joy, but unable to restrain my emotions
> longer, I put my hands to my face and wept like a school
> boy. However, my condition was much better than many
> of my comrades as quite a number were without a stitch of
> clothing and had to be wrapped in sheets and blankets.
>
> As we reached the top of the hill we were put in ambu-
> lances and carriages and taken to various hospitals and other
> institutions. I was taken to the Overton Hospital, where we
> received the best of treatment, not only by the medical fra-
> ternity but by the nurses and attendants as well.[42]

Other survivors shared their own memories. Sixteen-year-old
Private McFarland, who had teased the drunken "seven-footer" from
Tennessee on the hurricane deck before the boat left Memphis, came
across the same man in the water. "A guilty conscience needs no accuser,"
McFarland said, "and I supposed he would drown me if he caught me.
I began swimming away from him." Captain Friesner encountered the
tall Tennessean in memorable fashion: He was "a powerful man, whose
massive, naked chest stood out of the water nearly to the waist. His
eyes shone with excited brilliancy and his actions were uncanny, as with
no apparent malice or purpose he would move up to a swimmer who
seemed to be making his escape and strike him under. If two struggled
and parted, he would strike both. He seemed to enjoy his powerful
deeds as amusements. I have no doubt that he was insane."[43]

McFarland was eventually rescued by a yawl from the steamboat
Silver Spray. To his horror, "the next person the yawl approached

was my long Tennessee friend, who was comfortably seated on a log." Unbelievably, the man was still roaring drunk. McFarland continued,

> He asked how far it was to Memphis, and when told only a mile, he said to the crew, "Go to hell with your boat; if you couldn't come to help me before now you had better have stayed away," and with that he slid from his log and began swimming down the river. When the survivors arrived at Memphis that morning, all the hacks and omnibuses in the city were at the wharf to convey us to the Overton Hospital. The seven-foot Tennessean had arrived at the landing . . . still under the influence of liquor. . . . They tried to force him into a hack, but in the shuffle two or three soldiers were knocked down. A guard was detailed to march him through the streets to the hospital. On the way up we passed through a street inhabited mostly by Jews, who kept second-hand clothing establishments, etc., and as the hack in which I was riding was slowly passing along the street I could see that long Tennessean pulling off boots, shoes, hats, caps, and other articles from the signs hanging in front, and by the time he reached the hospital he had about a dozen Jews at his heels clamoring for their wares. . . . The Tennessean turned, and, glaring at the crowd, threw the lot at his feet, saying, "There, help yourselves," and as they rushed forward and stooped over the pile he began to knock them right and left.[44]

Overton Hospital handled ninety *Sultana* victims.

The Officers' Hospital, at the southeast corner of Front Street and Court, was strictly for officers, so only six survivors were sent there. Lieutenant Dixon was among them: "I was very poorly for several days and could not stand on my legs. I spit blood from being injured in my chest and swallowing so much water." Captain Friesner of the guard unit was likewise "taken to the Officers Hospital . . . and my wounds treated by the U.S. Surgeon in charge. Being exposed in the water so long I contracted a deep cold and my wounds were slow to heal. I remained in the Hospital until about the 13th of June."[45]

At least 260 soldiers were taken to the U.S. Sanitary Commission Soldiers' Home near the waterfront. Pvt. George H. Young (Co. A, 95th OH Inf) remembered being taken to "the Soldiers' Lodge on the river's bank. I stayed with them for a few days, nursing my burned arm and keeping quiet. For many days and nights I was so nervous that I could not sleep, and when any of the boats were near and puffing, I shook as if seized with an ague. Night after night would I jump up on hearing any noise, and I had to change my sleeping-place from a bunk to a cot, for I had bumped my head till it was sore." Cpl. Albert P. Varnell (Co. I, 3rd TN Cav) was also taken to the Soldiers' Home. "While there I was unconscious two or three days, and when I came to myself I found that the left side of my face was scalded so as to put out my eye, or nearly so."[46]

Private Walker ended up at the Soldiers' Home as well. When he came ashore, slightly scalded, he was given a pair of drawers and an undershirt by the Sanitary Commission and taken to Washington Hospital. He "remained there but a short time, however, as an officer called for volunteers to go to the Soldiers' Home in order to make room in the hospital for the more seriously injured. Since my injuries were not of a serious nature, I volunteered to go; and again seated on top of a cab with no clothing but the white drawers and undershirt, I was driven through the city to the Home." Corporal Elder showed up at the Soldiers' Home in strange attire. He was completely naked when taken on board a rescue vessel. He searched around and "found an old pair of knee pants belonging at one time to a boy, but which was being used by the engineer to clean off his machinery. I asked his permission to put them on, so when we arrived at Memphis, I had to go through the streets wearing nothing but the knee pants. A red shirt was given me by the sanitary commission, and with that on my arm, I started to the soldiers' home. I must have aroused the sympathy of a man, for he called me into his store and gave me a pair of trousers, canvas shoes, and a hat. That with my red shirt completed my costume."[47]

Among the citizens of Memphis who aided in the rescue was young Richard F. Hostin, who helped three other boys carry a man to Adams Hospital. "The poor fellow was in a dreadful condition, with both legs broken above the ankle and the bones protruding through the flesh." The "poor fellow" was civilian passenger Daniel McLeod, the man Captain Elliott had carried from the main saloon and thrown overboard at McLeod's request. McLeod had "floated down the river about two miles and lodged in the brush on Cheek's Island, above Memphis." Captain Elliott, already on board the *Jenny Lind*, recalled McLeod's rescue. "Just after boarding this boat, I saw a 'dugout,' paddled by a citizen, coming out of the woods, and in the bottom there lay McLoyd [McLeod], I helped lift him on board and lay him on deck and gave him a tumbler of whiskey." In his own account, McLeod wrote, "In the morning I was picked up and taken to Memphis and placed in Adam's Hospital [where the surgeon told me] it was no use trying to save my right leg as it was in such a condition from the previous wound [at Shiloh] that it would be practically impossible to save it and that he would have to cut it off above the old wound. This he did and set the broken bones of the other leg, and soon both were healed."[48]

In addition to the hundreds of injured, exhausted, and chilled individuals who were rushed to the hospitals and the Soldiers' Home, the recovered bodies of the dead, per Dr. Irwin's instructions, were collected together at one spot on the wharf. Coffins for them were brought from all over the city. After the coffins ran out, the bodies were lined up side by side and covered with blankets. When he got off the *Jenny Lind*, Captain Elliott met Private Safford and discovered that he had been separated from his father after leaving the wreck. "Together he and I opened more than a hundred coffins on the wharf, hoping to have the satisfaction of giving him a burial," recalled Elliott. Private Safford learned the next day that his father had been rescued near President's Island, and father and son were soon reunited.[49]

Pvt. Samuel Pickens, who was on the *Sultana* with his older brother William (Pvt. William Cowan Pickens, Co. B, 3rd TN Cav), also searched among the dead. The day after his rescue, Samuel wrote home, "i must Con fess tha to the best of mi noledg brother William is A mong the lost. i hav not hurd of him Sens the explosion took plase an i hav no hop of ever hering of him eney more."[50] Such letters went home to hundreds of families.

20

THE
LONG-AWAITED
DAYBREAK

Although the burned-out remains of Hopefield, Arkansas, across the river from Memphis were underwater, the small collection of buildings known as Mound City, five miles above Memphis on the Arkansas side, were high and dry.[1] The town's few residents had all the reason in the world to hate Union soldiers. On the night of January 16, 1863, Union authorities had burned a number of structures in the town as punishment after saboteurs burned two steamboats there.[2] In spite of that, the citizens did not hesitate to come to the aid of the *Sultana* victims.

Seven-year-old Louis Perkins Berry was sound asleep when shouts from his father, Sheriff James Garrett Berry, woke him. Louis' account is one of the best we have of what the people ashore witnessed in the aftermath of the *Sultana* explosion. "[M]y father awakened to find the whole premises lightened to almost the brightness of midday. Going out, he called back to my mother that a steamboat was afire up the river and a thousand people were drowning." Louis and his mother,

Mary Susan Berry, quickly dressed. The family went down "to the bank of the river, which was lighted, as it seemed to me for miles in all directions, [and] we saw, about a mile up the river, the burning boat." The twin paddlewheel housings had fallen away and the *Sultana* had turned completely around by the time the Berrys saw her. They watched as the fire broke through the firebreak formed by the fallen deck. "The flames were leaping and plunging and breaking like the waves of the ocean. We could see what looked like hundreds of men on the main deck for'd, and as the flames, wafted by the morning breeze, reached forward, those near the flames would push away, forcing those in front to either fall or jump into the water, and I saw numbers of men either crowded off or pushed into the river."

As the sun began to rise, Louis saw that the submerged trees along the riverbanks were crowded with survivors. "My father, a discharged Confederate soldier, and Capt. George Malone . . . rescued more than 100, for whom a cousin and I built fires to warm and dry as they came out of the water. Our cook brought a big boiler of coffee and everyone did what he or she could to relieve the suffering."[3]

Franklin H. Barton, formerly a soldier in the Confederate 23rd Arkansas Cavalry, also lived near Mound City. When he heard the cries of the *Sultana* victims, he put on his Confederate jacket and raced to get the dugout canoe that he had hidden from the *Pocahontas* crew. Barton began snagging survivors from the treetops. Among them was Corporal Atchley, who remembered that "a confederate soldier . . . came to my relief, and took me to a house nearby, and gave me something to eat, and I felt something like myself again. . . . The said confederate soldier worked hard to save the lives of the drowning men, and brought to shore in his little dugout about fifteen of them."[4]

Also among those Barton brought out of the treetops were Private Young and a comrade who had clung to a log throughout the dark night. "In all directions we could hear the sounds of struggling and shouting human beings," Young later said. Eventually they heard the voice of Frank Barton calling to them. Young continued,

> With his canoe it was difficult for him to come to us, through the dense brush, so he directed us to come to him.

Following his directions we waded toward him, at one place
falling completely under water, but a few minutes after
we were oh, how thankful our hearts, how cheering the
thought! in his canoe. . . . [W]ith a long pole he pushed
through the shallow water to the cabin of which he had
spoken, but by the time we arrived there we were so stiff
from the cold and long continued bath that we could only
get out of the canoe by his assistance. [W]e passed into
the cabin, where we found two ladies sitting on a "trussel,"
two soldiers, badly scalded and burned, lying on a bed, and
two others, somewhat injured, lying on the floor. The men
on the bed were in dreadful agony, and could not repress
their groans, as the wind would at times blow through the
cracks between the logs on their writhing bodies. One of
the ladies was scantily dressed, and, like all others who had
any clothing, hers was dripping with water. The little room
gave some evidence of being used for a shelter, so I looked
about hoping to find some cloth of any kind to put on my
scalded arm. On looking into a barrel I discovered some
flour, and asked if I could have a little to cover over my
burns. No one seemed to have any ownership in the flour,
but several of those present spoke up at once and urged me
to take what I might want. I did so, covering the burned
parts thickly with flour, and in a few minutes my suffering
from that source was much diminished.[5]

One of the women inside was undoubtedly Jennie Perry. Corporal
King, who had aided her in the water, recalled that they were taken to
a "shanty nearby where quilts and blankets were thrown over us and
we were placed in front of a fire. Several others were brought in soon
after." When Mrs. Perry had warmed up a little, King said, "she drew
a ring from her finger, handed it to me saying that all the valuables she
had with her on the *Sultana* were lost excepting that ring and it was all
she could at the time offer me as a token of reward."[6]

Eventually, Private Young stepped out onto the porch and "found
two or three new arrivals, one of whom was a one-armed comrade

who was entirely naked, poor from a long prison life, and shivering in the wind." The one-armed man was Private Hamblin, who recalled, "I never was as cold in all my life; I shook until I thought I would shake their shanty down." Private Young gave Hamblin his "drawers, and then he was willing to go into the cabin into the presence of the ladies, from whose sight he had before shrunk."[7]

While Frank Barton, the Berrys, and others were plucking survivors from the swirling waters, the burning hulk of the *Sultana* continued to drift downstream in the strong current. The flames had consumed most of the superstructure above the main deck. The hundreds of people who had taken refuge on the bow before the *Sultana* had turned completely around had been forced into the water. Once the bow was clear and the flames seemed to die down, a few stalwart individuals climbed back on board the burning hulk.

The first person back on board was Sergeant Peery:

> I climbed up on the boat [and] found a space on the bow of the boat that had not been burned. The rest of the boat had burned down except the large timbers which were still burning, but soon burned down to the hull of the boat and continued to burn. The fire was so hot it caused me to turn around and around. I picked up a pair of pants and put them on to help protect me from the heat of the fire [which] affected me, so for a little while I was very weak. I soon recovered but was on the boat alone. There were two spars or long mast poles lying with one end on the boat and the other end in the river, just to the left side of the boat not far from the bow. Two men in the river who saw me on the boat climbed the spars and got onto the boat and now we began to work. The floor was covered with clothing that had been carried there. . . . We threw the clothing into the river, for it was catching fire.[8]

Following a few others who climbed up one of the spars was Private Hamilton: "Seeing several of the boys had got back on the bow of the boat, I swam to where one of the spars was lying with one end in the water and the other end on the bow of the wreck. I climbed it and got back on the bow." Also getting back on board was Pvt. Thomas Pangle (Co. K, 3rd TN Cav), who recalled that the men immediately began "throwing water on the burning coal, etc."[9]

"When the clothes were all thrown off," Sergeant Peery wrote, "the other men pulled up several men by letting down ropes to men in the river. I helped them and we pulled up a good many. Some were so weak we would double the rope and get them to place the rope under their arms, and in that way we pulled them up." Two of the men pulled up in this fashion were Farrier Thrasher and his friend Private Rhodes, who had hung below the bow "until the cabin burned down." The men on the bow "threw down a rope which we put under our arms and they drew us up to the hull of the burning steamer," Thrasher wrote. "After all were back on the hull we went to work and put out the fire, so that it would not sink so quickly."[10]

Twenty-six-year-old William Durkan, an Irish-born deckhand on the *Sultana*, was another man helped up onto the bow. A Memphis newspaper reported that he was "terribly burnt in the hands and face, and had a horrid gash on the face, the nose being completely severed." Private Hamilton added, "His nose was torn off, all except a small particle of skin."[11]

Private Patterson was floating nearby when he "observed men drawing their fellow victims out of the water by means of ropes. Availing myself of this opportunity, I grasped one of these with a death-like grip, but feeling my utter exhaustion, I put my arms through the noose of the rope and was thus drawn up into the portion of the boat which had not yet sunk."

Corporal Fast had floated downriver and lodged in what he took to be some partially submerged brush, bewildered that he could not touch the bottom. Finally, he realized that he was not in bushes at all: "Looking about me, I noticed that there was as much as from forty to sixty acres of water surface covered with small bushes and twigs, and these were but the tops of small cottonwood and willow trees, whose roots were from ten to twenty feet below the surface of the water." Eventually, Fast spotted the still-burning hull of the *Sultana*.

About a quarter of a mile down the river, I saw the hull of the vessel, the upper decks all burned off, slowly turning round and round in an eddy. I made my way from bush to bush down to it. On it were several men. The only way of making our way from the water to the top of the hull . . . was by a rope and a chain let down by the boys already on the craft. . . . It was about sunrise, I think, when I made my first trial, and perhaps half-past seven when I got on the boat. This remnant of the boat was then about three fourths of a mile from the Arkansas shore, and from two to four miles from the Tennessee shore, and I think about five miles from Memphis. On the remnant of the boat was from two to three feet of debris coal, wood, etc. all afire and alive with intense heat, save and except about twenty feet of the floor nearest the prow.[12]

When Fast got back on board the *Sultana*, "there was about twenty-five persons on it, about twenty of whom were able-bodied, the balance scalded or maimed. We pulled up out of the water about twelve more, making in all thirty-seven, I think, who linked their fortunes, for the time, to the burning boat in its last struggle."[13]

The burning hull eventually floated into the submerged trees at the head of Hen Island (Island No. 41) of Paddy's Hen and Chicken Islands (Nos. 41–45). Sergeant Peery recalled that "[t]he boat was floating down the river and passing an island" when deckhand Durkan "told us if we would tie the cable rope to the timber, we could pull the boat and draw it and cause it to swing around on the timber." While the men were working at securing the boat, they spotted Sgt. Michael J. Owens (Co. I, 13th IN Cav) and Pvt. Riley Moore (Co. D, 7th KY Cav) floating nearby. "We called to them to come and get the cable rope and take it to the timber." Corporal Fast "threw Owens a small rope. I tied to this a big rope, and Owens pulled up to the island of brush, hauled the big rope out, and tied it to the limb of a fallen tree."[14]

Following Durkan's instructions, the men began winching the boat toward shore. "We would pull and wrap around a post, and pull and wrap, and kept working," Peery said. "We saw it was drifting toward timber, but at last the boat stopped and [Durkan] said it had struck land or something and I don't think it moved any further. But I think the bow of the boat rested on land and kept the boat from sinking sooner." The hull had come to rest at the head of Hen Island, close to Fogleman's Landing near the opening of the Mound City Chute, a narrow passage that ran past Mound City before flowing back into the Mississippi. John Fogleman lived nearby. "[T]he burning mass of what had been the fine steamer *Sultana*, floated slowly down with the current until within a few hundred yards of Mr. Fogleman's residence," the *Memphis Argus* reported, "when it grounded on the Arkansas shore."[15]

John Fogleman owned approximately two thousand acres and a plantation house near Mound City. "On being aroused by the noise and seeing the burning steamer, he hastily constructed a rude raft" and went to rescue the men on the bow. Since the crew of the *Pocahontas* had destroyed all the small boats they could find along the Arkansas shore, Fogleman and his sons Dallas (20) and Leroy (17) used the material at hand to construct the raft. Corporal Fast described it as "two hewn logs lashed together. The logs were about one foot square and ten or twelve feet long."[16]

Fogleman "came within about six rods of us and our burning boat," Fast said, "and then stopped for a parley. He said that he could carry only six of us, and if more got on we would all drown. He was afraid to come nearer lest all should leap overboard and get on to his logs. The crisis was getting desperate. Finally, a comrade, whom I called all the morning 'Indiana,' and myself stepped to the edge of the burning hull, and declared in the most solemn manner that if he would approach we would not get on his logs, and would not permit over six persons to get on." Assured that he would not be overwhelmed, Fogleman pushed closer to the bow of the burning boat.[17]

Private Davenport was among the first to get on the raft. "We . . . started for the shore but there was a large sickmore tree standing sum little distance from us. We told our frends two take us to the tree and we could get on the limes [limbs] and sta until tha could get the rest away from the burning boat and so we puld our little bark to the tree we all got on the tree verey easey as the watter was among the limes." Corporal Fast confirmed Davenport's account: Fogleman "approached, six got on, he took them about half-way to the Arkansas shore, and they climbed some trees, the branches of which was above the water, most of their trunks beneath. He came and went several times, always taking six, and leaving them in the tree-tops."[18]

"By this time the floor was getting hot," Sergeant Peery wrote. "I had seen a man and his two sons come and get men on a log and push the log before them and take one or two out at a time. I heard the boat crack several times and I saw it was breaking in two and the ends settling down." Figuring that they would have to do something to save themselves while they waited for Fogleman to take them all away, Peery and some of the others

> pushed the two spars or mast poles off the boat and one man got down and got on the end farthest from the boat. I swung down and let loose of the boat and dropped down on the poles. They started to turn and it was all the other man at the end could do to get them stopped. It looked as if they would drown me. I finally got up on the poles and one of the citizens came along and pushed us up on a log and now the men on the bow of the boat threw us down some small ropes and we tied all three together. Then the men on the boat got down on our raft. I don't know how many there were, somewhere between twelve and twenty.

Fogleman had been taking small groups of men to the treetops during this time, but finally, Fast said,

> he said, the men were too much exhausted, and it took too long to climb a tree, so he began taking the remainder to shore, the men always paddling with their hands and feet so as to speed the trip. All this took time, and more desperate became the chances of those of us still on the burning hull. After a while the floor . . . burned through at a place near the rear. Then the flames swept clean through under us and up through the large hole near the prow, which operated

like a chimney. So it was fire on both sides and under our feet. We feared our fate must be death by burning, yet we hung blankets and blouses about us, dipped up water with our quart coffee-cups, with ropes attached, and poured over our heads, keeping the clothing and blankets on us saturated. We fought the fire and still hoped to get the last man off before she sank or burned completely.[19]

There were still thirteen men on the bow when Fogleman returned with his log raft. Knowing that seven men would have to go this time or the next, Corporal Fast helped six men onto the raft and then jumped on himself. "We landed, the raft went back, [and] got the other six off almost overcome with heat and smoke. The raft had got only about six rods from the burning hull when it sank, leaving nothing but the jack-staff sticking above water to mark where she went down."[20]

Farrier Thrasher wrote that he "and one of the 3rd Tennessee Cavalry were the last to leave the boat, and had not been off the hull but a short time when it went down." Pvt. Michael Dougherty (Co. M, 13th PA Cav), the only soldier from Pennsylvania on the *Sultana*, watched the death of the steamboat from the Arkansas shore: "Before they landed the last man, the hull of the '*Sultana*' went down, its hot iron sending the hissing water and steam to an enormous height." The *Memphis Daily Bulletin* reported that the *Sultana* sank in "twenty-six feet of water."[21]

John Fogleman had been aided in his efforts not only by his sons Dallas and Leroy but also by his wife, Sarah, and his younger children Frances K. "Fannie" (15) and Gustavus "Gus" (12). The Foglemans used their home as "a temporary hospital for the sufferers, and every possible care and attention were bestowed upon them by Mr. Fogleman's family."[22]

Sergeant Peery was one of those at the Foglemans' house. Among the other *Sultana* passengers he saw there was Sgt. Lewis Milton Kidd (Co. A, 3rd TN Cav). "He had been holding onto a cable rope all the time, the same rope that saved my life," Peery said. "He was nearly drowned. I gave him some tobacco I found in the pants I put on. They also brought out a girl; she had on a life preserver [Elizabeth "Lizzie" Spikes]. She was dead. She looked as if she was asleep. Her brother [DeWitt Clinton Spikes] got out with us. He cried." Private Hamilton also witnessed the grief of young Spikes: "The men that rescued us brought ashore the bodies of two dead women, mother and daughter, who were of a family of about eight persons, all of whom were drowned except a grown son who was frantic with grief at the sight of his dead mother and sister."[23]

Out of the nine members of the Spikes family who had boarded the *Sultana* at New Orleans, only nineteen-year-old DeWitt survived, although the *Memphis Argus* on April 30, 1865, published a report that a younger brother "has been rescued by some Confederate soldiers on the Arkansas shore." Though devastated by the loss of his entire family, DeWitt pushed aside his grief and went to work helping to save others. "[F]inding that he could not save any of his own family, with a noble courage that is beyond all praise, notwithstanding his exhausted condition he used every effort to assist his fellow sufferers, and succeeded in saving no less than thirty lives." Only the bodies of his mother, Elethia Spikes, and his young sister Lizzie were ever recovered. They were later buried in Elmwood City Cemetery in Memphis.[24]

By the time the sun was up, the many steamboats at Memphis that had been frantically building up pressure within their boilers had finally set out to rescue anyone they could find. The first boat out was the *Silver Spray*, which began picking people up close to Memphis. Private Walker was one of them. "In my struggle for self-preservation," he later said, "I had discarded my clothing but others had done the same and thus we were taken from the water and finally when 85 struggling soldiers had been gathered out of the murky water of the river we were taken to Memphis where the Christian commission supplied us with clothing as could be had." The *Silver Spray* also picked up Senator-elect Snow.[25]

Pvt. Truman Smith, only seventeen years old, remembered the crew handing him whiskey. "The first thing after we got on the boat they brought me a tin cup of whiskey which I drank. I had got so that I could walk by this time. We kept going up the river, picking up

men and making them comfortable as possible." Among those rescued from the top of a tree was his good friend Pvt. Manly White,
who recalled,

> I was rescued by the steamer *Silver Spray*, after being in
> my tree about three hours. We were treated kindly on the
> boat. Bedclothes were taken from the state-rooms and
> given to the boys to wrap around them. We soon landed
> in Memphis. The excitement was intense. It seemed that
> everyone in the city was down to the wharf, and nearly
> every hack in the city was in charge of a soldier, backed
> down to the wharf-boat ready to take us to the hospital as
> fast as we were ready. As we stepped from the gangplank
> into the wharf-boat, to greet us were ladies of the Sanitary
> Commission and Sisters of Charity (God bless them), who
> handed to each of us a red flannel shirt and drawers. As fast
> as we donned our red suits we stepped into a carriage and
> was driven rapidly to the hospital, where all was done for us
> that could be to make us comfortable.

Certainly he was more comfortable than he had been in the treetops,
where "the buffalo gnats were so thick that they nearly ate us up."[26]

Leapfrogging past the *Silver Spray*, the *Jenny Lind* reached a group
of twenty-three soldiers standing on the roof of a submerged stable.
Among the group were the few men who had managed to hang onto
the second large stageplank. Sergeant Karns was one of them:

> While standing on the roof of our little shanty fighting off
> the pesty mosquitoes, I noticed the black curling smoke of
> a steamer as it circled up over the tree tops some distance
> below. Soon a boat made its appearance around the bend of
> the river and soon another and another, until five boats were
> busily engaged picking up the survivors, some on logs, others
> in trees. As the boats hove in sight, the shouts of the survi-
> vors could be heard far and near on both sides of the river.
>   A small boat called the *Jenny Lind* came over to our
> rescue. As we went on board . . . the captain met us with

a bucket of whisky and gave each a good "jag," which I believe was beneficial to us at the time. After standing around the warm boilers a short time, I became drowsy, went in the cabin and threw myself on a cot, and was soon lost to everything around me.[27]

Private Brady was on the stable roof as well:

> The steamer came as close as she dared to and sent out little boats to take us in. I had now become so stiff that I could not move and my friend, with some of the boat's crew, carried me down into a little boat and took me over to the large one, which proved to be the *Jenny Lind*. There was a doctor on board and he gave us something to make us throw up the water, but I did not throw any up. They carried me in the cabin, and that was the last I knew until about four o'clock in the afternoon. When I awoke there was one of the Sisters of Charity trying to pour a hot sling down my throat with a teaspoon, for I found that I was in a hospital at Memphis, Tenn. After waking up it was not long until I opened my mouth, and I think there was about a gallon of water ran out of it.[28]

Like the *Silver Spray* and the *Jenny Lind*, the *Marble City* concentrated on gathering people from the flooded treetops. Sergeant Nisley "was picked up by the steamer *Marble City* about 9 o'clock next morning from some driftwood. I could find no shore, I think I could see about forty on the driftwood around me, they had all got to places of safety. The forty men on the driftwood around me were picked up by the *Marble City*."[29]

Shortly after the *Marble City* left the wharf, the *Grey Eagle* arrived "with some two or three hundred of the *Sultana*'s victims, who were placed in ambulances and taken to the several United States Hospitals." David A. Prosser, a citizen of St. Louis who had helped rescue "about a dozen" people, wrote of Captain Ray's little steamboat. "The *Grey Eagle* made at least another trip to the wreck, and through the untiring efforts of her gallant officers, many, very many, lives were saved."[30]

The *Bostona*, having unloaded the 100–150 people she had rescued near the burning *Sultana*, set out from Memphis again. Ames Fisher, the *Bostona*'s clerk, recalled, "as soon as we landed them all, we went immediately back up the river again to pick up any that might be lodged on jams of driftwood, or in the bushes on the shore, the water at the time being over the banks; we got back to Memphis a little after noon, and discharged our second load; I think we must have saved some three or four hundred in all." Corporal Hulit was one of those rescued during the second trip, as was Sergeant Rush, who had managed to get on top of some driftwood. When daylight came, Rush determined that he "was then about two miles from Memphis." He "remained there until about 7 o'clock, when the steamer *Bostona* came to my rescue. Many drowned right there, who had not strength enough to help themselves onto the wood."[31]

Another person rescued during the *Bostona*'s second trip was Captain Friesner, commander of the guard unit on the *Sultana*, who had left the burning boat clinging to his frock coat and vest. He still had them when he was rescued.

> I saw a small rowboat as it pulled a man out of the water. I called and it started toward me. Oh, such a feeling of gladness—but lo, it crossed some distance in front of me, picking up another man. I shouted again as I steered straight for the boat. They again passed me within 15 or 20 feet. . . . I again shouted. Although looking, they could not find me. . . . To be lost at the feet of deliverance, in the presence of safety and all it seemed unbearable, and as they passed me on their return I cried out, "If you intend to save me, you must do it now. I can't hold out longer." . . . About this time . . . a brawny hand pulled me on board. My stiff fingers had clung to my coat and vest and a gruff voice said, "This is a pretty time to be saving clothes."[32]

Departing from the Memphis waterfront after the others were the ferry *Rosedella* and the steamboat *Rose Hambleton*. The *Rosedella* picked up the body of J. D. Fontaine, later identified by his embroidered shirt, and "one dead man [who] . . . was so horribly scalded that not the size of half a dollar of skin was left on the whole body." The *Rosedella* also picked up the passengers—living and dead—whom William Boardman, R. K. Hill, and young William Woodridge had pulled from the water. The crew of the *Rose Hambleton* recovered the Spikes family Bible and took on board "the body of a young lady apparently about twenty years of age. She was of medium height, say about five feet five inches, with a fine head of long brown hair, blue eyes, and a slight scar across the chin. She was dressed in the night attire of a respectable lady; she wore on her bosom a neat breastpin of plain jet set in gold; she was a very handsome lady." Three envelopes found on her person identified the woman as Sarah "Sallie" Bowman Woolfolk of Lexington, Kentucky.[33]

After the *Bostona* and the *Grey Eagle*, it was the small steamboat *Pocahontas* that picked up the greatest number of survivors. When the night watchman informed Henry Seman, the pilot, of a bright light on the water far above Memphis, Seman immediately "knew some steamer had caught fire." While the *Pocahontas* built up steam, the captain sent out her small boats to rescue the passengers. The *Memphis Argus* reported that "the pilot and an engineer went out with a yawl and picked up five or six."[34]

When Captain McDougal finally had enough steam in his boilers the *Pocahontas* set out for the scene of the disaster carrying some soldiers from the 113th Illinois who were assigned to the boat. Corporal Rosselot had managed to "climb a sapling tree and roost there" and was trying "to keep the mosquitoes from eating me up" when he spotted the first of the rescuing steamboats. "When the first steamboat made its appearance it cheered up the poor boys and we shouted, but it stopped way below us, so did the second, third and fourth, but the fifth one, the little picket boat [*Pocahontas*], came boldly up to where we were and sent out its boats and picked us all up."[35]

Sgt. Edward Burns (Co. G, 18th MI Inf) was also being eaten alive by mosquitoes. Burns had stripped off his clothes before leaving the burning boat and was naked when he climbed into a submerged treetop and perched "himself on a branch that swayed to and fro with his weight." The *Pocahontas* found him "whisking his body vigorously

with a bush to keep off the mosquitoes and buffalo gnats who had covered him with bloody punctures." When the picket boat approached,
Burns sang out, "Bully boys—here's your mule—I couldn't have stood
it five minutes longer—Lord ain't the mosquitoes big."[36]

Pvt. Joseph Burr Norton (Co. C, 51st OH Inf) had also managed to reach a submerged treetop. "All the time I was holding onto
the brush in the water I could hear the boys that had got into trees,
as it began to get daylight, crowing like roosters, and crying 'here's
your mule!' It was about seven o'clock before I was able to crow. I
was picked up by the United States picket-boat *Pocahontas* about ten
o'clock a.m. April 27, without a stitch of clothing on my back, and
pretty well tired out as well as peppered by bites of buffalo gnats."[37]

Sgt. Lewis Wolf McCrory (Co. A, 100th OH Inf) was clutching
an "old fashioned iron bound" pocketbook with more than $100 in it
between his teeth when the *Pocahontas* picked him up. "My pocketbook kept my mouth partially open so that I took in some water," he
admitted. After being rescued, McCrory was given some whiskey. "I
took a big drink, but it was not enough, so I went up to the bar of the
boat and called for brandy." Having saved his pocketbook, McCrory
was in the unique position of being able to buy another drink. "The
bartender set down a bottle and a small glass but I called for a large
one. He then set down a big beer tumbler. I filled this brimming full
and drank it, then offered to pay for it, but he refused to take pay, saying 'it is free to *Sultana* survivors.' I told him that when he disposed of
it by wholesale he ought to charge something."[38]

After plucking people from the treetops, the *Pocahontas* picked
up those the Foglemans had rescued. "About eleven o'clock, a boat,
whose mission it was to gather survivors, came along, and a little
body of about fifty gathered together on the Arkansas shore [and]
boarded her," Corporal Fast remembered. From Fogleman's Landing,
the steamboat went a mile upriver and picked up the people ex–
Confederate soldier Frank Barton had rescued in his dugout canoe.
Private Young, one of the men who boarded the *Pocahontas* at the
Barton place, "found many comrades who had been picked up previously, and our number so filled the boat that she could rescue no more,
and at once started down the river to Memphis."[39]

Before the *Pocahontas* left the Barton residence, Private Homer, who had been rescued from a treetop along with the *Sultana's* pilot, George Cayton, witnessed a tragic sight. "Finally they landed and I walked out on the plank," Homer reported, "and to my astonishment I saw eight women all in a row on the ground, whom they had taken off the [*Sultana*], burned or scalded to death." Also rescued by the *Pocahontas* was Samuel Clemens, the *Sultana's* second engineer. "The engineer on the *Sultana*, scalded all over, was rolled in cotton and oil but died a few minutes later," Corporal Sharp recalled. In fact, Clemens lived long enough to make it back to Memphis to speak with Nathan Wintringer and give a statement to authorities.[40]

In addition to crew members Cayton and Clemens, the *Pocahontas* also picked up Thomas Butler, a watchman on the *Sultana*, and the body of deckhand William Durkan, who had finally succumbed to his painful scalds and horrible facial wounds after being taken from the bow of the *Sultana*. Butler was suffering terribly. "He was very badly burned in the face and hands, and his left leg broken. He was alive when picked up, but died after being taken on the boat."[41]

While the *Pocahontas* was still near the Barton residence, the steamboat *Rose Hambleton* hove into view, carrying C. W. Christy and Dr. Benjamin Woodward of the Sanitary Commission and "a number of citizens who had supplied themselves with stimulants, sweet oil, flour, &c." Christy reported that "Dr. Woodward, with a large number of citizens and soldiers, and most of the stores, was transferred to [the *Pocahontas*]. The aid thus afforded was most timely, and, of itself, well repaid us all for the trip."[42]

When the *Pocahontas* finally arrived back at Memphis, she was carrying 146 survivors and a number of recovered bodies. One-armed Private Hamblin, who had been rescued by Frank Barton, remembered his arrival in town. "It was quite embarrassing for me when I got off the boat at the wharf. I was still in the same condition as when I leaped into the water—entirely naked. When we reached the warehouse the United States Sanitary Commission gave me a pair of red drawers and undershirt, when I felt comparatively happy. I was then taken to the Soldiers' Home at Memphis, and there fitted out with a full suit and cared for like a human being."[43]

Throughout the day, the members of the Sanitary Commission passed out much-needed items to new arrivals. In all, the commission gave out "Shirts, 670; drawers, 720 pairs; quilts, 40; socks, about 100 pairs—exact number unknown; towels and handkerchiefs, 200." A number of local stores and citizens helped out, too. "One store . . . gave fifty pairs of shoes," reported Dr. Woodward. Private Morgan, who had received a red shirt and drawers from the Sanitary Commission, recalled, "One man gave me a pair of shoes, another a pair of trousers and another a hat, and in this condition I went home."[44]

While the Memphis hospitals admitted approximately 518 victims from the *Sultana* and the Soldiers' Home took in about 260 (total 778), some survivors were taken to private residences. Jennie Perry received "the utmost kindness at the hands of the Mayor of Memphis [Provisional Mayor Capt. Channing Richards of the Union Army] and his wife." Sergeant Sprinkle was rescued from the river in front of Memphis, and "citizens afterwards took me home with them and gave me a suit of clothes. I stayed with them about nine days." Pvt. John Albert Naus (Co. B, 101st IN Inf) had been hit in the head by a shutter when the *Sultana* exploded and was in great pain when pulled out of the river. Because the hospitals were full, a private family took him in.[45] The number of survivors taken to private residences is unknown, so it cannot be added to the tally.

Whether taken to a hospital, the Soldiers' Home, or a private residence, all of the *Sultana* victims agreed that the people of Memphis treated them well. "[W]e received every possible attention from the citizens, in the way of food, clothing and hospitality," Private Johnston said. "No people could have shown more compassion and kindness."[46]

21

MORNING IN MEMPHIS

Many of those rescued from the river and taken to the Soldiers' Home or a hospital returned to the riverfront looking for relatives and comrades. Cpl. Jesse F. Millard (Co. G, 3rd TN Cav) went to look for his brother, Pvt. Elcana K. Millard (Co. G, 3rd TN Cav). When he got there, "[t]hey were forming some troops across the way from me and I heard his name above all that was going on, and I knew he was alive. He was soar [*sic*] and tired but O.K."[1]

As he stepped off the steamboat that brought him into Memphis, Pvt. Nathan Samuel Williams (Co. B, 5th IN Cav) saw "the bodies of the dying, wounded and scalded . . . on every hand." He was taken to the Soldiers' Home but decided to leave and look for his friends. "I must have made a fine show with nothing on but a shirt and drawers, bare headed and bare footed. I did not go very far in this manner before a clothier called me in and gave me a fair suit of clothes. I then went on but did not find many of my company; most of them were lost in the deep waters of the Mississippi or had been consumed by the flames."[2]

Sergeant Mavity left the Soldiers' Home after one day to search for his friends. "[T]hat evening I saw a squad of boys coming up the street and recognized the features of one of my company, Bill Harden

[Pvt. William H. Harden, Co. H, 9th IN Cav]. I managed to hobble to him and to hear his glad cry, 'My God! Mavity, Is that you? I thought all were gone but me.' I replied that I had reached the same conclusion regarding myself." Out of the nine men of Company H, 9th Indiana Cavalry, only one other person, Pvt. Hermon B. Stoops, survived.[3]

Sergeant Jones of Company C of the 115th Ohio Infantry, which had forty-seven officers and men on board the *Sultana*, wrote to his brother on April 29,

> Yesterday I was busy all day visiting Soldiers' Home and different hospitals in search of survivors of Co. C. Of those I could find but 17 out of 42 [*sic*] who were on board at the time of the explosion. . . . We are still in hopes that more of our boys will yet be found, but it is very doubtful. Those of us who are left can only mourn their loss, and deeply sympathize with their friends and relatives. It will indeed be a great blow to those who were daily expecting their boys, fathers, and husbands home, many of them having been absent for years, others for months. After all their suffering in Southern prisons, getting safely within our lines, on our route homeward, congratulating ourselves on the good news and the times we were to have at home, all this, and to have this terrible calamity, hurling so many into eternity, it makes me shudder as I write.[4]

Only twenty-one of the forty-seven members of Company C survived.

On April 30, three days after the disaster, Teamster Solomon Franklin Bogart wrote to his sister regarding the fate of her husband, Teamster Henry Marshall Misemer (both Co. F, 3rd TN Cav) and their brothers Pvt. Levi Morrison Bogart (Co. K, 3rd TN Cav) and Pvt. Charles Harrison Bogart (Co. F, 3rd TN Cav): "[A]moung the lost was H M Misemer. I did not See either of the boys [Levi or Charles] after the alarm commenced. The names of all that was saved is in the papers and there is neither of their names there. . . . I hav ben all over this town in evry Hospital and neither of the boys is here they are all lost and their Remains to day lay in the bed of the Mississippi

River. horid thought."[5] Henry Misemer, Levi Bogart, and Charles Bogart all perished.

To aid the survivors and their family and friends at home, the two major Memphis newspapers, the *Argus* and the *Daily Bulletin*, published the names of those taken to the different hospitals. Additionally, the two papers published the names of the Ohio soldiers known to have been put on board the *Sultana* and a partial list of the men from Indiana. Apparently, these were the only lists Capt. Frederic Speed and his aides at the parole camp finished before Captain Williams suggested placing all of the remaining men at Camp Fisk on the *Sultana* and compiling the rolls afterward.

Corporal Winters, who had been slightly scalded on his face, neck, left arm, hands, and feet, was taken to Adams Hospital. The following day, he "was scarcely able to move; every muscle in my body was sore. I felt as though someone had beaten me all over the body with a club." While he was in the hospital Winters gave his name and regiment to a reporter. Corporal Sharp, who was admitted to Overton Hospital with chills, noted that "the newspaper men got the survivors names, company, and regiment and they were sent broadcast to the press and published at 2 p.m." Unfortunately, in their haste to get the names out, the papers sometimes got it wrong. Private Pottle saw himself listed as "one of the drowned."[6]

Two St. Louis newspapers, the *Daily Missouri Democrat* and the *Daily Missouri Republican*, went a step further and published the hospital lists along with the reason the person had been admitted— "Exhaustion," "Seriously scalded," "Fracture of left clavicle," and so on. Copying the Memphis newspapers, the *Cincinnati Daily Commercial* and the *Cincinnati Daily Gazette* published the hospital lists with only the name, regiment, and company, but omitted the condition of each individual.[7]

Since Jennie Perry had been taken in by a private family, only one woman passenger was named on the hospital lists. Ann Annis was taken to Gayoso Hospital "very ill from injuries and exhaustion." On April 29, the *Memphis Argus* published an appeal: "It is hoped that the generous ladies of Memphis will take some interest in the case of this lady, who needs their aid. She lost everything, and is in need of clothing and other necessaries." Not to be outdone, the following day the *Memphis Daily Bulletin* informed its readers that Mrs. Annis "is in destitute circumstances, owing to the loss of her clothing and money, here is an object for the charitably disposed ladies of Memphis, and we trust they will not be lacking in their usual liberality. We doubt not that donations of clothing sufficient to enable the unfortunate lady to pursue her journey homeward would be acceptable."[8]

Of the seventeen or so female passengers and unknown number of female crew members on the *Sultana*, only a few survived. Private Rush came up with his own total: "Of all the seventeen lady passengers on board only one was saved, and several of the wives of the deck hands were also lost, which, I think, made a total of twenty-two ladies lost." Although Corporal Winters thought there were fewer women than that on board, he also thought that three or four women survived.[9] There were several children and perhaps one infant on the boat. None survived.[10]

Although hundreds of dead bodies were pulled from the river, the majority of the *Sultana* victims were never found. The river was at flood stage, reaching back over the banks for more than three miles in some places, and many of the bodies may have been left high and dry miles from the river when the water eventually receded. When a body was recovered, chances are it went unidentified. "Yesterday the towboat *Home* brought down two bodies which were not recognizable," the *Memphis Argus* reported on April 28. "They were taken from the ruins of the *Sultana*, and were burned to a crisp. One of them was a mere jumble of black cinders, and the other's legs were burned off up to the knees, but the upper part of the body had the form of a man, but there was nothing in the features that would enable an acquaintance to recognize it, as it merely showed the outline of a face." The day following the disaster the "*Rose Hambleton* brought down three dead, the *Pocahontas* five, the *Home* two, the *Grey Eagle* three, and the crew of the *Essex* four."[11]

The bodies of the female passengers were buried on April 28. "Two benevolent ladies of Memphis, Mrs. Goodman and Mrs. Carlisle, finding that several of the drowned lady passengers of the *Sultana* were not likely to receive the funeral care and attention due to their sex, took charge of the matter, and collecting a small subscription to aid them, procured the needful articles, and making them up had the bodies . . . buried yesterday in a fitting manner."[12] Sallie Woolfolk was buried at Elmwood Cemetery, but she was soon reinterred beside her husband in Lexington Cemetery in Lexington, Kentucky.[13]

Bodies continued to turn up during the week following the disaster. The *Jenny Lind* brought in seven bodies on May 3 and another twenty-eight on May 4. That same day, when William Thornburgh, part owner of the *Sultana*, and Capt. Frank Dozier, brother-in-law of Captain Mason, came down from St. Louis and visited the wreck, they "found that some thirty bodies had risen." It was speculated "that a salvo of artillery fired over the wreck about this time would cause a general rising of bodies."[14]

In addition to William Thornburgh and Captain Dozier, many relatives of *Sultana* victims descended upon Memphis. On May 13, John P. Mason, brother of Captain Mason; Zadock Inghram, father of pilot Henry Inghram; and survivor Seth Hardin went downriver on the *Jenny Lind* looking for their loved ones. Although they recovered a few bodies, none were the ones they sought. "At times we could see tears rolling down Mr. Inghram's face when he would pick up a body, and then think of his son the pilot; he is, without doubt, very much affected and grieved by the loss of his son. As evidence of this, he has been for the past two weeks every day engaged in searching for his son's body. But it seems like vain work, and the chances of his finding his son are small."[15]

Notices were placed in the Memphis newspapers offering rewards for the recovery of certain individuals. A reward of $200 each was offered for the bodies of Captain Mason and the two clerks, William Gambrel and Willie Stratton. Seth Hardin and Zadock Inghram offered $100 rewards for their wife and son, respectively. The brother of Major Fidler offered a reward for the recovery of Fidler's body. Several rewards were placed through the Indiana military agent for the recovery of the bodies of certain Indiana soldiers.[16] None of the rewards was ever collected.

Since soldiers did not yet wear identification tags and the armed services kept no fingerprint and dental records, there was no way to identify many of the recovered bodies. Some soldiers were identified

through letters or items in their possession, but most of the men had
stripped off their clothing before jumping into the water, leaving
behind any items that might have been used to identify them. The
recovery teams searched the victims still wearing uniform pants or
jackets, which led to rumors of looting of the dead. "In some cases
where the bodies were found with clothing on, it is alleged that the
pockets were cut out and all valuable taken," the *Memphis Daily
Bulletin* reported on May 7. "This matter may be a slanderous impu-
tation on the persons engaged in the recovery of bodies." Two days
later, the same paper published a number of statements from people
searching for loved ones "fully refuting rumors to the prejudice of the
benevolent persons who have been untiring in their work of mercy.
The persons whose names are given here nearly all lost relatives and
friends, and have been present at the search for bodies, and they all
unite in commending in the warmest terms the humanity, the untiring zeal, unselfish labors" of those helping recover the bodies.[17]

More bodies were found as the floodwaters receded. "Many bodies
are now rising from the vicinity of the wreck of the *Sultana*, and a
few have drifted down past the landing," the *Memphis Daily Bulletin*
reported on May 6. "About forty-five were picked up yesterday and
brought ashore." A passenger on the steamboat *Indiana*, which was
heading downriver from Memphis to New Orleans two days after the
disaster, said that "for two days they were scarcely ever out of sight
of dead bodies . . . who were floating down the stream." In mid-May,
the *Pauline Carroll*, on her first trip downriver since leaving Vicksburg
with only seventeen passengers while the *Sultana* was being overcrowded, reported "passing among the rising dead" all the way from
Memphis to Helena, Arkansas. Between Helena and the White River,
a distance of about eighty river miles, the crew of the *Pauline Carroll*
were "literally sailing among the dead! It has been a sight too horrible
to describe. The bodies were bloated with the gases of putrifaction
[*sic*], and floating like bags of cotton upon the surface."[18]

Many, many bodies floated the ninety miles downriver to Helena.
Capt. Thomas J. Abel (Co. B, 56th US Colored Infantry), the provost
marshal of the District of Eastern Arkansas, wrote, "A few days after
the catastrophe floating bodies of passengers and crew began to make

their appearance. A patrol was placed above and below the town with instructions to secure and bury the bodies. About 200 corpses were thus gathered up and buried along the shore. The last taken up were in such a state of decomposition that canvas had to be wrapped about them in the water."[19]

As the bodies moved further downriver, the crews of some boats ignored them. Phineas D. Parks, acting engineer on the ram *Vindicator* near the mouth of the Red River, 313 river miles below Memphis, wrote,

> I wish to say that the most horrible sights I saw during my whole service was immediately after [the *Sultana* disaster]. The *Vindicator* was a powerful side-wheeler, and while at anchor in the Mississippi River would catch the drift-wood, which made it necessary to clear her wheels every day. When clearing the wheels after the *Sultana* disaster we would find them clogged with dead bodies from the *Sultana*. The crew of the *Vindicator* were mostly old soldiers, and there came very nearly being a revolt because we were not allowed to bury the bodies which lodged on our wheels.[20]

Such heartlessness was not unique. Pvt. James R. Clark (Co. C, 100th IL Inf), serving on the tinclad *Cricket* at the mouth of the White River, 350 river miles below Memphis, wrote home on May 12,

> The ill fated Soldiers that was on the *Sultana* there bodys keep floating down Every day and do you just think our Captain won't allow one of us to Pick up one of them. I have seen the poor fellows Float right at my feet Where all I Would have had to do just put my hand out and pull them aboard[.] I am sure there is not one of the deck hands but would be willing to dig a Grave for the Poor men that have Fought and Bled for there country but no we must just let them Float Past us like as many dogs[.]

The *Daily Bulletin* reported that when some of the passengers on the steamboat *Mississippi* spotted the body of a *Sultana* victim floating in the water, the captain supposedly said, "Oh no, it is only a soldier, let him go. . . .We hope that there is no truth in the statement."[21]

Some of the bodies that floated downriver fell prey to animal scavengers. An army officer who arrived in Memphis from Vicksburg reported seeing crows feeding on some of the bodies in the river. When the bodies washed ashore, animals devoured the decaying flesh. "Reliable, well informed parties who arrived from below inform us that many bodies of the victims of the *Sultana* catastrophe can be seen floating in the river, and lying on the banks and in the driftwood on both sides," the *Memphis Argus* reported on May 12. "Many of them, owing to the temperature, are too much decomposed to be moved. Some of them have been made the prey of dogs and hogs, and doubtless other animals. Fifteen miles below the city, on the east bank of the Mississippi, near the head of Cow Island, the nude and putrified body of a lady was seen. Hogs were eating the body."[22]

The bodies of the soldiers pulled from the river at Memphis were buried at Fort Pickering Cemetery.[23] The *Memphis Argus* lamented, "A Funeral of Eleven—Yes, a funeral of eleven noble dead, was to be seen yesterday on their way to their last earthly abiding place. Not drawn in eleven different hearses followed by great many carriages filled with mourning and sobbing friends, inclosed in finely trimmed and beautiful coffins, but in rude coffins piled on one another in a rough Government wagon drawn by four horses through the busy streets, nobody taking any notice whatever."[24]

Bodies continued to rise over the next few days: "counted 38 on one barge," "About fifty dead bodies were recovered yesterday," "thirty-two bodies of the lost *Sultana*'s passengers were found yesterday in the vicinity of the wreck." For the week ending May 7 the *Argus* reported 133 bodies recovered from the river. Eleven days after the disaster, Sergeant Aldrich was still in Memphis. He "went down to the landing where they were boxing up the dead and there I saw two hundred of my comrades lying in rows and in the same shape they were taken out of the water, after rising and floating on top."[25]

Among the bodies recovered was that of George Slater, the second steward of the *Sultana*. "The Stewards' Association immediately set about the charitable object of having him decently interred, for which purpose a collection was made among the stewards of this city, and a sufficient amount of money was raised to buy the deceased a very nice coffin and a lot in the Elmwood Cemetery; also, to hire carriages for the funeral, which was very well attended by all the stewards now in the city."[26]

On April 28, 1865, one day after the disaster, the *Argus* placed the number of dead at "no less than twelve or fifteen hundred persons," and the *Daily Bulletin* reported "Not Less Than 1,400 Lives Lost." Picking up on details from the Memphis papers, the *Daily Missouri Democrat* in St. Louis reported that "the lives lost will not exceed 1,400," while the *Daily Missouri Republican* said that "the actual loss may reach 1,600." By the time the news reached the East Coast on May 3, the *New York Times* was reporting that "nearly 1,700 persons were lost by the disaster. All reports agree that not less than fifteen hundred were lost."[27]

Brevet Brig. Gen. William Hoffman, the commissary general of prisoners, began an investigation into the *Sultana* disaster in Vicksburg on May 7. Hoffman traveled to Memphis, Cincinnati, Columbus, and Pittsburgh to interview people connected to the disaster. In his summary report to Secretary of War Stanton on May 19, Hoffman wrote that there were 1,886 soldiers, 70 cabin passengers, and 85 crew personnel on the *Sultana* when she exploded, a total of 2,021 people; 765 soldiers and 18 crew and passengers had survived; 1,101 soldiers and 137 passengers and crew members had perished, "making the total loss 1,238."[28]

Unfortunately, Hoffman's total of 1,886 soldiers was wrong. The transportation pass Captain Kerns' clerk issued to the *Sultana*, as stipulated by Captain Williams, was for 1,966 officers and men.[29] The adjusted number would make the grand total of people on board the *Sultana* 2,121. Subtracting Hoffman's 783 survivors, the official number of deaths was 1,338.

That number changed less than two years later after Joseph Holt, the judge advocate general of the Army, had studied the collected ledgers, rolls, and material investigators had turned up. On February 25, 1867, Holt wrote that "the loss [was] eleven hundred lives." That number was the "official" total until 1880, when the 51st Congress, in conjunction with the War Department and the Pensions and Records Department, adjusted the casualty number to 1,259 paroled prisoners of war.[30] Adding in the 137 dead passengers and crew brought the total to 1,396. Throughout the mid-1880s, the *Sultana's* death toll stood at 1,400, although it occasionally jumped to 1,700 or 1,800. In an article published in 1904, survivor John A. Kurtz (Co. F, 7th OH Cav) claimed that "between 1,800 and 2,000 were killed."[31]

After the RMS *Titanic* sank on April 14–15, 1912, with the loss of 1,517 lives, newspapers began to list the *Sultana* death toll as somewhere between 1,500 and 1,700 lives, as if competing with the ocean liner. "More Lives Lost in Mississippi River," the *Alton Evening Telegraph* proclaimed five days after the *Titanic* sank: "The metropolitan newspapers are heralding the disaster of the steamer *Titanic* as being the greatest maritime disaster in the history of the world, but we believe they are mistaken. If we are correctly informed the blowing up of the *Sultana* on the Mississippi river near Memphis, Tenn., in March, 1865, when more than 1800 discharged soldiers lost their lives and only three hundred were saved out of 2100 lives was far worse than the recent accident of the great steamer, the *Titanic*." Likewise, the *Pensacola Journal* shouted in bold black letters, "Disaster More Appalling than *Titanic* Wreck," claiming, "But few of the soldiers were saved, about 1,900 going down."[32]

Now that a great many of the old reports and other sources are available on the Internet, numerous websites have offered death totals, with most settling at 1,800, although one website in April 2019 claimed that "as many as 2,000 men died either in the explosion and fire or in hospital beds following the tragedy."[33]

Nobody at the time seemed to know how many people were actually on board the *Sultana* on April 24–27, 1865. And, like the death toll, the numbers reported went up and up as time went on. On April 28, 1865, one day after the disaster, the *Argus* reported that there were 2,100 on board, and the *Daily Bulletin* placed the number at 2,200. For the most part, the 2,100–2,200 figure remained consistent until the late 1880s/early 1890s, when the number increased slightly. Survivor James Walter Elliott wrote in 1887 that there were "2,500 human beings on board." Five years later, survivor Alexander

C. Brown wrote that the boat's first clerk, William Gambrel, had told him there were "2,400 soldiers, 100 citizen passengers, and a crew of about eighty—in all over 2,500."[34]

When survivor Chester Berry published his book *Loss of the* Sultana *and Reminiscences of Survivors* in 1892, most of the survivors whose stories he included placed the number on board at between 2,200 and 2,300. After the *Titanic* went down in 1912, the number climbed slowly to just above 2,300. Ten years later, the *Sandusky Star Journal* increased the number to "about 2,500 civil war soldiers."[35] That seems to be the highest number ever stated.

As estimates of the number of deaths and the number of people on board the *Sultana* have gone up over the last 150-plus years, the number of survivors reported has steadily decreased. One day after the disaster, the *Daily Bulletin* reported that "thus far 780 have been found alive. . . . It is probable that a hundred other persons will be found alive," suggesting that there may have been as many as 900 survivors. A few days later, the *Daily Missouri Democrat* reported: "Up to two o'clock P.M., there had been received into the [Memphis] hospitals 518 persons who were rescued. Of those who received no injury and are at the Soldiers' Home, there are from 200 to 300." Within a month, the number of rescued settled at 786.[36]

That number remained the unofficial number of survivors until 1880, when the 51st Congress evaluated the number of survivors receiving pensions and concluded that 931 passengers had survived.[37] Nevertheless, newspapers in the late 1880s and early 1900s were reporting that "not 400 were saved" or that there were "four hundred survivors of the wreck." The *Sandusky Star Journal* stated in 1911 that "about 300 were saved"; and a year later, after the *Titanic* went down, survivor Levi G. Morgan calculated that, "about 464 were saved," far fewer than the number of *Titanic* survivors. In 1922, survivor Vincent Malone, who believed that there were some 2,500 people on board the *Sultana*, concluded that "only a few more than five hundred were saved." Most historians and websites today put the number of survivors at between 500 and 600.[38]

The obvious question, then, is which numbers are correct?

In 2015 I undertook a comprehensive study of all available material connected with the *Sultana* and spent three years trying to determine the true numbers connected with the disaster. The first challenge was to determine exactly how many people were on board the steamboat between April 24 and 27, 1865. While it is known that some people got off at Memphis, their numbers should still be included on the *Sultana*'s manifest since they experienced the crowded conditions and the dangers of the grossly overcrowded vessel for at least the first two days of the trip. Once it was determined how many people were on board, verifying the presence of each person from multiple sources, the determination had to be made as to who survived and who did not.

Utilizing 140 different sources, including government documents, pension records, adjutant generals' reports from the different states, lists from the various 1865 newspapers, and so on, I have identified 1,953 paroled prisoners (1,918 enlisted men and 35 officers), all 22 guards of the 58th Ohio Infantry, 47 of the 70 paying passengers, and 25 of the 85 crew members. Out of a total number of 2,135 people that I can place on board the *Sultana* between April 24 and April 27, 1865, I have positively identified 2,052. The 83 unidentified individuals are crew members and civilian passengers who may never be identified.

Lieutenant Colonel Compton and the fourteen members of the Chicago Opera Troupe, including acting manager T. H. Williams, disembarked at Memphis, so while their numbers are included on the manifest of the *Sultana*'s last trip, they are not counted among the people on board when she exploded. Still, Senator-elect Snow, who boarded at Memphis, spoke to William Gambrel just a few hours before the disaster and was told that "there were 70 Cabin Passengers and 85 hands belonging to the boat."[39] So, at the time of the explosion there were 70 cabin passengers, 85 crewmembers, 1,953 paroled prisoners, and 22 guardsmen, a total of 2,130 individuals.

Extensive research identified among the survivors 906 paroled prisoners, 6 guards, 21 civilian passengers, and approximately 28 crew personnel, a total of 961 people. The *Daily Missouri Republican* of April 29, 1865, reported that "several cabin boys, firemen, and deck hands have been saved. The names, under the excitement, it is almost impossible to ascertain." That same date, the *Cincinnati Commercial Tribune* wrote that in addition to Pilot George Cayton, First Engineer Nathan Wintringer, and First Mate William Rowberry, nineteen deckhands and four of the cabin crew were rescued, a total of twenty-six crew members. The *Chicago Tribune* reported that eighteen deckhands and nine cabin crew were rescued in addition to Cayton, Wintringer, and Rowberry, for a total of thirty.[40] This author places the number of surviving crew personnel directly in the middle at twenty-eight.

Interestingly, on May 31, 1865, after a month of studying and investigating the disaster, the authorities in Memphis stated that "976 of the passengers and crew have been found alive."[41] That number corresponds nicely with the 961 survivors determined by recent research and is not far from the number of 931 determined by the 51st Congress and the War Department Pensions and Records Department in 1880.

With a total of 2,130 people on board at the time of the explosion and 961 survivors, the true number of deaths is 1,169, which, again, is not far from the 1,259 deaths determined by Congress and the War Department in 1880. It is also close to the 1,110 deaths quoted by Judge Advocate Holt during the court-martial of Capt. Frederic Speed in 1866. Although the death toll of 1,169 is far below the 1,500–1,800 that is generally bandied about, the *Sultana* disaster still ranks as the deadliest maritime disaster in U.S. history. (The second costliest is the burning and sinking of the excursion steamer *General Slocum* in New York City's East River on June 15, 1904, with the loss of 1,021 lives.)[42]

If the number of dead *soldiers* from the *Sultana* disaster (1,047) is compared with the number of Union soldiers killed in major battles of the Civil War, the *Sultana* disaster ranks twelfth, behind such large battles as Gettysburg (3,155 Union dead), Wilderness (2,246 Union dead), Antietam (2,108), Cold Harbor (1,845), Shiloh (1,754), Stone's River (1,677), and Chancellorsville (1,606). The number of Union soldiers killed on the *Sultana* exceeds the number of Union dead on the battlefields of Spotsylvania (753), Chattanooga (753), the May 22, 1863, assault on Vicksburg (502), and First Bull Run (481).[43] Also, it should be remembered that most of the *Sultana* deaths occurred within a span of only seven hours, while some of the deadliest battles went on for two or three days.

Some might argue that the total of 1,169 deaths does not include those who later died in the Memphis hospitals. Lt. Elbert Squire, a *Sultana* survivor, claimed that "a large number" of those who were

rescued "afterward died of their injuries and exposure." In 1892, survivor Alexander C. Brown concluded that "about 200 of the rescued
died soon after from the injuries received at the time of the accident."
The latter number has apparently stuck.[44] However, a careful study
has found the names of only thirty-one who died after being admitted.

I used the same criteria in arriving at the number thirty-one that
the U.S. government used in 1865. Any person who left a Memphis
hospital or the Soldiers' Home and made his or her way north is considered a survivor, even if that person had to be admitted to a hospital
at home and died there. Any soldier who remained in a Memphis
hospital but died of dysentery or diarrhea or some other ailment, most
likely contracted while in prison, was not listed as a *Sultana* victim.

Two seriously scalded men who survived were the ever-observant
Louis Bean, who was taken to Adams Hospital, and Pvt. William
Montgomery (Co. F, 6th KY Cav), who was admitted to Gayoso
Hospital and listed as "very seriously scalded [and] femur fractured
at middle third." Brothers 1st Sgt. William D. Wade (Co. B, 3rd TN
Cav) and Cpl. Silas W. Wade (Co. C, 3rd TN Cav) were both taken to
Adams Hospital with severe scalds. Both survived and shared in the
$1,183.90 collected from the people of Memphis and city establish-
ments, and raised from a benefit performance by the Chicago Opera
Troupe. The money was divided among twenty-three *Sultana* victims,
including Ann Annis and Daniel McLeod, and ten soldiers.[45]

Not all of the soldiers who died in Memphis hospitals or shortly
thereafter should be counted as victims of the *Sultana*, even though
they had suffered just as much as the others. Pvt. James T. Marshall
(Co. C, 2nd KY Cav), who died at Gayoso Hospital on May 19,
1865, from chronic diarrhea is not considered a *Sultana* casualty.
Pvt. Henry F. Taylor (Co. L, 1st TN Cav), who died on June 15,
1865, of "congestion of liver" at Gayoso Hospital, is likewise not
listed as a *Sultana* victim. Sgt. Nelson D. Voglesong (Co. F, 18th
MI Inf) actually made it all the way home to Wright, Michigan,
before dying on June 25, 1865, "from diseases contracted in rebel
prisons." His name is also not on the official list of people who died
in the disaster because his death was not related to the disaster
itself.[46]

The *Sultana* docked at the St. Louis waterfront, circa 1864. This is one of only two known photographs of the *Sultana* (No. 5).
Courtesy of the Herman T. Pott National Inland Waterways Library of the St. Louis Mercantile Library at the University of Missouri–St. Louis

James Cass Mason, captain and part owner of the *Sultana*. Mason died in the disaster.
Courtesy of the Ohio History Connection

Officers of Camp Fisk, Exchange Camp, near Vicksburg, Mississippi.
Seated: Capt. Archie C. Fisk, assistant adjutant general, Post and District
of Vicksburg (*left*), and Lt. Col. Howard A. M. Henderson, exchange
agent, CSA. *Standing (left to right)*: unknown Union soldier with white
flag; Maj. William R. Walls, 9th Indiana Cavalry; unknown; Lt. Frederick
A. Roziene, 49th USCT; Maj. Frank Ellis Miller, 66th USCT; 1st Lt.
Edwin L. Davenport, assistant commissary of exchange; Col. Nathaniel G.
Watts, exchange agent, CSA; Capt. Reuben Benton Hatch, chief quartermaster, Dept. of Mississippi; Rev. Charles Kimball Marshall, CSA;
unknown Confederate soldier with white flag.
Library of Congress

Recently identified image of Capt. Reuben Benton Hatch, chief quartermaster, Department of Mississippi.
Library of Congress

Capt. Frederic Speed, assistant adjutant general, Department of Mississippi.
Courtesy of Sultana *Disaster Museum, Marion, AR*

The grossly overcrowded steamboat *Sultana* at Helena, AR. This photograph, usually shown cropped, was taken by Thomas W. Bankes less than twenty-four hours before the *Sultana*'s boilers exploded.
Courtesy of Sultana *Disaster Museum, Marion, AR*

Union picket boat *Pocahontas*. On the day of the disaster, the crew rescued 146 survivors.
Library of Congress

The steamboat *Bostona* (No. 2). Coming downriver on her first voyage after being refurbished, the *Bostona* pulled about 250 people from the waters of the Mississippi.
Courtesy of the Collection of Cincinnati and Hamilton County Public Library

Steamboat boiler explosion, 1860s. The only known photograph of a steamboat that has suffered a boiler explosion. Similar to the damage on the *Sultana*, one smokestack has fallen forward, crushing the upper deck down onto the middle deck.

Courtesy of Sultana *Disaster Museum, Marion, AR*

Capt. Legrand Winfield Perce, assistant quartermaster, Department of Mississippi. A lawyer before the war, he represented Captain Speed during his court-martial.

Library of Congress

Lt. Col. Norman Shepard Gilson, judge advocate, Department of Mississippi. Gilson was the prosecutor in Captain Speed's court-martial. *From* The History of Fond du Lac County, Wisconsin. *Chicago: Western Historical Company, 1880*

Civilian passenger Ann Annis, survived.
Courtesy of Helen Chandler

Civilian passenger Sallie
Bowman Woodfolk,
perished.
*Courtesy Woodford
County Historical Society,
Versailles, KY*

Pvt. John Henry King,
Company F, 9th Indiana
Cavalry, survived. This
photo was taken after
King was released
from Cahaba Prison,
still wearing his prison
clothes.
Courtesy of Robert Smith

Second Lt. Thomas B. Reeves, Company C, 10th Indiana Cavalry, perished.
Courtesy of the Reeves Family

Pvt. James Zeek, Company B, 57th Indiana Infantry, perished. *Courtesy of* Sultana *Disaster Museum, Marion, AR*

Maj. William H. Fidler, Regimental Command, 6th Kentucky Cavalry, perished. He was in charge of the paroled prisoners on the *Sultana*. *Courtesy of* Sultana *Disaster Museum, Marion, AR*

Cpl. James Warren Bradish, Company A, 18th Michigan Infantry, perished.
Courtesy of Sultana *Disaster Museum, Marion, AR*

Cpl. Jeremiah Spring, Company A, 18th Michigan Infantry, perished.
Courtesy of Sultana *Disaster Museum, Marion, AR*

Cpl. William Lester Faurot, Company G, 18th Michigan Infantry, perished.
Courtesy of J. Michael Joslin

Pvt. Abraham Cassel, Company B, 21st Ohio Infantry, survived. *Courtesy of* Sultana *Disaster Museum, Marion, AR*

Pvt. Levi G. Morgan, Company B, 21st Ohio Infantry, survived. *Courtesy of* Sultana *Disaster Museum, Marion, AR*

Pvt. Peyton Shields, Company D, 31st Ohio Infantry, survived. *Courtesy of* Sultana *Disaster Museum, Marion, AR*

Cpl. Albert W. King, Company D, 100th Ohio Infantry, survived. He helped save Jennie A. Perry, one of the two female civilian passengers who survived. *Courtesy of* Sultana *Disaster Museum, Marion, AR*

Pvt. Harrison Spafford, Company B, 102nd Ohio Infantry, survived. *Courtesy of* Sultana *Disaster Museum, Marion, AR*

Pvt. Daniel Garber, Company E, 102nd Ohio Infantry, survived.
Courtesy of Carol and Karen Lundquist

Pvt. John F. Kauffman, Company K, 102nd Ohio Infantry, survived.
Courtesy of Sultana *Disaster Museum, Marion, AR*

Pvt. Peter Weaver, Company C, 115th Ohio Infantry, perished.
From the Timothy R. Brookes collection

Pvt. Daniel Myers, Company G, 115th Ohio Infantry, perished.
Courtesy of Sultana *Disaster Museum, Marion, AR*

Pvt. Isaac Anderson and Pvt. Gilford Canon Morrison, Company L, 3rd
Tennessee Cavalry. Both brothers perished in the disaster.
Courtesy of Gene Fort

Of all those pulled from the river and sent to the Memphis hospitals or the Soldiers' Home, it seems reasonable to assume that those who were destined to die had already perished, and those who were destined to live were still alive. A person who could survive scalding, burns, and hypothermia for almost seven hours before being rescued was likely to survive. Indeed, with only 31 of the 519 people admitted to Memphis hospitals dying, the survival rate was just above 94 percent.

With 488 people surviving the various Memphis hospitals and another 259 of the less seriously injured going to the Soldiers' Home, the total number of survivors from the various institutions totals 747. However, pension records, invalid pension declarations, and so forth indicate that 961 people survived the *Sultana*. The most likely explanation is that the 214 people whose names do not appear on one of the lists of people taken to a hospital or to the Soldiers' Home were either taken to private residences, as Jennie Perry was, or ended up at a hospital after the lists were compiled, such as Pvt. Chester Berry, who suffered a fractured skull and was eventually taken to Washington Hospital but whose name does not appear on any of the published lists.

If, as some survivors suggested, between 150 and 200 men did not get back on the *Sultana* before she left Memphis near midnight on April 26, 1865, there would be no reason for their names to appear among the survivors at either the Soldiers' Home or any of the hospitals. They, of course, were the lucky ones.

In 1866, the federal government established a national cemetery near Memphis on 32.64 acres of land 7 miles northeast of the city "upon the east side of the Memphis & Ohio Railroad." Work on the Mississippi River National Cemetery commenced in February 1867, with crews collecting the bodies of Union soldiers up and down the Mississippi River from as far away as Helena, Arkansas, and Hickam, Kentucky. Each body was placed in a wooden coffin, if necessary, and brought to the new national cemetery. The *Memphis Public Ledger* on February 4, 1867, reported that "those whose business or pleasure called them yesterday in the neighborhood of the Memphis and Ohio depot were much annoyed by a horrible stench that proceeded from a couple of freight cars containing a large number of coffins. They contained Federal dead that had been collected along the river for internment in the National Cemetery."[47]

One of the myths that has lingered around the *Sultana* disaster is that the dead Union soldiers were originally buried in Elmwood City Cemetery in Memphis and then exhumed and reinterred in the national cemetery. The story goes that each man's name was written in chalk on the top of his wooden coffin, but before the coffins could be reburied, a torrential rainstorm washed off or obscured many of the names. That, the myth claims, is the reason why so few of the *Sultana* soldiers are identified in the Memphis National Cemetery and why there are more than eight thousand soldiers buried there in "unknown" graves. Like many stories associated with the *Sultana*, this tale does not hold up under scrutiny.

Sultana historian Jerry O. Potter called this story "a legend that never happened." In fact, the bodies of the soldiers who died in the *Sultana* disaster were never buried at Elmwood Cemetery, which was a civilian cemetery. Instead, they were buried at Fort Pickering Cemetery. The *Lafayette Daily News* in 1867 reported, "Their mortal remains were gathered up, all that could be found of them, and interred at Fort Pickering, near Memphis and they have been exhumed and laid in their final resting place in the national cemetery at that city." Many of them could not be identified because they were burned or scalded beyond recognition or wore no clothing that might indicate who they were.[48]

Only twenty-eight *Sultana* soldiers have identifying headstones in the national cemetery, which changed its name to Memphis National Cemetery in May 1871.[49] Four of them died before reaching a hospital. The other twenty-four died in the Memphis hospitals over a span of three weeks and were buried at Fort Pickering Cemetery. The bodies of the remaining seven soldiers who died in Memphis hospitals were claimed by their families and taken home for burial at a local cemetery.

22

SPREADING THE WORD

Word of the disaster spread quickly. The *Marble City*, after helping with the rescues, departed Memphis on the afternoon of April 27 carrying city newspapers reporting the story. She reached New Madrid, Missouri, site of a telegraph office, on April 28, and the news of the *Sultana* disaster was flashed to St. Louis and elsewhere. Near 7:30 p.m., the steamboat glided up to the Cairo wharf boat. News went out that "the *Marble City*, just arrived, brings the sad intelligence of the explosion and burning of the steamer *Sultana*, some eight or ten miles above Memphis, at a little past two o'clock on the morning of the 27th. Her Memphis [newspapers], of the 27th . . . [contain] many interesting particulars connected with the explosion of the *Sultana*. She brought the mate [William Rowberry] and nineteen of the crew."[1]

Telegraphs spread the terrible news to every part of the nation. Newspapers in the important river towns of St. Louis and Cincinnati picked up the story on April 28. Papers in New York, Philadelphia, Boston, Cleveland, Chicago, and Washington, DC, proclaimed the news the next day, received through "Special Dispatch" from Cairo and St. Louis. The *Daily Eastern Argus* in faraway Portland, Maine, proclaimed, "Terrible Accident on the Mississippi"; while the *Daily Illinois State Journal* from President Lincoln's hometown of Springfield was informing readers of a "Terrible Steamboat Accident." The edition, heavily bordered in bold black ink, also reported the movement of Lincoln's funeral train, which was now at Cleveland, Ohio.[2]

The news went west at the same time. On April 29 readers in Sacramento and San Francisco, California, and Gold Hill, Nevada, read about the *Sultana* disaster. On May 3, the *Denver Rocky Mountain News* ran the story; one day later, people in Atchison, Kansas, and Auburn, Nebraska, were reading it. Having only weekly newspapers, the people of Helena, Montana, and Eugene, Oregon, had to wait until May 13 to read about the disaster.[3]

Indianapolis received the news on April 29, as did Columbus and Cleveland. The *Detroit Free Press* ran the headline "Terrible Explosion on the Mississippi River" on April 29. The *Milwaukee Sentinel* and the *Daily Milwaukee News* ran similar headlines and stories that same date. The readers in Davenport, Iowa, had the story by May 1, while farther north in Minnesota the weekly *St. Cloud Democrat* published the story on May 4 in the first edition that came out after the disaster.[4]

Although there were no telegraphic communications with towns below Memphis, the news spread rapidly via steamboat. People in Helena, Arkansas, eighty-five miles downriver, heard quickly, and in spite of the flooded streets, the *Helena Western Clarion* ran a story on April 29 on the "Horrible Disaster on the River." The news reached Vicksburg that same date. The *Vicksburg Daily Herald* published a Sunday supplement on April 30 containing a "List of Paroled Prisoners from Camp Fisk, on Board the Ill-fated Steamer *Sultana*," furnished by Captain Speed. One day later, on May 1, the *New-Orleans Times* ran the story about the "Loss of the Steamer *Sultana*," scooping the *Times-Picayune*.[5]

Even inside the old Confederacy, word of the *Sultana* disaster spread quickly. The citizens and Union soldiers in the captured city of Richmond, Virginia, read the news on May 6 in the very first issue ever published of the *Commercial Bulletin*. In Georgia, the *Daily Constitutionalist* from Augusta had the story the same date, while the *Atlanta Weekly Intelligencer* waited until May 10 to proclaim "Terrible

Steamboat Accident." Six days later, readers of the *Macon Telegraph* heard about the terrible event. In Charleston, South Carolina, birthplace of the Civil War, the *Charleston Courier* told its readers about "The *Sultana* Disaster" on May 12.[6]

On April 29, two days after the disaster, word reached the first foreign city when the *Halifax Citizen* in Halifax, Nova Scotia, Canada, ran an article titled "Disastrous Steamboat Explosion." On May 1, the *Montreal Herald and Daily Commercial Gazette* had the story, and a day later the citizens in far-off New Westminster, British Columbia, near Vancouver, were reading about the "Explosion of the Steamboat *Sultana*." The English-speaking people of Quebec had to wait until May 5. Getting the news via the British and Irish Magnetic Telegraph, a transatlantic cable, the *London Express* reported about the "Frightful Steamboat Disaster" on May 10, scooping the *London Guardian* and *The Times* by one day. With no underwater cable connecting them to the United States, readers in Australia had to wait until July 17 before the *Melbourne Age* told them about the "Terrible Steamboat Explosion" in America.[7]

Harper's Weekly, a leading illustrated New York City journal, ran a short article titled "The Wreck of the *Sultana*" on page 291 of its May 13 edition. (The pages were numbered consecutively from the first edition of 1865, published on January 7.) The next week, in the May 20 edition, a half-page illustration appeared on page 316 showing a steamboat engulfed in flames with hundreds of people struggling in the water around it. Titled "Explosion of the Steamer *Sultana*, April 28, 1865," the illustration included no further remarks. There was no accompanying story to explain what had happened or where it had taken place. The editors of *Harper's Weekly* were relying on their readers to be well informed from the week before.[8]

Over the years, the belief has arisen that the *Sultana* got little print in the newspapers of the day, swept aside by such events as the procession of President Lincoln's funeral train, the hunt for and death of John Wilkes Booth, the hunt for and capture of Jefferson Davis, and the surrender of the second largest Confederate army in the field under General Joseph Johnston on April 26, 1865. In fact, it received significant coverage in some of the top newspapers of the era. The

New York Tribune, the *Chicago Tribune*, and the *Boston Herald* devoted extensive space to the story throughout May. The same three newspapers covered the Battle of Shiloh (fought on April 6–7, 1862) and the Battle of Chancellorsville (May 1–4, 1863) for about the same length of time, although in more depth.

Horace Greeley's *New York Tribune*, perhaps the leading newspaper of the day, reprinted a small article from the Memphis newspapers on April 29. Another small article followed on May 1 and then a large article on May 2. On May 3, the paper reported the findings of former congressman John Covode of Pennsylvania, who had traveled to Memphis to investigate the disaster and came away with the information that the *Sultana* "was overloaded" and that "other good boats" had been available to take an overflow of paroled prisoners. As far as the *Tribune* was concerned, however, Covode's biggest finding was that "no troops belonging to States East of Ohio were lost." Still, small stories appeared in the *New York Tribune* on May 5, 9, 10, and 12, with an extensive story on May 13, and more short stories on May 22, 23, and 26. A final large article on May 31 published the findings of an investigative committee appointed to look into the disaster.[9]

In Washington, DC, the *Daily National Intelligencer* first reported the incident on April 29 and followed up with eight separate articles throughout May. During that same month, the capital's *Daily National Republican*, which likewise broke the story on April 29, covered the *Sultana* a total of seven times. *The Boston Herald* ran the story nine times after its initial article on April 29, while the two Philadelphia newspapers, *The Age* and *The Press*, each provided coverage seven times after breaking the news on April 29. Even the *Hartford Daily Courant* in Connecticut splashed the news through its pages nine different times.[10] While some people claim that the eastern papers lost interest in the *Sultana* immediately after Covode reported that no soldiers from states east of Ohio died in the disaster, that simply is not true.

In the Midwest, the *Chicago Tribune* first told of the *Sultana* with a big front-page article on April 29 and then carried the story for the next seven straight days, with large articles on May 3, 4, 5, and 6. The May 3 article included the publication of the Memphis hospitals and Soldiers' Home lists. Small articles appeared on May 9, 10, 15, 18, and 22, and large articles on May 11 and 13. The *Tribune* published the findings of the investigative commission on May 24, and in its last article on the subject, on May 30, reported the number of recovered bodies that had been buried in Memphis in the past month.[11]

Understandably, the news was never far from the front pages of the *Daily Missouri Democrat* and *Daily Missouri Republican* of St. Louis. The *Cincinnati Daily Enquirer* in the *Sultana*'s birthplace opened its coverage with long articles on April 29 and May 1 and 2, and then ran smaller articles every other day for the next two weeks. The paper reported the findings of the investigating commission on May 24, and then followed up with shorter articles on May 25 and 26 and June 2.[12]

Not surprisingly, since 635 of the paroled prisoners came from Ohio, the *Cleveland Leader* and the *Cleveland Plain Dealer* each covered the disaster eleven different times over the thirty-five days between April 29, when they both broke the story, and June 2. The *Daily Ohio Statesman* in Columbus, near Camp Chase, the final destination of the *Sultana* soldiers, ran big stories on April 29 and May 1 and then, on May 3, published the entire list of Ohio soldiers known to have been on board the *Sultana*. Stories about the disaster remained in the *Statesman* on May 4, 5, 9, 10, 16, 19, and 25, then disappeared from its pages after the findings of the investigative commission were published.[13] Of the 635 Ohioans on the *Sultana*, 342 never came home.

Many paroled prisoners from the 64th and 102nd Ohio Infantry regiments, as well as a sprinkling of men from the 15th and the 65th Ohio Infantry and McLaughlin's Ohio Cavalry Squadron, came from Richland County, in the middle of the state. In an article titled "The Greatest Accident of the Age," the *Ashland Union* wrote, "When the dispatch was first received, we indulged the hope that there might be some mistake, for the number lost was perfectly inconceivable." Of the 167 paroled prisoners from Richland County, 99 lost their lives. Later it would be reported that the *Sultana* disaster "cast a gloom over the county, as the lost soldiers were all residents and were soon expected home."[14]

Surprisingly, with 407 confirmed soldiers from Indiana on the *Sultana* and 224 deaths, the Indianapolis newspapers covered the disaster for only a few days. The *Indianapolis Star* and the *Daily State*

Sentinel both published only seven articles apiece. On May 3, the *Indianapolis Daily Gazette* published a list of the Indiana men who had been rescued. Perhaps because of its location on the Ohio River, the *Evansville Daily Journal* gave eight days of coverage to the tragedy. However, the best coverage in Indiana came from the weekly newspaper in Richmond, Indiana, about seventy-five miles east of Indianapolis. Two Richmond area units—the 57th and the 124th Indiana Infantry—lost men on the *Sultana*, twenty-two from the 57th and eighteen from the 124th, and the *Richmond Palladium* gave heavy coverage to the tragedy with every issue in May and one in June.[15] Only five soldiers from the 57th and seven from the 124th returned home.

Michigan lost 129 of the 258 soldiers from that state confirmed on board the *Sultana*. The weekly *Detroit Advertiser and Tribune* ran the story throughout the month of May and into the first week of June. On May 30, the paper published a list of all the known soldiers from Michigan who had been on board. The *Detroit Free Press* ran the story almost daily from April 28 to May 5, then ran seven more articles between May 6 and May 30. The *Free Press* published the findings of the investigative commission on May 31 and wrapped up its coverage on June 15 with a list of all known Michigan soldiers who had been on board.[16]

The *Hillsdale Standard* from Hillsdale, Michigan, began coverage on May 2. Hillsdale was home to many of the paroled prisoners from the 18th Michigan Infantry, which was captured almost intact at Athens, Alabama, on September 24, 1864, and had 118 men on board the *Sultana*. The paper hung to the story tenaciously for six more weeks, even reprinting letters written home by a few of the survivors.[17] In all, the 18th Michigan lost sixty-seven soldiers on the *Sultana*.

Kentucky lost 119 of the 194 men from that state on board the *Sultana*, the largest percentage at 61 percent, perhaps because the Kentuckians had been on the last train and had been crowded around the boilers and engines. The *Louisville Daily Journal* covered the news extensively, starting on April 29 and continuing for almost two weeks straight. On May 3, the paper published "a list of Kentucky soldiers who were rescued from the fatal wreck of the *Sultana*, and are now in

Memphis." The list contained sixty-three names, giving hope to many homes but bringing tears in many others.[18]

Tennessee had the second largest contingent of paroled prisoners on the *Sultana* with 429 men. The vast majority, 360, belonged to the 3rd Tennessee Cavalry, which had been recruited around Knoxville and captured almost intact at Athens and Sulphur Creek Trestle, Alabama. On May 17, after many other stories on the disaster, the weekly *Brownlow's Knoxville Whig and Rebel Ventilator* published a list of 3rd Tennessee Cavalrymen who were in the Memphis hospitals and at the Soldiers' Home. Two weeks later the paper published another list, this one identifying 174 survivors who had reached Camp Chase, Ohio, as of May 15, 1865. Surprisingly, the *Nashville Daily Union* in the state capital spent only a few days covering the *Sultana*, instead concentrating on the hunt for Jefferson Davis.[19]

As is the case with most appalling disasters, positive changes followed the tragedy. On May 2, after word reached Washington that the *Sultana* had exploded, killing a large number of Union soldiers, the quartermaster general of the army, Montgomery C. Meigs, issued a circular to all his quartermasters: "As it is probable a large number of troops will be returning to their homes the *strictest attention* should be given to prevent the use of any but *perfectly safe Transports* under experienced and careful masters, provided with everything necessary for the safety and comfort of troops." He especially wanted each quartermaster to be sure that the transports "*are not overloaded*" (emphasis in original). It was too late for the *Sultana* victims, but perhaps it would prevent injury or death to others.[20]

Many steamboat captains took matters into their own hands and organized their crews into fire brigades, then drilled them in their duties. Today, steamboat crews follow strict U.S. Coast Guard–mandated drills and emergency procedures that "train the vessel's personnel on the use of fire equipment, and instruct them on the safe and proper methods of assembling and caring for guests."[21]

Unfortunately, fire drills and inspections could do nothing about the poor design of tubular boilers. It was only after the tubular boilers on the *Sultana* exploded on April 27, 1865, with the loss of 1,169 lives; on the *Missouri* on January 30, 1866, killing 65; and on the *W. R. Carter* on February 9, 1866, costing 125 lives, that tubular boilers were pulled from the lower Mississippi. On March 3, only four weeks after the explosion of the *Carter*, steamboat owners began to remove the dangerous boilers from their boats. The *Cincinnati Daily Enquirer* reported on March 10, 1866, that the *Linnie Drown* "has had her tubular boilers taken out, and in their place substituted the old-style reliable ones."[22]

Within days, several other steamboats ran advertisements proclaiming that their boats did not have tubular boilers. An advertisement on March 13 announced, "For the benefit of the nervous we would state that the *Doubloon* does not carry tubular boilers." On April 3, 1866, the Atlantic and Mississippi Steamship Company published a large advertisement announcing that the steamers *W. R. Arthur*, *Mississippi*, *Mollie Able*, and *Lady Gay* would all have their tubular boilers replaced with standard flue boilers: "The A.&M.S.S. Company, determined to meet the wishes of the public as soon as those wishes were known, [are] having all the tubular boilers taken out of their steamers, and putting in their places boilers of the old and safest construction, and best material. . . . No boats of the line, other than those mentioned, have tubular boilers."[23]

The frenzy to replace tubular boilers lasted the rest of the year. In December 1866, the *Louisville Daily Courier* reported, "Now that the tubular boilers are dispensed with, the next best move will be to make it a part of the duty of the inspectors to test, or prove, all boiler iron before it is made into boilers." Beyond the design of the boilers, mechanics and engineers were beginning to question the integrity of the iron being used in the construction of boilers, tubular or otherwise. At the St. Louis Steamboatmens' Convention in May 1867, it was pointed out, "At present no marked or equitable distinction is allowed for superior qualities of iron or steel, little more than the thickness of the sheet; diameter of the shell and flue being taken into consideration. Under this practice commercial economy enforces the purchase and usage of such as will pass muster. The most costly, the best, will not be manufactured." In other words, steamboat owners might have replaced their tubular boilers, but the replacement boilers were still made of inferior iron.[24]

In spite of the proven problems with tubular boilers, some steamboats—and some factories—continued to use them, sometimes with deadly results. On November 6, 1867, "two tubular boilers in the cotton mill of S. & J. Lees, exploded, and tore the brick building house to fragments." The myth that tubular boilers were safe if used on land, where they were not subject to the up-and-down and side-to-side yawing of a steamboat, proved fatal to two men. Six weeks later, on January 4, 1868, a tubular boiler on the steamboat *Harry Dean* exploded on the Ohio River, dispelling the myth that the tubular boilers would explode only in the muddy waters of the lower Mississippi. More factories and steamboats pulled their tubular boilers. The last mention of a steamboat getting rid of its tubular boilers came on March 3, 1869, almost four years after the loss of the *Sultana*, when a Cincinnati newspaper reported that the "tugboat *Kate Ellis* has had her tubular boilers taken out, and will receive new 6-flued boilers."[25] A positive outcome had finally been realized.

The horrible loss of life from the explosions of the *Sultana*, *Missouri*, and *W. R. Carter* also brought about another positive outcome. On June 30, 1866, two young Hartford businessmen, Jeremiah M. Allen and Edward M. Reed, established the Hartford Steam Boiler Inspection and Insurance Company. "The principle upon which the company operated," noted *The Weekly Underwriter* on January 15, 1887, "was that with proper inspection and management, disastrous boiler explosions might be guarded against." When it became known that Hartford Company inspectors checked boilers in factories, locomotives, and especially steamboats, and insured them only after they passed stringent tests, the public regained confidence that the boilers were safe and reliable.[26]

Finally, in 1871, Congress decided to strengthen the Steamboat Act of 1852. Among the additions and corrections was the Act of February 28, 1871, creating the Steamboat Inspection Service. "The requirements for the inspection and equipment of steamboats were laid down with greater care and in more detail," steamboat historian Louis Hunter noted. "New precautions were introduced for the prevention of explosions, fires, and collisions." Perhaps linked directly to the *Sultana* disaster, the act also stipulated that not only engineers and pilots had to be licensed, but the captain and chief mate as well. Conceivably realizing that Captain Mason had put thousands of lives in jeopardy by not adhering to existing steamboat laws and prohibiting the overcrowding, and that First Mate Rowberry had failed to properly redistribute the top-heavy cargo after the hogsheads of sugar had been removed from the hold, Congress now sought to make such actions criminal. And, like pilots and engineers, captains and chief mates could now have their licenses revoked or suspended for negligence or carelessness.[27]

Although it was too late for the victims of the *Sultana* disaster, the many changes that followed ensured that such a disaster was less likely to happen again.

23

DISCHARGED

The fact that the *Sultana* exploded only seven miles above a major city undoubtedly saved the lives of many of those on board. Had she been thirty miles farther upriver from Memphis, or twenty, or even ten, the number of survivors might have been substantially less. Memphis was an important Union citadel with several top-notch hospitals, an efficient Soldiers' Home, and many willing hands ready to help. First-rate medical attention doubtless saved the lives of many. Likewise, since the disaster had occurred so close to Memphis, it did not take long for the first man, Pvt. Wesley Lee, to float downriver and give the first warning of the terrible explosion. And it did not take long for the numerous steamboats docked in the city to send out their small boats and then, once they had built up enough steam, to go themselves and begin plucking people out of the treetops and off the roofs of submerged buildings. While an unknown number of people undoubtedly died from hypothermia, that number might have been greater had the men and women from the *Sultana* been forced to remain in the cold water another two or three hours.

As fortunate as they were to be rescued and taken to Memphis, however, one problem remained: the paroled prisoners were only halfway home. Cairo, their original destination, was still 246 river miles away, and the survivors would have to take a train from there to

Camp Chase, outside Columbus, Ohio. The surviving prisoners still had a three-day trip ahead of them.

"[T]he thoughts of getting on another boat was a horror to me," First Sergeant Karns admitted. "If it had been reasonable that I could have made the trip through afoot I never would embark on another boat." One survivor who did walk home was blacksmith Caleb Rule (Co. K, 3rd TN Cav), who had lost his brother, Cpl. John Rule (Co. K, 3rd TN Cav), in the disaster. Many years later, his great-grandson explained, "Caleb was supposedly offered passage on another steamer going up the river, but declined to accept. He started walking. Along the way somewhere he found a grapevine growing around [a] small tree and cut it to use as a cane since he had a bad leg. So, Caleb walked from Memphis to Knoxville on a bum leg with a grapevine cane to assist."[1]

On April 29, less than forty-eight hours after the disaster, Captain Friesner of the guard unit was placed in command of a group of survivors who were more than ready to leave Memphis. About 280 men, most of them from Indiana, Ohio, and Michigan, were placed on board the one-year-old *Belle St. Louis*, commanded by Capt. Alexander Ziegler.[2]

"In a day or two we got some new clothing and blankets and then were taken aboard the *Belle of St. Louis* [sic] and steamed up to Cairo, Ill.," Corporal Rosselot wrote. More precisely, Corporal Sharp reported that "two hundred and eighty of us got renewed transportation, and boarded the steamer *Bell St. Louis* at 5 p.m. and were on our way home again."[3]

Many of the men were understandably apprehensive about getting on another steamboat. Commissary Sergeant Mavity admitted that "it was with more foreboding that I boarded the second boat, and when night came I could not close my eyes with such a feeling of safety as before." First Sergeant Karns boarded the boat, went up to the bow, "lay down in a coil of rope, and never got out of there until we reached Cairo the next day." Charles B. Ziegler, son of the captain of the *Belle St. Louis*, remembered that the prisoners "were all affected by their experience" and "settled down and moved about very little on the trip."[4]

Rather than being afraid, Private Garber was amused at the men's behavior: "Some of the more timid were springing up at every little noise, thinking there was going to be another explosion. At one time we supposed that they were having a race with another boat, and one comrade said if he had a gun he would shoot the captain."[5]

Quartermaster Sergeant Wells kept track of dates and times: "Saturday the 29 at 5 PM I left memphis on the Boat *Bell of St. Louis* [*sic*] for Cairo. arive at cairo the nex day at 6 oc PM." Corporal Rosselot "could not repress a shout of joy, when I again set my foot on land, for I was afraid of boats and water." Karns was off the boat as soon as it "touched the shore . . . and the gangplanks in order."[6]

Having arrived late in the evening of April 30, the men had to lay over at Cairo until the next day before catching a train to Camp Chase. Karns remembered, "We only remained [at Cairo] over night, boarding a freight train the next morning for Mattoon, Ill., via the Illinois Central Rail Road." The men were surprised that word of their approach had preceded them. Private Hamilton noted, "On arriving at Mattoon we were met by the citizens of the surrounding country with wagonloads of provisions, the best that the country afforded. The vast multitude manifested their sympathy for us through speeches made by chosen orators. Never shall I forget seeing the tears shed by the stoutest hearts on that occasion."[7]

Karns was equally moved by their reception.

> As soon as the citizens of Mattoon learned that the survivors of the ole *Sultana* were in town, they turned out with their baskets of pies, buns, cakes, pickles, and everything good to eat. We had not been received with such hospitality on all the route, nor did we on the remainder of our journey but it was not long before we bid the good people of Mattoon goodbye, with the many good wishes that they might be rewarded some day for their kindness. Our freight train soon pulled out and we were soon flying through the beautiful prairies of central Illinois. I cannot express my joy as I sat on top of a box car viewing the beautiful country as we sped along.[8]

At Mattoon the men caught the St. Louis, Alton and Terre Haute Railroad east toward Columbus. Their next stop was Terre Haute, where they arrived at 10 p.m. Corporal Chelf remarked that they "were treated well by the citizens." From Terre Haute the group continued on to Indianapolis, where Private Garber remembered stopping for "part of the day. From there we went to Camp Chase, Ohio." The people of Indianapolis were also welcoming. While they were waiting for another train to be prepared, Karns said, "a number of passengers and citizens made up a purse and bought eatables for us which we devoured in short order. After a few hours delay we boarded another freight train on the P.C.&St.L [Pittsburgh, Cincinnati, and St. Louis Railroad] for Columbus, Ohio. After arriving at Columbus we were taken to Camp Chase to await our discharge." Sergeant Wells' notes said: "[W]e arved at camp chase Clumbus O Wendnesday May 3 at 4 oc P M."[9]

On May 3, the *Cincinnati Commercial Tribune* announced the arrival at Camp Chase of 210 Ohio and 20 Michigan *Sultana* survivors. The group did not include the fifty men from Indiana who had started out with them. During the layover at Indianapolis, Indiana governor Oliver P. Morton had seen the physical condition of the Indiana survivors and decided that they had had enough, so he telegraphed the War Department in Washington and obtained permission to remove the Indiana men from the train. The *Morgan County Gazette* of Martinsville, Indiana, reported that Secretary of War Stanton "consented to allow . . . [s]oldiers who were injured in the *Sultana* disaster [to be] . . . furloughed or discharged at this point, without the necessity of reporting at Camp Chase."[10]

When the Ohio and Michigan men arrived at Camp Chase, Gov. John Brough of Ohio made them welcome. "Immediately on learning of the arrival of these men, Governor Brough directed the Quartermaster and Surgeon General to repair to the spot and provide all things for their wants, which was cheerfully and promptly done, and the men were suitably cared for."[11] Once at Camp Chase, however, the men had to wait to be officially mustered out of the service before they could go home, a process that would take a couple more weeks.

A second contingent of survivors left Memphis on May 1 on the five-year-old *Belle Memphis*, commanded by Capt. Daniel Mussleman. Ironically, James Cass Mason had commanded the *Belle Memphis* in May 1863 when she had beaten the *Sultana* in her first ever race. Leading the survivors was Capt. James Walter Elliott, at the men's request. "I was hailed at every turn," Elliott stated. "'Captain, they have left us. You must get transportation for us to take us home.' So I gathered up the boys—all who were able to be moved, about 250— and shipped them for Cairo. We had a dozen or more scalded men laid on the cabin floor, and nursed them."[12]

Private Bringman was among this second group. "I was at the hospital about four days when an order came to discharge all that were able to go home. I got up and walked around to show that I was able to go, but I suffered terribly before I got very far." On the way upriver from Memphis, the *Belle Memphis* passed the sunken remains of the *Sultana*. "We saw the jack-staff, a sentinel on duty, marking the spot where lay the remains of the *Sultana*," Corporal Fast noted.[13]

Captain Mussleman did everything in his power to make the trip enjoyable. The *Indianapolis Journal* reported that officers and enlisted men alike "were treated, by her whole souled commander, with as much conciliation as if they had been millionaires, eating at his table and partaking of the best his abundant larder afforded." "As the boat was not very crowded," Private Eldridge noted happily, "my comrades and I got a good stateroom to stay in while on the boat."[14]

The *Belle Memphis* reached Cairo about 6 p.m. on Wednesday, May 3, 1865. "She brought up 327 survivors of the *Sultana* disaster, en route for Camp Chase, only ten or twelve of whom are wounded," the *Daily Missouri Republican* reported.[15] Because they arrived after dark, Captain Elliott "placed the well in barracks and the wounded in hospitals for the night." Additionally, a few went to the Cairo Soldiers' Home. According to Private Brady,

> Most of the boys went to the barracks as they were afraid they would get left, but I, with a few others, stopped at the Soldier's home, where we received the finest of treatment, a good supper (something we had not had for three

long years), and a nice bed. It was not long before I was sound asleep, and I knew no more until [the next morning when] I got a gentle shake from one of the attendants that awoke me. . . . I got up feeling greatly refreshed, dressed and washed myself and sat down to a breakfast that was good enough for a king.[16]

On May 4, the second group of survivors climbed on board the Illinois Central and headed north to the rail junction at Mattoon, 190 miles away. "At every station at which we stopped large crowds of people were waiting to see the survivors of the great *Sultana* disaster," Corporal Hulit said. "They had baskets well filled with roast chicken, boiled ham, cake, pies, eggs, and steaming hot coffee. This was repeated at every station." Private Johnston agreed that the men "received every consideration possible from the citizens along the route."[17]

By the time the train reached Mattoon, word that a second large group of *Sultana* survivors was approaching had spread throughout the area. "O, what a sight we witnessed!" Private Brady said. "The platform at the depot was crowded, from one end to the other, with the citizens of Mattoon and surrounding country, with baskets filled to overflowing with everything you could think to eat. As fast as a basket was empty it was refilled, and after we had eaten all we could it seemed as though the baskets hadn't been touched. Let me say that during my entire term of service I never received such treatment as while in the State of Illinois." Private Homer "should like to have stayed a month there. Why the citizens just fed us on biscuit and chicken and sweet cake and pie and hot coffee, almost everything imaginable in the eating line, and I send ten thousand thanks to them . . . for their kindness."[18]

Although the *Sultana* survivors were scheduled to board an eastbound train at 4 p.m. they had an unexpected delay. When the townspeople learned that the men would not be leaving until early the next morning, Brady remembered, they "called a meeting in a new hotel, which was not completed inside yet. That evening the local speakers of the town made several patriotic speeches to us, but what was the nicest thing of all there were about forty ladies, dressed in red, white, and blue, that sang several patriotic songs. But all things have an end, and so at one o'clock [on May 5] we started for Columbus, the capital of the great and glorious state of Ohio." Traveling east through the darkness, the men reached Terre Haute just after sunup. Indiana-born Captain Elliott proudly proclaimed, "Terre Haute gave us a dinner worthy of my grand old native State." A couple of hours later, the train reached Indianapolis, where they "found ambulances in waiting for the disabled, and a good supper prepared for all."[19]

As he had done with the earlier group, Governor Morton had the seventy-one Indiana soldiers removed from the train at Indianapolis and given furloughs. As far as he was concerned, they were home. "Governor Morton saw to it that the Indiana boys got off at Indianapolis and were restored to their family and friends," noted Captain Elliott, although the others had to continue on to Camp Chase.[20]

The soldiers who had to wait at Camp Chase for their paperwork to be completed had an abrupt return to reality. "[O]h, what a change," Brady complained, "instead of being treated like lords, as we were in Illinois, we were treated more like so many dogs than human beings. Myself and a few others could not endure this kind of treatment, so we took French leave [went AWOL] and went home." Sergeant Fies was another Ohioan who went AWOL. Upon arriving in Columbus, Fies complained, "right in sight of the capitol of our own glorious state of Ohio[,] we were treated more like brutes than soldiers, and were almost starved to death by some inhuman, dishonest scoundrel, in the employ of the government. I had too much grit to put up with such treatment and took 'French leave' and left for home, where I soon received notice to return immediately to be mustered out of the service May 30, 1865, under a special telegraphic order from the war department."[21]

Corporal Hulit, from Mansfield, Ohio, also felt the need to leave:

> After spending a week in camp I was very anxious to get home to see my wife and baby. So I took what was called in those days a French furlough. I anticipated some difficulty in traveling on the cars without either a ticket or pass, but

conductors and trainmen were very lenient when I would explain to them that I was an ex–prisoner of war and a survivor of the steamer *Sultana*, and I had not received any pay for eight months. I was carried from Columbus, Ohio, to Mansfield on my word of honor. In one week orders came for survivors of the steamer *Sultana* to report at once to Camp Chase, Ohio, to be mustered out by reason of a telegram from the war department. On the 20th day of May, 1865, I received a final discharge from the service of the United States army, and returned to my home rejoicing that I was still alive and once more a free man.[22]

After the departure of the two large groups, totaling about 600 survivors, approximately 350 *Sultana* people remained in Memphis hospitals or private homes. Lieutenant Dixon remained at the Officers' Hospital for about one week, "spitting up a bloody froth . . . caused by the injury in my breast," before he and several other survivors boarded another steamer and started upriver toward Cairo. The men's frayed nerves were put to the test when a fire broke out on board. "This boat took fire and came near burning up between Memphis and Cairo, but was saved without loss of life," wrote Dixon. Pvt. David Eddleman (Co. I, 64th OH Inf) explained that the boat "was draped in mourning for Lincoln, and near Cairo the mourning caught fire." Fortunately, the fire was quickly extinguished, and the unnamed steamer reached Cairo safely.[23]

As with the other groups that had preceded them, the Indiana men were removed from the train in Indianapolis. Governor Morton gave them "transportation to our various homes, with instructions to report to him at Indianapolis in ten days, which we did, and was mustered out with our regiments." Private Eddleman, from Ohio, continued on and finally reached Columbus. He and the others had to walk the four miles from the train depot to Camp Chase.[24] Like those before them, the newly arrived *Sultana* survivors would have to wait a bit longer before being discharged and sent home.

Following close on the heels of Lieutenant Dixon's group was a large group of survivors that included Private Walker:

After remaining in Memphis at the Soldiers' Home for several days, we were placed aboard a boat [the *City of Alton*] bound for Cairo, Illinois, and I must confess that we had some misgivings about again boarding a steamboat. On one occasion those of us who had just had such a thrilling experience became greatly alarmed when the boat ran aground in a shortcut the captain undertook to make through the woods; but he assured us that everything was all right and that we should be off again in a few minutes, which we were. The captain then remarked that that was the last boat which would pass through there during the rise, as the river was then falling.

The *City of Alton* reached Cairo without further incident. The men boarded freight cars for the trip to Indianapolis where they spent the night at Camp Morton. The next morning, minus the men from Indiana, they boarded another train and headed east to Camp Chase to await their final discharge.[25]

Corporal Winters, who had been admitted to Adams Hospital with slight burns, complained, "It seems hard to get out of a hospital when you once get in one." He was finally released with a small group of other survivors on May 10. He wrote to his parents from Cairo on May 13, "I left Memphis three days ago, and arrived here yesterday evening. We had a very pleasant trip from Memphis here on the steamer *Marble City*; it is a fine boat, and we were not crowded, as there was but few soldiers aboard." Later, Winters admitted that "we *Sultana* boys would jump every time the engineers would try his water gauges, fearing another explosion."[26]

On May 14, the men caught the Illinois Central Railroad north to Mattoon and then transferred to an eastbound P.C.&St.L train toward Columbus, riding all day and all night. As they were coming into Indianapolis, they "received the cheering news that Jeff Davis had been captured. . . . The news raised quite an excitement on the train, and we began to think now that surely peace was near for our unhappy country." When they finally arrived at Camp Chase, Corporal Winters and his companions joined the other *Sultana* survivors awaiting the completion of their paperwork. "The time passed very slowly," Winters said; "every day seemed a week."[27]

Eventually, only a few soldiers remained in Memphis. Private Young, with only an injured left hand, should have gone with the first group but admitted, "I had such a dread of going on to a boat, that I thought best to stay till my nerves got more quiet and my hand got well." After two weeks in Washington Hospital, Young finally left Memphis and traveled safely to his home in Columbus. "No words can portray the joy of the restoration to my family, both to my parents and to myself."[28]

Sixteen-year-old Private McFarland was likewise reluctant to get on another steamboat. Finally overcoming his anxiety, he boarded a boat bound for Evansville, Indiana: "Adopting what I supposed was the safest plan, I crawled into the yawl hanging over the stern of the boat (as all sidewheel packets have) and never left my quarters until I arrived at the wharf at Evansville." Private Haines and Pvt. Nathan D. Everman (Co. F, 40th IN Inf) stayed in Memphis for two weeks before finally boarding a steamboat. "We were afraid to try the boats again and waited for the train to go North," Haines recalled. "We received word that they would not run any trains for several weeks. We were too anxious to get home to wait any longer, so we again tried the water. This time we succeeded in getting to Cairo, Ill." Like the other survivors from Indiana, both Haines and Everman were furloughed at Indianapolis and were soon home.[29]

The survivors stuck at Camp Chase finally gained their release under General Orders No. 77, issued by the War Department on April 28, 1865. Private Davenport "was glad to here that welkem word distarge call. I thought I would sune get home to meet with my loved ones thare. it had bin sixteen monts sence I had herd from them."[30]

Most of the Tennessee men were sent to Nashville on May 17. About half of them received their discharge on June 10, including a large number of the 3rd Tennessee Cavalry. When Private Collins arrived in Nashville, he "found the remainder of our regiment, the third Tennessee cavalry, and we were mustered out together, after which each fellow struck out for his own, dear sweet home, happy." Private Eldridge, also from the 3rd Tennessee Cavalry, arrived in

Nashville on June 9. "We got our discharge and money the next morning and started that evening for home." The other half of the Tennesseans, including Sergeant Wolverton of the 6th Tennessee Cavalry, were sent from Camp Chase to Pulaski, Tennessee, about seventy-five miles south of Nashville, and were mustered out on August 3.[31]

Survivors from Michigan were also sent home in mid-May. The *Jackson Citizen Patriot* announced the glad news: "Arrival of Michigan Soldiers Saved from the *Sultana*." The article stated, "Yesterday, seventy survivors of the wreck of the ill-fated steamer *Sultana*, all Michigan soldiers, arrived here and were sent to Camp Blair to be mustered out." Quartermaster Sergeant Wells, with his usual attention to detail, noted that "wee lef camp chas on the 16 [of May] arived at Jackson of the 17th. on the evning of the 18th I got a furlow and lef for home. I arived home on the morning of the 19 May 1865." Leaving about the same time was Private Koon: "I do not know exactly how long I remained at [Camp Chase], but we were sent from there to Jackson, Mich. where we remained about a week until we got leave of absence from Detroit, when I was permitted to go home, where I arrived on the 20th of May."[32]

Most of the men sent home from Jackson eventually had to report to Detroit for their official release. Private Van Vlack was among them. He was "discharged from the service on the 1st of July, 1865 as a private." Private Johnston "received a furlough to go home and remain until I received orders to report to be mustered out. On July 6 I received orders to go to Detroit, where I was mustered out the next day—July 7, 1865."[33]

For the Kentucky soldiers, Lady Luck smiled on a few of the early arrivals at Camp Chase when, around May 9, they were sent across the Ohio River to Louisville for immediate mustering out. The majority, however, like the soldiers from Tennessee and Michigan, were released on May 17. For some unknown reason, it took longer for the Kentucky soldiers to be mustered out once they returned to their native state. Some were not released until June or July. Corporal Clinger was sent from Cairo to Camp Chase to Louisville and "discharged from the service on the 17th day of June 1865." Farrier Thrasher of the 6th

Kentucky Cavalry was sent to Louisville and then to Nashville, where he was mustered out on July 23.[34]

Of the twenty West Virginians and one Virginian on the *Sultana*, eleven West Virginians and the sole Virginian survived. Most of the West Virginians who arrived at Camp Chase before May 7 were immediately sent on to Wheeling, West Virginia, to be mustered out. The few late arrivals were sent to Wheeling around May 17. As with the Kentucky survivors, the West Virginia discharges were scattered over three months, with a handful coming in May, a few in June, and one man, Pvt. Taylor Woodyard (Co. F, 4th WV Cav), receiving his discharge on July 26.[35] The lone Virginian, Pvt. William Bull (Co. A, Loudoun County Independent Rangers), traveled perhaps the longest distance to be discharged: "After being in the hospital for a time at Memphis, I was sent to Cairo, Ill., and thence to Camp Chase, Ohio, and from there to Washington, D.C., where I was mustered out." Bull actually traveled to Bolivar, West Virginia, just east of Harpers Ferry, where he rejoined his unit and was mustered out on May 31, 1865, having traveled almost one thousand miles.[36]

Private Dougherty, the sole Pennsylvania soldier on board the *Sultana*, also traveled a great distance. From Camp Chase he was forwarded to Annapolis, Maryland, arriving "tired and worn out" on May 6. From there he went to Philadelphia and finally to Spring Mills, Pennsylvania, where he was discharged on June 27, 1865.[37]

One Ohio survivor never made it to Camp Chase and never received a discharge, but he got home just the same. After he was interviewed in Memphis by a committee looking into the disaster, Private Rush and Pvt. George Washington Stewart Jr. (Co. D, 40th IN Inf) "smuggled our way on board a steamer, and, being out of money, begged our way home, telling our story as we went. I reached my home, Kelley's Island, O., on May 5th, 1865, at one o'clock in the morning, having rowed across Lake Erie in a row-boat, a distance of twelve miles from Sandusky City."[38] As it turned out, Private Rush was one of the first Ohioans to reach home.

Most of the Ohio survivors were discharged during the last two weeks of May. Corporal Horner, one of the first to be released, wrote that he was in Columbus for three weeks before he was "mustered out of the service by order of the War Department May 15, 1865." Among the last Ohio survivors to be discharged was Private Walker, who was discharged on May 28 and, with his fellow Ohioans, "returned home to the life of ordinary citizens."[39]

The surviving crew members and civilian passengers had also been leaving Memphis, of course. First Mate William Rowberry and nineteen other crew members came upriver on the *Marble City*, arriving at Cairo on April 28. At St. Louis, the five deckhands who had fled the burning *Sultana* in the sounding yawl were quickly arrested and sent back to Memphis for trial. "Further particulars of the destruction of the steamer *Sultana* put the conduct of five of the deck hands in a most diabolical light," reported a Milwaukee newspaper. "They have very properly been arrested and put in irons." Added an Ohio newspaper, "These men were arrested by the military, the charges being that they launched the yawl and saved themselves, without making an effort to save any of the passengers." While the arrested deckhands were being sent back to Memphis, First Engineer Nathan Wintringer made his way upriver to his home in Steubenville, Ohio, while Pilot George Cayton traveled in the opposite direction, arriving at his hometown of New Orleans on May 1.[40]

Senator-elect Snow may have been among those traveling on the *Marble City* with Rowberry and the others. He reached Cairo on April 28. Over the next few weeks, most of the civilian passengers, including Jennie Perry, Seth W. Hardin Jr., and James M. Safford Sr., headed north to their homes. Nineteen-year-old DeWitt Clinton Spikes spent many days in Memphis attending to the burial of his mother and sister and looking for the bodies of the rest of his family. When the *Memphis Argus* reported that "one of the Spikes family, who was supposed to have been lost, has been rescued by some Confederate soldiers on the Arkansas shore," Spikes set out almost immediately to discover the truth. Unfortunately, the report was in error. Eventually, the sole surviving member of the Spikes family, which had lost $17,000 in gold on the *Sultana*, was given $200 out of the fund collected for the *Sultana* victims. The $200 was the largest amount awarded to a survivor or family member.[41]

Perhaps the most celebrated civilian survivor was Ann Annis. Tenderly cared for at Gayoso Hospital, she slowly began to improve in both body and mind. The *Argus* noted that "several ladies have been soliciting aid for her among our citizens, and it is earnestly requested that they will forward what they have obtained to Capt. F. W. Fox's residence, No. 71, Union street, by 3 o'clock today." With ample clothing and gifts received from the women of Memphis, Mrs. Annis finally left for home in Oshkosh, Wisconsin, on May 11.[42]

Only a few *Sultana* victims were still in the Memphis hospitals by the end of May. Seventeen-year-old Private Lesley, who had been sleeping near the boilers and had been severely scalded, was the last of the survivors to leave the hospital. After his release on June 7, he "traveled by boat from Memphis to Cairo, Ills., thence to Paducah, Ky, thence to Columbia, Tenn., and last to Nashville, Tenn., where I was honorably discharged from the service on June 10th, 1865." On June 28, Pvt. George Washington Dawson (Co. G, 30th IN Inf.), who had been severely scalded, died in Overton Hospital, the last *Sultana* victim in Memphis.[43]

24

THE
INVESTIGATIONS

The *Sultana* victims were still being pulled from the river when Maj. Gen. Cadwallader Washburn, commander of the District of West Tennessee in command at Memphis, issued Special Orders No. 109: "A Court of Inquiry is hereby appointed to meet at these Hd. Qrs. as soon as practicable to investigate the facts and circumstances connected with the burning of the steamer *Sultana* on the Mississippi River near this city and also give their opinion upon the facts which may be developed."[1] Lt. Col. Thomas McLelland Browne (7th IN Cav), a lawyer by profession, was placed in charge of the three-man team of investigators, assisted by Maj. Raphael Guido Rombauer (Battery G, 1st IL Lt. Art) and Capt. Asher Robbins Eddy (asst. QM US Army).[2]

Next, Washburn sent a telegraph to Secretary of War Stanton in Washington. "Will you please order an inquiry to be made at Vicksburg to ascertain why 2,000 released Federal prisoners were crowded on board the ill-fated steamer *Sultana*, against the remonstrance of the captain of the boat and when two other large steamers were in port at the same time, bound up river, with very few passengers?"[3] Washburn's telegram made Captain Mason appear an innocent victim in the overcrowding of the *Sultana* when in fact he had been more than willing to get as many men on board his vessel as possible. It would take a couple more days, but Secretary Stanton would order the inquiry.

The Washburn Commission began interviewing survivors at 11:30 a.m. on April 27, 1865. They started with George Cayton, the surviving pilot of the *Sultana*, who was followed shortly thereafter by First Mate William Rowberry. Each man was asked about the loading of the vessel and the patching of the boiler at Vicksburg, the number of soldiers on board, and the details of the explosion. Along with his other testimony, Cayton stated that the "boat was running at her usual rate about nine or ten miles per hour."[4]

The next person interviewed was Senator-elect Snow, who told of his conversations with First Clerk William Gambrel regarding the number of people on the *Sultana* and Gambrel's apprehension that a calamity might occur as a result. Snow also detailed his escape from the burning boat. Capt. J. V. Lewis, who had once been the transportation quartermaster of Memphis, came next. Lewis testified that "the *Sultana* in my opinion, ought not to have taken on board more that twelve or thirteen hundred men." Lewis did stipulate that federal authorities often ignored the legal carrying capacity of a vessel when shipping troops.[5]

The three commissioners had to hurry to get a three-sentence statement from the mortally scalded Samuel Clemens, who had been the engineer on duty at the time of the explosion. Clemens managed to tell them that the *Sultana* had been "carrying about one hundred thirty-five (135) pounds of Steam," and that he "considered the boilers safe after the repairs at Vicksburg." He added, "Though the work was apparently well done [I] think it very probable the explosion was caused by defective repairs." He ended by saying, "The boat rolled considerably owing to her being very light."[6]

Lieutenant Colonel Browne and his fellow investigators next interviewed the first mate from the *Bostona* (No. 2), who explained that vessel's part in the rescue; and then spoke to William H. Geins, who had been a passenger on the *Pauline Carroll* and had witnessed the loading of the *Sultana* at Vicksburg. Geins was the first person to mention Capt. Reuben Hatch in connection with the loading.[7] Before the end of the day, the three investigators had also spoken to Captain Friesner and Sergeant Nisley. On April 28 and 29, the investigators interviewed two more survivors, Captain Hake and Private Rush.[8]

The newspapers were following all aspects of the investigation, and they soon began to offer opinions and ask questions of their own. On April 29, *The Age* editorialized, "It seems impossible that the disaster could have been an accident—with nobody to blame. The *Sultana* was evidently out of order and overloaded. On every consideration of humanity, a most thorough investigation of the causes of the tragedy should be made, and if parties are found guilty of negligence or recklessness, they should meet with the sternest and severest punishment."[9]

The next day, after learning that other steamboats had been on hand to take some of the men, the *Memphis Argus* reported,

> There were other boats in port at Vicksburg. The *Pauline Carroll* and *Lady Gay* were lying in port, both bound up the river, both almost without freight, and yet these boats, which could easily have taken a portion of the returned prisoners, were suffered to proceed; without any large list of passengers, or heavy invoices of freight. Why was it so? Why was it that these steamers were not required to take a portion of the freight of precious ones, and thus lessen the risk of human life? There must have been a screw loose somewhere. . . . Who is responsible? There must be someone.[10]

On April 30, Secretary of War Stanton ordered an official "inquiry be made at Vicksburg" to investigate "all facts touching the shipment of passengers on board the steamer *Sultana* and the explosion of the boilers of that vessel and the destruction of life in consequence of such explosion." He instructed Washburn to "cause the investigation to be deliberately and vigorously prosecuted. Have all parties guilty of neglect or improper conduct in the matter arrested and report, that speedy trial and proper punishment may be had." Washburn now had the authority to arrest all guilty parties.[11]

In addition to his instructions to General Washburn, Stanton wrote up Special Orders No. 195 instructing General Hoffman, the commissary general of prisoners, "to proceed without delay to Memphis, Tenn., and such other points in the vicinity as may be necessary, to investigate and report upon the circumstances connected with the destruction of the steamer *Sultana*, and the loss of life among the paroled prisoners of war consequent thereto."[12]

On May 1, in Washington, DC, General Grant issued Special Orders No. 79 ordering yet another investigation: "Brevet Colonel Adam Badeau, Military Secretary, will proceed without delay to the Department of the Mississippi, and make a full investigation of all the facts and circumstances connected with the loss of life of released Federal prisoners by the recent explosion of the steamboat *Sultana* on the Mississippi river."[13] Colonel Badeau, a member of Grant's personal staff, set out immediately.

Lieutenant Colonel Browne's investigators next met on Tuesday, May 2, 1865. At 9 a.m. they interviewed Capt. William C. Postal, an agent with the St. Louis and Memphis Packet Company. On Sunday, April 30, Postal and a few others had taken the steam tug *Little Giant* up to the site of the sunken *Sultana*. They searched among the debris and found "portions of fire brick, pieces of coal, and a piece of Shell." Postal remarked that "the piece of Shell looked to me as if it had been subjected to a Severe heat. The mark[s] on the outside show that the Shell in my opinion has been in a coal fire recently."[14]

Captain Postal's discovery of a shell fragment was corroborated by the next person interviewed, John Curtis of the Memphis Quartermaster Department, who had accompanied Postal. Curtis spoke of a "piece of shell which from its appearance I judge to have been recently exploded." These two interviews, following close on the heels of a statement attributed to Rowberry published on April 29 that he thought "a torpedo shaped like a lump of coal must have caused the explosion," would instantly give rise to speculation that the *Sultana* had been sabotaged by Confederate agents. The *Memphis Daily Bulletin* reported on May 2 that the men on the *Little Giant* had "found a piece of a shell weighing nearly a pound among some brick near the starboard guard knee."[15]

In Washington, DC, General Parsons, chief of rail and river transportation, wrote up a circular on May 2 to be distributed to the many

Army quartermasters warning them to use only the best boats when sending soldiers home from the South. General Meigs, the quartermaster general, forwarded the circular to Secretary Stanton that same day, thereby "showing the action taken by this Department relative to the disaster by the Transport *Sultana* on the Mississippi River."[16]

On May 2, General Washburn received Stanton's Special Orders No. 114, which stated: "The Court of Inquiry convened to investigate the cause of the disaster to the Steamer *Sultana* will forthwith proceed to Vicksburg, Miss., there to take such testimony pertinent to the subject as can be collected which may enable them to make a complete report."[17] Around that same date, steamboat inspector John Witzig arrived in Memphis from St. Louis. The *Memphis Daily Bulletin* reported, "When he can examine the wreck he will be able to determine whether the explosion was caused by a shell or not. He inclines to think that the fearful disaster was not the result of fiendish malice, but accidental, and mainly caused by the overcrowding of the boat and her consequent careening when crossing the current." On Friday, May 5, Colonel Badeau arrived in Memphis to start his own investigation.[18]

Capt. William Thornburgh, a one-quarter owner of the *Sultana*, and Captain Dozier, Captain Mason's brother-in-law, visited the wreck on May 4: "Capt. Thornburg [*sic*] intends to have every boiler and fragment of boiler taken from the wreck for the purpose of an examination. He thinks the explosion was from external causes, and has much faith in the story that it was from a shell or shells among the coal."[19] If Thornburgh could prove that sabotage caused the explosion, he and the other owners would be absolved of any financial responsibility toward the *Sultana* victims and survivors. On May 6, part owner William D. Shanks, formerly an assistant clerk on the *Sultana* and now a part owner, arrived in Memphis. Shanks wrote to the editors of the *Memphis Daily Bulletin*: "You will please publish in your paper that all claims against the steamer *Sultana* must be presented to Dameron Bros., commission merchants, St. Louis, for payment within thirty days, or they will not be paid."[20] Most of the survivors had already left Memphis, of course, and others were unable to get to St. Louis, so no claim was ever filed against the remaining owners of the *Sultana*.

At 9 a.m. on May 5, 1865, General Washburn's three-man team began their investigation in Vicksburg. They quickly discovered that General Dana had begun his own investigation. The Dana Commission was headed by Brig. Gen. Morgan Smith, assisted by Col. Michael W. Smith (66th US Colored Inf), Maj. George Delachaumette Reynolds (6th US Colored Heavy Art), Capt. Legrand Winfield Perce (asst. QM), and Lt. Porter A. Ransom (Co. E, 72nd IL Inf).[21]

By the time Lieutenant Colonel Browne and his two associates reached Vicksburg, the Dana Commission had already interviewed Captain Kerns and Capt. L. S. Mitchell, a steamboat captain and acquaintance of Captain Mason. General Smith provided copies of the interviews to Browne, and the Washburn people then interviewed George Dunton, the chief clerk in the Quartermaster Department (and Hatch's friend); William C. Jones, the agent for the Atlantic and Mississippi Steam Ship Company; and 2nd Lt. William Tillinghast, the acting assistant quartermaster under Hatch. Although all three were questioned about suspected bribery, only Lieutenant Tillinghast admitted to accepting a bribe.[22]

At 9 a.m. on May 6, the Washburn trio, with the officers of the Dana Commission sitting in, began the first of three very important interviews for that date. The first man they spoke to was R. G. Taylor, the boiler mechanic who had repaired the *Sultana*'s leaky boiler. Taylor told the investigators all that had transpired during his twenty hours of work. The second person was Capt. George Williams, who told the team about his trip out to Camp Fisk with Captain Speed and then of his later actions in loading the *Sultana* among suspicions of bribery. There were no follow-up questions.[23]

Capt. Reuben Hatch was the third man interviewed on May 6. It was the only interview that Hatch would ever give regarding the *Sultana* disaster. Perhaps already feeling the pressure, and aware that people were pointing fingers at the Vicksburg Quartermaster Department, Hatch tried to implicate Capt. William Kerns, the one man who had tried repeatedly to get the prisoners divided and placed on two boats. Hatch began the interview with the false claim that Captain Kerns had "failed to report the arrival of the *Olive Branch*" to his office on the night of April 22.

Hatch next tried to shift the blame for the overcrowding to Capt. Frederic Speed, stating that he felt that he had been under the orders of Captain Speed during the prisoner exchanges. "He is presumed to act and order by the authority of the Comdg. General," Hatch said. "I consider that I have the control of the shipment of troops unless that duty is taken from me by a superior officer." It is ridiculous to think that Hatch, the chief quartermaster at Vicksburg, would consider Speed, an assistant adjutant general, a "superior officer."

Continuing his attack on Speed, Hatch said that he had "objected to sending so many troops on the steamer *Sultana*," claiming "my telegram to Capt. Speed [out at Camp Fisk] shows that I thought too many were going on that boat." This was a bold-faced lie. Hatch's telegram to Speed was sent around 10 a.m. on April 24, before the first trainload of soldiers had even left Camp Fisk. At that time, both Captain Speed and Captain Williams, who were together at Camp Fisk, were operating under the false impression that there were only about 1,400 prisoners left in the camp, a number small enough to go on one boat. The steamboat *Henry Ames* had already taken 1,315 men, so 1,400 was not an unreasonable number. Hatch's telegram to Speed sent around 10 a.m. and asking: "Is there more prisoners than can go on the *Sultana*?" was evidence that he had not objected to the number of troops being placed on the *Sultana* and that he did not think "too many men were going on that boat." Hatch was playing fast and loose with the facts.

Although Hatch testified that he thought "the *Sultana* ought not to have carried more than fifteen hundred troops," nothing he did on the date of the loading indicated that. When Captain Kerns repeatedly implored him to come down to the waterfront and see for himself how overcrowded the boat was getting, Hatch did nothing. "I did start to see if there was sufficient room on the boat," he admitted, "but effecting that the business was taken out of my hands [by Speed], I turned about and left her." All of the special orders dealing with the shipment of prisoners had included the phrase, "The Quartermaster Department will furnish transportation." Hatch, who was the senior officer in charge of transportation in that department, now claimed that he had nothing to do with furnishing the transports.

Finally, when asked, "Do you know of any bribes being offered to any officers in the U.S. service or to any employee of the Govt. by any person for the privilege of transporting troops?" Hatch simply stated, "I do not."[24]

With the finger of guilt turning toward Captain Speed, the Washburn people, again with the officers of the Dana Commission sitting in, began their May 7 interviews by questioning Speed himself. Speed told of his involvement in the release of the paroled prisoners, not only for the *Sultana* but also the *Henry Ames* and the *Olive Branch*. When he was asked, "Did you make any requisition upon the Quartermaster Dept. for the transportation of the troops referred to?" he answered, "Special orders were given in each case to Capt. Kerns for the movement of each detachment from the beginning of the movement to the end." Lieutenant Colonel Browne asked, "Why did you give the order to Capt. Kerns instead of [Capt.] Hatch, the quartermaster on Genl. Dana's staff?" Speed responded, "Simply because it has been the custom to send the order directly to Capt. Kerns[,] and [Capt.] Hatch intimating that he did not care to see this class of orders."[25]

This was another indication of how little responsibility Captain Hatch was willing to take in his own department. As chief quartermaster, Hatch should have been involved with every shipment, and yet he refused even to receive the information involving the transactions. When it came to the shipment of men on the *Sultana*, however, Hatch made sure that boat was selected, because he was getting a kickback from her captain.

When Speed was asked directly, "Who gave the order for the troops to go on the *Sultana*?" he responded, "I think it was [Captain] Hatch. I did not give any orders for the troops to go on board."[26] Speed had been out at Camp Fisk when the first two trainloads of men were placed on the *Sultana* and had eventually gone to the riverfront only because Lieutenant Davenport asked him to.

When he arrived in Vicksburg from Washington, General Hoffman discovered that the Washburn Inquiry and the Dana Commission were cooperating in the investigation. "The court and the commission were about closing their proceedings when I arrived at Vicksburg,"

Hoffman reported, "and finding upon a perusal of their records that all the testimony taken would be useful to me in forming an opinion as to the merits of the case, I determined to avail myself of a copy of them."[27]

On May 8, Hoffman asked General Dana to provide him with a report "regarding the shipment of paroled Federal prisoners from here." Dana responded with a long letter describing the events concerning the loading of the *Henry Ames*, the *Olive Branch*, and the *Sultana* but failed to point the finger toward any guilty party. When Hoffman asked, "Will General Dana please state what officer or officers he considers responsible for the shipment of the paroled troops within referred to, and for the proper character of the transportation?" Dana responded, "Captain Speed was intrusted with the transfer and shipment of the prisoners, and assumed full and active management and control of it, and I therefore consider him fully responsible therefor. The quartermaster's department was ordered to provide the transportation, and I consider Captain Kerns, quartermaster in charge of transportation, responsible for the character of it."[28]

With just a few sentences General Dana had picked the two least culpable officers as being the most responsible for the overcrowding of the *Sultana*. Throughout the date of the loading, April 24, Captain Kerns had tried repeatedly to have the men divided and put on different vessels, even taking the responsibility of ordering the *Olive Branch* to remain in port until the third trainload of prisoners was on the *Sultana*. And Captain Speed had at first refused to send any prisoners on the *Sultana*, claiming that he had not yet completed the rolls. It was Hatch and Williams who had insisted that the rolls could be completed later and that the remaining men at Camp Fisk could all be sent on Mason's boat.

The Washburn commissioners and the Dana Commission met together again on May 8 and recalled Captain Williams, who ended his short session with a statement that placed Captain Speed's head on the chopping block. It was Captain Speed, Williams said, who "attended to the making up the rolls, exchanging the men, and having the rolls signed. I signed no rolls of exchange whatever."[29] In other words, Williams said he had nothing to do with any of it.

Interestingly, the next two interviews were with General Smith and Captain Perce, both members of the Dana Commission. General Smith testified that Captain Kerns had protested the overcrowding of the *Sultana*. He explained that because of his own experience with steamboating, however, he thought that the prisoners on the *Sultana* "could be comfortable with the exception of cooking and privy accommodations." He had not personally seen the overcrowded boat, he admitted, although he had received numerous requests to go down to the waterfront to see the overcrowding firsthand.

Smith was next asked if he felt that the two-year-old boilers on the *Sultana* were "more liable to explode than if [they] had been new and perfect." It was at this point that he became the only witness to state that a boiler full of water was just as dangerous as one that was partially full. His statement was not pursued.[30]

The only question posed to Captain Perce, an experienced quartermaster, was whether he had "ever known of a larger number of troops having been placed on one steamer in proportion to her capacity than were in this instance shipped on the *Sultana*." Although he cited one instance when a boat took as many, and one instance when a boat took more, he admitted that "these cases were all, as far as my knowledge extends, of absolute necessity," whereas the overcrowding of the *Sultana* was not.[31]

After returning to Memphis, the last person the Washburn commissioners interviewed before they concluded their investigations was John J. Witzig, the supervising inspector of steamboats. Witzig began by explaining that the *Sultana*'s boilers had been properly inspected in St. Louis prior to her last trip. When asked "What cause do you assign to the explosion?" Witzig told the assembled investigators that "the piece of boiler found at the wreck gives unmistakable evidence that the lower portion of that boiler had been burned, that the portion corresponding with the fracture showed evidence that the waterline was ten inches below the fire line. In my opinion the explosion was caused by excess of steam." Unwilling to drop the sabotage theory, the commissioners next asked, "Supposing about half pound of powder had been thrown in the fire under the boilers and there exploded. What manner would such explosion affect the boilers of the steamboat?" Witzig answered, "In my opinion, it would have spread the boilers. It may have punched a hole through them but could in no case cause such an explosion as took place on the *Sultana*."[32] In other words, had there been a coal torpedo, it could not have caused the damage done to the *Sultana*.

On May 8 the Dana Commission interviewed three more witnesses, asking them mainly about bribes.[33] After these short interviews, General Smith and the other commissioners concluded their investigation. The only people still looking into the disaster were General Hoffman in Vicksburg and Colonel Badeau in Memphis.

The next day, General Hoffman got short statements from three people, including Captain Kerns and Edward D. Butler, the superintendent of military railroads at Vicksburg.[34] Hoffman also got written statements from Captain Williams and Captain Speed clarifying whether either of them had inspected the *Sultana* prior to her being loaded (they had not), and from Speed as to "who selected her." To that question Speed responded: "[Captain] Hatch selected the boat, so far as I know."[35]

On May 5, a scathing editorial appeared in the *Chicago Tribune*. "Shocking as were our first accounts of the *Sultana* disaster, it appears upon a fuller investigation that those accounts failed altogether to bring to light the enormity of the crime which resulted in this fearful sacrifice of seventeen hundred lives." After repeating the story that the *Lady Gay* and *Pauline Carroll* had stood by, ready to take an overflow of men, the editors stated, "The necessary inference at the time was that the captain of the *Sultana* obtained them by corrupt means." Finally, someone was mentioning the culpability of Captain Mason.

The *Tribune* went on to point out that the *Sultana*'s boilers had not been inspected after they were patched, and that she may have been running with a higher amount of steam pressure than allowed by law: "These facts are sufficient to give the lie to the canard, started by the mate, that the explosion must have been arisen from an infernal machine. The infernal machine that exploded the boiler and sent so many souls into eternity, carrying bereavement and mourning into thousands of Western homes, was undoubtedly, the bribe—the greenbacks paid by the officers of the *Sultana* to the Quartermaster for the transportation of the troops."

The *Chicago Tribune* had figured out that Captain Mason and Captain Hatch had been working together to overload the *Sultana*, with Captain Hatch accepting money from Captain Mason for sending the men to that boat. It was not sabotage but greed and corruption that had led to those deaths.

The editorial concluded by stating, "Enough has already transpired to justify the charge that the appalling calamity is traceable to the cupidity of the officers in charge. This being true, the community will watch closely the investigation, and will demand that an example be made, which, though it cannot retrieve the past, may at least protect us in the future."[36]

On May 10, the Washburn commissioners and John J. Witzig accompanied survivor Seth Hardin and others on the steam tug *Little Giant* back to the site of the *Sultana*. While searching about the wreck, they "managed to get a piece of the boilers (which, it was impossible to tell), which showed evidence of the terrible power of pent up steam—it being straightened out and then bent back and torn in several places by the explosion. These gentlemen said this piece of the boilers dissipated the idea that a shell was the cause of the explosion, as one end of this piece is very badly burned, proving, beyond doubt, that the boilers were in very bad condition."[37]

Hard evidence was showing that the *Sultana*'s boilers had been operating with insufficient water, something Corporal Elza had suggested after noting Samuel Clemens expelling hot water from the boilers. The hard evidence was also showing that the *Sultana* was not the victim of sabotage. The *Argus* article added, "If, when the river falls, the rest of the boilers tell the same tale as this piece somebody will have to suffer for this unparalleled disaster."[38]

Still conducting interviews, General Hoffman returned to Memphis on May 11 and spoke to some of the survivors who remained in the city's hospitals. He saw Ann Annis and Sergeant Hites at Gayoso Hospital, and Louis Bean at Adams Hospital. He also was given a copy of the testimony of Captain McCown at Officers' Hospital that had been taken by Colonel Badeau. Each survivor told of conditions on the vessel prior to the explosion and of their individual fight to survive.[39]

Finished with his work in Memphis, Hoffman set out for Washington on the *Marble City*. Accompanying him was John Witzig, who was taking the recovered piece of boiler back to St. Louis for further analysis. On the way, the two men showed the piece to W. B. Richardson, chief engineer of the *Marble City*. After examining the piece, Richardson gave a statement about the power of steam, about the effects of careening, and about the possibility that the *Sultana*'s boilers lacked sufficient water. The piece showed signs of being "heated to redness." Still, Richardson admitted, "as the boat was burned up after the explosion, it is possible that this piece of iron may have been heated by being exposed to the fire of the burning boat."[40] He could come to no positive conclusion regarding the cause of the explosion.

While the *Marble City* was northbound, the *Memphis Argus* published its own conclusion about the cause of the accident: "From indications about the wreck, and upon examination of the fragments of bodies raised, the idea advanced by some that her blowing up was from effects of the bursting of a shell, is exploded as is also that it was caused by the way in which she was loaded and the number of human beings on board. The true reason, as near as can be ascertained from ocular proof, is that the water was too low in her boilers and her fires too hot, hence this sad calamity."[41] There was no coal torpedo, and the fact that the *Sultana* was top-heavy after the hogsheads of sugar were removed from the hold made no difference. It was low water in the boilers, plain and simple.

On May 12, in Vicksburg, Major General Dana received General Orders No. 78, issued by General Grant in Washington, relieving him of command: "Maj. Gen. N. J. T. Dana, U.S. Volunteers, is relieved from command of Department of Mississippi, and Maj. Gen. G. K. Warren, U.S. Volunteers, is assigned to the command of that department." The order instructed Dana to "proceed to his place of residence" to await further orders. Dana immediately sent a telegram to Adjutant General Lorenzo Thomas: "In view of the immediate close of the war and with the opinion that my services will not now be longer required I request that this my resignation be accepted." Dana was trying to resign his commission before he could be officially relieved of command. While he waited for a response, he went home to Portsmouth,

New Hampshire. On May 27, he received word that his resignation had been accepted.[42]

When the *Marble City* with General Hoffman and Inspector Witzig reached Cairo, the general stayed on board and headed west along the Ohio River while Witzig took the piece of boiler and returned to St. Louis. On May 14, Hoffman reached Cincinnati and spoke to engineer and boilermaker Isaac West, who gave his "views in relation to the causes of the bursting or exploding of steamboat boilers in general, and especially in the case of the *Sultana*." Hoffman traveled from there to Camp Chase and on May 15 spoke to survivors Corporal Mahoney, Sergeant Barker, Lieutenant Dickinson, and Lieutenant Squire about their experiences on the *Sultana*.[43]

On May 16, General Hoffman went to Pittsburgh and concluded his investigation by interviewing Nathan Wintringer, the *Sultana's* first engineer. Wintringer told of the repair to the boiler, of his actions prior to and after the explosion, and of speaking to the mortally scalded Samuel Clemens after both were rescued. When asked about careening, Wintringer said, "The boat was frequently careened to one side or the other, even before the sugar was taken out, but never so much so as to cause the water in any of the boilers to be so much lowered as to expose any part of it to the fire unprotected by water." He concluded, "I do not think the cause of the explosion can be conjectured until the boilers can be inspected."[44]

While General Hoffman was en route to Washington, he received a telegram from General Washburn in Memphis telling him that "twelve commissioned officers and 757 enlisted men make the total of paroled prisoners saved from the steamer *Sultana*."[45] Washburn's total did not include the civilian survivors or the surviving crew members, yet 769 survivors would be the official figure for a long time.

On May 19, after reaching Washington, Hoffman wrote up the results of his investigation for Secretary of War Stanton. In his second paragraph, Hoffman noted that

> a proper order was issued by the general commanding the department [Dana] for the embarkation of the paroled prisoners, and there were four officers of his staff who were

responsible that this order was properly carried out, viz. [Capt.] R. B. Hatch, captain in the quartermaster's depart- ment, chief quartermaster; Capt. Frederic Speed, assis- tant adjutant general, U.S. Volunteers, adjutant-general Department of Mississippi; Capt. George A. Williams, First U.S. Infantry, commissary of musters and in charge of paroled prisoners, and Capt. W. F. Kerns, assistant quar- termaster, U.S. Volunteers, and master of transportation. If there was anything deficient or unsuitable in the character of the transportation furnished, one or more of these offi- cers should be held accountable for the neglect.[46]

In spite of all the testimony he had heard and read, Hoffman erred when naming the person who selected the *Sultana*: "She was provided by the master of transportation [Kerns], with the approval of the chief quartermaster [Hatch]." Kerns had nothing to do with the selection of the *Sultana*. He first learned of it when Captain Mason came to his office on the morning of April 24. And Captain Hatch had not *approved* the selection, he had *made* the selection. After cutting his deal with Captain Mason on April 17, Hatch did everything he could to get a large group of prisoners placed on board the *Sultana*. It was Hatch, not Kerns, who "provided" the *Sultana*.

In naming the officers he thought most responsible for the over- crowding, General Hoffman pointed to "[Captain] Hatch and Captain Speed." He thought that Captain Williams "was assisting Captain Speed and seems to have felt that there was no special responsibility resting on him," although he added, that "there was manifest propri- ety in [Williams'] knowing the number embarked, and if there was a deficiency of transportation, he should have reported it."

Hoffman next rebuked Captain Kerns because he "made no inspec- tion of the steamer to see if she was properly fitted up . . . [and] made no report of the repairing of the boilers, which he seems to have been aware was going forward." However, he praised Kerns for trying to get the men divided onto other vessels. "[Kerns] did report her to [Captain] Hatch, and also to General Smith, as being insufficient for so many troops, and his report should have been noticed."

In the same paragraph, Hoffman mentioned Lieutenant Tillinghast, the acting assistant quartermaster of Camp Fisk, and Gen. Morgan L. Smith. Of Tillinghast he wrote, "It is shown by his own testimony that a bribe was proffered to him to induce him to use his influence in having some of the troops shipped on the *Pauline Carroll*, which he showed a willingness to accept—at least he did not reject it." Smith, Hoffman wrote, "had nothing officially to do with the shipment of the troops; yet as it was officially reported to him by Captain Kerns that too many men were being put on the *Sultana*, it was proper that he should have satisfied himself from good authority whether there was sufficient grounds for the report, and if he found it so he should have interfered to have the evil remedied. Had he done so the lives of many men would have been saved."

As to what caused the boilers to explode, General Hoffman admitted, "The testimony which I have been able to collect does not enable me to form a positive opinion." He noted the repairs done at Vicksburg and that the boiler mechanic had pronounced the work "a good job," though "not perfect." Hoffman also told Stanton that Wintringer had watched the patched boiler carefully after leaving Vicksburg and had found that "it did not at any time show the least sign of giving way" and that Samuel Clemens had stated before dying that "the boilers were all right and full of water."

In touching on the careening story, General Hoffman wrote, "There is nothing to show that there was any careening of the boat at the time of the disaster, or that she was running fast; on the contrary, it is shown that she was running evenly and not fast." After describing his inspection of the piece of boiler that Witzig had recovered from the wreck, Hoffman stated, "It is the common opinion among engineers that an explosion of steam boilers is impossible when they have the proper quantity of water in them, but the boilers may burst from an over-pressure of steam when they are full of water, owing to some defective part of iron." This statement would be proved 150 years later by engineer Patrick Jennings. Since the boiler water contains most of the energy, a full boiler is more dangerous than a partially full boiler. If a small tear occurs on a boiler full of water, the resulting escape of steam is catastrophic. Continued Hoffman, "One engineer, who is said to be the most reliable on the river, says that even in such a case the great power of steam, having once found a yielding place, tears everything before it, producing the effect of an explosion."[47]

Those who continue to believe that the *Sultana* was sabotaged point out that General Hoffman did not address the coal torpedo theory. He did not mention the theory because there was no need to. By the time Hoffman made his report to Stanton on May 19 it had long been disproven. Although Hoffman was not sure what had caused the explosion, he was positive that it was not a coal torpedo.

In conclusion, Hoffman told Stanton that there were "1,866 troops on board the boat, including 33 paroled officers, 1 officer who had resigned [Lt. Annis], and the captain in charge of the guard [Friesner]." Of course, Hoffman's total, like that of Captain Williams before him, was short 100 men. He believed that 765 soldiers were saved and 1,101 lost. When he added in the lost passengers and crew, he came to a "total loss [of] 1,238," a number much smaller than the 1,500 or 1,700 the various newspapers and even some of the survivors were bandying about.[48] It is also very close to the 1,169 identified by this author.

On May 23, Secretary Stanton received the report and the testimonies taken by the Washburn Court of Inquiry. One day later, the *Cincinnati Commercial Tribune* published the report. It began by mentioning the repair to the larboard boiler, saying only, "This work was done well, so far as it went, but sufficient repairs were not made." The report likewise described the journey from Vicksburg to Memphis in a single sentence. Oddly enough, although it mentioned the stops at Memphis and at the coal barges, the Washburn Inquiry's report did not mention the removal of the hogsheads of sugar. Of the explosion of the *Sultana*'s boilers the report said, "Soon afterward the boat caught fire, and was totally destroyed." Of those on board, "only about 800 persons were saved."

The three investigators disbelieved the careening theory because "the men were all, or for the most part, asleep. . . . Good order prevailed, and the men were as comfortable as could be." They added, "The safety of the boat was not particularly endangered by the number of men on board, but there was no military necessity for placing them upon one boat." Acknowledging that the *Pauline Carroll* was at Vicksburg during the overcrowding, the investigators agreed that "[t]he men should have been divided."

The report went on to say that "the Quartermaster's Department at Vicksburg [i.e., Captain Hatch and Captain Kerns] is censurable for not insisting on its rights, and for permitting others, without urgent protest to the General commanding [i.e., General Dana] to perform its duties, and the Adjutant General of the Department of Mississippi [i.e., Captain Speed] is censurable for taking upon himself duties not properly belonging to him." The investigators were quick to point out, however, that "there was no part . . . on the part of the officers referred to, to do any injustice to the soldiers on board the *Sultana*." The Washburn report concluded, "The cause of the explosion, from the evidence, was by there not being sufficient water in the boilers."[49]

The report did not assign responsibility to any officer by name but did imply that Hatch, Speed, and Kerns deserved censure. Surprisingly, Captain Williams, who had stood at the foot of the wharf boat and stubbornly worked hard to have all the men crowded onto the *Sultana*, received no blame for the overloading.

In his cover letter accompanying the report General Washburn stated his conclusion that "the explosion was occasioned by the want of water in the boilers. It is also shown that the boilers were defective and known to be so." He mentioned that the Court of Inquiry had censured the Quartermaster Department at Vicksburg "for not having remonstrated with greater earnestness against the placing of so many men on one boat when there were other boats present and anxious to take a portion of the soldiers on the same terms." In his opinion, "this censure is not deserved. It is plain that [Captain] Hatch, chief quartermaster of the department, and Captain Kerns, master of transportation, said all that was necessary for them to say, to have a portion of the troops placed upon the steamer *Pauline Carroll*, and that they interested themselves to such an extent as to draw upon themselves the accusation of receiving bribes from parties interested in the boat, of which there is no proof."[50]

Washburn's conclusions are inaccurate or incomplete in several respects. While Captain Speed made the mistaken accusation to

General Dana that Captain Kerns was taking a bribe, Captain Hatch was never mentioned in connection with bribery. Although he was up to his eyeballs in schemes to get kickbacks from the various steamboat captains, he somehow managed to keep that hidden. And while Kerns *did* say "all that was necessary . . . to have a portion of the troops placed upon the steamer *Pauline Carroll*," Hatch had said nothing about doing so. Hatch's telegram to Captain Speed at Camp Fisk at about 10 a.m. on April 24 did not demonstrate that Hatch was doing "all that was necessary" to get the men divided. In fact, Hatch did not want the men divided. Neither the testimonies of those the commissioners interviewed nor the facts supported Washburn's statements.

Washburn did not mention Captain Williams or Captain Speed in his cover letter, but there was an offhand reference to Captain Mason and Second Engineer Clemens as being responsible for the overcrowding and for the explosion. "All the parties to the boat who were in any wise responsible for the disaster," Washburn noted, "lost their lives at the time of the explosion or have since died."[51]

After publishing Washburn's report, the *Commercial Tribune* of Cincinnati ripped into it: "It is unsatisfactory. We do not understand from it, very definitely, what occasioned the explosion, and perhaps it was impossible to clearly determine that point. Some censure is placed at the door of the officer [Speed], who crowded sixteen hundred soldiers on board this boat, but it is, to say the least, drawn very mild." The *Tribune* hinted at the suspected bribery, noting, "While the commission show that no necessity existed for such a cramming and crowding of men on the transport, they don't appear to have inquired how it happened that the *Sultana* should have been particularly and overabundantly favored, while other equally good and trustworthy transports, were lying idle in port. It might have been profitable to look into it."

"The conclusion arrived at," the *Tribune* went on to say, "is as near a verdict of 'nobody to blame' as it was, perhaps, prudent to approximate. It strikes us, that a disaster so fearful in its character and consequences, demands a more rigid investigation than seems to have been given it."[52]

Although Hatch, Kerns, Speed, and Williams were repeatedly mentioned in the testimonies and reports as being the most culpable for the overcrowding of the *Sultana*, which may or may not have contributed to the destruction of the vessel, only one of the four was singled out for court-martial. As May came to a close, it was clear to Capt. Frederic Speed that he was being set up to be the sacrificial lamb.

25

SCAPEGOAT

Instead of waiting for the hammer to fall, Captain Speed decided to strike first. On May 26, Speed wrote to Michigan senator Jacob M. Howard, a longtime friend of the Speed family, asking him to ask President Johnson for a court of inquiry to look into his role in the *Sultana* disaster. Senator Howard wrote to the president on June 5. Eventually, the request ended up on the desk of General Grant.[1]

After writing to Senator Howard, Speed wrote to Lieutenant Colonel Browne, who had been in charge of the Washburn Commission: "I have read in the papers what purports and undoubtedly is the finding of the commission of which you were the presiding Officer, to investigate the *Sultana* disaster. I have, I confess, been much surprised and mortified at the result, for I must say that I did not expect it, and still think that I have done nothing to deserve censure."

Speed wondered how the Washburn Commission had come to the conclusion that he was responsible for the selection and loading of the *Sultana*. "I *request* you to inform me in what way I took upon myself duties which did not properly belong to me to perform. . . . I should like to know, in general terms, in what manner I exceeded my duties. . . . I did nothing before the arrival of Captain Williams which did not meet with [Captain] Hatch's approval. After Captain

Williams arrived, and especially after he took upon himself the duty of shipping the men, I did not consider myself responsible."

Speed commented on his conversation with Captain Kerns on the wharf boat when Kerns had approached him and suggested that the *Sultana* was becoming too crowded and wondered if the men should be divided. "I had nothing to do, officially, although I carried his suggestion, to divide the men, to Captain Williams, who overruled it. It may be that the commission thought that I should have had nothing to do with the prisoners, and I should not have had, if I had not been ordered to do so and upon this ground [the Washburn investigators] based their finding."

Speed was perplexed that he was being chastised for being involved with the prisoner exchange. "If this is the ground for the actions of the commission, it does me great injustice, but if, on the contrary, it was thought that I, in any way, interfered with shipping the men, or did, or said, anything to prevent the men from being divided further than to say that it would be inconvenient to do so and to express an opinion that one boat could carry all the men before I knew their exact number I do not think that the facts justify the finding."[2] Speed wanted answers but got none.

Colonel Badeau, General Grant's military secretary, had arrived in Memphis and gone up to the wreck of the *Sultana* on May 7. Afterward he returned to the city to interview a few steamboat captains and engineers, and to speak to a few of the survivors still languishing in Memphis hospitals. On May 12, he traveled to Vicksburg and "heard the several statements of those implicated," including Captain Speed. Upon his return to Washington, he sent a report to General Grant, who forwarded the report to Secretary Stanton. On June 17, Assistant Secretary of War Charles A. Dana contacted Grant regarding Speed's earlier request for a court of inquiry. Although Grant had already marked the first request "Disapproved," he followed up his one-word response with a formal statement on June 19. "Respectfully returned with the information that the application of Captain Speed for a Court of Inquiry in his case was recieved [sic], and that the same disapproved. I have not, and donot [sic] at present recommend the dismissal of Capt. Speed."[3] Instead of getting an inquiry, Speed would get a court-martial.

While Speed waited for Senator Howard's response, he began thinking of his future. On June 3, he wrote to his father in Maine and told him that he wanted to remain in the South after the war and open an ice business.[4] That same date, he wrote to his older sister Anna, "I do not know what I shall do and cannot tell until I hear from any application from a Court of Inquiry, in regard to the august imputations of [the] Memphis Commission to investigate the *Sultana* disaster—If a favorable answer is received I shall resign at once that the decision of the Court is in."[5] Speed was still hopeful that a court of inquiry specifically established to look into his actions in the disaster would exonerate him.

Also on June 3 in Washington, Quartermaster General Meigs, who had a deep-seated distrust and dislike for Captain Hatch because of Hatch's earlier dishonesty while at Cairo, finally received and approved the recommendation of the New Orleans quartermaster's examining board from February 1865 that Hatch was "totally unfit to discharge the duties of assistant quartermaster" and should be dismissed from the service. After signing the recommendation, Meigs forwarded the papers to Secretary of War Stanton for action by President Johnson.[6] Unfortunately, the report had come five weeks too late for the people who had been killed, injured, or otherwise affected by the explosion of the *Sultana*.

A few days later, Captain Speed was transferred to New Orleans and the Department of the Gulf. Although the war was winding down and other officers were leaving the service, Speed refused to leave. "I shall not resign until I hear from the *Sultana* matter, when that is settled I am off in a moment," he wrote home on June 9. Eight days later, Speed was transferred to Mobile, Alabama.[7]

On June 16, Quartermaster General Meigs sent General Washburn's cover letter and the "Report of the [Washburn] Court of Inquiry" to Adjutant Brig. Gen. Charles Thomas. Pointing out that the court found "the Quartermaster's Department at Vicksburg is censurable for not insisting on its rights, and for permitting others . . . to perform its duties," Meigs recommended that "the officers of the Quartermaster's Department . . . be ordered before a Court Martial for trial." Since the Washburn Report failed to identify a single officer by name, General Meigs provided them: "Capt. R. B. Hatch, A.Q.M. Chief Q.M. Dept. of Miss.; Capt. W. F. Kerns, A.Q.M. in charge of Transportation."[8] While Hatch undoubtedly deserved a court-martial, Kerns did not. Neither officer, however, would ever face a military tribunal.

At Vicksburg on June 16, Maj. Gen. Morgan Smith, who was still suffering from the hip wound he had sustained in 1862, submitted a letter of resignation to the Adjutant General's Office. Six days later he was granted a leave of absence. General Grant approved Smith's resignation on July 8, and Secretary Stanton endorsed it on July 12.[9] Another officer connected with the *Sultana* was gone, and one was about to leave.

On June 26, Captain Hatch, who had been relieved of command as chief quartermaster at Vicksburg, boarded the steamboat *Atlantic* at Vicksburg, bound for St. Louis, carrying $14,490 in government funds. Hatch apparently reasoned that he was still responsible for the funds of the Vicksburg Quartermaster Department and could not leave them behind with his replacement. He intended to hand them over to the chief quartermaster in St. Louis. The assistant quartermaster general, Maj. Gen. Robert Allen, disagreed with that reasoning, concluding that Hatch had violated army regulations by not turning the funds over to bonded quartermasters at Vicksburg.[10] Upon boarding the steamboat, Hatch reportedly placed the funds in the safe alongside $22,000 in private funds belonging to other passengers.[11]

During the trip upriver, the safe was robbed. After a thorough search, two suspected thieves were arrested. All of the private funds were recovered, but only $5,948 of the government funds was found; $8,542 was still missing. A Board of Survey immediately looked into the loss and deemed Hatch "personally responsible" for the missing funds since he had not turned the money over to the proper authorities at Vicksburg.[12] No one at the time realized how big a part the robbery on the *Atlantic* would play in the upcoming court-martial of Captain Speed. On July 28, 1865, Reuben Benton Hatch was honorably mustered out of the service. In spite of two arrests and numerous accusations against him, he had never spent a single moment in front of a military court-martial.[13]

Another officer connected to the loading of the *Sultana* left the service under more disgraceful circumstances. In July, Lieutenant Tillinghast, who had admitted to the Washburn investigators that he had accepted a bribe to help put prisoners on both the *W. R. Arthur* and the *Pauline Carroll*, went absent without leave. On August 10 he was arrested in Natchez and faced a court-martial for desertion. Tillinghast, who had been arrested in Chicago for forgery before he ran away to join the service, practiced his skills once more. On September 11 he forged some orders and deserted. Although military authorities pursued him as "a deserter & a forger," he was instead arrested by civilian authorities and sent to Chicago to face the consequences for his earlier forgery and for skipping bail in 1864.[14]

On June 27, Captain Speed wrote a letter to his sister Lotty complaining about the lack of letters from home:

> There has been no time since I parted from those most dear to me that I have [been more in] need [of] good comforting letters, than since the terrible accident to the *Sultana* of which you have had the full particulars. But you know that my spirits are so abundant that I cannot long remain depressed, yet there is something so very mean in the finding of the commission appointed to investigate a affair that I cannot refer to it without feelings of sadness and I fear anger, sometimes—I have now waited so long that I have no hope of hearing from my application for a court of inquiry.

Knowing that many of the Vicksburg officers involved in the disaster were resigning and going their separate ways, he complained that "most [of the] important witnesses are now unattainable and this too greatly to my prejudice."[15]

Twelve weeks after the *Sultana* explosion, on July 20, 1865, Judge Advocate Joseph Holt drafted charges and specifications toward the court-martial of Capt. Frederic Speed. Charge No. 1 was for "Conduct prejudice to good order and military discipline," with three specifications. Specification 1 stated that Speed "did without authority assume to order and did order that a large number of . . . paroled prisoners of war . . . be embarked on board the steamer *Sultana*" and that Speed "well knew that it was the duty of the Quartermaster Dept. to provide the transportation for the said paroled prisoners."

Specification 2 said that Speed "did . . . load or cause to be loaded upon the steamer *Sultana*, a Mississippi River steamboat, with defective boilers" a large number of paroled Union prisoners and that because of this large number "the boiler or boilers of said boat did explode causing the deaths of a great number." The specification ended with the sentence, "That Capt. Speed well knew the defective condition of the boiler or boilers of said boat [at] the time of placing the paroled prisoners of war on board."

Specification 3 stipulated that Speed did "assume unwarranted authority in directing the arrangements for the transportation of a large number of paroled persons . . . and did without authority board a large number . . . upon one boat, to wit, the steamer *Sultana* where at the same time other and better constituted steamboats, to wit, the *Pauline Carroll* and the *Lady Gay*, were at the post of Vicksburg aforesaid, and whose officers were anxious to take a portion of the said paroled prisoners." The specification added that Captain Kerns had informed Speed that the *Pauline Carroll* wanted to take a portion of the men, but "Capt. Speed, against the remonstrances of the said Capt. Kearns [*sic*] . . . did cause the whole number . . . to be placed upon the steamer *Sultana*."[16]

Shockingly, Charge No. 2 was "Manslaughter." According to the single specification, Speed "freely and with no authority assumed to direct and manage the business of transporting a larger number" of paroled prisoners and did "greatly neglect to procure the proper and safe number of steamboats upon which to safely transport the paroled prisoners aforesaid but did negligently and carelessly cause the whole number . . . to be loaded upon the steamer *Sultana*." The specification charged that Speed knew that the *Sultana* had defective boilers, and yet, "against the remonstrances of the officer of the QM Dept. to wit [Capt.] R. B. Hatch and Capt. Kearns [*sic*] against placing the whole number of paroled prisoners aforesaid upon one boat, [did] load or cause to be loaded upon the steamer *Sultana* the whole number of persons." According to the specification, it was the "large load of passengers" and the defective condition of the boilers that caused the deaths of almost 1,200 people.[17]

Although the charges had been formalized, another four months passed before they were preferred against Captain Speed. However, he knew they were coming. On September 17, he wrote to his father,

> I . . . have ascertained that I am to be tried by a General Court Martial on account of the part I played in the *Sultana* disaster—I do not fear the result, although I do not court the notoriety which I must gain. The charges are serious and much time must be consumed in the trial, and I fear not a little money. I am glad to observe that all who have any acquaintance with the case are on my side. . . . I have not yet been served with a copy of the charges but have seen a memorandum of them and therefore know that they will be very strongly drawn and although easily disapproved yet of a nature too serious to warrant any mistake on the part of the defense.[18]

Two days later, an anxious Speed wrote his father again, this time referencing the trial of Henry Wirz, the commandant of Andersonville prison, who was being tried in Washington for mistreatment of prisoners. Many, including perhaps Speed, felt that Wirz was being set up as a scapegoat for the conditions at Andersonville to appease an angry public. "There is a disposition manifested to make [my court-martial] another Wirtz trial, greatly to my prejudice," Speed wrote. "[My commanding officer] who has read all the evidence told me I would be acquitted—every one says this, but the order from Mr. Stanton is to try every one implicated in the matter and the Judge Advocate thinks that he can make a great thing for himself out of it and so he takes advantage of the ample order of Mr. S— to make it a Wirtz trial, if possible." Although Speed was confident that he would prevail, he was nervous lest something go wrong.

On September 22, Captain Speed again wrote to his father. "No progress has yet been made in my trial, indeed the charges have not been determined upon as yet, but it is certain that they will be as strong as the Judge Advocate dare to make them. It only makes my defense the more elaborate and serves to cater to the public feeling which is making the Wirtz trial so attractive to the class of men who

delight in murder trials and you know that it is easier to charge than
to disapprove."[19]

That same date, Speed wrote to his mother,

> God only knows how gladly would I have the cup turned
> from my lips, if it could be done, with honor, but as the
> issue stands we must abide by it, as best we may. I only ask
> that the charges shall be fairly put and a competent court
> appointed, which I have no good reason to doubt will be
> the case, although, the charges, so far as determined upon,
> are unjust and not according to good sense, and, perhaps,
> malice have its share in their composition. However we will
> not complain but look to God for the victory, praying that
> as we do not fear to stand before earthly courts so shall we
> not fear the arraignment before that most high and mighty
> Judge eternal, when each poor mortal shall stand forth to
> render his account of the deeds done in the flesh.[20]

By the time Speed was formally charged, the manslaughter charge
had been dropped completely and the first charge had been cut down
to two specifications. Charge No. 1 had been changed from "Conduct
prejudice to good order and military discipline" to "Neglect of duty,
to the prejudice of good order and military discipline." Specification
1 now recognized that General Dana had appointed Speed to the
temporary job of overseeing the prisoner exchange, and Speed had
not acted "without authority." The new Specification 1 stated that
"Captain Speed did neglect to avail himself of the services of Captain
Ruben [sic] B. Hatch . . . and Captain W. F. Kerns . . . [and] did himself assume to discharge the duties properly belonging to the aforesaid Officer of the Quartermasters Department . . . by deciding and
directing that a large detachment of the paroled prisoners" should all
be placed on the *Sultana*, "against the advice and remonstrances" of
Captain Kerns. The paroled prisoners "would not have so lost their
lives but for the misconduct of the said Captain Speed, in overloading
said steamer *Sultana*."[21]

Specification 1 included several inaccuracies. Speed had not
selected the *Sultana*; Captain Hatch had. Speed had actually argued

against loading prisoners on the *Sultana* at all, stating on the night of April 23 to Captain Williams, Captain Hatch, and even Captain Mason that the rolls for the men were not complete. After Captain Williams suggested that the rolls could be made up later and the *Sultana* had been selected, Speed had no hesitation in placing all of the remaining men on one boat, believing that there were only about 1,400 left at Camp Fisk. When he finally reached the *Sultana* on the late afternoon of April 24 at the head of the third trainload, after Williams had already placed two trainloads on board, Speed indeed heeded the "advice" of Captain Kerns and asked Williams if the men should be divided. Suspecting that Kerns, and possibly even Speed, had been bribed to put some of the men on another boat, Williams had emphatically stated that everyone was going on the *Sultana*. It had not been Speed's decision.

Specification 2 stipulated that Speed "did assume unwarrantable authority, in directing the arrangements for the transportation of a large number of paroled prisoners . . . and did (without authority) load and cause to be loaded, a large number . . . on one boat, the steamer *Sultana*," which was "largely in excess of the number which the steamer *Sultana* could carry with safety, and when at the same time, other and better conditioned steamboats, to wit *Pauline Carroll* and *Lady Gay*, were at the port . . . whose officers were ready and anxious to take a portion of the said paroled prisoners on board the boats." The specification further stated that Captain Speed, "against the remonstrances of . . . Captain W. F. Kerns, A.Q.M., against crowding so many men on one boat, did with criminal neglect and carelessness cause the whole number . . . to be placed upon the said steamer *Sultana*, and afterward, from the effects of which large load of paroled prisoners," the *Sultana* "did explode, from the effects of which explosion, eleven hundred and ten . . . paroled prisoners . . . were scalded, burned, and drowned, until they were dead."[22]

But Speed did not "assume unwarranted authority" or act "without authority" during the loading of the prisoners. He had been ordered by General Dana to take over the job of exchanging the prisoners accumulating at Camp Fisk in Captain Williams' absence. His activities had been authorized. Nor had Speed acted "against the remonstrances"

of Captain Kerns. He had taken Kerns' suggestion that the troops be
divided to Captain Williams, whom Speed thought was actually now
in charge of loading. It had been Captain Williams who had made the
final decision to put every last man on board the *Sultana*.

The officer who would prosecute that case against Captain Speed
was twenty-six-year-old Lt. Col. Norman Shepard Gilson (58th
USCT), the judge advocate of the Department of Mississippi since
October 17, 1865.[23] On October 27, as those involved in the disaster continued to leave the army, Brig. Gen. Edward D. Townsend,
the assistant adjutant general in Washington, sent a telegram to Maj.
Gen. Peter J. Osterhaus, the new commander of the Department
of Mississippi, in Vicksburg. Realizing that several key witnesses
in the Speed trial had already left the service, Townsend instructed
Osterhaus to have Judge Advocate Gilson "issue summons for civil
witnesses" since they were no longer "within military control." After
mentioning a few witnesses who should be summoned, Townsend
said, "No orders can be given Lieut. W. H. Tillinghast, 66th U.S.C.I.
He is confined by civil authorities of forgery."[24]

On November 1, 1865, Osterhaus issued Special Orders No. 89
calling for a general court-martial "for the trial of Captain Frederic
Speed . . . and such other persons as may be properly brought before
it." The trial was set for "the first Monday in December."[25]

Lieutenant Colonel Gilson "at once informed the major general
commanding that it would be impossible to procure the witnesses in
time to proceed with the trial at the time specified in the order, as they
were scattered over the whole country from New Jersey to Montana
Territory." On November 14, Maj. Gen. Thomas J. Wood assumed
command of the Department of the Mississippi and three days later
issued Special Orders No. 103 delaying Speed's court-martial until
January 8, 1866.[26]

The delay hurt Captain Speed. In addition to many key witnesses
leaving the service, some of the officers assigned to preside at the trial
also left, including the ranking officer, who was the only one with
a legal background. When the court finally sat, the ranking officer
would be Brevet Brig. Gen. Charles Allen Gilchrist, a civil engineer.
Of the eight officers who composed the court-martial panel, only

Swiss-born Col. Hermann Lieb (5th USC Art. [Hvy]), who had emigrated to the United States in 1856, had been a lawyer before the war.[27]

Speed's choice for defense counsel was twenty-nine-year-old Capt. Legrand Perce, an assistant quartermaster at Vicksburg who had been a member of the Dana Commission and had provided a statement to the Washburn Commission. Perce had graduated from law school in Buffalo, New York, and had been admitted to the New York bar in 1857. An ardent abolitionist, he was practicing in Chicago when the war came. Like Speed, he planned on remaining in the South after the war and hoped to open a law practice in Natchez.[28]

Speed was using his own money to bring defense witnesses back to Vicksburg and board them in city hotels, and the delay added to his expenditures. On December 13, Speed wrote to Colonel Badeau, General Grant's personal investigator. After thanking him for the "kindness you displayed and patience with which you heard the several statements of those implicated, while here last spring," Speed brought up the delayed trial:

> However much I desired a trial *immediately* after the accident, I cannot look forward to it now with the same confidence, because of the utter impracticability of assembling the necessary witnesses. I greatly fear that some of these persons cannot be found and that others will not obey the summons of the court, one [Hatch] has written as much. General Dana is in Nevada and it is doubtful if he will come, even if the summons reaches him. . . . Tillinghast, the fellow who started all the stories about the bribery, and as it proved, was the only one who was offered a bribe is now in jail, at Chicago, charged with forgery. You can judge of the likelihood of his coming.[29]

Still, Speed remained confident.

"I now am also in possession of a list of persons," Speed told Badeau, "who, at various times, were present at the several consultations I had with Capt. Hatch, upon the subject of transportation for the paroled prisoners and can fully establish the fact, which I have always insisted upon, that I complied with the customs and regulations of the service in securing transportation for these men." Speed was certain that the court would recognize that it was Captain Hatch who had selected the *Sultana*. "[W]ith all I have to discourage me I am not at all alarmed about the final result of my trial, because it is absolutely out of the question for the prosecution to make a case—nearly every witness which is important to them is of greater importance to me."[30]

Unfortunately, as Speed mentioned in his letter to Badeau, a key witness for both the prosecution and the defense was refusing to cooperate. On November 18 and again on November 20, Lieutenant Colonel Gilson, acting on the advice to "issue summons for civil witnesses," sent subpoenas to Reuben Hatch in Quincy, Illinois, requesting his appearance in Vicksburg on January 8, 1866. On December 12, 1865, Hatch's attorney Jackson Grimshaw—Hatch's good friend and brother-in-law—responded that Hatch could not be in Vicksburg on that date because he had been subpoenaed as a key witness in the trial of *United States v. Atlantic and Mississippi Steamship Company* regarding the missing $8,542.17 stolen from the safe on the *Atlantic*. "There is a good deal of money involved in the case," Grimshaw explained. "Hatch's presence is absolutely necessary for its prosecution successfully. . . . The U.S. Dist. Atty . . . cannot spare Hatch . . . and will be compelled to issue an attachment if needed to keep him here." In layman's terms, Grimshaw was threatening to have a U.S. marshal physically detain Hatch (writ of attachment) to keep him in Illinois. Since the *Atlantic* case was scheduled to begin on the same date as the Speed trial, Grimshaw doubted that Hatch would be able to appear in Vicksburg before the "1st March or at least until case is disposed of." He did, however, suggest that Hatch would be willing to give a deposition.[31]

As the new year arrived, Captain Speed must have been at least somewhat apprehensive over his upcoming court-martial. Although Speed was confident that he would prevail, he knew that it would be a tough go. As January 8, 1866, approached, Speed no doubt hoped for a quick trial so he could quit the service and get on with his life.

26

COURT-MARTIAL

At 10 a.m. on Monday, January 8, 1866, the court-martial of Capt. Frederic Speed commenced in the second-story courtroom of the Vicksburg Courthouse. After being read the single charge and two specifications, Speed officially pleaded "not guilty" to all. Judge Advocate Gilson then called his first witness, Capt. George Augustus Williams, who was still on duty as commissary of musters at Vicksburg. Over the course of the following two and one-half days, Williams testified that he had been in charge of the paroled prisoners prior to his departure from Vicksburg, but that upon his return on the night of April 23, he felt himself subordinate to Captain Speed, who had been performing Williams' duties in his absence. Throughout his testimony Williams seemed to be splitting hairs. He reiterated time and again that he had never placed a single prisoner on the *Sultana*. "I did not place them on the *Sultana*. They were delivered at the wharf boat for transportation," he stipulated. Although Captain Williams did not state outright that Captain Hatch had been the one to select the *Sultana*, he did say, "Neither I nor Captain Speed had anything to do with transportation. It was the duty of the quartermaster entirely."[1]

On January 9, Gilson had General Wood send another subpoena to Reuben Hatch. Wood wrote to Maj. Gen. Edward O. C. Ord, commanding the Department of Ohio, which included Illinois: "I would most respectfully request that you will cause the enclosed

315

subpoenas to be served on R. B. Hatch, late Captain and Assistant Quartermaster, Chief Quartermaster, Department of Mississippi. The trial of Captain Speed for the *Sultana* disaster has commenced, which makes Hatch's presence necessary as he is an indispensable witness." In an enormous understatement, Wood said, "Hatch was somewhat concerned in loading the *Sultana* so that he may not wish to appear before the Court Martial if he can find a convenient excuse for not doing so."[2]

The next person called before the court-martial was Capt. William F. Kerns, who had left Vicksburg in October and had been mustered out in St. Petersburg, Minnesota, on December 13, 1865. Now a civilian, Kerns returned to Vicksburg and spent three days on the stand explaining how he had gone to many different officers trying to get the paroled prisoners divided between boats but had faced opposition at every level. When asked if he knew who selected the *Sultana*, Kerns was quick to state, "It was not done by me, nor from my office. I do not know who did it."[3]

The second week began with William C. Jones, steamboat agent of the Atlantic and Mississippi Steamship Company, taking the stand. In answering a question regarding who arranged for a load of prisoners to go on Captain Ben Tabor's *Olive Branch*, a steamboat that did not have a government transportation contract, Jones said, "My impression is that the arrangement was made between Captain Tabor and [Captain] Hatch."[4]

The next two witnesses were survivors of the disaster: Captain McCown, aide to Major Fidler, and Captain Friesner, who had been in charge of the guard detachment. McCown told how the men were prepared at Camp Fisk and loaded on the *Sultana*. Both men spoke of their experiences on the crowded vessel and of the explosion and their survival. Lieutenant Colonel Irwin, the medical director and superintendent of U.S. hospitals at Memphis, followed and answered a few questions about the rescue and treatment of the *Sultana* victims.[5]

On Thursday, January 17, John J. Witzig, the supervising inspector of steamboats from St. Louis, appeared. He told how he had visited the wreck shortly after the disaster and had recovered and examined a "piece of boiler, about seven feet long and about twenty-three or twenty-four inches wide." He then astounded the court when he announced that "about October 20, the superintendent of the wrecking company [doing salvage work on the *Sultana*], told me they had removed one boiler, which was the only one unharmed, and that the other three were blown to atoms." Miraculously, in spite of the massive explosion, one boiler had remained intact.[6]

On September 4, 1865, the *St. Louis Daily Missouri Democrat* had reported that "the wrecking boat *Salvor* [commanded by Captain Gudgeon] was . . . to proceed to the scene of the *Sultana* disaster, with a view to the recovery of her engines and whatever of value may be still about the river." By October it was being reported that Captain Gudgeon had recovered "most of the boat machinery, and will soon have it all out." Apparently, one of the items taken from the wreck was an intact boiler—in fact, one of the inside boilers. "Both of the outside boilers exploded," Witzig told the court. When asked how he could account for the fact that an inside boiler had remained intact while the others had disintegrated, he said, "Only in one way. That this boiler might have been better preserved than the other. They might all have been overheated but this boiler might have been better cleaned. Sometimes one is kept cleaner. Or this might have had less sediment in it."[7]

Witzig informed the court that he believed that the careening of the boat and the lack of water inside the boilers had caused the explosion. When one of the judges asked if he could see the waterline inside the recovered intact boiler, wanting to know if the water inside the boiler had been below the top horizontal tubes, Witzig answered, "The inside I couldn't see, as it was full of sand."[8]

Witzig was asked, "Can the explosion of the boiler be attributed to any other cause but to the pressure of steam? For instance, to the bursting of a shell in the furnace?" An examination of the many pieces of boilers recovered from the wreck and the testimony of hundreds of eyewitnesses had already made it clear that the explosion had originated in the top rear of the boilers, and not in the furnace area. Further, Witzig was aware that on February 6, 1862, during the Union gunboat attack on Fort Henry, Tennessee, a shell had gone straight through the boiler of the *Essex* without causing an explosion.[9]

He responded accordingly: "I think this was demonstrated that a shell struck the *Essex* and passed through the furnace and boiler but didn't burst the boiler. I think a shell might pass through a boiler and then not burst it as steam would."[10] The coal torpedo theory, as far as Witzig and most others were concerned, did not hold up under scrutiny.

Memphis steamboat agent Joseph Elliott followed Witzig and spoke of the removal of the hogsheads of sugar from the *Sultana*; then Elias Shull, a clerk for Captain Kerns, took the stand and spoke briefly about the arrival and loading of the *Sultana*. Next came Lieutenant Colonel Compton, who had been a passenger on the *Sultana* from New Orleans to Memphis. He reported on the repairs to the boiler and the crowded conditions after the prisoners had been put on board. On Monday, January 22, Edward D. Butler, the superintendent of U.S. railroads at Vicksburg, told how he had accompanied Captain Speed and Captain Williams out to Camp Fisk. Butler also stipulated that three separate trainloads of paroled prisoners came in from Camp Fisk on the day of the loading.[11]

At that point Judge Advocate Gilson requested that the court-martial be postponed until March 3, when he believed that Reuben Hatch would appear before the court. Two days earlier, on January 20, Gilson had received a telegram from General Ord notifying him that the provost marshal general in Illinois was attempting to serve the second subpoena on Hatch. Gilson wanted the court to wait for Hatch because "R. B. Hatch is a material and important witness . . . [and] is cognizant of certain facts relative to the detention and loading of the *Sultana*." Gilson believed that Hatch's testimony would prove his case that Speed had neglected "to avail himself of the services of the officers of the Quartermaster's Department" in selecting the *Sultana* and had placed the paroled prisoners on the *Sultana* "against the advice and remonstrances of the officers of the Quartermaster's Department."[12]

Speed's counsel, Captain Perce, objected "most strenuously" to the delay. He complained that the prosecution had been given five months to prepare for the trial, and during all that time Captain Speed "has been kept idle, in suspense, his time lost, his pecuniary interests entirely sacrificed [by putting witnesses up in hotels], and now after preparing for trial, and after being engaged in the trial for two weeks, is called upon again to postpone the case, to wait, to sacrifice his time and money, to go to further expense in his defense, because the prosecution have not fully prepared to try the case." Furthermore, Perce argued, the judge advocate should not have been surprised that Hatch had ignored the subpoenas. "The prosecution not only should have known that [Captain] Hatch would not appear, but it did actually know that [Captain] Hatch would not appear upon his subpoena."

If the prosecution had wanted a delay, Perce said, Gilson should have asked for a postponement before the trial had begun; a delay now would make it "impossible for the Court to remember the testimony of the witnesses, their appearance on the stand, the interest manifested for, or against, the Accused, or many of the little things which go to make up the degree of credit attached to a witness testimony." Perce assured the court that he was just as anxious as Gilson to have Hatch on the stand, and in fact had told Gilson before the trial "that if he would give him (the Accused) official notice that [Captain] Hatch would not appear upon the subpoena served upon him, that he would take upon himself to procure [Captain] Hatch's attendance before the Court."[13] Each side knew how important Hatch was to its case, and each side wanted him in court. Hatch, of course, had no intention of helping either side.

When Gilson asked Perce why he had refused to take a deposition from Hatch rather than requiring him to appear, Perce answered that Speed "has been anxious to have him here, here before the Court, where the members could look upon him as he gave his testimony. But where his testimony is read upon deposition before the Court; where the members cannot see the manner of the witness, the character of his actions, the way he gives his testimony, the interest he manifests for or against the Accused, all of which the Court are bound to weigh and consider with the evidence, the Accused most seriously objects." Hatch's body language and speech patterns, in other words, would help the members of the court determine whether he was telling the truth or lying, while the written, well-thought-out, well-conceived answers of Reuben Hatch would not.

Captain Perce then hit the nail squarely on the head. Captain Hatch, he said,

is an interested witness. He is one of the parties ordered to
be brought to trial, upon similar charges as the Accused, by
the Secretary of War. If he can convict Speed, or Williams,
or Kerns, or anyone, he clears his own skirts. He is bound to
convict someone or he convicts himself. . . . He has already
been proven to have had knowledge of the intended shipment; that he not only had knowledge but that he made the
arrangement for the men to be shipped on the *Sultana*; that
he sent Captain Mason and Miles Sells to Captain Speed
to see how many men could he get ready.[14]

Indeed, Hatch was the officer who had selected the *Sultana*. There was
no way he was going to appear before the Vicksburg court-martial.

General Gilchrist and the other officers sided with Judge Advocate
Gilson and postponed the "case until the third (3rd) day of March,
1866," a delay of forty days.[15]

On January 30, a week after the decision was made to postpone
the trial, the provost marshal in Illinois served Hatch with a second
subpoena. Hatch told the officer who served him "that a subpoena in
this case had already been served on him but that he was restrained
from leaving" Illinois because he was a material witness in the steamboat *Atlantic* suit, "and as the case has not yet been called for trial,
it is not known how long he will be detained."[16] Although *United
States v. Atlantic and Mississippi Steamship Company* had been scheduled to begin at the same time as Speed's court-martial, by January
30, twenty-two days after the Speed court-martial had begun, it
had yet to start. During those twenty-two days Hatch could have
traveled to Vicksburg, given his testimony, and returned to Illinois
while waiting for the other trial to begin. If the *Atlantic* trial had
begun while Hatch was in Vicksburg, other witnesses could have
been called until Hatch was finished testifying before the Speed
trial. It was readily apparent that Hatch had no intention of appear-
ing before the court-martial trial in Vicksburg, no matter how long
the *Atlantic* trial was delayed.

On February 2, still hoping to entice Hatch to appear, General
Wood advised General Oakes in Illinois that the Speed trial had been

postponed until March 3 for the express purpose of giving Hatch time to appear. Six days later, on February 8, General Oakes reported that Reuben Hatch had been notified of the delay and "that he stated to the officer, who served the notice, that he would appear on the first of March in compliance with the subpoena."[17] Both Gilson and Perce must have jumped for joy at the news. Still, both had to be thinking, "I'll believe it when I see it."

When the Speed trial resumed on March 3, Reuben Hatch was not present. The first witness to appear after the forty-day delay was Nathan Wintringer. Although the *Sultana's* first engineer answered questions and spoke at length about the repair done to the *Sultana's* outside larboard boiler, he said that he could give no definite cause for the explosion because he had been off duty at the time.[18]

Immediately after Wintringer's testimony, Judge Advocate Gilson asked General Wood to "ask the Secretary of War to compel the attendance of the said Hatch before the Court." Wood immediately telegraphed Secretary Stanton "that Hatch has disregarded the subpoenas issued from this Court and asked that Hatch be arrested and sent to this place."[19] The next day, after the court heard the testimony of 1st Lt. Joseph McHarg, who had assisted with the loading of the first train at the parole camp, Gilson requested another postponement for a few days.[20]

Once again Captain Perce objected. Every delay hurt Captain Speed, he said. Speed's "honor and fair name is in the hands of the Court, and upon those strings, the Judge Advocate is playing," he announced. "Already his name is bandied from mouth to mouth, as a criminal. The papers are spreading his name broadcast over the land and soon whether the decision of this Court be favorable or not, will be a matter of indifference. He will have been already damned by a cruel, useless and unprecedented delay of justice."[21]

Perce tried to reason with the court regarding the appearance of Reuben Hatch. "The delay asked for is useless [because] Captain Hatch cannot be forced to come before this Court against his will. He is not in the military service, and is not within the jurisdiction of the Court. He is a citizen of the State of Illinois and as such is entitled to all the right and immunities of a citizen of that state and cannot be forced to leave it."[22] Perce was wrong. Hatch *could* have been compelled to appear before the military court.

After Perce argued that a further delay would still not produce Hatch but would merely cost Captain Speed additional money to retain his witnesses in Vicksburg, the court agreed. The next day, March 9, the court-martial resumed as scheduled, with Speed's roommate, William H. H. Emmons, an assistant adjutant general in the Department of the Mississippi, taking the stand. During two days of testimony Emmons told of Hatch coming to see Speed in the early morning hours of April 24 and said that "when Captain Hatch departed, that he and Captain Speed was agreed that the prisoners should go on the steamer *Sultana*." Emmons also said, "I considered Captain Hatch responsible for furnishing transportation on orders issued from Department Headquarters."[23]

While the case was continuing, General Wood informed Judge Advocate Gilson that he had finally heard from Washington, DC. Assistant Adjutant General R. Williams had sent a telegram to General Wood informing him that "Instructions have been sent General Ord [to] cause the attendance of R. B. Hatch."[24] General Williams did not specify how Hatch would be forced to appear.

On Monday, March 12, Joseph Warren Miller, an assistant adjutant general at Vicksburg who had worked with Captain Speed, was questioned. The takeaway moment in his testimony came when he recalled how Captain Williams had stormed into department headquarters with the accusation that Captain Speed was taking bribes to delay the men at Camp Fisk in order to put some of the men on a boat other than the *Sultana*. "Captain Williams thought they all ought to go on the *Sultana* and thought, at that time that Captain Speed was trying to prevent it." Williams had said that "they could, and should all go on the *Sultana*."[25] According to Miller, the final decision to put all of the prisoners on one boat had been made by Captain Williams, not Captain Speed.

The next day, having gone through all of his witnesses except Reuben Hatch, Gilson asked for a ten-day postponement, believing that General Williams would indeed manage to get Hatch to Vicksburg. Captain Perce was ready with a response. He laid out eight reasons why a postponement should not be granted. The trial had been postponed twice already, he said, and a further delay would "be an outrage upon the rights of the Accused to a speedy trial." He pointed out that should military personnel arrest Hatch and drag him before the court, the army "would commit an outrage upon an individual in direct contravention to his constitutional and lawful rights as a citizen of the United States." (Perce was still working under the false belief that civilians could not be forced to appear before a military tribunal.) His eighth point stipulated that many of the witnesses would leave Vicksburg if the trial was further delayed and would "be lost to [Speed]."[26]

Over the next two days, the prosecution fought back. Hatch must and would be compelled to appear before the court, Gilson insisted. "It [is] inconsistent with my duty as prosecutor to close the case on the part of the government without securing the testimony of [Captain] Hatch in some shape were it possible to do so." When making his request for the first postponement, Gilson had believed that Hatch would comply with the subpoenas, he said. Clearly, however, Hatch's actions "indicate very strongly that he has willfully and intentionally disregarded the subpoena duly served upon him."

Gilson spelled out how he had pursued Hatch through two more subpoenas, actually receiving word from General Oakes that Hatch would be present on March 1. "Was this not sufficient ground to believe that Mr. Hatch would be here on the third day of March?" Gilson asked. "There was nothing left but to wait until the 3rd of March to see whether Mr. Hatch would be here, as he had given his word that he would be, in obedience to his summons." After March 3, Gilson and all the others involved with the Speed court-martial knew the value of Hatch's word.

Gilson pointed out that Perce was wrong in asserting that the military could not force a civilian to appear before a court-martial. "We have word from the War Department, from one of its officers [General Williams], that Hatch has been ordered sent down here, and it's presumed that the Secretary of War has acted advisedly and that his order will be enforced. Judge Advocate General Holt states that, '(12) The jurisdiction of a General Court Martial being coextensive with that of the United States Government, a summons may be sent to any witness within the limits of the Federal Domain.'"[27]

Gilson fully expected Hatch to testify. A subpoena is a legally binding document whether issued by a civilian judge or a military judge. Hatch had been in contempt of court the moment he did not appear in response to the first subpoena. It was now up to military authorities to enforce the subpoena and compel Hatch to appear in Vicksburg.

"There is no one that can supply Hatch's place—his position, his duties, his acts, in connection with this affair can alone be told by him," Gilson continued.

> His testimony is indispensable to a full, complete and exhaustive investigation of the charges against the Accused. While I lay so much stress on the importance of Hatch's testimony, it is not because I consider it would inevitably result in the conviction of the Accused, for it may secure his full acquittal, but to the great end that the truth, and the whole truth, may be got at in relation to loading the *Sultana*, as far as the Accused is concerned, if at all.
>
> If the terrific and appalling calamity, whereby over eleven hundred (1,100) brave men were lost, was the result of carelessness and misconduct, either directly or indirectly, on the part of any man, or set of men, this Court and the Country want to know who that man or set of men were, and more particularly do this Court want to know whether the Accused is that man. This subject is of as deep and vital interest to the Accused as to the government so that, if he is innocent, that this Court can say so with emphasis and reason, so that no one in this land will dare to dispute or gainsay their decision, pronounced with a full knowledge and thorough understanding of all the facts in the case that he may be punished for his official acts or that he may be so completely vindicated that no one, in the future, can cast a spot or a cloud upon his character. . . . This trial will close the matter forever.[28]

Speed's counsel presented a few more arguments against a continuation before the court recessed to deliberate. A short time later, the court granted the postponement. The court-martial of Capt. Frederic Speed was scheduled to resume on March 25.[29]

Over the next eleven days, Colonel Gilson, General Wood, and others did everything in their power to get Reuben Hatch to Vicksburg. On March 15, General Wood telegraphed General Ord and wanted to know "what measures have been taken to secure the attendance of R. B. Hatch as witness before Court Martial in *Sultana* case. . . . When will he probably be here?" Two days later, Ord responded. "R. B. Hatch refused to obey [my] orders to attend the Court, which refusal is telegraphed to Washington." General Wood also wrote to Washington. On March 19 he wrote to General Townsend, the assistant adjutant general, informing him that "R. B. Hatch refuses to obey the order to report here. Will Hatch be compelled to come?" Judge Advocate General Joseph Holt, the top military judge, sent a telegram back to General Wood. "Has Captain Hatch been regularly summoned, if he has, and refuses to attend, a process should be issued to compel him."[30]

On March 20, in response to Holt's question of whether Hatch had been "regularly summoned," General Wood responded that Hatch had been "regularly summoned by the Judge Advocate three separate times, twice notified by the authorities of the Dept. of Ohio, to appear before the Court, [and] he has refused to obey each and all of these summons and notifications." After telling Holt that the "Court has twice continued this case and waited two months for Hatch," Wood asked, "Has the War Department no authority to compel his attendance?"[31]

Holt wrote back on March 22,

If Capt. Hatch's testimony is indispensable his attendance should be enforced under section twenty-five of act of third March eighteen sixty-three. The Court should state on its record that this witness has been regularly summoned and refuses to obey the summons. And it should thereupon order the Judge Advocate to issue a process of attachment against him which should be directed to such officer as the Secretary of War may designate to execute it, and should

command such officer to bring the body of the witness
before said Court to give his testimony in the case named
and also to show cause why he should not be fined for a
contempt of Court in refusing to obey its summons.[32]

Holt was instructing General Gilchrist, as the head of the court, to
order Judge Advocate Gilson to send a U.S. marshal to the home of
Reuben Hatch to literally attach himself to Hatch and bring him to
Vicksburg. Holt also thought that Hatch should be fined for "contempt
of Court" for his wanton refusal to obey three subpoenas. Holt con-
cluded with the statement, "Let this process be sent to the Adjutant
General here [in Washington] who will secure the designation of the
Secretary of War and will see that the process is executed."[33]

On March 27, General Gilchrist and the court commanded Gilson
"to issue a process of attachment against said R. B. Hatch and bring
him before this Court." In response, Gilson asked for another postponement, until May 10, so that "the said process may be issued and
the attendance of R. B. Hatch be enforced by bringing the body of the
said Hatch before this Court to give his testimony." Although Speed's
counsel objected, the postponement was granted. The court-martial
of Captain Speed would be delayed for another forty-four days.[34]

In those same six weeks, the only officer on the Speed court-martial
panel with any law experience, Colonel Lieb, was relieved from the
trial. Henceforth, General Gilchrist and the remaining six officers
would rely on their own judgment, without legal experience and
instruction, to determine the fate of Captain Speed.[35]

On May 24, when the court-martial trial resumed after another
short delay because Speed was ill, Gilson told the court that although
a writ of attachment against Reuben Hatch had been forwarded to
Secretary of War Stanton on March 29, "No return has been made
from the writ nor has any information been received as to the action
of the Secretary of War thereupon." After many months of delay
and several postponements, Gilson had to admit that Reuben Hatch
was not coming. "Everything possible having been done to procure the attendance of the witness R. B. Hatch without success, the
Prosecution is compelled to close the case without his testimony."[36]

Reuben Hatch was nowhere to be found when the U.S. marshal came looking for him. He would never spend a day in court in connection to the *Sultana* disaster.

Captain Perce, as counsel for the accused, called his first witness on May 24. Howard A. M. Henderson, the Confederate exchange commissioner, now working as an editor for a Demopolis, Alabama, newspaper, told the court how Camp Fisk was established and how it was run. Then, after stating that he recognized Captain Williams as the officer assigned to facilitate the transportation of the prisoners to the North, Henderson was asked if there were any other officers who acted in Williams' stead. "If they did, I always recognized them as agents of Captain Williams," Henderson answered. When asked point-blank, "Who did you recognize as Commissioner of Exchange upon the part of the United States Government the day the paroled prisoners were sent to Vicksburg to be shipped aboard the *Sultana?*" Henderson replied, "Captain G. A. Williams." General Gilchrist asked, "During your official action in the delivering of the paroled prisoners, did you ever recognize another officer as Commissioner of Exchange upon the part of the United States other than Captain G. A. Williams? If so, whom?" Once again, Henderson was adamant. "No sir. I regarded all others as agents, adjutants, or clerks of Captain Williams. No other one having been appointed, I always recognized him, of course."[37]

Although Gilchrist was undoubtedly fishing for the name of Captain Speed, Colonel Henderson was not biting. As the Confederate exchange commissioner, he had always recognized Captain Williams as the man in charge. Although Speed had taken over while Williams was gone, Henderson had considered him a temporary replacement. When Captain Williams returned on the night of April 23, 1865, he had immediately resumed his duty as the U.S. exchange agent.

Having elicited strong testimony that Speed was not in charge of the prisoner exchange on April 24, Captain Perce called his second witness, 1st Lt. Edwin Davenport, who had assisted Captain Williams as acting assistant commissioner of exchange. During his two days of testimony, when he was asked who he recognized as being in charge on the date of the loading of the *Sultana*. Davenport responded, "I understood Captain George A. Williams to be." Davenport's greatest contribution to the defense came when he told how Captain Speed had wanted to get off the train at Cherry Street to return to headquarters but could not do so because of the steep grade of the tracks at that point. After the train reached the depot, Davenport said, Speed still intended to go straight to headquarters, because he believed his business with the prisoners was concluded. "What induced him to go to the *Sultana*?" Captain Perce asked. "I asked him to go down," Davenport answered.[38]

Had it not been for Davenport, Speed would have returned to headquarters without ever visiting or seeing the *Sultana* on April 24. A simple request from Lieutenant Davenport had sent Speed to the riverfront, where Captain Kerns had approached him and asked if the men should be divided. One simple request had changed Captain Speed's life forever.

Following on the heels of Davenport was George J. Cayton, the surviving pilot of the *Sultana*. During his one day of testimony Cayton stipulated that the *Sultana* "was not overloaded in amount of tonnage. . . . The tonnage of the steamboat was about twelve hundred (1,200) tons. She could carry twelve hundred (1,200) tons easy." Without actually saying it, Cayton was indicating that the combined weight of 2,136 people could never amount to 1,200 tons. He added, however, "I don't think she should have over a thousand (1,000) men on her."[39]

As part of Specification 1 against Captain Speed, Judge Advocate Gilson had to prove that the prisoners "would not have so lost their lives but for the *misconduct* of the said Captain *Speed*, in *overloading* said steamer *Sultana*."[40] Gilson tried to prove that the overcrowding had caused the *Sultana* to careen, which caused the boilers to explode. In cross-examination, Gilson asked Cayton, "Does the careening of a boat have a tendency to weaken the boilers and make them more liable to explosion?" Cayton replied, "Well, yes, sir. It is rather dangerous." When Gilson later asked, "In your opinion as a steamboat man, did the number of men on board the steamer *Sultana* cause the explosion of her boilers?" Without hesitation Cayton said, "No, sir." Perhaps taken aback, Gilson pressed, "In your judgment, was there not sufficient men aboard the boat to cause her to careen sufficiently if the men went to one side of the boat to cause the explosion, and what were your means of information that they did not do so?" Cayton responded, "There was enough men to do so if they went to one side. The explosion took place at two or three o'clock in the morning and the men were asleep. The men were in their quarters and therefore the boat was setting level on the water."[41] Careening, according to Cayton, had had little to do with the explosion of the *Sultana's* boilers, and the overcrowding of the vessel did not cause the boat to career on the night of the disaster.

Before the appearance of the next witness, Captain Perce read the deposition of Jameson Cox into the court records. Cox, the orderly who had accompanied Captain Speed and Captain Williams to the parole camp on April 24, had been deposed on January 24 and testified to the loading of the three trains at Camp Fisk and coming into Vicksburg with Speed.[42] Perce then called Dr. Henry Clay Huntsman, the physician stationed at Camp Fisk on the day the men were loaded on the trains. Huntsman testified that he had examined all the men as they went to board the trains and insisted that there would have been no sick prisoners on board the *Sultana* had some of them not hidden themselves on the trains.[43]

After Dr. Huntsman left the stand, Captain Perce read two more depositions into the record. The first one, from Dr. George S. Kemble taken on November 22, 1865, explained how he had prevented a large number of sick men from going on board the crowded boat. His deposition reiterated that the sick men were never on the official roster for the trip and should not be counted among those placed on board the *Sultana*. The second deposition was from Maj. Frank E. Miller taken on March 28, 1866. Major Miller, who had been in charge of the guards at Camp Fisk, told of some of his interactions with the officers who were loading the men on the trains on April 24.[44]

The last witness to appear in person was Joseph Warren Miller, who had earlier testified for the prosecution. Miller testified about some entries in a special orders book.[45] On Tuesday May 29, after Counsel Perce read seventeen special orders into the official records, the case against Captain Speed came to a close.[46] All that remained now were the closing statements.

Captain Perce gave his closing statement for the defense on Friday, June 1. "No man will say, or suppose for a moment, that Captain Speed was actuated by any but the best motives through-out his entire connection with these prisoners," Perce began. "His constant desire and efforts was to promote their welfare and hasten them on their way from loathsome prisons to comfortable homes. Their ease, comfort, and welfare were ever uppermost in his mind, and his sole aim and object in first taking the duties on himself, and throughout was to gain this desired end." If Speed was guilty of anything, Perce said, it was being "too zealous in the performance of duties assigned him."

After restating the charge and specifications against Speed, Perce said, "The questions then to be decided are; First Specification, did Captain Speed put the men on board the steamer against the advice and remonstrances of Captains Hatch and Kerns; Second Specification, did Captain Speed cause the explosion of the boilers of the steamer *Sultana*?" Perce pointed out that in spite of the conflicting evidence, the boat was almost certainly not careening at the time of the explosion, so overcrowding was not the cause of the explosion. Specification 2, then, had been proven wrong.

As to whether Speed had availed himself of the services of the Quartermaster Department, Perce pointed out that the only person Speed needed to interact with was Captain Hatch, since Kerns was Hatch's subordinate. "The parties principally concerned in the ship-ment of the prisoners upon the *Sultana* are, first, Captain Hatch; sec-ond, Captain Williams; third, Captain Speed," Perce emphasized. He then went on to prove that Hatch, and only Hatch, had selected the *Sultana*. He reminded the court that Captain Mason and Miles Sells, Mason's steamboat agent, had gone to Hatch on the night of April 23 after getting an earlier promise from Hatch that the *Sultana* would get a load of prisoners. "Before Speed knew of her arrival, Hatch had selected the *Sultana* and bargained with her captain, that she should have all the men that could be got ready."[47]

When Hatch, Williams, and Speed had met on the night of April 23, Perce pointed out, it was Speed who said that he could have no more than five hundred men ready to go on the *Sultana*. "Captain

Speed objected to sending all the men and consequently it was either Captain Hatch or Captain Williams who decided, or suggested, that the names of the men should be checked off on the rolls." Focusing on Hatch, Perce said, "[The next morning,] Hatch notified Speed that he had transportation for the men, designated the steamer, and made all the necessary arrangements for the boat[,] and how anyone can claim on this testimony, that the duties of the quartermaster's department were usurped by either Speed or Williams, stresses all understanding." It was Hatch, and Hatch alone, who had selected the *Sultana* for transportation.[48]

As to Captain Williams, Perce insisted that Speed had resumed his role as Williams' subordinate as soon as Williams returned from Cairo. Perce pointed out many of the inconsistencies in Williams' statements. Perce knew that Captain Williams was a career army officer who wanted to remain in the service, and in fact had been promoted to major on March 15, 1866. He would do anything and say anything to push suspicion away from himself. "The testimony of Williams is a marvel," Perce stated. "It is a standing monument of caution. The workings of his mind, as he studied whether his statement would or would not militate against himself are pictured in his evidence. He is not testifying for or against Speed, but for himself."[49]

When Captain Perce was finished, it was Judge Advocate Gilson's turn for closing remarks. After reiterating the specifications against Speed, Gilson said, "It is most true that the proposition that the accused loaded or caused to be loaded the *Sultana* is the foundation of these specifications, the objective point against which we must marshal the force of evidence for its support, or else falls the whole superstructure. There must be clear and unequivocal proof of this." While the defense had identified first Hatch, then Williams, and then Speed as the parties most responsible for the overcrowding, Gilson disagreed: "[T]he parties principally concerned in the shipment on the *Sultana* are first: Captain Speed; second: Williams; third: Captain Kerns, and lastly, if at all, Captain Hatch."[50]

This is an incredible statement. Reuben Hatch had failed to answer three subpoenas issued by Gilson himself, and yet, in spite of the testimony from dozens of witnesses, Gilson was saying that Hatch was just a peripheral player in the selection and loading of the *Sultana*.

To show how Speed had continued to act as commissioner of exchange even after Williams had returned from Cairo, Gilson reminded the court, "Upon application to the Accused for the books and papers, indispensable before he could do any single act, [Williams] was told by Speed that there were but thirteen or fourteen hundred men at the Camp, and that as he was familiar with the affairs and Williams was not, he proposed that he should continue and finish up the work. Williams assented. He laid down his office at the feet of the Accused." According to Gilson, Williams had never reclaimed his title as commissioner of exchange. He had let Speed continue in that capacity until the last of the men were gone from Camp Fisk. "Speed recognized [Williams] as a superior in no manner whatsoever," Gilson insisted.

Gilson went on to recount the loading of the prisoners onto the first train, when both Williams and Speed were present: "Williams was not an actor, but a spectator, and was ever spectator more silent? He must have been watching the transportations and operations of the Parole Camp, not being familiar with them, that he might conduct the duties of Commissioner of Exchange understandingly when he should be permitted to take charge, if ever."

Gilson insisted that when the first train was loaded and ready to take the men into town, it was Speed, still acting as the commissioner of exchange, who asked Williams to count the men as they went on board the wharf boat. "Williams was going to town at all event, and, had he not been requested to perform the counting he would, in my opinion, have disappeared from the scene all together." Gilson then reminded the Court that just before the first train left Camp Fisk, Speed had loaded on another 150–200 men, against the advice of Edward D. Butler, the superintendent of U.S. railroads at Vicksburg. "Is this the harbinger of deeds to be reenacted in the case of the steamer, no less culpable but far more destructive, as the sequel proved? Here the cry of too many men is first raised. The first protest to overloading is made to be first overruled and trampled down."[51] According to Gilson, Speed had been negligent from the start.

In trying to prove that Speed had assumed the duties of the Quartermaster Department as well, Gilson told the court "it was not [Hatch's] duties to provide the transportation for these men transferred by the Accused on the 24th of April, unless specially directed. I assert that he was not so directed as the order for transportation was sent direct to Captain Kerns as the quartermaster to provide it by the selection of the transports." As Gilson presented it, Speed had selected the *Sultana* and had sent an order direct to Captain Kerns informing him that the prisoners were to go there. "Hatch does not appear to perform the act of providing transportation, and we are allowed by the law of evidence to presume that he was not so ordered. How far, if at all, the Accused neglects to avail himself of the services of Hatch, leaves the Court to judge."[52]

What Gilson failed to point out, however, was that Special Orders No. 140 ordering the remaining prisoners at Camp Fisk to be sent to Camp Chase, and every previous order connected to the movement of the prisoners, included the phrase, "The Quartermaster's Department will furnish transportation." Those six words constituted a direct order. As head of the Quartermaster Department, Hatch was being ordered to provide transportation for the prisoners. He would be in dereliction of duty if he did not. Additionally, although Gilson did not say so, the transportation order had been sent directly to Captain Kerns because Hatch had already made it clear "that he did not care to see this class of orders."

As proof that Speed had assumed unwarranted authority over the shipment of the prisoners, which was the basis of the charge and specifications against him, Gilson summarized,

> He tells Williams he will remain in charge and finish up the work. He issues an order the same evening for a guard to report on the *Sultana* at noon the next day, and another in the morning to the Quartermaster's Department to furnish transportation. He directs the calling [of] the rolls and loading the trains at Camp. He directs and controls the running of the trains; overloads them against the protest of the superintendent of the road. Requests Williams to come

in and count the men. Comes in himself in the evening to decide that the men cannot be divided; and that they must all go together on the *Sultana*. Whenever and wherever we find Speed and Williams together on that day we find Speed controlling and directing. At the cars in the morning, at the Parole Camp at noon and at the *Sultana* in the evening.[53]

It was plain and simple: Speed had been in command and should suffer the consequences.

Gilson concluded by touching on the cause of the disaster: "Of the theory that the load per se on the *Sultana* caused the explosion of her boilers, there is reasonable doubt. Whether the huge mass of persons reeling from side to side at landings, and in the course of the river 'causing' the boat to career would weaken her boilers, thereby producing explosion of them, experts have failed to tell us. They cannot speak positively, but say, 'It is dangerous.'"[54] In spite of all of the testimony and proffered theories, in June 1866 nobody was sure what had caused the *Sultana*'s boilers to explode.

Having heard the closing statements of both the accused and the prosecution, the court met for the last time on June 5, 1866, to render a verdict. The court-martial of Frederic Speed had spanned 149 days, with numerous postponements. At 10 a.m., General Gilchrist and the other six sitting officers announced their findings. Judge Advocate Gilson had begun the court-martial trying to prove Speed guilty of one specific charge and two specifications. Counselor Perce had fought hard to prove that his client had not violated the specific charge and specifications. In the end, the court ruled that Captain Speed was guilty on all counts—but only if the wording in the one charge and its two specifications was changed.

While Specification 1 had charged Speed with neglecting to avail himself of the services of *both* Hatch and Kerns, the court now decided that Speed had interacted sufficiently with Hatch. Therefore, to make the specification fit, the court simply removed any reference to Hatch. Likewise, Specification 1 stipulated that Speed had ignored the "advice and remonstrances" of Captain Kerns. It having been shown in the trial that Kerns had never objected to Speed about the overcrowding, the court removed the word "remonstrances" to make the specification fit. With these changes, Speed was found guilty of Specification 1: ignoring the "advice" of Captain Kerns.

To make Specification 2 fit, the Court also removed words or phrases that contradicted the evidence. Speed had been authorized by General Dana to perform the duties of acting commissioner of exchange while Captain Williams was away; that was not in doubt. It was not proven that the *Lady Gay* or the *Pauline Carrol* had been "better conditioned" than the *Sultana*, nor had there been any "remonstrances" from Captain Kerns. Colonel Gilson had failed to prove that the actions of Captain Speed on April 23 and 24, 1865, had been "criminal," and he had also failed to prove that the "large loads of paroled prisoners" had contributed to the boiler explosion. So, once again, the court simply modified the wording of the specification, which led to a finding of guilty on the single charge of "Neglect of duty, to the prejudice of good order and military discipline."[55]

Having been found guilty on both specifications and the single charge, Capt. Frederic Speed was sentenced "to be dismissed [from] the service of the United States" with a dishonorable discharge and a blot on his record for the rest of his life.[56]

As he was required to do, General Gilchrist sent the findings and sentence to General Wood, the department commander, for verification and implementation. Instead of dismissing Speed from the army then and there, on June 8 General Wood forwarded the "proceedings, findings and sentences" to the "Secretary of War for final action." In a cover letter to General Townsend, Wood stated that although he endorsed the court-martial's findings and sentencing, he had "deferred exercising my authority" to dismiss Speed since the "orders were originally issued from the War Department to bring to trial the officers implicated in the *Sultana* disaster[,] . . . and besides the questions involved in this trial are so grave and numerous of such vital interest to the accused, and of general public interest to those states which lost a large number of brave men on the *Sultana*, that I deem it important that the record should be submitted for the reviews of the Judge Advocate General of the Army before the findings and sentence of the Court are published."[57] Since the decision to put Speed on trial had come from Secretary of War Stanton and Judge Advocate Holt, Wood was passing the buck back to Washington.

For the next two weeks Holt pored over the transcripts of the trial. On June 21 he sent his conclusion to Secretary Stanton. After listing the charge and the two specifications, and the findings of the court, Judge Holt wrote, "It is the opinion of this Bureau [of Military Justice], after a careful study of the record, that Capt. Speed took no such part in the transportation for the prisoners in question as should render him amenable to punishment; that his connection with the events which preceded the disaster to the *Sultana* was a wholly subordinate one." Holt further stated that if read carefully, "the evidence point[s] out with distinctness those officers, whose indifference . . . resulted in, though without causing, the deaths of over eleven hundred of their numbers." He chastised General Gilchrist and his court for changing the specifications and charge to fit the evidence: "An examination of the findings of the Court, contrasted with the specifications as orig-inally laid, will show indeed that this was in fact the opinion of the officers who comprised it." In other words, the Speed court knew that the "specifications as originally laid" could not be sustained, so they changed them.[58]

Holt wrote flatly that "the evidence shows that the *Sultana* was selected by Capt. Hatch" and that "Capt. Williams . . . was present when the men were put on the *Sultana*, counted them as they went aboard, declared them to be comfortable, and insisted in a conversa-tion with Capt. Kerns that none should go on any other boat. What ground remains for visiting Capt. Speed with a dishonorable and life-long punishment, in view of the light in which the Court regards his acts, is difficult to discern."[59]

Holt summarized his views of the evidence and the court's verdict as follows:

> The evidence shows that Accused was appointed verbally by Gen. Dana to act as Commissioner of Exchange during the temporary absence of Capt. Williams; that Capt. Williams returned the day before the men were sent to Vicksburg to

go North; and that he immediately resumed the duties of his office. It is shown that Capt. Kerns advised with Capt. *Williams* against so many men going on one vessel, and that the latter insisted very angrily that they should all go by the *Sultana*; and it is further shown by abundant evidence that the boat, though over-crowded, was not overloaded . . . that the *Sultana* ran smoothly on the trip, and finally that the explosion was owing, not to the excess in the numbers of men she was carrying, but to the fact that . . . her boilers had been burnt, through the probable carelessness of her engineers, and had been repaired imperfectly with a patch of thinner iron.[60]

"Terrible as was the disaster to the *Sultana*," Holt continued, "there is no evidence that it was caused by the over-crowding of her decks; and it is therefore difficult to say upon whom the responsibility for the loss of eleven hundred lives should really rest."

Holt went on to chastise Nathan Wintringer for permitting inadequate repairs to the leaking boiler: "[H]is criminality in risking the lives of so many men, knowing as he did the condition of his boat, was great and without [excuses]." Holt concluded, "Whoever should be regarded as meriting punishment for his connection with the event, it is believed that it is not Capt. Speed."[61]

Holt agreed with Captain Perce that Hatch and Williams were the officers most culpable for the selection and overcrowding of the *Sultan*:

The selection of the *Sultana* is shown to have been made by Capt. Hatch, the Chief Quartermaster; not by the accused. Capt. Speed is shown to have been in frequent communications with Capt. Hatch; who, moreover, is proved to have previously promised a full load to the captain of the *Sultana*, and to have sent the latter to Capt. Speed in reference to the matter. Capt. Williams is known to have taken abreast the entire direction of affairs on his return from the North, and to have insisted that the prisoners should not be divided; and Capt. Speed, the Accused, is proven to have believed the control of the arrangements to be so completely taken out of his hands, that he went to the *Sultana* while the men were going on board only through an accident, and performed no services while there; convinced that his duties had exited when he brought the prisoners from "Four Mile Bridge" to Vicksburg, and that to the Commissioner of Exchange, Capt. Williams, and the officers of the Q.M. Dept. belonged the additional duty of shipping them to the North.[62]

Once again chastising the Speed court, Judge Holt wrote that "the Court have by its findings so unarticulated the allegations of the charge as to absolve the Accused of all responsibility for the catastrophe. How then, however, they could proceed to inflict upon the Accused a punishment so terrible for offences of which they virtually find him not guilty this Bureau fails to understand."[63]

Holt "recommended that the sentence be disapproved, and that Capt. Speed be publicly exonerated from the charges which have been made against his character as an officer."[64] He went on to conclude that Captain Williams' actions on the date of the loading could be excused because he had been led to believe that someone had taken a bribe to put the prisoners on other boats, and also because, like Speed, he had been led to believe that there were only 1,400 men at Camp Fisk. Finally, although Williams was clearly in charge of the loading of the *Sultana*, he could be excused for the overcrowding "by the extreme difficulty of effecting a division at so late a period."[65] Perhaps Holt was cutting Williams some slack because he was a West Point graduate and Regular Army. Whatever Holt's reasoning, Williams should have been held accountable for his actions on April 24, 1865, and Judge Holt was doing the army, and the nation, an injustice by whitewashing his actions.

Holt left his most scathing attack for last: "That Capt. Hatch felt a consciousness of the responsibility for the disaster, is believed to be shown by the fact that though three times subpoenaed to give testimony at the trial, and though the trial was prolonged three months that his presence might be secured, he refused to obey the summons;

and that notwithstanding every effort was made to compel his presence, the Secretary of War being finally appealed to to order his arrest as guilty of contempt, it was found necessary to finish the trial without his evidence."[66] Although Holt was sure that Hatch was the person who should be prosecuted, Hatch would never be brought to trial. In fact, other than Captain Speed, not one single person would stand trial for the worst maritime disaster in American history.

On June 25, four days after Judge Holt wrote up his remarks, the War Department rendered its decision: "It is recommended that the sentence be disapproved, and that Capt. Speed be publicly exonerated from the charges which have been made against his character as an officer." Capt. Frederic Speed was honorably discharged on September 1, 1866, almost a year and a half after the *Sultana* disaster.[67]

Unfortunately for Speed, Lieutenant Colonel Gilson was never convinced of his innocence. In 1903 he was still insisting that "Captain Frederic Speed was found guilty of overloading the steamer *Sultana* by court martial which tried him at Vicksburg and was sentenced to be dismissed from the service." He admitted that "the findings were forwarded to Washington for review and the sentence of the court martial was set aside," but then he made an unwarranted allegation. "The uncle of Captain Speed was the Attorney General in President Johnson's cabinet at the time. I do not know, however, that he had anything to do with the case in securing the setting aside of the findings of the court martial." Gilson was wrong on two counts: Attorney General James Speed of Kentucky was no relation to Frederic Speed, and James Speed had not influenced the decision of Judge Advocate Holt and Secretary of War Stanton.

Unfortunately, public opinion was hard to change. In 1962, almost one hundred years after the disaster, in one of the first full-length books written about the *Sultana*, author James W. Elliott, the grandson of survivor Capt. James Walter Elliott, wrote that Speed "had caused or contributed to the death of some 1,500 of his fellow soldiers." Elliott called Judge Holt's report "a classic of confusion and self-contradiction from beginning to end" and said that Holt had issued an "illogical but spirited defense of Speed [that] was completely out of character." Following in Gilson's footsteps, Elliott concluded,

"Perhaps someone pulled one of the myriad wires of Washington influence to have the convicted captain exonerated."[68]

Like so many others over the years, Elliott had failed to review the firsthand evidence of the Washburn, Dana, and Hoffman investigations and the Speed court-martial papers. He wrote that after Holt finished his review, "an orderly in Holt's office gathered up the leavings of the game, the great heap of records and reports, the mass of unwanted documents which chronicled the last voyage of the *Sultana*. He wrapped them neatly and tied them securely for delivery to the War Department Archives. On the outside of the package, as was customary in such cases, he scrawled the instructions, *For file—not to be re-opened*. But on this particular package a slightly different legend would have been more appropriate; *For file: Never to be remembered*."[69] Again, not true on all counts. Unfortunately, however, the damage was done. Because of Elliott's account, a new generation believed Speed to be the main culprit in the *Sultana* disaster.

And so it remained until 1978, when Memphis attorney Jerry O. Potter and I began independently researching the disaster. Potter went to the National Archives and without difficulty retrieved copies of the Washburn, Dana, and Hoffman investigations and the transcripts of the Speed court-martial. He shared copies with me, and both separately and together we saw Speed in the same vein as Judge Advocate Holt had done—as a scapegoat in the *Sultana* disaster—and decided that Reuben Hatch and George Williams were those most culpable. It has been a long road, and it is still being traveled.

27

AFTERMATH

Most of the people who suffered through the *Sultana* disaster or were touched in some way by the event went on to lead normal lives; a few did not. Not one of them, however, whether victim, rescuer, or witness, ever forgot the horrors of that early Thursday morning on April 27, 1865.

The deaths of men who were expected home after having survived battle, capture, and prison pen were very hard on family and friends. Private Collins, who lost his father on the *Sultana*, knew how his mother—and all the other mothers and loved ones—would react: "When the news of that awful tragedy was sent abroad, many a home was darkened with grief and sorrow that had been happy in anticipation of the home-coming of a father, a son, or perhaps a brother or sweetheart."[1]

The great-great-niece of eighteen-year-old Pvt. Eli Finley Provines (Co. A, McLaughlin's OH Cav) told the story that "a person from the military appeared at my great-great grandparents' home [on July 15, 1865] to inform them of their young son's death. My Great-great-grandfather arose from his chair at the dinner table, went to a daybed, and suffered a heart attack and died." Pvt. James C. Cook's father "spent the balance of his life going out the walk and looking for his son to come from the [river]. At least four or five times a day was this kept up for years, or while he lived."[2]

The deaths of brothers Pvt. Gilford Canon and Pvt. Isaac Anderson Morrison (both Co. L, 3rd TN Cav) so affected their father that he became "deeply depressed and talked of killing himself." The family kept a constant watch on him, but on April 30, 1868, three years and three days after his two boys died, Pleasant Morrison got his way. He was plowing a field with a young grandson watching over him. "Pleasant asked the grandson for his Barlow knife to repair the reins. The grandson forgot, as he had been told, to ask his grandfather to return the knife. Pleasant plowed to the other end of the field, stopped, sat down under a tree, and cut his throat. He died in the back of a wagon on the way to a doctor."[3]

Comrades who had lost friends on the *Sultana* were likewise affected. Sgt. Andrew McBath Rule had been on the boat with blacksmith John H. Campbell (both Co. A, 3rd TN Cav). Rule told Campbell's family that their son had survived the explosion, "but as [with] so many others in the water that night, John H. was constantly being grabbed by other soldiers who could not swim. Mr. Rule said he kept hearing John H. tell them, 'Let go, let go, I've got to get home to my little children.' Mr. Rule said that [John] was eventually pulled under and drowned." Rule was forever haunted by memories of Campbell's death. John Campbell left a wife and two young children.[4]

Pvt. Michael Conrad likewise never got over the loss of his dear friend Pvt. Adam Philip Schneider (both Co. C, 183rd OH Inf). Both had been captured at Franklin, Tennessee, and held in Andersonville prison. Placed on board the *Sultana* together, Conrad survived while Schneider, who was forty-one years old with three young daughters, did not. "[Conrad] could not be wakened on any other night," wrote one of Schneider's daughters, "but April 27th always brought him to our house, and cry, cry like a baby."[5]

The wife and two young children of Cpl. Gideon Harrington Jr. (Co. H, 102nd OH Inf) were waiting for his return so they could open the last jar of cherries he had helped can in 1862 before joining the army. After word arrived that Harrington had perished in the disaster, his widow "left the jar of cherries unopened in memory of her husband."[6]

Time in a Confederate prison combined with the *Sultana* disaster broke many men. Pvt. Billy Morrow died only a short time after reaching his home in Piqua, Ohio. His best friend, Private Walker, recalled, "He had contracted a severe cold from the many hardships of army and prison life, so with the added exposure of the *Sultana* experience his health gradually failed, and death came to him in a short time after our discharge." Morrow died October 2, 1865, at age twenty-three. "Thus was severed a beautiful and trusted friendship," Walker lamented.[7]

Although he eventually married and had three children, Private McIntosh, the Illinois soldier who had stowed away on the *Sultana* at Memphis, came home a "mental and physical wreck." By January 1868 he was unable to do manual labor. He began traveling about the country playing music and writing and selling songs and poetry. "I was discharged at Springfield, Ills., June 30th, 1865 and have been under the doctor's care ever since," he wrote. "I now travel for my health and sell my photos to defray expenses. . . . I also sell my songs with music." He died penniless on July 26, 1927, at the National Military Home in Leavenworth, Kansas.[8]

Private Eldridge was also much debilitated by his time in prison and his experience on the *Sultana*. On arriving home,

> My mother was greatly surprised when she found out who it was, you see I hadn't had a chance to let her know I was coming so it was a complete surprise to her. She came running out and lifted me clear off the ground hugging me and said "Why Charley, you arent as big as you were two years ago when you left home." I told her "No, Mother, I have been just about dead for the last three months." She wanted to carry me in the house, I told her that I could walk, and when we got in the house she sat there ever so long before she said anything. She said I looked so poor and weak she couldn't bare to look at me, and when my sisters came in they had to have their rounds over me so it was a great day with me, after two years of hardships and suffering that no one could describe, to be at home again with those I loved

better than my own life. . . . I only weighed 70 pounds and hardly able to stand up. It was two years before I got able to work.[9]

Corporal Horner's friends and relatives were equally surprised when he suddenly appeared at home in mid-May. "The people at home looked at me as one of the dead, as they had learned that I was on the boat and they did not expect to see me alive again, but they did not know that I had learned to swim since they last saw me. If I had not learned to swim I should, without any doubt, have drowned." The family of Pvt. James H. Brown (Co. D, 3rd TN Cav) believed that he too had died on the *Sultana*. "[H]is wife was out in the garden working and had her gun out there when she saw him come walking up," reported a granddaughter. "[S]he got the gun and pointed it at him and told him to stop or she would shoot. He called her name and said 'this is your husband, Jim,' she said 'no it isn't he is dead.' But he had a missing finger before he had gone in the army so he showed her this and she knew then it really was her husband. I suppose he looked a lot different after all he had been thru."[10]

War and the *Sultana* experience had also changed the appearance of seventeen-year-old Pvt. Truman Smith. When he reached Kalamazoo, Michigan, Smith stopped at a local hotel to reintroduce himself to some friends and heard his own father's voice coming from the adjoining barroom. "[H]e went in and spoke to his father, asking the latter if he did not know him," reported a local newspaper. "Three times the elder Smith looked at him, as he stood hanging to the door casing, and then he picked him up, for he was reduced to a 96-pound skeleton. 'You're my boy, but I don't know which one,' he said." Truman Smith and three of his brothers had gone off to war. All four returned.[11]

Many *Sultana* victims suffered for the rest of their lives from the injuries they received on the steamboat and were forced to apply for invalid pensions. Pvt. Darius Isaac Minier (Co. G, 183rd OH Inf) floated ten miles downriver after leaving the *Sultana*. He succinctly reported, "Caught cold settled in my head Caused my deafness." The pension application of Pvt. William Henry Ross (Co. A, 102nd OH

Inf) noted that he was "struck by something in his skull bone. . . . 5 pieces of his skull bone was taken out by a surgeon. . . . As a result of said injurie, he is unable to work."[12]

Corporal Learner received "severe scalds" and spent about a month in a Memphis hospital before being "sent home on crutches, but he never recovered fully from the injuries." A hometown newspaper reported that "Mr. Learner was scalded so badly that the flesh came off of his left leg. He was so weak from the injury that for three months he was unable to feed himself. During the ensuing years he often battled for his life when poisoning would arise from the old wound which never healed but gave him incessant pain." His application for an invalid pension in 1870 noted, "Left leg badly scalded veins bursted rendering him unable to perform manual labor . . . his physical condition is leg swollen ulcerating and by using leg causes blood to gush out[,] veins being bursted and growing worse." His injuries still bothered him in 1903, and he was said to be "confined to his home." When he died in 1925, Learner's obituary noted, "An injury received by Mr. Learner in the explosion which destroyed the *Sultana* and snuffed out the lives of several hundred men, was really the cause of his death. . . . The hurt was one that never healed; though he lived nearly sixty years after receiving it. Always it was threatening to him, and finally it brought on the condition which resulted in his death." It was reported, "Burns suffered in the explosion, which never healed, led to his death from septic poisoning."[13]

Although newspapers reported that Pvt. Sanford P. Ames (Co. E, 7th IN Cav) was admitted to Adams Hospital suffering from "exhaustion," he was apparently badly injured in the explosion. One of his relatives wrote, "He came near death, but lived several years an invalid." He died four years after the disaster on August 23, 1869, at age thirty. Another survivor who appeared to have come through the disaster uninjured and was taken to the Soldiers' Home instead of a hospital was Pvt. Joseph H. Gray Jr. (Co. B, 9th IN Cav). Even though he died in 1904 at age sixty-seven, he suffered every day of his life. His obituary, titled, "Victim of the *Sultana*," read in part, "The cause of his death was injuries received when the boat *Sultana* exploded. He was badly injured, and since then never had had first-class health."[14]

Pvt. Joel Frank Nevins (Co. F, 18th MI Inf.) applied for an invalid pension in 1880 and after telling of his suffering in Cahaba and on the *Sultana* said: "Since my discharge, I have not been able to perform manual labor more than one third of the time." Private Rush lived until 1902, but his time in Cahaba and on the *Sultana* had broken him. "All these hardships, besides a wound caused by a bullet which went through his lungs [at Shiloh], left his health shattered for the rest of his life."[15]

In addition to physical injuries, many soldiers suffered afterward from post-traumatic stress disorder. Pvt. Payton Baines Shields (Co. D, 31st OH Inf) was pulled from the Mississippi five hours after the disaster "more dead than alive." An article published in 1886 noted, "Ever since the fearful experience of that night, he has been periodically afflicted with water fits, in which he involuntarily strikes with his arms and feet as he did on the terrible night in the turbid waters of the Mississippi." Pvt. John Henry King lost some teeth to scurvy in prison and injured his back on the *Sultana*. King became an alcoholic, but he managed to hide his affliction and traveled around the country lecturing on temperance. "That sight I shall never forget," he wrote of his *Sultana* experience in 1892, "I often see it in my sleep, and wake with a start." King died of acute alcohol poisoning on May 22, 1893, at age sixty-two.[16]

Capt. William George McElrea (Co. I, 5th IA Cav), the lone representative from Iowa on the *Sultana*, was so shaken by what he had seen—and perhaps done—on April 27, 1865, that he never spoke of the matter. A local newspaper reported after his death in 1915, "His hardships following the explosion appear to have so preyed upon his mind that he would never discuss the horrors of that night with any-one, not even the members of his family." Sergeant Aldrich likewise suffered from post-traumatic stress disorder. "There are scenes in the lives of everyone that are impressed indelibly upon the mind by reason of some accident," he wrote years after the disaster. "I shall never for-get the cries and groans of my drowning comrades . . . they sleep the sleep of death, and the Mississippi furnished the most of them with shrouds and graves."[17]

Pvt. Charles H. Herberth (Co. C, 115th OH Inf) survived the *Sultana* with no apparent physical disability but was torn apart mentally over the deaths of twenty-six men from his company, many of them close friends. In 1887, after suffering twenty-two years with the horrible memories, Herberth walked into the rear of a beer garden and shot himself in the head. Inside his coat pocket was a card with the message, "Dear father, and mother, and sister: Forgive me for what I am going to do." Attached to his vest was a pin for the Memorial Post of the Grand Army of the Republic (GAR), a veterans' group to which he belonged.[18]

Near the beginning of the Civil War, Congress passed the Act of July 14, 1862, a general pension law for veterans who had sustained war-related disabilities. In time, pensions became available to widows, minor children, and dependent relatives of soldiers who had died from war-related injuries. Originally, a totally disabled veteran received $8 per month.[19]

Before a soldier could receive a pension or invalid pension, however, he had to provide "the sworn statement of a commissioned officer or two comrades who were eyewitnesses to the injury."[20] Eyewitnesses were almost impossible to obtain for soldiers who had sustained injuries on the *Sultana*. Private Raudebaugh, for example, explained,

> I was blown off the boat when sound asleep and injured in my breast and groin, and am suffering from it every day I live, but I cannot tell how it was done, nor what did it, much less can anyone else. When the explosion occurred we were sound asleep, and were blown up into the air among one another along with pieces of the wreck, and scarcely two of us were taken out at the same place; hence we cannot help one another as we could had we been injured in battle, in camp, or on the march.[21]

Some of the *Sultana* soldiers found it nearly impossible to obtain a pension. QM Sgt. Henry Tolbert Linginfelter (Co. I, 3rd TN Cav) applied for his pension around 1890:

> I cannot furnish the evidence comissioned [sic] officer, Surgeon, Assistant Surgeon, nor Hospittle Steward for the following reason, I was a Prisoner of War on my way from

the Rebel prison Cahaba, Alabama to Camp Chase Ohio to be exchanged as I thought, when I received the injuries that I claim. I was blown from the boat by the explosion and was in water several hours holding to somthing like a piece of a Cracker Box. I faintly remember of being taken from the water. I do not know who it was that took me from the water. When I came to conscious again I found myself in a private house in the City of Memphis badly crippled in my hips and back with a roaring in my head which resulted in total deafness in one ear and partial deafness in the other. . . . I have no recollection of passing one day without suffering more or less pain since I was blown up with the explosion of that boat and especially when trying to work. I have been often so that I could not put on or pull off my clothes myself and sometimes I could not get out of my bed without help, the result of the injuries I received while in the service of the United States.[22]

Cpl. Alexander Howard Perry (Co. G, 115th OH Inf), who suffered a scalded face and a "contused wound of spine" on the *Sultana*, was given a $10 per month pension in 1889. Ten years later, he applied for an increase because of the deterioration of his spine and the development of "severe tremors of right hand and arm"; the increase was rejected because the deterioration had not originated in the service. Perry pursued his case as his body worsened into "a very dilapidated condition, not only in a physical but also in a mental sense." Eventually, in 1901, Congress increased his pension to $30 per month. He died eight years later.[23]

James Augustus B. Butterfield had been a sergeant in the 2nd Illinois Cavalry but had mustered out in August 1864. Instead of returning home, he had "remained in the service of the Government," working in Louisiana. He boarded the *Sultana* at New Orleans and lost his life in the disaster. His dependent mother, a widow, applied for a Mother's Pension soon after the disaster, but her "papers were lost or misplaced." In 1888, when she was eighty-eight years old, Congress finally approved the pension, but President Grover Cleveland vetoed it "upon the ground that there is no proof that the soldier was in the service of the country when he lost his life." On August 12, 1888, the *New York Tribune* scolded, "But whether he was in the service or out of the service at the known moment when the *Sultana* exploded matters not. His aged mother, whose only child he was, and who had given her all to her country, is entitled to the sympathy and support of its Government. Of all the cruelties that Mr. Cleveland has inflicted upon his country's defenders and their dependents none was more heartless than his veto of Mrs. Butterfield's claim."[24]

Ann Annis had a tough time with the Pension Bureau as well because Harvey Annis was not in the army when he died. He had resigned due to illness two months before the family boarded the *Sultana* at Vicksburg. In 1877, Congress granted her a lump sum of $235 to cover the time from her husband's resignation on February 24, 1865, until April 27, 1865, the date of the disaster, and even paid her a monthly pension. However, in 1886, Congress declared, "it is clear that [Lieutenant Annis] was at the time [of his death] a *discharged* officer, and not then in the service of the United States. If so, then the widow was certainly paid for thirty-three days after Lieutenant Annis was out of the service, and three days *after he was drowned*, and the pension is an absolute gratuity, for it cannot be claimed that Lieutenant Annis either died in the service or that he died from any incident of the service." Although Congress recommended denying Ann's pension application, she eventually received a widow's pension of $17 per month.[25]

Ann Annis had an interesting background even before she boarded the *Sultana*. Born in England in 1816, she had been a maid-in-waiting at Queen Victoria's coronation. She married an English sea captain in 1840, and the two were shipwrecked on an island six months after their marriage. Ann survived; he did not. She married another sea captain three years later, and the couple had three children before he died at sea in 1849. With her parents, brother, and children, Ann moved to the United States and settled in Wisconsin. In 1850 she married her third husband, Harvey Annis, a carpenter. They had four children together. Living far away from either ocean, Ann probably never imagined that her third husband and her youngest daughter would also die in a maritime disaster.

After spending two weeks in a Memphis hospital, Ann returned to Wisconsin only to discover that her oldest and second-oldest sons had run off to join the army (both boys survived the war). Ann rented out rooms in her home while trying to obtain the government pension money owed to her. Four of her seven children, including seven-year-old Isabella, died before her. She passed away at age eighty-four in 1900. She never remarried.[26]

Another survivor who never remarried was Seth W. Hardin Jr. The twenty-nine-year-old Chicago banker had been returning from his honeymoon trip when he lost his young wife, Hannah, on the *Sultana*. He returned to Chicago afterward, worked in banking for a few years, and then went into the real estate and loan business. He survived the Great Chicago Fire of 1871 but died in 1880 of typhoid pneumonia at age forty-four. He is buried in an unmarked grave in Chicago's Graceland Cemetery.[27]

The fact that nobody knew exactly how many soldiers had been on the boat, who they were, or who had survived made it difficult for some men to claim a pension. Pvt. Martin Van Buren Simmerman (Co. C, 86th IN Inf) was treated at Overton Hospital for a "contusion [of] left foot," but the Indiana Adjutant General's Report for 1865 listed him as "Supposed to have been lost on the str. *Sultana*." Because of this one sentence he had difficulty convincing the Pension Bureau that he was alive, and he did not receive a pension until 1885. Reported a hometown newspaper, "This record, we are informed, did give him difficulty in getting a pension."[28]

Pvt. Chester Berry, whose skull was fractured in the explosion, was taken to Washington Hospital.

> I gave my name, company and regiment to a reporter, and also to the hospital steward, yet about two or three months afterward my mother received official notice from Washington that her son was killed upon the *Sultana*; and my name stands today upon the Michigan Adjutant General's Report for 1865 as killed by the explosion of the steamer *Sultana*. Yet, when in after years, I applied for a pension for that fractured skull, which was so bad that the

surgeon at Washington hospital told the man in the next bunk to mine that I could never get well, I was obliged to prove that I was upon the *Sultana* and that I was hurt or had my skull fractured at that time.

He added sarcastically, "Such is the ease with which pensions are procured, and such the liberality of the government officials when they have the official evidence in government reports before them." Berry finally received an invalid pension in 1880.[29]

Senator-elect William Snow reached Washington shortly after the disaster only to discover that he would not be seated because Arkansas had yet to be readmitted into the Union. He went to Paris to study civil law, then returned to the United States and settled in Brooklyn, New York. In 1874, he invented and patented three devices dealing with electricity. A year later he graduated from Columbia Law School and was admitted to the New York Bar. A successful lawyer, inventor, newspaper publisher, and poet, he died in 1910 in Hackensack, New Jersey at age seventy-eight.[30]

Three of the *Sultana*'s senior crew members survived the disaster. First Mate William Rowberry was living in St. Louis in 1867 and working as a "riverman." On December 2, 1885, he died at age fifty-eight of "congestion of the Brain." His partner in the pilothouse, George J. Cayton, had a very successful career after the *Sultana* explosion. In August 1865 Cayton became the pilot on the brand-new steamboat *Magnolia* alongside his brother Frank, also a pilot, and ex-*Sultana* mate William B. Alvord Jr. In June 1866, after the *Magnolia* burned completely to the waterline at St. Louis, the resilient Cayton set out to find another boat.[31]

Over the next few years Cayton worked on several different boats, often alongside his brother. By late 1876 he was suffering from rheumatism caused by long hours in the pilothouse and the bruising he had suffered during the explosion. On March 28, 1877, Cayton passed away in Cincinnati at age forty-two from "consumption superinduced by exposure" from the *Sultana* disaster. The Cincinnati, St. Louis, and New Orleans Pilots' Association held a memorial service for the "well-known and highly esteemed" pilot, "a companion whose kind and genial disposition was a mark of affection for everyone who knew him."[32]

First Engineer Nathan Wintringer had his license revoked by Supervising Inspector John Witzig shortly after the disaster. Wintringer fought back, pointing out that he was not on duty at the time of the explosion, although he ignored the fact that he had cajoled boiler mechanic R. G. Taylor into putting a temporary patch on a bad boiler. He also ignored the fact that he knew his boilers were in bad shape and said nothing to any of the federal officers involved with loading the prisoners. In March 1866, Witzig's decision was overruled and Wintringer's license was reinstated. He returned to the water but remained mainly on the Ohio River. In February 1878 he moved from chief engineer to captain of the steamboat *Abner O'Neal* when the owner of the *O'Neal* suddenly died. That August, Wintringer came near dying himself when he was poisoned after ingesting a handful of "Carter's pills" which turned out to have "strychnine in their composition." It was a full month before he was well enough to take over the *Abner O'Neal* again.[33]

In 1879, Captain Wintringer built his own boat, the *C. W. Batchelor*, and entered the Wheeling-to-Pittsburgh trade on the upper Ohio River. On October 12, 1886, Wintringer came home from a fishing trip, complained of a "terrible pain in his head," and dropped dead on his kitchen floor. It was later surmised that he had died from heart disease. He was fifty-five years old.[34]

Of the four Union officers most involved with the overcrowding of the *Sultana*, only one remained in the service after the war. In spite of a nagging oblique inguinal hernia, George Williams was promoted to major on March 15, 1866, and was given command of the 6th U.S. Infantry in Charleston, South Carolina, in August. During the beginning of Reconstruction, he was an assistant commissioner in the Freedmen's Bureau in North and South Carolina, and in early 1869 he was placed in command of the 20th U.S. Infantry and Fort Totten in northern Dakota Territory. His hernia worsened, and Williams finally retired from the army in December 1870 and moved to Newburgh, New York. On April 2, 1889, he died at his home from "congestion of the lungs" (i.e., pneumonia) at age fifty-eight.[35]

William Franklin Kerns left the army in December 1865 and returned to Minnesota. He married in 1869, had one child, and moved to St. Joseph, Missouri, where he clerked in a hardware store. By the 1880s he was working as a secretary and traveling salesman. He died of "Gastro Intestinal Catarrh" on February 17, 1894, at age fifty-four.[36]

After leaving the army in September 1866 with an honorable discharge, Frederic Speed settled in Vicksburg, where he was praised for "the work of reconciliation and the bringing about [of] kindly relations" between the North and South.[37] Perhaps spurred on by his own court-martial, Speed read law and was admitted to the bar in 1868. In 1869 he became editor of the conservative *Vicksburg Times* and made an unsuccessful run for state senator. He eventually resigned his editorial job but two years later married the daughter of the late owner of the newspaper, Esther Adele Hillyer. They would have five children.[38]

In 1880 Speed and a partner purchased sixty-nine acres just south of Vicksburg. "Speed's Addition" was soon known as "one of [Vicksburg's] most beautiful suburbs." In 1905, the city of Vicksburg annexed Speed's Addition after promising to provide "light, water, and other municipal services."[39] Speed died on March 11, 1911, of Bright's disease at age seventy. He was accorded full Masonic honors as the only thirty-third degree Mason in Mississippi and was laid to rest "amid the loving circle of the hundreds of citizens and Masons who had cherished him in his long and useful life's work."[40]

After managing to avoid the sheriff and the writ of attachment, Reuben Hatch continued to have trouble with the *Atlantic* steamboat case. In an ironic twist of fate, one of his key witnesses had moved out of Illinois and could not be found. The trial stretched on until June 1867 before the United States and Hatch eventually prevailed and forced the Atlantic and Mississippi Steamship Company to pay the missing $8,542.[41]

On January 24, 1867, during the middle of the *Atlantic* trial, Hatch and two other men became lessees in the state penitentiary in Joliet, Illinois. Hatch's lessee fee was $8,391.43.[42] Eventually the penitentiary deal went sour and his two partners bowed out, losing their entire investment. Hatch, however, refused to go quietly and sued the two men and the state of Illinois. In the end, nothing came of the lawsuits.[43]

Perhaps out of pity, Hatch's father-in-law hired him to supervise the construction of a three-story brick building in downtown Pittsfield. The "large, new brick building . . . was totally demolished" by a severe storm that tore through Pittsfield on the night of June 18, 1871. Considering his past history, Hatch may have cut corners by buying cheap building material, with the difference going into his pockets.[44] Hatch died on July 24, 1871, at age fifty-two of "congestion of the brain superinduced by alcoholism."[45]

The gallant *Bostona*, which had come upon the burning *Sultana* shortly after the explosion and whose crew had rendered invaluable service to the victims by throwing everything into the river that would float and then outfitting those they rescued with sheets, blankets, and spare clothing, remained in Memphis for at least a week afterward because she "was not in a fit condition to proceed on her voyage." Clerk Ames Fisher explained that "the *Bostona* lost a great deal in the shape of doors, blinds, staging-planks, bucket-planks, wood, hay-bales, rigging cut up &c., &c.; also, in damage to the cabin carpet and furniture; also, in mattresses, pillows, and bed-clothes." Captain Watson filed a requisition with the U.S. government for compensation for those items. On February 19, 1872, he was awarded $3,962 "in full compensation for his expenditures and losses in rescuing United States officers and soldiers from the disaster of the steamboat *Sultana*."[46]

In early 1866, long before Watson received the payout, the *Bostona* was laid up in Cincinnati for unpaid debt and "offered for sale at auction" by the U.S. marshal. The boat was in St. Louis for dismantling when a fire broke out on board at 1 a.m. on June 2, 1866, and spread to two nearby steamboats. "It was but a few moments after the alarm was sounded, before the three vessels were one mass of flames."[47] The "Gallant *Bostona*" was gone.

The other vessels involved in the rescue met various fates. The *Pocahontas* hit a snag and sank on the Missouri River on August 9, 1866, while carrying supplies to the South Dakota Territory. The *Silver Spray*'s boilers exploded thirty miles above Memphis on April

10, 1870, killing nine people. The boat was a total loss. The *Rose Hambleton* was eventually bought by a wrecker and was dismantled on September 30, 1869, to be used in "pumping out coffer-dams in the construction of bridges in the Upper Ohio." The *Marble City* was dismantled in 1873; her hull became a coal barge, which sank during a hurricane in September 1879. The steam ferry *Rosedella* ran the Mississippi until 1869 and then disappeared from the river, her fate unknown.[48]

The *Lady Gay*, whose captain had wanted to take some of the paroled prisoners from Vicksburg, blew a cylinder head on one engine in February 1867. "The piston rod speared through the body of an engineer, killing him." Three years later, in January 1870, the *Lady Gay* struck an underwater obstacle near Chester, Illinois, "and sank 30 yards from shore." The *Pauline Carroll*, which had been detained for long hours waiting for an overflow of prisoners that never came, ran successfully for many years and was finally sold at St. Louis in 1875. She was stripped down, and her hull was used as an ice barge.[49]

The *Henry Ames*, the first steamboat to take a large group of paroled prisoners north, hit a snag near Waterproof, Louisiana, in August 1874 and sank with the loss of two lives. The *Olive Branch*, the second steamer to take a large group of prisoners, was going downriver just below St. Louis in July 1871 when she hit a hidden stump that tore out her bottom. She sank in only one and a half minutes.[50]

Three military vessels sent out crews to help in the rescue of *Sultana* victims. The tinclad *Grosbeak* was actually the sidewheel steamboat *Fanny* (No. 2) that had been sold to the military in December 1864, fitted out as a tinclad, and rechristened the *Grosbeak*. A short time after the *Sultana* disaster, the boat was sold, stripped of her armament, and renamed the *Mollie Hambleton*. She eventually operated out of Galveston, Texas, and in June 1871 was sunk and lost on the Trinity River.[51]

The ironclad *Essex* had been the centerwheel snagboat *New Era* before the war. She was purchased by the U.S. government, rechristened the *Essex*, and had a splendid Civil War career, even surviving a Confederate shot through her boiler while attacking Fort Henry, Tennessee, in February 1862. She was decommissioned in July 1865, after her crew had helped rescue the *Sultana* victims, and in November was sold to "private interests" and renamed *New Era*. In December 1870, she was dragged ashore near Mound City, Illinois, and burned for scrap.[52]

The timberclad *Tyler* had also been a commercial boat before the war. Originally the sidewheel steamboat *A. O. Tyler*, she had actually been sunk and raised in early 1860 before the U.S. government bought her. Covered with a heavy layer of timber and armed with several heavy guns, she took part in the battles of Fort Henry and Fort Donelson, Shiloh, and Helena, Arkansas, and participated in the attack on the Confederate ram *Arkansas*. Several months after the *Sultana* disaster, the *Tyler* was sold at Mound City for a mere $6,000, probably for scrap.[53]

As for the *Sultana* herself, she was in "fifteen feet of water" with only "her jackstaff and part of her ribs" visible above the Mississippi on May 7 when Colonel Badeau visited the site. A few months later, when the floodwaters receded, Hen Island, where the *Sultana* had been snagged and sank, became clearly visible. Effinger M. Stapleton visited the site around July 1865: "The disaster had occurred some miles above, but she floated down and sank there. There was a low stage of water at the time and we considered ourselves the first to go aboard the sunken hulk. It was a lonely spot and no habitation was near. The island was well wooded and about the size of a small farm."[54]

Each year the Mississippi rose with the spring floods and deposited silt across the top and along the sides of the sunken steamboat. Each year, less and less of the boat was visible when the floodwaters receded. Somewhere along the way, the jackstaff disappeared. Charles W. Stewart, who worked for the Navy Department, recalled in 1902, "[I] surveyed the banks and channel near the wreck . . . which was very plain in 1890. Since that time the caving has eaten into the Tennessee side and the bar grown out correspondingly from the Arkansas side, so that the site of the wreck is probably now covered with cottonwood trees."[55]

The wreck of the *Sultana* acted like a cork at the opening that led into the Mound City Chute on the Arkansas (west) side of Hen Island. The northern end of the chute was eventually blocked as the silt and mud piled up against the wreck. In 1890 "the boat sank in the channel, and around the old hull a bar soon began to form. It enlarged from year to year, and soon changed the channel of the river. The bar thus formed about the sunken hull is now an island of considerable size, and completely shuts off Mound City from the river. So, as it has no river trade, and the railroads taking the freight to the interior, [Mound City] is now nothing more than the barest remembrance of what it used to be."[56] The *Sultana* was responsible for another death.

In 1898 parts of the *Sultana* were still visible above the surface of the Mississippi during low water. That year George R. Wilson, a woodworker from the Cochran Lumber Company in Memphis, was hired to put together a memorial relic board as a sixtieth birthday present for Capt. William S. Friesner, who had been in charge of the guard unit on the *Sultana*. Wilson recovered a piece of "board . . . from the lower section of the *Sultana*" as well as several metal artifacts, including a door latch, an S-hook, and the metal tip of a bayonet scabbard, and mounted the artifacts on the board. The finished piece was given to Captain Friesner by his friends at GAR Post 140 in Logan, Ohio.[57]

The wreck was still in the news, and perhaps still accessible, in 1915, the fiftieth anniversary of the disaster. The Indianapolis Chamber of Commerce took out a newspaper advertisement warning "against probable visits of peddlers . . . who claim their wares as 'salvage from the wreck of the steamship *Sultana*.' It is said the peddlers take orders but fail to make deliveries."[58]

By the sixtieth anniversary of the explosion, the *Sultana* was gone and the river had cut a new path east of the wreck site. "The spot where the *Sultana* sank now is inland as a result of a shifting of the river channel," the *Little Rock Arkansas Gazette* reported in 1925. Two years later, the cottonwood trees had been removed and Paddy's Hen Island was fertile farmland. An article in the *Commercial Appeal* of Memphis noted: "The point where the hulk of the *Sultana* drifted while on fire and sank, has been under cultivation many years. It is now Barton's plantation in Crittenden County, Arkansas, and up until a few years ago, some of the boat's timbers could be seen." A follow-up article written nine years later explained, "The spot where the *Sultana* sank after her hulk drifted into the Arkansas shore, is now three miles inland, or part of the old Barton plantation about two and a half miles northeast of Marion, [Arkansas,] seat of Crittenden County."[59]

The *Sultana* remained hidden and forgotten under the cultivated field until 1982, when Clive Cussler, author of *Raise the* Titanic and founder of the National Underwater and Marine Agency (NUMA), a naval research foundation, set out to locate the *Sultana* and two sunken Confederate gunboats. Cussler was working with Memphis attorney Jerry O. Potter and Arkansas farmer Sam Oliver, owner of the land above the *Sultana*. Potter had become interested in the *Sultana* six years earlier, and by studying old river maps and Civil War records had been able to determine how the course of the river had changed since 1865. He and Oliver had already located several artifacts that they thought belonged to the *Sultana*.

NUMA "searched the area where the artifacts were found" and did locate and excavate other artifacts. Cussler was concerned, however, that "according to [an 1871] pilot's chart, we were working almost four hundred yards too far south of the marked wreck site." Indeed, what the searchers had found was the debris pile left atop Hen Island when the salvage wrecker had excavated the wreck in September 1865. Anything brought up by Captain Gudgeon considered not of value was simply tossed onto Hen Island. When the April rains forced NUMA to postpone the excavation, Cussler laid out a grid for Potter to search, "including [his] preference for the *Sultana*'s grave," and then left to look for the two sunken gunboats.[60]

Potter and his wife, Janita, continued the search, with landowner Oliver using metal detectors in the area laid out in the grid. When they felt they were near, they switched to a more powerful magnetometer and found "a strong magnetic field . . . in an area about 100-by-300 feet"—an area large enough to contain the 40-by-260-foot *Sultana*. The searchers used a water probe and managed to find "bits of mortar . . . unburned coal and charred wood" about twenty feet down. Potter was excited by the find because he knew that the *Sultana* had taken on one thousand bushels of coal just prior to leaving Memphis. "That is what we had been looking for all along," he said.[61]

Cussler and NUMA announced that the *Sultana* had been found, but also cautioned that "there is no way we can come out and say definitely we have it unless we dig up a sign that says 'Here lies the *Sultana.*' We do have a 19th Century steamer down there. There are no other wrecks in the area, and it looks like a 99 per cent chance that we've got it." When Potter was asked if he would work to get the steamboat excavated, he responded, "If you destroy it, it's gone forever. We are walking a fine line. We have removed some artifacts but only those that were in a plow zone."[62] Most of the descendants and others associated with keeping alive the story of the *Sultana*, myself included, feel that the site should not be disturbed. Instead, it will remain an undisturbed buried memorial to those who died on the Mississippi River so many years ago.

28

REUNIONS AND
REMEMBRANCE

n April 6, 1866, Union veterans started the Grand Army of
the Republic (GAR), an organization open to all "honorably
discharged [Union] veterans." Over the next few years, individual armies, corps, divisions, and regiments began having reunions.
In April 1874, the National Union of Andersonville Survivors was
organized in Worchester, Massachusetts. In 1883 the organization
changed its name to the National Association of Ex–Union Prisoners
of War, thereby welcoming all "survivors of Rebel Military Prisons."
Two years later, in 1885, "a convention of the survivors of the disaster resulting from the explosion of the steamer *Sultana*" was held at
Fostoria, Ohio. Organizer and survivor Samuel Raudebaugh said,
"All survivors are earnestly requested to be present, as there will be
measures taken looking to their interests."[1] By "interests," of course,
Raudebaugh meant pensions. Although many *Sultana* survivors were
already members of the GAR and the National Association of the
Ex–Union Prisoners of War, they would now have an organization
dedicated solely to their needs.

Twenty survivors attended the Fostoria convention, most from
Ohio units but one each from Kentucky and Tennessee. A Cleveland

newspaper reported that the survivors were meeting "to effect a permanent organization and to make arrangements for annual reunions to be held in the future." After agreeing to meet annually, they chose the name *Sultana* Survivors' Association and elected Raudebaugh president. The association immediately set up a goal: "Whereas, All the survivors of the *Sultana* are suffering more or less as a result of injuries received; Resolved, That a committee appointed to prepare a memorial to Congress to grant all survivors of the *Sultana* a pension." Next, a measure was passed to work "on book publication" to keep the world informed about the worst maritime disaster in American history. The next meeting was scheduled for the twenty-first anniversary of the disaster, April 27, 1886, in Toledo, Ohio, and invitations went out to all the known survivors.[2]

Although only some thirty *Sultana* survivors attended the second meeting, it was said to be "a very enthusiastic and thrilling affair" with many of the survivors telling of their wartime and *Sultana* experiences. Hoping to boost attendance and bring in some attendees from Kentucky, Indiana, and Tennessee, the next meeting was scheduled to be held in Dayton, Ohio. Secretary William Fies immediately placed an announcement in the *National Tribune*, a Washington, DC, weekly published for Civil War veterans and their families.[3]

The meetings continued year after year, with more and more survivors attending. Attendance peaked at two hundred in 1890, the twenty-fifth anniversary of the disaster. Each new attendee was asked to provide his story. In 1892, survivor Rev. Chester D. Berry published *Loss of the* Sultana *and Reminiscences of Survivors*, a compilation of the stories of 133 survivors, 3 rescuers, and 1 former employee who had left the *Sultana* just prior to her fateful trip. In 1895, one of the guest speakers at the reunion was Howard A. M. Henderson, the conscientious commander of Cahaba Prison and one of the architects of Camp Fisk. "The speaker was tendered a magnificent ovation and in turn delivered an address that will not be forgotten by those who heard it," reported an Ohio newspaper. Meetings were also held in Michigan and Indiana but eventually settled around the Toledo area. In each town where the survivors met, residents gave them "a grand reception," often with parades, banquets, songs, speeches, and evening bonfires.[4]

On May 29, 1886, the southern survivors, mostly men from the 3rd Tennessee Cavalry from the Knoxville area, held their own reunion in the Knoxville courthouse "for the purpose of organizing a branch of the Ohio survivors of the ill-fated vessel" because of the expense of traveling so far to an annual reunion in northern Ohio. The southern survivors began their own annual meetings, almost exclusively in the Knoxville region. Attendance peaked at about one hundred in 1901. The northern and southern groups came together in 1896 for the dedication of a new GAR hall in Knoxville. The two groups kept in touch, with both advocating for an increase in pension money for the survivors and for the erection of a national monument.[5] In 1889, President Raudebaugh, who now went by the title "Colonel," explained their wants to the *National Tribune*: "First, a suitable monument be erected by the Government somewhere along the Mississippi River near the place of the disaster in memory of the poor heroes who lost their lives in that most fearful disaster; and second, a special pension of about $50 a month be given to the suffering survivors."[6] Regarding the monument, Raudebaugh asked, "should they not have as good a monument as any General?"[7]

Ironically, the first bill introduced in Congress concerning the *Sultana* disaster was H.R. 5742, submitted by Representative John Ford (D-TN) in April 1882, seeking compensation for the "owners of the steamer *Sultana*." Since the steamboat had been in the employ of the federal government when she exploded, the owners felt that the government owed them compensation for the loss of the vessel. The bill was passed to the House Committee on Claims.[8] The next year, in April 1883, Senator George Graham Vest (D-MO) introduced S. 1678 seeking "relief of the legal representatives of the owners of the steamer *Sultana*," which was sent to the Senate Committee on Claims.[9] When the bill stalled in committee, Senator Vest introduced an exactly worded bill, S. 211, in December, which also was sent to the Committee on Claims. All three bills died in committee, and no federal compensation was ever paid to the surviving owners of the *Sultana*.[10]

In January 1886, Senator John A. Logan (R-IL), who had been the second commander in chief of the GAR, was the first congressman to present a petition to place the "survivors of the *Sultana* disaster . . . on the pension rolls." The petition was referred to the Senate Committee on Pensions. In 1890, Congress passed an act granting all soldiers and sailors a pension if they were "incapacitated for the performance of manual labor." Over the next few years, several of the *Sultana* survivors applied for this additional pension.[11]

When the Fifty-First Congress opened on December 2, 1889, Representative Erastus J. Turner (R-KS) wasted no time introducing H.R. 350 calling for "the relief of the survivors of the *Sultana.*" H.R. 350 was referred to the House Committee on Claims. One month later, in January 1890, Senator Preston B. Plumb (R-KS) introduced S. 1722 asking "for the relief of the widows and orphans caused by the explosion of the steamer *Sultana.*" This bill was referred to the Senate Committee on Military Affairs.[12] Had the two bills passed into law, not only the survivors but also the widows and orphans of the disaster would have had lifelong compensation. Unfortunately, both bills died in committee.

On May 10, Sen. John Sherman (R-OH) introduced S. 3789 "providing for the special pension of $25 a month to the surviving soldiers . . . who were on board the *Sultana* when she exploded her boilers." That bill was sent to the Senate Committee on Pensions. Five days later, Rep. William E. Haynes (D-OH) introduced H.R. 10210, an identical bill, in the House. It was sent to the House Committee on Invalid Pensions.[13] Again, both bills died in committee.

Beginning in 1896, the Tennessee representative from the Second District, which included Blount and Knox Counties and the city of Knoxville, where many *Sultana* survivors resided, began calling for "a Bill to do justice to the survivors of the shipwreck *Sultana.*" Rep. Henry R. Gibson (R-TN) introduced H.R. 3296 in 1896, H.R. 1981 in 1897, H.R. 1932 in 1899, H.R. 4966 in 1901, and H.R. 5486 in 1903. None passed into law. When Representative Gibson retired in 1904, his replacement, Rep. Nathan W. Hale (R-TN) continued the campaign. In 1905 Hale introduced H.R. 1614 "seeking justice" for the survivors, and in 1907 he introduced H.R. 3061. After Hale was defeated for reelection in 1908, the new representative for the Second District, Richard W. Austin (R-TN), introduced *Sultana* survivor pension bills in 1909 (H.R. 5961), 1911 (H.R. 742), 1913 (H.R. 1895), 1915 (H.R. 953), and 1917 (H.R. 398). Each bill died in committee.[14] By 1917, the United States was at war, and Congress had more to worry about than providing "justice" for the two hundred or so surviving *Sultana* soldiers who were already receiving some form of government pension. The call for an enhanced pension was never brought up again.

Attempts to have the government build a monument commemorating the *Sultana* disaster met a similar fate. Sen. Chauncey M. Depew (R-NY) presented a petition by the "*Sultana* Survivors' Association . . . for the erection of a monument in memory of the soldiers who lost their lives by the destruction of the steamboat *Sultana*" on February 2, 1900. The petition was referred to the Senate Committee on the Library. In March 1902, "Colonel" Raudebaugh traveled to Washington to lobby Congress for the monument and the funds. By April, a bill had been prepared to appropriate $50,000 for the construction of a monument "in memory of the 1,457 soldiers ex-prisoners of war from Andersonville and Cabala [*sic*] who lost their lives" on the *Sultana*. On April 22, a few days before the thirty-seventh anniversary of the disaster, Sen. Joseph B. Foraker (R-OH) introduced the bill on the Senate floor calling for a monument in Washington, DC, "in memory of those who lost their lives on the steamer *Sultana*." The *Washington Times* reported, "The sum of $50,000 is appropriated for the purpose. A committee is appointed . . . which shall select a site and supervise the construction of the monument."[15]

A few days later, survivor Joseph Stevens, who had appeared before the committee, felt confident "that success will probably come to the movement under way. . . . The measure should receive the support of every congressman. It will carry down to history the explosion and the men whose lives were sacrificed by it."[16] Unfortunately, Stevens was wrong. While the *Sultana* survivors were pushing for their monument, Congress was also considering the appropriation of funds for the construction of a monument for President McKinley, who had been assassinated on September 6, 1901. In the end, neither would be built. A stock market crash in May 1901 and the resulting 1902–4 recession made Congress unwilling to appropriate funds for any national monument.[17]

In 1914, one last attempt was made to get a national monument for the *Sultana* victims. H.R. 12300 was introduced on January 26 by Rep. Frank B. Willis (R-OH). Willis did not want the memorial built in Washington, but instead "on the shore of the river near the scene of the great calamity." The bill was sent to committee, where it quickly died. In 1919, survivor James Kimberlin wrote in disgust,

> Our association twenty-five years ago appointed a monument committee to go before Congress and ask that an appropriation be made for the erection of a suitable monument to those dead martyrs, and every Congress has been appealed to, but the committee has as often met with the same cold indifference. For men who had endured the torments of a hell on earth, starved, famished from thirst, eaten with vermin, having endured all the indignities, insults, and abuses possible for an armed bully to bestow upon them, to be so soon forgotten does not speak well for our government or the American people.[18]

After witnessing failure after failure with the federal government, Ohio state representative James A. Welker (R) proposed a bill in April 1904 to the Ohio legislature "appropriating $25,000 for the erection of a monument in the statehouse park to the Ohio soldiers who perished in the wreck of the steamer *Sultana*." Gov. Myron T. Herrick (R), a nonveteran, vetoed the expensive bill. Two years later, state senator Robert A. Pollock (R) tried again, lowering the requested funds to $15,000. This time, under newly installed governor and Civil War veteran Andrew L. Harris (R), the bill was approved. On July 24, 1906, Governor Harris appointed a three-man commission that included survivors William P. Madden and John J. Zaiser to arrange and finalize the construction of a *Sultana* memorial "on the Capitol grounds in Columbus."[19]

Zaiser submitted a design for a monument that was twenty-one feet tall, "of gray granite and octagonal in shape." The shaft would have a globe on top surmounted by "a Goddess of Liberty." Surrounding the column would be "statues typifying the four branches of service, infantry, cavalry, artillery, and marines. Sketches of the *Sultana* will adorn the monument, and in the inside will be placed tablets containing the names of the victims of the explosion." With Zaiser's design in hand, the commissioners hired a New York granite firm to handle the construction.[20] Everything progressed smoothly for a while.

Then, amid accusations that the New York firm had bribed the commissioners to approve the contract, Governor Harris put the whole thing on hold. Ohio attorney general Wade H. Ellis investigated and decided that the commissioners had gone beyond their "legal authority" in selecting a firm to construct the monument. Since the state was paying the bill, the commissioners should have put out a call for bids. Ellis also ruled that "the act creating the commission does not specifically grant authority to place the monument on the state capitol grounds." The *East Liverpool Evening Review* reported: "*Sultana* Monument Act Fails to Provide Legally for a Site." On Christmas Day 1906, the three commissioners were relieved of their jobs, and the endeavor to build a memorial to honor the men from Ohio who perished in the disaster came to an end.[21] Although the northern *Sultana* Survivors' Association would try again in 1915 on the fiftieth anniversary of the disaster, and a private industrialist would try in 1917, it would all be for naught. A monument to the memory of the *Sultana* disaster would never be erected in Columbus.[22]

Perhaps disgusted with affairs in Washington and Ohio, the Tennessee survivors decided to erect their own monument. Survivor John Harrison Simpson, who was only seventeen years old on the night of the disaster, spearheaded the effort, and a beautiful monument, made from a light pink crystalline limestone found only in Tennessee, was erected in Mount Olive Cemetery, south of Knoxville, and unveiled on July 4, 1916. The names of 365 Tennessee soldiers who were on the *Sultana* and a replica of the *Sultana* herself are carved into the limestone. The entire monument cost the southern survivors only $379 because a local company donated the stone. Among the hundred or so people who attended the unveiling were four survivors from the Knoxville area, including "Colonel" Simpson and a representative from the northern *Sultana* Survivor's Association who gave a short speech on behalf of the aging survivors from the North who could not attend.

The keynote speaker for the unveiling was former representative Henry R. Gibson, now a judge, who had fought so hard and long to get the federal government to erect a monument in Washington. After retelling the story of the disaster, Judge Gibson concluded: "The monument . . . is built here on the banks of Knob creek whose waters run into the Tennessee, from the Tennessee into the Ohio, and from the Ohio into the Mississippi, and the rain that falls here upon this monument will find its way into Knob creek, and thence will spread far and wide over the Mississippi, and cover the very place where lie the remains of any soldiers, whose bones yet lie unburied in the oozie bottom of the mighty Mississippi."[23] What the federal government couldn't or wouldn't do, the survivors from Tennessee had done themselves.

The two *Sultana* Survivors' Associations continued to meet year after year. In 1912, the two groups held their meetings only two weeks after the RMS *Titanic* sank with the loss of 1,517 people. Newspapers began to compare the two disasters, many claiming falsely that the American disaster was worse than the English tragedy.[24] In the eyes of American newspaper reporters and editors, the *Sultana* was *the* greatest maritime disaster in history, and if the number of deaths had to be raised every time there was a worse disaster, so be it. William Madden urged both groups to rise above the newspapers' petty squabbling: "There is a kindred feeling, however, that only exists between those who shared the affliction of [those] terrible time[s]."[25]

In April 1925, near the sixtieth anniversary of the *Sultana* disaster, Rep. James Willis Taylor (R-TN) announced his plan to introduce a bill to the next Congress "to provide funds for the construction of a government park and suitable monument in Crittenden County, Arkansas, in memory of the 1,400 Union soldiers who lost their lives when the steamer *Sultana* exploded." Taylor even proposed building a highway to the park. There is no evidence in the *Congressional Record* that such a bill was ever introduced.[26]

As time went by and the survivors passed away, attendance at the meetings of the two *Sultana* Survivors' Associations dwindled. A single survivor attended the last meeting of the southern group, held in 1930. Pleasant Keeble showed up at Rockford Presbyterian Church near Knoxville, walked down the aisle, gave a silent prayer, and then returned home. A Knoxville newspaper reported, "The famous Association of *Sultana* Survivors is no more." Keeble died March 4, 1931, five weeks before the sixty-sixth anniversary of the disaster.[27]

Two members of the northern group, Robert Gilbreath and Andrew Jackson McCormack (private, Co. E, 9th IN Cav), met informally at McCormack's home near Cadiz, Ohio, in 1933. "There probably will never be another reunion," said Mrs. Theodore Warren, daughter of "Colonel" Samuel Raudebaugh, who had passed away in 1931. "The few boys who are left are too old."[28] Gilbreath died April 4, 1934, and McCormack died a year and a day later on April 5, 1935. The very last known survivor of the *Sultana* disaster, Charles M. Eldridge, died in Denison, Texas, at age ninety-six on September 8, 1941, seventy-six years after the disaster and just three months before the United States entered World War II.[29]

At his last reunion in 1931, Plez Keeble expressed the hope that future generations would carry on the memory of the *Sultana*. Speaking about his best friend and fellow survivor John Simpson, Keeble said, "Mr. Simpson died hoping that our descendants would continue the *Sultana* anniversary services after the last survivor had passed away. I hope so too. . . . It's just that such a tragic event of history should be remembered."[30] More than fifty years passed before Knoxville attorney and Civil War enthusiast Norman Shaw wondered if any descendants of *Sultana* survivors still lived in the area. In 1987 he held an informal meeting at the Tennessee *Sultana* monument in Mount Olive Cemetery, and forty to fifty people showed up. After that simple meeting, Shaw, who had no relative on the *Sultana*, founded the Association of *Sultana* Descendants and Friends, open to anybody with a love of history and a commitment to perpetuate the memory of the *Sultana*. The group has met annually each year since 1988, ensuring, as John Simpson hoped, "that such a tragic event of history should be remembered."[31]

In 1990, with the assistance of *Sultana* historian Jerry O. Potter, a Tennessee state memorial plaque was erected near Memphis' cobblestone wharf, the *Sultana*'s last stopping point before she headed upriver toward disaster. Over the next several years, dedicated markers and monuments were placed in Marion, Arkansas; Muncie, Indiana; Hillsdale, Michigan; Vicksburg, Mississippi; Mansfield and West Alliance, Ohio; in Memphis' Elmwood Cemetery; and on the Cincinnati waterfront. Monuments to individual regiments that lost men on the *Sultana* were erected in Adrian, Lime Creek, and Franklin Township, Michigan; and Cuyahoga Falls and West Alliance, Ohio. In 2015, the *Sultana* Disaster Museum was opened in Marion, Arkansas, the closest city to the site of the buried remains of the *Sultana*. John Simpson's dream lives on. The *Sultana* will always be remembered.

29

NO SABOTAGE

When Jerry Potter wrote *The* Sultana *Tragedy* in 1992 and I wrote *Disaster on the Mississippi* in 1996, neither of us spent much time discussing or disproving the possibility that the *Sultana* had been sabotaged by a Confederate agent, because neither of us put much credence in the theory. We both felt that the issue had been put to rest long ago. Unfortunately, that proved not to be the case.

In recent years, a faction of *Sultana* enthusiasts has begun promoting the idea that the boilers on the *Sultana* were exploded by a Courtenay coal torpedo. Such theories of sabotage do arise now and then among those who rely on secondary sources. Let us put the sabotage theories to rest once and for all by looking at what the primary sources say.

The sabotage/coal torpedo theorists say that investigators spent very little time "in Memphis seeking the exact cause of the explosion before moving to concentrate on who was responsible for so overloading the boat in Vicksburg."[1] Not true. Three investigative bodies spent at least a month looking into the cause of the explosion, and each did consider sabotage. When hard evidence and expert testimony determined that the torpedo theory did not hold up, the investigators concentrated on other, more plausible causes.

First Mate William Rowberry was among the first to promote the sabotage theory. On April 27, 1865, Rowberry was interviewed on the steamboat *Marble City* shortly after he was rescued. In a sworn statement, he testified,

> I was Chief Mate of the Steamer *Sultana* and at the time of the accident I had charge of the boat and was in the Pilot House with Mr. Cayton. We were about seven miles up the river when the boilers exploded and I found myself in the river. I and five others got hold of a plank and was picked up by the Steamer *Bostonia* [*sic*]. The boilers were tested in St. Louis, on this our last trip and pronounced good, and the boat had the usual certificates. Mr. Schaffer at St. Louis was the inspector. There was a little patch put on the boilers at Vicksburg, I believe the boat at the time was running as usual about nine or ten miles per hour. We were not "running against time." No boat left with us.
>
> The boiler leaked some twelve hours before we reached Vicksburg and the Engineer [Nathan Wintringer] said he would go no farther until it was repaired. We laid at V— about thirty-three hours, most of this time was taken up repairing the boiler and the Engineer said it was a good job. It was done by regular mechanics at Vicksburg, we had no trouble with the boiler after leaving Vicksburg.
>
> The patch was put on the larboard side of the larboard boiler, the Second, or third sheet from the forward end. The patch was made necessary by the leaking of the boilers. There was not to my knowledge any fears expressed by crew or passengers as to the safety of the boat. I had no fears of the boat, have been on the *Sultana* about four months. Have been on the river with Captain Mason, master of the *Sultana*, for about five years, he was a perfect gentleman. There was no carousing on the boat amongst crew or passengers. Capt. Mason was in his room, the 1st Engineer [Wintringer] in his, and the 2nd Engineer [Clemens] on watch. We had no cargo on the boat except about 60 head of mules and horses.[2]

Rescued only hours after the explosion, with events very fresh in his mind, Rowberry made no reference to sabotage or a coal torpedo.

The next day, the *Memphis Daily Bulletin* summarized Rowberry's statement: "Rowberry . . . can give no idea of the cause of the accident; says the boat was going at ordinary speed, and that all seemed well up to the moment the explosion occurred." On April 29, however, Rowberry spoke with a reporter for the *St. Louis Daily Missouri Republican* in Cairo, and a different story emerged: "I conversed with the 1st mate of the ill-fated steamer, Wm. Rowberry . . . and he thinks there must have been some infernal machine put in the coal, as boat at the time was running very steady and so little steam on that explosion was impossible." After Rowberry had given a sworn statement in which he claimed that he could "give no idea of the cause of the accident" and did not mention an "infernal machine," a reporter was now claiming that Rowberry was blaming sabotage as the cause of the accident.[3]

That same date, April 29, the *Cincinnati Commercial Tribune* published a story headlined "Suspicion that the Explosion was Caused by a Torpedo in the Shape of a Lump of Coal." The accompanying story read, "Mate Paberry [*sic*] says the steam was not near as high on the *Sultana* as it was usually carried. He thinks a torpedo shaped like a lump of coal must have caused the explosion."[4] Neither newspaper quoted Rowberry directly. As is usually the case with the sabotage theory, the story was secondhand, reported by someone claiming to have spoken to the eyewitness.

Only a few hours after being rescued, Rowberry had "no idea of the cause of the accident." Within thirty-six hours, however, newspapers were claiming that Rowberry believed a "torpedo shaped like a lump of coal" was responsible. What happened within those thirty-six hours to change his mind?

During their investigations on April 27, General Washburn's inquiry team had learned that the *Sultana* had offloaded 225 hogsheads of sugar from the hold during her stop at Memphis. As first mate, Rowberry was responsible for the distribution of weight on the steamboat. He would have known that the *Sultana* would be top-heavy after the removal of the sugar, and he should have redistributed the weight of the soldiers from the upper deck, perhaps by having those on the hurricane deck move down into the empty hold for the one-day trip to Cairo. This he did not do. With early suspicion centering on the probability that the explosion was caused by the careening of the top-heavy vessel, it was only a matter of time before fingers would begin to point at Rowberry for not doing his job. It seems highly likely that Rowberry concocted the coal torpedo story to divert suspicion away from himself. The explosion had nothing to do with his negligence, he claimed; an "infernal machine," a "torpedo shaped like a lump of coal," was the cause.

Three days later, on May 2, the *Memphis Daily Bulletin* reported that "a witness before the investigating committee swore that he saw the doors of the furnace blown open, just before the explosion." A careful study of all the statements taken by the Washburn Commission, as well as numerous statements made to the two Memphis newspapers, has failed to find any such sworn statement or to identify the "witness." Likewise, a careful examination of the 227 first-person accounts of survivors I have collected over the course of 30 years of researching the disaster has failed to identify any person who "swore that he saw the doors of the furnace blown open, just before the explosion." Further, this statement fails to take into account the fact that the explosion originated on the top, back of the boilers, and not in the furnace.

The next person to lend credence to the sabotage theory was Capt. William Postal, the agent with the St. Louis and Memphis Packet Company. When he visited the wreck of the *Sultana* on April 30, Postal found a "piece of a Shell" among the rubbish of the sunken decks.[5] This finding actually supports the argument that a coal torpedo was *not* used. The Courtenay coal torpedo, designed by Thomas E. Courtenay, was fabricated to look like a lump of coal, not a regular Civil War artillery shell. The torpedo, about the size of a man's fist, was "a block of cast-iron" containing "about four ounces of black gunpowder." Not all coal torpedoes looked alike. Patterns for them "were fashioned from random pieces of coal and sized so that they would not require trimming by a fireman before shoveling into the furnace. After the shell body was filled with powder and plugged, it was dipped into a boiling mixture of coal tar, resin or beeswax, and pulverized coal, and then plunged into cold water, leaving a final product resembling a lump of coal in weight, smell, and general appearance."[6] No one could ever confuse a Courtenay coal torpedo with a Civil War artillery shell. In fact, it was specifically made to look nothing like an artillery shell.

What Captain Postal found on the deck of the *Sultana* may have been a piece of a shell, but it had nothing to do with the explosion of the boilers, and it was definitely not a piece of a Courtenay coal torpedo.

"Was It a Fiendish Atrocity?" the *Memphis Daily Bulletin* for May 2, 1865, asked. A "well-informed machinist who was aboard the *Sultana* says there were three distinct explosions" suggesting "that the *Sultana* was intentionally blown up by someone." According to the newspaper, this possibility was corroborated by the "fragments weighing a pound, of bombs" found on the *Sultana* that "seemed to have been subjected to intense heat." Initially, one has to wonder if the fragments mentioned in the article and Captain Postal's "piece of a shell" were one and the same. Examples of the Courtenay coal torpedo found in the office of Confederate president Jefferson Davis weighed less than a pound. If the fragment found on the wreck of the *Sultana* weighed a pound, then there is no possibility that any of these "fragments" could have been from a Courtenay coal torpedo.

Once again, the "well-informed machinist" was not identified, and only two survivors ever mentioned more than one explosion. Private Rush recalled what "seemed to be two distinct explosions. The first awakened us, and by the time we were on our feet, the hot steam was coming up through the deck, and immediately another explosion followed." This second explosion occurred long after the boilers had exploded. It was definitely not connected with a coal torpedo. Ann Annis clung for a time to the rudder of the *Sultana* to adjust her lifebelt. While she was hanging there she "heard a second explosion which seemed to be made up of three great reports like the explosion of shells or gunpowder."[7] Again, this second explosion came long after the initial blast. It was not connected to a coal torpedo.

Analysis of the sabotage theory continued on May 4 when Supervising Inspector of Steamboats John Witzig arrived in Memphis to investigate the cause of the disaster. "When he can examine the wreck he will be able to determine whether the explosion was caused by a shell or not," the *Memphis Daily Bulletin* predicted.[8] If anyone had a reason to claim that the boilers were exploded by a coal torpedo it was Witzig. Inspectors working out of his office in St. Louis had signed off on the safety of the *Sultana*'s boilers on April 12, only two weeks before the explosion. By claiming that a coal torpedo had caused the explosion he would have exonerated his two inspectors and thrown the blame elsewhere.

By the beginning of May 1865, Union troops had fully occupied Richmond, the capital of the Confederacy. On May 4, the *Washington National Republican* broke the story that "a torpedo, prepared to represent a lump of coal" had been found "in Jeff. Davis' house, in his cabinet of curiosities." The newspaper mentioned that the Confederate government had a "Bureau of Infernal Machines" and that it was believed that one of these "specimens" had been "the cause of the explosion of the steamer *Sultana*, near Memphis, and the loss of about 1,500 lives." There was no hard evidence to point to this conclusion, only conjecture and a piece of a supposed artillery shell that did not resemble a coal torpedo in shape or weight. But the theory had been suggested, and now there was proof that a Courtenay coal torpedo did exist. The sabotage theorists continued their speculation.

The *Memphis Daily Bulletin* reported on May 5 that Capt. William Thornburgh, one of the co-owners of the *Sultana*, and Capt. Frank Dozier, Captain Mason's brother-in-law, had visited the wreck hoping to recover "every boiler and fragment of boiler." With a fiduciary interest in the vessel, and possibly facing multiple lawsuits if it was proven that Mason, Rowberry, or Wintringer had been negligent in the boiler repairs and the placement of the paroled prisoners, Thornburgh and the other owners were hoping to prove that the explosion had been caused by a "shell or shells among the coal." All they found at the wreck, however, was thirty bodies.[9]

That same date, the *Chicago Tribune* ran an article calling Rowberry's alleged statement about an "infernal machine" an outright fabrication. The overcrowding of the *Sultana*, a steamboat that had "a boiler which had not been examined or tested since its last patch," was at fault, the *Tribune* said, and the "necessary inference at the time was that the Captain of the *Sultana* obtained [his passengers] by corrupt means. The infernal machine that exploded the boiler and sent so many souls into eternity, carrying bereavement and mourning into thousands of Western homes, was undoubtedly, the bribe—the greenbacks paid by the officers of the *Sultana* to the Quartermaster for the transportation of the troops."[10] In the *Tribune*'s estimation, it was the overcrowding of the boat, plus bad boilers, that had caused the explosion, not an "infernal machine."

On May 7, 1865, Washburn's investigators finally got a chance to question Witzig, who had examined a portion of the boiler pulled from the wreck. Witzig told them that the explosion had been caused by an "excess of steam," not by an "infernal machine."[11] The coal torpedo theory had taken another hit.

Two days later, a newspaper article reported that "a portion of one of the boilers of the *Sultana* was taken from the wreck" and examined. The piece "showed evidence of the terrible power of pent up steam—it being straightened out and then bent back and torn in several places by the explosion." The *Memphis Argus* summarized, "This piece of the boilers dissipated the idea that a shell was the cause of the explosion, as one end of this piece is very badly burned, proving, beyond doubt, that the boilers were in very bad condition."[12] On May 13, *Argus* readers were told that the boilers had exploded because "the water was too low in her boilers and her fires too hot," and not "from effects of the bursting of a shell."[13] Two more strikes against the sabotage theory, this time from physical evidence.

The sabotage theory took another hit on May 14 when expert engineer and boilermaker Isaac West pronounced "that the explosion took place from a deficiency of water in the boilers," and not from a coal torpedo. Picking up on West's conclusion, the *Chicago Tribune* on May 15 reported, "It is believed there really exists no grounds for supposing the explosion of the *Sultana* was occasioned by a torpedo placed in the coal. The wreck has been visited and pieces of the boilers recovered, which were badly burned, proving beyond doubt or denial, that the boiler was in very bad condition."[14]

After three weeks of looking into the sabotage/coal torpedo theory, as well as the other possible causes for the explosion, most of the investigators had concluded that the *Sultana*'s boilers had exploded because of a lack of water, not a Confederate plot. Although General Hoffman admitted that he could not be certain about the cause, he mentioned only the "lack of water" and the "careening" theories in his letter to Secretary of War Stanton on May 19, 1865.[15]

On May 26, the *Cincinnati Commercial Tribune* summarized the findings of the three investigative commissions succinctly:

> [The] facts are: 1st. That the steamer *Sultana* was badly out of repair at the time she lay at the port of Vicksburg. 2d. That the repairs to her boilers, while effectual, so far as completed, were insufficient. 3d. That the want of thorough repairs, while not endangering the general seaworthiness of the boat, did not warrant a high pressure of steam. 4th. That the immediate cause of the explosion was the want of sufficient water in the boilers. The inference from these facts, is that a boat, sadly overcrowded, and but partially repaired, was put under high pressure, and the water in the boiler exhausted more rapidly than supplied.[16]

The sabotage theory popped up now and again in 1865, but nobody gave it much credence. In January 1866, during the Speed court-martial, Witzig drove another nail into the sabotage theory's coffin when he was asked if the *Sultana*'s boilers would have exploded from the "bursting of a shell in the furnace." Witzig pointed out that a Confederate shell had gone completely through a boiler on the iron-clad *Essex* during the naval attack on Fort Henry, and while steam and boiling water had escaped, there was no explosion.[17] The explosion of a torpedo in the furnace under the boiler might have sent fragments of the shell into the boiler, and perhaps even entirely through the boiler, causing an escape of boiling water and steam, but it would not have caused the boiler to explode.

The sabotage/coal torpedo theory was mostly forgotten until April 1880, the fifteenth anniversary of the disaster, when survivor George Schmutz was interviewed by an Ohio newspaper and brought up the topic once again. Schmutz noted, "It was conjectured that in loading up coal at Memphis, a torpedo was taken in with the coal and was put in the furnace, and thus burst the boilers." He was quick to point out, however, that he was "ignorant of the cause of the explosion."[18]

Six years later, and a few months after the first meeting of the *Sultana* Survivors' Association, survivor William French Dixon brought the sabotage theory back to life. In a March 6, 1886, article published in the *Evansville Journal*, Dixon wrote, "Many think, and have good grounds for the belief, that a torpedo had been placed in the coal, which was thrown into the furnace causing all this death and destruction, and I am inclined to the opinion that this is the correct theory."[19]

Two months later, on May 20, 1886, an Iowa veteran wrote to the *National Tribune* that a friend claimed to know the identity of the person who had smuggled the coal torpedo on board the *Sultana*. As was always the case with such thirdhand stories, the person said to be the saboteur was long since dead and could not be asked to verify the story.

In that same *National Tribune* article, veteran Boynton T. Chapman professed that he had been "informed some time ago by a friend that Lieut. Barnett, of the 12th Ky., who was on board the steamer *Sultana* at the time of the explosion, confessed that he was the man who caused the disaster, being bribed by certain parties in Louisville to do the damnable work for $80,000. The miscreant did not get the money, and in a fit of despair and remorse blew out his brains."[20] It was an interesting story, but what had caused Chapman to come forward now, twenty-one years after the disaster, and how much of it, if any, was true?

The second *Sultana* Survivors' Association meeting was held on April 27, 1886, three weeks before Chapman's article came out. The *National Tribune* and many other major newspapers had run articles announcing the forthcoming reunion. The *Sultana* was a hot topic again and back in the eyes of the public. That may have been what sparked Chapman to come forth with his story.

"Lieut Barnett, of the 12th Ky." was in fact 2nd Lt. James T. Worthington Barnett (Co. B, 12th KY Inf). Born in 1817, he had fought in the Mexican War and in July 1861, at age forty-four, had organized "Capt. Barnett's Co., 1st Reg't Kentucky Vols.," which subsequently became Company K, 3rd Kentucky Infantry. In October 1861 Captain Barnett was court-martialed for an unspecified reason, and in February 1862, while awaiting sentencing, resigned. On May 23, 1863, however, he was "Appointed by Gov. of Ky." as a second lieutenant in Company B, 12th Kentucky Infantry. A year later,

Barnett was in trouble again, court-martialed for drunkenness on two separate occasions, for using "loud, boisterous and indecent language" in the quarters of a fellow officer, and for playing cards and dice with the enlisted men. While awaiting the verdict, Barnett was captured at the Battle of Franklin, Tennessee, on November 30, 1864, and sent to Andersonville prison. He spent the next four months suffering with his fellow prisoners before he was released and sent to Camp Fisk. He went on board the *Sultana* with the other Kentucky prisoners and was rescued at Fort Pickering after the disaster. The *Pocahontas* took him back to Memphis, where he was admitted to the Memphis Officers' Hospital suffering from a "Slight Bruise."

Lieutenant Barnett reached Camp Chase on May 3, 1865, and was "mustered out and honorably discharged" effective May 15, 1865. Five months later, on October 20, he died at age forty-eight of unknown causes. He was given a government headstone and buried in Gilmore Cemetery in Somerset, Kentucky.[21]

Although Barnett had a spotty career early in the war, Kentucky governor James Fisher Robinson had thought well enough of Barnett to appoint him a second lieutenant in 1863. Likewise, in spite of his problems in his second regiment, Barnett fought well at Franklin and was honorably discharged at the end of the war. The injuries he suffered on the *Sultana* and the fact that he floated about nine miles downriver to Fort Pickering attest to the fact that he was on board the *Sultana* when she exploded. It is hard to believe that he blew up the boat while he was on it, then had to fight his way through the struggling, clinging, drowning crowd and float nine miles downriver in icy cold waters hoping to be rescued so he could collect his $80,000. Also, one must wonder how "certain parties in Louisville" managed to entice Barnett to blow up the *Sultana* after he had just spent four months in a Confederate prison and one month recuperating at Camp Fisk. By the time these "facts" were made public, Lieutenant Barnett had been dead for almost twenty-one years and could not answer to the charge. Still, the sabotage theorists now had a name to add to the deed.

J. W. Chrisinger responded to the *National Tribune* article by writing, "I see a good deal of nonsense in regard to the *Sultana* disaster. I was in Memphis at the time and assisted in rescuing the few survivors. I know just about how and why it happened." Chrisinger diagrammed the layout of the interconnected boilers and described the overcrowding. He then explained how the *Sultana* might have careened when moving from one side of the river to the other. "If there was any one to blame for this sad disaster, it was either the captain of the boat or the officer in charge of the paroled men—the former for overloading the boat, the latter for allowing it done."[22] To Chrisinger and most others, the sabotage theory was still dead.

The second annual meeting of the *Sultana* Survivors' Association held at Dayton, Ohio, on April 27, 1887, made national news both before and after the gathering. Not long afterward, a "society of survivors" was organized in St. Louis in September 1887 during the twenty-first annual GAR encampment. Although the society elected a president and secretary, only one survivor, Jacob Rush, was actually in attendance, along with Dr. Jesse Hawes, a former prisoner of war who was writing a book about Cahaba that would include several firsthand accounts from *Sultana* survivors. The information about this meeting was published in the November 10, 1887, edition of the *National Tribune*.[23]

The *Sultana* Survivors Association held its third reunion on April 27, 1888, at Hillsdale, Michigan. Once again, newspapers were full of survivors' accounts and stories about the *Sultana*. On May 3, the *National Tribune* published an article restating the Barnett story, but this time claiming that the *Sultana* had been destroyed by "a Kentuckian, who enlisted in the Union army and took passage on that steamer for the purpose of destroying it." Three days later, the bombshell story that would become the linchpin of the sabotage theory was published in the *St. Louis Globe Democrat* under the headline "Blew up the *Sultana*."[24]

The May 6, 1888, article began: "The recent publication of a number of statements from survivors of the explosion of the Mississippi River steamer *Sultana* twenty-three years ago, has led to the cause of the disaster." The article stated that in an interview, William C. Streetor, who "was employed as a clerk in the Gratiot and Myrtle street prisons" during the war, had stated, "Yes, I know something about the *Sultana* disaster. . . . I can give the cause of the explosion. A torpedo in a lump of coal was carried aboard the steamer in Memphis and deposited in the coal pile. . . . The man who placed the torpedo on the boat is my authority, for I had the statement from his own lips." That man, according to Streetor, was Robert Louden.[25]

Streetor said that Louden "was a painter by trade, and he worked in the same shop with me for William H. Gray, some three years after the close of the war." He described Louden as "a young, vigorous daredevil. He possessed bravery of a certain kind, I think, equal to that of any man who ever lived. He was cool and calculating in his disposition, but at times he drank heavily, and when in his cups was disposed to talk a little too much for a man with a record like he had. It was while he was drinking one day that he and I got to talking about the war, and the burning of so many boats by the Confederate agents came up." Louden claimed to have "fired no less than half a dozen steamboats on the Mississippi." Added Streetor, "I asked him in an offhand way what he knew about the *Sultana* explosion. Then he told me the story of the torpedo in the coal, and, using his own expression, 'It had got to be too—ticklish a job to set the boat afire and get away from her.'" Streetor ended by saying that Louden "died in New Orleans during the yellow fever epidemic along in the latter part of the '60s."[26] The sabotage theorists now had a more substantial story on which to base their beliefs. But does the story stand up under careful examination?

When looked at carefully, there are many holes in Streetor's story. Streetor claimed that he worked with Robert Louden "some three years after the close of the war" (i.e., 1868). However, Louden died in New Orleans on September 13, 1867, a year and a half after the war. Streetor also said that Louden claimed that he had burned "no less than half a dozen steamboats on the Mississippi." Although the theorists claim that Confederate "boat-burners" destroyed more than sixty steamboats, hard evidence points to perhaps thirty-one, all of which were set afire and not exploded. Louden was probably responsible for one of those.[27]

Streetor also claimed that Louden said he had carried the coal torpedo "aboard the steamer at Memphis and deposited [it] in the

coal pile in front of the boilers." Louden indeed could have boarded
the boat when she was docked at Memphis amid the confusion with
the unloading of the sugar and the coming and going of the prisoners.
However, had he placed a coal torpedo in the coal bin at that time, the
torpedo would have been buried under a ton of coal shortly thereafter
when the steamer moved upriver at midnight to take on one thousand
bushels from the coal barges. If that were the case, the coal torpedo
would not have been shoveled into the furnace until the boat was hundreds of miles upriver from Memphis, not seven miles.

Louden might have meant that he put the coal torpedo on the
boat while she was docked at the coal barges, but that seems unlikely.
He would have had to row out to the barges simply to reach them,
since they were anchored far from the Tennessee shore. It was pointed
out at the time that the employees working on the coal barges "were
loyal union men" and certainly would have noticed, and perhaps chal-
lenged, anyone approaching in the darkness. Everyone was aware of
Confederate saboteurs and guerrillas. Two days before the disaster,
on April 25, 1865, the Union picket boat *Pocahontas* had gone up and
down the river destroying every boat they could find in an effort to
stop the sabotage.[28] Although not impossible, it would have been very
difficult for Louden to obtain a rowboat during the few hours that the
Sultana was at Memphis.[29]

There are many more problems with Streetor's statement. He said,
for example, that Louden "drank heavily" and was "in his cups" when
he admitted to destroying the *Sultana*. Also, the story of the *Sultana*
had been in the newspapers repeatedly for the past few years, and
one person had already claimed that he knew who had exploded the
Sultana. Streetor might have decided to garner some of the attention
by announcing that a known Confederate saboteur had told him that
he had caused the greatest maritime disaster in U.S. history. Streetor
may have actually admired the "vigorous daredevil." In any case, there
was no way to prove or disprove Streetor's story, because Louden had
been dead for twenty-one years.

On May 7, 1888, one day after the Streetor story broke, Henry
J. Lyda, formerly a steward on the *Sultana*, wrote a scathing rebut-
tal: "Permit me to reply to an article regarding the explosion of the

steamboat *Sultana*. No person can induce me to believe that 'old chestnut' about a torpedo being the cause of the explosion of said steamer. The explanation of the real cause is simple. She had tubular boilers, the most dangerous form of boiler ever known by man for use on the Mississippi river." The tubular boilers "were not only dangerous," Lyda wrote, "but defective as well. The crew of the *Sultana* imagined that she was a much faster boat than she really was, and every pound of steam her boilers were thought capable of standing was carried for the purpose of making the fastest time possible." Having worked on the *Sultana*, Lyda was "perfectly familiar with the above facts."[30]

On May 8, after "making inquiries concerning the matter," the *Memphis Avalanche* reported that a number of the civilian passengers on board the *Sultana* had been placed there by the firm of Kernan, Sayers & Blessing. Michael J. Blessing, a lifelong resident of Memphis and the only partner still alive in 1888, "at once denounced [Streetor's claim] as unfounded." "I was aboard the *Sultana* but a short time before the explosion. . . . I knew Lowden [*sic*] well and am positive he was not then in Memphis or anywhere in the surrounding country. The *Sultana* disaster was caused by an explosion of the steamer's boiler."[31] Here was first-person testimony from an eyewitness who actually knew Louden. Blessing was certain that Louden had not been in or near Memphis on April 26, 1865.

The *Memphis Avalanche* pointed out that the *Sultana* had gone upriver from Memphis to take on coal "from Brown & Jones' fleet of coal barges. Members of the firm of Brown & Jones and all of the attaches of the barge fleet were loyal union men, and a confederate blockade runner and spy would never have been harbored on them." In short, if Louden had attempted to board the *Sultana* when she was docked at Memphis unloading the hogsheads of sugar, Blessing would have noticed him; and if Louden had tried to put a coal torpedo onto the *Sultana* from the coal barges, the employees would have spotted him and prevented it.[32]

That same date, Justice John J. Barry of Memphis called Streetor's story "perfectly ridiculous." He explained, "I'm the man that coaled the boat. At the time of the disaster, I was checking clerk on the coal fleet. . . . We put aboard her 800 or 1,000 bushels of coal. It was

Pittsburg nut coal, and not a lump of it was larger than a man's fist. . . .
I checked every box that went aboard of her myself." As to the cause of
the explosion, Judge Barry said, "The *Sultana* was . . . fitted with those
murderous tubular boilers that are now forbidden on passenger boats,
and all her steam-pipes leaked. . . . The story told by the St. Louis
man Streeter [*sic*] is absurd. The fuel taken on here was all Pittsburg
nut coal, and hiding a cartridge in one of the lumps would have been
impossible."[33]

Rebuttals to Streetor's story continued. On May 13, Henry A.
Richards, an assistant engineer on the *Sultana* who had gone on leave
just before the fatal trip, contacted a *Chicago Tribune* reporter. "He
scouts the torpedo idea," the reporter said. "The greatest care, he says,
was exercised in firing, and the coal was broken into small bits for the
reason that a tip had been furnished that there would be an effort to
blow up the vessel. The negroes who shoveled the coal were especially
careful, as they were filled with dread that some such fiendish effort
would be made. [Richards] is not, therefore, inclined to credit the St.
Louis story."[34] Another eyewitness testimonial from a man who had
worked on the boilers of the *Sultana* and knew how her crew operated.

In 1902, another former *Sultana* engineer, Robert D. Long, came
forward to refute Streetor's claim. "She ran like a snake in the water
and made steam so easily that the firemen sat on the coal and sang
but the river water was so riley that her boilers would get scaley and
go to leaking," Long said. "The tubular boilers had been condemned
but she was using them. We had plugs in the aft ends of them to keep
them from leaking and they were in bad shape."[35] Both Richards and
Long had intimate knowledge of the *Sultana*'s boilers and crew. Both
had come forward to refute Streetor's sabotage story, instead blaming
the explosion on the tubular boilers. Their eyewitness testimonials
could not be easily dismissed.

When Chester Berry published his book of reminiscences in 1892,
only three survivors mentioned the coal torpedo theory; two believed
the theory and one did not. The latter, Henry J. Lyda, once again
reiterated that "it was carelessness on the part of the captain and engineer that caused the disaster. The *Sultana*'s boilers were not fit for
duty." In October, the Chicago *Daily Inter Ocean* reported, "There is

no foundation whatever for [the coal torpedo] story, and those who were on the vessel at the time, and survived the wreck, assert that the overcrowding of the steamer was the sufficient and sole cause of the disaster."[36] Within four years, following several firsthand statements refuting the secondhand statement of William C. Streetor, most of the people, including the survivors, had already forgotten about Robert Louden and his coal torpedo. It would be years before another sabotage theory was proposed.

In May 1903, a man from West Virginia declared that *he* knew the real cause of the *Sultana* disaster because he had been told "by the perpetrator of the deed thirty-eight years ago." The perpetrator's name was never mentioned. The West Virginian explained, "An old farmer living some distance below Vicksburg, and who kept a wood yard for many years, was greatly annoyed by Union gunboats and transports taking the wood without compensation." The old farmer took no part in the war but was considered "a 'rebel' by the officers and marines on the gunboats. . . . [He] was frequently arrested and charged with disloyalty, called a rebel, traitor, etc." After one of the farmer's servants died after mistreatment by Union authorities and some Confederate soldiers had been killed on his property, the farmer plotted revenge.

The old farmer cut a large amount of wood, in spite of the fact that the Union gunboats and transports kept taking it without payment,

> select[ed] a large round stick of ash, . . . split it with an axe, hollowed it out and carefully put two pounds of gunpowder in a strong bottle, which he wrapped with copper wire, put a fuse in it, placed it in the hollowed out ash log, put the pieces together and wrapped with copper wire, drawing it tight that the bark might hide the wire as much as possible, then muddied the whole stick well to conceal everything and placed it in the middle of one of the cords of wood. That night the *Sultana* steamed up the river and "wooded" at his landing. That particular stick was not heaved under the boilers till the *Sultana* reached Cat Island [*sic*], twelve miles above Memphis, where such awful havoc was made of human life.

Unfortunately, the West Virginian admitted, "the old planter has been dead for years."[37]

Survivor Joseph Taylor Elliott was quick to debunk the "exploding cordwood theory," writing on May 16: "As a matter of fact the story of the stick of wood with the bottle of powder concealed in it will not hold good. The *Sultana*, on that trip at least, did not burn wood."[38] Elliott was wrong. Sticks of cordwood were tossed in with the coal to help aerate the mixture. A few survivors mentioned the cordwood piled alongside the coalbins, and some saved themselves by clinging to the wood in the water. The "exploding cordwood theory" has at least one major flaw, however, that makes it highly unbelievable.

According to the West Virginian, the old farmer's wood yard was located "some distance below Vicksburg." The *Sultana* did not stop at any wood yard on her way upriver between New Orleans and Vicksburg. In fact, the *Sultana* had sprung a leak when she was about ten hours below Vicksburg, and Wintringer immediately reduced the steam pressure "and worked along moderately" the rest of the way. With the steamboat limping along with a leaking boiler, Wintringer had no intention of stopping for cordwood. Fortunately, the "exploding cordwood theory" never caught on and was quickly forgotten.

As the last of the *Sultana* survivors passed away in the 1930s, articles about the disaster became fewer, and talk about the coal torpedo theory died out. Although the recent sabotage theorists who espouse the coal torpedo theory say that it was never strongly investigated, it should be clear that it was. The three different sabotage claims considered above were all based on secondhand information. All three of the supposed saboteurs were long dead by the time the claims were made public, making it impossible to interrogate them. Why the proclaimers waited so long to make the claims is unknown and leads to even more questions. In any case, the sabotage theorists tend to overlook one glaring fact. The explosion of the boilers did not originate in the firebox under the front of the boilers, it came from the top, back of the boilers, far away from where an "infernal machine" of any sort might have exploded.

The *Sultana* was destroyed by greed and arrogance aided by faulty boilers of shoddy construction filled with the dirty Mississippi water, and perhaps from low water. In any case, the *Sultana* should not be remembered for the way she died. She should be remembered for the many survivors who fought the odds in the chilling waters of the Mississippi on the morning of April 27, 1865, and won. The *Sultana* should be remembered for the 1,169 innocent people who died with her or because of her. Survivor James R. "Jack" Collins understood the magnitude of the tragedy as well as anyone:

> And those poor fellows who died in that awful catastrophe! They had gone through four long years of war, had undergone countless hardships, and suffered hunger, pain, and sickness, on the battlefield, and in the prison, and after all these, they were now going home to loved ones, their hearts filled with a great shout of joyous thanksgiving that all war and strife and danger were over, and that they could once more greet the dear ones at home who they knew were waiting anxiously for their return.
>
> But for many a poor fellow on that boat, this dream was not to come true. Seventeen hundred of them were either burned to death or went down into a watery grave at the bottom of the great river.[39]

"They sleep the sleep of death," Cpl. Winfield Colvin mourned, "and the Father of Waters is their shroud, their coffin, and their grave."[40]

Remember the *Sultana*.

NOTES

CHAPTER 1. THE SULTANAS

1. "Burning of the *Sultana*," *New Albany Daily Ledger*, March 18, 1857, 3.

2. *Louisville Price-Current*, April 25, 1840, 1; "The Gentleman in Black," *Times-Picayune*, March 12, 1837, 2; "A Perfect Steamboat," *Times-Picayune*, April 19, 1838, 2; "A Crack Steamer," *Illinois Weekly State Journal*, May 26, 1838, 2; Lloyd, *Lloyd's Steamboat Directory*, 279; various advertisements, *Times-Picayune*, 1838–43; steamboat advertisement, *Times-Picayune*, February 26, 1843, 4; Paskoff, *Troubled Waters*, 174.

3. "The *Sultana*," *Times-Picayune*, October 15, 1843, 2.

4. The *Sultana*," *Times-Picayune*, March 3, 1844, 2; "Quick Trip," *Times-Picayune*, April 11, 1844, 2; Lloyd, *Lloyd's Steamboat Directory*, 280; "The Steamboat *Sultana* . . . " *Tri-weekly Maysville Eagle*, April 2, 1845, 3.

5. "The *Sultana*," *Weekly Advocate*, December 1, 1847, 2; "The New Steamer *Sultana*," *Concordia Intelligencer*, March 11, 1848, 2.

6. "Immense Cargo," *Wabash Courier*, March 31, 1849, 2.

7. "Burning of the *Sultana*," *Madison Daily Banner*, June 16, 1851, 2.

8. "The New *Sultana*," *Times-Picayune*, February 26, 1852, 2; "River Items," *Times-Picayune*, February 4, 1853, 2; "Marshal's Sale," *Times-Picayune*, June 2, 1853, 3; *Times-Picayune*, July 6, 1853, 2; *Times-Picayune*, November 11, 1853, 1; "Boats Lying Up," *New Albany Daily Ledger*, September 9, 1854, 2; various steamboat advertisements, *Times-Picayune*, 1855 and 1856; "*Sultana*," *New Orleans*

Price-Current and Commercial Intelligencer, December 17, 1856; "*Sultana* Burned," *New Albany Daily Ledger*, March 27, 1857, 3.

9. "Miscellaneous," *Cincinnati Daily Commercial*, January 5, 1863, 2; "Miscellaneous," *Cincinnati Commercial Tribune*, February 4, 1863, 4; "River News," *Memphis Daily Bulletin*, May 4, 1865, 3.

10. "Miscellaneous," *Cincinnati Daily Commercial*, January 5, 1863, 2; "Miscellaneous," *Cincinnati Commercial Tribune*, February 4, 1863, 4; "River News," *Memphis Daily Bulletin*, May 4, 1865, 3.

11. *History of Cincinnati and Hamilton County, Ohio*, 774–75.

12. Bates, *The Western Rivers Steamboat Cyclopoedium*, 30, 35–36, 46, 48, 50–54, 62, 67, 70–73, 80–81; Watson, *Paddle Steamers*, 28–30, 34–37, 53–55; Hunter, *Steamboats on the Western Rivers*, 93.

13. "Miscellaneous," *Cincinnati Commercial Tribune*, February 4, 1863, 4; "River News," *Daily Missouri Democrat*, July 22, 1863, 4. Although the Cincinnati newspaper stated that *Sultana* (No. 5) drew only "thirty-four inches of water" when fully loaded, on July 22, 1863, the *Daily Missouri Democrat* mentioned that *Sultana* (No. 5) was "drawing about 5 feet."

14. "Tubular Boilers," *Daily Missouri Democrat*, February 10, 1866, 2.

15. "Miscellaneous," *Cincinnati Commercial Tribune*, February 4, 1863, 4; "Inspector's Certificate," Exhibit G, Civil War, *Sultana* Disaster, April 1865, *The Proceedings and Report of the Court-Martial of Capt. Frederick Speed*, 3, www.fold3.com (hereafter cited as *Court-Martial*).

16. "Inspector's Certificate," Exhibit G, *Court-Martial*, 3; Jennings, "What Happened to the *Sultana*?" Presentation before the National Board of Boiler and Pressure Vessel Inspectors, April 27, 2015.

17. "Miscellaneous," *Cincinnati Commercial Tribune*, February 4, 1863, 4.

18. "Miscellaneous"; *Williams' Cincinnati Directory*, 158, 177, 201, 223, 228, 262, 196; letter, Dickey to Belle, September 8, 1863.

19. "Inspector's Certificate," Exhibit G, *Court-Martial*; Bates, *The Western Rivers Steamboat Cyclopoedium*, 90.

20. "Inspector's Certificate."

21. Hunter, *Steamboats on the Western Rivers*, 237–38.

22. Hunter, 239–40.

23. Hunter, 241; Watson, *Paddle Steamers*, 80.

24. Hunter, 260–62.

25. Hunter, 262–63.

26. Watson, *Paddle Steamers*, 87.

27. Watson, 88; Hunter, *Steamboats on the Western Rivers*, 383.

28. Hunter, 446–47, 451.

29. "Miscellaneous," *Cincinnati Commercial Tribune*, February 4, 1863, 4.

CHAPTER 2. THE FIRST TWO YEARS

1. "Arrivals and Departures," *Cincinnati Commercial Tribune*, February 11, 1863, 4; "River Correspondence," *Daily Missouri Republican*, February 19, 1863, 4; Rutter, "Bewitching News," 12.

2. Hunter, *Steamboats on Western Rivers*, 314, 523–24.

3. Hunter, 526–27, 529, 532–35; Havinghurst, *Voices on the River*, 146.

4. Redfield, *Letter to the Secretary of the Treasury on the History and Causes of Steamboat Explosions and the Means of Prevention*; Rusk quoted in Rives, *Congressional Globe*, vol. 24, pt. 3, 2426.

5. Lloyd, *Lloyd's Steamboat Directory*, 215, 223, 240–45, 268, 287–89, 290–91, 296, 327–28; Hunter, *Steamboats on the Western Rivers*, 537, 542–43; Havinghurst, *Voices on the River*, 147.

6. Lloyd; Hunter, 537, 542–43.

7. Hunter, 548–61; Perce and Speed, Washburn Inquiry, 145–46, 253; Witzig, *Court-Martial*, 135–36.

8. Parsons, *Reports to the War Department*, 6, 7, 45.

9. Parsons, 7, 8.

10. Griffith, *Rates of Passage of Northern Line Packet Company*.

11. Parsons, *Reports to the War Department*, 9, 58; Hunter, *Steamboats on the Western Rivers*, 375, 381, 420.

12. Steamboat advertisements, *Daily Missouri Republican*, various dates, February, March, and April 1863; steamboat advertisements, *Cincinnati Commercial Tribune*, various dates, February, March, and April 1863; "Arrivals and Departures," *Wheeling Daily Intelligencer*, various dates, March and April 1863; Rutter, "Bewitching News," 12; "From the 2nd Ohio Cavalry," *Cleveland Leader*, April 11, 1863, 2.

13. "River News," *Daily Missouri Republican*, May 9, 1863, 4.

14. "River News," *Daily Missouri Republican*, May 16, 1863, 4; "River News," *Daily Missouri Democrat*, May 12, 1863, 4.

15. Asboth to Hurlbut, May 11, 1863, U.S. War Department, *The War of the Rebellion*, 1st ser., vol. 23, pt. 2, 323–24 [hereafter cited as ORs]; Report of Acting Lt. Smith, May 18, 1863, U.S. Navy Department, *War of the Rebellion*, ser. 1, vol. 25, 4 [hereafter cited as Navy ORs].

16. *Hancock Jeffersonian*, May 29, 1863, 1; *Springfield Republican*, May 29, 1863, 4; *Boston Traveler*, May 29, 1863, 2; "The Steamer *Sultana* Reported Lost," *Daily National Republican*, May 29, 1863, 2; *Daily Missouri Democrat*, May 30, 1863, 2; *Chicago Tribune*, June 6, 1863, 2.

17. *Chicago Tribune*, June 10, 1863, 2; "From Memphis," *Louisville Daily Democrat*, June 19, 1863, 1; *Cincinnati Commercial Tribune*, July 6, 1863, 4; *Daily Missouri Republican*, July 18, 1863, 4.

18. "River News," *Daily Missouri Democrat*, July 22, 1863, 4; Stillwell, *The Story of a Common Soldier of Army Life in the Civil War*, 149–50; "The War in the Southwest," *Philadelphia Press*, August 10, 1863, 1; "From the Southwest," *Joliet Signal*, August 4, 1863, 2; *Daily Missouri Democrat*, August 3, 1863, 1, and August 5, 1863, 4; "Arrivals and Departures," *Daily Missouri Republican*, August 5, 1863, 4.

19. "Ho, for Vicksburg," *Daily Missouri Democrat*, August 5, 1863, 4; *Daily Missouri Democrat*, August 10, 1863, 4; *Times-Picayune*, August 19, 1863, 4.

20. "From Cairo and Below," *Chicago Tribune*, October 3, 1863, 1; "Special Dispatch to the Missouri Democrat," *Louisville Daily Democrat*, October 4, 1863, 3, and October 6, 1863, 3; "Gleanings from Our Exchanges," *Cincinnati Commercial Tribune*, August 13, 1863, 4.

21. *Cincinnati Commercial Tribune*, November 16, 1863, 4; *Daily Missouri Republican*, November 18, 1863, 4; Hopkins, *Under the Flag*, 84–85, 87.

22. "Cairo Letter," *Daily Missouri Democrat*, January 12, 1864, 4; U.S. Navy Department, *War of the Rebellion*, ser. 1, vol. 25, 206; steamboat advertisement, *Cincinnati Commercial Tribune*, January 23, 1864, 4; *Times-Picayune*, February 4, 1864, 2; Vessels bought, sold, and chartered by the United States, 218.

23. "River Matters," *Louisville Daily Democrat*, March 1, 1863, 3, and March 31, 1864, 4; *Cincinnati Commercial Tribune*, March 3, 1864, 4; Form C Enrollment, National Archives, Washington, DC.

24. "Missouri History Recalled during the Past Week," *Sikeston Herald*, January 9, 1936, 4; "River and Steamboat News," *Cincinnati Daily Enquirer*, May 2, 1865, 4; Way, *Way's Packet Directory*, 403; *Daily Missouri Democrat*, October 11, 1861, 3.

25. *Daily Missouri Democrat*, June 16, 1862, 4, and February 20, 1863, 4; "The Contraband Trade," *Cincinnati Commercial Tribune*, February

14, 1863, 3; "Seizure of Steamers," *The World*, New York, February 24, 1863, 2.

26. *Cincinnati Commercial Tribune*, March 4, 1863, 4; *Daily Missouri Democrat*, March 12, 1863, 1; "United States of America, Southern District of Illinois," *Daily Illinois State Register*, March 20, 1863, 3.

27. "Steamboats and Machinery at Public Auction," *Cincinnati Commercial Tribune*, July 21, 1863, 4.

28. "For Memphis," *Daily Missouri Democrat*, March 30, 1863, 4; "River News," *Daily Missouri Democrat*, February 6, 1864, 4; "Lost—$200 Reward," *Memphis Daily Bulletin*, April 28, 1865, 3.

29. "Sherman's Expedition," *Wisconsin Daily Patriot*, Madison, March 11, 1864, 1; *Daily Missouri Democrat*, March 10, 1864, 4; Form C Enrollment; "Departure of Two Regiments of African Descent to the Field," *Daily Missouri Democrat*, March 14, 1864, 4; *Cincinnati Commercial Tribune*, March 15, 1864, 4, and April 4, 1864, 4; Vessels bought, sold, and chartered by the United States, 218; *Joliet Signal*, April 5, 1864, 2; "The Campaign in Louisiana," *Milwaukee Sentinel*, April 15, 1864, 3.

30. Parsons, *Reports to the War Department*, 63.

31. Parsons, 63.

32. *Cincinnati Commercial Tribune*, April 7, 1864, 4; *Daily Missouri Democrat*, April 7, 1864, 4, and April 8, 1864, 4; *Louisville Daily Democrat*, April 9, 1864, 4, and May 14, 1864, 2; *Daily Missouri Democrat*, April 14, 1864, 4, April 29, 1864, 4, and April 30, 1864, 4; *Cincinnati Daily Enquirer*, April 27, 1864, 4; "River News," *Evansville Daily Journal*, May 13, 1864, 3; Vessels bought, sold, and chartered by the United States, 218.

33. *Daily Missouri Democrat*, May 16, 1864, 4; "From Cairo," *Cincinnati Commercial Tribune*, May 27, 1864, 3; *Commercial Appeal*, Memphis, May 29, 1936; "River Intelligence," *Daily True Delta*, June 19, 1864, 3.

34. "River News," *Daily Missouri Democrat*, July 4, 1863, 4, and July 16, 1864, 4; "River News," *Evansville Daily Journal*, July 8, 1864, 3; "River Intelligence," *Daily True Delta*, July 12, 1864, 3; *Cleveland Plain Dealer*, July 14, 1864, 3.

35. "River News," *Daily Missouri Democrat*, July 23, 1864, 4.

36. "Editors *Missouri Democrat*," *Cincinnati Commercial Tribune*, August 1, 1864, 4; *Daily Missouri Democrat*, July 30, 1864, 4, August 1, 1864, 4; "Our Cairo Correspondence," *Daily True Delta*, August 9,

1864, 1. The *Henry Ames* was eventually raised and returned to the Mississippi River trade.

37. *Cincinnati Daily Enquirer,* August 20, 1864, 4; *Daily Missouri Democrat,* August 18, 1864, 4, August 24, 1864, 4, September 3, 1864, 4, and September 8, 1864, 4; *Daily True Delta,* September 15, 1864, 3 and 4.

38. *Daily Missouri Democrat,* September 23, 1864, 4, September 29, 1864, 4, and October 6, 1864, 4.

39. *Louisville Daily Democrat,* October 20, 1864, 3; *Cincinnati Commercial Tribune,* October 31, 1864, 4; *Daily Missouri Democrat* October 31, 1864, 4; *Cincinnati Daily Enquirer,* November 4, 1864, 4; "Receipts," *Daily True Delta,* November 11, 1864, 3; "Another Line of Steamers between St. Louis and New Orleans," *Daily True Delta,* November 30, 1864, 2.

40. "Another Line of Steamers between St. Louis and New Orleans," *Daily True Delta,* November 30, 1864, 2, and November 28, 1864, 4; *Cincinnati Commercial Tribune,* November 30, 1864, 4.

41. *Daily Missouri Democrat,* December 31, 1864, 4.

CHAPTER 3. HARD FINANCIAL TIMES

1. Steamboat advertisement, *Daily Missouri Democrat,* January 5, 1865, 4; *New-Orleans Times,* January 14, 1865, 8, and February 12, 1865, 8; "River and Steamboat News," *Cincinnati Daily Enquirer,* February 8, 1865, 4.

2. *Cincinnati Daily Enquirer,* February 8, 1865, 4. All advertisements and newspaper stories concerning the *Sultana* spell the first clerk's name William Jordan Gambrel, although the headstones for his wife and children spell the last name Gambrell. I use "Gambrel," the spelling preferred by the first clerk.

3. Nanson, Washburn Inquiry, 245; memorial and family information for Ida Rodes Brown Gambrell, www.findagrave.com website; biography of Mrs. Ida R. Gambrell, Arrow Rock Township Biographies, Saline County, Missouri MOGenWeb Project, https://cousin-collector.com/projects/index.php/saline-county/biographies/1679-arrow-rock-township-biographies.

4. "From Cairo," *New-Orleans Times,* February 14, 1865, 7; "Miscellaneous," *Daily Missouri Democrat,* February 8, 1865, 4.

5. "River Intelligence," *New-Orleans Times*, February 13, 1865, 8; *Daily Missouri Republican*, February 14, 1865, 4; *Cairo News*, February 20, 1865, 3; *Daily Missouri Republican*, February 21, 1865, 1; *Daily Missouri Democrat*, February 23, 1865, 4; "River News," *Times-Picayune*, March 5, 1865, 3.

6. "River Intelligence," *New-Orleans Times*, March 4, 1865, 8, March 5, 1865, 8, and March 7, 1865, 8; *Daily Missouri Republican*, March 17, 1865, 1.

7. "The *Olive Branch* and the *Sultana*," *New-Orleans Times*, March 10, 1865, 8.

8. *Daily Missouri Republican*, March 17, 1865, 1; "The *Olive Branch* and the *Sultana*," *New-Orleans Times*, March 10, 1865, 8; *New-Orleans Times*, March 5, 1865, 8, and March 7, 1865, 8; *Daily Missouri Democrat*, March 18, 1865, 4; Lyda in Berry, *Loss of the* Sultana, 28; Hunter, *Steamboats on the Western Waters*, 263.

9. "Tubular Boilers," *Daily Missouri Democrat*, February 10, 1866, 2; Hunter, *Steamboats on the Western Waters*, 263.

10. *Memphis Argus* reports published in *Tri-Weekly Missouri Republican*, March 22, 1865, 1; *Cincinnati Commercial Tribune*, March 27, 1865, 4.

11. "Veterans Commemorate Greatest River Disaster," *Cleveland Plain Dealer*, January 27, 1918, 4; "The *Sultana* Disaster by a Survivor of One of the Civil War's Greatest Tragedies," *Kansas City Star*, May 14, 1909, 1; White in Hawes, *Cahaba*, 177-80.

12. Nanson, Washburn Inquiry, 245; memorial and family information for Ida Rodes Brown Gambrell, www.findagrave.com website; biography of Mrs. Ida R. Gambrell; "The *Sultana* Disaster," *Daily Missouri Democrat*, April 29, 1865, 4.

13. "The *Sultana* Disaster"; "River News," *Memphis Daily Bulletin*, May 6, 1865, 3. The *Daily Missouri Democrat* incorrectly listed William D. Shanks as "Wm. Shands."

14. "River News," *Daily Missouri Democrat*, March 23, 1865, 4, and March 25, 1865, 4; *Cincinnati Commercial Tribune*, March 27, 1865, 4.

15. Steamboat advertisement, *Tri-Weekly Missouri Republican*, March 20, 1865, 1; *Daily Missouri Democrat*, March 29, 1865, 4; *Cincinnati Commercial Tribune*, March 27, 1865, 4; "River Intelligence," *New-Orleans Times*, April 2, 1865, 8, and April 4, 1865, 8; "Cairo

News," *Daily Missouri Republican*, April 10, 1865, 3; "Miscellaneous," *Cincinnati Commercial Tribune*, February 4, 1863, 4.

16. The elk's antlers are visible on the lower set of chimney bracings in the photograph taken at Helena, Arkansas, on April 24, 1865, when the boat was crowded with the paroled Union prisoners of war.

17. *Tri-Weekly Missouri Republican*, April 5, 1865, 1, 3.

18. "From Vicksburg," *Daily Missouri Republican*, April 1, 1865, 2; "Paroled Prisoners," *Daily Missouri Democrat*, April 4, 1865, 10, 13, 19, 20, 21.

19. Speed, Tillinghast, and Williams, Washburn Inquiry, 210–11, 220, 231.

20. "Inspector's Certificate," Exhibit G, *Court-Martial*.

21. Lyda in Berry, *Loss of the* Sultana, 28; Henry J. Lyda, All Titles, Navy Survivors' Certificates, L, Ly, Lyda, Henry J (#1894), 3, www.fold3.com; "The *Sultana* Explosion Again," *Hutchinson Daily News*, May 10, 1888, 8.

22. "The *Sultana* Disaster," *Daily Missouri Democrat*, April 29, 1865, 4; Cayton and Rowberry statements in *Memphis Daily Bulletin*, April 28, 1865, 1; Wintringer, *Court-Martial*, 168; Cayton, *Court-Martial*, 317.

23. *War Eagle*, April 14, 1865, 1, 2; "Cairo Port List," *Cincinnati Commercial Tribune*, April 17, 1865, 4.

CHAPTER 4. MESSENGER OF DEATH

1. Swanson, *Manhunt*, 44–45, 57–60, 78–79, 102–3, 138.

2. *Tri-Weekly Missouri Republican*, April 17, 1865, 1; "Explanatory," *War Eagle*, April 15, 1865, 2.

3. *Cincinnati Commercial Tribune*, April 21, 1865, 4; *Times-Picayune*, April 19, 1865, 4.

4. *Daily Missouri Republican*, April 18, 1986, 3.

5. "From Memphis," *Missouri Republican*, April 18, 1865, 3, and April 21, 1865, 2; *Cincinnati Commercial Tribune*, April 21, 1865, 4.

6. "Special Correspondence: Burning of the *Sultana*," *Cincinnati Commercial Tribune*, April 21, 1882, 7.

7. The records often refer to Reuben Hatch as Colonel Hatch or Lieutenant Colonel Hatch; however, as late as April 21, 1865, his commanding officer, Maj. Gen. N. J. T. Dana, was requesting that Hatch be promoted "with the rank of Lieut. Colonel" (Dana to

Christensen, April 21, 1865, www.fold3.com, Civil War, Letters Received by Commission Branch, 1865, D-140 Dana). During testimony before the Washburn Inquiry, Hatch himself stated, "My name is R. B. Hatch, my rank is Captain" (Hatch, Washburn Inquiry, 223). Sells, *Court-Martial*, 121.

8. Sells, 121.
9. Berry, *Loss of the* Sultana, 47; Karns, "Karns' Reminiscences of the Late War," *Lewisburg Leader*, March 30, 1898, 8.
10. Kerns, *Court-Martial*, 62; Parsons, *Reports to the War Department*, 63–64.
11. Sells, *Court-Martial*, 121.
12. "Fire in Griggsville," *Daily Illinois State Journal*, November 21, 1863, 3.
13. Sells, *Court-Martial*, 121, 122.
14. Sells, 121; Smith, Washburn Inquiry, 250.
15. Hobart, "Assassination of Lincoln," *National Tribune*, June 7, 1900, 7; Hobart, *Semi-History of a Boy-Veteran of the Twenty-Eighth Regiment Illinois Infantry Volunteers in a Black Regiment*, 34.
16. Baton Rouge headlines quoted in *Times-Picayune*, April 19, 1865, 4; Baton Rouge newspaper quotations in *Daily Missouri Democrat*, April 27, 1865, 1.
17. "Office of the Picayune," *Times-Picayune*, April 20, 1865, 10; "Midnight Walk on Deck of the Steamer *Sultana*, Opposite Vicksburg, in April, 1865," *New-Orleans Times*, April 20, 1865, 1.
18. Steamboat advertisement, *New-Orleans Times*, April 20, 1865, 8; "The River News," and "Boats Leaving," *Times-Picayune*, April 21, 1865, 1; "Memoranda of *Olive Branch*," *Cleveland Leader*, May 1, 1865, 1.
19. "A Sad Case," *Memphis Daily Bulletin*, April 28, 1865, 2.
20. "The Washington Woman," *Evening Star*, September 26, 1868, 1; "A Struggle for Life," *Cincinnati Commercial Tribune*, May 11, 1865, 2.
21. "Supposed Recognition," *Memphis Argus*, April 28, 1865, 3; 1850 Census Records, Mississippi, Yazoo County, www.ancestry.com; Mississippi, Compiled Census and Census Substitute Index, 1805–1890 MS 1950 Slave Schedule, www.ancestry.com; *Daily Missouri Republican*, May 1, 1865, 1; "Portraits Donated to Society," 17–18.
22. "Acts of Daring—Noble Deeds of Noble Men," *Memphis Argus*, April 28, 1865, 3; Nanson, Washburn Inquiry, 244–45; St. Louis, MO, City Directory, 1865, U.S. City Directories, 1822–1995, www.

ancestry.com; "Nanson, Joseph S.," Hyde and Conrad, ed., *Encyclopedia of the History of St. Louis*, vol. 3, 1613–14.

23. U.S. Congress, *Mrs. Anna Butterfield*, H. Rep. 1607; Reese, *Report of the Adjutant General of the State of Illinois*, vol. 7, 488; Fletcher, *The History of Company A, Second Illinois Cavalry*, 170–71.

24. McLeod in Berry, *Loss of the* Sultana, 254–55; 1900 U.S. Federal Census, Missouri, City of St. Louis, 285.

25. U.S. Congress, Elizabeth Hackleman, H. Rep. 207; 1850 U.S. Federal Census, Indiana, Rush County, District 97, www.ancestry.com; 1860 U.S. Federal Census, Indiana, Rush County, Anderson, www.ancestry.com.

26. Enoch Bent biography, www.ancestry.com; Wisconsin, Wills and Probate Records, Bent, Enoch, www.ancestry.com; 1860 U.S. Federal Census, Wisconsin, Kenosha County, Town of Randall, 88, www.fold3.com; letter from William A. McKesson to Clerk of Circuit Court, April 12, 1866, Kenosha County Historical Society and Museum.

27. Compton, *Court-Martial*, 147; Compton obituary, *Los Angeles Herald*, July 21, 1909; Special Order No. 42, ORs, 1st ser., vol. 48, ch. 60, pt. 1, sec. 1, 811.

28. "Incidents of the Disaster," *Memphis Argus*, April 29, 1865, 3; "Statement of Mr. William Long, a Passenger," *Memphis Argus*, April 28, 1865, 3; Cloghen to Learner, May 1, 1924.

29. "Personal Experience of Jacob Homer as a Prisoner of War," in Schmutz, *History of the 102d Regiment, OVI*, 239; Mahoney, Civil War, *Sultana* Disaster, April 1865, Quartermaster vessel file relating to the *Sultana*, 165, www.fold3.com (hereafter cited as Hoffman Investigation); "The *Sultana* Disaster," *Daily Missouri Democrat*, June 19, 1865, 4; J. T. Elliott, *Court-Martial*, 143; Cayton statement in *Memphis Daily Bulletin*, April 28, 1865, 1.

30. "The Waters," *Vicksburg Daily Herald* quoted in *Times-Picayune*, April 28, 1865, 1.

31. "River News," *Daily Missouri Democrat*, April 24, 1865, 4.

32. Wintringer, Hoffman Investigation, 170; "The Steamer *Sultana*," *Larned Chronoscope*, August 20, 1886, 3; "*Sultana*: by a Survivor," *Lyons Tribune*, August 23, 1888, 1; Lock, "Women on the *Sultana*," *National Tribune*, May 31, 1923, 6.

33. Wintringer, Hoffman Investigation, 170; Compton and Cayton, *Court-Martial*, 148, 321.

34. Wintringer, 170; "The *Sultana* Disaster," *Daily Missouri Democrat*, June 19, 1865, 4; Sharp, "The *Sultana* Disaster," *National Tribune*, November 21, 1912, 7.

35. "The *Sultana* Disaster," *Daily Missouri Democrat*, June 19, 1865, 4; Taylor, Washburn Inquiry, 215; Sells, *Court-Martial*, 120.

CHAPTER 5. THE VICKSBURG OFFICERS

1. New Hampshire, Birth Index, 1659–1900, www.ancestry.com; advertisement for R. B. Hatch, Meredosia store, *Illinois Weekly State Journal*, February 1846–October 1849; Illinois, Compiled Marriages, 1790–1860, www.ancestry.com; wedding announcement, *Daily Illinois State Journal*, February 25, 1847, 6; Massie, *Past and Present of Pike County, Illinois*, 165.

2. Massie, 247; "Congressional Convention—7th District," *Daily Illinois State Journal*, August 8, 1850, 2; *Hatch v. Preston & Wightman*, Case File ID: L01138, www.lawpracticeofabrahamlincoln. org; *Wightman & Preston v. Hatch*, Case File ID: L011380, www. lawpracticeofabrahamlincoln.org; George Merrick Hatch obituary, *Herald Lethbridge*, January 30, 1929, 1, 6; Pease, *The Diary of Orville Hickman Browning*, vol. 1, 125, 169; letter of O. M. Hatch to Lamon, March 18, 1861, in Lamon, *Recollections of Abraham Lincoln*, 316; Military Record of Col. Reuben B. Hatch, Records of the Adjutant General's Office, Record Group 94 (hereafter cited as Hatch Military Records); Lincoln to Cameron, in Basler, *The Collected Works of Abraham Lincoln*, vol. 4, 461; *Cleveland Leader*, August 2, 1861, 2; "Correspondence, from Cairo," *Daily Illinois State Journal*, June 5, 1861, 2.

3. Ellen Hatch, Dr. J. H. Ledlie, Dr. E. M. Seeley, and James S. Grigsby testimonies, all in Ellen Hatch Pension Application Papers, Hatch Military Records.

4. Taylor and Edwards testimonies in U.S. Congress, *Reports of Committees of the House of Representatives*, 37th Cong., 2nd sess., 28, 49; "Vindication of Capt. Hatch," *Illinois State Journal*, January 16, 1862, 1; "Buying Lumber for Cairo—the False Invoice System," *Chicago Tribune*, December 12, 1861, 4; Hillyer to Grant and Grant to Kelton, December 15, 1861, in Simon, *The Papers of Ulysses S. Grant*, vol. 3, 323–27, 420; "More Frauds—Arrests," *Cincinnati Daily Press*, January 17, 1862, 3; "Cairo Contracts," *Chicago Tribune*,

January 16, 1862, 2; Wilcox testimony in U.S. Congress, House of Representatives, *Purchase of Army Supplies, Report of Committees of the House of Representatives*, 37th Cong., 2nd sess., 1133; Pease, *The Diary of Orville Hickman Browning*, vol. 1, 526, 527; Dunton to Browning, January 20, 1862, Grant to Meigs, January 22, 1862, Browning to Stanton, January 27, 1862, Meigs to Stanton, January 31, 1862, Halleck to Thomas, January 31, 1862, Grimshaw to Lincoln, January 31, 1862, and Hatch to Oglesby, all in Simon, *The Papers of Ulysses S. Grant*, vol. 4, 52, 58–59, 82–83.

5. *Personal Histories of Volunteer Officers in the Quartermaster's Department, 1861–1865*, vol. 3, 144, 146; U.S. Congress, *War Claims at St. Louis*, 37th Cong., 2nd sess., H. Rep. 94, p. 24; Lincoln's endorsement of letter to Lee, March 20, 1862, Meigs endorsement of Lincoln's letter to Lee, March 21, 1862, Richardson to Lincoln, August 29, 1862, Grimshaw to Lincoln, August 29, 1862, Browning to Lincoln, undated, Lincoln to Stanton, September 27, 1862, Department of Tennessee Special Orders No. 39, all in Simon, *The Papers of Ulysses S. Grant*, vol. 4, 83–84, 297–98; Lincoln to Stanton, April 2, 1862, in Basler, *The Collected Works of Abraham Lincoln*, vol. 5, 177; "Report of Davis, Holt and Campbell," *Chicago Tribune*, April 8, 1862, 1, 2; U.S. House of Representatives, "Testimony, Part II," *Purchase of Army Supplies, Report of Committees of the House of Representatives*, 37th Cong., 2nd sess., House of Representatives, 10, 13–15, 17–19, 23–29, 48–50; "Captain R. B. Hatch," *Daily Illinois State Journal*, April 23, 1862, 3; Dana, *Recollections of the Civil War*, 11–14; Lincoln, Logan, and Hatch to Miller, July 11, 1859, in Nicolay and Hay, *Abraham Lincoln Complete Works*, vol. 1, 536; Cert. 176,861, Ellen D. W. Hatch, widow of Reuben B. Hatch, Hatch Military Records; Tuttle to Thomas, October 16, 1862 (T604), and Meigs to Thomas, November 8, 1862 (Q104), Letters Received by the Adjutant General's Office, 1862, www.fold3.com.

6. O. M. Hatch to Lincoln, March 4, 1863, Prentiss to Lincoln, March 4, 1863, Cullom to Lincoln, March 4, 1863, and Grimshaw to Lincoln, March 15, 1863, Hatch Military Records; "Fire in Griggsville," *Daily Illinois State Journal*, November 21, 1863, 3.

7. Thomas to Meigs, December 11, 1863, Hatch Military Records; Lincoln to Stanton, January 14, 1864, in Simon, *The Papers of Ulysses S. Grant*, vol. 7, 115, 298; Dana to Nicolay, February 6, 1864, and Meigs to Nicolay, February 6, 1864, in Hatch Military Records;

Daily Illinois State Journal, March 23, 1864, 3; "Promoted," *Daily Illinois State Journal*, April 21, 1864, 3; Kiper, *Major General John Alexander McClernand*, 7–8; *Army and Navy Official Gazette, 1863–64*, vol. 1, 671.

8. General Orders No. 16, ORs, ser. 1, vol. 34, pt. 3, 141; "Ellen De Witt Hatch," 52nd Cong., 1st sess., H. Rep. 2009; Jackson Grinshaw testimony in Ellen Hatch Pension Application Papers, Hatch Military Records.

9. Grant to Meigs, July 31, 1864, and Lincoln to Meigs, August 1, 1864, in Simon, *Papers of Ulysses S. Grant*, vol. 11, 357; Ellen Maria Hatch, www.ancestry.com; Hatch to O. M. Hatch, January 4, 1865, Hatch Military Records.

10. Although Hatch was promoted to lieutenant colonel of volunteers in March 1864, after his return to the service in January 1865 he was recognized as a captain in the Quartermaster's Department.

11. *Personal Histories of Volunteer Officers in the Quartermaster Department, 1861–1865*, vol. 3, 148.

12. Stone, *Army and Navy Official Gazette, 1864–65*, vol. 2, 606.

13. *Thirty-Eighth Annual Reunion of the Association of the Graduates of the United States Military Academy at West Point, New York, June 13, 1907*, 31–34; U.S. Wall of Honor, Civil War, "Napoleon Jackson Tecumseh Dana," Stories, www.fold3.com.

14. General Orders No. 30, ORs, ser. 1, vol. 48, ch. 60, pt. 1, sec. 2, 1121; Speed to Anna, March 29, 1865, Frederic and William Speed papers, William L. Clements Library, University of Michigan; "Arrival of Gen. Dana," *Natchez Daily Courier*, March 16, 1865, 5.

15. H. W. Smith to B. F. Wade, March 22, 1862, Civil War, Letters Received by the Adjutant General 1861–70, 1862; Smith, Morgan L., www.ancestry.com.

16. Civil War, Letters Received by the Adjutant General 1861–70, 1862, and 1864, Smith, Morgan L., www.ancestry.com; "Smith, Morgan Lewis," in Grant, *Appleton's Cyclopaedia of American Biography, 1600–1899*, vol. 5, 580–81; ORs, ser. 1, vol. 41, ch. 52, pt. 3, 5, 34; Special Orders, No. 177, ORs, ser. 1, vol. 39, ch. 51, pt. 3, 726.

17. Cullum, *Biographical Register of the Officers and Graduates of the U.S. Military Academy at West Point, N.Y.*, 3d ed., 503–4; Appointment, Commission, and Personal file for Capt. George Augustus Williams (2553 ACP 1889), "Exhibit A," Civil War, *Sultana* Disaster, April 27, 1865, www.ancestry.com.

18. Lash, *A Politician Turned General,* 137; Simon, *Papers of Ulysses S. Grant,* vol. 11, 88n; ORs, ser. 2, vol. 7, sec. 1, 404, 407; General Orders No. 45, ORs, ser. 1, vol. 41, ch. 55, pt. 4, 219.

19. Lufkin, *History of the Thirteenth Maine Regiment,* 3, 9, 20, 65; Civil War, Civil War Service Records, Union Records, Maine (Index Cards), Speed, Frederic, www.ancestry.com; Byrne, *Prophet of Prohibition,* 93; Speed to his father, August 3, 1861, Speed to his family, November 3, 1862, Speed papers; Report of Col. N. A. M. Dudley, ORs, ser. 1, vol. 15, ch. 27, 411, 523, 627–28; Report of Col. N. A. M. Dudley on action at Plains Store, LA, ORs, ser. 1, vol. 26, ch. 38, pt. 1, 122; Report of Col. N. A. M. Dudley on engagement at La Foche, LA, ORs, ser. 1, vol. 26, ch. 38, pt. 1, 209; General Orders No. 5, ORs, ser. 1, vol. 34, ch. 46, pt. 2, 101; Speed to Reynolds, August 12, 1864, and Special Orders No. 100, ORs, ser. 1, vol. 41, ch. 53, pt. 2, 663, 743; Special Orders No. 59, and Dana to Christensen and General Order No. 30, ORs, ser. 1, vol. 48, ch. 60, pt. 1, sec. 2, 1121.

20. "Minnesota, Territorial and State Censuses, 1857," www.ancestry.com; "Census, U.S. Federal 1860, Mankato Township, Minnesota," www.fold3.com, 6; Returns from Military Posts, 1808–1916 through June 1863, Post at Saint Peter, MN, www.ancestry.com; Moore to Stanton, November 19, 1863; Tibbetts to Stanton, November 4, 1865; and Moore to Stanton, November 19, 1865; "Army Registers, 1798–1969: 1865," www.fold3.com, All Titles, 66; *Annual Report of the Adjutant General of the State of Minnesota,* 425; U.S. War Department, *Army and Navy Official Gazette,* vol. 2, 14; Kerns, *Court-Martial,* 77; Speed, Washburn Inquiry, 239.

CHAPTER 6. CAPTURED

1. McFarland in Berry, *Loss of the* Sultana, 247; "Louis Shirmeyer One of Seventeen Survivors of Burning of Steamship *Sultana,* Most Disastrous of Marine Horrors," *Fort Wayne Journal-Gazette,* April 28, 1912, 8.

2. Middleton, ed., *History of Champaign County, Ohio,* vol. 2, 870; "Up and Down the State," *Indianapolis News,* April 11, 1930.

3. Dunnavant, *The Railroad War,* 48–49.

4. Dunnavant, 49–56.

5. Dyer to his wife and children, March 27, 1865; Eldridge, unpublished reminiscence from 1926, 8.

6. Dunnavant, *The Railroad War*, 61–65.

7. Homer, "Every Fellow for Himself," *Civil War Times*, March 2002, 23, 68.

8. Aldrich, *Cahawba Prison*, 1; Lockhart, unpublished manuscript, 6.

9. Dunnavant, *The Railroad War*, 71–82.

10. Ohio Roster Commission, *Official Roster of the Soldiers of the State of Ohio in the War of the Rebellion, 1861–1866*, vol. 9, 505.

11. "A *Sultana* Survivor," *Indianapolis News*, September 6, 1893, 13; "War's Experiences," *Indianapolis News*, February 18, 1888, 4.

12. Nevin, *Sherman's March*, 96–105, 112–18.

13. Horner, "No Scriptural Authority," *National Tribune*, June 3, 1909, 7.

14. Winters, *In the 50th Ohio*, 121.

15. Ely, unpublished diary, various dates December 1864.

16. Robert D. Farmer, email message to author, April 8, 1997; Chelf in Berry, *Loss of the* Sultana, 84.

17. Eldridge, unpublished reminiscence from 1926, 8–9.

18. Aldrich, *Cahawba Prison*, 2.

19. Jordan, "On the *Sultana*," *National Tribune*, July 31, 1913, 7.

CHAPTER 7. PRISONERS

1. "The Northern Prisoners," *Macon Telegraph*, May 6, 1862, 2; "Shiloh's Captives," *Sioux City Journal*, July 17, 1895, 2; Pulis, "The Story of a Soldier Who Died a Prisoner of War," *National Tribune*, August 24, 1899, 7; "E. B. Fisher Has Crossed Divide," *Florence Bulletin*, July 7, 1921, 1; Bryant in Walker, *Cahaba Prison*, 17–21.

2. Bryant, 20–23.

3. Walker, *Cahaba Prison*, 9.

4. Walker, 23–24; "Myth: Grant Stopped the Prisoner Exchange," Andersonville National Historic Site, National Park Service, https://www.nps.gov/ande/learn/historyculture/grant-and-the-prisoner-exchange.htm.

5. "Myth: Grant Stopped the Prisoner Exchange."

6. Walker, *Cahaba Prison*, 4.

7. Eldridge, unpublished reminiscence from 1926, 10; Homer, "Every Fellow for Himself," 70.

8. Christine reminiscence in Schmutz, *History of the 102d Regiment*, 249; Homer, 70.

9. "Findlay Survivor Tells Story of *Sultana* Wreck," *Toledo Daily Blade*, May 1, 1912, 10; Commodore Smith in Berry, *Loss of the Sultana*, 319.

10. Rosselot [misspelled Roselot] in Berry, *Loss of the* Sultana, 304; Homer, "Every Fellow for Himself," 70; Aldrich in Walker, *Cahawba Prison*, 5.

11. Walker, *Cahaba Prison*, 16; Bryant in Walker, *Cahaba Prison*, 37–38. In May 1883, Rev. Howard A. M. Henderson presided over the funeral of Hannah Simpson Grant, the mother of general and president Ulysses S. Grant.

12. ORs, ser. 2, vol. 7. sec. 2, 1176–77.

13. "Had a Varied Experience," *National Tribune*, July 22, 1897, 3.

14. Garber in Berry, *Loss of the* Sultana, 145.

15. "Life in a Rebel Prison," unknown Hudson, MI, newspaper, March 28, 1884.

16. Rosselot in Berry, *Loss of the* Sultana, 304; Williams to home, March 19, 1865.

17. Collins, unpublished Civil War reminiscence, 1.

18. Miller, *Photographic History of the Civil War*, pt. 7, 74; Karns, "Karns' Reminiscences," *Lewisburg Leader*, September 22, 1897, 8.

19. Karns, 8.

20. McFarland in Berry, *Loss of the* Sultana, 247–48; Davenport, "Story of the *Sultana* Steamboat," unpublished manuscript.

21. Karns, "Karns' Reminiscences," *Lewisburg Leader*, January 26, 1898, 1.

22. Berry, *Loss of the* Sultana, 45.

23. Karns, "Karns' Reminiscences," *Lewisburg Leader*, March 16, 1898, 1.

24. "Thrilling Experiences," *Coffeyville Weekly Journal*, October 9, 1891, 7; McIntosh biography on photocard.

25. Horan, "A Sketch of My 15 Months in C.S.A. Prison," March 27, 1865; Davenport, "Story of the *Sultana* Steamboat."

26. Stevens in Berry, *Loss of the* Sultana, 338; Davenport.

27. Miller, *The Photographic History of the Civil War*, pt. 7, 76; Raudebaugh in Berry, *Loss of the* Sultana, 292.

28. J. W. Elliott, "By Fire and Flood," 2; Wells, unpublished manuscript, 5.

29. "History of the Andersonville, Prison," Andersonville National Historic Site, National Park Service, https://www.nps.gov/ande /learn/historyculture/camp_sumter_history.htm; Horan, "A Sketch of My 15 Months in C.S.A. Prison"; Ely, unpublished diary, January 23, 1865.
30. Elliott, "By Fire and Flood," 2.
31. "A Nut for Capt. Wirz," *Pantagraph*, October 5, 1865, 1; J. T. Elliott, "The *Sultana* Disaster," 164.
32. Horan to McCutchan, April 18, 1865.

CHAPTER 8. CAMP FISK

1. Penfield, "Unique Plan of Exchanging War Prisoners," *Sun*, March 21, 1915, 6.
2. Headquarters District of Mississippi, February 21, 1865, ORs, ser. 2, vol. 8, 284–85.
3. Maury to Granger, March 4, 1865, Bullock to Watts, March 10, 1865, Bullock to Watts, March 12, 1865, Parkhurst to Whipple, March 15, 1865, ORs, ser. 2, vol. 8, 355–56, 378, 382, 402.
4. Camp Townsend, Aubrey Territory, March 16, 1865, ORs, ser. 2, vol. 8, 404–5.
5. Penfield, "Unique Plan of Exchanging War Prisoners"; Civil War, Civil War Service Records, Union Records, Colored Troops, 56th–138th Infantry, 66th U.S. Colored Infantry, M, Miller, Franklin E., www.fold3.com.
6. Stubberfield, *Loss of the* Sultana, 347; Eldridge, unpublished reminiscence from 1926, 14.
7. Eldridge, 14. Although Eldridge wrote that he arrived at the Big Black River on March 19, it was actually March 16.
8. Stewart in Berry, *Loss of the* Sultana, 343.
9. Eldridge, unpublished reminiscence from 1928, 27.
10. Carver, "Letters from Home," 3; Eldridge, unpublished reminiscence from 1928, 28.
11. Goodrich in Berry, *Loss of the* Sultana, 154; Winters, *In the 50th Ohio*, 154.
12. Winters, 154–56.
13. Winters, 154–56; Walker, *Cahaba Prison*, 16.

14. Williams, Washburn Inquiry, 218; Smith to Dana, March 23, 1865, ORs, ser. 2, vol. 8, 425–26; Henderson, *Court-Martial*, 278; "Important from Vicksburg," *Times-Picayune*, April 4, 1865, 3.

15. Winters, *In the 50th Ohio*, 161; Speed to his father, April 4, 1865, Frederic and William Speed papers, William L. Clements Library, University of Michigan.

16. J. W. Elliott in Berry, *Loss of the* Sultana, 114.

17. Elliott, 114–15; Horan, "A Sketch of My 15 Months in C.S.A. Prison," March 27, 1865.

18. Karns, "Karns' Reminiscences," *Lewisburg Leader*, March 30, 1898, 1.

19. Speed and Williams, Washburn Inquiry, 219, 228–29; Henderson, *Court-Martial*, 275; Dana to Adjutant General U.S. Army, ORs, ser. 2, vol. 8, 477.

20. Special Orders No. 126, *Court-Martial*, 342-3; Dana to Hoffman, April 14, 1865, ORs, ser. 2, vol. 8, 492–93; Speed to his father, April 4, 1865, Speed papers; Special Orders No. 128, *Court-Martial*, 345; Speed to Davenport, April 11, 1865, ORs, ser. 2, vol. 8, 486–87.

21. Speed to Watts, April 13, 1865, ORs, ser. 2, vol. 8, 488–89.

22. Poysell to his wife, April 7, 1865; Dyer to his wife and children, April 9, 1865; Foley to his sister, April 15, 1865.

23. Poysell to his wife, April 7, 1865; Misemer to his wife, March 28, 1865.

24. "Relief for the *Sultana* Sufferers," *Memphis Daily Bulletin*, May 4, 1865, 3; "Letters from Mr. Woodward," 189.

25. Dyer to his wife and children, March 27, 1865; Foley to his sister, April 8, 1865.

26. Winters, *In the 50th Ohio*, 156; Misemer to his wife, March 24, 1865; J. T. Elliott, "The *Sultana* Disaster," 167; Hinds to his father and mother, March 19, 1865.

27. Foley to his sister, April 13, 1865; Ely, unpublished diary, April 13, 1865, entry.

28. Joseph Miller, *Court-Martial*, 215–16; Dana to Hoffman, May 8, 1865, Civil War, *Sultana* Disaster, April 27, 1865, Quartermaster vessel file relating to the *Sultana*, 72–76, www.fold3.com.

29. Speed to Colonel, May 28, 1865, Speed papers; Emmons, *Court-Martial*, 190–91; Dana to Hoffman, May 8, 1865, Civil War, *Sultana* Disaster, April 27, 1865, Quartermaster vessel file relating to the *Sultana*, 72–76, www.fold3.com.

30. Speed, Washburn Inquiry, 242.

31. Dana to Hoffman, May 8, 1865, Civil War, *Sultana* Disaster, April 27, 1865, Quartermaster vessel file relating to the *Sultana*, 72–76, www.fold3.com.
32. Special Orders Nos. 132 and 133, *Court-Martial*, 346–47; Ely, unpublished diary, April 16, 1865, entry.
33. Dana to Hoffman, May 8, 1865, Civil War, *Sultana* Disaster, April 27, 1865, Quartermaster vessel file relating to the *Sultana*, 72–76, www.fold3.com.
34. Dunton, Washburn Inquiry, 204.

CHAPTER 9. HIDDEN OFFERS

1. Adams, Dana Commission, Civil War, Sultana Disaster, April 1865, Quartermaster vessel file relating to the *Sultana*, 135, www.fold3.com (hereafter cited as Dana Commission).
2. Dunton, Washburn Inquiry, 204; Adams, Dana Commission, 135.
3. "River Intelligence," *Times-Picayune*, April 18, 1865, 8; "Marine Intelligence," *New-Orleans Times*, April 18, 1865, 8.
4. McGuire, Dana Commission, 136–37; Jones, Washburn Inquiry, 206; Civil War, Service Records, Union Records, Illinois (index cards), T, TI, Tillinghast, William H., www.fold3.com.
5. "Police Matters—Forgery," *Chicago Tribune*, February 14, 1864, 4; Civil War, Civil War Service Records, Union Records, Colored Troops, 56th–138th Infantry, 66th US Colored Infantry, T, Tillinghast, William H., 5, www.fold3.com.
6. McGuire, Dana Commission, 137; Tillinghast, Washburn Inquiry, 209.
7. Tillinghast, 209.
8. Tillinghast, 209.
9. Dana to Hoffman, May 8, 1865, Civil War, *Sultana* Disaster, April 27, 1865, Quartermaster vessel file relating to the *Sultana*, 72–76, www.fold3.com.
10. Tillinghast, Washburn Inquiry, 210.
11. Tillinghast, 211.
12. Special Orders No. 138, *Court-Martial*, 359; Exhibit N—Deposition of Cox, *Court-Martial*.
13. Jones, *Court-Martial*, 89–90.
14. Jones, 90.
15. Cox deposition, Exhibit N, *Court-Martial*.

16. Speed and Hatch, Washburn Inquiry, 224, 232.
17. Speed, Washburn Inquiry, 232; Dana to Hoffman, May 8, 1865, Civil War, *Sultana* Disaster, April 27, 1865, Quartermaster vessel file relating to the *Sultana*, 72–76, www.fold3.com.
18. "From Cairo and Below," *Cincinnati Commercial Tribune*, April 27, 1865, 3; "From Cairo and Below," *Daily Missouri Democrat*, April 27, 1865, 1.
19. Dana to Hoffman, May 8, 1865.
20. Speed, Washburn Inquiry, 233; Kerns, *Court-Martial*, 62–63.
21. Kerns, 62–63.
22. Speed, Washburn Inquiry, 239–40; Sells, *Court-Martial*, 127; Sells, Dana Commission, 139.
23. Taylor and Dunton, Washburn Inquiry, 201, 212.
24. Dana to Hoffman, May 8, 1865.
25. Sells, Dana Commission, 139–40.
26. Sells, 139–40; Sells, *Court-Martial*, 122.
27. Sells, *Court-Martial*, 122, 125; Sells, Dana Commission, 139–40; Speed, Washburn Inquiry, 229–30.
28. Speed; Sells, *Court-Martial*, 119.
29. Speed, 230; Sells, 123.
30. Taylor, Washburn Inquiry, 215–16; McLeod in Berry, *Loss of the Sultana*, 255.
31. Williams, *Court-Martial*, 12; Speed, Washburn Inquiry, 230.
32. Speed, 230; Sells, *Court-Martial*, 124.
33. Williams and Sells, *Court-Martial*, 30, 41, 42, 124.
34. Williams, 14.
35. Williams, 13; Speed, Washburn Inquiry, 231.
36. Williams, 22, 27.
37. Williams, 14; Speed, Washburn Inquiry, 231.
38. Davenport, *Court-Martial*, 283.
39. Dana to Hoffman, May 8, 1865.
40. Special Orders No. 139, *Court-Martial*, 361.

CHAPTER 10. THE LOADING BEGINS

1. Emmons, *Court-Martial*, 193; Speed, Washburn Inquiry, 244.
2. Special Orders No. 140, and Joseph Miller, *Court-Martial*, 55, 217, 221.
3. Kerns and Joseph Miller, *Court-Martial*, 80, 221.

4. Schmutz, *History of the 102d Regiment, OVI*, 239; Karns, "Karns Reminiscences," *Lewisburg Leader*, March 30, 1898, 8.

5. McCown, *Court-Martial*, 95, 98.

6. Davenport, *Court-Martial*, 284; Cox deposition, Exhibit N, *Court-Martial*, 284.

7. Taylor, Washburn Inquiry, 216, 217.

8. Wintringer, *Court-Martial*, 166, 169.

9. Taylor, Washburn Inquiry, 215–16; Witzig, *Court-Martial*, 130.

10. Tillinghast, Washburn Inquiry, 211.

11. Tillinghast, 211.

12. Jones, Washburn Inquiry, 213–14. Throughout this book I use Hatch's Quartermaster Department rank of captain in quoted material.

13. Kerns, Washburn Inquiry, 194.

14. Kerns, 194; Kerns, *Court-Martial*, 47.

15. Williams, *Court-Martial*, 28–29; Cox deposition, Exhibit N, *Court-Martial*, 28–29.

16. Speed, Washburn Inquiry, 231–32.

17. Cox deposition, Exhibit N, *Court-Martial*.

18. Davenport, *Court-Martial*, 285.

19. Williams and Davenport, *Court-Martial*, 30, 105, 306; Cox deposition.

20. Henderson, *Court-Martial*, 281; "Wreck of *Sultana*," *Galveston Daily News*, May 13, 1895, 7.

21. Huntsman, *Court-Martial*, 323–24.

22. "William S. Friesner," *Logan Daily News*, Sesquicentennial Edition, June 27, 1966, 25.

23. Kerns, Washburn Inquiry, 194.

24. Kerns and Dunton, Washburn Inquiry, 194, 203.

25. Kerns, *Court-Martial*, 48.

26. Edward Butler, *Court-Martial*, 154.

27. Williams, Edward Butler, and Henderson, *Court-Martial*, 13, 153, 280; Cox deposition.

28. "Dayton has a *Sultana* Survivor," *Dayton Daily News*, October 7, 1928, 75; "William S. Friesner."

29. Williams and Edward Butler, *Court-Martial*, 13, 16, 25, 152.

30. Boor and Jones in Berry, *Loss of the* Sultana, 57, 190.

31. Brown in Berry, *Loss of the* Sultana, 76.

32. Brown, 76–77.

33. "*Sultana* Disaster: A Survivor Tells of a Terrible Experience and His Escape," *National Tribune*, May 10, 1900, 7. The placement of the different units is based on comparison of first-person accounts of 149 survivors.
34. McHarg, *Court-Martial*, 174, 175, 177.
35. Speed, Washburn Inquiry, 233; Cox Deposition, Exhibit N, *Court-Martial*.
36. Cox deposition.
37. Williams, Washburn Inquiry, 221; Williams, *Court-Martial*, 13.
38. Kemble deposition, Exhibit O, *Court-Martial*.
39. Kemble deposition.
40. Kemble deposition.
41. Williams and Davenport, *Court-Martial*, 42, 293, 311.
42. Davenport, *Court-Martial*, 311, 312.
43. Speed, Washburn Inquiry, 233–34.
44. F. E. Miller deposition, Exhibit P, Washburn Inquiry.
45. Edward Butler, *Court-Martial*, 152; Nisley, Washburn Inquiry, 125.
46. "*Sultana* Disaster: A Survivor Tells of a Terrible Experience and His Escape"; Baker in Berry, *Loss of the* Sultana, 37; "The *Sultana* Disaster," *Daily Missouri Democrat*, June 19, 1865, 4.
47. J. W. Miller, *Court-Martial*, 219, 221.
48. Dana to Hoffman, May 8, 1865, Civil War, Sultana Disaster, April 27, 1865, Quartermaster vessel file relating to the Sultana, 72–76, www.fold3.com.
49. Dana to Hoffman, May 8, 1865.
50. J. W. Miller, *Court-Martial*, 218, 219–20.

CHAPTER 11. LIKE DAMNED HOGS

1. McCown, *Court-Martial*, 104.
2. Cox and F. E. Miller depositions, Exhibits N and P, *Court-Martial*.
3. Speed, Washburn Inquiry, 233; Dana to Hoffman, May 8, 1865, Civil War, *Sultana* Disaster, April 27, 1865, Quartermaster vessel file relating to the *Sultana*, 72–76, www.fold3.com.
4. Kerns and Jones, *Court-Martial*, 49, 89.
5. Geins and Hatch, Washburn Inquiry, 121–22, 226.
6. Hatch, 226.
7. Kerns, *Court-Martial*, 49.
8. Kerns, 49–50.

9. Kerns, 50.

10. Kerns, 50–51.

11. Smith, Washburn Inquiry, 250.

12. McGuire, Dana Commission, 138.

13. Dunton and Hatch, Washburn Inquiry, 202, 224–25.

14. Dunton and Speed, Washburn Inquiry, 203, 234.

15. Speed and Dickinson, Washburn Inquiry; McCown, *Court-Martial*, 94, 95, 98; Cox deposition, Exhibit N, *Court-Martial*; Aldrich in Walker, *Cahawba Prison*, 14.

16. Davenport, *Court-Martial*, 288; Cox deposition, Exhibit N, *Court-Martial*.

17. Edward Butler, Emmons, and Davenport, *Court-Martial*, 152, 208, 290, 310.

18. Kemble deposition, Exhibit O, *Court-Martial*.

19. McCown and Davenport, *Court-Martial*, 33, 290; Davenport, "Story of the *Sultana* Steamboat," unpublished manuscript; Sharp, "The *Sultana* Horror," 7.

20. Kerns, *Court-Martial*, 51, 61–62.

21. Speed, Washburn Inquiry, 235.

22. Speed, 235.

23. Williams, Washburn Inquiry, 221–22; Kerns, *Court-Martial*, 51–52.

24. Tillinghast, Washburn Inquiry, 211–12; McGuire, Dana Commission, 138.

25. Jones, Washburn Inquiry, 212–13; Kerns, *Court-Martial*, 52.

26. William Butler and Bean, Hoffman Investigation, 148, 156.

27. Mahoney, Hoffman Investigation, 165.

28. Chicago Opera Troupe advertisement, *Vicksburg Daily Herald*, April 20, 1865, 2; J. T. Elliott, "The *Sultana* Disaster," 168; "The *Sultana* Disaster," *Piqua Daily Call*, September 30, 1885, 2; J. W. Elliott, "By Fire and Flood," 2.

29. Annis, Hoffman Investigation, 152; Ann Annis, Widow's Claim for Pension, May 6, 1872, National Archives.

30. Annis, Hoffman Investigation, 152.

31. Morgan in Berry, *Loss of the* Sultana, 258; "The Steamer *Sultana*," *Kokomo Daily Gazette Tribune*, February 7, 1893, 4.

32. Bean, Hoffman Investigation, 158; McCown, *Court-Martial*, 101.

33. Mahoney, Hoffman Investigation, 164; Eldridge, "Some Events at Close of the Civil War," 6.

34. "McMinn Countian Recalls Escape from the *'Sultana'* Fifty-Eight Years Ago When 1,238 Lost Lives," *Knoxville Sentinel*, Dec. 8, 1923; Collins, unpublished Civil War reminiscences, 2.

35. Taylor, Washburn Inquiry, 217.

36. Benjamin Davis and Ira Horner in Berry, *Loss of the* Sultana, 105, 180, 225; Warner Ogden, "1700 Died When *Sultana* Sank 64 Years Ago," *Knoxville News-Sentinel*, April 28, 1929, 23.

37. Clinger in Berry, *Loss of the* Sultana, 97; "Story of the *Sultana*," *Chicago Tribune*, April 22, 1888, 25.

38. Vannuys in Berry, *Loss of the* Sultana, 362; "The *Sultana* Disaster," *Piqua Daily Call*, 2.

39. McCown, Hoffman Investigation, 155.

40. McCown, *Court-Martial*, 101.

41. Tillinghast, Washburn Inquiry, 207; Williams, *Court-Martial*, 13–14.

42. Williams, 13, 15.

43. Williams, Washburn Inquiry, 222.

44. Speed, Washburn Inquiry, 236; Williams, *Court-Martial*, 17.

45. Williams, *Court-Ma*rtial, 17, 43; Speed, Exhibit C2, *Court-Martial*.

46. Speed, Washburn Inquiry, 237.

47. Kerns, *Court-Martial*, 52–53.

48. Kerns, 59.

49. Kerns, 53.

50. William Butler, Hoffman Investigation, 149; Geins, Washburn Inquiry, 123.

51. Shull, *Court-Martial*, 145, 146, 147.

52. Friesner, *Court-Martial*, 110.

53. Speed, Washburn Inquiry, 237; Davenport, *Court-Martial*, 73.

54. Kerns, *Court-Martial*, 73; Karns, "Karns' Reminiscences," *Lewisburg Leader*, April 6, 1898, 1; "The Sultana Disaster," *Piqua Daily Call*, 2.

55. Hiram Wells, unpublished manuscript, n.p.; William Wells, Hoffman Investigation, 151.

56. Cayton, Washburn Inquiry, 109; Foglesang in Berry, *Loss of the* Sultana, 135.

CHAPTER 12. ON THE RIVER

1. Winters, *In the 50th Ohio*, 163.

2. Brown in Berry, *Loss of the* Sultana, 77–78.

3. Karns, "Karns' Reminiscences," *Lewisburg Leader*, April 6, 1898, 1.

4. "Story of Sinking of Ill-Fated *Sultana*," *Liberty Express*, August 30, 1918, 7.

5. "The Loss of the Steamer *Sultana*," *Hancock Democrat*, August 26, 1913, 4; J. T. Elliott, "The *Sultana* Disaster," 169, 170; Squire to L. W. Day, March 29, 1886.

6. J. T. Elliott, 169.

7. Bean, Hoffman Investigation, 158.

8. Eldridge, unpublished reminiscence from 1928, 29.

9. Squire to L. W. Day, March 29, 1886; Ely, unpublished diary, April 25, 1865, entry.

10. McCown, *Court-Martial*, 99, 107; Barker, Hoffman Investigation, 166.

11. McCown, 99, 106; Bean, Hoffman Investigation, 158.

12. McCown, 102; Barker and Hites, Hoffman Investigation, 159, 166.

13. Bean, Hoffman Investigation, 157; Wintringer, *Court-Martial*, 163.

14. Squire, Hoffman Investigation, 168; McCown, *Court-Martial*, 99.

15. "Like Ververa: Two County Commissioners Have Been in Marine Disasters," *Cleveland Plain Dealer*, March 4, 1895, 5.

16. Kerns and Bean, Hoffman Investigation, 150, 157; Tillinghast, Washburn Inquiry, 208.

17. Photo of the *Sultana* at Helena, AR, taken April 26, 1865, by Thomas W. Bankes.

18. McCown, Hoffman Investigation, 155.

19. Dana to Hoffman, May 8, 1865, Civil War, *Sultana* Disaster, April 27, 1865, Quartermaster vessel file relating to the Sultana, 72–76, www.fold3.com.

20. Taylor to Tucker, April 24, 1865, ORs, ser. 1, vol. 48, pt. 2, , 176; Tucker to Dana, April 24, 1865, ORs, ser. 1, vol. 48, pt. 2, , 175; Dana to the Adjutant General of the Army, April 28, 1865, ORs, ser. 1, vol. 48, pt. 2, 232; Dana to Tucker, April 28, 1865, ORs, ser. 1, vol. 48, pt. 2, 233.

21. Morgan Smith, Washburn Inquiry, 252.

22. Curtis, "Only Living Eye-Witness Details *Sultana* Explosion," *Commercial Appeal*, January 25, 1920, 3.

23. Barker, Mahoney, and Dickinson, Hoffman Investigation, 165, 166, 169.

24. McCown, *Court-Martial*, 100; Bean, Hoffman Investigation, 154; "An Old Veteran Dead," *Journal Gazette*, January 5, 1905, 5.

25. Sanders in Berry, *Loss of the* Sultana, 309.

26. Berry, *Loss of the* Sultana, 10; Michael, "Explosion of the *Sultana*," 253.
27. "Not True," *Chicago Tribune*, May 2, 1865, 4.
28. Walker, *Cahaba Prison*, 26; Rush in Hawes, *Cahaba*, 194; "The Field of Battle," *Argos Reflector*, May 28, 1903, 6; George C. Loy to Frank Loy, April 28, 1865.
29. Rush, Washburn Inquiry, 128; Aldrich in Walker, *Cahawba Prison*, 16; "The Wreck of the *Sultana*," *News-Leader*, October 8, 1896, 1; Karns, "Karns' Reminiscences," *Lewisburg Leader*, April 6, 1898, 1; "Escaped Flaming *Sultana* on Door," *Cleveland Plain Dealer*, April 10, 1927, 43; *Daily Missouri Democrat*, April 29, 1865, 3.
30. Bean, McCown, and Mahoney, Hoffman Investigation, 154, 158, 165; Rush and Rowberry, Washburn Inquiry, 112, 128–29.
31. "Large Arrival of Paroled Prisoners," *Daily Missouri Republican*, April 26, 1865, 3; "From New Orleans," *Cleveland Leader*, April 25, 1865, 2.
32. Lugenbeal in Berry, *Loss of the* Sultana, 225.
33. Bean, Mahoney, and Annis, Hoffman Investigation, 153, 157, 165; "The Field of Battle," *Argos Reflector*, May 28, 1903, 6; McCown, *Court-Martial*, 99.
34. Bean and McCown, Hoffman Investigation, 156, 157.
35. McCown, *Court-Martial*, 101; J. T. Elliott, "The *Sultana* Disaster," 169.
36. Wintringer, Hoffman Investigation, 172–73.
37. McCown, Hoffman Investigation, 154; "The *Sultana* Slaughter," *Indianapolis Daily Journal*, May 4, 1865, n.p.
38. Hake, Washburn Inquiry, 127; Wintringer and Squire, Hoffman Investigation, 168, 173.
39. Fox quoted by Erastus Winters in Winters, *In the 50th Ohio*, 167; "The Explosion of the Sultana," *Iola Register*, November 23, 1888, 8.
40. "The Steamer *Sultana*," *Kokomo Daily Gazette Tribune*, February 7, 1893, 4.
41. Story of Sinking of Ill-Fated *Sultana*," *Liberty Express*, August 30, 1918, 7; Friesner, *Court-Martial*, 115.
42. Collins, unpublished Civil War reminiscences, 2.

CHAPTER 13. HELENA AND MEMPHIS

1. "William S. Friesner of Logan Commanded Detail on Ill-Fated *Sultana*," *Logan Daily News*, June 27, 1966, 25; "Explosion of the Sultana," *Iola Register*, December 14, 1888, 8.

2. Winters, *In the 50th Ohio*, 163.

3. Brown in Berry, *Loss of the* Sultana, 77; "Terrible Steamboat Disaster," *Lebanon Patriot*, May 4, 1865, n.p.

4. McCown, Hoffman Investigation, 154–55.

5. "Special Correspondence: Burning of the *Sultana*," *Cincinnati Commercial Tribune*, April 21, 1882, 7; Foglesang in Berry, *Loss of the* Sultana, 135; Aldrich, *Cahawba Prison*, 14.

6. "Reminiscence of the War," *Wayne County Democrat*, April 28, 1880, n.p.; J. T. Elliott, "The *Sultana* Disaster," 169.

7. "William S. Friesner of Logan Commanded Detail on Ill-Fated *Sultana*."

8. Palmquist, *Pioneer Photographers*, 86; Thomas W. Bankes advertisements, *Southern Shield*, January 28, 1860, 1, and February 8, 1862, 1.

9. J. W. Elliott, "By Fire and Flood," 2.

10. Friesner, Washburn Inquiry, 124; Friesner, *Court-Martial*, 112.

11. "*Sultana*: by a Survivor," *Lyons Tribune*, August 23, 1888, 1.

12. Descriptions gleaned from a close study of the image of the *Sultana* taken by photographer Thomas W. Bankes, Helena, AR.

13. Foglesang in Berry, *Loss of the* Sultana, 135; Aldrich, *Cahawba Prison*, 14.

14. "William S. Friesner of Logan Commanded Detail on Ill-Fated *Sultana*."

15. Curtis, "Only Living Eye-Witness Details *Sultana* Explosion," *Commercial Appeal*, January 25, 1920, 3.

16. "River News," *Cleveland Leader*, April 27, 1865, 2; "Memoranda of Olive Branch," *Cleveland Leader*, May 1, 1865, 1.

17. "Awful *Sultana* Disaster: A Symposium."

18. LaPointe, "Military Hospitals in Memphis, 1861–1865."

19. "The Rescue," *Winchester Randolph Journal*, October 11, 1876, 1.

20. "Escaped Flaming *Sultana* on Door," *Cleveland Plain Dealer*, April 10, 1927, 43; "The Explosion of the *Sultana* in 1865," *Times-Picayune*, May 10, 1888, 4.

21. Foglesang and Porter in Berry, *Loss of the* Sultana, 135, 286.

22. Truman Smith and Stevens in Berry, *Loss of the* Sultana, 325, 341; "Story of Another Survivor," *Chicago Tribune*, April 12, 1888, 25.

23. "Letter from Mr. Christy," 187.

24. "A Sultana Survivor," *Indianapolis News*, September 6, 1893, 13; J. T. Elliott, "The *Sultana* Disaster," 169; Boner obituary, *Commercial News*, December 17, 1921, n.p.

25. "Like Ververa: Two County Commissioners Have Been in Marine Disasters," *Cleveland Plain Dealer*, March 4, 1895, 5; Raudebaugh in Berry, *Loss of the* Sultana, 293; Gilbreath reminiscence in Hazzard, *Hazzard's History of Henry County, Indiana*, 610; "*Sultana* Survivor Seeks Companion in Radio Plea," *Columbus Dispatch*, April 27, 1926, 6.

26. Aldrich, *Cahawba Prison*, 15.

27. Gaston in Berry, *Loss of the* Sultana, 150; Winters, *In the 50th Ohio*, 164.

28. Compton, *Court-Martial*, 148; "A Sultana Survivor," *Indianapolis News*, September 6, 1893, 14; "The Chicago Opera Troupe," *Memphis Daily Bulletin*, April 29, 1865, 2, 3.

29. Snow obituary, *New York Times*, February 12, 1910, n.p.; U.S. Congress, *Compilation of Senate Election Cases*, 302.

30. J. T. Elliott, "The *Sultana* Disaster," 170.

31. J. T. Elliott, 170.

32. J. W. Elliott, "By Fire and Flood."

33. Snow, Washburn Inquiry, 113.

34. Porter in Berry, *Loss of the* Sultana, 287.

35. McFarland, in Berry, *Loss of the* Sultana, 248–49.

36. Pierce, Volunteer Enlistment record, Civil War Service Records, www.fold3.com.

37. McIntosh in Berry, *Loss of the* Sultana, 252.

38. Friesner, Washburn Inquiry, 124; Friesner, *Court-Martial*, 112.

39. "Story of Another Survivor," *Chicago Tribune*, April 12, 1888, 25.

40. Boner obituary; Kinzer and Kline in Berry, *Loss of the* Sultana, 206, 210.

41. "Commemoration of Heroic Deeds on Ill-Fated Boat," *Knoxville Sentinel*, April 27, 1912, n.p.; "The *Sultana* Disaster," *Daily Missouri Democrat*, June 19, 1865, 4.

42. "The Rescue," *Winchester Randolph Journal*, October 11, 1876, 1.

43. Bean and Mahoney, Hoffman Investigation, 158, 165; "A Survivor from the *Sultana*," 124.

44. Wintringer, Hoffman Investigation, 172; "The *Sultana* Disaster," *Daily Missouri Democrat*, June 19, 1865, 4.
45. Walker, *Cahaba Prison*, 17–18.
46. Fies in Berry, *Loss of the* Sultana, 126; Rush, Washburn Inquiry, 129.

CHAPTER 14. EXPLOSION: THE CAUSE

1. "Terrible Steamboat Disaster," *Lebanon Patriot*, May 4, 1865, n.p.; "Veterans Commemorate Greatest River Disaster," *Cleveland Plain Dealer*, January 27, 1918, 4.
2. "Explosion of the *Sultana*," *Iola Register*, December 14, 1888, 8.
3. Clarkson in Berry, *Loss of the* Sultana, 95.
4. Davis, Ben, and McLeod in Berry, *Loss of the* Sultana, 103, 256.
5. Cayton, *Court-Martial*, 138; Guernsey and Alden, *Harper's Pictorial History of Civil War*, 429; "When the *Sultana* Blew Up," *Mulvane Record*, August 11, 1892, 5.
6. "Dayton has a *Sultana* Survivor," *Dayton Daily News*, October 7, 1928, 75.
7. "Commemoration of Heroic Deeds on Ill-Fated Boat," *Knoxville Sentinel*, April 27, 1912, n.p. Elza gave a similar account in "He Was Awake and Realized that the Explosion was Coming," *Knoxville Sentinel*, April 27, 1894, 2.
8. "When the *Sultana* Blew Up."
9. Ben Davis in Berry, *Loss of the* Sultana, 103.
10. "Personal Experience of Jacob Homer as a Prisoner of War," in Schmutz, *History of the 102d Regiment, OVI*, 243; Vannuys in Berry, *Loss of the* Sultana, 362.
11. Jennings, "The *Sultana*—Part 5: What Caused the *Sultana* Disaster?" https://blog.hsb.com/2016/04/27/sultana-disaster-cause/.
12. Barr, *Practical Treatise on High Pressure Steam Boilers*, 22.
13. Jennings, "The *Sultana*—Part 5."
14. Jennings, "What Happened to the *Sultana*?"; "Engineer on the *Sultana*," *Fort Wayne Journal-Gazette*, May 5, 1902, 5.
15. "Tubular Boilers: Are They Peculiarly Dangerous?" *Daily Missouri Democrat*, February 10, 1866, 2.
16. "Explosion of the *Carter*," *Spirit of Democracy*, February 14, 1866, 3; Way, *Way's Packet Directory*, 321, 326–27, 409, 464, 477; "Explosions of Steam-Boilers," *New York Tribune*, February 17, 1866, 10.

17. Clemens, Washburn Inquiry, 118; Wintringer, Hoffman Investigation, 173.
18. Wintringer, 173.
19. "Explosions of Steam-Boilers."
20. West, Hoffman Investigation, 162.
21. Witzig, *Court-Martial*, 135.
22. Hunter, *Steamboats on the Western Rivers*, 292.
23. Bates, *The Western Rivers Engineroom Cyclopoedium*, 9.
24. Taylor, Washburn Inquiry, 216.
25. Hoffman to Stanton, May 19, 1865, ORs, 1st ser., vol. 48, pt. 1, 216–17; Jennings, "What Happened to the *Sultana*?," presentation before the *Sultana* Disaster Conference, April 27, 2019.
26. Jennings, "The *Sultana*—Part 2: How Do Boilers Go Boom?" https://blog.hsb.com/2015/04/06/sultana-boiler-explosion/.
27. Smith, Washburn Inquiry, 252.
28. Witzig, *Court-Martial*, 133; Neal, Washburn Inquiry, 246–47; Wintringer, Hoffman Investigation, 172.
29. Cayton, *Court-Martial*, 318.

CHAPTER 15. EXPLOSION: THE STRUCTURAL DAMAGE

1. Homer, "Personal Experience of Jacob Homer as a Prisoner of War," in Schmutz, *History of the 102d Regiment, OVI*, 245; William Norton to his parents, April 27, 1865, https://www.ancestry.com/mediaui-viewer/tree/54068443/person/13609360180/media/89ad5b59-4f20-4a06-a413-0ff7212e6704.
2. Witzig, *Court-Martial*, 131, 139; Wintringer in Berry, *Loss of the Sultana*, 27; Wintringer, Hoffman Investigation, 170; "The *Sultana* Disaster," *St. Louis Missouri Democrat*, June 19, 1865, 4.
3. *Memphis Argus*, April 28, 1865, 3.
4. Squire to L. W. Day, March 29, 1886.
5. "The Explosion of the *Sultana*," *Iola Register*, November 23, 1888, 8.
6. Maes and Vanscoyoc in Berry, *Loss of the Sultana*, 234–35, 366.
7. "Veterans Commemorate Greatest River Disaster," *Cleveland Plain Dealer*, January 27, 1918, 4; "Reminiscence of the War," *Wayne County Democrat*, April 28, 1880.
8. Gilbreath reminiscence in Hazzard, *Hazzard's History of Henry County, Indiana*, 610.
9. John Norton and Ray in Berry, *Loss of the Sultana*, 270, 297.

10. Asa Lee in Berry, *Loss of the* Sultana, 219; "The Steamer *Sultana*," *Kokomo Daily Gazette Tribune*, February 7, 1893, 4.

11. Eldridge, "In the *Sultana* Disaster"; Anderson in Berry, *Loss of the* Sultana, 35.

12. White in Berry, *Loss of the* Sultana, 374.

13. Kline, in Berry, *Loss of the* Sultana, 210.

14. Berry and Clinger in Berry, *Loss of the* Sultana, 51, 98.

15. Wintringer, Washburn Inquiry, 171–72.

16. "Story of the Sultana," *Chicago Tribune*, April 22, 1888, 25; "Personal Experience of Jacob Homer as a Prisoner of War," 244.

17. Rowberry, Washburn Inquiry, 111; Sharp, "The *Sultana* Disaster"; Cayton statement, *Daily Memphis Bulletin*, April 28, 1865, 1.

18. Deerman in Berry, *Loss of the* Sultana, 108; "*Sultana* Disaster: A Survivor Tells of a Terrible Experience and His Escape."

19. "*Sultana* Wreck: A Canton Survivor Tells the Story of His Escape," *Repository*, October 17, 1897, 10.

20. Madden in Berry, *Loss of the* Sultana, 229–30.

21. Crisp to Wolverton in C. M. Elliott and Moxley, *Tennessee Civil War Veterans Questionnaires*, 151.

22. Wesley Lee in Berry, *Loss of the* Sultana, 220; "The *Sultana* Disaster by a Survivor of One of the Civil War's Greatest Tragedies," *Kansas City Star*, May 14, 1909, 1.

23. "The *Sultana* Disaster by a Survivor of One of the Civil War's Greatest Tragedies"; Wesley Lee and Rosselot in Berry, *Loss of the* Sultana, 220, 305.

24. Walker, *Cahaba Prison*, 18; "The Loss of the Steamer *Sultana*," *Hancock Democrat*, August 26, 1913, 4; Albert Norris in Berry, *Loss of the* Sultana, 266; J. W. Elliott, "By Fire and Flood"; J. T. Elliott, "The *Sultana* Disaster," 171.

25. Crisp to Wolverton.

26. Gaston in Berry, *Loss of the* Sultana, 150; Peacock reminiscence in Hazzard, *Hazzard's History of Henry County*, 617–18.

27. "Escaped Flaming *Sultana* on Door," *Cleveland Plain Dealer*, April 10, 1927, 43; King and Smith in Berry, *Loss of the* Sultana, 200, 201, 319.

28. "Civil War Reminiscences," *Plainville Times*, May 28, 1908, 2; Shumard in Berry, *Loss of the* Sultana, 315.

29. "Andrew T. Peery's Story of the Sinking of the *Sultana*," *Maryville Enterprise*, April 30, 1975, 3.

30. Friesner, *Court-Martial*, 112; Annis, Hoffman Investigation, 152; "The Wreck of the *Sultana*," *News-Leader*, October 8, 1896, 1; J. W. Elliott, "By Fire and Flood"; "*Sultana* Disaster: A Survivor Tells of a Terrible Experience and His Escape."

31. White in Hawes, *Cahaba*, 177; Chelf, Haines, and Truman Smith in Berry, *Loss of the* Sultana, 88, 158–59, 326.

32. J. T. Elliott, "The *Sultana* Disaster," 171; "Statement of W. D. Snow," *Memphis Daily Bulletin*, April 28, 1865, 1; "Terrible Steamboat Disaster," *Lebanon Patriot*, May 4, 1865; "A *Sultana* Survivor," *Indianapolis News*, September 6, 1893, 13.

33. Annis, Hoffman Investigation, 152; "The *Sultana* Disaster by a Survivor of One of the Civil War's Greatest Tragedies"; "The *Sultana* Disaster," *Piqua Daily Call*, Sept. 30, 1885, 2.

34. Winters, *In the 50th Ohio*, 165; Rush, Washburn Inquiry, 275; Rush in Hawes, *Cahaba*, 192.

35. McCown, Hoffman Investigation, 155; James M. McCown, Invalid Pension Application, March 14, 1888; McCown, Invalid Pension Application, September 19, 1892.

36. Garber in Berry, *Loss of the* Sultana, 146; Van Buren Jolley, Invalid Pension Application, March 20, 1879.

37. Squire to L. W. Day, March 29, 1886; Berry and John E. Norton in Berry, *Loss of the* Sultana, 49, 271; Sharp, "The *Sultana* Disaster."

38. "Sultana Disaster Is Recalled to Mind," *Athens Daily Messenger*, May 3, 1912, 1; Cayton statement in *Memphis Daily Bulletin*, April 28, 1865, 1.

39. King and Morgan in Berry, *Loss of the* Sultana, 201, 259.

40. Fies and William Norton in Berry, *Loss of the* Sultana, 127.

41. "Civil War Reminiscence," *Plainville Times*, May 28, 1908, 2; "William S. Friesner of Logan Commanded Detail on Ill-Fated *Sultana*," *Logan Daily News*, June 27, 1966, 26; Karns, "Karns' Reminiscences," *Lewisburg Leader*, April 6, 1898, 8.

CHAPTER 16. THE EXODUS

1. Rush, *Cahaba*, 192–93; "The *Sultana* Disaster," *Piqua Daily Call*, September 30, 1885, 2.

2. Fast and Rush in Hawes, *Cahaba*, 167, 193.

3. Rush, 193; "Statement of W. D. Snow, Congressman-Elect from Arkansas," *Memphis Daily Bulletin*, April 28, 1865, 1; Ross, *History of the 102d Regiment, OVI*, 244.

4. Karns, "Karns' Reminiscences," *Lewisburg Leader*, April 6, 1898, 1.

5. Hamblin in Berry, *Loss of the* Sultana, 161–2.

6. Bardon in Berry, *Loss of the* Sultana, 40.

7. "The Explosion of the *Sultana*," *Iola Register*, November 23, 1888, 8; "Disaster of the *Sultana* Recalled by a Survivor," *Steubenville Herald*, May 1, 1903, 5.

8. "The Loss of the Steamer *Sultana*," *Hancock Democrat*, August 26, 1913, 4.

9. Brady, Albert King, and Chelf in Berry, *Loss of the* Sultana, 64, 88, 201.

10. "A *Sultana* Survivor Who Feels All the Bitterness of the Past," *National Tribune*, June 3, 1909, 7; James McKendry, Invalid Pension Application, December 5, 1887; Oxley in Berry, *Loss of the* Sultana, 278, 279–80.

11. "Civil War Reminiscence," *Plainville Times*, May 28, 1908, 2; Kochenderfer in Berry, *Loss of the* Sultana, 212.

12. J. T. Elliott, "The *Sultana* Disaster," 172; "The *Sultana* Disaster," *Piqua Daily Call*.

13. Benjamin Davis in Berry, *Loss of the* Sultana, 103.

14. Patterson and Porter in Berry, *Loss of the* Sultana, 283, 288; "The Wreck of the *Sultana*," *News-Leader*, October 8, 1896, 1.

15. "The Wreck of the *Sultana*"; Rosselot in Berry, *Loss of the* Sultana, 305; "A Survivor from the *Sultana*," 124.

16. Boor in Berry, *Loss of the* Sultana, 58; "The Field of Battle," *Argos Reflector*, May 28, 1903, 6.

17. "Survivor Recalls *Sultana*'s Sinking," *Cleveland Plain Dealer*, April 15, 1923, 11; Gaston, Jones, and Maes in Berry, *Loss of the* Sultana, 151, 192–93, 235.

18. William Norton and Robinson in Berry, *Loss of the* Sultana, 275, 276, 301.

19. Fast in Hawes, *Cahaba*, 169; Patterson in Berry, *Loss of the* Sultana, 283.

20. Karns, "Karns' Reminiscences," *Lewisburg Leader*, April 6, 1898, 1.

21. "The *Sultana* Disaster," *National Tribune*, November 21, 1912, 7.

22. Winters, *In the 50th Ohio*, 165–66.

23. Brunner, *Loss of the* Sultana, 81; Karns, "Karns' Reminiscences."

24. "Had a Varied Experience," 3.
25. Karns, "Karns' Reminiscences"; Walker, *Cahaba Prison*, 19; Fies in Berry, *Loss of the* Sultana, 127.
26. Karns, "Karns' Reminiscences"; Walker, *Cahaba Prison*, 19.
27. Gambill in Berry, *Loss of the* Sultana, 143.
28. Ray in Berry, *Loss of the* Sultana, 297.
29. Wintringer, in Berry, *Loss of the* Sultana, 27.
30. "The *Sultana* Disaster by a Survivor of One of the Civil War's Greatest Tragedies," *Kansas City Star*, May 14, 1909, 1; "Letter from Mr. Rush," *Sandusky Register*, May 10, 1865, 3.
31. "Story of the *Sultana*," *Chicago Tribune*, April 22, 1888, 25; "The Steamer *Sultana*," *Kokomo Daily Gazette Tribune*, February 7, 1893, 4; Rush in Hawes, *Cahaba*, 194.
32. Annis, Hoffman Investigation, 152; "In the River Wreck: The *Sultana* Disaster Recalled to Mind," *Oshkosh Northwestern*, March 30, 1880, 1.
33. "In the River Wreck."
34. "In the River Wreck"; Annis, Hoffman Investigation, 152–53; Helen Chandler, email message to author, June 21, 1997.
35. "A Struggle for Life," *Chicago Tribune*, May 13, 1865, 2; "The Washington Woman," *Washington Evening Star*, September 26, 1868, 1.
36. McLeod in Berry, *Loss of the* Sultana, 256; J. W. Elliott, "By Fire and Flood."
37. "A Sad Case," *Memphis Daily Bulletin*, April 28, 1865, 2; "Wreck of *Sultana* Cost More Lives than the *Titanic*," *Denver Post*, April 23, 1912, 3.
38. "When the *Sultana* Blew Up," *Mulvane Record*, August 11, 1892, 5.
39. Van Vlack in Berry, *Loss of the* Sultana, 368; "Statements of Parties on Board—Incidents, etc., etc.," *Memphis Argus*, April 28, 1865, 3 [Alvord misnamed Fred Albeck]; "Statement of W. D. Snow," 1.
40. "The *Sultana* Disaster," *Piqua Daily Call*.
41. McFarland in Berry, *Loss of the* Sultana, 249.

CHAPTER 17. THE GROWING FIRE

1. Friesner, *Court-Martial*, 113.
2. Fies in Berry, *Loss of the* Sultana, 127–28.
3. Squire to L. W. Day, March 29, 1886; Squire reminiscence in Day, *Story of the One Hundred and First Ohio Infantry*, 343.

4. Colvin to Wolverton, in C. M. Elliott and Moxley, *Tennessee Civil War Veterans Questionnaires*, 147–48.

5. "Statement of W. D. Snow, Congressman-elect from Arkansas," *Memphis Daily Bulletin*, April 28, 1865, 1.

6. Leak in Berry, *Loss of the* Sultana, 218; Walker in Hawes, *Cahaba*, 20–21.

7. Leak, 218; Walker, 20–21.

8. Cayton statement, *Memphis Daily Bulletin*, April 28, 1865, 1; Clemens, Washburn Inquiry, 109–10; "The *Sultana* Disaster," *Daily Missouri Democrat*, June 19, 1865, 4.

9. Rowberry and Wintringer, Washburn Inquiry, 112, 171; Cayton statement; "The *Sultana* Disaster," *Daily Missouri Democrat*, June 19, 1865, 4; Wintringer, *Court-Martial*, 167–68; Wintringer in Berry, *Loss of the* Sultana, 27.

10. Rush in Hawes, *Cahaba*, 194; Helminger in Berry, *Loss of the* Sultana, 170.

11. Homer, "Personal Experience of Jacob Homer as a Prisoner of War," in Schmutz, *History of the 102d Regiment, OVI*, 244; Rush, Washburn Inquiry, 280.

12. Stevens in Berry, *Loss of the* Sultana, 341.

13. "William S. Friesner of Logan Commanded Detail on Ill-Fated Sultana," *Logan Daily News*, June 27, 1966, 26.

14. "Memphis, April 27, 1865, To the Editor of the Republican," *Daily Missouri Republican*, April 30, 1865, 2; Nisley in Berry, *Loss of the* Sultana, 263; Nisley, Washburn Inquiry, 125; "Lost—$200 Reward," *Memphis Daily Bulletin*, April 28, 1865, 3.

15. Davis and Horner in Berry, *Loss of the* Sultana, 105, 179–80; Ogden, "1700 Died When *Sultana* Sank," *Knoxville News-Sentinel*, April 27, 1929, 23.

16. Lugenbeal in Berry, *Loss of the* Sultana, 225–26.

17. Lugenbeal, 225–26; wooden cane and curio box, both decorated with the words "Saved by a Alligator," on display in *Sultana* Disaster Museum, Marion, AR.

18. "*Sultana* Wreck: A Canton Survivor Tells the Story of His Escape," *Repository*, October 17, 1897, 10

19. Martin in Berry, *Loss of the* Sultana, 238.

20. "A *Sultana* Survivor," *Indianapolis News*, September 6, 1893, 13; Rush in Hawes, *Cahaba*, 193.

21. Karns, "Karns' Reminiscences," *Lewisburg Leader*, April 13, 1898, 1; "Story of Sinking of Ill-Fated *Sultana*," *Liberty Express*, August 30, 1918, 7.

22. Lockhart reminiscence in Baughman, *History of Ashland County, Ohio*, 218; Sprinkle in Berry, *Loss of the* Sultana, 331; Homer, "Personal Experience of Jacob Homer as a Prisoner of War," 245.

23. Commodore Smith in Berry, *Loss of the* Sultana, 319–21.

CHAPTER 18. THE RIVER

1. Rush, Washburn Inquiry, 280–81; Eldridge, unpublished reminiscence from 1926, 15.

2. Summerville in Hawes, *Cahaba*, 180; "Reminiscence of the War," *Wayne County Democrat*, April 28, 1880; Schmutz in Berry, *Loss of the* Sultana, 310.

3. Anderson in Berry, *Loss of the* Sultana, 35.

4. Horn reminiscence in Howells, "Wooster Men Tell of Civil War Horror," *Canton Daily News*, June 5, 1927, 50; "Veterans Commemorate Greatest River Disaster," *Cleveland Plain Dealer*, January 27, 1918, 4.

5. McIntosh reminiscence in Boggs, *Eighteen Months a Prisoner*, 85; McIntosh in Berry, *Loss of the* Sultana, 253–54.

6. Atchley in Berry, *Loss of the* Sultana, 36.

7. "Terrible Steamboat Disaster," *Lebanon Patriot*, May 4, 1865; Thrasher in Berry, *Loss of the* Sultana, 356–57.

8. "Escaped Flaming *Sultana* on Door," *Cleveland Plain Dealer*, April 10, 1927, 43.

9. "Survivor of the *Sultana*," *Olympia Daily Recorder*, May 22, 1912, 3; Eldridge, "Some Events at Close of the Civil War," 6; Madden in Berry, *Loss of the* Sultana, 231.

10. "A *Sultana* Survivor," *Indianapolis News*, September 6, 1893, 13; J. T. Elliott, "The *Sultana* Disaster," 173; Bringman in Berry, *Loss of the* Sultana, 71.

11. Clapsaddle in Berry, *Loss of the* Sultana, 94; Summerville in Hawes, *Cahaba*, 181; Wolverton to *Memphis Commercial Appeal*, January 29, 1920, in C. M. Elliott and Moxley, *Tennessee Civil War Veterans Questionnaires*, 146.

12. McIntosh reminiscence in Boggs, *Eighteen Months a Prisoner*, 86.

13. "Hypothermia," Patient Care & Health Information, Diseases & Conditions, Mayo Clinic, https://www.mayoclinic.org/diseases-conditions/hypothermia/symptoms-causes/syc-20352682.

14. Walker, *Cahaba Prison*, 23; Bringman and Mayes in Berry, *Loss of the* Sultana, 72, 239–40.

15. Dixon, "Aboard the *Sultana*," 38; "*Sultana* Disaster: A Survivor Tells of a Terrible Experience and His Escape," *National Tribune*, May 10, 1900, 7.

16. "Want a *Sultana* Monument," *Fort Wayne Evening Sentinel*, April 30, 1902, 5; Walker, *Cahaba Prison*, 22; Commodore Smith in Berry, *Loss of the* Sultana, 208.

17. Christine in Schmutz, *History of the 102d Regiment, OVI*, 251; J. T. Elliott, "The *Sultana* Disaster," 175.

18. Kinzer in Berry, *Loss of the* Sultana, 208.

19. Annis, Hoffman Investigation, 153.

20. Albert W. King in Berry, *Loss of the* Sultana, 202; "*Sultana* Blast Survivor Dead," *Cleveland Plain Dealer*, February 14, 1929, 3.

21. "A Struggle for Life," *Chicago Tribune*, May 13, 1865, 2.

22. "A Struggle for Life"; Albert W. King in Berry, *Loss of the* Sultana, 203.

23. William Norton in Berry, *Loss of the* Sultana, 272.

24. Stevens in Berry, *Loss of the* Sultana, 341–42.

25. Van Vlack in Berry, *Loss of the* Sultana, 368; Wells, unpublished manuscript, 16–17.

26. Fies and Hodges in Berry, *Loss of the* Sultana, 127, 173.

27. J. T. Elliott, "The *Sultana* Disaster," 174; Robinson in Berry, *Loss of the* Sultana, 301–2.

28. "*Sultana* Wreck: A Canton Survivor Tells the Story of His Escape," *Repository*, October 17, 1897, 10.

29. Oden, "1700 Died When *Sultana* Sank."

30. "Best Bargain He Ever Made Was to Trade a Live Horse for a Dead One," Judith Deaderisle to Jerry Potter, April 24, 1984, courtesy of Jerry O. Potter; Robinson in Berry, *Loss of the* Sultana, 302.

31. "Andrew T. Peery's Story of the Sinking of the *Sultana*," *Maryville Enterprise*, April 30, 1975, 3.

32. J. T. Elliott, "The *Sultana* Disaster," 178–79.

33. Gilbreath reminiscence in Hazzard, *Hazzard's History of Henry County, Indiana*, 611.

CHAPTER 19. THE RESCUES

1. J. H. Curtis, "Only Living Eye-Witness Details *Sultana* Explosion," *Commercial Appeal*, January 25, 1920, 3; "Two Brave Fellows," *Memphis Daily Bulletin*, April 28, 1865, 2.
2. Alvord, Washburn Inquiry, 118–19.
3. Ames Fisher testimony in U.S. Congress, John T. Watson, 43rd Cong., 1st sess., H. Rep. 65, February 4, 1874; *Memphis Argus*, April 28, 1865, 3.
4. Ames Fisher testimony in U.S. Congress, John T. Watson.
5. Rush, Washburn Inquiry, 278–79; Rush in Hawes, *Cahaba*, 196.
6. Karns, "Karns' Reminiscences," *Lewisburg Leader*, April 13, 1898, 1.
7. Alvord and Rowberry, Washburn Inquiry, 111, 119.
8. "*Sultana* Survivor Seeks Companion in Radio Plea," *Columbus Dispatch*, April 27, 1926, 6; Rush, Washburn Inquiry, 278.
9. "Story of the *Sultana*," *Chicago Tribune*, April 22, 1888, 25; Karns, "Karns' Reminiscences," 8.
10. "The *Sultana* Disaster" and "River News," *Daily Missouri Democrat*, December 12, 1871, 4; "River News," *Daily Missouri Democrat*, December 16, 1871, 4.
11. Ames Fisher testimony in U.S. Congress, John T. Watson.
12. Cook in Berry, *Loss of the* Sultana, 101.
13. "The *Sultana* Explosion," *Daily American*, May 9, 1888, 1.
14. Wesley Lee in Berry, *Loss of the* Sultana, 221; Eldridge, "In the *Sultana* Disaster," 7.
15. Fenton Andrew Hussey to his parents, April 30, 1865, *Abraham Lincoln Presidential Library*; "Horrible Disaster on the River," *Memphis Daily Bulletin*, April 28, 1865, 1.
16. "Reminiscence of the War," *Wayne County Democrat*, April 28, 1880; Schmutz in Berry, *Loss of the* Sultana, 311.
17. "The Field of Battle," *Argos Reflector*, May 28, 1903, 6.
18. Floyd, "The Burning of the *Sultana*," 71.
19. "The *Sultana* Tragedy," *Evening Star*, May 17, 1890, 8; Ackley, *Log, January 9–September 25, 1865*, 103; U.S. Congress, Frances L. Ackley, 57th Cong., 1st sess., S. Rep. 1050; U.S. Congress, Frances L. Ackley, 57th Cong., 1st sess., H. Rep. 1160.

20. "The *Sultana* Tragedy," *Evening Star*, May 17, 1890, 8; Michael, "Explosion of the *Sultana*," 257.
21. Michael, unpublished handwritten statement, n.d.; U.S. Congress, Frances L. Ackley, S. Rep. 1050; U.S. Congress, Frances L. Ackley, H. Rep. 1160; Ackley, *Log, January 9–September 25, 1865*, 62; *Davenport Daily Leader*, June 18, 1902, 6.
22. Michael; Frances L. Ackley, S. Rep. 1050; Frances L. Ackley, H. Rep. 1160; Lahue in Berry, *Loss of the* Sultana, 215.
23. "Story of the Loss of the Transport *Sultana*," *Fort Wayne Evening Sentinel*, April 29, 1902, 8.
24. "The Rescue," *Winchester Randolph Journal*, October 11, 1876, 1.
25. Love in Berry, *Loss of the* Sultana, 223.
26. Love, 223; "The Rescue"; "In the River Wreck: The *Sultana* Disaster Recalled to Mind," *Oshkosh Northwestern*, March 30, 1880, 1.
27. J. W. Elliott, "By Fire and Flood," 2; "The *Sultana* Disaster," *Piqua Daily Call*, September 30, 1885, 2.
28. "Work of the Crew of the Gunboat *Essex*," *Memphis Argus*, April 28, 1865, 3; "Veterans Commemorate Greatest River Disaster," *Cleveland Plain Dealer*, January 27, 1918, 4; Horn reminiscence in Howells, "Wooster Men Tell of Civil War Horror," *Canton Daily News*, June 5, 1927, 50.
29. Horn reminiscence in Howells, "Wooster Men Tell of Civil War Horror," *Canton Daily News*, June 5, 1927, 50; "Story of the Loss of the Transport *Sultana*," 8.
30. "Story of the Loss of the Transport *Sultana*."
31. "Story of the Loss of the Transport *Sultana*"; Gilbreath reminiscence in Hazzard, *Hazzard's History of Henry County, Indiana*, 611; Ray in Berry, *Loss of the* Sultana, 297–98; "Letter from Mr. Christy," *Sanitary Reporter*, 187.
32. Horner and Truman Smith in Berry, *Loss of the* Sultana, 180, 327–28.
33. Eldridge, "Some Events at Close of the Civil War," 6; Eldridge, unpublished reminiscence from 1926, 16–17; Eldridge, unpublished reminiscence from 1928, 30–31.
34. J. W. Elliott, "By Fire and Flood," 2; Warner Ogden, "1700 Died When *Sultana* Sank 64 Years Ago," *Knoxville News-Sentinel*, April 28, 1929, 23.
35. Kochenderfer in Berry, *Loss of the* Sultana, 213; "A Survivor from the *Sultana*," 125.
36. Anderson, *The Story of Aunt Lizzie Aiken*, 131–33.

37. Winters, *In the 50th Ohio*, 171–72; Fies in Berry, *Loss of the* Sultana, 131; "Recall *Sultana* Disaster," *Canton Daily News*, April 13, 1930, 31.
38. Irwin, *Court-Martial*, 117.
39. "Nurse Hays Still Living," *Osage City Free Press*, August 24, 1905, 7; "To the Ladies of Memphis," *Memphis Daily Bulletin*, April 30, 1865, 2; Hamilton in Berry, *Loss of the* Sultana, 166.
40. Walker in Hawes, *Cahaba*, 24–25; Thomas Dunn Moore to his parents, April 27, 1865.
41. Foglesang in Berry, *Loss of the* Sultana, 139.
42. Karns, "Karns' Reminiscences," *Lewisburg Leader*, April 20, 1898, 1, 8.
43. McFarland in Berry, *Loss of the* Sultana, 250; "William S. Friesner of Logan Commanded Detail on Ill-Fated *Sultana*," *Logan Daily News*, June 27, 1966, 26.
44. McFarland, 250–51.
45. Dixon, "Aboard the *Sultana*," 39; James M. McCown, Invalid Pension Application, March 14, 1888.
46. Young in Hawes, *Cahaba*, 190; Varnell in Berry, *Loss of the* Sultana, 370.
47. Walker in Hawes, *Cahaba*, 25; "*Sultana* Disaster Is Recalled to Mind," *Athens Daily Messenger*, May 3, 1912, 1.
48. "Scattering," *National Tribune*, August 16, 1906, 3; J. W. Elliott, "By Fire and Flood," 2; McLeod in Berry, *Loss of the* Sultana, 256–57.
49. Elliott, 2.
50. Samuel Pickens to Cynthia and Mary Pickens, April 28, 1865.

CHAPTER 20. THE LONG-AWAITED DAYBREAK

1. Cheek to Maj. Gen. Curtis, Com. Porter, and Maj. Gen. Hurlbut, n.d., Civil War, Union Citizens File, Cheek, Elijah, p. 2, www.fold3.com.
2. "Mound City Destroyed," *Commercial Appeal*, February 3, 1863, 3; Judge King to A. Johnston, May 5, 1863, Civil War, Union Citizens File, Cheek, Elijah, 12, www.fold3.com.
3. "Sunday Is Anniversary of *Sultana* Explosion," *Evening Times*, April 25, 1969, 10.

4. Civil War, Civil War Service Records, Confederate Records, Arkansas, Miscellaneous, Arkansas, A-I, B, Barton, F H, www.fold3.com; Atchley in Berry, *Loss of the* Sultana, 36.

5. Young in Hawes, *Cahaba*, 188–90.

6. Albert W. King in Berry, *Loss of the* Sultana, 203–4.

7. Young in Hawes, *Cahaba*, 190; Hamblin in Berry, *Loss of the* Sultana, 163.

8. "Andrew T. Peery's Story of the Sinking of the *Sultana*," *Maryville Enterprise*, April 30, 1975, 3.

9. Hamilton and Pangle in Berry, *Loss of the* Sultana, 166, 281.

10. "Andrew T. Peery's Story"; Thrasher in Berry, *Loss of the* Sultana, 357.

11. "A Horrid Scene," *Memphis Argus*, April 28, 1865, 3; Hamilton in Berry, *Loss of the* Sultana, 166.

12. Fast in Hawes, *Cahaba*, 170–71.

13. Fast, 171–72.

14. Fast, 172; "Andrew T. Peery's Story."

15. "Andrew T. Peery's Story"; "A Visit to the Wreck," *Memphis Argus*, April 28, 1865, 3.

16. John Fogleman tax assessment, 1861; Porteous, "Great Mystery of River: 1450 Died in Sinking of *Sultana*," *Press-Scimitar*, April 26, 1946; "Sunday Is Anniversary of *Sultana* Explosion"; Fast in Hawes, *Cahaba*, 172.

17. Fast, 172.

18. Fast, 172–73; Davenport, "Story of the *Sultana* Steamboat," unpublished manuscript, n.d.

19. Fast, 173–74.

20. Fast, 174.

21. Thrasher in Berry, *Loss of the* Sultana, 357; Dougherty, *The Prison Diary of Michael Dougherty*, 68; "River News," *Memphis Daily Bulletin*, May 2, 1865, 4.

22. "River News."

23. "Andrew T. Peery's Story"; Hamilton in Berry, *Loss of the* Sultana, 166.

24. "Acts of Daring," *Memphis Argus*, April 28, 1865, 3; "Charitable," *Memphis Daily Bulletin*, April 29, 1865, 3.

25. "John L. Walker, Hamilton's Sole Survivor of the *Sultana* Horror," *Butler County Democrat*, July 1, 1905, 3; "Statement of W. D. Snow, Congressman-Elect from Arkansas," *Memphis Daily Bulletin*, April 28, 1865, 1.

26. Truman Smith in Berry, *Loss of the* Sultana, 328; White in Hawes, *Cahaba*, 179–80.

27. Karns, "Karns' Reminiscences," *Lewisburg Leader*, April 20, 1898, 1.

28. Brady in Berry, *Loss of the* Sultana, 66–67.

29. Nisley, Washburn Inquiry, 126.

30. "River News," *Daily Missouri Democrat*, December 21, 1871, 4; "The *Sultana* Disaster," *Daily Missouri Democrat*, December 22, 1871, 4.

31. Ames Fisher testimony in U.S. Congress, John T. Watson, 43rd Cong., 1st sess., H. Rep. 65, February 4, 1874; Hulit in Berry, *Loss of the* Sultana, 184; "Letter from Mr. Rush," *Sandusky Register*, May 10, 1865, 3.

32. "William S. Friesner of Logan Commanded Detail on Ill-Fated *Sultana*," *Logan Daily News*, June 27, 1966, 26. Two buttons from Friesner's coat are on display in the *Sultana* Disaster Museum, Marion, AR.

33. "Horrible Disaster on the River," "Caring for the Living and the Dead," and "Horribly Scalded," *Memphis Daily Bulletin*, April 28, 1865, 2; "A Touching Incident," *Memphis Argus*, April 28, 1865, 3; "Supposed Recognition," *Memphis Daily Bulletin*, April 29, 1865, 3.

34. "Statement of Mr. Henry Seman," *Memphis Argus*, April 29, 1865, 3.

35. "Statement of Mr. Henry Seman"; Bracken, "The *Sultana* Disaster," 3; Rosselot in Berry, *Loss of the* Sultana, 306–7.

36. "A Plucky Sergeant," *Memphis Daily Bulletin*, April 28, 1865, 2.

37. Joseph Norton in Berry, *Loss of the* Sultana, 269.

38. McCrory in Berry, *Loss of the* Sultana, 244–46.

39. Fast in Hawes, *Cahaba*, 176.

40. Homer, "Personal Experience of Jacob Homer as a Prisoner of War," in Schmutz, *History of the 102d Regiment, OVI*, 245; Sharp, "The *Sultana* Horror," *National Tribune*, July 7, 1921.

41. "A Horrid Scene," *Memphis Argus*, April 28, 1865, 3.

42. "Letter from Mr. Christy," *Sanitary Reporter*, 187.

43. Hamblin in Berry, *Loss of the* Sultana, 163–64.

44. "Relief for the *Sultana* Sufferers," *Memphis Daily Bulletin*, May 4, 1865, 3; "*Sultana* Disaster Is Recalled to Mind," *Athens Daily Messenger*, May 3, 1912, 1; "Findlay Survivor Tells Story of *Sultana* Wreck," *Toledo Daily Blade*, May 1, 1912, 10; "Commendable," *Memphis Daily Bulletin*, April 29, 1865, 3.

45. "A Struggle for Life," *Chicago Tribune*, May 13, 1865, 2; Sprinkle in Berry, *Loss of the* Sultana, 332; "Death of Columbus *Sultana* Survivor," *Repository*, July 6, 1906, 13.

46. "*Sultana* Disaster: A Survivor Tells of a Terrible Experience and His Escape," *National Tribune*, May 10, 1900, 7.

CHAPTER 21. MORNING IN MEMPHIS

1. P. Steve Millard to author, January 8, 1994.
2. Nathan Williams in Berry, *Loss of the* Sultana, 378–79.
3. "Terrible Steamboat Disaster," *Lebanon Patriot*, May 4, 1865.
4. Jones to his brother, April 29, 1865, "The *Sultana* Affair—Further Particulars," *Summit County Beacon*, May 5, 1865, 2.
5. Solomon Bogart to Mrs. M. S. Misimer, April 30, 1865.
6. Winters, *In the 50th Ohio*, 172; Sharp, "The *Sultana* Horror," *National Tribune*, July 7, 1921; Feagin, "God Forgive Them, I Can't," *Dayton Daily News*, January 1906, www.ancestry.com.
7. Various hospital lists, *Memphis Argus*, April 28 and 29, 1865; *Memphis Daily Bulletin*, April 28, 1865; *Daily Missouri Democrat*, May 1, 1865; *Daily Missouri Republican*, May 1, 1865; *Cincinnati Daily Commercial*, May 2, 1865; *Cincinnati Daily Gazette*, May 2, 1865.
8. "Appalling Marine Casualty," *Memphis Argus*, April 28, 1865, 3; "Mrs. Lieutenant Ennis," *Memphis Argus*, April 29, 1865, 3; "To the Ladies of Memphis," *Memphis Daily Bulletin*, April 30, 1865, 2; "A Laudable Enterprise," *Memphis Daily Bulletin*, May 3, 1865, 3.
9. Rush in Hawes, *Cahaba*, 194; Winters, *In the 50th Ohio*, 169.
10. "Incidents of the Calamity," "Drowning of a Little Girl," and "A Woman and Child," *Memphis Daily Bulletin*, April 28, 1865, 2; "Incidents of the Burning of the *Sultana*," *Sandusky Register*, May 17, 1865, 2
11. "A Horrid Scene" and "The Number of Dead Found," *Memphis Argus*, April 28, 1865, 3.
12. "Charitable," *Memphis Daily Bulletin*, April 29, 1865, 3.
13. Sarah Woolfolk, www.findagrave.com; Woolfolk obituary, *Lexington Observer*, May 20, 1865, np.
14. "Local News—Bodies Found," *Memphis Daily Bulletin*, May 4, 1865, 3; "Local News—Bodies Found" and "River News—The Wreck," *Memphis Daily Bulletin*, May 5, 1865, 3.

15. "Another Search after *Sultana* Victims," *Memphis Argus*, May 13, 1865, 3.

16. "Reward" and "Lost," *Memphis Daily Bulletin*, April 28, 1865, 3; "Reward," *Memphis Daily Bulletin*, April 30, 1865, 3; "$200 Reward," *Memphis Daily Bulletin*, May 2, 1865, 3; "$100 Reward," *Memphis Daily Bulletin*, May 3, 1865, 3; "$100 Reward," *Memphis Daily Bulletin*, May 13, 1865, 2; "A Liberal Reward," *Memphis Daily Bulletin*, May 13, 1865, 3; "$200 Reward," *Memphis Daily Bulletin*, May 23, 1865, 3.

17. "The Wreck of the *Sultana*: Shameful Conduct," *Memphis Daily Bulletin*, May 7, 1865, 3; "The Dead of the *Sultana*: Their Treatment," *Memphis Daily Bulletin*, May 9, 1865, 3.

18. "River News—Rising," *Memphis Daily Bulletin*, May 6, 1865, 3; "The *Sultana* Disaster," *Evansville Daily Journal*, May 11, 1865, 2; "Wayside Glimpses," *Boston Traveler*, May 25, 1865, 1.

19. "*Sultana* Disaster Is Recalled by Capt. Abel, the Provost Marshal," *Decatur Herald*, April 21, 1912, 16.

20. Parks, "The *Sultana* Disaster," 6.

21. Clark to Helen, May 12, 1865; "Heartless if True," *Memphis Daily Bulletin*, May 19, 1865, 3.

22. "Dead Bodies Below," *Memphis Argus*, May 11, 1865, 3; "From Below," *Memphis Argus*, May 12, 1865, 2.

23. "Explosion of the *David White*," *Lafayette Daily Journal*, February 23, 1867, 1.

24. "A Funeral of Eleven," *Memphis Argus*, May 6, 1865, 3.

25. Clough, "Burning of the Flagship *Black Hawk*," 3; "The Wreck of the *Sultana*," *Memphis Daily Bulletin*, May 7, 1865, 3; "River News" and "Health Report," *Memphis Daily Bulletin*, May 9, 1865, 3; Aldrich, *Cahawba Prison*, 18.

26. "The Body of George Slater," *Memphis Argus*, May 10, 1865, 3.

27. "Twenty-One Hundred Souls on Board," *Memphis Argus*, April 28, 1865, 1; "Over a Thousand Lives Lost," *Memphis Daily Bulletin*, April 28, 1865, 2; "Special Dispatch to the *Missouri Democrat*," *Daily Missouri Democrat*, April 29, 1865, 1; "The *Sultana* Disaster," *Daily Missouri Republican*, April 29, 1865, 2; *New York Times*, May 3, 1865, 1.

28. Hoffman to Stanton, May 19, 1865, ORs, ser. 1, vol. 48, pt. 1, 216–17.

29. Williams and Shull, *Court-Martial*, 13–14, 144.

30. Holt to the Adjutant General, February 25, 1865, Civil War, *Sultana* Disaster, April 27, 1865, Quartermaster vessel file relating to the *Sultana*, 68–69, www.fold3.com; "Report in the Case of Survivors of the Steamer *Sultana*," 51st Cong., 1st sess., War Department, Civil War, *Sultana* Disaster, April 27, 1865, Enlisted Branch file (HAAQ 981 EB 1865), 80, www.fold3.com.

31. Aldrich, "Cahawba Prison," *National Tribune*, July 31, 1884, 7; "The Dear Old Flag," *Coshocton Semi-Weekly Age*, February 12, 1886, 1; J. W. Elliott, "By Fire and Flood"; "*Sultana* Survivors Meet," *Newark Daily Advocate*, April 28, 1888, 1; "Sultana Survivors," *Asheville Citizen*, April 27, 1901, 1; "The Story of the Loss of the Transport *Sultana*," *Fort Wayne Evening Sentinel*, April 29, 1902, 9; Warner Ogden, "1700 Died When *Sultana* Sank 64 Years Ago," *Knoxville News-Sentinel*, April 28, 1929, 23.

32. "*Titanic* Victims," Titanic *Facts: The Life & Loss of the RMS* Titanic *in Numbers*, https://titanicfacts.net/titanic-victims/; "More Lives Lost in Mississippi River," *Alton Evening Telegraph*, April 20, 1912, 7; "*Sultana* Disaster Greater than *Titanic*," *Elkhart Daily Review*, April 29, 1912, 3; "Disaster More Appalling than *Titanic* Wreck," *Pensacola Journal*, May 25, 1912, 3.

33. Wright, "Ghosts of Cahaba."

34. "Twenty-One Hundred Souls on Board," 1; "Over a Thousand Lives Lost," 1; J. W. Elliott, "By Fire and Flood," 2; Bardon and Brown in Berry, *Loss of the* Sultana, 39, 77.

35. Berry, Clinger, Benjamin G. Davis, Gaston, Kinzer, McFarland, Raudebaugh, George F. Robinson, Schmutz, Commodore Smith, Van Nuys, and Varnell in Berry, *Loss of the* Sultana, 8, 97, 103, 150, 206, 248, 291, 301, 310, 319, 360, 370; "Commemoration of Heroic Deeds on Ill-Fated Boat," *Knoxville Sentinel*, April 27, 1912; "Findlay Survivor Tells Story of *Sultana* Wreck," *Toledo Daily Blade*, May 1, 1912, 10; "Soldiers' Home," *Star Journal*, April 1, 1922, 7; "Only Survivor *Sultana* Disaster at Soldiers' Home Tells Experience," *Register*, April 16, 1922, 16.

36. "Not Less than 1,400 Lives Lost," *Memphis Daily Bulletin*, April 28, 1865, 2; "Special Dispatch to the *Missouri Democrat*," 1; "The *Sultana* Disaster," *New York Times*, May 1, 1865, 1; "The *Sultana* Disaster," *Cincinnati Daily Enquirer*, May 3, 1865, 1; "The *Sultana* Disaster," *Cincinnati Daily Commercial*, May 4, 1865, 2.

37. "Report in the Case of Survivors of the Steamer *Sultana*."

38. "Larned Chronoscope," *Topeka Daily Capital*, April 21, 1886, 3; "The Story of the Loss of the Transport *Sultana*," *Fort Wayne Evening Sentinel*, April 29, 1902, 7; "*Sultana* Survivors," *Sandusky Star Journal*, April 27, 1911, 8; "Findlay Survivor Tells Story of *Sultana* Wreck," *Toledo Daily Blade*, May 1, 1912, 10; "Only Survivor *Sultana* Disaster."

39. Snow, Washburn Inquiry, 113.

40. "River News," *Daily Missouri Republican*, April 29, 1865, 3; "Second Dispatch," *Cincinnati Commercial Tribune*, April 29, 1865, 3; "Terrible Disaster," *Chicago Tribune*, April 29, 1865, 2.

41. "The Great Disaster," *Spirit of Democracy*, May 31, 1865, 2.

42. "Charges and Specifications," *Court-Martial*, 5–7; "A Horrible Holocaust!," *Evening Tribune*, June 15, 1904, 1; "1,000 Lives May Be Lost in Burning of Excursion Boat *Gen. Slocum*," *New York Times*, June 15, 1904, 1; G. King, "A Spectacle of Horror—the Burning of the *General Slocum*."

43. All figures taken from Miller, *The Photographic History of the Civil War*, pt. 10, 142, 144.

44. Squire to L. W. Day, March 29, 1886; Brown in Berry, *Loss of the Sultana*, 79; LaPointe, "Military Hospitals in Memphis, 1861–1865," 341.

45. Adams Hospital and Gayoso Hospital lists, *Daily Missouri Democrat*, May 1, 1865, 3; Adams Hospital and Gayoso Hospital lists, *Daily Missouri Republican*, May 1, 1865, 3; "Minstrel Concert on Behalf of the *Sultana* Sufferers," *Memphis Daily Bulletin*, April 29, 1865, 3; "Relief Fund for the Sufferers by the *Sultana* Disaster," *Memphis Argus*, May 27, 1865, 3, and *Memphis Daily Bulletin*, May 27, 1865, 3. The ten severely scalded soldiers who received relief money were Pvt. John Archer (Co. F, 90th OH Inf), $25; Louis Bean (Co. A, 6th KY Cav), $50; Sgt. Charles C. Curry (Co. D, 6th KY Cav), $48; Pvt. Seth J. Green (Co. K, 9th IN Cav), $10; Cpl. Benjamin Franklin Learner (Co. G, 57th IN Inf), $50; Pvt. John William Norcutt (Co. D, 18th MI Inf), $10; Pvt. Thomas S. Smith (Co. E, 18th MI Inf), $25; Cpl. Silas W. Wade (Co. C, 3rd TN Cav), $50; 1st Sgt. William D. Wade (Co. B, 3rd TN Cav), $100; and Cpl. James E. White (Co. D, 11th TN Cav), $15.

46. *Register of Deaths of Volunteers, 1861–1865*, Kentucky, L–Z, Marshall, 44, www.ancestry.com; "Certificate," Civil War, Civil War Service Records, Union Records, Tennessee, First Cavalry, T, Taylor,

Henry F., 17; "Nelson D. Voglesong . . . ," *Detroit Advertiser and Tribune*, July 11, 1865, 5.

47. "Decidedly Unpleasant," *Public Ledger*, February 4, 1867, 3; "Honors to Loyal Dead," *Memphis Evening Post*, June 1, 1868, 5; U.S. Veterans Administration, *Memphis National Cemetery*, 1.

48. "Explosion of the *David White*," 1; Potter to author, July 30, 2019.

49. "Union Soldiers Interred in Southern Cemeteries," *New York Herald*, October 27, 1869, 7; "Decoration Day," *Daily Arkansas Gazette*, May 31, 1871, 1.

CHAPTER 22. SPREADING THE WORD

1. "Latest by Telegraph," *Cleveland Leader*, May 1, 1865, 1; "Frightful Steamboat Explosion," *The Age*, April 29, 1865, 2.

2. "Appalling Calamity! 1400 Lives Lost!," *New York Tribune*, April 29, 1865, 8; "Miscellaneous News," *New York Herald*, April 29, 1865, 5; "Frightful Steamboat Explosion"; "Horrible Steamboat Disaster!," *Boston Daily Advertiser*, April 29, 1865, 1; "Terrible Casualty," *Boston Herald*, April 29, 1865, 2; "Explosion of the *Sultana*," *Cleveland Leader*, April 27, 1865, 1; "Appalling Steamboat Disaster near Memphis," *Chicago Tribune*, April 29, 1865, 2; "Terrible Loss of Life on a Mississippi Steamer," *Daily National Republican*, April 29, 1865; "Steamboat Explosion on the Mississippi," *Evening Star*, April 29, 1865, 1; "Terrible Accident on the Mississippi," *Daily Eastern Argus*, April 29, 1865, 2; "Terrible Steamboat Accident," *Daily Illinois State Register*, April 29, 1865, 1.

3. "Steamer Accident and Loss of Life," *Sacramento Bee*, April 29, 1865, 4; "Miscellaneous Items," *San Francisco Bulletin*, April 29, 1865, 2; "Terrible Steamboat Explosion," *Gold Hill Daily News*, April 29, 1865, 3; "The News," *Denver Rocky Mountain News*, May 3, 1865, 2; "Latest News by Telegraph," *Weekly Champion and Press*, May 4, 1865, 2; "The Most Fearful Steamboat Accident," *Nebraska Advertiser*, May 4, 1865, 3; "Telegraphic News," *Montana Post*, May 13, 1865, 2; "Telegraphic News," *Oregon State Journal*, May 13, 1865, 1.

4. "From Memphis," *Indianapolis Star*, April 29, 1865, 3; "Terrible Accident on the Mississippi," *Daily Ohio Statesman*, April 29, 1865, 3; "Explosion of the *Sultana*," *Cleveland Leader*, April 29, 1865, 1; "Steamer Blown Up—Terrible Loss of Life," *Cleveland Plain Dealer*, April 29, 1865; "Terrible Explosion on the Mississippi River,"

Detroit Free Press, April 29, 1865, 1; "Terrible Explosion," *Milwaukee Sentinel*, April 29, 1865, 4; "Terrible Accident," *Daily Milwaukee News*, April 29, 1865, 1; "Terrible Accident on the Mississippi River," *Daily Davenport Democrat*, May 1, 1865, 2; "Latest News," *St. Cloud Democrat*, May 4, 1865, 3.

5. "Horrible Disaster on the River," *Western Clarion*, April 29, 1865, 2; "List of Paroled Prisoners from Camp Fisk, on Board the Ill-fated Steamer *Sultana*," *Vicksburg Daily Herald* supplement, April 30, 1865; Civil War, *Sultana* Disaster, April 1865, *Cincinnati Daily Commercial*, May 2, 1865, and *Vicksburg Daily Herald*, 7–10, www.fold3.com; "Loss of the Steamer *Sultana*," *New-Orleans Times*, May 1, 1865, 1; "The Steamer *Sultana*," *Times-Picayune*, May 3, 1865, 3.

6. "Terrible Steamboat Accident," *Commercial Bulletin*, May 6, 1865, 4; "Terrible Steamboat Accident," *Daily Constitutionalist*, May 6, 1865, 1; "Terrible Steamboat Accident," *Atlanta Weekly Intelligencer*, May 10, 1865, 3; "Awful Steamboat Disaster," *Macon Telegraph*, May 18, 1865, 1; "The *Sultana* Disaster," *Charleston Courier*, May 12, 1865, 1.

7. "Disastrous Steamboat Accident," *Halifax Citizen*, April 29, 1865, 2; "By Telegraph—General Press Dispatches," *Montreal Herald and Daily Commercial Gazette*, May 1, 1865, 3; "Explosion of the Steamer *Sultana*," *New Westminster British Columbian*, May 2, 1865, 3; "Explosion of the Steamer *Sultana*," *Quebec Gazette*, May 5, 1865, 2; "Frightful Steamboat Explosion," *London Express*, May 10, 1865, 2; "Summary of News—Foreign," *London Guardian*, May 11, 1865, 2; "Latest Intelligence—America," *The Times*, May 11, 1865, 7; "Terrible Steamboat Explosion," *Melbourne Age*, July 17, 1865.

8. "The Wreck of the *Sultana*," *Harper's Weekly*, May 13, 1865, 291; "Explosion of the Steamer *Sultana*, April 28, 1865," *Harper's Weekly*, May 20, 1865, pl. 316.

9. *New York Tribune*, April 29, May 1, 2, 3, 5, 9, 10, 12, 13, 22, 23, 26, 31, 1865.

10. *Daily National Intelligencer*, April 29, May 1, 2, 4, 5, 6, 8, 9, 11, 1865; *Daily National Republican*, April 29, May 1, 2, 4, 9, 19, 27, 1865; *Boston Herald*, April 29, May 1, 2, 3, 8, 9, 11, 16, 20, 27, 1865; *The Age*, April 29, May 1, 2, 3, 10, 17, 25, 30, 1865; *The Press*, April 29, May 1, 2, 3, 5, 9, 10, 26, 1865; *Hartford Daily Courant*, April 29, May 1, 2, 3, 5, 6, 11, 13, 15, 1865.

11. *Chicago Tribune*, April 29, 30, May 1, 2, 3, 4, 5, 6, 9, 10, 11, 13, 15, 18, 22, 24, 30, 1865.

12. *Cincinnati Daily Enquirer*, April 29, May 1, 2, 4, 6, 8, 9, 10, 11, 17, 24, 25, 26, June 2, 1865.

13. *Cleveland Leader*, April 29, May 1, 2, 3, 4, 6, 9, 10, 11, 16, 25, 1865; *Cleveland Plain Dealer*, April 29, May 1, 2, 3, 4, 8, 10, 24, 25, 27, June 2, 1865; *Daily Ohio Statesman*, April 29, May 1, 3, 4, 5, 9, 10, 16, 19, 25, 1865.

14. *Ashland Union*, May 3, 10, 24, June 14, 1865; Graham, *History of Richland County, Ohio*, 365.

15. *Indianapolis Star*, April 29, May 1, 2, 4, 10, 11, 1865; *Daily State Sentinel*, April 29, May 1, 2, 4, 10, 11, 1865; *Indianapolis Daily Gazette*, May 3, 1865; *Evansville Daily Journal*, May 1, 4, 5, 8, 9, 10, 12, 20, 1865; *Richmond Palladium*, May 4, 11, 17, 25, June 1, 1865.

16. *Detroit Advertiser and Tribune*, May 16, 23, 30, June 6, 1865; *Detroit Free Press*, April 29, 30, May 1, 2, 4, 5, 9, 10, 11, 20, 26, 29, 30, 31, June 15, 1865.

17. *Hillsdale Standard*, May 2, 9, 16, 23, 30, June 6, 13, 1865.

18. *Louisville Daily Journal*, April 29, 30, May 2, 3, 7, 9, 10, 11, 1865.

19. *Brownlow's Knoxville Whig and Rebel Ventilator*, May 17, 31, 1865; *Nashville Daily Union*, May 3, 4, 1865.

20. "Quartermaster General Circular, May 2, 1865," Civil War, Sultana Disaster, April 1865, Quartermaster vessel file relating to the *Sultana*, 64–65, www.fold3.com.

21. "Adventure on a Western River," *Indianapolis Journal*, December 27, 1903, 2; "On a Western River," *Hutchinson Daily News*, January 29, 1890, 1; American Queen Steamboat Company, *Essential Travel Guide*, 14–15.

22. "In relation to the *Sultana*," *New-Orleans Times*, July 2, 1865, 8; Way, *Way's Packer Directory*, 327–27, 477; "The *Linnie Drown*," *Cincinnati Daily Enquirer*, March 10, 1866, 4.

23. "The *Doubloon*," *Times-Picayune*, March 13, 1866, 3; advertisement for *Planter*, *Times-Picayune*, March 15, 1866, 11; "More about Tubulars," *Daily Missouri Democrat*, April 3, 1866, 3.

24. "Cause of Boiler Explosions," *Louisville Daily Courier*, December 29, 1866, 4; "The Steamboatmens' Convention at St. Louis," *Evening Argus*, May 18, 1867, 3.

25. "At Coshocton, Pa.," *Richmond Palladium*, November 21, 1867, 5; "Terrible Steamboat Disaster," *Memphis Daily Avalanche*, January 7, 1869, 3; "River News," *Cincinnati Daily Gazette*, March 26, 1869, 4.

26. "The *Sultana* Disaster," company history on back of 1990 vacation calendar of the Hartford Steam Boiler Inspection and Insurance Company; "Hartford Steam Boiler Inspection and Insurance Company," *Weekly Underwriter*, 58.

27. Hunter, *Steamboats on the Western Rivers*, 544.

CHAPTER 23. DISCHARGED

1. Karns, "Karns' Reminiscences," *Lewisburg Leader*, April 27, 1898, 1; W. Rule, "The Long Walk Home," 3. The grapevine cane is still in the Rule family.

2. Friesner, *Court-Martial*, 114; "River News: Arrivals," *Memphis Daily Bulletin*, April 29, 1865, 3; "River News: Departures," *Memphis Argus*, April 30, 1865, 3; "Port List," *Daily Missouri Democrat*, May 1, 1865, 4.

3. Lugenbeal and Rosselot in Berry, *Loss of the* Sultana, 227, 307; Sharp, "The *Sultana* Disaster."

4. "Terrible Steamboat Disaster," *Lebanon Patriot*, May 4, 1865; Karns, "Karns' Reminiscences," 1; "River's Shifting Sands Uncover Grim Reminder of the Mississippi's Most Terrible Tragedy," *St. Louis Post-Dispatch*, February 8, 1920, 75. Karns stated that he was taken to Cairo on the *Belle Memphis*, but the actions of the survivors and the timeline for their arrival at Cairo coincide more with the group of survivors who traveled on the *Belle St. Louis*.

5. Garber in Berry, *Loss of the* Sultana, 148.

6. Rosselot in Berry, *Loss of the* Sultana, 307; Wells, unpublished manuscript, 19.

7. Hamilton in Berry, *Loss of the* Sultana, 166–67.

8. Karns, "Karns' Reminiscences," 8.

9. Karns; Chelf and Garber in Berry, *Loss of the* Sultana, 91, 148–49; Wells, unpublished manuscript, 19.

10. "From Columbus," *Cincinnati Commercial Tribune*, May 4, 1865, 2; "Items of State News," *Morgan County Gazette*, May 6, 1865, 2.

11. "From Columbus."

12. J. W. Elliott, "By Fire and Flood."

13. Bringman in Berry, *Loss of the* Sultana, 72; Fast in Hawes, *Cahaba*, 174.

14. *Indianapolis Journal* quoted in "A Generous Deed," *Memphis Daily Bulletin*, May 10, 1865, 2; Eldridge, unpublished reminiscence, 1928, 34.

15. "Cairo Port List," *Daily Missouri Republican*, May 3, 1865, 3; "*Sultana* Disaster: A Survivor Tells of a Terrible Experience and His Escape," *National Tribune*, May 10, 1900, 7; Karns, "Karns' Reminiscences," 1.

16. Brady in Berry, *Loss of the* Sultana, 67; Karns, 1.

17. J. W. Elliott, "By Fire and Flood"; Karns; "The *Sultana* Disaster by a Survivor of One of the Civil War's Greatest Tragedies," *Kansas City Star*, May 14, 1909, 1; "*Sultana* Disaster: A Survivor Tells of a Terrible Experience and His Escape," 7.

18. Brady in Berry, *Loss of the* Sultana, 67–68; Homer, "Personal Experience of Jacob Homer as a Prisoner of War," in Schmutz, *History of the 102d Regiment, OVI*, 246.

19. J. W. Elliott, "By Fire and Flood"; Brady, 68.

20. "A *Sultana* Survivor," *Indianapolis News*, September 6, 1893, 14; "The Steamer *Sultana*," *Kokomo Daily Gazette Tribune*, February 7, 1893, 4; "From Indianapolis," *Cincinnati Daily Enquirer*, May 9, 1865, 3; "Items of State News," *Morgan County Gazette*, May 6, 1865, 2.

21. Brady and Fies in Berry, *Loss of the* Sultana, 68, 132–33.

22. "The *Sultana* Disaster by a Survivor of One of the Civil War's Greatest Tragedies."

23. "Soldier's Reunion," *Evansville Journal*, March 6, 1886, 4; "Survivor of the *Sultana* Disaster Lives Over Terrible Experience," *Repository*, September 17, 1911, 13.

24. "Soldiers' Reunion"; "Survivor of the *Sultana* Disaster Lives Over Terrible Experience."

25. Walker, *Cahaba Prison*, 28–29; James King Ashley, Civil War manuscript, n.d., 112.

26. Winters, *In the 50th Ohio*, 173, 176–77.

27. Winters, 177–79.

28. Young in Hawes, *Cahaba*, 191.

29. Haines in Berry, *Loss of the* Sultana, 160.

30. "From Washington," *The Age*, April 29, 1865, 2; Davenport, "Story of the *Sultana* Steamboat," unpublished manuscript, n.d.; Linginfelter letter from pension file in the National Archives, n.d.

31. "Civil War Reminiscence," *Plainville Times*, May 28, 1908, 2; Wolverton to *Memphis Commercial Appeal*, January 29, 1920, in C. M. Elliott and Moxley, *Tennessee Civil War Veterans Questionnaires*, vol. 1, 146; Eldridge, unpublished manuscript, 1928, n.p.

32. "Arrival of Michigan Soldiers Saved from the *Sultana*," *Jackson Citizen Patriot*, May 18, 1865, 1; Wells, unpublished reminiscence, 19; Koon reminiscence from the Hudson, MI, paper of March 28, 1884, http://www.bksphoto.com/p344726312/h47d82551#h47d815d.

33. Van Vlack in Berry, *Loss of the* Sultana, 369; "*Sultana* Disaster: A Survivor Tells of a Terrible Experience and His Escape," 7.

34. Clinger and Thrasher in Berry, *Loss of the* Sultana, 99, 357–58.

35. Civil War, Civil War Service Records, Union Records, West Virginia, Fourth Cavalry, W, Woodward, Taylor, www.fold3.com.

36. Civil War, Civil War Service Records, Union Records, Virginia, Loudon County Rangers, A-Mi, B, Bull, William, www.fold3.com; Bull reminiscence in Fluharty, *On the Way Home*, 132.

37. Dougherty, *The Prison Diary of Michael Dougherty*, 68; Sharp and Dunnigan, *Congressional Medal of Honor*, 765.

38. Rush in Hawes, *Cahaba*, 199.

39. Bringman and Horner in Berry, *Loss of the* Sultana, 72, 181; "John L. Walker, Hamilton's Sole Survivor of the *Sultana* Horror," *Butler County Democrat*, June 1, 1905, 11; Winters, *In the 50th Ohio*, 178; Walker, *Cahaba Prison*, 29.

40. "Frightful Steamboat Explosion," *The Age*, April 29, 1865, 2; "Further Particulars," *Milwaukee Sentinel*, May 4, 1865, 1; "Home Items," *Holmes County Farmer and Free Press*, May 4, 1865, 4; "The Sultana Disaster," *Daily Missouri Democrat*, June 19, 1865, 4; "River News," *Memphis Daily Bulletin*, May 6, 1865, 2.

41. "The *Sultana* Explosion—Some New Developments," *Memphis Argus*, April 30, 1865, 3; "Relief Fund for the Sufferers by the *Sultana* Disaster," *Memphis Argus*, May 27, 1865, 3, and *Memphis Daily Bulletin*, May 27, 1865, 3.

42. "A Laudable Enterprise," *Memphis Daily Bulletin*, May 3, 1865, 3; "Laudable," *Memphis Daily Bulletin*, May 5, 1865, 3; "Contributions," *Memphis Argus*, May 11, 1865, 3.

43. "McMinn Countian Recalls Escape from the '*Sultana*' Fifty-Eight Years Ago When 1,238 Lost Lives," *Knoxville Sentinel*, December

8, 1923; Huddle and Huddle, *History of the Descendants of John Hottel*, 667.

CHAPTER 24. THE INVESTIGATIONS

1. Special Orders No. 109, April 27, 1865, *Court-Martial*, 46.
2. "Browne, Thomas McClelland," *U.S. Politicians—All Your United States Politicians*, https://www.unitedstatespolitics.org/thomas-mclelland-browne/; Pivany, *Hungarians in the American Civil War*, 19, 58; Rombauer, Maj. Raphael Guido, memorial information, https://www.findagrave.com/memorial/116037267/raphael-guido-rombauer; Cullom, *Biographical Register of the Officers and Graduates of the U.S. Military Academy at West Point*, vol. 2, 194; Lash, *A Politician Turned General*, 136.
3. Washburn to Stanton, April 28, 1865, ORs, ser. 1, vol. 48, pt. 2, 233.
4. Cayton and Rowberry, Washburn Inquiry, 109–12.
5. Snow and Lewis, Washburn Inquiry, 112–18.
6. Clemens, Washburn Inquiry, 118.
7. Alvord and Geins, Washburn Inquiry, 118–23.
8. Friesner, Nisley, Hake, and Rush, Washburn Inquiry, 124–29; Parsons to Thomas, April 29, 1865, Civil War, *Sultana* Disaster, April 27, 1865, Quartermaster vessel file relating to the *Sultana*, 61–62, www.fold3.com.
9. "The Disaster on the Mississippi," *The Age*, April 29, 1865, 2.
10. "The *Sultana* Disaster," *Memphis Argus*, April 30, 1865, 2.
11. Stanton to Washburn, *Court-Martial*, 45.
12. Special Orders No. 195, April 30, 1865, ORs, ser. 1, vol. 48, pt. 2, 247.
13. Simon, *The Papers of Ulysses S. Grant, May 1–December 31, 1865*, 533.
14. Postal, Washburn Inquiry, 130–31.
15. Curtis, Washburn Inquiry, 131–2; "Was It a Fiendish Atrocity?" and "River News," *Memphis Daily Bulletin*, May 2, 1865, 4; "Latest by Telegraph—Second Dispatch," *Cincinnati Commercial Tribune*, April 29, 1865, 3.
16. "Circular—Quartermaster General's Office," May 2, 1865, and Meigs to Stanton, May 2, 1865, Civil War, *Sultana* Disaster, April 27, 1865, Quartermaster vessel file relating to the *Sultana*, 64–65, 90, www.fold3.com.
17. Special Orders No. 114, May 2, 1865, *Court-Martial*, 66.

18. "The *Sultana* Disaster," *Memphis Daily Bulletin*, May 4, 1865, 3; "Lt. Col. Badeau," *Memphis Daily Bulletin*, May 6, 1865, 2.

19. "River News—The Wreck," *Memphis Daily Bulletin*, May 5, 1865, 3. The article incorrectly lists Mason's brother-in-law as "Captain Osier."

20. "Editor Memphis Bulletin," *Memphis Daily Bulletin*, May 6, 1865, 3.

21. Dana Commission, 134; Washburn Inquiry, 193.

22. Kerns, Mitchell, Dunton, Jones, and Tillinghast, Washburn Inquiry, 193–211.

23. Taylor and Williams, Washburn Inquiry, 212–23.

24. Hatch, Washburn Inquiry, 223–27.

25. Speed, Washburn Inquiry, 228, 239.

26. Speed, 239.

27. Hoffman to Stanton, May 19, 1865, ORs, ser. 1, vol. 48, pt. 2, 213–17; Butler, Hoffman Investigation, 148–49.

28. Dana to Hoffman, May 8, 1865 (no. 1), Hoffman to Dana, May 8, 1865, and Dana to Hoffman, May 8, 1865 (no. 2), ORs, ser. 1, vol. 48, pt. 2, 210–12.

29. Williams, Washburn Inquiry, 248–49.

30. Smith, Washburn Inquiry, 249–52.

31. Perce, Washburn Inquiry, 252–53.

32. Witzig, Washburn Inquiry, 254–55.

33. Adams, Maguire, and Sells, Dana Commission, 134–41.

34. Kerns, Wells, and Butler, Hoffman Investigation, 149–52.

35. Williams and Speed, Hoffman Investigation.

36. "The *Sultana* Tragedy," *Chicago Tribune*, May 5, 1865, 2.

37. "Investigation of the *Sultana* Disaster," *Memphis Argus*, May 11, 1865, 3.

38. "Investigation of the *Sultana* Disaster."

39. Annis, Hites, McCown, and Bean, Hoffman Investigation, 152–59; Hoffman to Stanton, May 19, 1865, ORs, ser. 1, vol. 48, pt. 2, 217.

40. Richardson, Hoffman Investigation, 160–61; "River News," *Evansville Daily Journal*, May 20, 1865, 3; "From Cairo," *Cincinnati Commercial Tribune*, May 13, 1865, 4.

41. "More concerning the *Sultana* Disaster," *Memphis Argus*, May 13, 1865, 3.

42. General Orders No. 78, May 1, 1865, ORs, ser. 1, vol. 48, pt. 2, 280; Dana to Adjutant General, May 12, 1865, Civil War, Letters

Received by Commission Branch, 1874–1894, D, Dana, Napoleon Jackson Tecumseh, 92–93, 106, www.fold3.com.

43. West, Mahoney, Barker, Dickinson, and Squire, Hoffman Investigation, 162–69.
44. Wintringer, Hoffman Investigation, 170–74.
45. Washburn to Hoffman, May 14, 1865, ORs, ser. 1, vol. 48, pt. 2, 440.
46. Hoffman to Stanton, May 19, 1865, ORs, ser. 1, vol. 48, pt. 2, 214.
47. Hoffman to Stanton, 213–17.
48. Hoffman to Stanton, 217.
49. "The *Sultana* Disaster," *Cincinnati Commercial Tribune*, May 24, 1865, 1.
50. Washburn to Stanton, May 23, 1865, May 14, 1865, ORs, ser. 1, vol. 48, pt. 2, 212–13.
51. Washburn to Stanton, 213.
52. "The *Sultana* Disaster," *Cincinnati Commercial Tribune*, May 24, 1865, 2.

CHAPTER 25. SCAPEGOAT

1. Simon, *The Papers of Ulysses S. Grant*, vol. 15, 533.
2. Speed to Colonel (Browne), May 28, 1865, Frederic and William Speed papers, William L. Clements Library, University of Michigan.
3. "The Wreck of the *Sultana*" and "Personal," *Memphis Daily Bulletin*, May 7, 1865, 3; "More concerning the *Sultana* Disaster," *Memphis Argus*, May 13, 1865, 3; Speed to Badeau, December 13, 1865; Simon, *The Papers of Ulysses S. Grant*, vol. 15, 533.
4. Speed to his father, June 3, 1865, Speed papers.
5. Speed to Anna, June 3, 1865, Speed papers.
6. *Personal Histories of Volunteer Officers in the Quartermaster's Department, 1861–1865*, vol. 3, 148.
7. Speed to his father, June 9, 1865, Speed papers; Special Orders No. 161, June 17, 1865, ORs, ser. 1, vol. 48, pt. 2, 909.
8. Meigs to Adjutant General of the Army, June 16, 1865, Civil War, *Sultana* Disaster, April 27, 1865, Quartermaster vessel file relating to the *Sultana*, 92–93, www.fold3.com.
9. Smith to Adjutant General of the Army, June 16, 1865, Civil War, Letters Received by Commission Branch, 1874–1894, S, Smith, Morgan L., 19–20, www.fold3.com; Slocum, *The Life and Services of Major-General Henry Warner Slocum*, 322.

10. *Personal Histories of Volunteer Officers in the Quartermaster's Department, 1861–1865*, vol. 3, 148; Allen to Quartermaster General's Office, January 24, 1872, Hatch Military Records.

11. "Robbery of the *Atlantic*'s Safe," *Times-Picayune*, July 8, 1865, 1; "Money Found," *Daily Missouri Democrat*, July 6, 1865, 5; "The Safe," *Daily Illinois State Journal*, July 7, 1865, 3; "Mississippi River Steamboat Robbed of $57,000," *Chicago Tribune*, July 7, 1865, 4. Newspaper accounts vary from a low of $36,000 in the safe to a high of $57,000. I have used $40,000, the amount that appeared in two different newspapers.

12. "Robbery of the *Atlantic*'s Safe"; "Money Found"; "Mississippi River Steamboat Robbed of $57,000"; "Personal," *Daily Missouri Democrat*, July 14, 1865, 4; "Generals," *Daily Inter Ocean*, July 15, 1865, 1; Allen to Quartermaster General's Office, January 24, 1872, Hatch Military Records.

13. Simon, *The Papers of Ulysses S. Grant*, vol. 23, 115.

14. Civil War, Civil War Service Records, Union Records, Colored Troops, 56th–138th Infantry, 66th US Colored Infantry, T, Tillinghast, William H., 13, 17, 25, 26, www.fold3.com; Townsend to Osterhaus, October 27, 1865, *Court-Martial*, 229–30.

15. Speed to Lotty, June 27, 1865, Speed papers.

16. "Original Draft of C & S Preferred against Capt. Frd. Speed," *Court-Martial*, 638–44.

17. "Original Draft of C & S Preferred against Capt. Frd. Speed," *Court-Martial*, 644–47.

18. Speed to his father, September 17, 1865, Speed papers.

19. Speed to his father, September 22, 1865, Speed papers; U.S. Congress, *Biographical Directory of the United States Congress*, 1995.

20. Speed to his mother, September 22, 1865, Speed papers.

21. "Charges and Specifications," *Court-Martial*, 5–7.

22. "Charges and Specifications," *Court-Martial*, 7–9.

23. Hobart, *Semi-History of a Boy-Veteran*, 49; Civil War, Civil War Service Records, Union Records, Colored Troops, 56th–138th Infantry, 58th US Colored Infantry, G, Gilson, Norman S., 5, 10, 19, 21, 34, www.fold3.com.

24. Townsend to Osterhaus, October 27, 1865, *Court-Martial*, 229–30.

25. Special Orders No. 89 and No. 103, *Court-Martial*, 119–20.

26. Gilson, *Court-Martial*, 233–34; Hobart, *Semi-History of a Boy-Veteran*, 49.

27. Special Orders No. 129, *Court-Martial*, 121–22; various entries, www.Ancestry.com.

28. Johnson, "Legrand Winfield Perce," 331–56.

29. Speed to Badeau, December 13, 1865.

30. Speed to Badeau.

31. Grimshaw to Gilson, December 12, 1865, *Court-Martial*, 235–36.

CHAPTER 26. COURT-MARTIAL

1. Williams, *Court-Martial*, 10–45.

2. Wood to Ord, January 9, 1866, *Court-Martial*, 238–39.

3. Kerns, *Court-Martial*, 45–84.

4. Jones, *Court-Martial*, 84–91.

5. McCown, Friesner, and Irwin, *Court-Martial*, 92–118.

6. Witzig, *Court-Martial*, 131.

7. Witzig, 139–40; "Port List," *Cincinnati Commercial Tribune*, September 5, 1865, 3; "River and Steamboat News," *Cairo Evening Times*, September 4, 1865, 5; "Captain Gudgeon," *Daily Missouri Democrat*, October 3, 1865, 4.

8. Witzig, *Court-Martial*, 140.

9. Cunningham, *Shiloh and the Western Campaign of 1862*, 50.

10. Witzig, *Court-Martial*, 138–39.

11. Elliott, Shull, Compton, and Butler, *Court-Martial*, 141–54.

12. Gilson, *Court-Martial*, 155–56.

13. Perce, *Court-Martial*, 156–58.

14. Perce, 158–59.

15. Decision of the court on postponement, *Court-Martial*, 159.

16. Oakes to Wood, February 1, 1866, *Court-Martial*, 240.

17. Oakes to Wood, February 8, 1866, *Court-Martial*, 242–43.

18. Wintringer, *Court-Martial*, 161–70. Wintringer gave his testimony on Monday, March 5, 1866. When the Speed trial had resumed on Saturday, March 3, one of the members of the court was not present and the trial was delayed two more days until Monday.

19. Gilson, *Court-Martial*, 181–82.

20. Gilson, 182, 183.

21. Perce, *Court-Martial*, 184.

22. Perce, 185.

23. Emmons, *Court-Martial*, 189–213.

24. R. Williams to Wood, March 10, 1866, *Court-Martial*, 227–28.

25. Miller, *Court-Martial*, 214–25.

26. Gilson and Perce, *Court-Martial*, 226–31.

27. Gilson, 231–47.

28. Gilson, 247–49.

29. Decision of the court on postponement, *Court-Martial*, 255.

30. Wood to Ord, March 15, 1866, Ord to Wood, March 17, 1866, Wood to Townsend, March 19, 1866, and Holt to Wood, March 19, 1866, all in *Court-Martial*, 260–62.

31. Wood to Holt, March 20, 1866, *Court-Martial*, 262–63.

32. Holt to Wood, March 22, 1866, *Court-Martial*, 263–64.

33. Holt to Wood, 264.

34. Decision of the court on postponement, *Court-Martial*, 266–67.

35. Special Order from General Wood, *Court-Martial*, 269.

36. Gilson, *Court-Martial*, 272–73.

37. Henderson, *Court-Martial*, 274–81.

38. Davenport, *Court-Martial*, 282–90.

39. Cayton, *Court-Martial*, 319.

40. "Charges and Specifications," *Court-Martial*, 5–7.

41. Cayton, *Court-Martial*, 318–20.

42. Depositions of Cox, Exhibit N, *Court-Martial*, 323.

43. Huntsman, *Court-Martial*, 321.

44. Depositions of Kemble and Frank Miller, Exhibits O and P, *Court-Martial*, 323–24.

45. Joseph Warren Miller, *Court-Martial*, 325.

46. Various special orders, *Court-Martial*, 339–64.

47. Perce, Closing Statement, Exhibit R, 1–13 (www.fold3.com, Civil War, *Sultana* Disaster, April 1865, The proceedings and report of the *court-martial* of Capt. Frederick [*sic*] Speed, *court-martial* case MM3967, 523–35).

48. Perce, *Court-Martial*, 17 (www.fold3.com, 539).

49. Perce, 18–56 (www.fold3.com, 540–78).

50. Gilson, closing statement, Exhibit S, 1–14 (www.fold3.com, Civil War, *Sultana* Disaster, 587–600).

51. Gilson, *Court-Martial*, 14–24 (www.fold3.com, 600–10).

52. Gilson, 25–32 (www.fold3.com, 611–18).

53. Gilson, 32–43 (www.fold3.com, 618–29).

54. Gilson, 44–50 (www.fold3.com, 630–36).

55. *Court-Martial*, 370.

56. *Court-Martial*, 371.

57. *Court-Martial*, 372; Wood to Townsend, June 8, 1866, *Court-Martial*, 11–12.

58. Holt to Secretary of War, June 21, 1866, www.fold3.com, Civil War, *Sultana* Disaster, 34–36, 38, 41.

59. Holt, *Court-Martial*, 42–43.

60. Holt, 43–44.

61. Holt, 44.

62. Holt, 31.

63. Holt, 32.

64. Holt, 32.

65. Holt, 33.

66. Holt, 33.

67. "Officers of the 13th Maine Infantry (Cont.), Assistant Adjutant General Frederic Gordon Speed," *13th Maine Infantry Regiment*, http://maine13th.com/moreoff-3.html#speed-fg.

68. Elliott, *Transport to Disaster*, 219–22.

69. Elliott, 223.

CHAPTER 27. AFTERMATH

1. "Civil War Reminiscence," *Plainville Times*, May 28, 1908, 2; Madden in Berry, *Loss of the* Sultana, 233.

2. Isenogle to Potter, May 31, 1989; Cook in Berry, *Loss of the* Sultana, 101; "James Cook of Kent was on the *Sultana*," *Cleveland Plain Dealer*, October 20, 1938.

3. "Not All *Sultana* Related Deaths Were Immediate," *The* Sultana *Remembered* (summer 2008): 5.

4. Biography of John H. Campbell, www.ancestry.com.

5. Braunmart to Sirs [*Sultana* Survivors' Association], April 24, 1901.

6. Raynor, "A Memory Preserved," *Northern Ohio Live* (May 1994): 108.

7. Walker, *Cahaba Prison*, 29.

8. McIntosh, "Autobiography," "This Skeleton Photo," "This Photo," and "Camp Fire and Reunion Song Book," circa 1868.

9. Eldridge, unpublished manuscript, 1928; Eldridge, "In the *Sultana* Disaster," 7.

10. Horner in Berry, *Loss of the* Sultana, 181; Norwood to author, August 10, 1990.

11. "Eight Comrades at Company's Reunion," *Kalamazoo Gazette*, January 13, 1909, 3.

12. Darius Isaac Minier, Invalid Pension Application, December 8, 1893; William Henry Ross, Invalid Pension Application, June 29, 1875.
13. Declaration of Original Pension of an Invalid for Benjamin F. Learner, September 14, 1870; Benjamin F. Learner obituary, unknown Indiana newspaper, February, 1925; "One Man from Howard Died on *Sultana*," *Kokomo Daily Tribune*, April 29, 1915, 1; "Sultana Survivor Dead," *Call-Leader*, February 2, 1925, 2; "B. F. Learner Passes Away at Age of 82," *Kokomo Daily Tribune*, January 31, 1925, 1.
14. Brown, "Memories of Our Family"; "Victim of the *Sultana*," *Indianapolis News*, April 11, 1904, 13.
15. Joel Frank Nevins, Invalid Pension Application, December 28, 1880; "Jacob M. Rush," *Sandusky Daily Register*, February 3, 1902, 8.
16. "Neighboring Counties," *Athens Daily Messenger*, September 2, 1886, 1; Smith, *Indiana and the* Sultana *Disaster*; King in Berry, *Loss of the* Sultana, 64.
17. "Iowa *Sultana* Survivor Dead," *Waterloo Evening Courier and Reporter*, November 27, 1915, 2; Aldrich, *Cahawba Prison*, 19.
18. "A Salesman's Suicide," *Cleveland Plain Dealer*, July 14, 1887, 8.
19. Gorman, "Civil War Pensions," *Essential Civil War Curriculum*, https://www.essentialcivilwarcurriculum.com/civil-war-pensions.html; "Union Pension Records," https://www.familysearch.org/wiki/en/Union_Pension_Records.
20. Raudebaugh, "The *Sultana* Disaster," 4.
21. Raudebaugh, 4.
22. Linginfelter letter from pension file in the National Archives, n.d.
23. U.S. Congress, Perry H. Alexander, 57th Cong., 1st sess., S. Rep. 1033.
24. U.S. Congress, Mrs. Anna Butterfield, 50th Cong., 1st sess., H. Rep. 1607; "A Heartless Pension Veto," *New York Tribune*, August 12, 1888, 16.
25. U.S. Congress, In the Senate of the United States, 45th Cong., 3d sess., S. Rep. 647; U.S. Congress, Ann Annis, 49th Cong., 1st sess., S. Rep. 2242; Chandler, email message to author, April 13 and June 21, 1997; Mathews to author, February 25, 1997.
26. Chandler, email message to author, April 13 and June 21, 1997; Mathews to author, February 25, 1997.

27. *City Directory of Chicago*, 1862–80; "Seth William Hardin, Jr.," *U.S. Federal Census Mortality Schedules, 1850–1885*, all on www.ancestry.com.

28. Overton Hospital List, *Daily Missouri Republican*, May 1, 1865, 1; *Report of the Adjutant General of the State of Indiana*, vol. 6, 392; "Martin Simmerman," *Attica Daily Ledger*, June 17, 1907, 5.

29. Berry in Berry, *Loss of the* Sultana, 55–56.

30. U.S. Government, *Specifications and Drawings of Patents, 1874*, 613, 615, 616; "William Dunham Snow," *New York Tribune*, February 12, 1910, 7; "William D. Snow," in Harvey, *Genealogical History of Hudson and Bergen Counties New Jersey*, 500.

31. "River News," *Daily Missouri Democrat*, August 5, 1865, 5; "Burning of the Steamer *Magnolia*," *Daily Missouri Democrat*, June 15, 1866, 4.

32. "River News," *Cincinnati Daily Gazette*, March 29, 1877, 7; "Deck Sweepings," *St. Louis Globe Democrat*, April 2, 1877, 7; "The Memphis Scimitar Says," *Courier Journal*, May 9, 1890, 3.

33. "The *Sultana* Disaster," *Daily Missouri Democrat*, October 31, 1865, 5; "John Magwire," *Daily Missouri Democrat*, March 12, 1866, 4; "Editors *Missouri Democrat*," *Daily Missouri Democrat*, March 13, 1866, 7; "Poisoned," *Wheeling Register*, August 15, 1878, 4; "We Met Capt. . . . ," *Daily Intelligencer*, August 29, 1878, 2.

34. "Contract Awarded," *Wheeling Register*, January 25, 1879, 4; "The New Wheeling and Pittsburgh Packet," *Daily Intelligencer*, April 26, 1879, 5; "Sudden Death," *Wheeling Intelligencer*, October 12, 1886, 5; "Ohio News Condensed," *Cleveland Leader*, October 12, 1886, 2.

35. Cullum, *Biographical Register of West Point*, 503–4; "Major George A. Williams," *New York Tribune*, April 4, 1889, 7.

36. U.S. Census 1870, Missouri, www.genealogybank.com; St. Joseph, Missouri, City Directory, 1882, 1887, 1888, 1889, 1890, 1893, www.ancestry.com; "William F. Kerns," *Mount Mora Cemetery*, http://www.mountmora.org/findagrave/main.asp?page=search_details&id=7700.

37. *Biographical and Historical Memoirs of Mississippi*, vol. 2, pt. 2, 807.

38. "Meddling in Politics," *Vicksburg Daily Times*, January 28, 1868, 2; "Today the *Vicksburg Times* . . ." *Vicksburg Daily Herald*, July 20, 1869, 2; "*Vicksburg Times*," *Oxford Falcon*, July 31, 1869, 4; "A Correspondent of the *Chicago Post*," *Portland Daily Press*, August 25, 1869, 3; "Jackson, Miss. . . . ," *Louisiana Democrat*, September 15, 1869, 4; "Warren—The Conservatives of Warren . . . ," *Clarion*

Ledger, November 4, 1869, 2; "Letter from the 'Free State,'" *Clarion*, November 18, 1869, 2; "Public Speaking To-Night," *Tri-Weekly Clarion*, November 18, 1869, 2; "Captain Frederic Speed . . . ," *New Orleans Republican*, July 31, 1870, 5.

39. "The Late Giles M. Hillyer," *Times-Picayune*, April 26, 1871, 9; *Mississippi Marriages, 1800–1911*, www.familysearch.org; *Biographical and Historical Memoirs of Mississippi*, vol. 2, pt. 2, 806; U.S. Department of the Interior, National Park Service, *National Register of Historic Places Registration Form, South Cherry Street Historic District*, September 30, 2003, 49.

40. "Judge Speed Laid to Rest," *Port Gibson Reveille*, March 23, 1911, 8; "Judge Frederic Speed Crosses the Dark River," *Vicksburg Evening Post*, March 11, 1911, 1; *Biographical and Historical Memoirs of Mississippi*, vol. 2, pt. 2, 807.

41. Hatch to Circuit Court of the United States of America, Southern District of Illinois, June 17, 1867, *United States v. Atlantic and Mississippi Steamship Company*, National Archives, Chicago Branch; "River Matters," *Commercial Appeal*, June 7, 1867, 5.

42. "Legislature," *Daily Inter Ocean*, June 27, 1867, 1; *Journal of the Senate of the Twenty-Fifth General Assembly of the State of Illinois, Second Session*, June 11–28, 1867, 27–28, 53, 158–59.

43. *Journal of the Senate*, June 11–28, 1867, 27–28, 53, 158–60; "The Penitentiary Investigation," *Chicago Tribune*, June 22, 1867, 2; "The Penitentiary," *Daily Inter Ocean*, July 25, 1867, 1; "A Bill in Chancery. . . ," *Wilmington Independent*, August 14, 1867, 2.

44. "Damage by the Storm on Sunday," *Daily Illinois State Register*, June 20, 1871, 4; "Storm at Pittsfield," *Quincy Daily Whig*, June 24, 1871, 4; Dr. J. H. Ledlie and D. D. Hicks testimonies, Ellen Hatch Pension Application Papers, Hatch Military Records.

45. Dr. Francis M. Casel and Dr. J. H. Ledlie testimonies, Ellen Hatch Pension Application Papers, Hatch Military Records.

46. Ames Fisher testimony in U.S. Congress, John T. Watson, 43rd Cong., 1st sess., H. Rep. 65, February 4, 1874; U.S. Congress, John T. Watson. 42nd Cong., 2d sess., H. Rep. 1548.

47. "River News," *Wheeling Daily Register*, May 16, 1866, 5; "From St. Louis—Burning of two Valuable Steamers," *Chicago Tribune*, June 4, 1866, 2; Way, *Way's Packet Directory*, 59.

48. Way, 374, 427; "Port Items," *Cincinnati Daily Enquirer*, July 26, 1869, 7.

49. Way, 275, 364.

50. Way, 211, 355.

51. Way, 162, 201, 328.

52. Way, 154, 343; Donovan, *Ironclads of the Civil War*, 76, 78, 80, 104, 105; Wideman, *Naval Warfare*, 48, 49, 50, 89.

53. Way, 2–3, 461; Wideman, 48, 51, 85, 87.

54. "The Wreck of the *Sultana*," *Memphis Daily Bulletin*, May 7, 1865, 3; "The *Sultana*'s Grave," *National Tribune*, December 6, 1923, 2.

55. "Story of the *Sultana*," *Fort Wayne Evening Sentinel*, April 30, 1902, 2.

56. *Biographical and Historical Memoirs of Eastern Arkansas*, 398.

57. The relic board is on display in the *Sultana* Disaster Museum in Marion, AR. On the back is a handwritten note stating, "The Friesner family said this board came from the lower section of the *Sultana*. This relic was made by G. R. Wilson of Memphis, Tenn." A metal plaque attached to the back of the board reads "GAR Post 140."

58. H. J. Brademeyer, "The Wreck of the *Sultana*," 7; "The Vigilance Committee . . . ," *Carthage Citizen*, July 23, 1915, 1.

59. "Solon Would Build Government Memorial Park in Arkansas," *Arkansas Gazette*, April 23, 1925, 9; Curtis, "Fire of Hate Brands Boat of Early Days," *Evening Appeal*, May 13, 1927; Curtis, "Burning of *Sultana* in 1865 Recalled," *Commercial Appeal*, May 29, 1936.

60. "Battle of Memphis," NUMA, https://numa.net/expeditions/battle-of-memphis/.

61. "Wreckage of Sunken Civil War Steamer Believed Found in Arkansas Soybean Field," *Arkansas Gazette*, July 5, 1982, 4; "Search to Resume for Steamboat on Which 1,500 Died," *Huntsville Times*, February 18, 1983, 7; "'Swapper, Trader' Hopes He's Tripped over What's Left of Historic Riverboat," *Arkansas Gazette*, March 3, 1983, 13–14.

62. "Search to Resume for Steamboat on Which 1,500 Died," *Huntsville Times*, February 18, 1983, 7.

CHAPTER 28. REUNIONS AND REMEMBRANCE

1. Nye, *The Official Souvenir of the Fortieth National Encampment of the Grand Army of the Republic*, 11; Beath, *History of the Grand Army of the Republic*, 680; "Survivors of the *Sultana*," 10.

2. "*Sultana* Survivors," *Cleveland Leader*, December 31, 1885, 2.

3. "A. W. King . . . ," *Defiance County Express*, April 29, 1886, 11; "The Disaster Almost Forgotten," *Corpus Christi Caller-Times*, May 9, 1886, 8; "Wm. Fies . . . ," *National Tribune*, May 13, 1886, 6.

4. "The *Sultana* Survivors," *Newark Daily Advocate*, April 25, 1887, 1; "The *Sultana* Survivors' Association," *Chicago Tribune*, April 28, 1888, 5; Berry, *Loss of the* Sultana; "*Sultana* Survivors," *Defiance Republican Express*, May 2, 1895, 4; "*Sultana* Survivors Meet," *Piqua Daily Call*, May 1, 1900, 5.

5. "The *Sultana* Survivors," *Daily Journal and Tribune*, May 31, 1889, 4; "*Sultana* Explosion," *Daily Inter Ocean*, May 16, 1901, 4.

6. Raudebaugh, "The *Sultana* Disaster," 4.

7. Raudebaugh, 4.

8. U.S. Congress, *Congressional Record* 13, pt. 3, 2735.

9. U.S. Congress, *Congressional Record* 13, pt. 3, 2752.

10. U.S. Congress, *Congressional Record* 15, pt. 1, 18.

11. U.S. Congress, *Congressional Record* 17, pt. 1, 965; U.S. Congress, *Congressional Record* 21, pt. 2, 1045; U.S. Congress, *Congressional Record* 21, pt. 4, 3478, 3592, 3593, 3652, 3957.

12. U.S. Congress, *Congressional Record* 21, pt. 1, 237, 387; U.S. Congress, *Congressional Record* 21, pt. 5, 4065.

13. "House Resolution 3296," Civil War, *Sultana* Disaster, April 1865, H.R. 3296, 1–4; *Congressional Record*, 51st Cong., 1st sess., 4443, 4750; "Senator Sherman . . . ," *Charlotte News*, May 12, 1890, 2.

14. U.S. Congress, *Journal of the House of Representatives, First session, Fifty-Fourth Congress*, 91; *Fifty-Fifth Congress*, 42; *First session, Fifty-Sixth Congress*, 51; *First session, Fifty-Seventh Congress*, 107; *First session, Fifty-Eighth Congress*, 42; *First session, Fifty-Ninth Congress*, 172; *First session, Sixtieth Congress*, 42; *First session, Sixty-First Congress*, 112; *First session, Sixty-Second Congress*, 122; *First session, Sixty-Fifth Congress*, 28; U.S. Congress, *Congressional Record* 53, pt. 1, 35.

15. U.S. Congress, *Congressional Record* 3, pt. 2, 1663; "Rev. S. H. Raudebaugh," *Sandusky Star Journal*, March 26, 1902, 3; "To the Men of the *Sultana*," *Sandusky Star Journal*, April 1, 1902, 1; "Victims," *Butler County Democrat*, April 3, 1902, 6; "In Memory of a Tragedy," *Washington Times*, April 23, 1902, 3; U.S. Congress, *Congressional Record* 35, pt. 5, 4512.

16. "Want a Monument for *Sultan*'s [sic] Victims," *Evansville Courier and Press*, April 27, 1902, 9.

17. "Extra—President Shot," *Evening Star*, September 6, 1901, 1; "Wonderful Growth of Business in Stock Market," *New York Times*, November 6, 1904, 23.

18. U.S. Congress, *Congressional Record* 51, pt. 3:2356; "Memorial Proposed for the Survivors of the *Sultana* Disaster," *Journal News*, January 27, 1914, 4; Kimberlin, "The Destruction of the *Sultana*," unpublished manuscript, 1919.

19. "The House Passed . . . ," *Cambridge Jeffersonian*, April 28, 1904, 2; "Monument Passed," *East Liverpool Evening Review*, January 20, 1906, 5; "Columbus, July 24," *Hamilton Daily Democrat*, July 24, 1906, 1; "The Memorial Commission . . . ," *Defiance Express*, August 8, 1906, 8.

20. "Like Zaiser's Plan," *Canton Morning News*, August 18, 1906, 17; "*Sultana* Survivors," *Canton Morning News*, October 1, 1906, 3.

21. "*Sultana* Commissioners Charge Bribery," *Defiance Express*, November 9, 1906, 1; "*Sultana* Monument Commission Scandal," *Defiance Express*, November 10, 1906, 1; "Ellis Using the Probe," *Massillon Independent*, December 12, 1906, 3; "Flaw in *Sultana* Act," *Athens Daily Messenger*, December 21, 1906; "Fatal Defect Discovered," *East Liverpool Evening News*, December 21, 1906, 1; "*Sultana* Monument Is Held Up," *Defiance Express*, December 22, 1906, 1; "*Sultana* Commission," *Morning News*, December 26, 1906, 1.

22. "Wants State to Erect Monument," *Elyria Evening Telegram*, April 9, 1915, 1; "Ray Ball Heads Monument Board," *Sandusky Star Journal*, April 29, 1927, 22.

23. "*Sultana* Monument Unveiling," *Journal and Tribune*, July 4, 1916, n.p.; "*Sultana* Victims' Shaft Unveiled," *Knoxville Sentinel*, July 4, 1914, 2; "Beautiful Monument Unveiled to Memory of the *Sultana*'s Men," *Knoxville Journal*, July 5, 1916, 8.

24. "Louis Schirmeyer One of Seventeen Survivors of Burning of Steamship *Sultana*, Most Disastrous of Marine Horrors," *Fort Wayne Journal-Gazette*, April 28, 1912, 8a; Lynch, *Titanic: An Illustrated History*, 193; "Recalls *Sultana* Disaster," *Bad River News*, May 2, 1912, 9.

25. "A *Sultana* Survivor," *Defiance County Republican and Express*, June 27, 1890, 7.

26. "Solon Would Build Government Memorial Park in Arkansas," *Arkansas Gazette*, April 23, 1925, 9.

27. "Lone *Sultana* Survivor Here Has Anniversary," *Knoxville News-Sentinel*, April 27, 1930, n.p.; "Last *Sultana* Man Closes Association," *Knoxville News-Sentinel*, April 28, 1930, n.p.

28. "Two *Sultana* Survivors Celebrate Anniversary," *Greenfield Daily Reporter*, May 5, 1933, 1; "Anniversary of River Tragedy That Killed 1,750 Unobserved," *Coshocton Tribune*, April 28, 1933, 4.

29. "River Tragedy Survivor Dies; Civil War Vet," *Dallas Morning News*, September 10, 1941, 5.

30. "Lone *Sultana* Survivor Here Has Anniversary," *Knoxville News-Sentinel*, April 27, 1931, n.p.

31. Shaw, "*Sultana* Association Revived," *The* Sultana *Remembered* 1, no. 1 (summer 1990): 2; "*Sultana*," Camp Talk, *Blue & Gray Magazine* 5, no. 5 (May 1988): 41.

CHAPTER 29. NO SABOTAGE

1. Rule, Sultana: *A Case for Sabotage*, 6.
2. Rowberry, Washburn Inquiry, 47–50.
3. "Horrible Disaster on the River," *Memphis Daily Bulletin*, April 28, 1865, 1; "From Cairo," *Daily Missouri Republican*, April 29, 1865, 3.
4. "Latest by Telegraph, Second Dispatch," *Cincinnati Commercial Tribune*, April 29, 1865, 3.
5. Postal, Washburn Inquiry, 130–31.
6. Scharf, *History of the Confederate States Navy*, 762; "Coal Torpedoes," *The Times*, December 30, 1875, 4; Thatcher, *Confederate Coal Torpedo*, 88–89.
7. Rush in Hawes, *Cahaba*, 192; Annis, Hoffman Investigation.
8. "The *Sultana* Disaster," *Memphis Daily Bulletin*, May 4, 1865, 3.
9. "River News," *Memphis Daily Bulletin*, May 5, 1865, 3.
10. "The *Sultana* Tragedy," *Chicago Tribune*, May 5, 1865, 2.
11. Witzig, Washburn Inquiry, 254.
12. "Miscellaneous," *Memphis Daily Bulletin*, May 10, 1865, 3; "Investigation of the *Sultana* Disaster," *Memphis Argus*, May 11, 1865, 3.
13. Richardson, Hoffman Investigation, 160; "More concerning the *Sultana* Disaster," *Memphis Argus*, May 13, 1865, 3.
14. West, Hoffman Investigation, 162–64; "From Cairo and Below," Cairo, May 13, *Chicago Tribune*, May 15, 1865, 2.
15. Hoffman to Stanton, May 19, 1865, ORs, 1st ser., vol. 48, pt. 1, 216–17.

16. "The *Sultana* Disaster," *Cincinnati Commercial Tribune*, May 26, 1865, 2.
17. Witzig, *Court-Martial*, 138–39.
18. "Reminiscence of the War," *Wayne County Democrat*, April 28, 1880.
19. "Soldier's Reunion," *Journal*, March 6, 1886, 4.
20. "Condensed Letters," *National Tribune*, May 20, 1886, 3.
21. Barnett, James T. W., Civil War, Civil War Service Records, Union Records, Kentucky, Third Infantry, A–Br, B, Barnett, James T. W., www.fold3.com; Barnett, James T. W., Civil War, Civil War Service Records, Union Records, Kentucky, Twelfth Infantry, A–Bo, B, Barnett, James T. W., www.fold3.com; "Barnett, James T. W.," Headstones Provided for Deceased Union Civil War Veterans, 1861–1904, www.ancestry.com.
22. Chrisinger, "The *Sultana* Disaster," 3.
23. "Random Shots," 3.
24. "The *Sultana* Survivors Association," *Chicago Tribune*, April 28, 1888, 5; "*Sultana* Survivors Meet," *Newark Daily Advocate*, April 28, 1888, 1; "*Sultana* Survivors," *Hillsdale Standard*, May 1, 1888, 1.
25. "Blew Up the *Sultana*," *St. Louis Globe Democrat*, May 6, 1888.
26. "Blew Up the *Sultana*."
27. Robert Louden, 1833–1867, www.ancestry.com; J. H. Baker to C. A. Dana, April 25, 1865, ORs, ser., 1, vol. 48, pt. 2, 194–95. The thirty-one steamboats supposedly destroyed by the "boat-burners" were the *Admiral, Belle Creole, Black Hawk, Catahoula, Champion, Chancellor, Cherokee, Daniel G. Taylor, E. M. Ryland, Edward F. Dix, Empire Parish, Fawn, Forest Queen, Glasgow, Hiawatha, Imperial, J. H. Russell, Jesse K. Bell, Laurel Hill, Louisiana Belle, Meteor, Northerner, Philadelphia, Post Boy, Robert Campbell Jr., Robert Lee* (towboat), *Ruth, Stephen Bayard, Sunshine, Time and Tide*, and *Welcome*. All of the boats were set on fire; none of them exploded from a Courtenay coal torpedo. Parsons, *Report to the War Department*, 30–39.
28. Curtis, "Only Living Eye-Witness Details *Sultana* Explosion," *Commercial Appeal*, January 25, 1920, 3.
29. Curtis, 3.
30. "News in General," *Springfield Daily Leader*, May 9, 1888, 1.
31. "The Explosion of the *Sultana* in 1865," *Times-Picayune*, May 10, 1888, 4.
32. "The Explosion of the *Sultana* in 1865."

33. "Ancient History," *Public Ledger*, May 8, 1888, 5; "The *Sultana* Explosion," *Daily American*, May 9, 1888, 1.

34. "Current Bits of Gossip," *Chicago Tribune*, May 13, 1888, 24.

35. "Engineer on the *Sultana*," *Fort Wayne Journal-Gazette*, May 5, 1902, 5.

36. Lyda, Horn, Nisley, and Ray in Berry, *Loss of the* Sultana, 28, 177, 264, 296; "The Explosion of the *Sultana*," *Daily Inter Ocean*, October 15, 1892, 11.

37. "*Sultana* Survivor Denies Latest Story," *Indianapolis News*, May 16, 1903, 23; "Secret of the *Sultana* Explosion Which Killed a Steubenvillian," *Steubenville Herald*, June 12, 1903, 1.

38. "*Sultana* Survivor Denies Latest Story," *Indianapolis News*, May 16, 1903, 23.

39. "Civil War Reminiscence," *Plainville Times*, May 28, 1908, 2.

40. "The Wreck of the *Sultana*," *News-Leader*, October 8, 1896, 1.

BIBLIOGRAPHY

NEWSPAPERS

The Age (Philadelphia, PA)
Alton (IL) Evening Telegraph
Argos (IN) Reflector
Arkansas Gazette (Little Rock, AR)
Asheville (NC) Citizen
Ashland (OH) Union
Athens (OH) Daily Messenger
Atlanta (GA) Weekly Intelligencer
Attica (IN) Daily Ledger
Bad River News (Philip, SD)
Bismarck (ND) Weekly Tribune
Boston (MA) Daily Advertiser
Boston (MA) Herald
Boston (MA) Traveler
Brownlow's Knoxville (TN) Whig and Rebel Ventilator
Butler County Democrat (Hamilton, OH)
Butler (MO) Weekly Times
Cadiz (OH) Sentinel
Cairo (IL) Evening Times
Cairo (IL) News
Call-Leader (Elmwood, IN)
Cambridge (OH) Jeffersonian

Canton (OH) Daily News

Canton (OH) Morning News

Carthage (IN) Citizen

Charleston (SC) Courier

Charlotte (NC) News

Chicago (IL) Tribune

Cincinnati (OH) Commercial Tribune

Cincinnati (OH) Daily Commercial

Cincinnati (OH) Daily Commercial Tribune

Cincinnati (OH) Daily Enquirer

Cincinnati (OH) Daily Gazette

Cincinnati (OH) Daily Press

Clarion (Jackson, MS)

Clarion Ledger (Jackson, MS)

Cleveland (OH) Leader

Cleveland (OH) Plain Dealer

Coffeyville (KS) Weekly Journal

Columbus (OH) Dispatch

Commercial Appeal (Memphis, TN)

Commercial Bulletin (Richmond, VA)

Commercial News (Danville, IL)

Concordia Intelligencer (Vidalia, LA)

Corpus Christi (TX) Caller-Times

Coshocton (OH) Semi-Weekly Age

Coshocton (OH) Tribune

Daily Alta California (San Francisco, CA)

Daily American (Nashville, TN)

Daily Arkansas Gazette (Little Rock, AR)

Daily Constitutionalist (Augusta, GA)

Daily Davenport (IA) Democrat

Daily Eastern Argus (Portland, ME)

Daily Illinois State Journal (Springfield, IL)

Daily Illinois State Register (Springfield, IL)

Daily Intelligencer (Wheeling, VA)

Daily Intelligencer (Wheeling, WV)

Daily Inter Ocean (Chicago, IL)

Daily Journal and Tribune (Knoxville, TN)

Daily Milwaukee (WI) News

Daily Missouri Democrat (St. Louis, MO)

Daily Missouri Republican (St. Louis, MO)

Daily National Intelligencer (Washington)

Daily National Republican (Washington)

Daily Ohio Statesman (Columbus, OH)

Daily State Sentinel (Indianapolis, IN)

Daily True Delta (New Orleans, LA)

Dallas (TX) Morning News

Dayton (OH) Daily Empire

Dayton (OH) Daily News

Decatur (IL) Herald

Defiance County (OH) Express

Defiance County (OH) Republican

Defiance County (OH) Republican and Express

Defiance (OH) Express

Defiance (OH) Republican Express

Denver (CO) Post

Denver (CO) Rocky Mountain News

Detroit (MI) Advertiser and Tribune

Detroit (MI) Free Press

East Liverpool (OH) Evening Review

Elkhart (IN) Daily Review

Elyria (NY) Evening Telegram

Empire (Sydney, New South Wales, Australia)

Enquirer (Cincinnati, OH)

Evansville (IN) Courier and Press

Evansville (IN) Daily Journal

Evening Appeal (Memphis, TN)

Evening Argus (Rock Island, IL)

Evening Star (Washington, DC)

Evening Times (West Memphis, AR)

Evening Tribune (New York, NY)

Florence (KS) Bulletin

Fort Smith (AR) New Era

Fort Wayne (IN) Evening Sentinel

Fort Wayne (IN) Journal-Gazette

Fort Wayne (IN) Sentinel

Galveston (TX) Daily News

Gold Hill (NV) Daily News

Greenfield (IN) Daily Reporter

Halifax Citizen (Halifax, Nova Scotia, Canada)

Hamilton (OH) Daily Democrat

Hancock Democrat (Greenfield, IN)

Hancock Jeffersonian (Findlay, OH)

Hartford (CT) Daily Courant

Herald (New York, NY)

Hillsdale (MI) Standard

Holmes County Farmer and Free Press (Millersburg, OH)

Huntsville (AL) Times

Hutchinson (KS) Daily News

Illinois State Journal (Springfield, IL)

Illinois Weekly State Journal (Springfield, IL)

Indianapolis (IN) Daily Gazette

Indianapolis (IN) Daily Journal

Indianapolis (IN) Journal

Indianapolis (IN) News

Indianapolis (IN) Star

Iola (KS) Register

Jackson (MI) Citizen Patriot

Joliet (IL) Signal

Journal (Evansville, IN)

Journal and Tribune (Knoxville, TN)

Journal Gazette (Mattoon, IL)

Journal Gazette (West Plains, MO)

Journal News (Washington, DC)

Kalamazoo (MI) Gazette

Kansas City (MO) Star

Knoxville (TN) Journal

Knoxville (TN) News-Sentinel

Knoxville (TN) Sentinel

Kokomo (IN) Daily Gazette Tribune
Kokomo (IN) Daily Tribune
Lafayette (IN) Daily Journal
Larned (KS) Chronoscope
Lebanon (OH) Patriot
Lethbridge (Alberta, Canada) Herald
Lewisburg (OH) Leader
Lexington (KY) Observer
Liberty (IN) Express
Logan (OH) Daily News
London (England) Express
London (England) Guardian
Los Angeles (CA) Herald
Louisiana Democrat (Alexandria, LA)
Louisville (KY) Daily Courier
Louisville (KY) Daily Democrat
Louisville (KY) Daily Journal
Louisville (KY) Price-Current
Lyons (KS) Tribune
Macon (GA) Telegraph
Madison (IN) Daily Banner
Maryville (TN) Enterprise
Massillon (OH) Independent
Melbourne Age (Melbourne, Victoria, Australia)
Memphis (TN) Argus
Memphis (TN) Commercial Appeal
Memphis (TN) Daily Avalanche
Memphis (TN) Daily Bulletin
Memphis (TN) Evening Post
Milwaukee (WI) Sentinel
Montana Post (Helena, MT)
Montreal Herald and Daily Commercial Gazette (Montreal, Quebec, Canada)
Morgan County Gazette (Martinsville, IN)
Morning News (Canton, OH)
Mulvane (KS) Record

Nashville (TN) Daily Union

Nebraska Advertiser (Auburn, NE)

New Albany (IN) Daily Ledger

New-Leader (Springfield, KY)

New Orleans (LA) Price-Current and Commercial Intelligencer

New Orleans (LA) Republican

New-Orleans (LA) Times

New Westminster British Columbian (New Westminster, British Columbia, Canada)

New York (NY) Herald

New York (NY) Times

New York (NY) Tribune

Newark (OH) Daily Advocate

News-Leader (Springfield, KY)

Olympia (WA) Daily Recorder

Omaha (NE) Daily Bee

Orange Leader (Orange, New South Wales, Australia)

Oregon State Journal (Eugene, OR)

Osage City (KS) Free Press

Oshkosh (WI) Northwestern

Oxford (MS) Falcon

Pantagraph (Bloomington, IL)

Pensacola (FL) Journal

Piqua (OH) Daily Call

Plainfield (KS) Times

Port Gibson (MS) Reveille

Portland (ME) Daily Press

The Press (Philadelphia, PA)

Price-Current and Commercial Intelligencer (New Orleans, LA)

Public Ledger (Maysville, KY)

Public Ledger (Memphis, TN)

Quebec Gazette (Quebec City, Quebec, Canada)

Quincy (IL) Daily Whig

Register (Sandusky, OH)

Repository (Canton, OH)

Richmond (IN) Item

Richmond (IN) Palladium

Sacramento (CA) Bee

San Antonio (TX) Express

Sandusky (OH) Daily Commercial Register

Sandusky (OH) Daily Register

Sandusky (OH) Register

Sandusky (OH) Star Journal

San Francisco (CA) Bulletin

Sikeston (MO) Herald

Sioux City (IA) Journal

Southern Shield (Helena, AR)

Spirit of Democracy (Woodfield, OH)

Springfield (MA) Republican

St. Cloud (MN) Democrat

St. Louis (MO) Globe Democrat

St. Paul (MN) Daily Globe

Star Journal (Sandusky, OH)

Steubenville (OH) Herald

Summit County (OH) Beacon

Sun (New York, NY)

The Times (London, England)

Times Herald (Port Huron, MI)

Times-Picayune (New Orleans, LA)

Toledo (OH) Daily Blade

Topeka (KS) Daily Capital

Tri-Weekly Clarion (Meridian, MS)

Tri-Weekly Maysville (KY) Eagle

Tri-Weekly Missouri Republican (St. Louis, MO)

Tri-Weekly Ohio Statesman (Columbus, OH)

Van Wert (OH) Weekly Bulletin

Vicksburg (MS) Daily Herald

Vicksburg (MS) Daily Herald Supplement

Vicksburg (MS) Daily Times

Vicksburg (MS) Evening Post

Wabash Courier (Terre Haute, IN)

War Eagle (Cairo, IL)

Washington (DC) Times
Waterloo (IA) Evening Courier and Reporter
Wayne County (OH) Democrat
Weekly Advocate (Baton Rouge, LA)
Weekly Champion and Press (Atchison, KS)
Western Clarion (Helena, AR)
Wheeling (WV) Daily Register
Wheeling (WV) Register
Wilmington (IL) Independent
Winchester (IN) Journal
Winchester (IN) Randolph Journal
Wisconsin Daily Patriot (Madison, WI)
World (New York, NY)

PRIMARY SOURCES

Ackley, Charles. *Log, January 9–September 25, 1865.* Inland Rivers Library, Public Library of Cincinnati and Hamilton County, Ohio.

Aldrich, Hosea C. *Cahawba Prison: A Glimpse of Life in a Rebel Prison.* N.p., 18—?

Annual Report of the Adjutant General of the State of Michigan for the Years 1865–66. 3 vols. Lansing: John A. Kerr & Company, 1866.

Annual Report of the Adjutant General of the State of Tennessee for the Years 1865–66. Nashville, 1866.

Annual Report of the Adjutant General of the State of West Virginia for the Year Ended December 31, 1865. Wheeling: John Frew, 1866.

Ashley, James King. Civil War manuscript, n.d. University of Kentucky Special Collections. https://exploreuk.uky.edu/fa/findingaid/?id=xt7r 7s7hsb3t.

Bankes, Thomas W. Photograph of overcrowded *Sultana* docked at Helena, AR, April 26, 1865. *Sultana* Disaster Museum, Marion, AR.

Barr, William M. *A Practical Treatise on High Pressure Steam Boilers: Including Results of Recent Experimental Tests of Boiler Materials.* Indianapolis: Yohn Brothers, 1880.

Baughman, A. J. *History of Ashland County, Ohio.* Chicago: S. J. Publishing, 1908.

Beath, Robert B. *History of the Grand Army of the Republic.* New York: Willis McDonald & Company, 1888.

Bent, Enoch. Wisconsin, Wills and Probate Records. www.ancestry.com.

Berry, Chester D. *Loss of the* Sultana *and Reminiscences of Survivors.* Lansing, MI: Darius D. Thorp, 1892.

Boggs, Samuel S. *Eighteen Months a Prisoner under the Rebel Flag.* Lovington, IL: Privately printed, 1887.

Collins, James Robert. Unpublished Civil War reminiscences.

Court-Martial. The Proceedings and Report of the Court-Martial of Capt. Frederick Speed, Court-Martial Case. MM3967, Civil War, *Sultana* Disaster, April 1865. www.fold3.com.

Dana, Charles A. *Recollections of the Civil War.* New York: D. Appleton and Company, 1913.

Dana Commission. "Records of the Commission Conducted by General Napoleon Jackson Tecumseh Dana." Records of the Adjutant General's Office, Record Group 153, National Archives.

Davenport, Isaac Noah. "Story of the *Sultana* Steamboat." Unpublished manuscript.

Day, Lewis W. *Story of the One Hundred and First Ohio Infantry.* Cleveland: Privately printed, 1894.

Dougherty, Michael. *The Prison Diary of Michael Dougherty.* Bristol, PA: C. A. Dougherty, 1908.

Eldridge, Charles M. Unpublished reminiscence, 1926.

———.Unpublished reminiscence, 1928.

Elliott, Colleen Morse, and Louis Armstrong Moxley, eds. *The Tennessee Civil War Veterans Questionnaires.* 3 vols. Easley, SC: Southern Historical Press, 1985.

Ely, John Clark. Unpublished diary.

Fletcher, Samuel H. *The History of Company A, Second Illinois Cavalry.* Privately printed, 1912?

Form C Enrollment, March 24, 1865. Official Steamboat Enrollment in Conformity to an Act of Congress of the United States Entitled "Act of Enrolling and Licensing Ships or Vessels," Approved February 18, 1793, and of "An Act to Regulate the Admeasurement of Tonnage of Ships and Vessels of the United States," Approved May 6, 1864. National Archives.

Gilson, Norman S. Civil War, Civil War Service Records, Union Records, Colored Troops, 56th–138th Infantry, 58th US Colored Infantry, G, Gilson, Norman, S. www.fold3.com.

Griffith, Thomas H. *Rates of Passage of Northern Line Packet Company.* St. Louis, MO, March 31, 1863.

Hatch, Reuben Benton. Military Records, National Archives.

Hawes, Jesse. *Cahaba: A Story of Captive Boys in Blue*. New York: Burr Printing House, 1888.

Hazzard, George. *Hazzard's History of Henry County, Indiana, 1822–1906*. New Castle, IN: George Hazzard, 1906.

Hobart, Edwin L. *Semi-History of a Boy-Veteran of the Twenty-Eighth Regiment Illinois Volunteer Infantry Volunteers in a Black Regiment*. Denver, 1909.

Hoffman Investigation. "Records of the Investigation Conducted by General William Hoffman." Records of the Adjutant General's Office, Record Group 153, National Archives.

Homer, Jacob. "Every Fellow for Himself." *Civil War Times*, March 2002.

Hopkins, Owen Johnston. *Under the Flag of the Nation: Diaries and Letters of a Yankee Volunteer in the Civil War*. Columbus: Ohio State University Press, 1968.

Horan, Thomas W. "A Sketch of My 15 Months in C.S.A. Prison." Unpublished memoir, March 27, 1865.

Inspector's Certificate of *Sultana*, April 12, 1865. Records of the Adjutant General's Office, Record Group 153, National Archives.

Lloyd, James T. *Lloyd's Steamboat Directory and Disasters on the Western Waters*. Cincinnati: James T. Lloyd, 1856.

Lockhart, William Columbus. Unpublished manuscript.

Lufkin, Edwin B. *History of the Thirteenth Maine Regiment*. Bridgton, ME: H. A. Shorey & Sons, 1898.

McIntosh, Epenetus W. "Autobiography," "This Skeleton Photo," "This Photo," and "Camp Fire and Reunion Song Book." Circa 1868.

Michael, William H. C. "Explosion of the *Sultana*." *Civil War Sketches and Incidents*. Vol. 1. Omaha: Commandery, 1902.

———.Unpublished handwritten statement, n.d.

Minnesota, Adjutant General's Office. *Annual Report of the Adjutant General of the State of Minnesota*. St. Paul: Pioneer Printing Company, 1866.

Newsom, Earl. *Sergeant Wade's Letters, 1863–1865*. Salisbury, CT, 1968.

Nicolay, John G., and John Hay, eds. *Abraham Lincoln: The Complete Works*. Vol. 1. New York: Century, 1894.

Nye, Wallace G. *The Official Souvenir of the Fortieth National Encampment of the Grand Army of the Republic*. Minneapolis: Hahn & Harmon, 1906.

Parsons, Lewis B. *Reports to the War Department by Brev. Maj. Gen. Lewis B. Parsons, Chief of Rail and River Transportation*. St. Louis: George Knapp & Company, 1867.

Quartermaster Vessel File relating to the *Sultana*. Civil War, *Sultana Disaster*, April 27, 1865. www.fold3.com.

Record of Service of Michigan Volunteers in the Civil War, 1861–1865. Kalamazoo, MI: Ihling Bros. & Everard, 1905.

Schmutz, George S. *History of the 102d Regiment, O.V.I.* Wooster, OH, 1907.

Simon, John Y., ed. *The Papers of Ulysses S. Grant*. Vols. 3, 4, 11, 15, 21, and 23. Carbondale: Southern Illinois University Press, 1971.

Speed, Frederic, and William Speed Papers. William L. Clements Library, University of Michigan, Ann Arbor.

Stillwell, Leander. *The Story of a Common Soldier of Army Life in the Civil War*. Kansas City, MO: Franklin Hudson, 1920.

Stone, Lincoln R. *Army and Navy Official Gazette, 1864–65*. Vols. 1 and 2. Washington, 1864.

U.S. Sanitary Commission. *The Sanitary Reporter*. Vols. 1 and 2. May 15, 1863, to August 15, 1865. New York, 1866.

Walker, John L. *Cahaba Prison and the* Sultana *Disaster*. Hamilton, OH: Brown & Whitaker, 1910.

Washburn Inquiry. "Records of the Inquiry Conducted by Major General Cadwallader C. Washburn." Records of the Adjutant General's Office, Record Group 153, National Archives.

Wells, Hiram C. Unpublished manuscript, 1886 or 1887.

Winters, Erastus. *In the 50th Ohio Serving Uncle Sam*. East Walnut Hill, OH: Erastus Winters, 1905.

BOOKS AND ARTICLES

American Queen Steamboat Company. *Essential Travel Guide*. 2018.

Anderson, Galusha. *The Story of Aunt Lizzie Aiken*. Chicago: Jansen, McClurg & Company, 1880.

"A Survivor from the *Sultana*." *Indiana History Bulletin* 32, no. 7 (July 1955): 124.

"Awful *Sultana* Disaster: A Symposium." *National Tribune*, May 10, 1923, 3.

Bacon, W. P. *Septennial Meeting of the Class of Fifty-Eight, Yale College*. New Haven, CT: Tuttle, Morehouse & Taylor, 1865.

Basler, Roy P., ed. *The Collected Works of Abraham Lincoln*. Vol. 5. New Brunswick, NJ: Rutgers University Press, 1953.

Bates, Alan L. *The Western Rivers Engineroom Cyclopoedium*. Louisville, KY: Cyclopoedium Press, 1996.

————. *The Western Rivers Steamboat Cyclopoedium.* Leonia, NJ: Hustle Press, 1968.

Biographical and Historical Memoirs of Eastern Arkansas. Chicago: Goodspeed Publishing, 1890.

Biographical and Historical Memoirs of Mississippi. Vol. 2, pt. 2. Gretna, LA: Pelican, 1999.

Boatner, Mark M., III. *The Civil War Dictionary.* New York: David McKay, 1959.

Bracken, William. "The *Sultana* Disaster." *National Tribune,* March 18, 1886, 3.

Brademeyer, H. J. "The Wreck of the *Sultana.*" *National Tribune,* September 17, 1908, 7.

Bridgeman, Burt Nichols, and Joseph Clark Bridgeman. *Genealogy of the Bridgeman Family, Descendants of James Bridgeman.* Springfield, MA: Clark W. Bryan Company, 1894.

Byrne, Frank L. *Prophet of Prohibition: Neal Dow and His Crusade.* Madison: State Historical Society of Wisconsin, 1961.

Carver, Ruth. "Letters from Home: Adam Farmer, 3rd Tennessee Cavalry." *The* Sultana *Remembered,* Newsletter of the Association of *Sultana* Descendants and Friends (summer 2003): 3.

Chrisinger, J. W. "The *Sultana* Disaster." *National Tribune,* July 15, 1886, 3.

Clough, B. F. "Burning of the Flagship *Black Hawk.*" *National Tribune,* September 3, 1885, 3.

"Condensed Letters." *National Tribune,* May 20, 1886.

Cullum, George W. *Biographical Register of the Officers and Graduates of the U.S. Military Academy at West Point, N.Y.* 3rd ed. Boston: Houghton Mifflin, 1891.

Cunningham, O. Edward. *Shiloh and the Western Campaign of 1862.* New York: Savas Beatie, 2007.

Dixon, Lt. William F. "Aboard the *Sultana.*" *Civil War Times Illustrated* 12, no. 10 (February 1974).

Donovan, Frank. *Ironclads of the Civil War.* New York: American Heritage, 1964.

Dunnavant, Robert, Jr. *The Railroad War.* Athens, AL: Pea Ridge Press, 1994.

Eldridge, Charles. "In the *Sultana* Disaster." *National Tribune,* June 16, 1924, 7.

————. "Some Events at Close of the Civil War." *National Tribune,* August 1, 1929, 6.

Elliott, James W. "By Fire and Flood." *National Tribune*, June 30, 1887, 2.

——.*Transport to Disaster.* New York: Holt, Rinehart and Winston, 1962.

Elliott, Joseph Taylor. "The *Sultana* Disaster." *Indiana Historical Society Publication* 5, no. 3 (1913): 161–99.

"Explosion of the Steamer *Sultana*, April 28, 1865." *Harper's Weekly* 9, no. 438, May 20, 1865, pl. 316.

Floyd, William B. "The Burning of the *Sultana*." *Wisconsin Magazine of History* 11 (1927–28): 70–76.

Fluharty, Linda Cunningham. *On the Way Home: West Virginia Soldiers on the* Sultana. Linda Cunningham Fluharty, 2003.

Graham, A. A. *History of Richland County, Ohio.* Ashland, OH: A. A. Graham & Company, 1880.

Guernsey, Alfred N., and Henry M. Alden. *Harper's Pictorial History of Civil War.* New York: Fairfax Press, 1977.

"Had a Varied Experience." *National Tribune*, July 22, 1897, 3.

Harvey, Cornelius Burnham, ed. *Genealogical History of Hudson and Bergen Counties New Jersey.* New York: New Jersey Genealogical Publishing Company, 1900.

Havinghurst, Walter. *Voices on the River.* New York: Macmillan, 1964.

Henderson, Howard A. M. "Lincoln's Assassination and Camp Fisk." *Confederate Veteran* 15 (April 1907): 170–71.

History of Cincinnati and Hamilton County, Ohio. Cincinnati: S. B. Nelson & Company, 1894.

Hobart, Edwin. "Assassination of Lincoln." *National Tribune*, June 7, 1900, 7.

Horner, Ira B. "No Scriptural Authority." *National Tribune*, June 3, 1909, 7.

Huddle, Rev. W. D., and Lulu May Huddle. *History of the Descendants of John Huddle.* Strasburg, VA: Shenandoah Publishing House, 1930.

Hunter, Louis C. *Steamboats on the Western Rivers.* New York: Dover, 1993.

Hyde, William, and Howard L. Conrad, eds. *Encyclopedia of the History of St. Louis.* Vol. 3. New York: Southern History Company, 1899.

Illinois. Military and Naval Department. *Report of the Adjutant General of the State of Illinois.* 8 vols. Springfield: Baker, Bailhache & Company, 1867.

Indiana. Adjutant General's Office. *Report of the Adjutant General of the State of Indiana.* 8 vols. Indianapolis: A. H. Conner, 1865–69.

"In Dread Cahaba." *National Tribune*, October 20, 1898, 2.

Jennings, Patrick. "What Happened to the *Sultana*?" Presentation before the National Board of Boiler and Pressure Vessel Inspectors, Colorado Springs, CO, April 27, 2015.

———."What Happened to the *Sultana*?" Presentation before the *Sultana* Disaster Conference, Marion, AR, April 27, 2019.

Johnson, Kenneth R. "Legrand Winfield Perce: A Mississippi Carpetbagger and the Fight for Federal Aid to Education." *Journal of Mississippi History* 34, no. 4 (November 1972): 331–56.

Jordan, Montgomery. "On the *Sultana*." *National Tribune*, July 31, 1913, 7.

Kentucky. Adjutant General's Office. *Report of the Adjutant General of the State of Kentucky.* 2 vols. Frankfort: Kentucky Yeoman Office, 1866–67.

Kiper, Richard L. *Major General John Alexander McClernand.* Kent, OH: Kent State University Press, 1999.

Lamon, Ward Hill. *Recollections of Abraham Lincoln, 1847–1865.* Lincoln: University of Nebraska Press, 1994.

LaPointe, Patricia M. "Military Hospital in Memphis, 1861–1865." *Tennessee Historical Quarterly* 43, no. 4 (1983): 325–42.

Lash, Jeffrey. *A Politician Turned General: The Civil War Career of Stephen Augustus Hurlbut.* Kent, OH: Kent University Press, 2003.

Leonard, Elizabeth D. *Lincoln's Forgotten Ally: Judge Advocate General Joseph Holt of Kentucky.* Chapel Hill: University of North Carolina Press, 2011.

Lock, G. Monroe. "Women on the *Sultana*." *National Tribune*, May 31, 1923, 6.

Lynch, Don. Titanic: *An Illustrated History.* New York: Hyperion, 1992.

Massie, Melville D. *Past and Present of Pike County, Illinois.* Chicago: S. J. Clarke, 1906.

McCammon, Charles S., ed. *Loyal Mountain Troopers: The Second and Third Tennessee Volunteer Cavalry in the Civil War.* Maryville, TN: Blount County Genealogical and Historical Society, 1992.

Middleton, Evan P., ed. *History of Champaign County, Ohio: Its People, Industries and Institutions.* Vol. 2. Indianapolis: B. F. Bowen & Company, 1917.

Miller, Francis Trevelyan, ed. *The Photographic History of the Civil War.* 10 parts. New York: Castle Books, 1957.

Nevin, David. *Sherman's March: Atlanta to the Sea.* Alexandria, VA: Time-Life Books, 1986.

"Not All *Sultana* Related Deaths Were Immediate." *The* Sultana *Remembered* (summer 2008): 4.

Ohio Roster Commission. *Official Roster of the Soldiers of the State of Ohio in the War of the Rebellion, 1861–1866*. 12 vols. Akron, OH: Werner Company, 1886–95.

Palmquist, Peter E., and Thomas R. Kailborn. *Pioneer Photographers from the Mississippi to the Continental Divide: A Biographical Dictionary, 1839–1865*. Stanford: Stanford University Press, 2005.

Parks, Phineas D. "The *Sultana* Disaster." *National Tribune*, January 3, 1889, 6.

Paskoff, Paul F. *Troubled Waters: Steamboat Disasters, River Improvements, and American Public Policy, 1821–1860*. Baton Rouge: Louisiana State University Press, 2007.

Pease, Theodore Calvin. *The Diary of Orville Hickman Browning*. Vol. 1. Springfield: Illinois State Historical Library, 1925.

Pivany, Eugene. *Hungarians in the American Civil War*. Cleveland: Dongo, 1913.

"Portraits Donated to Society." *Woodford Heritage News* (Woodford County Historical Society, Lexington, KY) 25, no. 1, 17–18.

Potter, Jerry O. *The Sultana Tragedy*. Gretna, LA: Pelican, 1992.

Pulis, Wash B. "The Story of a Soldier Who Died a Prisoner of War." *National Tribune*, August 24, 1899, 7.

"Random Shots." *National Tribune*, November 10, 1887, 3.

Raudebaugh, Samuel H. "The *Sultana* Disaster." *National Tribune*, April 18, 1889, 4.

Raynor, Jessie. "A Memory Preserved." *Northern Ohio Live* (May 1994): 108.

Record of Service of Michigan Volunteers in the Civil War, 1861–1865. 46 vols. Kalamazoo, MI: Ihling Bros. & Everard, 1905.

Rule, D. H. Sultana: *A Case for Sabotage*. Ramsey, MN: Variations on a Theme, 2013.

Rule, Walt. "The Long Walk Home: A Survivor's Story." *The Sultana Remembered* (spring 1998): 3.

Rutter, J. W. "Bewitching News." *S & D Reflector* 2, no. 3 (September 1965): 3.

"Scattering." *National Tribune*, August 16, 1906, 3.

Scharf, J. Thomas. *History of the Confederate States Navy from Its Organization to the Surrender of Its Last Vessel*. New York: Rogers & Sherwood, 1887.

Sharp, Thomas R. "The *Sultana* Disaster." *National Tribune*, November 21, 1912, 7.

Sharp & Dunnigan. *The Congressional Medal of Honor: The Names, the Deeds*. Chico, CA: Sharp and Dunnigan, 1984.

Shaw, Norman. "*Sultana* Association Revived." *The* Sultana *Remembered* 1, no. 1 (summer 1990).

Slocum, Charles Elihu. *The Life and Services of Major-General Henry Warner Slocum*. Toledo, OH: Slocum Publishing Company, 1913.

Smith, Robert. *Indiana and the* Sultana *Disaster*. Indianapolis: IBJ Book Publishing, 2015.

"*Sultana*." Camp Talk, *Blue & Gray Magazine* 5, no. 5 (May 1988): 41.

"*Sultana* Disaster: A Survivor Tells of a Terrible Experience and His Escape." *National Tribune*, May 10, 1900, 7.

"The *Sultana*'s Grave." *National Tribune*, December 6, 1923, 2.

"Survivors of the *Sultana*." *National Tribune*, December 17, 1885, 10.

Swanson, James L. *Manhunt: The 12-Day Chase for Lincoln's Killer*. New York: HarperCollins, 2006.

Tennessee. Adjutant General's Office. *Report of the Adjutant General of the State of Tennessee, of the Military Forces of the State, from 1861 to 1866*. Nashville: S. C. Mercer, 1866.

Thatcher, Joseph, and Thomas H. Thatcher. *Confederate Coal Torpedo: Thomas Courtenay's Infernal Sabotage Weapon*. Fredericksburg, VA: Kenerly Press, 2011.

Thirty-Eighth Annual Reunion of the Association of the Graduates of the United States Military Academy at West Point, New York, June 13, 1907. Saginaw, MI: Seeman & Peters, 1907.

U.S. Sanitary Commission. "Letter from Mr. Christy." *Sanitary Reporter*, no. 4, May 15, 1865, 187.

———. "Letters from Mr. Woodward." *Sanitary Reporter*, no. 4, May 15, 1865, 189.

———. "What the U.S. Sanitary Commission Is Doing in the Valley of the Mississippi." *Sanitary Reporter*, no. 1, May 15, 1863, 1.

Watson, Ken. *Paddlewheel Steamers*. New York: W. W. Norton, 1985.

Way, Frederick, Jr. *Way's Packet Directory*. Athens, OH: Sons and Daughters of Pioneer Rivermen, 1983.

The Weekly Underwriter, an Insurance Newspaper. Vol. 36, January 1 to June 25, 1887. New York: Underwriter Printing & Publishing Company, 1887.

Wideman, John C. *Naval Warfare: Courage and Combat on the Water*. New York: Metro Books, 1997.

"William Fies." *National Tribune*, May 13, 1886, 6.

Wilson, James Grant, and John Fiske, eds. *Appleton's Cyclopaedia of American Biography, 1600–1899.* Vol. 5. New York: D. Appleton, 1898.

"The Wreck of the *Sultana.*" *Harper's Weekly* 9, no. 437 (May 13, 1865): 291.

GOVERNMENT DOCUMENTS AND PUBLICATIONS

1850 U.S. Federal Census, Indiana, Rush County, District 97. www. ancestry.com.

1860 U.S. Federal Census, Indiana, Rush County, Anderson. www. ancestry.com.

Annis, Ann. Widow's Claim for Pension, May 6, 1872. National Archives.

Appointment, Commission, and Personal file for Capt. George Augustus Williams (2553 ACP 1889). Exhibit A. Civil War, *Sultana* Disaster, April 27, 1865. www.fold3.com.

Barnett, James T. W. Civil War, Civil War Service Records, Union Records, Kentucky, Third Infantry, A–Br, B, Barnett, James T. W. www.fold3.com.

———.Civil War, Civil War Service Records, Union Records, Kentucky, Twelfth Infantry, A–Bo, B, Barnett, James T. W. www.fold3.com.

———. Headstones Provided for Deceased Union Civil War Veterans, 1861–1904. www.ancestry.com.

Barton, Frank H. Civil War, Civil War Service Records, Confederate Records, Arkansas, Miscellaneous, Arkansas, A–I, B, Barton, F. H. www.fold3.com.

Buck, George M. *Compilation of Senate Election Cases from 1789 to 1903.* Washington: Government Printing Office, 1903.

Bull, William. Civil War, Civil War Service Records, Union Records, Virginia, Loudon County Rangers, A–Mi, B, Bull, William. www.fold3.com.

Dana, N. J. T. All Titles, Letters Received by Commission Branch, 1863–1870, 1865, D7-D194, D140—Dana, N J T, 3. www.fold3.com.

Dana, Napoleon Jackson Tecumseh. U.S. Wall of Honor, Civil War. www.fold3.com.

Illinois State Senate. *Journal of the Senate of the Twenty-Fifth General Assembly of the State of Illinois, Second Session, June 11–28, 1867.* Springfield: Baker, Bailhache & Company, 1867.

"Inspector's Certificate." Exhibit G. *The Proceedings and Report of the Court-Martial of Capt. Frederick Speed, Court-Martial Case MM3967,* Civil War, *Sultana* Disaster, April 1865. www.fold3.com.

Jolley, Van Buren. Invalid Pension Application, March 20, 1879. National Archives.

Jones, Josias W. Pension Application. National Archives.

Learner, Benjamin F. Declaration of Original Pension of an Invalid, September 14, 1870. National Archives.

Letters Received by the Adjutant General. 1861–70. Civil War. www.fold3.com.

Letters Received by Commission Branch. 1874–1894. Civil War. www.fold3.com.

Lindley, Henry C. Invalid Pension Application, April 4, 1882. National Archives.

Lingenfelter, Henry Tolbert. Letter in Pension File, n.d. National Archives.

McCown, James M. Invalid Pension Applications, March 14, 1888, and September 19, 1892. National Archives.

McKendry, James. Invalid Pension Application, December 5, 1887. National Archives.

Military Record of Col. Reuben B. Hatch. Records of the Adjutant General's Office, Record Group 94, National Archives.

Miller, Franklin Ellis. Civil War, Civil War Service Records, Union Records, Colored Troops, 56th–138th Infantry, 66th U.S. Colored Infantry, M, Miller, Franklin E. www.fold3.com.

Minier, Darius Isaac. Invalid Pension Application, December 8, 1893. National Archives.

Nevins, Joel Frank. Invalid Pension Application, December 28, 1880. National Archives.

Parsons, Lewis B. *Reports to the War Department, by Brev. Maj. Gen. Lewis B. Parsons, Chief of Rail and River Transportation.* St. Louis, MO: George Knapp & Company, 1867.

Personal Histories of Volunteer Officers in the Quartermaster's Department, 1861–1865, vol. 3. National Archives.

Redfield, W. C. *Letter to the Secretary of the Treasury on the History and Causes of Steamboat Explosions and the Means of Prevention.* 25th Cong., 3d sess., Doc. No. 21. New York: William Osborn, 1839.

"Report in the Case of Survivors of the Steamer *Sultana*." 51st Cong., 1st sess. War Department, Civil War, *Sultana* Disaster, April 27, 1865, Enlisted Branch file (HAAQ 981 EB 1865), 80. www.fold3.com.

Rives, John C. *The Congressional Globe: New Series: Contains the Debates, Proceedings, and Laws of the First Session of the Thirty-Second Congress.* Vol. 24, pt. 3. Washington: John C. Rives, 1852.

Ross, William Henry. Invalid Pension Application, June 29, 1875. National Archives.

Smith, Morgan L. Civil War, Letters Received by the Adjutant General 1861–1870. www.fold3.com.

Speed, Frederic. Civil War, Civil War Service Records, Union Records, Maine (Index Cards), S, Sp, Speed, Frederic. www.fold3.com.

Taft, George S. *Compilation of Senate Election Cases from 1789 to 1885.* 49th Cong., 1st sess., Senate.

Tillinghast, William H. Civil War, Civil War Service Records, Union Records, Colored Troops, 56th–138th Infantry, 66th US Colored Infantry, T, Tillinghast, William H. www.fold3.com.

———. Civil War Service Records, Union Records, Illinois (Index Cards, T, Ti, Tillinghart, William H. www.fold3.com.

United States v. Atlantic and Mississippi Steam Ship Company. National Archives, Chicago, IL, Record Group 21, General Case Files, U.S. Circuit Court, Springfield, IL.

U.S. Census 1860. Wisconsin, Kenosha County, Town of Randall. www.fold3.com.

U.S. Census 1870. Missouri. www.genealogybank.com.

U.S. Congress. *Ann Annis.* 49th Cong., 1st sess., H. Rep. 2242. Washington: Government Printing Office, 1886.

———. *Biographical Directory of the United States Congress, 1774–2005.* Washington: Government Printing Office, 1885, 2005.

———. *Congressional Record Containing the Proceedings and Debates of the Forty-Second Congress, Second Session.* Vol. 3, pt. 2. Washington: Government Printing Office, 1875.

———. *Congressional Record Containing the Proceedings and Debates of the Forty-Seventh Congress, First Session.* Vol. 13, pt. 3. Washington: Government Printing Office, 1882.

———. *Congressional Record Containing the Proceedings and Debates of the Forty-Eighth Congress, First Session.* Vol. 15, pt. 1. Washington: Government Printing Office, 1884.

———. *Congressional Record Containing the Proceedings and Debates of the Forty-Ninth Congress, First Session.* Vol. 17, pt. 1. Washington: Government Printing Office, 1886.

———. *Congressional Record Containing the Proceedings and Debates of the Fifty-First Congress, First Session.* Vol. 21, pts. 1, 2, 4, and 5. Washington: Government Printing Office, 1890.

———. *Congressional Record Containing the Proceedings and Debates of the Fifty-Seventh Congress, First Session.* Vol. 35, pt. 5. Washington: Government Printing Office, 1902.

———. *Congressional Record Containing the Proceedings and Debates of the Sixty-Third Congress, First Session.* Vol. 51, pt. 3. Washington: Government Printing Office, 1914.

———. *Congressional Record Containing the Proceedings and Debates of the Sixty-Fourth Congress, First Session.* Vol. 53, pt. 1. Washington: Government Printing Office, 1916.

———. *Elizabeth Hackleman.* 43rd Cong., 1st sess., H. Rep. 207. Washington: Government Printing Office, 1874.

———. *Frances L. Ackley.* 57th Cong., 1st sess., S. Rep. 1050. Washington: Government Printing Office, 1902.

———. *Frances L. Ackley.* 57th Cong., 1st sess., H. Rep. 1160. Washington: Government Printing Office, 1902.

———. *In the Senate of the United States.* 45th Cong., 3d sess., S. Rep. 647. Washington: Government Printing Office, 1879.

———. *John T. Watson.* 42nd Cong., 2d sess., H. Rep. 1548. Washington: Government Printing Office, 1872.

———. *John T. Watson.* 43rd Cong., 1st sess., H. Rep. 65. Washington: Government Printing Office, 1874.

———. *Journal of the House of Representatives, First session, Fifty-Fourth Congress.* Washington: Government Printing Office, 1897.

———. *Journal of the House of Representatives, First session, Fifty-Fifth Congress.* Washington: Government Printing Office, 1898.

———. *Journal of the House of Representatives, First session, Fifty-Sixth Congress.* Washington: Government Printing Office, 1900.

———. *Journal of the House of Representatives, First session, Fifty-Seventh Congress.* Washington: Government Printing Office, 1902.

———. *Journal of the House of Representatives, First session, Fifty-Eighth Congress.* Washington: Government Printing Office, 1903.

———. *Journal of the House of Representatives, First session, Fifty-Ninth Congress.* Washington: Government Printing Office, 1906.

———. *Journal of the House of Representatives, First session, Sixtieth Congress.* Washington: Government Printing Office, 1908.

———. *Journal of the House of Representatives, First session, Sixty-First Congress.* Washington: Government Printing Office, 1909.

———. *Journal of the House of Representatives, First session, Sixty-Second Congress.* Washington: Government Printing Office, 1911.

——. *Journal of the House of Representatives, First session, Sixty-Fifth Congress.* Washington: Government Printing Office, 1917.

——. *Mrs. Anna Butterfield.* 50th Cong., 1st sess., H. Rep. 1607. Washington: Government Printing Office, 1888.

——. *Perry H. Alexander.* 57th Congress, 1st sess., H. Rep. 1033. Washington: Government Printing Office, 1902.

——. *Purchase of Army Supplies, Report of Committees of the House of Representatives.* 37th Cong., 2nd sess. House of Representatives. Washington: Government Printing Office, 1862.

——. *Reports of Committees of the House of Representatives.* 37th Cong., 2nd sess. House of Representatives. Washington: Government Printing Office, 1862.

——. *War Claims at St. Louis.* 37th Cong., 2nd sess., H. Rep. 94, Washington: Government Printing Office, 1862.

U.S. Department of the Interior. National Park Service. *National Register of Historic Places Registration Form, South Cherry Street Historic District.* September 30, 2003.

U.S. Navy Department. *Official Records of the Union and Confederate Navies in the War of the Rebellion.* 30 vols. Washington: Government Printing Office, 1894–1922.

U.S. Patent Office. *Specifications and Drawings of Patents Issued from the United States Patent Office for September, 1874.* Washington: Government Printing Office, 1875.

U.S. Quartermaster General's Department. *Roll of Honor (No. XXI): Names of Soldiers Who Died in Defense of the American Union Interred in the National Cemeteries at Memphis, Tennessee and Chalmette, Louisiana.* Washington: Government Printing Office, 1869.

U.S. Veterans Administration. *Memphis National Cemetery.* Pamphlet 40–26M, April 1983.

U.S. War Department. *The War of the Rebellion: A Compilation of the Official Records of the Union and Confederate Armies.* 70 vols. Washington: Government Printing Office, 1880–1901.

Vessels bought, sold, and chartered by the United States. Letter from the Secretary of War, transmitting, in answer to a resolution of the House of the 27 of January, a report by the Quartermaster General, relative to the number of vessels bought, sold, and chartered by the United States since April, 1861, July 16, 1868. Washington: Government Printing Office, 1868.

Williams, George Augustus. Appointment, Commission, and Personal file for Capt. George Augustus Williams. Civil War, *Sultana* Disaster, April 1865. www.fold3.com.

Woodward, Taylor. Civil War, Civil War Service Records, Union Records, West Virginia, Fourth Cavalry, W, Woodyard, Taylor. www.fold3.com.

INTERNET SOURCES

Andersonville National Historic Site. National Park Service. https://www.nps.gov/ande/index.htm.

Brown, Eunice Maria Lewis. "Memories of Our Family." 1890. http://www.silcom.com/~campbell/genealogy/lewishistory_brown.html.

City Directory of Chicago. 1862–80. www.ancestry.com. Last accessed August 14, 2002.

City Directory of St. Joseph (MO). 1882, 1887–90, 1893. www.ancestry.com.

"Confederate Prisoner of War Camps, Mississippi, Meridian." https://www.mycivilwar.com/pow/confederate.html.

Cussler, Clive. "Battle of Memphis." NUMA National Underwater and Marine Agency. https://numa.net/expeditions/battle-of-memphis/.

Department of Physics, University of Illinois at Urbana-Champaign. "Q & A: Water Expanding the Most." *Ask the Van*, October 22, 2007. https://van.physics.illinois.edu/qa/listing.php?id=1734.

Gorman, Kathleen L. "Civil War Pensions." *Essential Civil War Curriculum*, https://www.essentialcivilwarcurriculum.com/civil-war-pensions.html.

Jennings, Patrick. "The *Sultana*—Part 2: How Do Boilers Go Boom?" https://blog.hsb.com/2015/04/06/sultana-boiler-explosion/.

——. "The *Sultana*—Part 5: What Caused the *Sultana* Disaster?" https://blog.hsb.com/2016/04/27/sultana-disaster-cause/.

Kerns, William F. *Mount Mora Cemetery.* http://www.mountmora.org/findagrave/main.asp?page=search_details&id=7700.

King, Gilbert. "A Spectacle of Horror: The Burning of the *General Slocum*." *Smithsonian* magazine. Smithsonian.com, February 21, 2012. https://www.smithsonianmag.com/history/a-spectacle-of-horror-the-burning-of-the-general-slocum-104712974/.

Louden, Robert, 1833–1867. www.ancestry.com.

Mayo Clinic. "Hypothermia." Patient Care & Health Information, Diseases & Conditions. https://www.mayoclinic.org/diseases-conditions/hypothermia/symptoms-causes/syc-20352682.

Mississippi Marriages, 1800–1911. www.familysearch.com.

"Officers of the 13th Maine Infantry (Cont.), Assistant Adjutant General Frederic Gordon Speed." *13th Maine Infantry Regiment.* http://maine13th.com/moreoff-3.html#speed-fg.

Rombauer, Maj. Raphael Guido. Memorial information. https://www.findagrave.com/memorial/116037267/raphael-guido-rombauer.

"*Titanic* Victims." Titanic *Facts: The Life & Loss of the RMS* Titanic *in Numbers.* https://titanicfacts.net/titanic-victims.

"Union Pension Records." https://www.familysearch.org/wiki/en/Union_Pension_Records.

U.S. Federal Census Mortality Schedules, 1850–1885. www.ancestry.com.

U.S. Politicians—*All You United States Politicians.* https://bioguide.congress.gov/search/bio/B000958.

Williams' Cincinnati Directory. Cincinnati: Williams & Company, 1863. www.ancestry.com.

Woolfolk, Sarah. Memorial information. www.findagrave.com.

Wright, Gary. "Ghosts of Cahaba." *Porchscene: Exploring Southern Culture.* http://porchscene.com/2016/09/14/ghosts-of-cahaba/.

CORRESPONDENCE, INTERVIEWS, AND MISCELLANEOUS SOURCES

Note: Unless otherwise indicated, all sources are part of author's collection.

Bogart, Solomon Franklin. Letters to Mrs. M. S. Misimer, April 17 and April 30, 1865.

Braunmart, Mrs. Letter to Dear Sirs [*Sultana* Survivors' Association], April 24, 1901.

Chandler, Helen. Email message to author, June 21, 1997.

Cloghen, Agnes. Letter to B. F. Learner, May 1, 1924.

Deaderisle, Judith. Letter to Jerry O. Potter, April 24, 1984.

Dickey, Charlie H. Letter to Belle. September 8, 1863. *The* Sultana *Remembered*, Newsletter of the Association of *Sultana* Descendants and Friends (summer 1999).

Dyer, Samuel Abraham. Letter to his wife, March 18, 1865.

———.Letters to his wife and children, March 27 and April 9, 1865.

Farmer, Robert D. Email message to author, April 8, 1997.

Foley, Richard Jourdan. Letters to his sister, April 8, 13, and 15, 1865.

Hartford Steam Boiler Inspection and Insurance Company. Vacation desk calendar, 1990.

Hinds, Thomas Josiah. Letter to Dear Friends at Home, April 14, 1865.

———.Letter to his father and mother, March 19, 1865.

Horan, Thomas. Letter to his brother Vick, April 18, 1865.

Hussey, Fenton Andrew. Letter to his parents, April 30, 1865. Abraham Lincoln Presidential Library, Springfield, IL.

Isenogle, Ruth Provines. Letter to Jerry O. Potter, May 31, 1989.

Loy, George C. Letter to Frank Loy, April 28, 1865.

Mathews, Thomas. Letter to author, February 25, 1997.

McKesson, William A. Letter to Clerk of Circuit Court, April 12, 1866. Kenosha County Historical Society and Museum, Kenosha, WI.

Millard, P. Steve. Letter to author, January 8, 1994.

Misemer, Henry Marshall. Letters to his wife, March 24 and 28, April 14, 1865.

Moore, Thomas Dunn. Letter to his parents, April 27, 1865.

Norton, William. Letter to his parents, April 27, 1865. https://www. ancestry.com/mediaui-viewer/tree/54068443/person/13609360180/ media/7de68c23-668f-4bb2-9260-623f4aef025b?_phsrc=UxY820&_ phstart=successSource.

Norwood, Helen. Letter to author, August 20, 1990.

Pickens, Samuel. Letter to Cynthia and Mary Pickens, April 28, 1865.

Potter, Jerry O. Email message to author, June 30, 2019.

Poysell, Samuel W. Letter to his wife, April 7, 1865.

Squire, Elbert J. Letter to L. W. Day, March 29, 1886.

Williams, Spencer Harrison. Letter to home, March 19, 1865.

INDEX

mules on board, 128; on Mason assisting those in the water, 191; as prisoner, 52; on steering after explosion, 159; on sympathizers at Mattoon, 273–74; on throwing injured men overboard, 195

Hood, John Bell, 47, 48

Horan, Thomas W., 57, 58, 63

Horn, Philip L., 52, 148, 161, 198, 216–17

Horner, Ira B.: on the alligator, 112, 193; Confederates capture, 47; explosion injuries, 175; as homecoming surprise, 344; as Ohio survivor, 280–81; shot at by guards above Memphis, 217–18

horses on board, 127–28, 181, 205–6

Hosmer, Mrs. O. E., 127

Hostin, Richard F., 224–25

Howard, Jacob M., 303

Howard, Richard J., 25

Hulit, William A.: on anything to help stay afloat, 181; explosion and, 165, 166; on French leave in Ohio, 275–76; rescue of, 238; on sympathizers on the way home, 273

Hunnewell, Hill & Company, 4

Hunt, Harrison Parker, 56

Hunter, Louis C., 5, 7, 21–22, 155, 267–68

Huntsman, Henry Clay, 90, 329

Hurlbut, Stephen A., 42

hurricane deck: explosion and, 159, 161, 162, 165; fire from explosion and, 171; freight distribution and, 141; in Helena photograph, 135; lack of toilets on, 123–24; men on, 111; moving men from, 112–13; sagging down, 110; sleeping on, 121–22

Hussey, Fenton Andrew, 212

hypothermia, 200–201, 268

Indiana (steamboat), 248

Indianapolis Daily Gazette, 264

Indianapolis Journal, 272

Indianapolis Star, 263

infant on board, 127, 246

Inghram, Henry, 23, 25

Inghram, Zadock, 247

inspectors, steamboat, 10

investigations: *Chicago Tribune* editorial on, 293–94; Grant's orders to Badeau on, 286; Hoffman's, 295–99; sabotage considered during, 370; Stanton's orders on, 285–86; Washburn appoints Court of Inquiry, 283; Washburn questioning overcrowding, 283–84; Washburn report to Stanton, 299–300. *See also* Dana Commission; sabotage; Washburn Commission

iron: burned, Taylor on, 156; defective, boiler explosions and, 298; no.1 charcoal, 151; for replacement boilers, 266–67. *See also*

tubular boilers

Irwin, Bernard J. D., 220, 225, 316

Jackson Citizen Patriot, 279

Jennings, Patrick, 151–52, 156, 157, 298

Jennings and Jones, 108

Jenny Lind, 222, 225, 236–37, 247

Johnson, Andrew, 27, 303, 305

Johnston, Benjamin Franklin: on compassion of Memphis citizens, 242; on explosion sound, 168; hypothermia and, 201; mustering out in Michigan, 279; selecting place on *Sultana*, 98; on sympathizers on the way home, 273

Johnston, Joseph, 261

Jolley, Van Buren, 170

Jones, Arthur Alexander (Sgt.), 93, 244

Jones, Sam, 54

Jones, William C.: asking for men for *Pauline Carroll*, 102–3, 108–9; bribes and, 86–87, 102; former prisoner transport and, 70, 71, 72, 73; Kerns on no men for *Pauline Carroll*, 116; Speed's court-martial and, 316; Washburn Commission interview of, 288. *See also Olive Branch*

Jordan, Montgomery W., 49

Karns, Nicholas Homer: on *Belle St. Louis* for rest of trip home, 271, 438n4; *Bostona*'s passing by and, 209, 210; on explosion aftermath, 173; on fire from explosion, 171; on gangplank, 178; on getting on another boat for home, 270; on men trapped in the wreckage, 194–95; on order to ship north, 84; as prisoner, 55; prisoner exchange and, 63–64; on prisoner exchange remuneration, 29–30; rescue of, 222, 236–37; searching for place to sleep on board, 120; on stageplank launching, 179, 180; on *Sultana* underway, 118; on survivors met by multitude of sympathizers, 271; on train trip through Indiana, 272

Kate Ellis, 267

Keeble, John Harrison, 205

Keeble, Pleasant Marion, 205, 219, 367–68

Keeler, Lewis C., 142

Kemble, George S., 62–63, 95–96, 105–6, 329

Kennedy, Private, 139

Kerns, William Franklin: aftermath for, 353; background, 42–43; changing story of, 87–88; concerns on overloading, 115–16; Dana Commission interview of, 288; Dana on responsibility of, 291; on diverting overflow to another boat, 101, 106–8, 304; Hatch failure to notify when boats arrived,

ABOUT THE AUTHOR

Gene Eric Salecker is recognized as one of the leading authorities on the *Sultana* disaster and owns the largest collection of *Sultana* memorabilia. A retired police officer and middle-school teacher, he is currently the historical consultant for the *Sultana* Disaster Museum, Marion, Arkansas. Gene and his wife, Susan, live in River Grove, Illinois.